Introduction

Village London was first published in 1883 under the title 'Greater London'. Written by Edward Walford, a noted Victorian historian and antiquarian who was concerned to record the history and appearance of the hamlets, villages and market towns that made up the metropolitan area before they were overtaken by the urban sprawl that was then beginning to take place.

There was then a great deal of interest in London's history, but now, when there is little or nothing to differentiate between one district and another except the names on the railway stations, it has become even stronger.

Each village has its own history, in some cases stretching back to Roman or Saxon times and beyond. This is the story of these one-time villages and towns which grew up around coaching inns or river fords, or even Royal palaces — now long since demolished and ancient manors that are now tree lined suburban avenues. Every part of London has its own history and historical characters, ranging from Hampton Court's Cardinal Wolsey and Tooting's Daniel Defoe, to Enfield's Mother Wells. This book tells the fascinating story of Greater London's past, as distinct from its inner city; the battlefields — Epping, Barnet, and Brentford and many more; its palaces — Nonsuch, Croydon, Enfield and Hampton Court. But more importantly it recreates the atmosphere of the old villages, the inns and churches, the pastimes and pleasures of ordinary people as well as the rich and famous.

Edward Walford had the gift of writing history so that it would be of interest to the casual reader as well as the serious student and he brings the long lost days of rural London vividly to life.

VILLAGE LONDON

THE STORY OF
GREATER LONDON

by

EDWARD WALFORD, M.A.

PART 4 — South West

THE ALDERMAN PRESS

First published 1883/4 by Cassell & Co. Ltd.
under the title *Greater London*

Published in hardback by The Alderman Press
under the title *Village London Vol. 1* 1983

British Library Cataloguing in Publication Data.
Walford, Edward
    [Greater London]. Village London: The Story
    of Greater London.
    1. London (England) — History
    I. [Greater London] II. Title
    942.1   DA677

    ISBN 0-946619-11-5 (Pt.1)
    ISBN 0-946619-12-3 (Pt.2)
    ISBN 0-946619-13-1 (Pt.3)
    ISBN 0-946619-14-X (Pt.4)

This edition published 1985
The Alderman Press 1/7, Church Street,
Edmonton, London, N9 9DR.

Printed in Great Britain by
BAS Printers Limited, Over Wallop, Hampshire

CONTENTS.

---◆◆◆---

CHAPTER XXXIII.

CHESSINGTON, TALWORTH, LONG DITTON, THAMES DITTON, AND MOLESEY.

CHAPTER XXXIV.

ESHER AND CLAREMONT.

CHAPTER XXXV.

KINGSTON-ON-THAMES.

CHAPTER XXXVI.

KINGSTON-UPON-THAMES (continued).

CONTENTS.

CONTENTS.

LIST OF ILLUSTRATIONS.

GREATER LONDON.

THE "BALD-FACED STAG."

CHAPTER XXXIII.

CHESSINGTON, TALWORTH, LONG DITTON, THAMES DITTON, AND MOLESEY.

"The plain was grassy, wild, and bare—
Wide, wild, and open to the air."—TENNYSON.

Situation and Boundaries of Chessington—The Church—Charitable Bequests—Castle Hill—Descent of the Manor—Hook—Barwell Court—Talworth—Long Ditton—Population—The Church—Descent of the Manor—Situation and Boundaries of Thames Ditton—Railway Communication—Population, &c.—The Parish Church—Schools and Almshouses—William and Mary Howitt—Ancient Weapons found here—Boyle Farm—The Dandies' Fête—Lord St. Leonards—Ditton House—The Swan Tavern—Thames Angling Preservation Society—A Famous Angler—Lines composed by Theodore Hook in a Punt off Thames Ditton—Early History of the several Manors of Thames Ditton—Claygate—Imber Court—East Molesey—Population, &c.—The Church—The "Spa"—West Molesey—The Church—Cemetery—Molesey Hurst—Richard Baddeley the Actor—Molesey Grove—The Right Hon. J. Wilson Croker—Sir Robert Walpole—Other Residents—Apps Court.

THE long triangular tract of country which lies between Epsom and Kingston, for some reason best known to the natives of those parts, is but little known to Londoners. It has not the attractions of a breezy down, nor those of a rural valley; there is no navigable river to water it, acting at the same time as the pioneer of cultivation and civilisation. It lies between two lines of railways, and far away from any railway station, considering that as we walk across it we are within fifteen miles of Charing Cross, and are approaching one of the assize towns of Surrey. In fact, it may be doubted whether one in ten of our readers has heard of Chessington, or Talworth, or even Long Ditton. For between two and three miles this desert-like stretch of open country is traversed by an arm or feeder of the Hog's-mill or Ewell River, which, as we have stated in a previous chapter, unites with the Thames at Kingston.

Chessington, or, as it used to be called, Chesingdon, lies between Malden and Epsom, about three miles north-west from the latter town, and is a perpetual curacy, held along with the living of Malden, and therefore in the patronage of Merton College, Oxford. It lies so remote from railways and from the populous haunts of men, that its name is probably unknown to many of those who live at Croydon, Epsom, and Kingston-on-Thames. It is a quiet little village, extremely secluded, if not exactly the proverbial "five miles from anywhere." It consists of a church, the rectory adjoining it, and four or five small houses. From the churchyard is gained a lovely view of hill, vale, and down, with here and there a house peeping from sheltering trees. Few particulars of its church are given in either Manning's or in Brayley's "History of Surrey." The latter merely records the fact that "it originally consisted of a nave and chancel, and a small south transept, with a square wooden turret rising from the roof." In 1854 the fabric was "restored," and at the cost of nearly £2,000, Early English arches and windows being inserted in the place of square, wooden-framed windows which formerly gave light, and the building was lengthened. In the south wall of the chancel is an old piscina, and "in one of the chancel pews," writes Brayley, "is a small piece of oaken lattice-work, probably the remains of a confessional." The edifice consists of a nave, side aisle, and chancel. It is in the pointed Gothic style, with one of the insignificant spires so frequent in this part of Surrey. There are one or two small stained glass windows and an American organ. On the north wall is a tablet to the memory of Samuel Crisp, of Chiswick, with the following panegyric composed by C. Burney :—

"Reader, this cold and humble spot contains
 The much lamented, much revered, remains
 Of one whose wisdom, learning, taste, and sense,
 Good-humoured wit and wide benevolence,
 Cheered and enlightened all this hamlet round
 Whenever genius, worth, or want was found.

To few it is that courteous Heaven imparts
 Such depth of knowledge and such taste in arts,
 Such penetration and enchanting pow'rs
 Of bright'ning social and convivial hours:
 Had he through life been blest by nature kind
 With health robust of body as of mind,
 With skill to serve and charm mankind so great
 In arts, in science, letters, Church or State,
 His name the nation's annals had enrolled,
 And virtues to remotest ages told."

On each side of the east window is a beautiful fresco painting, the subjects being "The Annunciation" and "The Adoration of the Magi." Beneath the window is an elegantly-carved reredos.

In the vestry is another tablet, which records a benefactor to the parish : Henry Smith, Alderman of London, who died in the year 1621, and who in his lifetime gave to trustees a large portion of his real and personal estate for charitable uses here and elsewhere in Surrey.

From the estates of Worth and Balcomb, in the county of Sussex, the churchwardens receive annually certain moneys, to be distributed in meat, bread, or clothing among such poor persons as have resided in the parish for five years and bear a good moral character.

Near a small stream to the south of the church is an eminence which is evidently artificial, and which, with some four or five acres adjoining, is still called the Castle Hill, though all traces of a castle have long been effaced. It would seem, however, that Chessington was occupied by the Romans ; at all events, a large brass coin of the Empire was found there some years since.

There were here two manors, the one of which belonged to Richard de Tonbridge, and is thus described in "Domesday Book" :—"Robert de Wateville holds of Richard Cisendone what was held by Erding of King Edward. It was then assessed at five hides ; now at only half a hide. The arable land consists of two carucates. There are three 'villains' (*villani*) and one bordar, with one carucate. There is half a mill, valued at two shillings. The wood feeds thirty swine. In the time of King Edward the manor was estimated at £4, afterwards at 40s., and now at 70s." Apparently another manor of the same name existed here as well, for we read in "Domesday Book" that "Milo Crispin himself holds Cisedune, which Magno Swert held in the time of King Edward. It was then assessed at five hides ; now at one hide. Wigot had not possession of it when King William came into England. The arable land amounts to three carucates. The land lay in Bedinton ; it was in the tenure of villains. Now there is one carucate in demesne, and six villains, with two carucates." The latter manor seems to have been afterwards held by Richard, Earl of Cornwall, brother of King Henry III., as pertaining to the "honour" of Wallingford, whilst that belonging to Richard de Tonbridge was given to the Abbey of Boxley, near Maidstone. In the reign of Edward I. there was here a park, pertaining to the manor of Maldon, and belonging to the College of Merton. On the suppression of the monasteries this manor became vested in the greedy king, and it has since passed through various private hands, the Herveys, the Hattons, and the Northeys, to the family of Gosse, who now own it.

Chessington is intersected from south to north by the high road from Leatherhead; and on the western side of the road as we make our way towards Kingston we pass the hamlet of Hook, anciently called La Hoke, an assemblage of small cottages occupied chiefly by farm-labourers, and bordering a narrow byeway which winds westward towards Claygate. St. Paul's Church, at Hook, erected in 1833, is a small and poor structure, of red and yellow bricks intermingled. It is in the earliest Pointed style, lighted by narrow lancet-headed windows, and has a small open bell-turret rising from the roof.

The distance of this small hamlet, with its population of 500 souls, from the mother church of Kingston—nearly four miles, as we learn from Brayley—was the cause of its being separated into a distinct parish chapelry; independently of which the only place requiring notice is the manor of Berwell or Barwell Court, an ancient possession of the Priors of Merton, who, in the reign of Henry VIII., "had a charter of free warren throughout the same," paying six shillings yearly as a quit-rent to the corporation of Kingston. On the suppression of monasteries this manor escheated to the Crown, and was subsequently granted by Queen Elizabeth to Sir Thomas Vincent, of Stoke D'Abernon, who, towards the end of the sixteenth century, alienated it, together with the manor-house and its surroundings, to the Carletons of Stoke. This family later on obtained for themselves and their tenants a free right of pasture on the commons of Norbiton, Surbiton, &c., from the corporation of Kingston. The property has since undergone several changes of ownership, in various ways. Long tenanted as a farm, a considerable part of the old manor-house has been pulled down.

Far away to the north of Chessington, to which place we now retrace our steps, and on the high road connecting Ewell with Kingston and Long Ditton—indeed, forming part of the latter—lies the hamlet of Talworth, or Tolworth, one of those localities where town is still struggling with country. Long lines of villas stretch in every direction, and are gradually overcoming the rural character of the district. The church, dedicated to St. Matthew, is a very large and well-built edifice in the Pointed Gothic style, having nave, aisles, transepts, and chancel, the latter being semicircular in form, and containing five stained-glass windows.

The old manor-house, called Talworth Court, stands on the right of the road from Ewell, at the point where it crosses the Hog's-mill stream; it is now a farmhouse, and shows but little traces of its original architecture.

Long Ditton, which lies between Talworth and Esher, is a parish of some little historical interest, as that from which the Evelyns of Wotton took their origin. George Evelyn, son of John Evelyn, of Kingston-on-Thames, first settled here, but subsequently removed to Godstone, and ultimately to Wotton, where he died in 1603. He was largely engaged in the manufacture of gunpowder, an industry which he is said to have introduced into this country. Having obtained a patent from Queen Elizabeth, he continued these powder works with great profit until the civil wars of the reign of Charles I., when the family were deprived of their exclusive rights and privileges.

The parish, which comprises a population of about 2,000 souls, belongs to the Hundred of Kingston, and is bounded on the north-west by Thames Ditton.

Long Ditton Church, according to old Aubrey, originally consisted of a body and two aisles, and doubtless was a fair and goodly specimen of a country village church. But in the dreary reigns of Queen Anne and George I. it was spoilt by the mania for beautification which here and there swept over whole neighbourhoods. Little or nothing is known of it in detail, except that it was "newly ceiled and beautified" early in the last century, and that there were fresco paintings on the west wall, representing David playing on the Harp, with Time and Death on either side. But it contained some interesting monuments, including several to the Evelyns and to members of families with whom they were allied. It is enough to make one's blood run cold to read it coolly stated by Brayley, without one word of censure, that these "were removed when the church was re-built, and were never re-placed." Happily the inscriptions for the most part may be read in Aubrey's "Surrey," and in the History of the county by Manning and Bray.

The present church, which was built in 1880, is of stone, and in the mediæval style, consisting of chancel, nave, and aisles. It replaced a building which, though cruciform in plan, was a hideous brick structure, utterly nondescript in style. It had only four windows, one in each arm of the cross, and these were semicircular and near the roof—a feeble replica of the monstrosity on Paddington Green,* known as St. Mary's Church. On the floor of the present church is a sepulchral brass preserved from the former building, and representing a husband and wife in the attitude of prayer, and dressed in rather remarkable costumes.

The church and the burial-ground surrounding it having become unduly crowded, certain prohibitory regulations with regard to the future burials in those places were found necessary, and a new burial-place was consecrated at a short distance from the church. This also becoming filled, the present cemetery was inaugurated. The first interment took place in July, 1855. The cemetery, thirteen acres in extent, is tastefully arranged and planted, and the monuments, principally designed by local artists, are skilfully executed, and in good taste. The buildings consist of two chapels, both connected by an archway and surmounted by a spire.

There would seem to have been in Ditton two manors, namely, Ditton and Talworth—called in the "Domesday Book" Taleorde. In the reign of King John the manor of Long Ditton appears to have belonged to Geoffrey de Mandeville, Earl of Essex, and to have been granted by him to the Prior of the Monastery of St. Mary Without Bishopsgate. Edward VI. granted it, in 1553, to David Vincent, Keeper of the Wardrobe at Richmond, and afterwards one of the Gentlemen of his Bedchamber. The manor of Talworth, or Taleorde, according to Brayley, was, in the reign of Edward I., vested in the family of the Clares, Earls of Gloucester and Hereford. In the reign of Edward II. there was a separate manor here, called Turbervill, which, with another estate called Wyke, was subsequently united to Talworth. From a survey taken of the possessions of Hugh le Despenser, Earl of Gloucester, after his execution in 1327, and mentioned by Brayley, it appears that "there was at Talworth a 'capital messuage surrounded by a moat,' with various offices and farm buildings, 280 acres of arable land and ten of meadow, valued altogether at £3 15s. 10d. a year. At Wyke was a 'messuage for a family' with other buildings, 80 acres of arable and six of meadow, the whole valued at £1 2s. 5½d. At Turbervill was 'a messuage containing a chamber, with a chapel, covered with tiles, for the use of the lord on his coming,' with farm buildings, arable land, meadow, and pasture, &c." Both of

these manors were acquired by the Evelyns, who sold them to Lord Chancellor King, the ancestor of their present owner, the Earl of Lovelace. The Evelyns obtained one of these manors by marriage and the other by purchase.

Thames Ditton is so called to distinguish it from Long Ditton, which it adjoins on the south-west. The village lies near the southern bank of the river, and consists of a few straggling houses fringing the roadside, and·stretching away on the one hand to Weston Green and Imber, near which is Esher station on the South-Western Railway, and on the other hand to Gigg's Hill, an outlying hamlet on the Portsmouth road, about a quarter of a mile to the south. One side of the main street is formed by the mansion, outbuildings, and grounds of Boyle Farm, which extend down to the river-side. There is a station near the village, on the Hampton Court branch of the South-Western line. Much of the land in the parish is cultivated as market gardens, and the population, according to the latest return, is close upon 3,000 souls.

The church, dedicated to St. Nicholas, stands on the west side of the village, a little off from the street. It is said to be of "remote origin," but the building has been so much altered at different times, and enlarged by additional erections, that very little of the original work is visible. It was formerly a chapel-of-ease to Kingston, but was made parochial by Act of Parliament in 1769. It is an irregular building, chiefly constructed of rough stone, flint, and rubble-work ; and it consists of a chancel, with south aisle, nave, with north and south aisles, and a low massive tower, containing six bells, heightened with woodwork, and surmounted by a small octagonal spire of similar material. The nave is separated from the aisles by three low pointed arches, springing from heavy octagonal piers. The south aisle was added in 1864, from the designs of Mr. B. Ferrey, at which time the church was thoroughly restored, and the old-fashioned pews superseded by open benches. The font, apparently of very early Norman work, consists of a massive bowl, ornamented with rude carvings, and standing on a plain modern pedestal. Several of the windows are filled with stained glass.

Mr. Martin F. Tupper speaks of this church as being rich in brasses ; and he mentions as worthy of special notice one in memory of Erasmus Forde and his seventeen children. It is to be hoped that they were not all by one wife, but judging from the engraving on the brass, such would appear to be the case. The monument on which the above-mentioned brass is placed is built of freestone, and

---

is somewhat peculiar in construction, having more the appearance of sedilia. The upper part is embattled, and ornamented with sculptured flowers, quatrefoils, &c., in the cornice and facia, but the lower part is divided into two by low pointed arched recesses. Each of the recesses affords room for a human figure, from which circumstance, and from a small aperture being left in the separating wall, observes Brayley, it has been supposed that this monument was used in the Catholic times as a confessional. In one of the recesses is a large brass plate, engraved with a representation of a man in armour and his wife, each of whom is kneeling before a small altar whereon is an open book. In the centre is a coat-of-arms, with helmet, crest, and motto. On one side is Forde, with six sons, and on the other his wife, with eleven daughters. Erasmus Forde was treasurer to King Edward VI., and died in the year 1553, and his wife, Julyan, died six years later.

In the chancel are two or three other interesting brasses, notably one to William Notte and his wife, who died in 1576 and 1587 respectively, with their nineteen children—fourteen sons and five daughters. Their quiver also was full to overflowing.

Another brass is engraved with the small whole-length figures of a woman standing between two men in gowns, with their respective children, and underneath an inscription, stating that " Here within do rest the Bodyes " of Cuthbert Blakeden, serjeant of the confectionery to Henry VIII., John Boothe, one of the gentlemen ushers to Henry VIII. and Edward VI., and Juliana, " some time the wyf of the said Cuthbert and John," and who died in the year 1586.

On the south side of the chancel is a brass plate to the memory of Mr. Charles J. Corbett, of Imber Court, who died in 1882. A monument, with bust, commemorates Colonel Sidney Godolphin, Governor of the Scilly Isles, " who, after quitting the army, sat in Parliament for nearly fifty years as member for different constituencies in Cornwall, and who died, " the Father of the House of Commons," in 1732. There is also a memorial of Admiral Lambert, who died in 1836 ; and another, with medallion, to Vice-Admiral Rowley Lambert, C.B., who died in 1880.

Near the church are some well-built schools, and there are also almshouses for twelve poor persons. Six of the houses were founded early in the last century by Mr. Henry Bridges, of Imber Court.

William and Mary Howitt, the authors of " The Ruined Abbeys and Castles of Great Britain," the " Literature and Romance of Modern Europe," and of several works on country life, &c., lived for some time in this village. They have been mentioned at greater length in OLD AND NEW LONDON, under " Highgate." *

In the *Archæological Journal*, Vol. XIX. (1862), p. 364, are figured a long iron spear-head and some bronze weapons, in good preservation, which were found in the bed of the river at Thames Ditton, and which were presented to the British Museum by Lord Lovelace.

Boyle Farm was the residence of Lord De Ros, and afterwards of Lord St. Leonards, who retired hither when weary of his duties as Lord Chancellor. Here he sowed and planted ; here he entertained his legal and political friends, the chief of whom was Mr. Samuel Warren, Q.C., the author of " Ten Thousand a Year." The house is a large brick building, mostly covered with stucco, and, with its gables and battlements, has a picturesque appearance, particularly the older part, which fronts the river. The grounds, which descend to the water-side, are extensive, and well planted with trees, among them being some remarkably fine cedars.

Mr. Tupper speaks of Boyle Farm with almost a sneer, as " a place of some note, especially to aristocratical haymakers." We shall see presently why he does so.

The house was at one time occupied by Lord Henry Fitzgerald, brother to the Lord Edward Fitzgerald so deeply implicated in the Irish rebellion of 1798. Lord Henry married, in 1792, Charlotte, Baroness de Ros, to whose family the property belonged.

Horace Walpole, in a letter to the Earl of Strafford, dated from Strawberry Hill, July 28, 1787, writes :—" Mrs. Walsingham is making her house at Ditton (now baptized Boyle Farm) very orthodox. Her daughter, Miss Boyle, who has real genius, has carved three tablets in marble with boys, designed by herself. These sculptures are for a chimney-piece ; and she is painting panels in grotesque for the library, with pilasters of glass in black and gold." The Miss Boyle above referred to became in her own right Baroness de Ros, and married, as stated above, Lord Henry Fitzgerald.

In 1827 Boyle Farm became celebrated for a very gorgeous fête, somewhat after the style of that which took place at The Oaks, near Epsom.† It was given by five young men of fashion, one of whom was the son of Lady de Ros.

In the " Life and Correspondence of Thomas Slingsby Duncombe," edited by his son, in the chapter devoted to " Dinner-givers and Diners-out,"

---

* See " Old and New London," Vol. V., p. 412.   † See *ante*, p. 219.

the author writes :—"While treating of this subject, we must not forget the entertainments occasionally got up by members of the *beau monde*. Among the most successful was the one given jointly at Boyle Farm, the Lady de Ros's, on the banks of the Thames. The expenses were defrayed by a subscription of £500 each from Lords Alvanley, Castlereagh, Chesterfield, Robert Grosvenor, and Henry de Ros, and great taste was displayed in the arrangement. Pavilions on the bank of the river, a large dinner-tent on the lawn, capable of holding

of England. Born in London in 1781, Edward Sugden early in life devoted himself to the study of the law, and was called to the bar at Lincoln's Inn in 1807. Two years previously he had manifested his eminent qualifications for the profession he had chosen by the publication of "A Concise and Practical Treatise on the Law of Vendors and Purchasers of Estates." This work "was certainly the foundation of my early success in life," as he himself states in a thirteenth edition, published in 1857. It supplied a want, and it became a stan-

THAMES DITTON CHURCH.

four hundred and fifty, and a select table for fifty in the conservatory. Gondolas floated on the water, containing the best singers of the Italian Opera ; and in a boat, Vestris and Fanny Ayton, the one singing Italian and the other English. There were illuminations throughout the ornamental grounds, and character quadrilles were danced by the beauties of the season. This was long remembered as the Dandies' Fête. It was in every way a great success."

Lord St. Leonards, who afterwards became the owner of Boyle Farm, rose from a hairdresser's son in Duke Street, Piccadilly,* to be Lord Chancellor

dard work ; fresh editions were repeatedly called for, and, as his biographers tell us, "the author took care, by improving upon each, to add to his reputation, which also concurred to increase his practice as a conveyancer, to which branch of his profession he at first confined himself." In 1808 he published his "Practical Treatise on Powers," which has gone through several editions, and which derived its value from its author's knowledge and exposition of laws, orders, precedents, and decisions. Of a more popular character was his next work, "A Series of Letters to a Man of Property on Sales, Purchases, Mortgages, Leases, Settlements, and Devises of Estates," a small volume, published in 1809, which was followed two years

---

* See "Old and New London," Vol IV., p. 201.

later by " The Law of Uses and Trusts," a posthumous work of Chief Baron Gilbert, the principal value of which consists in the introduction and notes supplied by the editor. " The character of these various works," observes the writer of his memoir in the " English Cyclopædia," " had procured for him an extremely large business as conveyancer and chamber counsel, with frequent occasions for acting as counsel in the common law courts ; and he ceased to appear as an author, except in occasional pamphlets upon legal subjects, and in preparing new editions of his previous

House of Commons as member for Ripon ; and on Sir Robert Peel's accession to office again, in 1841, he resumed the duties of Lord Chancellor of Ireland, which he continued to perform till 1846, when Lord John Russell succeeded Sir Robert Peel. In 1849 Sir Edward Sugden published another work, entitled " A Treatise on the Law of Property as administered in the House of Lords," in which he examines and criticises the decisions given in the House of Lords when acting as a Court of Appeal ; and in 1851 he issued " An Essay on the New Real Property Statutes." In

" THE SWAN," DITTON.

works. In 1817 he gave up his chamber practice, and confined himself to that of the Chancery bar, where in a short time his assistance was eagerly sought in all the most complicated cases ; and when, in 1822, he was made king's counsel, he obtained the leading business in that court." In 1828 he entered Parliament as member for Weymouth. His legal knowledge made him a valuable acquisition to the House, and in 1829 he was appointed to the office of Solicitor-General, and received the customary honour of knighthood under the administration of the Duke of Wellington. His tenure of office lasted only till the accession of Earl Grey and the Whigs to power in 1831. In 1835, during the short administration of Sir Robert Peel, Sir Edward Sugden was Lord Chancellor of Ireland. He afterwards took an active part in the

February, 1852, on the accession of Lord Derby to the premiership, Sir Edward Sugden was appointed Lord Chancellor of England, and created a peer as Lord St. Leonards ; he had, however, again to resign the post at the close of the same year, but continued to take an active part in politics as an adherent of his party.

When Lord St. Leonards died, in the year 1875, no will could be found ; accordingly the succession to this place became a matter of family dispute, which eventually was settled on his second son, the Hon. and Rev. Frank Sugden, the present owner.

Ditton House adjoins the grounds of Boyle Farm on the east, and has a finely-wooded lawn, extending down to the water's edge. The mansion, which is now the property and residence of Mr. William

W. Fitzwilliam Dick, of Humewood, county Wicklow, was formerly the seat of a brother of the late Lord Darnley, the Hon. Edward Bligh, who died here in 1841.

In a secluded and pleasant nook of the river, close by Boyle Farm, stands the "Swan," a favourite inn for anglers. It commands a pretty view of the river, and of the palace and grounds of Hampton Court, on the opposite bank. The old tavern, with its contiguous grounds, abuts upon the water-side, and has long been famous in the annals of the angler. The Thames Angling Preservation Society have under their care two "deeps" at Ditton, one opposite Boyle Farm, rather more than 500 yards in length, and the other a little to the north, off Keene's Wharf, extending 250 yards.

One of the great lovers and haunters of this part of the Thames was that disciple of Izaak Walton, Mr. T. F. Salter, the author of the "Anglers' Guide," &c. Mr. Salter was originally a hatter in London, his shop being near Charing Cross. He there, by industry and indefatigable civility, amassed a competency, and was enabled to retire to a snug "box," within the influences, as it were, of his favourite haunts, the river Lea banks and two or three houses of call for fishermen, at which he was rejoiced to meet any brother-fisherman. The following tribute to this worthy, by a "brother of the angle," and written in imitation of the style of Pope and Dryden, was published a few years ago :—

"Ye who by silent waters take your stand,
  And poise the pliant rod with cautious hand,
  Your eye intent upon the wave to note
  Each flattering bubble of the buoyant float ;
  Or bolder tread the streamlet's bank to ply
  With agile arm the well-directed fly,
  As circling eddies ripple into spray,
  And mark where finny gluttons strike their prey ;
  Or ye who still, a band of brothers, meet
  In periodic pride in some retreat,
  Which Lea or Thames or royal Hampton bears
  To please the angler or to plume his wares.
  Pause for awhile amidst your pastime dear
  To give a sigh about our patriarch's bier !
  To him who was the Nestor of our art,
  Who joy'd its richest secrets to impart :
  Who taught us best our quiet course to run,
  Waved his light rod, and showed how trouts were won:
  Who shar'd our labours, and who join'd our play,
  Allured to exercise and led the way :
  Grieve that his shadow darkens not your door—
  That Salter, modern *Walton,* is no more ! "

Mr. S. C. Hall writes, in his " Book of the Thames ":—" Time out of mind Thames Ditton has been in favour with the punt-fisher, not alone because sport was always abundant there—its pretty aits, close beds of rushes, and overhanging osiers being nurseries of fish—but because the river is especially charming 'hereabouts,' and there are many associations connected with the fair scenery that greatly augment its interest to those who enjoy the recreation of the 'contemplative man.' All anglers, therefore, are familiar with the pleasures to be found in this quiet and attractive nook of the Thames. Our own memory," adds Mr. Hall, " recalls to us a day we cannot soon forget : it was passed in a punt with Theodore Hook—a lover of the gentle art, as many have been to whom 'society' and the gaieties of life were necessities. Hook was in strong health at that time—it was in the year 1834—the fountain of his wit was in full and uninterrupted flow ; it is not difficult to imagine, therefore, the stores of incident and humour that were opened up between the first cast of the plummet into the stream and the winding-up of the reel when the declining light gave notice that refreshment was provided at 'The Swan.'" Mr. Hall appends as a foot-note to the above some lines which Hook produced on that occasion. They were composed in the punt, afterwards written down, and they were printed, but not with Theodore Hook's name, in the *New Monthly Magazine* for July, 1834 :—

" When sultry suns and dusty streets
    Proclaim town's *winter* season,
  And rural scenes and cool retreats
    Sound something like high treason,—
  I steal away to shades serene,
    Which yet no bard has lit on,
  And change the bustling, heartless scene
    For quietude and DITTON.

" Here lawyers, free from legal toils,
    And peers released from duty,
  Enjoy at once kind Nature's smiles,
    And eke the smiles of beauty :
  Beauty with talent brightly graced,
    Whose name must not be written,
  The idol of the fane, is placed
    Within the shades of DITTON.

" Let lofty mansions great men keep—
    I have no wish to rob 'em—
  Not courtly Claremont, Esher's steep,
    Nor Squire Combe's at Cobham.
  Sir Hobhouse has a mansion rare,
    A large red house, at Whitton,
  But Cam with Thames I can't compare,
    Nor Whitton class with DITTON.

" I'd rather live, like General Moore,
    In one of the pavilions
  Which stand upon the other shore,
    Than be the king of millions ;

> For though no subjects might arise
>   To exercise my wit on,
> From morn till night I'd feast my eyes
>   By gazing at sweet DITTON.
>
> "The mighty queen whom Cydnus bore,
>   In gold and purple floated,
> But happier I when near this shore,
>   Although more humbly boated.
> Give *me* a punt, a rod, a line,
>   A snug arm-chair to sit on,
> Some well-iced punch, and weather fine,
>   And let me fish at DITTON.
>
> "The 'Swan,' snug inn, good fare affords
>   As table e'er was put on,
> And worthier quite of loftier boards
>   Its poultry, fish, and mutton ;
> And while sound wine mine host supplies,
>   With beer of Meux or Tritton,
> Mine hostess, with her bright blue eyes,
>   Invites to stay at DITTON.
>
> "Here, in a placid waking dream,
>   I'm free from worldly troubles,
> Calm as the rippling silver stream
>   That in the sunshine bubbles ;
> And when sweet Eden's blissful bowers
>   Some abler bard has writ on,
> Despairing to transcend his powers,
>   I'll *ditto* say for DITTON."

Thames Ditton contains within its bounds the manor of Claygate, the manor of Imworth, or Imber Court, and the manor, or reputed manor, of Weston; besides which, there are in the parish lands pertaining to the manors of Kingston, Molesey, and Sandon. In the "Domesday Book" it is stated that "Wadard holds of the Bishop (of Bayeux) *Ditone*, in the hundred of Kingstone ; " and it included the rich manors of Claygate and Weston, the former belonging to the abbots of Westminster, and the latter to the nuns of Barking.

Claygate, or Cleygate, as the name is sometimes written, is a pleasant and picturesque district, lying to the south of the village of Thames Ditton, having the hamlet of Hook and the parish of Chessington on its eastern side, and the parish of Esher, with the royal domain of Claremont—with which we shall deal presently—as its western boundary. In the "Domesday Book" it is stated that "the Abbot of Westminster holds Claigate." The manor appears to have been given to the abbot and convents of Westminster by Tosti, probably a son of Earl Godwin. Edward the Confessor confirmed the grant, and the confirmation was renewed by charters of Stephen, Henry. II., and Edward I. On the suppression of monasteries by Henry VIII., the conventual property fell into the hands of the king. Towards the end of the sixteenth century the manor of Claygate became the pro-

perty of George Evelyn, of Long Ditton, whose mother was the daughter of David Vincent, a former owner, who died seized of it in 1565. The estate continued in the possession of the Evelyns for about a century. It afterwards passed, through the marriage of an heiress, into the hands of Sir Stephen Glyn, who, according to Manning and Bray's "Surrey," in 1691 held a court here as lord of the manor in right of his wife. Later on, the manor was purchased by the Lord Chancellor King, whose descendant, Lord Lovelace, is the present owner.

The district is almost entirely agricultural ; but the hand of the builder is busy at work, and houses are beginning to spring up, with the result that its rural aspect is rapidly changing. The principal residence in this locality, Ruxley Lodge, is the seat of Lord Foley, who, next to Lord Lovelace, is the chief landowner in the neighbourhood. Ruxley Lodge, being situated on high ground, commands some extensive views over the surrounding country.

In 1841 Claygate was formed into a separate parish for ecclesiastical purposes, having been cut off from the civil parish of Thames Ditton. The church, dedicated to the Holy Trinity, is a stone building in the Decorated style. It was built in 1840, and enlarged in 1866. It is cruciform in plan, with a baptistery and tower, and some of the windows are filled with painted glass.

Manning, in his "History of Surrey," represents Imber as having been formerly included in Weston; but according to Brayley "it was certainly a distinct manor in the time of Henry III., when it belonged to a family designated from it, for in 1223 Ralph de Immeworth died seized of it and of the hundred of Emle-brigg." The manor was subsequently owned by the knightly family of Brewes, or Braose, and later on fell into the possession of Thomas, Duke of Norfolk, as heir general of that family. When Henry VIII. created the "honour" of Hampton Court, he obtained the manor of Imworth, either by exchange or purchase, and annexed it to the chase of Hampton Court. With respect to this transaction, we glean the following from Lysons' "Parishes of Middlesex" :—"The jurisdiction of the honour of Hampton Court extended over the parish of Thames Ditton, as well as several other parishes in Surrey and Middlesex, in the neighbourhood of the Thames. The chase was established by an Act of Parliament in 1538, for the especial convenience of the king (then grown old and corpulent), that he might enjoy his favourite amusement of hunting without going far from his palace of Hampton Court. It was enclosed with paling, and stocked with deer, to the great annoyance and injury of the agricultural population of the several parishes. During the remaining part of the reign of King Henry the grievance seems to have been borne without any attempt to obtain redress ; but soon after the decease of that prince, the inhabitants of Thames Ditton and other parishes joined in a petition to the Lord Protector Somerset and the Council of State for relief. The petitioners complained that their common meadows and pastures were taken in, and all the parishes overlaid with deer, many households let fall down, and families decayed, and the country made desolate, and that the king lost a great sum by the defalcation of yearly rents. In consequence of this application, a commission was issued to John Godewin and John Carleton, Esqrs., to examine twenty-four of the most substantial and discreet men on certain articles, devised by the Chancellor and the rest of the king's council. On the inquisition taking place, 'it was found that besides the damage to the king's subjects, the king lost in rents £84 1s. 2½d. ; and was besides charged with fees, annuities, costs of hay, &c., to the amount of £89 11s. 3½d. ; together with the loss of woods and coppices ; that this chase was lately erected in the latter days of the king, when he waxed heavy with sickness, age, and corpulency, and might not travel so readily abroad, but was constrained to seek his game and pleasure ready and at hand ; that his loving subjects were content, for his comfort and ease, to suffer, trusting of sufficient amends to be had after ; that within ten or twelve years the pale itself will decay, and that the making of the same new will be an importable cost, as it was thought in manner not possible to recover so much timber as may make the pale again in these parts of the realm.' In compliance with the prayer of this petition, the lands which had been enclosed were ordered to be de-chased ; the deer were removed to Windsor Forest or elsewhere ; and the estates included in the chase were restored to their former tenants at the old rents."

In 1630 the manor of Imber was granted to Dudley Carleton, Viscount Dorchester, who died in the following year, bequeathing it, together with Sandon, to his nephew, Sir Dudley Carleton, who resided at Imber Court in 1639, when he had a licence to erect a chapel on the south side of the parish church ; this, however, was not carried into effect. The estate soon after changed hands, and in 1720 it was settled by the then owner, Mr. Henry Bridges, on his niece, Ann Bridges, on her marriage with Mr. Arthur Onslow, afterwards Speaker of the House of Commons, and who made Imber Court

his principal country seat. His son, Lord Cranley, in 1784, sold the manor to a Mr. George Porter, who shortly after sold it to Sir Francis Ford. He in turn conveyed it to Mr. Robert Taylor, on whose death it devolved on Sir Charles Sullivan, in right of his wife, the only daughter of Mr. Taylor. In 1862 the property was purchased by the late Mr. Charles J. Corbett.

The Court, which, by the way, was for a time the residence of Sir Francis Burdett, is a large, square, brick-built mansion, stucco-fronted, with wings extending to the right and left of the principal front, the latter being added towards the end of the last century. The house stands well back from the roadway, the carriage-drive being approached through handsomely-wrought iron gates. The Mole flows through the grounds, on its way to join the Thames at East Molesey.

The roadway from Thames Ditton to Molesey skirts the palings of Imber Court, and winds along between flat, low-lying meadows and market-gardens, well watered by streams and narrow brooklets, whose sides are fringed with stunted willows. The Moleseys, East and West, are both included in Domesday Book, under *Molesham*, the "home or town by the Mole." The derivation of the present name of Molesey would seem to point to *ey*, an island, here formed by the river Mole dividing into two channels on entering the parish, and thus constituting a triangular tract of land near its junction with the Thames.

This would seem to be the best occasion to make a few remarks on the River Mole, which one poet calls " the silent," whilst no less a poet than Milton celebrates it as—

"The sullen Mole, that runneth underground."

Spenser, in his " Marriage of the Thames and Medway," writes :—

"And Mole, that like a mousling mole, doth make
His way still underground till Thames he overtake."

Drayton, too, thus sweetly mentions the fact of its junction with the Thames :—

" 'Gainst Hampton Court he meets the soft and gentle Mole,"

and is a little inclined to stay and dally with her. But this displeases the parents of Thames, who are anxious to hasten him on to his nuptials with the Medway.

" But Thames would hardly on ; oft turning back to show
From his much-loved Mole how loth he was to go.
The mother of the Mole, old Holmesdale, likewise beares
Th' affection of her childe as ill as they do theirs."

The river itself has its sources near Worth and Rusper, in Tilgate Forest, just over the Sussex border, and runs past Dorking, Leatherhead, and Cobham.

Antiquarians are at variance as to the real origin of its name. Some think that it comes from *Mola*, the Latin word for a mill, and that it was so termed from the number of mills that it turns—twenty of which are mentioned in "Domesday Book." But Latin words did not come into common use till the Norman Conquest, and the river was known as the Mole in the Anglo-Saxon times; and very few, if any, of our rivers bear Roman names—in this respect unlike our cities. Our poets, very naturally, have chosen the more poetical and symbolical derivation; and they, and historians and topographers after them, have made the most of the fact that the river does burrow underground occasionally. Thus, for instance, in a map in the Oxford edition of Camden's "Britannia," published in 1698, we find written under the entire sketch of the river, from near Leatherhead to Box Hill, the words "The river runneth underground." The burrowing propensities of this river, however, have been greatly over-stated.

Thus Camden bears testimony to this strange property of the river, that "after it has run several miles, being opposed by hills, it finds or makes itself a way under ground, and bursts out again so far off that the inhabitants thereabout boast, as the Spaniards do of their river the Anus, that they feed divers flocks upon a bridge."

Its eccentric flow is caused by the porous and cavernous nature of the chalky and gravelly soil over which it runs during several miles of its course below Dorking. When its waters are at their usual height no irregularity is noticed in its course; but in seasons of excessive drought its waters are absorbed through the hollows, or "swallows," as they are termed, and the channel is left dry, with the exception of a few stagnant pools. Near the bridge at Thorncroft the waters rise again to the surface, and flow on without further interruption.

"Soon after passing Esher the Mole separates into two branches: the one runs by Imber Court and near Thames Ditton, so favourite a resort of Thames anglers; the other flows towards Molesey Hurst, notorious in past days as the scene of many prize pugilistic encounters. The banks of the Mole here are low and marshy, and there is little more that is attractive in its course till its union with the Thames, nearly opposite Hampton Court. Near its termination we pass through the pretty rustic village of East Molesey, which takes its name from our river. Here it works a large factory-like and most unpicturesque mill. The termination of the Mole is a noble one. From its mouth the Thames, with Hampton Court on the opposite bank, forms a picture of surpassing beauty, and that magnificent palace is nowhere seen to greater advantage."

It was not on this river, as often stated, but on its neighbour, the Wey, that the first locks in this country were made.

The parish of East Molesey has the Thames for its northern boundary, and the Mole on the east and south-east, whilst on the south it borders upon Esher, and on the west it unites with West Molesey. The village is a straggling and scattered place, built principally by the sides of the road running westward through West Molesey to Walton-on-Thames. It lies opposite to Hampton Court, with which it is united by an iron girder-bridge, which we have already described in our account of Hampton Court.* The village has increased in population very considerably of late years, having risen from 2,400 in 1871 to 3,300 in 1881.

The Hampton Court Station, a terminus of a branch of the South-Western Railway, is in this village; near it a large number of new houses have of late years sprung up, and a new ecclesiastical district formed, known as Kent-Town-on-Thames. The church of this new district, dedicated to St. Paul, was built in 1856.

The old parish church, St. Mary's, was a mean-looking structure, rudely built, and consisting of a nave and chancel, with low wooden tower rising above the roof at the west end. The east windows, consisting of three divisions in the Pointed style, with smaller lights above, were somewhat of a relief to the otherwise humble appearance of the building. The church was considerably damaged by fire in 1863, and soon afterwards was entirely taken down, and a new and much larger church built in its place. The new church, built of flint and stone, is in the Early English style, and consists of a nave, chancel, and aisles, with a tower and spire at the north-west corner. The foundation stone of a new south aisle was laid in 1883. Some of the windows of the south aisle are filled with painted or stained glass, the east window containing a representation of the Ascension, among the others being the Good Shepherd, St. John, and St. Peter. The old church contained several sepulchral memorials and hatchments, some of which have been replaced in the new building. Among them is a brass to "Anthonie Standen, Gent. . . . Cupbearer to the King of Scotland, sometime Lord Darley (Darnley), father to King James, now of England, and also sworne Servant to his Majestie," who died in 1611. A handsome tablet, ornamented with emblems of

---

* See Vol. I., p. 135.

naval warfare, commemorates Admiral Sir John Sutton, who died in 1825; and another is in memory of Admiral Sir Edmund Nagle, and Mary, his wife, both of whom died at their residence at East Molesey, the former in 1830, and the latter six years afterwards. Another tablet recorded the burial here of Sir George (Blackman) Harnage, who was created a baronet in 1821, and who assumed the name of Harnage by royal licence, "in virtue of his maternal descent from an ancient family of

lars respecting the descent of the Manor of East Molesey:—"The Priory of Merton, in Surrey, was founded in the reign of Henry I. by Gilbert le Norman, who is supposed to have given this manor as part of the endowment of the convent, for which a quit-rent of 7s. 6d. a year was paid to the corporation of Kingston. . . . In 10 Henry VIII. the prior and convent demised to Sir Thomas Heneage, for sixty-six years, the manor of East Mulsey, with all their land and all their tithes in the

THE THAMES AT MOLESEY.

precinct of Est Mulsey and Thames Ditton, and their live stock there— namely, 11 oxen, price of each 12s.; 1 sow, 2s. 6d.; 2 hogs, each 2s. 8d.; 8 pigs, each 12d., and 5 pigs, each 4d.: for which he was to pay at Christmas and Easter, in money £12—namely, £6 at each festival, and to deliver at Christmas 6 capons, value 2s.; 6 geese, value 2s.; 6 hens, 1s. 6d.; 10 quarters of wheat, value £3 6s. 8d.; 10 quarters of rye, £2 10s.; 30 quarters of barley, £5; and 30 quarters of oats, £3; in all, £26 2s. 2d.

that name, who held a high rank in the county of Salop in the time of Edward III." He died in 1836.

The village of East Molesey was granted by Charles II. to Sir James Clarke, whose grandson had a ferry thence to Hampton Court, "in the room whereof he built a bridge, which, in 1753, was replaced by a light wooden structure." This latter bridge was superseded by a more substantial structure, also of wood, which has given place to the one above referred to.

At Molesey Park was formerly an extensive powder-mill, situated on the Mole, which flows through the grounds.

Brayley's "Surrey" gives the following particu-

"Henry VIII., when engaged in making the 'Chase' of Hampton, wished him to have possession of the manor and estate of East Molesey, or Molesey Prior, for which he gave in exchange to the fraternity of Merton lands, tenements, advowsons, &c., belonging to the priory of Calewiche, in Staffordshire. Thereon, 'John, Priour of the monastery of our Blessed Lady of Marten, in the county of Surrey, and the Convent in 27 Henry VIII., conveyed to the king all their manor of Est Mulsey, and all their titles, oblations, and profits in Est Mulsey, parcel of the parsonage of Kingston, and all their lands, &c., in Est Mulsey or elsewhere, reputed parcel of the said manor.'

"This Sir Thomas Heneage was counsel to the Prior of Merton, and resided at East Molesey, in a mansion he had himself erected. The estate, which he held on lease from the priory of Merton, becoming the property of the Crown, he resigned it, and obtained from the king a new grant of Molesey Prior. . . . . This lease expired in 1584; but in 1571 Anthony Crane obtained from Elizabeth the reversion of the manor, which included a mansion house, with 128 acres of land, at the same rent at which it was held by Sir Thomas Heneage." Subsequent grants of the manor for terms of years were made to different persons, and it is now held by a member of the family of Lord Hotham.

Mr. M. F. Tupper speaks of "tasting the Spa water near East Molesey." The chalybeate spring here referred to, which is generally called "the Spa," is situated in a meadow called Kemp's Eyot, and is walled in. It is on the road from East Molesey to Hampton Ferry, and is reported to have been formerly much visited by parties from Hampton Court.

JOHN WILSON CROKER.
(*From a Painting by S. Drummond, A.R.A.*)

Kemp's Eyot, or Ait—once a small island—was probably so named from a former landowner in this parish, a Mr. Thomas Kemp, of Laleham, Middlesex, who in 1730 bequeathed a rent-charge of 10s. for the young men of East Molesey "to ring and make merry with on the 6th of August yearly, in remembrance of the donor."

An annual amateur regatta is held here in July. The ferry serves as a communication between the village of Hampton and a broad flat space abutting upon the river, called Molesey Hurst, a spot formerly notorious for the pugilistic contests and duels fought there. Here, in 1807, was fought a great prize-fight between Cribb and Belcher, two celebrated pugilists, and resulted in the defeat of the latter. The fight was witnessed by a vast concourse of persons, the number being estimated at about 10,000, besides

"many hundreds of carriages, horses, carts, &c." Among the members of the aristocracy present were the Duke of Kent, Lord Archibald Hamilton, Lord Kinnaird, and Richard Brinsley Sheridan —the law-makers being also law-breakers. The Hon. Berkeley Craven acted as judge.

Molesey Hurst was at one time a famous spot for cricket matches, particularly between the years 1825 and 1840.* In August, 1775, if we may believe a newspaper, the place was "enlivened by an extraordinary cricket-match, played between six unmarried against six married women; it was won by the former, although one of the latter scored seventeen notches."

Mr. M. F. Tupper writes of the "dust-stained sod of Molesey Hurst, now happily better known as the Hampton Racecourse." The races take place annually in the summer, and bringing down large herds of betting men from London, are voted a nuisance by the neighbourhood.

West Molesey, as its name implies, is situated on the west side of the river Mole. The church, which stands in the centre of the village, is a plain, uninteresting building of brick, consisting of nave and chancel, with a tower, constructed of stone and flint, at the west end. The tower is the only remaining part of the old church, the rest having been rebuilt in 1843. A new aisle was added in 1859. A marble tablet on the north wall commemorates General Sir George Berkeley, a gallant Peninsular and Waterloo officer, who died in 1857, and was buried here. In the chancel are two small brasses of female figures, but the inscriptions are gone. The new cemetery for the united parishes of East and West Molesey is near the church. It is only about an acre in extent, and has a small mortuary chapel.

Mole Lodge, West Molesey, is the country seat of Alderman Sir Robert Walter Carden, one of the owners of the *Times*, and formerly Lord Mayor of London.

Robert Baddeley, the actor who left the bequest

* See Lillywhite's "Cricket Scores."

of £100 to Drury Lane for a twelfth cake to be washed down with wine, lived here in a house by the river-side, nearly opposite to Garrick's villa at Hampton. In addition to his above-mentioned bequest he left this villa to poor Thespians, "pensioners of the Theatrical Fund, who might not object to live together," thereby anticipating the Dramatic College at Woking. That their dignity might not be wounded by appearing dependent on charity, he left also a small sum to be distributed by these four recipients of his charity among their poorer neighbours. Altogether, Mr. Baddeley would seem to have been impregnated with the milk of human kindness, and to have possessed also a keen knowledge of the weaknesses of human nature. Mr. Robert Baddeley died in 1794. He is said to have been in early life a pastrycook, and to have been in the service of Foote, or to have had him as a customer and patron. In his day he made his mark on the stage, being the original representative of "Canton" in the *Clandestine Marriage*, and of "Moses" in the *School for Scandal.*

Sir Robert Walpole lived here, on a small estate which he had purchased, called Molesey Grove, a little to the west of the village, the same which, a century later, was occupied by John Wilson Croker. Dean Swift, calling one day on Sir Robert Walpole, said to the Minister:—"For God's sake, Sir Robert, take me out of that cursed country (Ireland), and place me somewhere in England." "Mr. Dean," answered Sir Robert, "I should be glad to oblige you ; but just look at that tree : I transplanted it from Houghton to the banks of the Thames, but it is good for little or nothing here." The company understood the allusion and laughed, while the dean turned on his heel without saying another word.

Molesey Grove is a plain, unassuming stucco-fronted house, on the left-hand side of the Walton road, about a quarter of a mile from the village, and it is shut in and almost hidden from view from the roadway by a heavy whitewashed wall.

The Right Hon. John Wilson Croker came to live here many years after the death of Walpole. Croker was one of the most remarkable literary and political characters of his time. He was for many years well known in St. Stephen's, but he refused, like Sir Charles Wetherell, to hold a seat in that august assembly after the passing of the first Reform Bill. The administration of the Admiralty was for many years in his hands. He was, however, better known as one of the most trenchant and merciless of *Quarterly Reviewers*, and his attacks on his contemporaries made for him

many enemies. He bitterly attacked Lady Morgan when known first to fame as the authoress of "The Wild Irish Girl," whom he accused of falsehood, impiety, &c., from motives of personal dislike. In Lady Morgan, however, Croker found his match, and her sketch of him as Counsellor Crawley in her "Florence Macarthy" is, perhaps, one of the best satiric portraits ever penned. Mr. Disraeli and Lord Macaulay both levelled their lances at the reviewer. He was the original of Mr. Rigby in the "Coningsby" of the former ; and Macaulay's critique on Croker's edition of "Boswell's Life of Johnson" is one of the best known and the most brilliant of his literary and political "Essays." Mr. Croker never quite forgave the attack, which certainly ruined the reputation of the book.

Mr. Raikes, in his "Journal" (1836), tells the following amusing anecdote about Mr. Croker :— "Lord Fitzgerald made us laugh at dinner to-day with a story about Croker, whose pertinacity of opinion is well known. He was laying down the law after dinner to the Duke of Wellington, and according to custom asserting the superiority of his own information on all subjects, having even flatly contradicted the duke, who had mentioned some incident that took place at the battle of Waterloo. At last the conversation turned upon the use of percussion-caps for the muskets of the army, when Croker again maintained a directly opposite opinion to that which was urged by the duke, who at last good-humouredly said to him :—' My dear Croker, I can yield to your superior information on most points, and you may perhaps know a great deal more of what passed at Waterloo than myself, but as a sportsman I will maintain my point about the percussion-caps.' Croker's view of politics has now for some years been of the most gloomy cast, and so far does his wish for infallibility supersede his patriotism, that he absolutely seems to rejoice at any partial fulfilment of his prophecies, though it may thwart his own views and those of his party. Fitzgerald once said to Lord Wellesley at the castle :—' I have had a very melancholy letter from Croker this morning.' 'Ay !' said Lord Wellesley ; 'written, I suppose, in a strain of the most sanguine despondency.' "

Mr. Croker died here in 1855, and his memory is perpetuated by a bust in the parish church, where he is buried.

About half a mile beyond Molesey Grove, on the right of the road to Walton, lies the estate of Apps Court, mostly enclosed within an old wall of red brick. The manor of Apps—or Abbs, as it was formerly called—to which we have already incidentally referred,* is really in the parish of Walton, but a small portion of the ground, as will be seen by a reference to the map which accompanies this work, lies within the bounds of the parish of West Molesey, and within the limits of our jurisdiction. At the commencement of the last century the property belonged to Charles Montague, Earl of Halifax, who is said to have bequeathed it to "Mrs. Catherine Barton, during her life," "together with the rangership, house, and lodge of Bushey Park." This lady was the daughter of Sir Isaac Newton's half-sister, and for many years lived in Sir Isaac's house. After the death of Lord Halifax, she became the wife of a Mr. Conduitt, Newton's suc-

cessor as Master of the Mint. Apps Court, however, was afterwards sold, and it has since passed into the hands of various persons whose names are of no public interest. Of the "capital mansion" which is said to have once stood here nothing now remains. The present house, constructed of white brick, was built by Mr. J. Hamborough early in the present century. It has no architectural character of importance. In front, in the centre, is a small semi-circular portico, on each side of which are bows extending to the roof and ends of the building. The grounds are flat, but there is a pleasant lawn, and some fine oaks, elms, and cedars diversify the scenery.

CHAPTER XXXIV.

ESHER AND CLAREMONT.

"Oh! who can paint in verse those rising hills,
    Those gentle valleys, and their silver rills;
    Close groves, and opening glades with verdure spread,
    Flowers sighing sweets, and shrubs that balsams bleed?"—Sir Samuel Garth.

Situation of Esher—Its Etymology—The Manor of Sandon, now called Sandown—Sandon Hospital or Priory—Sandown Racecourse—The "Travellers' Rest"—Anna Maria and Jane Porter—The old Parish Church—Christ Church—Esher Place—Wolsey's Tower—The Fall of Wolsey—Descent of the Manor of Esher—The Right Hon. Henry Pelham—Claremont—The Estate purchased by Sir John Vanbrugh—Holles, Earl of Clare and Duke of Newcastle—Lord Clive and subsequent Owners—Death of Princess Charlotte—The Grounds of Claremont.

THE village of Esher, with the royal domain of Claremont, which we now approach—although lying partly "over the borders" of the area embraced in "Greater London"—are invested with so much historic interest, that we may be pardoned for inviting the reader to accompany us in imagination over this classic ground—a spot which has been hallowed by the footprints of Wolsey, and in more recent times by those of the great Lord Clive, "to whose genius England owes her Indian empire." It is a spot, too, rendered sacred by having been the favourite home of Queen Victoria in her early years, and at the present time it is the residence of her Majesty's youngest son, Prince Leopold, Duke of Albany.

Esher is pleasantly situated on a hill to the south of Thames Ditton and Molesey, the lofty spire of its handsome new church rising above the trees with which it is surrounded, and being visible for miles round. The old Portsmouth road, in its course from Kingston and Thames Ditton, passes through the village, near which rise the woody heights of Claremont, and which, although but a few short miles from London, is still exceedingly rural and pretty.

Esher is so called from the old Saxon Æschealh—i.e., Ash-haugh (as Ashton is formed from Æsctun). The word "haugh" seems to denote a water-side pasture.* The name is mentioned by Shakespeare as Asher, and it appears to have been so spelt in the time of Henry VIII. In "Domesday Book" it figures as Aissela or Aissele, in the reign of John as Ashal, and in the following reign as Assere. It is suggested by a writer in *Notes and Queries* that the name may have been connected with the Welsh word Asserw, which meant "sparkling" or "glittering," in allusion to the river Mole. But the Mole is a sluggish, not a sparkling river, as it winds along through the meadows hereabouts to the west of the village, on its way to join the Thames at East Molesey. These meadows are green and pleasant in summer, but too apt to be flooded in winter.

On the north side of the parish, at Ditton Marsh, is the Esher and Claremont station of the South-Western Railway, whence the roadway skirting the grounds of Claremont leads up to the village, which is about three-quarters of a mile distant. Sandon Farm, close by the station, occupies the site of an hospital or priory which formerly stood here. The

---

* See Vol. I., p. 142.

* See *Notes and Queries*, March 26, 1881 p. 255.

Manor of Sandon (now called Sandown) lies partly in the parish of Esher, but extends into those of Walton, West Molesey, and Thames Ditton. It was conveyed to Henry VIII. in exchange for other lands in Essex; but in the first year of Edward VI. it was granted to John Dudley, Earl of Warwick. Coming, however, again into the hands of the king, Charles I. granted it, together with the manors of Imber, in Thames Ditton, as already stated, to Dudley Carleton, Viscount Dorchester.* After successive transfers, it was purchased, about the middle of the last century, by Mr. Arthur Onslow, Speaker of the House of Commons, then resident at Imber Court.

The hospital was dedicated to the Holy Ghost, though it was sometimes called the Hospital of St. Mary and All Saints. It was founded in the reign of Henry II. by Robert de Wateville, and was enriched by subsequent benefactions, one of which, by William de Percy, the founder of the Abbey of Salley, in Yorkshire, provided for the maintenance of six chaplains, and the keeping of "a lamp and candle of 2 lb. weight continually burning before the altar of the Virgin Mary in the hospital chapel (where the heart of William de Percy and the body of his consort Joan were interred), during the time that any mass was said at any altar in that chapel, on pain of the bishop's censure, and distress on their lands by the heirs of the founder." † In the middle of the fourteenth century the inmates of the hospital were swept down by a pestilence; and in 1436, on a plea of its reduced condition, it was united to the Hospital of St. Thomas, in Southwark, and at the Dissolution shared the fate of the other monastic establishments. In the reign of James I. the chapel of Sandon was granted to John, Earl of Mar, but it was afterwards re-annexed to the Crown. No vestiges of the building are now to be found. Part of the site of the priory is now occupied by a mansion, the property of Mr. James P. Currie, and the remainder, some 150 acres in extent, was, about the year 1870, formed into a racecourse, known as Sandown Park; it occupies some sloping ground close by the Esher railway station, and to the north of the high road.

Sandown has become known to the fashionable world of late years as the most select and exclusive racecourse in the kingdom. Here no "Derby" element intrudes itself: it is pre-eminently the ladies' racecourse. There are usually six meetings in the year: two in spring, two in summer, and two in autumn. The summer meetings are the best attended, and special trains are run on the

South-Western railway for the convenience of members. As there is considerable difficulty in being elected a member of the Sandown Club, and as members cannot admit male friends under any pretext whatever, the gatherings become altogether unique. Ladies are admitted by members on payment of ten shillings for the day, or they may become members of the Club themselves. On a hot day it is delightful to lounge beneath the trees, looking on at the races, and listening to the strains of the Hungarian Band, sometimes varied with that of a Highland regiment playing their bagpipes up in the wood; and it does not require any great stretch of the imagination to fancy oneself "hundreds of miles" from the smoke of town.

The members' stands and luncheon-rooms are most complete, and gaily decorated with scarlet and white—the club colours. There is a very pretty royal box in the members' enclosure, and the Prince and Princess of Wales are generally there, with other members of the Royal Family. The Prince is generally to be seen walking about, field-glass in hand, looking up his friends in his own cheery way. One particular feature of these gatherings is that the "correct cards of the races" are sold by pretty little girls verging on their teens, in fancy costume, sometimes as *Vivandières*, or fish-wives, or the Directoire dress, which is very becoming. In fact, one may say of Sandown Races that they more nearly resemble a garden-party on a large scale, with the racing thrown in.

On the slope of the hill, near the entrance to the village of Esher, is a small rustic building, constructed of flint and stone, which has been not inaptly named the "Travellers' Rest." In Mr. Howitt's "Visits to Remarkable Places" it is called Wolsey's Well; but from the initials, H. P., and the *buckle*, part of the family arms of Pelham, it would appear to have been erected by Mr. Pelham, brother of the Duke of Newcastle, by whom the neighbouring mansion of Esher Place was owned in the early part of the last century. The Travellers' Rest consists of three arched recesses, the centre one containing a seat for the weary wayfarer. Close by it is a well of clear and sparkling water.

Anna Maria Porter, the distinguished novelist, who lies buried in Esher old church, lived for many years with her mother in a small cottage in the village. Mr. S. C. Hall writes, in his "Book of the Thames":—"So far back as the year 1825 we visited the accomplished sisters, Jane and Anna Maria Porter, at their pretty cottage. . . . A tomb was erected by her daughters over the remains of Mrs. Porter; it gives the date of her birth

---

* See *ante*, p. 280.   † Dugdale's "Monasticon."

and death, and contains this memorable passage :—

'RESPECT HER GRAVE, FOR SHE MINISTERED TO THE POOR.'

It is in the churchyard; a cypress flourishes at the head of the grave. Not long after the death of her mother Anna Maria was laid by her side. . . . . While at Esher the sisters were in the wane of life, but having good health, and still occasionally writing, enjoying honourable repose, having obtained a large amount of fame, and being in easy and comfortable circumstances. Anna Maria, although the youngest, died first, Jane surviving her sister several years."

The old church, dedicated to St. George, has been left standing chiefly on account of the monuments which it contains. It is situated at the back of the "Bear" Inn, on the east side of the main street. It is small, consisting of a nave and chancel, with a projection on the south side, built by the Duke of Newcastle to contain the private sittings of the owners of Claremont and Esher Place. Among the monuments preserved here is one, by Flaxman, to the Hon. Mrs. Ellis, of Claremont, who died in 1803. Over the altar is a picture of the Saviour, which was painted by Sir R. Ker Porter, brother of the sisters Jane and Anna Maria mentioned above, the tomb of whose mother, "Jane Porter, a Christian widow," is in the churchyard. According to Mr. M. F. Tupper, the old church possesses a bell brought from San Domingo by Sir Francis Drake.

The new church, called Christ Church, stands by the Green, on the opposite side of the street. It was erected in 1853 by Mr. Benjamin Ferrey, F.S.A., and is large and cruciform, in the Early English style, the south transept serving the purpose of a private pew for the royal owners of Claremont. The windows of the chancel are filled with stained glass, and there is a handsome stone reredos, carved with a representation of the Resurrection, given by Mr. Robert Few, in memory of his wife, who died in 1878. At the west end of the church is a marble monument to Prince Leopold of Saxe-Coburg, the first King of the Belgians, who formerly resided at Claremont; this monument was removed hither from St. George's Chapel, Windsor, where it had been first erected by her Majesty Queen Victoria. Here also is a marble figure, in a kneeling posture, erected by Sir Francis Drake in memory of his father, Richard Drake, sometime equerry to Queen Elizabeth, who died in 1609. This was removed from the old church by Sir William Drake. The tower at the west end is surmounted by a tall spire. In the churchyard lies buried Mr. Samuel Warren, Q.C., many years M.P. for Midhurst and Recorder of Hull, and afterwards a Master in Lunacy. He was the author of "Ten Thousand a Year," "Now and Then," and other works. His son is now rector here.

On the high road, at the Green, is a handsome granite drinking-fountain, which was presented by the queen to the village to take the place of a disused pump given by the Comte de Paris; it bears the inscription :—"Presented to the Parish of Esher by her Majesty Queen Victoria, 1877."

The grounds of Esher Place extend from the village down to the banks of the Mole. Here, about a mile from Esher station, and in the rear of Sandown Park, stands a curious Gothic building, a castellated gateway, which is always styled in the neighbourhood "Wolsey's Tower." Though it was not built by that statesman, it was once tenanted by him, shortly before his fall from the king's good graces, and when he had begun to have reason to cry aloud—

"Farewell, a long farewell, to all my greatness."

And doubtless here he often walked at eventide; and on the grassy banks of the Mole, which flowed deep and full beneath his windows, mused upon the transitory nature of royal favour.

This gateway is all that remains of a house which, from a survey of the manor of Esher taken early in the reign of Edward VI., appears to have been "sumptuously built, with divers offices, and an orchard and gardens." There was also, we are told, a park adjoining, three miles in circuit, well stocked with deer.

In the early part of the last century the mansion of Esher Place—as its successor is still called—consisted of little more than the old tower, or gatehouse, above mentioned; but Mr. Henry Pelham, brother of the Duke of Newcastle, and then owner of the property, made considerable additions to the building, in a style supposed to correspond with the original, but it must be owned rather in the gingerbread Gothic fashion of Strawberry Hill. The additions, consisting of wings and offices, were designed by Kent, the architect of the eastern front of Kensington Palace; but they were inferior to the central part of the edifice, and, as Walpole himself remarks, "were proofs how little he conceived either the principles or graces of the Gothic architecture."

The name of Kent, however, whom Walpole styles "the inventor of an art that realises painting," has been inseparably connected by the poet with

"Esher's peaceful grove,
Where Kent and Nature vie for Pelham's love."

Several engravings of the house and grounds at Esher have been published at different times. One of the earliest is a bird's-eye view by Knyff and Kip, taken when the estate (with the manor of Esher) belonged to Mr. Thomas Cotton, in the reign of William and Mary. Another and larger plan, including both fronts of Mr. Pelham's mansion, together with four ornamental buildings, styled the Temple, Grotto, Hermitage, and Thatched House, was engraved by Rocque in 1737. Another

Aubrey, in his "Survey," tells us that Waynfleet, who held the see of Winchester from 1447 to 1486, erected a "stately brick mansion" on the banks of the Mole, within the park of Esher. It is described by Aubrey as "a noble house, built of the best burnt brick that I ever sawe, with a stately gate-house and hall. This stately house, a fit palace for a prince, was bought, about 1666, by a vintner of London, who is since broke, and the house was sold and pulled down to the ground about 1678."

WOLSEY'S TOWER.

view, showing the east front, was published in the same year by Buck; and in 1759 a large engraving of the west front was made by Luke Sullivan.

The gateway above mentioned, though it stands low, forms a most picturesque object when seen from the flat meadows on the opposite side of the stream, backed as it is by the dark foliage of the trees in the park which surrounds Esher Place; and it must be owned that it bears a striking resemblance to Wolsey's Gateway at Ipswich, and to the towers of Layer Marney and Leigh's Priory, in Essex. It owes its erection, however, to William of Waynfleet, Bishop of Winchester, nearly a century before the day of Wolsey's pride.

He adds :—"Over the gate-house, and on several other parts of the building he placed the armorial bearings of his own family and those of his see, sculptured in stone; and on the timber-work of the roof of the hall were carvings of angels supporting escutcheons, on which were inscribed in scrolls the words 'Tibi Christi,' and in the windows the sentence 'Sit Deo Gracia' was several times repeated." The interior of the tower comprises three storeys, but the apartments are small, and the floorings for the most part are so sadly decayed that it is dangerous to enter them. There is, however, within one of the octagonal turrets a very skilfully-wrought staircase of brick, in a good state of preservation, and in the roofing of which the principles of the construction of the oblique arch (a supposed invention of modern times) are practically exhibited. The windows, the door-frames, and the dressings, are of stone. In the character of the tower itself there are indications of an earlier period than that of Wolsey. Cavendish, in his "Life of Wolsey," speaks of the removal to Westminster (Whitehall) of "the new gallery which my lord had late before his fall newly set up at Asher;" and "the taking away thereof,"

other ventures in the way of building, gave instructions for the partial re-building of his house at Esher, which he fondly purposed to have made one of his residences after he had surrendered Hampton Court to his jealous sovereign. Many interesting circumstances relating to the last retirement of the great Lord Cardinal to Esher, on the declension of his favour with the royal tyrant, are mentioned by his biographers; but, unfortunately, there was no Pepys or Evelyn in the Tudor days

CLAREMONT.

he continues, "was to him corrosive—the which, indeed, discouraged him very sore to stay there any longer, for he was weary of that house at Asher, or with continual use it waxed unsavoury." This, it may be stated, is the only distinct notice which has appeared to connect Wolsey's name with any architectural works at Asher (or Esher) Place.

As might naturally be expected, the Bishops of Winchester occasionally resided on this pleasant spot, which was at the same time near the Court, and yet far removed from the bustle and strife of tongues. In fact, it was not their Lambeth, but their Addington. The historians of Surrey record the fact that Cardinal Wolsey, not content with his

to throw light upon his movements by the aid of a personal diary.

It may be remembered, however, that when the cardinal was at Whitehall, in the summer of 1529, and when the king sent the Dukes of Norfolk and Suffolk to demand back from him the Great Seal, Wolsey was ordered to retire to Esher; but the order being unaccompanied by any voucher of authority, the fallen chancellor refused to obey it until the return of the king's messengers next day with his Majesty's written commands. He then went by water to Putney, whence he rode leisurely to Esher. It was in the course of this journey that, being overtaken by one of the king's courtiers, who assured him that the storm would soon blow over, and that he stood really as high as ever in the tyrant's favour, he sent back his fool or jester, Patch, as a welcome present to his royal master.

For the rest of the story we have the "Chronicle" of "honest" John Stow to guide us. We read that Wolsey, having returned to Esher, continued there, with a numerous family of servants and retainers, for "the space of three or four weeks, without either beds, sheets, table-cloths, dishes to eat their meat on, or wherewithal to buy any; howbeit, there was good provision of all kinds of victual, and of beer and wine, whereof there was sufficient and plenty enough, but my lord was compelled of necessity to borrow of Master Arundell and of the Bishop of Carlisle plate and dishes both to drink in and to eat his meat in. Thus my lord, with his family, continued in this strange estate until after Halloweentide."

The cardinal then dismissed a large part of his attendants, and sent Thomas Cromwell, afterwards Earl of Essex, to London, to "take care of his interest at Court." But apparently Cromwell did not take much trouble in the matter, for though the charge of treason originally preferred against the cardinal was abandoned, Wolsey was subjected, as every reader of English history knows, to a *præmunire*, the result of which was to place him, with all his worldly goods and chattels, at the mercy of the king, his master.

During the next few weeks of Wolsey's existence our interest is fixed on the river-side at Esher. For it was here that, whilst his enemies were pursuing their plans for his destruction, the king sent him "gracious messages," betraying occasional symptoms of returning favour, first by Sir John Russell, and afterwards by the Duke of Norfolk; and it was whilst he was entertaining the duke here that Sir John Shelley, one of the judges, arrived for the purpose of obtaining—or, rather, of extorting—from Wolsey a formal cession of York House (Whitehall), the town mansion of the archbishops of that see.* We are told that the cardinal hesitated so much to execute this royal command that he put his pen to the parchment only upon being assured that the judges of the land considered it to be a lawful act and deed. It was thus, therefore, that, on finding all opposition vain, Wolsey did that which was required at his hands; but the deed threw him into a severe fit of illness. Dr. Butts, the Court physician, who came down to visit him here, was forced to go back to London with the news that his life was in danger; and it was here that, lying on his sick bed, Wolsey received the historic ring

which Henry, in a fit of ill-timed regret, sent to him with a "comfortable message." The latter was so far effectual, that the great statesman was somewhat cheered by the seeming kindness of his tyrannical master, and recovered for a time. It must, however, have been at Esher that the document was signed which alienated Whitehall from the prelates of York, and handed over that magnificent palace to the tender mercies of "Old Harry."

That he was "sick unto death" whilst here for the last time is clear from the cardinal's last letter to Stephen Gardiner, which is dated from Esher, and in which he writes:—"I pray yow at the reverens of God to helpe, that expedicion be usyd in my persu'ts, the delay whereof so replenyshth my herte with hevynes, that I can take no reste: not for any vague fere, but onely for the miserable condycion that I am presently yn, and lyclyhod to contynue yn the same, oneless that you, in whom ys myn assuryd truste, do helpe and releve me therein. For fyrst, contynuyng here in this mowest and corrup ayer, beyng enteryd into the passyon of the dropsy, *cum prostratione appetitûs et continuo insomnio*, I cannot lyve; wherefor, of necessyte I must be removyd to some other dryer ayer and place, where I may have comodyte of physycyans," &c.

A reference to Hume, or Froude, or to any other historian of the Tudor times, will serve to show the reader that only a few months subsequently the cardinal obtained permission from Henry to remove from Esher to Richmond, where he appears to have remained, making occasional expeditions to Esher, till his journey into Yorkshire, a few months previous to his death, which took place at the Abbey of Leicester, in November, 1530.

When Henry VIII. had resolved to constitute Hampton Court an "honour," and to make a "chase" around it, as stated above, he purchased several neighbouring estates, and among others that of Esher. In 1538, as we learn from Rymer's "Fœdera," Gardiner, Bishop of Winchester, conveyed to the king "his manor of Asher, in Asher, Ditton, Cobham, Kingston, and Walton, William Basyng, *alias* Kingswell, prior of the monastery and cathedral of St. Swithin, at Winchester, confirming the deed." In consequence of these acts, this manor, with other lands, was annexed to the "honour and chase of Hampton Court" in 1540. Ten years afterwards King Edward gave the office of chief keeper of the mansion of Esher, with its gardens and orchards, and that of Lieutenant of the Chace of Hampton Court, to John Dudley, Earl of Warwick, and John, Lord Lisle, his son, for their joint lives and the life of

* See "Old and New London," Vol. III., p. 68.

the survivor. The earl had a grant of the manor and park to himself and his heirs, but he soon reconveyed them to the king.

Bishop Gardiner obtained from Queen Mary the restoration to his see of this estate, described as the "lordship and manor of Eshere," with the park (part of the "honour" of Hampton Court), the rabbit warren, about 185 acres of land, and the land called Northwood, in Cobham, "to be held of the Crown in frankalmoigne."

In 1538 Queen Elizabeth bought this manor of the Bishop of Winchester, and very shortly afterwards granted it in the fee to Charles, Lord Howard of Effingham. The estate subsequently passed, probably by sale, to Richard Drake, Equerry to the Queen, who was in possession in 1603, in which year he died. His only son and heir, Francis Drake, held it in 1631, and five years later it had become the property of George Price, Esq. The manor was subsequently purchased by Thomas Pelham Holles, Earl of Clare, and afterwards Duke of Newcastle, Prime Minister to George II. and III., who built on part of the estate the mansion of Claremont, which, as we shall presently see, has since been rebuilt.

About the same time that the manor of Esher was sold to the Duke of Newcastle, the park and mansion-house of Esher, which had been separated from the manor, were disposed of to Mr. Peter de la Porte, one of the directors of the South Sea Company; but he possessed it only a few years, for on the breaking of that bubble the estates of the principal directors were seized under an Act of Parliament, and sold for the benefit of those proprietors of South Sea stock who had been deprived of their property by the practices of the general board. Esher Place was thereupon purchased by a Mr. Dennis Bond, who, in 1729, re-sold it to the Right Hon. Henry Pelham, brother of the Duke of Newcastle, who was celebrated as statesman in the reign of George II., and who soon made extensive alterations in the building. Few statesmen have been more highly eulogised by contemporary poets and other writers than Pelham. Thomson, in his "Seasons" (Summer), thus refers to

> "Claremont's terraced height and Esher's groves,
> Where in the sweetest solitude, embraced
> By the soft windings of the gentle Mole,
> From courts and senates Pelham found repose."

Edward Moore also, in an ode addressed to Pelham, and entitled "The Discovery," in which the goddess Virtue is portrayed as in search of an earthly abode, has sung the praises of the retired statesman in several stanzas. The two here quoted are selected as being peculiarly applicable to the place under notice :—

> "Long through the sky's wide pathless way
> The muse observed the Wand'rer stray,
>   And marked the last retreat ;
> O'er Surrey's barren heaths she flew,
> Descending like the silent dew
>   On Esher's peaceful seat.

> "There she beholds the gentle Mole,
> His pensive waters calmly roll
>   Amidst Elysian ground ;
> There through the windings of the grove
> She leads her family of Love,
>   And strews her sweets around."

By will, dated 1748, Mr. Pelham devised his lands in Esher to his eldest surviving daughter, Frances, on whose death, in 1804, they devolved on her nephew, Lewis Thomas, Lord Sondes. In the following year, however, his lordship sold the estate in parcels, by which means, according to the public prints of the day, he realised the good round sum of £37,000. Esher Place, and the park and other lands adjoining, were purchased by Mr. John Spicer, who pulled down what was left of the old house, with the exception of "Wolsey's Gateway," and with its materials erected a new mansion of brick, stuccoed in imitation of stone, on higher ground. The estate now belongs to Mrs. Wigram, the widow of Mr. Money Wigram, a member of the family of the late Sir Robert Wigram, of Walthamstow, Essex, merchant and Lord Mayor of London.

The new mansion commands extensive views, particularly towards the north-west and north-east points, the vale of the Thames, with all its delightful scenery, composing, as it were, the leading features of the intermediate landscape, whilst the hills of Harrow, Hampstead, and Highgate, unite with the horizon in the extreme distance. Independently of the extensive prospects obtained from the boldly-swelling heights of Esher, the home views in themselves possess great interest, both from variety and contrast. How far the creations of the landscape gardener may have contributed to this effect it is now too late to ascertain ; yet the natural undulations of the ground would seem to have required but little improvement from his conceptions. At all events, Kent, the landscape gardener, has the credit of having made alterations in conformity with the disposition of the ground and the range of scenery it commands. Within a sunken dell in that part of the grounds called the Wood is a large votive urn, standing on a pedestal of freestone, which, as it appears from the following inscription, was placed there as a grateful and be-coming record of the beneficence of Mr. Pelham by one whom he had patronised :—

> "HENRICO PELHAM, PATRONO SUO
> OPTIMO SEMPERQVE HONORATO,
> BENEFICIORVM GRATA VT DECVIT RECORDATIONE
> POSVIT.   J. R."

On the three other faces of the pedestal are bas-reliefs of Charon preparing to carry a disembodied spirit over the river Styx ; shepherds leaning upon a sarcophagus, on which are the words " Et in Arcadiâ Ego " ; and a mourning figure reclining against a column surmounted by a vase. The fol-lowing lines, adapted from the Odes of Horace, are annexed to these sculptures respectively :—

> " Tellus et Domus et placens Uxor linquenda.
> Nec Pudor aut Modus Desiderio.
> Debitâ spargens Lacrymâ Favillam."

The plantations of fir, beech, &c., which cover the heights, add much to the picturesque effect of the views in different parts, together with a remark-able holly-tree, the girth of which is between eight and nine feet. There are likewise several small ornamental buildings in the park ; but the prin-cipal feature of that description, as we have already shown, is the old brick tower, which formed part of " Asher Palace " when the estate belonged to the see of Winchester. The ivy by which it is now luxuriantly clothed was planted by the late owner, Mr. Spicer, when yet a boy.

The grounds of Esher Place adjoins those of Sandown Park, already described above.*

Claremont lies to the south of Esher, and has attained its high importance among the lordly demesnes of Surrey since the time of Queen Anne. In that reign an estate was bought here by Sir John Vanbrugh, the architect, who built a small brick house for his own residence. His dwelling, which stood on low ground and without any ad-vantages of prospect, was subsequently sold, as stated above, to the Earl of Clare, who " added a magnificent room for the entertainment of large companies when he was in administration," and greatly augmented the estate. He likewise erected on higher ground in the park which he had formed a " castellated prospect-house," and called it after his own title " Clare-mont," which afterwards came to be the general name of the property. The estate forms the subject of a somewhat lengthy and flattering poem by Sir Samuel Garth, the author of the once popular, though now forgotten, poem, " The Dispensary." It is entitled " Claremont,"

and was " writ upon giving that name to a villa now owned by the Earl of Clare." The preface adds that " the situation is so agreeable and sur-prising, that it inclines one to think that some place of this nature put Ovid at first upon the story of Narcissus and the Fountain." It deals largely, as might be expected, with the Newcastles and Pel-hams, and peoples the lawns and groves with sylvan goddesses, and ends with the line—

> " The place shall live in song, and Claremont be the name."

During the occupancy of the house by the Duke of Newcastle, the grounds were laid out under the direction of Kent, the landscape gardener, whose talents in this direction were, as above stated, also exercised in the grounds of Esher Place. On a tablet in the grounds is the following :—" Sir John Vanbrugh, Knight, owner of the estate, 1708. A dramatist and architect of celebrity. He built the first mansion, of which the gardens were laid out by Kent, by orders of Holles, Earl of Clare and Duke of Newcastle, Prime Minister to George II. and III., and bestowed on it the name of Clare-mont."

The mansion was the home of the Whig Duke of Newcastle after having retired from office, and here he lived in deep dejection, contemplating with bitter grief the changes in the administration which he could only lament, and not prevent, his influence having been superseded by that of Lord Bute.

In the *World*, No. 218, appear the following remarks with reference to the alterations effected in the estate by the Duke of Newcastle :—" If the noble duke who clothed the sands of Claremont with such exquisite verdure had made the same glorious experiment in Spain, he would have brought no less riches and much more happiness to the nation than the conquests of Philip or the discoveries of Columbus."

The Duke of Newcastle died in 1768, after which the duchess sold the manor, together with Esher-Wateville and the mansion and estate of Claremont, to Lord Clive, of Indian renown, who soon, however, ordered the house to be pulled down, and the present mansion built in its place, at a cost of £100,000, and the grounds remodelled. The work was carried out under the direction of the famous Mr. Lancelot Brown, better known as " Capability Brown." Claremont is said to be the only mansion that Brown ever built, although he altered many. It stands on the crest of a hill, sur-rounded by some fine trees, and with an ample slope of bright turf stretching before it. It forms an oblong square, measuring forty-five yards by

---

* See *ante*, p. 286.

nirty-four. The building is of brick, the window and door-frames and other dressings of stone. There is a stately Corinthian portico, and the pediment contains a large sculpture of Lord Clive's arms and supporters. The saloon is approached by a lofty flight of steps, ornamented by columns of scagliola marble. Among the more interesting pictures in the gallery are the full-length portraits (by Dawe) of the Princess Charlotte and Prince Leopold, a head of General Wolfe, and a view of the landing of the troops at Quebec. In the breakfast-room are two interesting portraits of her present Majesty as a child.

Lord Clive was not permitted to enjoy his purchase with any degree of comfort. He seems to have fallen upon evil times. His long trial and the fierce and persistent attacks upon his reputation rendered him gloomy, morose, and mistrustful, and ended in suicide, his lordship having died by his own hand at his residence in Berkeley Square, in November, 1774.*

His property at Esher was sold to Lord Galway, an Irish peer. He again disposed of the whole to the Earl of Tyrconnell, who made Claremont his residence until the beginning of the present century, when he re-sold the estate to Mr. Charles Rose Ellis, afterwards created Lord Seaford. In 1816 the property was conveyed by sale, for £66,000, to the Commissioners of his Majesty's Woods and Forests, for the purpose of providing a suitable residence for the Princess Charlotte on her marriage with Leopold, Prince of Saxe-Coburg. With the exception of a short time spent at Camelford House, Park Lane, the mansion continued their home during their few short months of married life in 1816-17. Baron Stockmar, who attended the prince to England, wrote to his friends :—" In this house reign harmony, peace, love—all the essentials, in short, of domestic happiness. My master is the best husband in the world, and his wife has for him an amount of love which in vastness can only be likened to the English National Debt."

But this happiness was destined to be rudely broken off by the sudden death of the princess in her first confinement, in November, 1817. The authentic account of the death of the princess had long been disputed, but the true state of the case was published in 1872, in the " Life of Baron Stockmar." The mother, though she had been delivered of a dead child, was doing for some four hours as well as could be expected or hoped, and the Ministers and others who had been summoned

had actually left for London, believing all danger to be past. But just at midnight Sir Richard Croft came to Stockmar, telling him that the princess was taken dangerously ill. Dr. Baillie was called in ; she was very restless, and Dr. Baillie continued plying her with wine. She called : " Stocky ! Stocky ! " breathed convulsively, and in an hour was no more. The sudden blow was felt all over and all through England. The hope of the country, who was but yesterday so full of health, vigour, and spirits, had passed away. Croft and Baillie, in fact, would not help Nature, but pulled their patient down, so that she died of exhaustion.

The Princess Charlotte died in a room in the south-west angle of the building, adjoining the breakfast-room. For a long time the apartment was kept closed and the furniture undisturbed ; but after Prince Leopold became King of the Belgians all the rooms were re-opened, and the mansion was occasionally occupied by the Duchess of Kent, and her daughter the Princess Victoria. It may be mentioned here that under the terms of the settlement the property of Claremont was vested in either survivor of the marriage. It remained, therefore, in the possession of Prince Leopold (who became King of the Belgians in 1831, and married, in 1832, Louise, eldest daughter of Louis Philippe of France) till his death, on the 10th of December, 1865 ; but he never cared to live there after the death of the princess, and eventually he gave it back into the hands of the sovereign. It is clear, from the Memoirs of Baron Stockmar, that the short residence of Prince Leopold here as a married man was extremely happy, and that his grief at the loss of his wife was very deep indeed. When, at the age of upwards of seventy, he drew up his reminiscences for his niece, the Princess Victoria, he wrote thus of himself :—" November (1817) saw the ruin of this happy home, and the destruction at one blow of every hope and happiness of Prince Leopold. He has never recovered the feeling of happiness which had blessed his short married life." Baron Stockmar confirms this statement by writing to a friend : " As long as grief found no expression, I was much alarmed for his health ; but now he is relieved by frequent tears and moans."

During the brief period above referred to, Queen Charlotte, the Prince Regent, and all the royal dukes then alive—whose physique and personal peculiarities are sketched in a very lively way by Baron Stockmar—also the Duke of Wellington, and Prince Nicholas afterwards Emperor of Russia, were among the illustrious visitors at Claremont.

---

* See " Old and New London," Vol IV., p. 332.

"Claremont," writes Mr. Martin F. Tupper, "is a sort of mausoleum to the memory of the Princess Charlotte : over all its statues and paintings, its bijouterie and bronzes, the spirit of that lamented lady seems to linger, as about her brief hour of maternal happiness. Numerous articles once belonging to her Royal Highness are still affectionately

The following lines were written by Princess Charlotte as an inscription for a *papier maché* snuff-box, intended as a present to Prince Leopold. The box had on the lid a portrait of her Royal Highness, from Hayter's excellent likeness. The inscription—which forms a parody or appropriation of the verses on Pelham, quoted above—was written

PRINCESS CHARLOTTE.   (*After A. E. Chalon, R.A.*)

preserved in the same state as when she looked upon them living ; and there is a sentiment of awe and sanctity about the whole deserted palace which seems to breathe around, 'Reverence the dead.' The pleasure-grounds, about sixty acres in extent, are replete with every charm that art can add to nature. 'Capability' Brown did his best with them, and he has since been considerably improved upon, especially by the flowering shrubs of America, and the several rustic memorials of the lamented princess, not to mention the Gothic alcove, now her mausoleum."

on white satin, and inserted on the inside of the lid :—

"To Claremont's terrac'd heights and Esher's groves,
 Where in the sweetest solitude, embraced
 By the soft windings of the silent Mole,
 From courts and cities Charlotte finds repose.
 Enchanting vale ! beyond whate'er the muse
 Has of Achaia or Hesperia sung ;
 A vale of bliss ! O softly-swelling hills,
 On which the power of cultivation lies,
 And joys to see the wonder of his toil !"

Among the objects of interest preserved at Claremont, observes a writer in the *Graphic*, April,

1871, are "two Indian cabinets (presented by the Marquis of Hastings, and containing a splendid collection of bijouterie), Sir W. Beechey's portrait of the Duchess of Kent and her infant daughter Princess Victoria, Lawrence's beautiful portrait of the Princess Charlotte, and a superb table, the service of which is of porcelain, covered with highly-finished paintings, among which are four views of the statue-gallery in the Louvre. This was presented by Charles X. of France to Prince Leopold."

During the early years of their married life Claremont was the favourite retirement of the Queen and Prince Albert. If Kensington Palace was the home of the infancy and childhood of the Princess Victoria, yet Claremont was the home of her girlhood; and in its pleasant glades she first learnt to sketch from nature—an art which she subsequently cultivated with much success, as we know from the views in "Our Home in the Highlands." For many years after her marriage, as we learn from

VIEW IN CLAREMONT PARK.

The pleasure-grounds occupy about sixty acres. There are long avenues of beech and elm trees, besides fir, spruce, pine, cedar, cork, and other exotic specimens. The park is about three miles and a half in circumference, and the chief entrance is near the village, on the Leatherhead road. It is surrounded by a ring fence, and includes about 300 acres; but the whole estate (to which gradual additions have been made) comprises not less than 1,500 acres.

Near the mount, on which stands the observatory built by the Duke of Newcastle, is an aged cork tree, beneath which her Majesty and the Prince Consort used frequently to breakfast in fine weather, with their children playing round them.

"The Early Years of the Prince Consort," the Queen and Prince Albert were in the habit of repairing from London and Windsor to Claremont, and of "seeking such short intervals of quiet and refreshment as they could snatch from the fatigue and excitement of London life."

"This place" (the Queen writes to her uncle Leopold, in January, 1843), "has a peculiar charm for us both, and to me it brings back recollections of the happiest days of my otherwise dull childhood, when I experienced from you, dearest uncle, kindness which has ever since continued. . . . Victoria* plays with my old bricks, &c., and I see

---

* The Princess Royal, now Princess Imperial of Germany.

her running and jumping in the flower garden, much as *old*, though, I fear, still *little* Victoria of former days used to do."

A quarter of a mile from the house, in a north-westerly direction, stands the mausoleum of the Princess Charlotte. It is built of freestone, in the Pointed style of architecture. It was originally designed by the princess for an alcove, or open summer house, but being unfinished at the time of her death, was converted into a mausoleum to her memory. The interior has painted windows and a groined ceiling enriched with tracery.

The lake covers five acres; on the north side is a luxuriant bank of rhododendrons, in the centre a finely-wooded islet, and on the south-west side some artificial rockwork connected with a ruined grotto. This grotto was formerly ornamented with spars and stalactites, but the majority of these were carried off as *souvenirs* by the public when re-admitted to the grounds after the death of Princess Charlotte. In the grounds, too, is a monument to the great Lord Clive, in the form of an obelisk.

When the French Revolution took place, in February, 1848, and Louis Philippe was compelled to seek refuge in this country, Claremont was placed at the disposal of his father-in-law by the King of the Belgians. The exiled monarch remained two years an inhabitant of the mansion, till his death in 1850. His venerable queen survived till 1866. They lived here a quiet and retired life, and were happy to find such a home when forced to fly from the Tuileries. They were both buried at the Roman Catholic chapel at Weybridge.

Claremont has since been the temporary abode of various members of the royal family. Here, in 1871, the Marquis of Lorne and his royal bride, the Princess Louise, came to spend a few days of privacy after their wedding. In 1882 the mansion was given up as a residence to her Majesty's youngest and favourite son, Prince Leopold, Duke of Albany, on his marriage with the Princess Helen of Waldeck. He lived here just long enough to gain the friend-ship of his neighbours. His sudden death in 1884 threw all England into mourning.

It must be admitted that the historic memories of Claremont are chiefly of a sorrowful character. "When we think of the Anglo-Indian potentate, broken-hearted in the midst of his wealth," remarks the writer in the *Graphic* above quoted, "of the gentle young princess, dying in the prime of her youth and beauty; and of the discrowned king re-turning to die amid the scenes which had afforded him shelter some forty years earlier, we are fain to exclaim with Burke, 'What shadows we are, and what shadows we pursue!'"

Adjoining Esher and Sandown are Walton-on-Thames and Weybridge, which I should have much liked to have included in this chapter, on account of the historic memories of Oatlands, an abode of royalty under the Stuarts, and more recently the home of the Duke and Duchess of York; but unfortunately these two parishes lie outside the area of the Metropolitan Police District, and we are obliged to pass them by with regret. The grotto at Oatlands, with the graves of the pet dogs of the Duchess of York, the quiet rural grave of their mistress in Weybridge churchyard, the tombs of Louis Philippe and his queen, all at Weybridge, and the grave of poor Maginn, and the scold's bridle at Walton, are among the things which would have afforded ample materials for a pleasant chapter. *Sed fata vetant.*

CHAPTER XXXV.
KINGSTON-ON-THAMES.

"Slow let us trace the matchless vale of Thames,
Far winding up to where the Muses haunt,
To Twickenham's bowers, to royal Hampton's pile."—THOMSON.

Situation and Boundaries of the Town—Nature of the Soil, and Health Qualities of the District—Water Supply—Acreage and Population of the Town—Early History—Discovery of Roman Antiquities—Origin of the Name of Kingston—The Coronation of Athelstan—Early Charters and Privileges Granted to the Townsmen—Curious Entries in the Chamberlain's and Churchwarden's Accounts—Loyalty of the Inhabitants—Death of Lord Francis Villiers in the Civil War—Frequent Discovery of Ancient Warlike Weapons at Kingston—The Castle—Supposed Evidences of a Roman Ford here—Archæological Discoveries—Kingston Bridge—The Old Bridge—Historical Remi-niscences—Tolls, &c.—The Ducking or Cucking Stool—Clattern Bridge—An Ancient Mill—The Parish Church—Crack-nut Sunday.

KINGSTON-ON-THAMES, so-called popularly, to dis-tinguish it from Kingston-on-Hull, Kingston-on-Sea, and half a dozen other Kingstons scattered up and down the country, is pleasantly situated on the southern bank of the Thames, and is surrounded by charming scenery which would lose nothing by comparison with that of other places boasting a greater reputation.

The town lies on the great road from London to Portsmouth, eleven miles from London Bridge, and, in spite of the fact that the high road to and from Hampton Court runs through it from end to end, it is the most irregular in plan of any town within a hundred miles of the metropolis.

Kingston is bounded by Petersham, Merton, Malden, Chessington, Long Ditton, and Surbiton; and it gives its name to the hundred in which it lies. For much of the information contained in the following account of the parish we must acknowledge our indebtedness to the admirable and interesting little "Handbook of Kingston" by Mr. W. Chapman.

The soil is chiefly gravel; and there is but little or no chalk. Mr. Brayley says that "the wild thyme which grows abundantly around is a sure and certain proof of the excellence of its atmosphere." The health qualities of the district are further proved by the death-rate, which for many years has not exceeded 20 per thousand; the general average for all England and Wales during the same period being 22·7. An important health element—excellent water—is not wanting to the other advantages of favoured Kingston. Hampton Court Palace was supplied with water brought through pipes from springs at Coombe Wood* in the neighbourhood of the town, the work of no less august a personage than Cardinal Wolsey. Dr. Hales observes that "the water left no incrustation on a boiler in the coffee house which had been in use for fourteen years, and that it is softer and will wash linen with a less quantity of soap than either the Thames water or that of the river which crosses Hounslow."

During the last century these and other springs in the district—notably those of Seething Wells—were considered very valuable from their medicinal properties. The hot spring at Seething Wells was even held to be an invaluable remedy in certain cases of ophthalmia. Perhaps the day may yet come when "the prophet shall have honour" even "in his own country," and the waters of Coombe and Seething be proved as healing as those of the more distant German or Belgian spa.

Kingston is a market and municipal town, and enjoys the privilege of electing its High Steward. The parish occupies an area of 47,650 acres, or nearly 7½ square miles, with a population, according to the last census, of 33,545 persons. The borough alone has a population of 19,875.

Kingston contests with Winchester its claim to have been the ancient capital of England. It is surrounded by historical and traditionary associations of a most interesting character. That at a very early period Kingston was a place of considerable importance is certain. This would naturally be the result of its being situated close to the first practical ford above the sea, for which reason some writers have referred to Kingston as the spot where Cæsar crossed the Thames when pursuing the Britons under Cassivelaunus.* However this may be, here probably was one of the ancient fords and ferries across the Thames.

That the Romans had a settlement either at Kingston or in the immediate vicinity is unquestionable, many antiquities belonging to the Roman era having been discovered hereabouts, particularly coins of Diocletian, Maximian, Maximus, and Constantine the Great.

"Kingston Hundred comes next in order," writes Mr. Martin F. Tupper, in his "Railway Glance at the County" [of Surrey], "and its chief town claims our first attention. This town dates from the earliest antiquity. Dr. Gale tells us, in his 'Commentary on the Itinerary of Antoninus,' that here was the ancient town of Tamesa, mentioned by the Geographer of Ravenna; and Leland tells us that 'yn ploughyng and diggyng hav (sic) very often been found foundations of waulls of houses and diverse coynes of brasse, sylver, and golde, with Romayne inscriptions, and paintid yerthen pottes; and yn one yn Cardinall Wolsey's tyme was found much Romayne money of sylver, and plates of sylver to coyne, and masses to bete into plates to coyne, and chaynes of sylver.' Delicious treasure-trove!"

The name of Kingston, he adds, dates from the coronations of the Anglo-Saxon kings within its walls—events which constituted it the King's Town, or at all events a King's Town. Anciently it was called Moreford, or the Great Ford, as stated by Camden. Alfred, Athelstan, Edwin, and Ethelred were crowned, or "hallowed," there, and the sacred stone on which they sat is still to be seen in the market-place. The coronation of our sovereigns in Westminster Abbey dates no earlier than the time of Harold.

Doctors, of course, disagree as to the origin of the name Kingston, some deriving it from the coronation stone, King's Stone, whilst others consider it to be due to the circumstance that the Saxon kings resided here, thus constituting it a "King's Town." This latter theory is probably the true one, for the town must have obtained its present designation long prior to the year 900, the date of the first recorded coronation, since in 838, a short time before the decease of King Egbert,

---

* See Vol. I., p. 142.

* See Vol. I., pp. 31 and 179.

a great council was held here, at which that prince, his son and successor, Ethelwulf, and many prelates, abbots, and nobles, were present, including Ceolnoth, Archbishop of Canterbury, who presided; and in the acts of that council it is stated to have been held "in loco famoso vocato Kyningestun." It follows, therefore, that Kingston must have been so called before the middle of the ninth century, and that its name could not have been imposed on account of the coronations of the Saxon kings after the termination of the Heptarchy.

A striking account of the coronation of Athelstan is given by Dean Hook, in his "Lives of the Archbishops of Canterbury." After alluding to the dislike felt by the Teutonic and German races to towns, the writer states:—"Athelstan accordingly, instead of proceeding to London, pitched the royal camp at Moreford, so called because there was a ford across the Thames, well known even in Roman times. This became the place where the Saxon kings were generally crowned, and it has retained the name of Kingston-on-Thames. It was of easy access to the multitudes who hastened to express their adherence to the decision of the Wessex Witan, and to fight under the banner of the son of Edward and the grandson of Alfred. The king stood before them, a thin spare man, thirty years of age, with his yellow hair beautifully interwoven with threads of gold. He was arrayed in a purple vestment, with a Saxon sword in a golden sheath hanging from a jewelled belt, the gifts of Alfred, from whom, on his coming of age, according to an old Teutonic custom, he had received the spear and shield. On an elevated platform in the Market Place, and on a stone seat, he took his place, the better to be seen of the multitude. He was received with shouts of loyalty, and elevated on a stage, or target; he was carried on the shoulders of his men, being from time to time, in their enthusiasm, *tossed into the air!* until they arrived at the door of the church. Here the Archbishop was standing to receive him, and the king, supported by two prelates on either side, proceeded to the steps of the altar, and prostrating himself, remained for some time in private prayer. When the king had finished his private devotions, the Archbishop proceeded to the coronation." Effigies of the kings crowned here formerly existed in the ancient Chapel of St. Mary, as we shall presently see.

In a charter of King Edred in 946,* Kingston is mentioned as "the royal town where consecration is accustomed to be performed;" whilst a

third charter, dated from "the royal town of Kingston," conveys numerous lands in Surrey.

King John often visited Kingston; and remains of a residence called his "dairy and stables" may still be seen in a house between Kingston and Surbiton. He granted the town its first and second municipal charters. Subsequent charters were granted by Henry III., amongst others that of an eight-day fair, "to be holden yearly on the morrow of All Souls, and seven days following, with all the usual liberties and free customs thereto belonging." This sovereign, indeed, was so lavish in the matter of charters that he gave three in four days. Edward III., Henry V., Henry VI., Edward IV., Philip and Mary, and Charles II., also granted charters and privileges to the townsmen of Kingston.

The second charter of King John, beautifully written, is in the possession of the town. The corporation surrendered their charter to Charles II. only a few weeks before his death.

There are in the chamberlains' and churchwardens' accounts many entries which would amuse the curious in such matters. For instance :—

"The churchwardens had to pay the sum of 20d. for mending the roads in September, 1599, when Queen Elizabeth passed this way from Wimbledon to her palace at Nonsuch."*

"A sum of 9d. was paid for ringing the bells when some traitors were taken."

"For setting of the torches gyven at the Quyne's burial from Hampton Court by water, 4d." This queen was Lady Jane Seymour, who died in giving birth to Edward VI.

"For a scarf and for a box for the late Queen Elizabeth, returned again to the seller, 5s. 9d."

"1601. To Thomas Haywarde for to pay for the Queen's gloves, 40s."

"Paid to the ryngers at the command of the master bayliff when word was brought that the Earl of Northumberland was taken, 20d."

"1624. To the ringers for joy of the prince's return out of Spain, 3s. 4d."

From these entries we may conclude that Kingston was a loyal town, as from its traditions and antecedents, and the near proximity of Hampton Court Palace, there was every reason to expect.

Here, too, great loyalty was shown to King Charles I.; when others had forsaken him, the men of Surrey petitioned, at great personal risk, in favour of "the king, their lawful sovereign," from whom they had experienced great favours. "In November, 1642, Sir Richard Onslow, one of the knights of

---

* *Vide* "Saxon Charters," edited by Mr. J. M. Kemble.

* See *ante*, p. 234.

the shire, went with the trained bands of Southwark to defend Kingston, but the inhabitants thereof showing themselves extremely malignant against them, would afford them no entertainment, calling them 'Roundheads,' and wished rather that the cavaliers would come among them; whereupon they left them to their malignant humours."

It is remarkable that during the Great Rebellion the first armed force we hear of was said to have assembled at Kingston under Colonel Linsford; and the dying struggle of the Royalist party took place close by the town. In a lane near Surbiton Common was fought the very last skirmish, in which Buckingham and Holland were defeated, and the handsome Lord Francis Villiers was slain.

The account of this unfortunate young man's death is full of interest. "He behaved with signal courage," we are told, "and after his horse had been killed under him stood with his back against a tree, defending himself against several assailants, till at length he sank under his wounds. The next day the lords, who had heard of the skirmish, and that Lord Francis Villiers was dangerously wounded, made an order that chirurgeons might be permitted to go to Kingston and take care of him if he were alive; but, as one of the journalists of that time observes, it was too late, for he was dead and stripped, and good pillage found in his pocket." His body was conveyed to York House, in the Strand, by water, and was buried in Henry VII.'s Chapel in Westminster Abbey. The initials of his name were inscribed on the tree under which he was slain, and remained till it was cut down, as Aubrey says, in the year 1680.

That Kingston has been oftentimes the theatre of war is known from history. Brayley writes, in his "History of Surrey":—"Many reminiscences of the hostile conflicts which have taken place in this neighbourhood from the earliest period of our history are occasionally brought to light here by excavations for new buildings; nor can this excite surprise when we advert to the position of the town on the banks of the Thames offering a strong point of defence, and also recollect that its old bridge (coeval with that of London) was in former times the only roadway between Staines and the capital by which the river could be crossed. Broken weapons and other remains of a warlike description, together with human bones, skeletons, and other vestiges of hasty inhumation, have been found at different times and places."

It is remarkable that no vestige remains of the ancient Castle of Kingston. It is supposed to have been connected with the Saxon palace, and to have stood near the corner of Heathen Street.

In the year 1264, Henry III., then at war with his barons, marched out of London, and took the castle of Keningston or Kingston, belonging to Gilbert Clare, Earl of Gloucester. The castle was, perhaps, then demolished. Another account states that the fortress afterwards belonged to the Nevills, Earls of Warwick. However this may be, it is certain that all traces of the building have been swept away—an unusual circumstance in the history of such edifices—and that its very site is simply a matter of tradition.

In the *Archæological Journal* for 1845 and 1848 are recorded discoveries of several Roman antiquities made in excavating the foundation for the new bridge at Kingston, among which is to be noticed a brass ring with eleven bosses; it lay near some weapons of bronze and iron celts, &c., which were also discovered, and which were regarded as evidences that Cæsar and the Roman invaders passed the Thames at the ford near that spot after a sharp conflict with the Britons. They were discovered at a depth of about six feet, under the gravel. There was also discovered "an elegantly ornamented object of bronze, with a spike which may have been intended to support a standard or Roman eagle. It measures about thirteen inches in length." Most of these were found near the Middlesex side, where we might expect that the fight, if the passage was contested, would be the most severe. Dr. Roots, a local antiquarian, is strong in his belief, in company with the learned Horsley, that this was the point where the river was crossed, and not at Cowey Stakes; and he urges in support of his belief the name of Moreford, "the great ford," by which the place was known before it became the King's Town. "That Cæsar," observes Dr. Roots, "should have paused for some little time in the vicinity after a fatiguing march is just what might fully be expected; and that he did so seems to be proved by the fine Roman encampment on the rising ground of Kingston, adjoining Wimbledon, and overlooking the valley of the Thames. An additional proof may be sought from the sepulchral interments, apparently made in haste, which were discovered at this spot, with bronze weapons and large masses of unwrought metal, of which a considerable quantity was found a few years since. This provision of metal seems to indicate the presence of an armourer's establishment, possibly for the purpose of refit, previously to the transit at the great ford below." Illustrations of these antiquities will be found in the *Archæological Journal* for 1848.*

---

* Page 327.

In 1863, in the course of some diggings in the George Gravel Pits, at Kingston Hill, Mr. Walter Tregellas made some discoveries, which he communicated to the Archæological Society. There were found some fragments of pottery, human teeth and bones, a boar's tusk, pieces of copper, and some burnt wheat. The discoveries are supposed to indicate the fact of a British settlement here. In 1868 the same gentleman exhibited some further relics before the Society—a sepulchral urn ten inches in height, and two smaller vessels. These were all discovered in the so-called "potholes," about three or four feet below the surface. "Excavations at Coombe Hill, in 1881," observes the *Athenæum*, "yielded numerous relics of the early British period. The *fictilia* include small cup-like vessels of coarse dark clay, hand-made, and not turned on a wheel, whorls, a mould, and a slab or tile pierced with rough holes ; the metal remains consist of pieces of unwrought bronze, spear-heads, and celts. In one of the food-vessels some grains of wheat still remain."

The modern Kingston Bridge is a very handsome structure, and forms a conspicuous ornament in the general landscape. The stone was laid by the Earl of Liverpool, High Steward of the Corporation, on the 7th November, 1825, with the usual formalities, and on the 17th July, 1828, the bridge itself was opened in grand procession by the late Queen Dowager Adelaide, then Duchess of Clarence.

The previous bridge, which stood a short distance lower down the stream, was undoubtedly the oldest on the lower Thames excepting London Bridge. It was composed almost entirely of wood, and presented a very singular appearance, having in all probability retained the original form in which it was known to the Saxons. This bridge, being almost the only passage over the Thames, was frequently liable to be destroyed during the time of any intestine commotions, in order to cut off the communication between Surrey and Middlesex. This is known to have occurred in the wars between the Houses of York and Lancaster, as well as in 1554, when Sir Thomas Wyatt, in arms against the government of Queen Mary in opposition to the Spanish marriage, led his followers to Kingston, and found the bridge so far broken down, by order of the Privy Council, that several hours were employed in repairing it to enable his men to cross the river. It has often been inferred from a passage in Dion Cassius that there was a bridge here at the time of the invasion of Britain by the Romans under Aulus Plautius, A.D. 43. But the earliest distinct notice of this bridge appears to be that which occurs in the Close Rolls of Henry III., where it is stated that in consequence of a representation made to the king of the bad condition of the bridge, he committed the custody and superintendence of it to Henry de St. Alban, and Matthew Fitz Geoffry de Kingston, and ordered the bailiffs of the town and the sheriff of the county to furnish them with materials for repairs of the structure whenever they should be requested.

Leland states that a new town was built here after the settlement of the Saxons in England, and adds that "yn the old tyme it was commonly reported that the bridge, which had served as a common passage over the Thames at olde Kingston, was lower on the ryver than it is now, and when men began a new toun yn the Saxon's times, they dug from the very clive of Coombe park side to builde on the Tamise side, and sett a new bridge hard by the same."

That there was no bridge between London and this place is shown by Tennyson in his *Queen Mary*, where the rebel Wyatt cries out—

> " On over London Bridge,
> We cannot stay, we cannot, we must round
> By Kingston Bridge."

The place of the former bridge is marked by an old " Bridge Street," narrow and curved, and lined with quaint old fishermen's and boatmen's cottages, more picturesque than cleanly in appearance.

In the seventh year of Queen Elizabeth, 1565, one Robert Hamond, a bailiff of the town, settled lands to the value of £40 per annum for the future support of the bridge, and for exempting it from tolls, in remembrance of which the following distich was inscribed on a rail about the middle of the bridge :—

> " 1565. Robert Hamond, gentleman, bailiff of Kingston
> heretofore,
> He then made this bridge toll-free for evermore."

Tolls are now no longer paid on the new bridge, having been abolished in March, 1870, when the freeing of it was celebrated with great rejoicing. The joint committee of the Metropolitan Board of Works and the Corporation of London paid the balance of the debt and interest, amounting to £16,200, and the trustees were accordingly enabled to resume the whole of the bridge property.

The ancient custom of punishing scolding females by immersing them in a river by means of a cucking or ducking stool, or chair fixed to a beam which was run out from the main arch or pier, was usually put in practice from the old bridge, and

KINGSTON, FROM THE RIVER.

numerous allusions thereto occur in the records of the corporation. Mr. Biden, in his "History of Kingston," thus describes the use of the cucking stool :—" In this basket those turbulent women who did not understand the proper regulation of their tongues were, after due admonition, seated, and the corporation servants forthwith proceeded to plunge them repeatedly beneath the water, until they were thought sufficiently cooled, or were induced to promise amendment ; " and he considers that this salutary operation would probably be more effective, and certainly far less expensive in stilling a few noisy voices of the present day than any length of imprisonment or amount of fine. The most recent instance mentioned by Brand of the use of the cucking-stool was at Kingston in 1745, but later instances have been discovered in other localities— at Liverpool, for example, in 1779. The following extract is taken from the *Universal Spectator* of Saturday, October 14th, 1738 :—" Last week, at the Quarter Sessions, at Kingston-on-Thames, an elderly woman, notorious for her vociferation, was indicted for a common scold, and the facts alleged being fully proved, she was sentenced to receive the old punishment of being ducked, which was accordingly executed upon her in the Thames by the proper officials, in a chair for the purpose, preserved in the town ; and to prove the justice of the court's sentence upon her, on her return from the waterside she fell upon one of her acquaintances, without provocation, with tongue, tooth, and nail, and, had not the officers interposed, would have deserved a second punishment even before she was dry from the first."

From the London *Evening Post* of April 27th, 1746, we learn a more recent instance of its employment. "Last week," observes a writer in that paper, " a woman that keeps the ' Queen's Head ' ale-house at Kingston was ordered by the Court to be ducked for scolding, and was accordingly placed in the chair and ducked in the river Thames, in the presence of 2,000 or 3,000 people."

The custom of ducking was not confined to England. Sir John Skene, in his " Regiam Majestatem," shows that it was a common mode of punishment in Scotland. In the " Burrow Lawes," chap. 69, in allusion to Browsters—that is, " wemen quha brewes aill to be sauld "—it is said :—" Gif she makes gude ail, that is sufficient ; bot gif she makes evill ail, contrair to the use and consuetude of the burgh, and is convict thereof, she sal pay ane unlaw of aucht shillinges, or sall suffer the justice of the burgh—that is, she sal be put upon the cock stule, and the ail sal be distributed to the pure folk."

Gay makes mention of the ducking stool in his Pastorals—

" I'll speed me to the pond, where the high stool
  On the long planks hangs o'er the muddy pool—
  That stool the dread of every scolding quean."

In addition to scolding wives and " Browsters," the " Barrators," or those gossips who made mischief between neighbours, received the punishment of the stool. The ways of our ancestors were rough-and-ready, and one can but regret that the punishment has not been retained for those backbiters and slanderers who are the curse of the neighbourhood in which they live.

Lysons, in his " Environs of London," and Brayley, in his " History of Surrey," give at full length a bill of expenses for making one of these machines, copied out of the churchwardens' and chamberlains' account books.

From local tradition we learn that the stool was not quite disused till very near the end of the last century. From the frequent entries relating to it in the parish books, it would seem that Kingston must have enjoyed a rather proud pre-eminence in respect of scolds and shrews, if we may judge from the sums of money laid out in the work of " taming " them. The cucking-stool was sometimes applied also to women who brewed and sold bad ale.

The antiquary Cole, in one of his MS. volumes, to be seen in the British Museum, gives a graphic sketch of this, or another, instance of the punishment. He writes :—" In my time, when I was a boy, I lived with my grandmother in the great corner house at the bridge foot, 'neath Magdalene College, Cambridge, and rebuilt since by my uncle, Joseph Cook. I remember to have seen a woman ducked for scolding. The chair was hung by a pulley fastened to a beam about the middle of the bridge, in which [he means the chair, of course, and not the bridge] the woman was confined, and let down under the water three times, and then taken out. The bridge was then of timber, before the present stone bridge of one arch was built. The ducking-stool was constantly hanging in its place, and on the back of it was [were] engraved devils laying hold of scolds, &c. Some time afterwards a new chair was erected in the place of the old one, having the same devices carved upon it, and well painted and ornamented. When the new bridge of stone was erected, in 1754, this chair was taken away ; and I lately saw the carved and gilt back of it nailed up by the shop of one Mr. Jackson, a whitesmith, in the Butcher's Row, behind the Town Hall, who offered it to me, but I did not know what to do with it. In October, 1776, I saw in the old Town Hall a third ducking-stool of plain oak, with an iron bar in front of it to confine the person in the seat, but I made no inquiries about it. I mention these things, as the practice of ducking scolds in the river seems now to be totally laid aside." Thus far Mr. Cole, who did not long survive this curious entry, as he died in 1782.

The Kingston scolds usually received the ducking from the old wooden bridge, but occasionally from Clattern Bridge, near the Surbiton entrance to the town. The practice of displaying a ducking stool against the residence of a notorious scold appears to have prevailed some years after the punishment by immersion or exposure had fallen into desuetude. The etymology of the name Clattern, or Clattering, may have some connection with the cucking-stool which was affixed to this bridge. This bridge is a brick structure of three arches, and was improved in appearance a few years ago by the substitution of an open iron railing, in imitation of Saxon workmanship, in lieu of the old brick parapet which formerly existed.

The Clattern Bridge spans the narrow river called the Hog's Mill, or, as it is now more generally styled, the New River, by the side of which, near the middle of the town, and not far from the market place, stands an ancient mill, the same which, in all probability, supplied the inhabitants with corn as far back as the Middle Ages. Tennyson's lines seem so appropriate that we must not omit them here :—

> " The brimming wave that swam
>   Through quiet meadows round the mill,
> The sleepy pool above the dam,
>   The pool beneath it never still ;
> The meal-sacks on the whitened floor,
>   The dark round of the dripping wheel,
> The very air about the door
>   Made misty with the floating meal."

The Thames here, especially in summer, is as fair to look upon as anywhere below Windsor and Maidenhead ; and the broad reach which runs from the bridge past Surbiton, and up to Hampton, is one of the favourite haunts of the amateur sculler and of the disciples of Izaak Walton. The banks are on both sides low, generally bordered with rushes, with occasional " aits," on which grow the " sallys," which supply so many of the basket-makers of London. The views in some parts might be aptly described in the lines of Tennyson :—

> " On either side the river lie
>   Long fields of barley or of rye,
> That clothe the wold and meet the sky ;
> And through the field the road runs by ;

> And up and down the people go,
> Gazing where the lilies blow,
> Round an island there below ;
> Willows whiten, aspens quiver,
> Little breezes dusk and shiver
> Through the wave that runs for ever
> By the island in the river."

The Portsmouth road, which leaves Kingston by the Clattern Bridge, winds to the south-west, by the river-side, on its way towards Thames Ditton and Esher. Pursuing our course by this road we pass on our left the houses and other buildings forming the pleasant suburb of Surbiton, the Italian Roman Catholic church, with its tall cross-surmounted campanile tower, forming a conspicuous object by the road-side. A broad esplanade, or public promenade, ornamented with grass-plats and flowering plants and shrubs, and separated from the roadway by a light railing and row of venerable elms, overlooks, on the right, the silvery-flowing Thames, on the opposite side of which stretches the broad acres of the park attached to Hampton Court Palace, with its avenues of stately trees.

At the far end of the esplanade are the reservoirs and filtering-beds, and the extensive ranges of buildings forming the works of the Chelsea and Lambeth Waterworks Company. The buildings are of light-coloured brick, and have tall campanile smoke and ventilating shafts. The locality in which the waterworks are placed is called "Seething Wells." The hot spring at Seething Wells was once thought an almost infallible remedy in certain cases of ophthalmia.* At Hampton, on the opposite side of the river, and just visible in the distance, are the pumping works of the Grand Junction, the West Middlesex, and the Southwark and Vauxhall Waterworks Companies. These companies, together with those at Kingston, have Parliamentary powers to draw from the Thames 100,000,000 gallons of water a day.

Kingston Church is cruciform in plan, and stands in the centre of the town, in the middle of a large churchyard. It is dedicated to All Saints. Its interior consists of chancel and a nave, with north and south aisles, from which it is separated by four pointed arches supported by low octangular columns. Outside it is in a most deplorable condition so far as taste is concerned, having been largely altered, and re-built from about the level of the window sills in the churchwardens' style of the eighteenth century. Inside, however, a wonderful revolution has taken place, the Gothic features of the building having been well brought out in the

---

* *Vide* Mr. S. C. Hall's " Book of the Thames."

restoration. The groining of the central tower is low, thus intercepting the view of the church from west to east; it stands at the intersection of the transepts with the main body. The spire, having twice been injured by lightning and wind, has not been rebuilt.

On Candlemas Eve, February 1st, 1444-5, the steeple of this church was fired by lightning in a storm which, considering the season of the year, was remarkably extensive, for at the same time the churches of Baldock, in Hertfordshire, Walden and Waltham, in Essex, and that of St. Paul's, in Lonnon, were also damaged.*

The peal of bells, ten in number, is very fine and sweet of tone. Near the vestry is a small piscina, and on the south side of the south chancel is another of a more imposing character beneath a Gothic canopy. There is also a third immediately adjoining the entrance to the tower staircase, where was originally a chapel.

The only part of the structure which exhibits a specimen of the antiquity of the whole is the south aisle of the chancel, which is built of chalk, irregularly intermixed with flints. Although probably no part of the present building is older than the fourteenth century, there is reason to suppose that a church was founded in this town during the very earliest existence of Christianity among the Saxons. There is mention in the "Domesday Book" of a church at Kingston.

The church can boast of many fine monuments, including a statue of the Countess of Liverpool, by Chantrey—very beautiful, although not very ecclesiastical. The ruthless Vandalism of the Cromwellites defaced or swept away some of the most ancient and interesting tombs and tablets, and almost all the brasses, of which, judging from the marks on the floor, there must have been many. Of those still remaining, that of Robert Skern and Joan, his wife, now placed beneath the wall near the north entrance, having been removed from the communion rails, by which it was partly covered, is well worthy careful inspection, on account of its execution and representation of the costume.

Some careful sexton would seem to have placed considerable value on this monument, for it has escaped alike the ravages of time and fanaticism which have destroyed other monuments. Robert Skern lived at Down Hall, on the banks of the Thames. His wife was a daughter of Edward III. and Alice Perrers. Against the south wall, under an arch, is the altar-tomb of Sir Anthony Benn,

formerly Recorder of Kingston, and at the time of his decease Recorder of London, who died on the 29th September, 1618. He is represented by a recumbent figure of alabaster, in his official gown, with a large ruff, and his head reposing on an embroidered cushion. In the nave of the church is an inscription to the memory of Thomas Cranmer, M.D., who died in August, 1748, John Cranmer, who died in 1723, and others of that family. Here, too, lie buried Thomas Agar, once mayor, and twelve times bailiff of Kingston, who died in 1703, aged 94; John Haywarde, ensign to Captain North, brother to the Lord North who died in Sir Walter Raleigh's last voyage, and Thomas Hayward, who died in 1655. The last-named is honoured by the following epitaph :—

"THOMAS HAWARD.
"Ashes on Ashes lie, on Ashes tread,
Ashes engrav'd these words, which Ashes read,
Then what poor thing is Man, when every gust
Can blow his Ashes to their kindred Dust?
More was intended, but a wind did rise,
And fill'd with Ashes both my mouth and eyes."

Dr. Bate, physician in succession to Charles I., Oliver Cromwell, his son Richard, and Charles II., also lies in Kingston Church, together with his wife, Elizabeth, whose death was accelerated by the Great Fire of London. The doctor appears to have had a happy facility for—not to put too fine a point upon it—adapting himself to circumstances.

Dr. Edmund Staunton, who was Vicar of Kingston, had ten children interred in the south chancel, with the following epitaph inscribed on a slab of brass :—

Here ly ye Bodies of

Frances	Richard	Children which ye Lord gave to EDMVND
Richard	Edmvnd	STAUNTON, Dr. of D., late Minister
Mary	Edmvnd	of Kingsto-vpon-Thames, now Presit.
Mathew	Sarah	of Corpus Christi Colledge, Oxon;
Mary	Richard	by Mary, his Wife, Daughtr. of Rich.
		Balthorp, Servant to ye late Qveene
		Elizab.

Ten Children in one grave! A dreadful sight.

a Iob 1. 2. Seven Sons and Daughters three, Job's number *a* right

b Eccl. 11. 10. Childhood *b* and Youth are vaine, Death reigns ouer all:

c Rom. 5. 14. Even those who never sin'd like Adams *c* fall :

d Rom. 5. 12. But why over all. In the first *d* Man every one Sin'd and fell, not He himselfe alone

e 1 Cor. 15. 22. } Our hope's *e* in Christ. The second Adam :
1 Tim. 1. 21. } He

f Mat. 1. 21. } Who saves *f* the Elect from sin and Misery.
Rom. 5. 9. 10. } What's that to Vs poore Children? This our Creed,

g Gen. 17. 7. God is *g* a God to th' faithfull and their seed.

---

* Mr. G. Roots says that on the occasion of this same storm a person died in the church through fear of a spirit which he saw there.

h 1 Thes. 4. 14. Sleepe *h* on deare Children, never that you
　　　wake
i Rev. 20. 12.　Till Christ doth raise *i* you and to Glory
　　　take.

The church contains some fine modern stained glass windows.

It is well known that in the olden times many holiday diversions, and even occasionally fairs, were held within the precincts of our parish churches. For instance, in the registers at Winchester there is to be seen a copy of a mandate from William of Wykeham, which forbids juggling, the performance of loose dances, ballad-singing, the exhibiting of profane shows and spectacles, and the celebration of other games, in the church and even in the churchyard of Kingston-on-Thames, on pain of excommunication. It would appear, however, that even this strong measure did not prevent the origin, or at all events the practice, of another ancient custom, of which little or nothing is known except that it is thought to have been peculiar to Kingston, but which was carried on in the church itself, even during the time of divine service, down to the end of the last century, if not to the beginning of this. The congregation, strange as it may sound, used to crack nuts during service on the Sunday next before the eve of St. Michael's Day. Hence that Sunday was called "Crack-nut Sunday." The custom was not restrained or confined to the younger branches of the congregation, but was practised alike by young and old ; and it is on record that the noise caused by the cracking was often so loud and so powerful as to oblige the minister to break off for a time his reading or his sermon until silence was restored.

The above custom is thought by one or two antiquaries to have been connected in some way or other with the choosing of bailiffs and other members of the corporate body on Michaelmas Day, and with the usual feast which attended that proceeding. Readers of Goldsmith, however, will not perhaps have forgotten a passage in the fourth chapter of the "Vicar of Wakefield," in which the good vicar, speaking of his parishioners, says : "They kept up the Christmas Carol, sent true-love-knots on St. Valentine's morning, ate pancakes at Shrove-tide, shewed their wit on the first of April, and religiously *cracked nuts* on Michaelmas Eve." It would be curious to learn whether this custom prevailed in other parts of the country, or whether Oliver Goldsmith made acquaintance with it in his wanderings through the south-west suburbs of London.

The churchwardens' and chamberlains' books here contain the earliest known allusion to the Morris Dance and its characters—Robin Hood, Maid Marian, Friar Tuck, &c. They range through the two last years of Henry VII. and the first of his successor.* The custom of acting plays in churches probably originated with the religious plays, or "mysteries," which were performed in the churches or churchyards more frequently than not on the Sunday, the subjects represented being usually the lives and miracles of the saints, or some of the leading events of Scripture. The practice was ultimately so abused, that in the reign of Henry VIII. Bonner, Bishop of London, issued a prohibition against "common plays, games, and interludes" in the churches.

The registers of Kingston preserved at the parish church commence in the year 1542. Among the entires frequent mention is made of individuals to whom were granted begging licenses, or briefs—permission, that is, to gather money for private distress, accorded to distressed persons and families by Queen Elizabeth. Amongst these entries is the following, dated 1571, by which we may see that history, and in particular the history of the sister isle, does but repeat itself :—" Sunday was here two women, mother and daughter, owte of Ireland, to gather upon the dethe of her husband, who was slayne by the Wild Iryshe, he being captain of the Gallyglasses."

Under date of March 10, 1673-4, is an entry of the burial of "Three Male Children, and one Female, unbaptized, of George Dennisses." The birth of these children was particularly recorded in a tract, which is supposed to have been written by Partridge the astrologer, entitled "The Fruitful Wonder ; or, a strange relation from Kinston-upon-Thames of a Woman who on Thursday and Friday, being the 5th and 6th days of this instant March, 1673-4, was delivered of Four Children at one Birth, viz., three Sons and one Daughter, all born alive, lusty children, and perfect in every part, which lived 24 hours, and then dyed, all much about the same time, &c. Published by J.P., Student in Physick. 4to. 1674." The following instances occur of extraordinary longevity:—

" Frances Phillips, widow, 110 years ould, buried Feb. 26, 1677-8."

" Winifred Woodfall, Gent., widow, agèd 108 years, buried Oct. 24, 1690."

Mention of another very prolific family is also to be found in Kingston Church, Mary Morton being interred there, widow of George Morton, and mother to three famous sons : Sir Robert Morton, sometime captain in the Netherlands, Sir Thomas

---

* See Chambers's "Book of Days," Vol. I. p. 631.

Morton, Knt. and colonel, and Sir Albert Morton, Knt., Principal Secretary of State to King Charles. Of Mrs. Morton's mother, Mrs. Honeywood, of Charing, in Kent, we are told that she was "the wonder of her sex and this age, for she lived to see near 400 issued from her loynes."

Dr. Nicholas West, vicar of Kingston in 1502, was a scholar of Eton and Fellow of King's College, Cambridge. He was consecrated Bishop of Ely in 1515, and died in 1533.

The Rev. Edmund Staunton was another distinguished vicar of Kingston. He was the son of General. He had retired from the bench about ten years before his death.

Besides the parish church, there are no less than eight other Protestant places of worship in or near the town. The church of St. John the Evangelist, Spring Grove, on the outskirts of the town, was built in 1873. It is constructed of Kentish rag, with Bath stone dressings, in the Early English style, and is cruciform in plan, with an apsidal chancel. Christ Church, in King Charles's Road, dates its erection from 1863, at which time the new ecclesiastical parish of Berrylands was formed.

KINGSTON MARKET PLACE.

Sir Francis Staunton, Knt., of Woburn, Beds., where he was born about 1600. Educated at Oxford, he became Fellow of Corpus Christi College, and proceeded D.D. in 1634, at which time, however, he was under suspension for refusing to read the declaration for allowing sports and pastimes to the people on Sunday. Rev. Richard Mayo, who succeeded Dr. Staunton as vicar of Kingston, was, like him, ejected on the passing of the Act of Uniformity. Dr. Thomas Willis, another vicar, was at one time chaplain to Charles II.

The Right Hon. Sir Robert Graham, one of the Barons of the Exchequer, who died in 1836, was buried at Kingston. He was a cadet of the noble house of Montrose, and was born at Dalston, Middlesex, in 1744. He was a great favourite with the Prince Regent, who made him his Attorney-

The church is built of brick, in the mixed or modern Gothic style, and most of the windows are of stained glass. In 1847 a cluster of dwellings which had sprung up close by the Robin Hood Gate, on the south side of Richmond Park, was formed into an ecclesiastical parish from the mother parish of Kingston. The church, dedicated to St. John the Baptist, is situated in Kingston Vale. It was erected in 1861, and is a small building, in the Early English style, consisting of nave and aisle and an apsidal chancel. The Nonconformists are also well provided with chapels and meeting-houses in the town and its outlying districts.

The Rev. John Townsend, the projector and partly founder of the Asylum for the Deaf and Dumb, was pastor of the Independent Chapel, in Eden Street, during rather more than three years.

THE "BALD-FACED STAG."

CHAPTER XXXVI.

KINGSTON-UPON-THAMES (*continued*).

"A praty town by Tamise ripe."—LELAND.

The Coronation Stone—Monarchs crowned here—The Town Hall—Historical Reminiscences of the Market Place—The Drinking Fountain—The Assize Court—Old Houses in the Town—The Drill Hall and Barracks—Public Free Library and Literary Institution—Cleave's Almshouses—Healthy Situation of the Town—Railway Communication—New Kingston—Modern Improvements—The Cemetery—St. Mary's Chapel—The Free Grammar School—Fairs—Public Amusements—The Fairfield—Thames Angling—Surbiton—St. Mark's Church—St. Andrew's—Roman Catholic Church of St. Raphael—Norbiton—Churches and Charitable Institutions—Residence of Lord Liverpool—Coombe Wood—Jerry Abershawe the Highwayman and the Doctor.

THE coronation stone, upon which seven—some say nine—of our Anglo-Saxon monarchs sat during the high ceremony by which their reigns were inaugurated, is by far the most interesting relic preserved at Kingston. All honour has been done to it by the Kingstonians, who have within the last thirty years given it a conspicuous position opposite the assize courts. It stands on a foundation of granite, and is surrounded by a handsome but massive railing, the granite pillars of which are surmounted by Saxon spear-heads. The seven sides of the base are inscribed with the names and dates of the kings crowned here. Previously to being set up in its present position, the stone had been preserved for ages in the church.

The date of the venerable relic is uncertain. It is quite possible that it was placed here during the Saxon Heptarchy; but if it is over a thousand years old, it may be two thousand years old, for all that is known to the contrary, and be a relic of the Roman occupation of this country. If so, the probable solution is that it was connected with the worship of the god Terminus, and used to mark a boundary. Thus Ovid writes:—

"Termine, sive lapis, sive es defossus in agro
  Stipes, ab antiquis sic quoque nomen habes."

"The Tounish men," writes Leland, "have certen knowledge of a few kinges crownid ther afore the Conqueste." In his commentary on the *Cygnea Cantio*, he gives the names of Ethelstan, Eadwin or Edwy, and Ethelred, as having been crowned here; and adds:—"I have been told that this was done in the midst of the market-place, a lofty platform being erected, that the ceremony might be seen from afar by a multitude of people: which, however, I do not state as a fact known with certainty."

According to Brayley and other historians, the earliest of the Saxon monarchs recorded to have been crowned here is Edward the Elder, son of Alfred the Great, A.D. 900; but the town must have obtained its present designation even previously to that, for in 838, before Egbert's death, a council was held here, at which that prince, his son and successor Æthelwulph, and many prelates, abbots, and nobles, were present, including Ceolnoth Archbishop of Canterbury, who presided. In the acts of that council it is stated to have been held "in loco famoso vocato *Kyningestun*." If the records of this council be authentic, it is evident, therefore, that Kingston must have been so called before the middle of the ninth century, and that its name could not have been imposed on account of coronations there of the Saxon kings after the termination of the Heptarchy. If so, then Kingston must mean the King's Town, not the King's Stone.

The following list of sovereigns crowned here is given by Lysons, on the authority of William of Malmesbury, Henry of Huntingdon, Roger Hoveden the Saxon chronicler, Holinshed, &c. :— "Edward the Elder, crowned A.D. 900; his son Athelstan, in 925; Edmund, in 940; Eldred, or Edred (said to have assumed the title of King of Great Britain), in 946; Edwy, or Edwin, in 955; Edward the Martyr, in 975; and Ethelred, in 978. Edgar, who succeeded to the throne in 959, is said to have been crowned either at Kingston or at Bath."

In an elaborate paper read before the annual meeting of the Surrey Archæological Society, held in Kingston, June 30th, 1854, Dr. W. Bell, dwelling at considerable length on the significance and early use of this and corresponding memorials in various and widely-distant countries, remarks that as stones must necessarily, in the earliest ages of society, have served as seats, so some of a particular form or in a peculiar situation were gradually elected from the mass as the royal throne of princes and kings, whence, when the pontiff and kingly power were united, they were deemed holy, and afterwards shed the halo of their sanctity on everything around or in contact with them, thus tracing the natural and gradual march of the human intellect from things common to select—from select to sacred and divine. In the East, for instance, the two ideas of stones and worship, or divinity, became almost identical, the terms being frequently synonymous, particularly with the Hebrews, whom we find giving the name of stone or rock to kings and princes—even to God Himself, as the Rock of Israel, where the stone metaphor was

intended to convey as much of sanctity as of security or endurance.

By a comparison of numerous Druidical stone circles in various parts of Europe, Dr. Bell assumes the probability that the above stone formed one of a smaller circle of thirteen, the latter, however, having all vanished before the requirements of an increasing population and the improvements in the construction of dwellings. But a reverence deeply seated in the minds of the people must have kept the principal and kingly stone from profanation or destruction.

The present Town Hall was built in the year 1840, at the expense of the Corporation, and at the cost of nearly £4,000. It is built of light-coloured brick with stone dressings, in the Italian style. At each angle, rising above the side pediments, is an ornamental turret; and over an embowered balcony in the south front is affixed a leaden statue of Queen Anne. It stands on the site of a much older building of the same kind, which, in its turn, no doubt, succeeded a still more ancient "Moot," or Town Hall. The venerable brick building, with its oak posts and frames, which gave place to the modern structure, was of Elizabethan style and date, although repaired and enlarged in the reign of Queen Anne. The arms of the maiden queen are still preserved in the Justices' Room; they were originally affixed to the eastern wall of the old building.

The hall also possesses a unique heraldic window, in which the arms and insignia of Roman emperors, heathen Britons, Christian Britons, Saxon, Danish, and Norman kings, Kings of Scotland, Wales, and Ireland, are exhibited with the more modern emblems of the Prince of Wales and the royal arms of England, as borne by Charles II. and James I. The lower and open portion of the building is devoted to the purposes of the markets, which are held here on Thursdays and Saturdays.

The corporation of Kingston is one of the oldest in England, its first charter having been dated by King John. The most valuable records of the town, from an antiquarian point of view, are still in existence in the Corporation muniment room. The civic regalia consist of a handsome silver-gilt mace of some antiquity; and also an elaborate SS collar, chain, and badge, worn by the mayor, which were presented to the Corporation by the senior member for the county, Sir Henry W. Peek, Bart.

It was in the market-place here, "when both parties were preparing for an appeal to the sword," that in January, 1641–42, the first attempt to assemble an armed force in the time of the Civil War was made by Colonel Lunsford and other Royalist officers for the purpose, as surmised, of seizing the "magazine of arms" then deposited in the town, and afterwards proceeding to Portsmouth to secure that fortress for the king. " Whatever was the actual design," observes Brayley, " it was defeated by the promptness of the Commons, who caused Lunsford to be arrested, and accused the Lord Digby of high treason, it having been given in evidence at the bar of the House that he came to Kingston ' in a coach and six horses from Hampton Court,' to which place his Majesty had retired from his palace of Whitehall a day or two previously to the meeting, ' and conferred with them a long time, and then returned again thither.' "

George Withers' libel on Sir Richard Onslow, entitled *Justiciarius Justificatus*, was ordered by the House of Commons, in August, 1646, to be publicly burnt in the market-place here on the market-day, as well as at Guildford.

In 1882 a drinking-fountain was set up in the market-place to the memory of Mr. Henry Shrubsole, who had been thrice in succession elected Mayor of Kingston, and who died while holding that official position.

Kingston is included in the Home Circuit, and both the Lent assizes and the Michaelmas sessions were formerly held in the Town Hall, but the inconveniences experienced were so great that it was deemed necessary to erect a new court-house. This was accordingly carried out, the new building being erected at a cost of about £10,000. This court-house stands at the lower end of the market-place, on the Surbiton side. The winter assizes are always held here. The two courts in which the Crown and Nisi Prius cases are tried are spacious and well lighted, and conveniently fitted up. In the Assize Court at Kingston was tried George Barnewell, the apprentice, for the murder of his uncle at Camberwell.*

Adjoining the law courts is a large mansion belonging to the Corporation, called Clattern House, in which the judges reside on their circuit in this town.

At one time Kingston must have been rich in old mansions. In the market-place there is a shop, kept by Mr. Chilcott, a tailor and draper, which looks as if it had been built since her Majesty's accession. Its walls and beams, however, are certainly as old as the reign of Elizabeth, though the panelling of the former is concealed by paper. The ground-floor rooms, now converted into a shop, are very low, and such is the case with the drawing-room, which contains a finely-carved oak chimney-piece. The glory of the house, however, is its staircase, a really noble specimen of late Elizabethan or early Jacobean work. It is broad and massive, and much resembles that in the former palace of the Howards at the Charterhouse,* though far richer in its details. The banisters are of the finest and most solid black oak, the handrails being carved with grotesque figures of beasts, birds, &c., and of children riding outside Bacchanalian casks or tuns. From this, and from the frequent recurrence of the initials E. B., I. B., C. B., &c., it is conjectured that the above figure is a "rebus," and that the house belonged to a family named " Boy-tun," or "Boyton." A part of the banisters represents an old castellated mansion, and may be intended as a representation of the original front.

In the centre of the town there still remain a few other quaint old houses with heavy beams of timber, massive timber mantelpieces, and richly-carved staircases ; but their number is diminishing gradually. Many of them have been re-fronted, so that, like ladies of a certain age, they disguise their antiquity. Many of the courts in the old part of the town still retain the quaint look which they wore, doubtless, in the days of the Stuarts.

The House of Correction was closed in 1852, on the completion of the county prison at Wandsworth. Additional buildings were subsequently erected for the accommodation of the Third Royal Surrey Militia. The drill hall, a spacious building, capable of accommodating between 2,000 and 3,000 persons, is occasionally used for public entertainments. It is the head-quarters of the 12th Surrey (Kingston) Rifle Volunteers. The interior is suitably decorated with banners, armorial shields, &c. Kingston is now a military depôt, and the head-quarters of the 31st Regimental District (East Surrey Regiment). The barracks are situate adjoining the King's Road, between Richmond Park and the Richmond Roads.

Kingston has its public free library and its literary institution. The latter is a handsome building, situated in Thames Street, and forms a conspicuous object in the approach to the town from the bridge. It is built of bricks of different colours, and consists of two storeys, surmounted by a stone coping, which partially conceals the roof. The institution was first established in 1839, and many useful lectures on various branches of art, science, and literature, have been delivered here.

Among the most important institutions of Kings-

---

* See "Old and New London," Vol. VI., p. 280.

* See "Old and New London," Vol. II., p. 383.

ton are the almshouses founded by Mr. William Cleave, an alderman of London, who died in 1667, and who bequeathed certain property in this parish for the maintenance for ever of six poor men and six poor women "of honest life and reputation." The almshouses originally consisted of twelve distinct dwellings, but from the accumulation of funds belonging to the charity, it was decided by the trustees, in 1880, to erect additional houses for four more inmates, two men and two women. Each house consists of an upper and a lower room under one roof, and in the centre of the row is a common hall, over the doorway of which are the founder's arms, with an inscription recording the erection of the building in 1668. The arms of the founder, engraven on a plate of silver, are worn on the sleeve by each inmate.

Though it lies so low, yet Kingston would seem to be a very healthy place. The soil generally is of a gravelly nature, and the wild thyme which grows abundantly around is a sure and certain proof of the excellence of its atmosphere. In December, 1883, an old woman in one of the almshouses died a centenarian—not the first centenarian of Kingston, as we have seen already.

Kingston-on-Thames is the terminus of Jonas Hanway's tour from Portsmouth, Southampton, &c., as recorded in his "Journal of an Eight Days' Journey," which he published in 1757, along with his celebrated "Essay on—or rather, in dispraise of—Tea," an essay which Dr. Johnson attacked with all the sledge-hammer force of an inveterate tea-drinker in a review in the *Literary Magazine* of that year.

The station on the South-Western line at Surbiton is the nearest railway approach on the south side of the town; but close to the north end of the town is the "New Kingston Station," on what is called the New Kingston line, which adjoins at Twickenham the Windsor branch of the London and South-Western Railway, and is worked in connection with the North London Railway. This line is carried on a high embankment through the lower part of the town to New Malden, where it joins the main line. The approach to Kingston by the North London line is through Richmond and Hampton Wick. By these several lines there is rapid and easy railway communication with almost all parts of London, from Waterloo terminus on the south side of the Thames, to Ludgate Hill and Moorgate Street stations on the north. Another line is in course of formation to connect Putney with Kingston and Surbiton, and to be continued to Cobham, and thence to Guildford.

The modern town of New Kingston rose into being, mushroom-like, immediately on the opening of the railway-station here. At first the building speculations were not successful; but since the extension of the South-Western Railway to Cannon Street it has been brought into such proximity to the City that it has become a favourite resort for merchants, whose charming residences add to the attractiveness of the place and neighbourhood. Indeed, within the last thirty years great and important improvements have taken place both in the town and its immediate neighbourhood. The green fields and lanes of Norbiton and Surbiton have given way to innumerable villas, streets, and thoroughfares, while the general aspect of the town has undergone a marked alteration through the removal of many antiquated buildings, and the substitution of handsome and substantial erections more in accordance with the modern idea of architectural arrangement.

The cemetery, on the north side of the town, is about fourteen acres in extent, and is tastefully laid out, and well planted with trees and shrubs. The two chapels are connected by an archway surmounted by a spire, which, owing to the elevated situation of the ground, is visible at a considerable distance. Sir William Bovill, Lord Chief Justice of the Common Pleas, who died in 1873, is buried here.

On the north side of the London road, to the east of the town, are the ruins of an old chapel, called St. Mary's, which for many years formed part of the grammar-school. In 1878 the school was removed to a new site on the other side of the road.

In this chapel were formerly to be seen the portraits of the Saxon kings who were crowned here, and also one of King John, from whom the town received its first charter of privileges as a body corporate. The windows and doors had long been boarded up, and the entire structure shored up to prevent it from falling, when, in 1882, it was decided to restore the building and once more utilise it as a chapel for the new school.

It is said, and traditionally received, that Dunstan placed the crown of England on the weak head of the youthful Ethelred, in A.D. 979, within the walls of St. Mary's Chapel. In the "Pictorial History of England" * is a view of St. Mary's Chapel as it must have appeared early in the present century; but it is clearly a Norman, not a Saxon structure, and could not, therefore, have been the building whose walls witnessed that ceremony.

After standing for eight centuries, part of the

building fell down. The particulars of the catas-trophe are related in a letter among Dr. Rawlin-son's MSS., in the Bodleian Library, dated "Kings-ton-on-Thames, March 4th, 1729-30." The sexton, who was digging a grave at the time, was killed on the spot, and his daughter, who was buried with him for three hours, was saved by the falling of a column over the grave in which she was helping her father. She subsequently succeeded him in his office. The portion of stone to which she owed her deliverance is still extant in the church, in-scribed : "Life Preserved, 1731." The portrait of the sextoness is in existence, representing a mas-culine female standing outside the church in a waistcoat and hat, with a pickaxe across her shoulder and her hand on a skull.

In the year 1540 the Chapel of St. Mary, with all its endowments, became forfeit to the Crown through the attainder of Charles Carew, the last warden or custos. The king shortly afterwards leased the site to Richard Taverner, Esq., of Nor-biton Hall, for twenty-one years, at a reserved rental of £12 12s. Queen Elizabeth, always liberal and ready in the cause of learning, in the third year of her reign founded, by charter, upon the ground once occupied by the chapel, a Free Grammar School, of which the bailiffs of Kingston were, then and for ever, to be governors. Three years later the queen endowed the school with "lands, tenements, and rents" yielding an income of £19 5s. 11d., and the bailiffs and freemen of the town were to pay annually twenty marks for the support of the masters. The endowment, since increased, amounts now to £200 per annum.

The school-room was, in point of fact, the interior of the ancient chapel, and is forty feet in length, twenty feet in breadth, and thirty feet in height. It is built in the Pointed style, and has a large and elegant east window. It is proposed to restore this fine room, which is said by competent judges to be the finest of any chantry in England with the exception of that at Wakefield.

William Walworth, the famous Lord Mayor of London during the rebellion of Wat Tyler, added to the endowment of the ancient chapel of St. Mary by gifts of lands and rents to support an additional chaplain. Walworth was said to be the apprentice of John Lovekyn, son of the founder, Edward Lovekyn. John was four times Lord Mayor of London. He rebuilt the chapel and adjoining mansion. His father was a native of Kingston ; hence the interest of both in the town.

We gather the following particulars of this school from Brayley's "Surrey" :—" It was established by Queen Elizabeth on the site of the ancient

Chapel of St. Mary Magdalen, founded in 1305 by Edward Lovekyn (a native of Kingston), in con-junction with his brother Richard, and endowed with ten acres of arable land, one acre of meadow, and five marks annual rent, for the support of a chaplain to pray for the souls of the founders and their relations. This benefaction was confirmed by letters patent of Edward II., dated 1309. John Lovekyn, fishmonger, four times Mayor of London, rebuilt the chapel, augmented the en-dowment for the maintenance of a second chaplain, and made regulations for its government, directing that one of the chaplains should be invested with the chief authority, and be styled the warden or custos. Lovekyn's charter relative to the dona-tions and statutes for the support of the chapel, ratified by himself in 1355, was confirmed by William, Bishop of Winchester. William Wal-worth, the famous Mayor of London in the reign of Richard II., said to have been the apprentice of John Lovekyn, added to the income of the estab-lishment by the gift of lands and rents for the sup-port of a third chaplain.

" The revenues of this chapel were valued at £34 19s. 7d. in 1534, and in 1540 escheated to the Crown, through the attainder of Charles Carew, the last master or warden. Not long after-wards the king granted the site with its appurte-nances to Richard Taverner, Esq., of Norbiton Hall, for twenty-one years, at a reserved rent of £12 12s. Soon after this property had reverted to the Crown, Elizabeth, by charter, founded a Free Grammar School here, and appointed the bailiffs of Kingston and their successors to be the governors. She also endowed the school with lands, tenements, and rents, yielding an income of £19 5s. 11d., in addition to which the bailiffs of the town were to pay twenty marks annually for the support of a master and an under-master."

Various endowments have since been added, and the funds at present derived from the Grammar School estate amount to about £200 per annum. In 1873 a new scheme for the management of this institution, was issued under the auspices of the Endowed Schools Commission, and under which the income is now regulated.

The new Grammar School accommodates one hundred boys, and not less than twelve boarders, at certain fixed fees. In 1878-9 two other schools were built in connection with the above scheme, each containing accommodation for 150 scholars, together with residences for the master and mistress.

William Burton, B.C.L., the author of several learned works, including a commentary on the " Itinerary " of Antoninus, so far as relates to

Britain, and who excelled as a critic, philologer, and antiquary, was master of the old school for some years prior to 1655.

The poet Hayley, Gibbon the historian, Lovibond the poet, George Alexander Stevens, author of the popular "Lecture upon Heads," George

to the south of the London road; but although allowed by charter to be continued for eight days, it has dwindled down to three days, the last being devoted exclusively to what is known as the pleasure fair. It is supposed that the fair was at an early period held in the church, since various enter-

ST. MARY'S CHAPEL.

Keate, George Charles Cholmondeley, and his relative the late Marquis of Cholmondeley, were all distinguished scholars of Kingston school; and to their names may be added others conspicuous for talent and learning.

Formerly three fairs were held yearly at Kingston—namely, on the Thursday in Whitsun week, on the 2nd of August and following day, and on the 13th of November and seven following days. The latter, locally termed the Great Allhallowtide fair, is now the only one kept up. It is held in a broad open space called the Fairfield, which lies

tainments as well as "miracle plays" were given in the building; but the proceedings were stopped by William of Wykeham in all churches in his diocese of Winchester. Kingston is now, however, in the diocese of Rochester.

Kingston-on-Thames has always been a place famous for its amusements. To this Butler refers in the second part of "Hudibras":—

> "Thus they pass through the market-place,
> And to the town green hye apace,
> Highly fam'd for its Hocktide games,
> Ycleped Kingston-upon-Thames."

It appears that Lilly used to ride over from his house at Hersham to Kingston every Saturday to play the quack among the market people.

Amongst the entries in the chamberlain's accounts are two or three concerning an extinct game called "the Kyngham," which would seem to have been of considerable importance. "Be yt in mynd," says the old chronicle, "that ye 19 yere of Kyng Harry ye 7, at the geveng out of the Kynggam by Harry Bower and Harry

in those days. It seems to have been a distinct thing from the May games, and to have been held later in the summer. Holinshed says that the young folks in country towns, in the reign of Edward II., used to choose a summer king and queen to dance about May-poles. The contributions to the celebration of the same game in the neighbouring parishes show that the Kyngham was not confined to Kingston.

Their favourite game of football will lose nothing

COOMBE HOUSE.

Nycol, cherchewardens, amounted clearly to £4 2s. 6d. of that same game." And again:—"23 Henry VII. Paid for whet and malt, and vele and motton and pygges, and ges and coks for the Kyngham, £0 33s. od." "Paid to Robert Neyle for goying to Wyndesore for Maister Doctor's horse ageynes the Kyngham day, 4s. od.; for baking the Kyngham brede, os. 6d.; to a laborer for bering home of the geere after the Kyngham was don, 1s. od."

The Kyngham appears to have been an annual game or sport conducted by the parish officers, who paid the expenses attending it, and accounted for the receipts. The clear profits, 15 Henry VIII. —the last time it is mentioned in the record— amounted to £9 10s. 6d., a very considerable sum

in the estimation of school-boys—normally a combative, not to say savage, race—by the tradition that it owed its origin to the celebration of a victory over the Danes by the townsmen of Kingston during the celebration of their Shrovetide or Hocktide sports, when a finer edge was put upon the enjoyment of the occasion by kicking the head of the Danish captain from one to another of the people. The tradition is supported by Dr. William Roots, whose opinion as an antiquary deserves great weight, and who quotes Salmon, the historian, on his side. Salmon says:—"Hock Tuesday is the day on which the Danes are said to have been generally massacred throughout England;" adding that "it is very reasonable to suppose a connection between the head of the Danish chief who had been slain by townsmen of Kingston, and the football sport at the same time."

The spacious Fairfield, where cricket, football, &c., are almost daily played, is about twenty acres in extent. The lower portion—about thirteen acres—is held on lease from various proprietors by the Corporation, and devoted to the purpose of recreation. The upper portion of the field is used for the cattle fair in the month of November, and is cultivated in small plots at other times.

Kingston has long been attractive to anglers —pike, barbel, roach, perch, chub, dace, and gudgeon, being abundant at this point in the Thames. Bream are also occasionally met with, and trout of a fair size are sufficiently plentiful. At a charge of ten shillings a day experienced fishermen with their punts will always be found who will supply every requisite, and thus save the angler coming from a distance the necessity of bringing with him a heavy burden, which, on a hot summer's day, is no small advantage. The river in this locality is strictly preserved by the Thames Angling Preservation Society, being under the immediate supervision of its officers, who are careful to prevent any infringement of the regulations.

Angling from the river bank is, of course, a favourite amusement, especially with the working classes. It may be mentioned as a singular incident that on a recent occasion a trout weighing no less than 7lbs. jumped voluntarily into a boat in which a boy happened to be sitting.

A curious contest, which at one time threatened to be serious, took place on a recent occasion between the officers of the Thames Conservancy and some members of the Kingston Corporation. The Conservancy desired to move the floating swimming baths, at present moored just above the "Anglers" Inn, to a site opposite the tan-yard; the Corporation, on the other hand, considered the site objectionable, and desired that the bath should remain where it is now fixed. An official, acting presumably on instructions from the Thames Conservancy, in command of the steam-tug *Queen*, attempted forcibly to remove it, and a scuffle ensued, in which an alderman received a severe thrust with a hitcher. After a *fracas* which lasted about an hour and a half the officers of the Thames Conservancy decided to give up the attempt, and withdrew their forces on board the tug, which steamed away amid the jeers of a large crowd attracted to the river-side by the extraordinary incident.

Surbiton (originally the South Barton), which stands on the high ground to the south of the town, is an extensive and somewhat fashionable suburb of Kingston, reaching westwards as far as Thames Ditton, southward to Long Ditton, and eastwards nearly as far as New Maldon. It was separated from Kingston by a private Act of Parliament, "The Surbiton Improvement Act," in 1855. It is scarcely old enough to have a history, and it is not even mentioned in Lewis's "Topographical Dictionary," as being originally only a hamlet in the parish of Kingston.

About the year 1845 a large plot of ground near the railway station was taken up by a speculative builder, who covered the greater part with houses, the name of Kingston New Town being given to the newly-formed district. The buildings, as fast as they were erected, were mortgaged, in order to obtain means for carrying out the designs; but the scheme not proving successful, the mortgagees took possession of the entire property. The unfinished houses were completed, others raised, a large space fronting the crescent was planted with trees, and a spacious church, St. Mark's, was erected on Surbiton Hill, near the bridge over the railway; and it was then decided that this increasing neighbourhood should in future be called Surbiton, it being wholly in that district.

The view from the top of the hill is one of great beauty. Looking eastward are to be seen Norwood and the Crystal Palace districts; descending the hill and looking northward over the town of Kingston, through the trees which form a beautiful margin to the landscape, the Hampstead and Highgate hills complete a very pleasing view.

There is a station here on the main line of the London and South-Western Railway, whence diverges a branch line for Hampton Court, with an intermediate station at Thames Ditton.

Surbiton is composed almost wholly of villas of the modern type, mostly standing in their own grounds; and the district is intersected by shady paths in every direction, and is peculiarly rich in woodland shrubs and wild flowers.

On the slope of the hill leading down to Kingston is an old wayside hostelry, a relic of other days, with the sign of the "Waggon and Horses," which has been a house of call for carriers for a couple of centuries or more.

The main street of Surbiton is composed of detached residences, and a few shops on each side of the high road. The first noticeable building is a fine red-brick Wesleyan chapel, which prominently shows the strength of the Dissenting element in the town; indeed, there are new churches and chapels in abundance.

St. Mark's Church, mentioned above, was built in 1845, on a site given by Lady Burdett-Coutts.

It is constructed chiefly of stone, and consists of a nave and chancel, short transepts, and a square tower rising from piers at the intersection. The aisles are separated from the nave by Pointed arches springing from octagonal columns. The ceiling is panelled, and ornamented with bosses; the pulpit is of stone, and is entered from the vestry, and most of the windows are filled with stained or painted glass.

In 1872 the church of St. Andrew, in Maple Road, was built as a chapel-of-ease to St. Mark's. It is a brick building, in the Italian style, and consists of chancel, nave, transepts, and a campanile.

On the western side of the town, close by the river, and opposite to the grounds of Hampton Court Palace, stands the Roman Catholic church dedicated to St. Raphael. It was built, in the Italian style, in 1846–7, at the expense of the late Mr. Alexander Raphael, of Surbiton Place, some time M.P. for St. Albans, on whose estate it stands. It consists principally of nave, aisles, and chancel, with a square tower of three storeys projecting from the centre of the west front. The external walls are chiefly of Bath stone, and the pulpit and font are of Sicilian marble. The door of the tabernacle is an ancient carved-oak panel, representing the Crucifixion, and supposed to date from the fourteenth century.

Norbiton is probably another suburb cut off from Kingston-on-Thames, and called *Nor*biton in contrast to *Sur*biton, from lying to the north, as the latter lies south of the parent town. It lies on the road towards London *viâ* Wimbledon, but, like the locality just described, it is scarcely old enough to have a history.

Norbiton was formed into a separate ecclesiastical parish in 1842. The church, dedicated to St. Peter, built by Sir Gilbert Scott, is a brick building, consisting of chancel, nave, and aisles, and a tower. The district of St. Paul's, Kingston Hill, was formed out of St. Peter's in 1881. The church, which is situated in Queen's Road, is of stone, and of Gothic design.

In this neighbourhood are several charitable institutions. The Children's Convalescent Institution, Kingston Hill, is one of the philanthropic features of this locality. It is in connection with the Metropolitan Convalescent Institution at Walton-on-Thames, and has for its object the relief of poor children recovering from serious illness, or suffering from complaints which require change of air and rest for their removal, and was erected from the design of Mr. Henry Saxon Snell, the architect. It contains 150 beds, and is open for children of either sex between the ages of two and fourteen, of whom more than 1,000 are admitted yearly.

Patients are admitted on the recommendation of annual and life subscribers only.

The Royal Cambridge Asylum for Soldiers' Widows, situated on the brow of a hill on the Cambridge estate at Norbiton, was opened in February, 1854. It is the only institution which provides for the soldier's widow, and was founded in memory of the late Duke of Cambridge. The Queen, the Prince of Wales, and other members of the royal family, are among its patrons; the Duchess of Cambridge is lady president, and the Duke of Cambridge, president, whilst many noblemen, ladies, and officers of distinction, assist in its management. The foundation-stone was laid by the late Prince Consort. The widows must be those of non-commissioned officers and privates of the army, not less than fifty years of age. Each widow has a furnished room, and receives 7s. weekly, besides a monthly allowance of 2s. 6d. for coals. The house has been enlarged, and is now capable of containing seventy widows. The building is of brick, in the Italian style, from a design by Mr. Thomas Allom, architect; and a chapel, detached from the main building, has been added. The funded income of the charity yields only £550, with an additional £50 from the Princess Mary's Fund for Nurses, to meet an estimated expenditure of £3,000 per annum. The inmates are admitted by election, the governors and subscribers voting by ballot for the election of candidates.

Not far off on the high ground stands Coombe House, the favourite residence of Lord Liverpool during his long premiership. Here he was frequently visited by the Prince Regent during the progress of the war against Napoleon. Here the Duke of Wellington dined and slept—in August, 1814—on his way to the Netherlands and to the field of Waterloo. The Prince Regent, the Emperor Alexander of Russia, the King of Prussia, and Generals Blucher and Platoff, were also hospitably entertained by the Earl here on their way to Portsmouth, in the same year. Here, too, in December, 1828, died the Earl of Liverpool, after lying ill from paralysis for about two years. His first wife has a monument in Kingston church. Lord Liverpool was Prime Minister of England under the Regency, and for the first seven years of the reign of George IV., and he divided his time at his country residence here and Fife House, Whitehall. He had lived, in his earlier days, at Addiscombe, near Croydon.

Coombe Wood is the name of a rather extensive property here, between Wimbledon, Richmond Park, and Kingston-on-Thames, belonging to His Royal Highness the Duke of Cambridge. Around it is a small park, surrounded by preserves, where the duke often entertains his friends with a day's pheasant shooting. The house is small and unpretending, but the grounds are well laid out. Coombe Warren belongs to Mr. W. B. Currie, whose refined taste in antiquarian and artistic matters is well known.

Here the Empress Eugénie lived for a few months, after leaving Chislehurst in 1881, before she could settle down into her new home at Farnborough.

Here also Mr. Gladstone found rest and change of air during the Parliamentary session of 1884.

Adjoining Coombe Springs, the seat of Sir Edmund Du Cane, are the gardens of Lord Londesborough, with a very extensive range of hot-houses, containing, amongst other choice productions, one of the best collections of orchids within the kingdom.

The united districts of Coombe and New Malden, which lie about two miles to the east of Kingston, were formed into an ecclesiastical parish in 1867. At New Malden is a junction of the Kingston branch line with the South-Western Railway. Close by the railway station stands Christ Church, which was built in 1866 on a site given by the Duke of Cambridge ; it is in the Early English style, and consists of chancel, nave, and north aisle.

The principal nurseries of Messrs. Veitch and Sons, the well-known horticulturists, are also in this neighbourhood. From the summit of Coombe Warren, a pleasant stroll on a summer day from Kingston, is gained a fine view of the Surrey hills, including Banstead and Epsom Downs, the chalk hills which divide the county into two parts, Paine's Hill, St. George's, St. Ann's, and the Marlow hills, with Windsor in the foreground—as pleasant and extensive a picture as any in the county.

On the Wandsworth approach to Kingston, a mile or two out, is a house which was formerly an inn called the "Bald-faced Stag," a hostelry well known in former times as having been the haunt and place of refuge of the notorious footpad, Jerry Abershaw, who long kept this part of the country in constant fear. There is a story related of this daring character that, on a dark and inclement night in the month of November, after having stopped every passenger on the road, being suddenly taken ill, he found it necessary to retire to the "Bald-faced Stag," and his comrades deeming it advisable to send to Kingston for medical assistance, Dr. William Roots (then a very young man) attended. Having bled him and given the necessary advice, he was about to retire home, when his patient, with much earnestness, said : "You had better, sir, have some one to go back with you, as it is a very dark and lonesome journey." This, however, the doctor declined, observing that he had "not the least fear, even should he meet with Abershaw himself," little thinking to whom he was making this reply.

It is said that the ruffian frequently alluded to this scene afterwards with much comic humour. His real name was Louis Jeremiah Avershawe. He was tried at Croydon for the murder of David Price, an officer belonging to Union Hall, in Southwark, whom he had killed with a pistol shot, having at the same time wounded a second officer with another pistol. In this case the indictment was invalidated by some flaw ; but on being again tried, and convicted for feloniously shooting at one Barnaby Turner, he was executed at Kennington Common in 1795, and his body afterwards hung in chains at Wimbledon, the scene of his marauding exploits.*

CHAPTER XXXVII.

HAM AND PETERSHAM.

"Ham's embowering walks,
Where polished Cornbury woos the willing muse."—THOMSON.

Situation and Boundaries of Ham-with-Hatch—Its Etymology—Descent of the Manor—Anne of Cleves—John Maitland, Earl of Lauderdale, and Lady Dysart—Ham House—The Interior of the Mansion—The "Cabal" Ministry—The Gardens and Grounds—Walpole's Description of the House—Queen Charlotte's Impression of the Mansion—Lady Dysart and Bishop Blomfield—Ham Walks—The Village and Church—National Orphan Home—Petersham—The Church—The Misses Berry—Gay's Summer-House—Catherine Hyde, Duchess of Queensberry—Petersham Lodge—Sudbrooke.

LEAVING the Vale of Kingston, with Norbiton, Kingston Hill, and Coombe Warren away to the right, we now break fresh ground by taking the road due north, and following partly the bend of the

river in its course towards Richmond. The village of Ham is located about midway between Kingston

---

* See "Old and New London," Vol. VI., pp. 334, 498.

and Richmond, between the Richmond road and the Thames, and adjoins Petersham. In official documents the place is called Ham-with-Hatch (derived from the Saxon word *house*, *vill*, or *home*), and Hatch, a *gate*.* It formerly constituted a subordinate manor in Kingston parish, but has in recent times been made into a "district chapelry." Lysons, quoting as his authority a charter in the British Museum, states that King Athelstan, in the year 931, granted lands at Ham to his minister Wulfar.

At the time of the "Domesday" Survey, as we learn from Brayley's "History of Surrey," this estate was included in the royal manor of Kingston; and Henry II. bestowed certain lands in Ham on Maurice de Creon, or Creoun, who, in 1168, was "charged with the sum of 43s. 4d. for his estate here, in aid of the marriage of Matilda, the king's daughter." The property eventually passed from this family to Sir Robert Burnell and his heirs, and from the latter it eventually devolved upon the Lords Lovel, in right of their maternal descent from Maud Burnell, whose first husband, John, Lord Lovel of Tichmarsh, died in 1315. Francis, the last heir male of the Lovels, was created a viscount by Edward IV., and he afterwards held the office of Lord Chamberlain of the Household to Richard III., and was constituted Chief Butler of England. After the battle of Bosworth Field, Lord Lovel sought refuge in Flanders, but as he was attainted of high treason by Henry VII., in his first Parliament in 1485, all his estates became forfeited to the Crown. With reference to this seizure of his inheritance by the king, Banks writes, in his "Dormant and Extinct Peerages":—"Aggrieved by this injustice, Lord Lovel espoused the cause of Lambert Simnel, and in 1487 he returned to England with the Earl of Lincoln and other Yorkists, accompanied by an army of two thousand foreign mercenaries, under the command of a German officer of talent, named Martin Schwarts. Met by the king's troops at Stoke, near Newark, a battle ensued, in which the invaders were completely defeated and most of the leaders slain. It was at first supposed that Lord Lovel had been killed, but the body not being found, it was concluded that he had been drowned in attempting to cross the Thames on horseback. From the discovery, however, about 1708, of the skeleton of a man in a secret chamber at Minster Lovel, in Oxfordshire, in a mansion belonging to the family, it has been since conjectured, with great probability, that this unfor-

tunate nobleman had sought an asylum at that place, and either through accident or treachery, had perished there from starvation."

But to return to Ham. Here the uncrowned queen, Anne of Cleves, spent part of her years, Ham, Petersham, and Shene having been among the manors settled on her by Henry VIII. on her divorce. All these manors subsequently reverted to the Crown, and were granted by James I. to his eldest son, Henry, Prince of Wales, and on his decease, in 1612, to his next son, Prince Charles. On the accession of the latter to the throne, this property was held by different persons on lease until 1671, when Charles II. granted the lordship of Petersham and Ham to John Maitland, Earl of Lauderdale, who in that year had married the Countess of Dysart, the then owner of Ham House. Lord Lauderdale was created Duke of Lauderdale, in Scotland, and Baron Petersham and Earl of Guildford, in England, in 1672. He was one of the confidential ministers of Charles II., and is known in history as one of the five obnoxious persons forming the "Cabal." He had been a Royalist in the time of the Civil War, and was present at the battle of Worcester, where he was taken prisoner. By his marriage with Elizabeth, Countess of Dysart, this estate, with other landed property, became vested in the heirs of that lady, and it has since remained in the possession of that family.

Ham House—the manor house—is located in Petersham parish, but belongs by position to Ham. It is situated on low ground near the banks of the Thames, opposite to classic Twickenham, and one of its avenues extends to Ham Common. Of this place Leigh Hunt observes, in his "Table Talk":—"Old trees, the most placid of rivers, Thomson up above you, Pope near you, Cowley himself not a great way off; I hope here is a nest of repose, both material and spiritual, of the most Cowleyian and Evelynian sort. Ham, too. . . . is expressly celebrated both by Thomson and by Armstrong; and though that infernal old Duke of Lauderdale, who put people to the rack, lived there in the original Ham House—he married a Dysart—yet even the bitter taste is taken out of the mouth by the sweets of these poets, and by the memories of the good Duke of Queensberry, and his good Duchess (Prior's Kitty), who nursed their friend Gay there when he was ill." Lytton-Bulwer writes of Ham House that it is "girt with stateliness of eld;" and it is probably this mansion that Tennyson speaks of as

"A Tudor-chimnied bulk
Of mellow brick-work on an isle of flowers."

The long avenues of majestic elms surrounding the mansion, in some places intertwining their branching arms, like the fan-traceried aisle of a cathedral, together with the grove of dark Scotch firs within the grounds, give the demesne a marked and peculiar character ; and the house itself, from almost every distant view, appears to be enshrouded in foliage. The Petersham avenue is about one-third of a mile in length ; the Ham walk, leading from the large folding iron gates which once formed

there are also arcade gradations between the central doorway and the inner side of the wings. In this front appears a range of busts (cast in lead, but painted stone colour), placed within oval niches constructed in the brickwork, between the basement and the first storey, and also in the side walls, which bound the lawn and extend to a gravelled terrace with iron gates, and a ha-ha separating the gardens from the adjacent meadows. On the middle of the lawn, raised upon a rocky pedestal

HAM HOUSE.

the main entrance, but are now disused, is almost a mile long, and terminates on Ham Common. The other avenues, which skirt the garden wall on the eastern side, and extend across the meadows near the Thames, are of a more limited range, but include many noble trees. In the fore-court forming the present entrance (near the stabling and out-buildings) are several time-worn and rugged elms of vast size.

The mansion is constructed of red brick, and has two fronts, along each of which a block cornice is continued the entire length, immediately below the parapet. The principal front faces the river, and at each end is a short projecting wing, with semi-hexagonal terminations extending to the roof ;

(on which is a small shield of the City arms), on steps, is a colossal statue of the Thames, sculptured in stone, and leaning upon a watery urn.

Tennyson's lines well describe the entrance to the mansion :—

"So by many a sweep
Of meadow smooth from aftermath we reached
The griffin-guarded gates, and passed through all
The pillared dusk of sounding sycamores,
And crossed the garden to the gardener's lodge,
With all its casements bedded, and its walls
And chimneys muffled in the leafy vine."

Built for Henry, Prince of Wales, elder brother of the ill-fated King Charles, the residence of the haughty Duchess of Lauderdale, and during her second husband's lifetime the head-quarters of the

"Cabal," the appointed asylum for the deposed James II., and the birthplace of the great states-man and general, John, Duke of Argyll, Ham well merits a prominent place in the rank of England's historic houses. It is full of memories, and its peaceful aspect on a bright summer's day, with the sunny meadows in front stretching down to the Thames, cannot fail to fill the beholder with a sense of mysterious longing to know the tales which its dark red walls enclose, and to recall the high walls, except where an apparently open space is guarded by some very handsome old iron gates, of admirable design and of great massiveness; and even were they opened—an operation which has not been effected for many long years— a sunk fence still prevents all access from the front. A small side door, however, answers the purpose, and admits the visitor who is fortunate enough to have his passport into the gravelled court.

TWICKENHAM FERRY.

powerful minds and stately figures who moved amid the shade of the trees which surround it, and soften while they throw out the bold and graceful outlines of the time-worn building. And yet Time's ruthless hand has here done less to mark its flight than in many another structure; the house has not been suffered to fall into decay, and the proofs of the magnificence of the period in which it was erected remain undisturbed and yet untarnished, for the work was well and solidly done, down to the minutest details.

The house does not stand high, and it is only on a near approach that its beauty is seen to advan-tage, and then it appears—as, indeed, it is—most difficult of entrance, for it is quite surrounded by

It was built in the beginning of the seventeenth century by Sir Thomas Vavasour, and though said to have been designed as a residence for Henry, Prince of Wales, it does not appear that he ever inhabited it—owing, possibly, to his early death, at the age of nineteen. The house would appear to have been finished in 1610, as that date, with the words "VIVAT REX," form a part of the orna-mental carvings on the principal door. Sir Thomas Vavasour held the post of Marshal of the House-hold to James I., and in 1611 he was appointed judge of the then newly-constituted Marshal's Court, conjointly with Sir Francis Bacon, then Solicitor-General, and afterwards Lord Chancellor. From Sir Thomas Vavasour it passed into the hands of the Earl of Holderness, whose family sold it to William Murray; and on the 22nd of May, 1651, it was surrendered to the use of Sir Lionel Tollemache, who had married Elizabeth, daughter of William Murray, who was created Countess of Dysart in her own right. From that day to this it has remained in the family of the Tollemaches, Earls of Dysart, who, as above stated, still retain it.

After the death of Sir Lionel the house underwent great alterations, and many additions were made to it by his widow, on whom the peerage was conferred; but it was furnished at great expense in the taste of the time of Charles II., and the parquet flooring in one at least of the drawing-rooms bears the monogram of this lady, in the double L, which formed her initials as Duchess of Lauderdale. The house and grounds, in fact, had at this time acquired some celebrity. Evelyn, in his "Diary," under date of 27th August, 1678, writes :—"After dinner I walk'd to Ham, to see the house and garden of the Duke of Lauderdale, which is indeede inferior to few of the best villas in Italy itselfe; the house furnish'd like a great prince's; the parterres, flower-gardens, orangeries, groves, avenues, courts, statues, perspectives, fountaines, aviaries, and all this at the banks of the sweetest river in the world, must needes be admirable."

Lady Dysart possessed great political influence even during Sir Lionel's life, through the intimacy existing between herself and the then Earl of Lauderdale, for, according to Burnet, "their correspondence was of an early date, and had given occasion to censure. For when he was a prisoner after the battle of Worcester, in 1651, she made him believe that he was in great danger of his life, and that he saved it by her intrigues with Cromwell. Upon the king's restoration, she thought the earl did not make her the return which she expected, and they lived for some years at a distance; but after her husband's death she made up all quarrels, and they were so much together that the earl's lady was offended at it, and went to Paris, where she died three years after. The Lady Dysart gained such an ascendency over him at length, that it lessened him in the esteem of the world, for he delivered himself up to all her humours and caprices." They were married in 1671, and then "she took upon herself to determine everything. She sold all places, and was wanting in no methods that would bring her money, which she lavished with the most profuse vanity. They lived at a vast expense, and she carried all things with a haughtiness that would not have been easily borne from a queen, and talked of all people with such ungoverned freedom, that she grew at length to be universally hated. She was a woman of great beauty, and of far greater parts. She had a wonderful quickness of apprehension, and an amazing vivacity in conversation. She had studied not only divinity and history, but mathematics and philosophy. She was violent in everything she set about: a violent friend, but a much more violent enemy. She had a restless ambition, was ravenously covetous, and would have stuck at nothing by which she might compass her ends." Such is the description of her in the pages of Burnet.

As scandal declared her to have been the duke's mistress long before he married her, and as before that she is said to have been the favourite of Oliver Cromwell, we need not wonder to find her not very creditably immortalised in a lampoon of the time :—

" She is Besse of my heart, she was Besse of Old Noll,
  She was once Fleetwood's Besse, and she's now of Atholl."

It was during the lifetime of her second husband that Clifford, Ashley, Buckingham, and Arlington met here, and in the house of their host —whose initial gave the last necessary letter to the notorious Cabal—formed those iniquitous schemes which have procured for Charles II.'s ministry the infamous reputation they have so long and justly borne.

On entering the house, the first of its many treasures that meets the visitor is a beautiful portrait, by Sir Joshua Reynolds, of a Countess of Dysart, so unfortunately placed that every time the hall door is opened wide its handle adds to the size of a hole which it has already made in a prominent part of the picture. The large hall in which it hangs contains several other good pictures. It occupies the whole of the centre of the house, and has round it a gallery, the upper walls of which are ornamented with more portraits: amongst them, one of General Tollemache, a stern-looking warrior, who was killed at Brest in 1694. Thereby hangs a tale which, if true, tarnishes the fame of the Duke of Marlborough. Tradition says that the great duke was jealous of the talents of this officer, whom he hated, and on whose ruin he was determined. When he summoned a council of war to consider the question of an attack on Brest, General Tollemache warmly opposed it as totally impracticable, which the duke, in his heart, also believed it to be; still he upheld the project, overruled the objections, and finally appointed General Tollemache himself to the command of the expedition in such a manner that he could not, consistently with honour, decline the proffered post. The duke, by this manœuvre, secured his defeat at least, and fortune granted even more, for not only was the attack completely repulsed, but the general himself died of a wound received during the fight.

Adjoining the hall is, perhaps, the very smallest chapel ever seen. Evidently the duchess, however large in most of her ideas, in spite of her divinity studies did not consider a chapel as an appendage of much importance to her mansion. Still it contains its point of interest, for the prayer-book was the gift of King Charles. Near the chapel door, in a sort of vestibule at the bottom of the staircase, hangs a large picture of the battle of Lepanto. A quaint and extraordinary picture it is. The name of the artist is unknown, which is unfortunate, as it does credit to his imagination and originality, if not to his truth and consistency. The broad stairs possess very handsome balusters of walnut wood, and up and down them the ghost of the Duchess of Lauderdale has been seen to walk, clad in the rustling silks and gorgeous fashions of Charles II.'s luxurious days. The large open hall is surrounded by suites of apartments, filled with beautiful furniture of the seventeenth century, and with rare cabinets; one of remarkable fineness is of ivory, and lined with cedar. Many of the chairs are of handsome carved wood, and the cushions are covered with old cut velvet of rich dark colours, and in all possible corners lurks the double L already mentioned. The ceilings are all painted, and by Verrio, and one of the rooms is hung with tapestry, remarkable for all the figures, in various fanciful dresses, having black faces and hands. There are many cabinets and shelves filled with a large quantity of china, chiefly of French make, and of no particular value, but even on them some double L's are to be found. One cabinet, however, contains a greater treasure, kept with care under lock and key—a crystal locket, and in it a lock of the hair of the Earl of Essex, Queen Elizabeth's ill-fated favourite. In a small room at the end of one of the suites is a recess, and in this recess stand the two arm-chairs of the Duke and Duchess of Lauderdale—not the easy low chairs of the present day, but solid and stiff uncompromising arm-chairs, with straight backs and carved wooden legs.

On the west side of the house is a gallery ninety-two feet long, and full of pictures, chiefly family portraits, looking grim and solemn in their dark dresses and total solitude. In a charming large window at one end it requires but little imagination to fancy the five ministers of Charles II. seated in the luxurious quiet of the country, concocting their three secret treaties with Louis of France, and devising means of replenishing their monarch's dissipated funds—a work in which, doubtless, they were ably assisted by the quick brain and ready wit of the duchess, their unscrupulous hostess. And there it was, no doubt, that the iniquitous scheme of shutting up the Exchequer was first conceived by Clifford or by Ashley—a measure which may have answered for the time, as it placed at the disposal of the ministers £1,300,000 of ready money : but surely this was dearly purchased by the loss of honour and reputation which it involved.* And the panic which it caused the commercial world, and the numbers of widows and orphans who were reduced to beggary, must have brought anything but a blessing on the heads of this council of five.

There they sit—Arlington,† originally Sir Henry Bennett, with his graceful, easy manner, ready flow of courtly language, covering the deepest cunning with the most insinuating address. That dark scar in his face, from a sabre cut, must have marred the beauty of his handsome countenance as much as his want of boldness detracted from his brilliancy of parts. He was a contrast to the man whom his patronage had raised to a level with himself; for Clifford, a privy councillor, treasurer of the household, and commissioner of the treasury, was brave, generous, and ambitious, constant in his friendship, and open in his resentment ; a minister with clean hands in a corrupt court, and endued with a mind capable of forming, and a heart ready to execute, the boldest and most hazardous projects. Next to him sits the pleasure-loving, extravagant Buckingham. One can fancy the duchess leaning over his chair with a serious and abstracted air, devising some fresh festivity for the evening, or arranging between them the shade of velvet for a gorgeous robe for the next fancy ball at court; while bold and sneering Lauderdale himself recalls the duke's attention to the business of the state, and attracts the observer's attention by his boisterous manner and ungainly appearance, to which even the rich materials of his dress and its massive gold embroidery fail to give the air of a gentleman. Arbitrary, sarcastic, and domineering, he was a bold man who stood in the duke's path, for he was never known to fail in attaining his object, be the means what they might.

Lastly comes Sir Anthony Ashley, soon to be made Earl of Shaftesbury, for some time a favourite of the king, who delighted in his singular fertility of invention, and sympathised but too strongly in

---

his reckless contempt of principle, and yet said of him, in a moment when he perhaps consulted his anger as much as his judgment, that he was "the weakest and wickedest man of his age." He it was who, from conceit of his own figure, insisted on riding on horseback in the procession to Westminster Hall on the occasion of his installation as Lord Chancellor, and further obliged all the law officers and the several judges to proceed in the same manner, instead of using the cumbrous carriages which they were accustomed to occupy, to the great annoyance of those reverend personages, one of whom, Mr. Justice Twisden, by the curveting of his horse, was laid prostrate in the mire.[*]

They had but little religion amongst them—all five—for while Buckingham scoffed openly at the subject, he was the only one who so much as called himself a Churchman. The others were Protestant or Roman Catholics, according to the fashion of the times, Ashley belonging to no Church whatever.

The haughty old Duchess of Lauderdale survived her husband by many years, and died in 1698. She was succeeded in her estates, and in her title of Dysart, by her eldest son by her first husband, Lionel, Lord Huntingtower. Her second son, General Thomas Tollemache, has already been mentioned as the victim of the Duke of Marlborough's hatred. The third son entered the navy, and having killed his opponent, the Hon. W. Carnegie, in a duel, died in the West Indies; while her eldest daughter, Elizabeth, married the first Duke of Argyll, and was the mother of the great Duke John, who, as before mentioned, was born at Ham in 1678. This duke was the victor of Sheriffmuir, and being no less distinguished in the council than in arms, is thus immortalised by Pope :—

> "Argyll, the state's whole thunder born to wield,
> And shake alike the senate and the field."

He bore the English title of Duke of Greenwich, which ceased with him, for he died without children in 1743, when he was succeeded in his Scottish honours by his brother Archibald, who was also born at Ham House.

At the meeting of the peers which took place at Windsor in December, 1688, the ultimate destination of the king (James II.) was discussed. It was deemed advisable that he should be sent out of London. "Ham," writes Lord Macaulay, "which had been built and decorated by Lauder-

dale, on the banks of the Thames, out of the plunder of Scotland and the bribes of France, and which was regarded as the most luxurious of villas, was proposed as a convenient retreat." But circumstances arose which prevented the design from being carried out.

Before taking leave of this place, we must mention the quiet beauty of the old-fashioned garden, where the large trees cast a welcome shade over the wide green terrace, enlivened by the side of the house with large beds of flowers—wild tangled beds, in keeping with the date of the house, for they speak of a far earlier period than the trimly-regulated lines of colour, disposed in the form of brilliant mosaics of the present day. Masses of roses and lavender, enormous pink peonies, and sweet mignonette, run at their own will over the space, and fill the air with fragrance. The sound of the jarring world is so completely shut out, that one can fancy oneself two hundred years back in the world's history, surrounded for miles with peaceful country scenes, meadows and fields sloping down to the river, which, fresh and pure, untainted by steam and the busy traffic of commerce, flows on to the great city of London, to bear on its bosom the barges of the great and noble, and the gay and voluptuous beauties and gallants of the time, some to jousts and revelry, some, more sadly and solemnly, to the Tower and the scaffold. But the river rolls on, caring little for the panorama of life that flows on along its banks, telling not a word of all that it has seen and known, taking no heed of all that is now passing before it, rolling steadily onwards into the future, to the time when we shall all be dust, and when Ham House and all its treasured memories will be forgotten.[*]

Horace Walpole, in a letter to Montagu, dated June 11, 1770, thus describes a visit which he paid to Ham House, when his niece, Charlotte Walpole, had become its mistress through her marriage with the Earl of Dysart :—

"I went yesterday to see my niece in her new principality of Ham. It delighted me and made me peevish. Close to the Thames, in the centre of all rich and verdant beauty, it is so blocked up, barricaded with walls, vast trees, and gates, that you think yourself a hundred miles off and a hundred years back. The old furniture is so magnificently ancient, dreary, and decayed, that at every step one's spirits sink, and all my pas-

---

[*] See Lingard's "History of England."

[*] For much of the above description of Ham House and its history we are indebted to an account of it which appeared in the *Gentleman's Magazine* (Vol. III., N.S., 1867), and which is reproduced by permission of the writer.

sion for antiquity could not keep them up. Every minute I expected to see ghosts sweeping by— ghosts that I would not give sixpence to see, Lauderdales, Tollemaches, and Maitlands. There is one old brown gallery full of Vandycks and Lelys, charming miniatures, delightful Wouvermans and Poelemburghs, china, japan, bronzes, ivory cabinets, and silver dogs, pokers, bellows, &c., without end. One pair of bellows is of filagree. In this state of pomp and tatters my nephew intends it shall remain, and is so religious an observer of the venerable rites of his house, that because they were never opened by his father but once, for the late Lord Granville, you are locked out and locked in, and after journeying all around the house, as you do round an old French fortified town, you are at last admitted through the stable-yard, to creep along a dark passage by the housekeeper's room, and so by a back door into the great hall. He seems as much afraid of rats as a cat, for though you might enjoy the Thames from every window of three sides of the house, you may tumble into it before you guess it is there."

Macaulay mentions this house as a symbol of wealth derived from dishonest statesmanship. He writes in his "History of England"* in the chapter which he devotes to a general view of the state of England in 1685: "The sumptuous palace to which the populace of London gave the name of Dunkirk House,† the stately pavilions, the fish-ponds, the deer park and orangery of Euston, the more than Italian luxury of Ham, with its busts, its fountains, and its aviaries, were among the many signs which indicated what was the shortest road to boundless wealth."

In the "Extracts of the Journal and Correspondence of Miss Berry" (Vol. II., p. 423) appears the following description of a visit to Ham House, and of the impression it made upon her, by Queen Charlotte, in a letter to one of her own family :—"The Rain having ceased, Ldy. Caroline wished to show me from Ham walks the View of the River, and likewise that of Lord Dysart's Place ; and as She has been favoured with a Key, She offered to carry us there. We walked, and most delightfull it was there, and saw not only the House, but all the Beautifull Old China, which a Civil Housekeeper offered to show us. It is so fine a Collection, that to know it and admire it as one ought to do would require many hours ; but when all the Fine Paintings, Cabinets of Excellent Workmanship, both in Ivory and Amber, also attract yr. Notice. Days

are required to see it with Advantage to oneself. The House is much altered since I saw it by repairing, and tho' the old Furniture still remains, it is kept so clean, that even under the Tattered State of Hangings and Chairs, One must admire the good Taste of Our forefathers, and their Magnificence. The Parqueté Floors have been taken up with great Care, cleaned, and re-laid, and in order to preserve them the Present Lord has put Carpets over them, but of Course not Nailed down. I saw this time also the Chapel, which is so dark and Dismal that I could not go into it. Upon the whole, the Place remaining in its old Stile is Beaufull and Magnificent, both within and without, but truly Melancholy. My Lord is very little there since the Death of His Lady, for whom he had the greatest regard and attention."

Lady Dysart died here in 1840, not far short of being added to the list of centenarians.

The following amusing story in connection with Ham House has been often told, but is worth repeating :—In 1829 old Lady Dysart asked Bishop Blomfield to dine here to meet the Duke of Clarence, afterwards King William IV. The duke, being offended with the bishop for having voted in favour of Catholic Emancipation, was so rude that he would hardly speak to him. At the end of the evening, however, the good dinner and the port wine had so far mellowed his feelings that he had quite condoned the offence ; and afterwards, when he came to the throne, few prelates stood higher with his Majesty than the Bishop of London.

The avenues and groves which occupy the meadows between Ham House and the river, extending as far as Twickenham Ferry, have long been known as "Ham Walks," under which name they have been celebrated by writers of the seventeenth and eighteenth centuries. The poet Thomson speaks of them, in his "Seasons," as

" Ham's umbrageous walks."

The spot was a favourite resort of Swift, Pope, and Gay. In our account of Twickenham * we have quoted from the *Daily Post* of June 4, 1728, the advertisement wherein Pope draws attention to a "scandalous paper cried about the streets under the title of 'A Pop upon Pope,'" intimating that he had been "whipt in Ham Walks on Thursday last," and notifying that he did not stir out of his house at Twickenham on that day, at the same time adding that the paper in question was "a malicious and ill-grounded report." Gay was often here whilst he lived in the house of the Duchess of Queensberry, close by. The Duchess herself lived here till 1777.

* "History of England," Chapter III.
† See "Old and New London," Vol IV., p. 274.

* Vol. I., p. 99.

Ham is a retired place, with a population of about 2,000. The village proper comprises a street of irregularly-built, commonplace houses, with a few of a better class, and several small cottages clustering round the sides of an extensive common, on the north side of which is one of the gateways of Ham House. Among the seats in the neighbourhood is Morgan House, which was some time the residence of the Duc de Chartres. The church, dedicated to St. Andrew, stands upon the common.

that fearful malady. It was rebuilt in 1861, and has been since enlarged. The object of this institution, which is under the patronage of the Duke of Cambridge, is "to receive orphan girls, without distinction as to religion, into a home where they can obtain a plain English education and practical instruction in the kitchen, house, and laundry, to fit them for domestic service." The charity is almost entirely dependent on voluntary donations and annual subscriptions.

PETERSHAM CHURCH.

It is a poor specimen of modern Gothic, being built of yellow brick, with stone dressings, in the Decorated style, and was first opened in 1832, but was considerably enlarged thirty years later. Close by are schools, which were built more recently.

On Ham Common Lord Mount Edgcumbe had a villa during the early part of this century, and Lady Brownlow records in her "Reminiscences of a Septuagenarian," her recollection of the volunteer corps that used to be drilled there in 1805, when the country was alarmed by the threatened invasion of "the great Napoleon."

The National Orphan Home was established on Ham Common in 1849, the "cholera year," to provide for orphan girls who had lost their parents by

Petersham adjoins Ham Common on the east and north, and is separated from the Thames by Ham Walks and the grounds of Ham House, whilst on the east it is bounded by Richmond Park. In "Domesday Book" the place is styled "Patricesham"—that is, the home or dwelling of St. Peter, it having belonged to the Abbey of Chertsey, of which St. Peter was the tutelary saint. The manor formed part of the original endowment of that institution, and it remained in the possession of the cloistered fraternity until early in the fifteenth century, when it was conveyed by Thomas, Abbot of Chertsey, to Henry V. The manor, as stated above, formed part of the estates granted to Anne of Cleves, who resigned the whole to Edward VI.

The property afterwards passed in the same way as the manor of Ham, already described.

Petersham gives its second title to the Stanhopes, Earls of Harrington; the previous Barony of Petersham, which formed one of the titles of the Duke of Lauderdale, having become extinct on the death of his Grace without issue, was revived in their favour in 1742.

The late Earl of Harrington was better known as Lord Petersham. He was a dandy of the first water under the Regency, and gave his name to the Petersham coat, which figures so constantly in George Cruikshank's and other comic sketches of life in the West End of London.

The church, dedicated to St. Peter, dates partly from the beginning of the sixteenth century. It is of land (Lysons.) The church was, as it is said, rebuilt in 1505. No doubt the roof of the chancel, the buttresses, and the windows, were renewed at that date, while the lancet windows, blocked up by a Jacobean monument, are remnants of the older structure, with probably most of the old walls of the chancel." The patronage was for several centuries attached to that of Kingston; but on the death of the Rev. Daniel Bellamy, in 1788, the chapelries of Kew and Petersham became a distinct vicarage: the livings are now disunited. One of the rectors here was the Rev. Caleb Colton, the author of "*Lacon; or, Many Things in Few Words,*" a work so popular at its first appearance, in 1820, that six editions were published in a twelvemonth. He was an Etonian, and took his

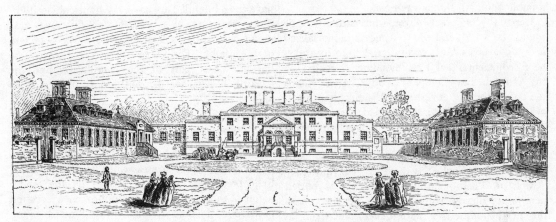

PETERSHAM LODGE. (*From a Contemporary Print.*)

built chiefly of brick, and consists of a nave and chancel, the latter being rough-casted over; a low tower at the western end forms the entrance. The chancel is the only part which dates back to mediæval times, the original nave having been superseded in the last century by a building placed transept-wise, extending north and south.

According to Brayley's "Surrey," there was a church here at the time of the Norman Conquest, and although the manor then appertained to Chertsey Abbey, and continued long in the possession of that house, the church belonged subsequently to Merton Priory. "In 1266, divine service having been discontinued in the Chapel of Petersham, an agreement was made between the Prior of Merton and the inhabitants of this parish that a chaplain should officiate there every Sunday, Wednesday, and Friday, on the following terms:— That the prior and convent should allow him a certain portion of grain annually out of the tithes, and that the parishioners, on their part, should give him a bushel of rye for every virgate, or ten acres

degree at King's College, Cambridge. Colton was an eccentric character. He is described by Alaric Watts as living in a miserable room over a ragshop, and yet able on occasion to produce a bottle or two of old Johannisberg for a guest if the occasion seemed to require it. Debts forced him to leave England, and he resided for some time in America and in Paris, where he was so successful a gamester that in two years he realised £25,000. In spite of thus finding himself once more "set upon his legs," he died by his own hand at Fontainebleau in 1832. We shall have more to say about him on reaching Kew.

Among the monuments that crowd the interior of Petersham Church, we may point out those of the following persons of rank and note:—namely, Vice-Admiral Sir George Scott, of Gala, who died in 1841; Sir Thomas Jenner, serjeant-at-law, who died in 1706, and who was the son of that high Tory judge in the reign of James II., Sir Thomas Jenner—the same who was excepted out of the Act of Indemnity in 1690. On the north side of the chancel, and partly within an arched recess flanked by Corinthian columns, and ornamented by cherubim, &c., are recumbent statues of George Cole, Esq., of the Middle Temple, and Frances, his wife : the former, who died in 1624, is habited in a long black gown, and has a roll of parchment in his hand. His wife, who is in the dress of the time, died in 1633. It appears from Cole's "Escheats" (Harleian MSS., No. 758) that the above George Cole died seized of a manor in Kingston parish called Harlington, held of the king *in capite* by the fortieth part of a knight's fee. It was afterwards enclosed in the new park at Richmond ; and Lysons, in his "Environs," says that " the proof of such a place having existed had considerable weight in determining the right of a public footpath through the park."

Captain George Vancouver, who made a voyage round the world, and whose name is immortalised in Vancouver's Island, was interred here in 1798 ; he is commemorated by a monument erected by the Hudson Bay Company. Sir Charles Stuart, the conqueror and governor of Minorca, fourth son of John, Earl of Bute, lies buried here, as also does his wife, Louisa, the daughter and co-heiress of Lord Vere Bertie. In the churchyard there is a handsome tomb, erected to the second Earl of Mount-Edgcumbe, with this inscription :— " Richard, Earl of Mount-Edgcumbe, is buried here, who, during a great part of his life, chose this neighbourhood for a residence, and dying at Richmond, desired that his mortal remains should not be borne to the distant tomb of his ancestors, but be deposited in this churchyard. Let us hope that his immortal part may mingle thus with rich and poor in that abode prepared by Christ alike for all who trust in Him." The date is 1839. On a tomb in the chancel, in memory of Lady Frances Caroline Douglas, daughter of the Marquis of Queensberry, are these lines :—

> " Dear as thou wert, and justly dear,
> 　　We will not weep for thee ;
> One thought shall check the starting tear :
> 　　It is that thou art free,
> And thus shall Faith's consoling pow'r
> 　　The tears of Love restrain.
> Oh, who that saw thy parting hour,
> 　　Would wish thee here again ?

> " Triumphant in the closing eye
> 　　The hope of Glory shone
> Joy breathed in thy expiring sigh
> 　　To think thy fight was won.
> Gently the passing spirit fled,
> 　　Sustained by Grace Divine,
> Oh, may such grace on me be shed,
> 　　And make my end like thine."

Poor Mortimer Collins was buried here ; and here also lie two celebrated literary characters, Agnes and Mary Berry, whom we have mentioned in our account of Twickenham as friends of Horace Walpole.* During the last twenty years of their lives the two sisters, Mary and Agnes Berry, spent the summer regularly in what they called their "retirement" at Petersham. In July, 1836, being at Paris, Miss Berry writes in her "Journal" :—" It is now that I figure Petersham and our quiet garden there as everything on earth that I most covet, and from which I no longer desire to wander. There, in the immediate neighbourhood of a friend more my child than any other can be—there I feel that I can patiently wait for the last stroke which is to send me to the neighbouring churchyard, where I have long intended to have my bones deposited." Some years, however, passed after this entry was made before the remains of Miss Berry were laid in the tomb. The grave of the two sisters is in the north-east part of the churchyard, and the inscription, from the pen of Lord Carlisle, runs as follows :—

"Mary Berry, born March, 1763 ; died Nov., 1852.
Agnes Berry, born May, 1764 ; died Jan., 1852.

" Beneath this stone are laid the remains of these two sisters, amidst scenes which in life they had frequented and loved. Followed by the tender regret of those who close the unbroken succession of friends, devoted to them with fond affection during every step of their long career."

These venerable and excellent ladies were among the last survivors of the literary set who had frequented Strawberry Hill in its palmy days, and worshipped at the shrine of its founder. Their diaries give an excellent picture of London society in the latter half of the Georgian era. They were the daughters of Mr. Robert Berry, a Yorkshire gentleman of fortune, and they and their father were Walpole's literary executors, so that it was under their friendly supervision that his works were introduced to the world of readers.

Walpole first became acquainted with them about the year 1780, when he met them, as is generally believed, at Lord Strafford's seat in Yorkshire, Wentworth Castle. Soon after, becoming his regular correspondents, they made a journey to Italy, and finally returned to the neighbourhood of London and Richmond, in order to be within reach and call of the prince of letter-writers. Both Mason and Lord Harcourt, it seems, were jealous of their influence over the Lord of

---

* See Vol. I., p. 123.

Strawberry Hill, who called them his "two wives," and seemed resolved to repeat in his own person the flirtations of Pope with Martha and Theresa Blount. The writer of the biography of Miss Berry in the *Gentleman's Magazine* remarks :—" He would write and number his letters to them, and tell them stories of his early life, and what he had seen and heard, with ten times the vivacity and minuteness which he employed towards his other friends. The ladies listened, and it was Walpole's joy

' Still with his favourite Berrys to remain.'

" Delighted with what they heard, they began to take notes of what he told them, and soon induced him, by the sweet power of two female pleaders at his ear and in his favourite ' Tribune,' to put in writing those charming ' Reminiscences of the Courts of George the First and his Son,' which will continue to be read with interest as long as English history is read."

When Walpole died, he left to these ladies, in conjunction with their father, the greater part of his papers and letters, and the charge of collecting and publishing his remains. The edition of his works, which appeared in five quarto volumes, was edited in 1768 by the father, who lived with his daughters at Twickenham and in South Audley Street for some years after Walpole's death. He died at a great age at Genoa, in 1817 ; but the daughters lived on in London, and for upwards of half a century entertained at their houses in South Audley Street and in Curzon Street, or at their summer residence near Richmond, two generations of literary men. " They loved the society of authors and of people of fashion also, and thought at times, and not untruly, that they were the means of bringing about them more authors of note, mixing in good society, than Mrs. Montagu or Lady Blessington, or any other ' Queen of Society,' had succeeded in drawing together."

It would have been strange if, with all their love and admiration for Horace Walpole, both or either of the Miss Berrys had escaped figuring as an authoress. Agnes escaped the infection, but Mary Berry was not equally fortunate. In 1840 she edited the sixty letters which Walpole had addressed to herself and her sister. It is much to her credit that her last literary undertaking was a vindication of his memory from the sarcasms of Lord Macaulay in his well-known article in the *Edinburgh Review*. Her scattered writings were collected by herself, in 1844, into two octavo volumes, entitled " England and France : A Comparative View of the Social Condition of both Countries from the Restoration of Charles the

Second ; to which are now added Remarks on Lord Orford's Letters, the Life of the Marquise du Deffand, the Life of Rachel, Lady Russell, and Fashionable Friends : a Comedy." " In these miscellanies—for by that name they should have been called "— writes Sylvanus Urban, " are to be found many keen and correct remarks on society, and on men and manners, with here and there a dash of old (*i.e.*, antiquarian) reading, and every now and then a valuable observation or two on the fashions and other minute details of the age in which Horace Walpole lived. . . . In his late years Walpole makes no better appearance than he does in his letters to Mary and Agnes Berry. He seems to have forgotten the gout, and Chatterton, and Dr. Kippis, and the Society of Antiquaries, and to have written like an old man no longer soured by the world, but altogether in love with what was good."

It will be seen that Mary Berry survived her sister only a few months. She is said to have felt her loss severely. For a time after the death of Agnes she was observed

" To muse and take her solitary tea;"

but she rallied again, and continued to cultivate the society of her living friends, as well as to dwell with pleasure on the reminiscences of that vanished society which she had once enjoyed, and of which she was the last survivor.

The celebrated Lady Dysart who afterwards became Duchess of Lauderdale, though she was both married and buried in Petersham Church, has no monument to her memory here. The following is the entry in the register referring to the marriage :—" The ryght honorable John, Earl of Lauderdale, was married to the ryght honorable Elizabeth, Countesse of Desert, by the Reverend Father in God (Walter) Lord Bishop of Worcester, in the church of Petersham, on the 17th day of Februarie, 1671—2, publiquely in the time of reading the common prayer, and gave the carpet, pulpit-cloth, and cushion."

Dr. Charles Mackay, in his " Thames and its Tributaries," writes thus, describing the scenery along the banks of the river between Ham Walks and Richmond :—" Among the most conspicuous of the places we pass there is a neat little rural hut, called ' Gay's Summer-house,' where, according to tradition, that amiable poet wrote his celebrated ' Fables ' for the infant Duke of Cumberland, currying court favour, but getting nothing but neglect for his pains. ' Dear Pope,' he wrote to his brother poet, ' what a barren soil have I been striving to produce something out of ! Why did

I not take your advice, before my writing fables for the duke, not to write them, or rather to write them for some young nobleman ? It is my hard fate—I must get nothing, write for or against them.' Poor Gay," he continues. "Too well he knew, as Spenser so feelingly sings in his 'Mother Hubbard's Tale' :—

> "What hell it was in suing long to bide,
>   To lose good days that might be better spent,
>   To waste long nights in pensive discontent ;
>   To speed to-day, to be put back to-morrow,
>   To feed on hope, to pine with fear and sorrow ;
>   To fret the soul with crosses and with cares,
>   To eat the heart through comfortless despairs,
>   To fawn, to crouch, to wait, to ride, to run,
>   To spend, to give, to want, to be undone.'

"Yet one cannot help thinking, after all, that it served him right ; for, according to his own confession, he was ready to wield his pen either for or against the court, as might be most profitable. Who is there but must regret that a man of his genius should ever have been reduced to so pitiful an extremity ? Who but must sigh that he should, even to his bosom friend, have made such a confession ? "

Gay's summer-house is (or used to be), observes Mr. Thorne, in his "Environs," pointed out by Thames boatmen to visitors as the place in which "Gay wrote Thomson's 'Seasons !' " It is a low-thatched, semi-circular or octagonal building.

On the north side of the parish, close to Petersham Lane, where the ground begins to slope up to Richmond Hill, there was in former time an estate and mansion called Petersham Lodge, which was sold to Charles I. by Gregory Cole, son of George Cole, whose monument in the church close by we have described. A lease of the property was granted by James II. to his nephew, Edward Hyde, Lord Cornbury, whom we have lately mentioned as the grandson of the great Lord Chancellor Clarendon , and it subsequently became the residence of his cousin, Henry, second and last Lord Rochester. Whilst in his possession, in 1721, the house was burnt down, and much of its rich furniture, family pictures, books, and manuscripts, including the valuable library which had belonged to the Chancellor, were destroyed. William Stanhope, who subsequently owned the property, and who was afterwards created Viscount Petersham and Earl of Harrington, rebuilt the lodge on the site of the former house, from the designs of Lord Burlington. The grounds were well planted with trees, among them being some fine cedars, many of which, still flourishing on the declivity of the hill, mark the site of the estate.

It is to this second Petersham Lodge that Thomson alludes when speaking of

> "——the pendant woods
>   That nodding hang o'er Harrington's retreat."

Lord Harrington's mansion in the middle of the last century was a great place for aristocratic *réunions*. Mrs. Montagu, who was among its frequent visitors, writes that "she could turn Pastorella here with great pleasure "—no doubt when she was tired of London.

Catherine Hyde, Duchess of Queensberry—Prior's "Kitty, beautiful and young," and Gay's "great protectress "—lived for many years at Petersham, whither she removed her share of the fine pictures which formerly belonged to her brother, Lord Clarendon. This collection, formed by the famous Lord Chancellor Edward Hyde, was known by the name of the Clarendon Portraits. They were about 100 in number, and on the sale of Clarendon* House, were removed to Cornbury House, in Oxfordshire, where, whilst in the possession of his lordship's son, Lord Cornbury, they were considerably reduced in number by executions and forced sales ; but they were eventually saved from further dispersion by the purchase of the house and its contents by Lord Cornbury's brother, Lord Rochester. On the death of Henry, the fourth earl, in 1752, his will, in which he had bequeathed his pictures, plate, and books, as heirlooms to the possessors of the estate, was contested by his surviving sister, the Duchess of Queensberry, and the bequest was set aside as far as related to the pictures. These were ordered to be divided between the Duchess and Lord Clarendon's eldest daughter, Lady Essex. The pictures selected by the duchess were taken first of all to her seat at Amesbury, in Wiltshire, but afterwards brought hither. On the death of the last Duke of Queensberry, in 1810, the pictures passed to Archibald, Lord Douglas, who removed them to Bothwell Castle, in Lanarkshire.

The following anecdotes, which we quote from the *Court Circular*, will be sufficient to justify the title of "witty and eccentric" which has been applied to the Duchess of Queensberry :—" Her Grace had been confined on account of mental derangement ; and her conduct in married life was frequently such as to entitle her to a repetition of the same treatment. She was, in reality—to say the least—most terribly eccentric, though the politeness of fashionable society and the flattery of her poetical friends seem rather to have attributed her extravagances to an agreeable freedom of

---

* See "Old and New London," Vol. IV., p. 273.

carriage and vivacity of mind. She was no admirer of Scottish manners. One habit she particularly detested—the custom of eating off the end of a knife, which is still too prevalent in this 'nation of gentlemen.' When people dined with her, and began to lift their food in this manner, she used to scream out, and beseech them not to cut their throats; and then she would horrify the offending persons by sending them a silver spoon or fork upon a salver. When in Scotland, she always dressed herself in the garb of a peasant girl. This she seems to have done in order to ridicule and put out of countenance the stately dresses and demeanour of the Scottish gentlewomen who visited her. One evening some country ladies paid her a visit, dressed in their best brocades. She proposed a walk, and they were, of course, under the disagreeable necessity of trooping off in all the splendour of full dress, to the utter discomfiture of their starched-up frills and flounces. Her Grace, at last pretending to be tired, sat down upon the dirtiest dunghill she could find at the end of a farmhouse, and invited the poor draggled ladies to seat themselves around her. They stood so much in awe of her that they durst not refuse. She had the exquisite satisfaction of spoiling all their silks. Let womankind conceive (as only womankind can) the rage and spite that must have possessed their bosoms, and the battery of female tongues that must have opened upon her Grace as soon as they were free from the restraint of her presence!

"When she went out to an evening entertainment, and found a tea-equipage paraded which she thought too fine for the rank of the owner, she would contrive to overset the table and break the china. The forced politeness of her hosts on such occasions, and the assurances which they made to her that no harm was done, delighted her exceedingly.

"Her custom of dressing like a *paysanne* once occasioned her Grace a disagreeable adventure at a review. On her attempting to approach the duke, the guard, not knowing her rank or relation to him, pushed her rudely back. This put her into such a passion, that she could not be appeased till he assured her that the men had been all flogged for their insolence." The story, if literally true, does not speak much for the tenderness of her heart.

"An anecdote scarcely less laughable is told of her Grace, as occurring at Court, where she carried to the same extreme her attachment to plain dealing and plain dressing. An edict had, it seems, been issued, forbidding the ladies to appear at the drawing-room in aprons. This was disregarded by the duchess, whose rustic costume would have been by no means complete without that piece of dress. The lord-in-waiting stopped her when she approached the door, and told her that he could not admit her in that guise, when she, without a moment's hesitation, stripped off her apron, threw it in his lordship's face, and walked on, in her brown gown and petticoat, into the brilliant circle!"

William, the third earl of Harrington, who succeeded to the property in 1779, shortly after sold it to Thomas Pitt, first Lord Camelford, from whom it subsequently passed by sale to the Duke of Clarence, afterwards William IV., who occasionally resided here. The estate was afterwards sold to Lord Huntingtower, the eldest son of Lady Dysart, who died in 1833. In the following year his executors sold the property to the Commissioners of Woods and Forests. All the buildings have since been pulled down, and the grounds have been annexed to Richmond Park.

Sudbrooke, close by, is mentioned as a hamlet of Petersham in a MS. of the thirteenth century preserved in the British Museum, but for nearly three centuries it has been reduced to a single building. In the time of George I. it was the property and seat of John, Duke of Argyll, from whom it descended to his eldest daughter and heiress, Lady Catherine Campbell, created Baroness of Greenwich in 1767, on whose death, in 1794, the estate was inherited by Henry, third Duke of Buccleuch, her son by her first husband, Francis, Earl of Dalkeith. Later on the mansion became the property of Sir Robert Wilmot Horton, formerly Governor of Ceylon, who made it his residence. The property was afterwards purchased by the Crown, and the greater part of the grounds annexed to Richmond Park. Sudbrooke House itself, a large three-storeyed building, has long been converted into a hydropathic establishment.

Bute House, near the village, was formerly the seat of Lord Bute, and is now a boarding-school. In the avenue leading to Ham House is Douglas House, at one time the residence of Lord Kerry, the eldest son of the third Lord Lansdowne. Here lived Gregory Cole, mentioned by John Evelyn as his "near kinsman," and whose monument is described among those in the church. This family are recorded as residents here in the old histories of Surrey. Here, too, Charles Dickens, flushed with the first success of "Nicholas Nickleby," enjoyed the quiet and repose of a rural cottage in the summer of 1839, where, to use the expression of Mr. John Forster, "the extensive garden-grounds admitted of much athletic competition." Here "bar-leaping, bowling, and quoits were . . . . carried on with the greatest ardour; and in sustained energy, in what is called keeping it up, Dickens certainly distanced every competitor. Even the lighter recreations of battledore and shuttlecock were pursued with relentless activity; and at such amusements as the Petersham races, in those days rather celebrated, and which he visited daily while they lasted, he worked much harder than the running horses did." This is probably an exaggeration; but it may be recorded that whilst residing here Charles Dickens much amused the children of the neighbourhood by starting a fire-balloon club for the benefit of the juveniles.

IN RICHMOND PARK.

CHAPTER XXXVIII.

RICHMOND.

"Say, shall we ascend
Thy hill, delightful Sheen? Here let us sweep
The boundless landscape: now the raptur'd eye
Exulting, swift to huge Augusta send;
Now to the sister hills that skirt her plain;
To lofty Harrow now; and now to where
Majestic Windsor lifts its princely brow."—THOMSON.

Change of the Name from Sheen to Richmond—Situation of the Town—Its Boundaries and Extent—Beauty of its Surrounding Scenery—Descent of the Manor of Shene—Earliest mention of the Palace—Death of Edward III.—The Palace Restored by Henry V.—Interview between Edward IV. and the "King-maker"—Camden's Account of the Palace—Vicissitudes of the Palace—A Royal Hoard—Visit of the Emperor Charles V.—The Princess Elizabeth entertained here by Queen Mary—Queen Elizabeth at Richmond—Her Death—Habits of the Queen—Her Burial at Westminster—Henry, Prince of Wales, son of James I., resident at Richmond Palace—Settlement of the Palace on Queen Henrietta Maria—A Survey of the Palace by Order of the Parliament—Decay and Demolition of the Palace—Asgill House—George III. and the Gatekeeper—The Monastery of Sheen—The Head of James IV., King of Scotland—The Convent of Observant Friars.

THE name of Richmond is suggestive of pleasant pictures, of shining green meadows and silver streams, of royal splendour and gentle poesy, of "Star and Garter" feasts and dainty "Maids of Honour," of four-in hands, and summer sunshine, and buoyant holiday spirits. Which of us has not some such pleasant or happy associations with the beautiful village on the banks of the Thames?

The place was anciently called Shene, or Sheen, the Saxon equivalent of brightness or splendour. The name was changed to Richmond in compliment to Henry VII. (Henry of Richmond), during whose residence here the palace was partly destroyed by fire. On its restoration the new style was adopted.

Richmond is beautifully situated on the banks of the Thames, by which it is bounded on the west, whilst it adjoins Kew and Mortlake on the

"Richmond Park," says the Vicomte d'Arling-court, in his work on "The Three Kingdoms," "is renowned for its scenery." This is a strong testimony from a Frenchman, who could hardly help contrasting it unfavourably with the far greater beauties of St. Cloud; whilst Cote, in his "Impressions of England," writes with enthusiasm of the spot.

"The English," he says, "though a proud people, are really very moderate in their appreciation o` the manifold charms of their incomparable isle.

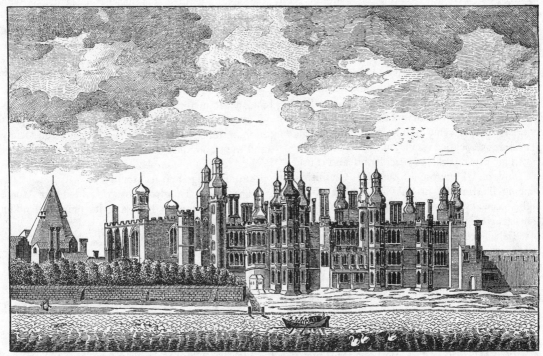

OLD RICHMOND PALACE, AS BUILT BY HENRY VII.
(*From a print Published by the Society of Antiquaries, 1765.*)

north, Mortlake on the east, and Petersham on the south. The soil is generally sandy, although some parts are clay and gravel.

The parish of Richmond contains about 1,200 acres, of which by far the larger proportion belongs to the Crown, comprehending a part of Kew Gardens and the paddocks adjoining, bounded by the river.

The beauty of the scenery in and around Richmond is celebrated in song and story. Alaric A. Watts thus sings of it :—

> "Let poets rave of Arno's stream,
> 　　And painters of the winding Rhine,
> I will not ask a lovelier dream,
> 　　A sweeter scene, fair Thames, than thine:
> As 'neath a summer sun's decline,
> 　　Thou 'wanderest at thine own sweet will,'
> Reflecting from thy face divine
> 　　The flower-wreathed brow of Richmond Hill."

When I surveyed the river view from Richmond Hill, I recalled the glorious waters of my own dear country, and many a darling scene which is imperishably stamped in my mind's eye, and asked myself whether indeed this was more delightful to the sight than those. I was slow to admit anything inferior in the scenery of the Hudson and Susquehanna, when I compared them with so diminutive a stream as the Thames, and I even reproved myself for bringing them into parallel; but over and over again was I forced to allow that

> 'Earth has not anything to show more fair'

than the rich luxuriance of the panorama which I then surveyed. A river whose banks are old historic fields, and whose placid surface reflects, from league to league of its progress, the towers of palaces and of churches which for centuries have been hallowed by ennobling and holy associations; which flows by the favourite haunts of genius, or winds among the antique halls of consecrated learning; and which, after sweeping beneath the gigantic arches, domes, and temples of a vast metropolis, gives itself to the burthen of fleets and navies, and bears them magnificently forth to the ocean: such an object must necessarily be one of the highest interest to any one capable of appreciating the mentally beautiful and sublime; but when natural glories invest the same objects with a thousand independent attractions, who need be ashamed of owning an overpowering enthusiasm in the actual survey?"

Charles Dickens also gives his testimony—less full and free, it is true, than the foregoing. "We grant," says he, "that the banks of the Thames are very beautiful at Richmond and Twickenham, and at other havens, often sought, though seldom reached, by cockney excursionists."

"The royal parks of Richmond and Bushey," we find in "Picturesque Europe," "furnish convincing illustrations of the manner in which art judiciously applied may be made to assist nature. The tangled brakes, plenteous ferns, flower dells, tastefully-bestowed shrubs, and trees great and small, are an untold boon to the City-pent thousands of the metropolis, and an attraction to visitors from every clime. In Richmond Park there is a marvellous intermingling of the old and new. By the sides of irregular groups of time-worn giants of the forest, carrying us back to those very early times indicated by the mention, in the reign of Henry VIII., of certain portions as 'the new park,' there stand vigorous plantations of maturing and matured trees that prove the fostering care of more recent guardians. It is possible, taking care that the keeper's eye is not upon us, to wander away into absolute solitude, where the thick underwood conceals hare, rabbit, and pheasant, and where the graceful hind and fawn repose in undisturbed confidence, with rare and luxuriant ferns and mosses as their carpet. . . . Ivy and lichens conceal the deep wrinkles of age upon the knotted pillars which uphold the latter; and in its season the foliage is sufficiently dense to provide unbroken shade. It may truly be said of all woods and forests that, as a rule, 'distance lends enchantment to the view;' and, happily for the visitor, the public pathways which intersect Richmond Park seem to have been specially designed to show off the wooded portions to the best advantage."

Another author writes:—"The amateur painter may also here find abundance of subjects on which to exercise his pencil or gratify his taste for nature and art: admiration of the former and knowledge of the latter being alike called into action by the scenery around him. The placid stream verifying Denham's description—

'Strong without rage, without o'erflowing, full'—

presents on one side emerald turf of the finest texture and brightest verdure, lofty elms, interspersed with chestnuts, poplars, acacias, and all the lighter shrubs, shading noble mansions with hanging gardens, and elegant cottages *ornée*; while on the other is seen the ancient village of Richmond, rising terrace-wise, and exhibiting every form of stately and of rural dwelling. A peculiar air of cheerfulness everywhere pervades the scene, which is alike remote from the noise and confusion attendant on the metropolis, and the sequestration which belongs to isolated dwellings in more remote districts. The pleasures of society and the tranquillity of retirement are nowhere better combined and completely enjoyed than in this beautiful village and its vicinity."

The poet Thomson, who resided for some years at Richmond, thus sang its praises in "The Seasons":—

"Which way, Amanda, shall we bend our course?
The choice perplexes. Wherefore should we chuse?
All is the same with thee. Say, shall we wind
Along the streams, or walk the smiling mead?
Or court the forest glades? or wander wild
Among the waving harvests? or ascend,
While radiant summer opens all its pride,
Thy hill, delightful Shene? Here let us sweep
The boundless landscape: now the raptured eye,
Exulting swift, to huge Augusta send;
Now to the sister-hills* that skirt her plain;
To lofty Harrow now; and now to where
Majestic Windsor lifts his princely brow.
In lovely contrast to this glorious view,
Calmly magnificent, then will we turn
To where the silver Thames first rural grows.
There let the feasted eye unwearied stray;
Luxurious there, rove through the pendant woods
That nodding hang o'er Harrington's retreat;
And stooping thence to Ham's embowering walks,
Beneath whose shades, in spotless peace retired,
With her the pleasing partner of his heart,
The worthy Queensberry yet laments his Gay,
And polished Cornbury woos the willing muse.
Slow let us trace the matchless vale of Thames;
Fair winding up to where the muses haunt
In Twit'nam's bowers, and for their Pope implore
The healing god; to royal Hampton's pile,
To Clermont's terraced height, and Esher's groves,
Where, in the sweetest solitude, embraced
By the soft windings of the silent Mole,

* Highgate and Hampstead.

> From courts and senates Pelham finds repose.
> Inchanting vale ! beyond whate'er the muse
> Has of Achaia or Hesperia sung !
> O, vale of bliss ! O, softly-swelling hills !
> On which the *Power of Cultivation* lies,
> And joys to see the wonders of his toil.
>
>   Heavens ! what a goodly prospect spreads around
> Of hills, and dales, and woods, and lawns, and spires,
> And glittering towns, and gilded streams, till all
> The stretching landscape into smoke decays."

The scenery of Richmond Hill has been the subject not only of much poetry, but also of many a *bon mot*. Thus, a certain French traveller, less magnanimous than the Vicomte d'Arlingcourt, once contemptuously observed that the Thames is merely "a little stream, which might be easily drained," a remark for which he was smartly reprimanded in the *Quarterly Review*. It is said that another foreign coxcomb, who had come to England for the special object of seeing this prospect, after gazing at it with an air of indifference, turned on his heel, saying : "Pretty enough, to be sure ; but, after all, take away the water and the verdure, and what is it ?"

The manor of Shene appears to have been comprehended in that of Kingston, which belonged to the Crown at the time of the Domesday Survey. Henry I. gave it to one of the family of Belet, to hold by the service, or sergeantry, of officiating as chief butler to the king. In the reign of Edward I. this property belonged to Robert Burnell, Bishop of Bath and Wells. The subsequent descent of the manor until it became vested in the Crown is rather uncertain.

"Both Lysons and Manning have asserted," says Brayley, "that the manor of Shene belonged to the Crown in the latter part of the reign of Edward I. ; but this seems inconsistent with the statements still existing in an ancient record relative to the holding of the manor by subjects in the reigns of Edward II. and Edward III. For though the first of our kings who held the entire manorial estate was Edward III., it appears that his father and grandfather occasionally resided at Shene, either as tenants of the lords of the manor or as owners of some portion of the property. A palace is said to have been erected by Edward III. on his manor of Shene ; and although some doubt is thrown upon the statement, it is certain that a royal mansion existed here in his time, for it was at the palace or mansion of Shene that death terminated his long and victorious reign, in 1377."

Baker, in his quaintly-worded "Chronicles," gives the following particulars of the death of Edward III. :—"The King, besides his being old and worn with the labours of War, had other causes that hastened his end : his grief for the loss of so worthy a Son, dead but ten months before ; his grief for the loss of all benefit of his Conquests in *France*, of all which he had little now left but only *Callice*. And oppressed thus in body and minde, he was drawing his last breath, when his Concubine, Alice Pierce, packing away what she could catch, even to the Rings of his Fingers, left him, and by her example other of his attendants, seizing on what they could come by, shift away ; and all his Counsellours and others forsook him when he most needed them, leaving his Chamber quite empty. Which a poor Priest in the house seeing, he approaches to the King's Bed-side, and finding him yet breathing, calls upon him to remember his Saviour, and to ask mercy for his offences, which none about him before would do. But now moved by the voice of this Priest, he shews all signs of contrition, and at last breath he expresseth the name of Jesus. Thus died this victorious King at his Manor of *Sheene* (now Richmond), the 21 day of *June*, in the year 1377, in the 64 year of his age, having reigned fifty years, four months and odd dayes. His body was conveyed from *Sheene* by his four Sons and other Lords, and solemnly interred within *Westminster* Church, where he hath his Monument, and where it is said the Sword he used in Battel is yet to be seen, being eight pound in weight, and seven foot in length."

His grandson and successor, Richard II., may be supposed to have passed much of his time at this place during the life of his first queen, Anne of Bohemia, for, as historians inform us, on her death, which happened at Shene in 1394, he was so violently afflicted, "that he, besides cursing the place where she died, did also for anger throwe downe the buildings, unto which former kings, being wearied of the citie, were wont for pleasure to resort."

The palace remained in ruins during the reign of Henry IV. ; but Henry V., soon after he ascended the throne, restored the edifice to its former magnificence. Thomas Elmham says it was "a delightful mansion, of curious and costly workmanship, and befitting the character and condition of a king." The second palace stood a little further from the river than the former had done.

Edward IV. was fond of the chase here, and it is at Sheen that Bulwer, in "The Last of the Barons," lays the scene of the stormy interview between Edward IV. and the "King-maker" relative to the betrothal of the king's sister, Margaret. In the previous chapter will be found a picturesque description of the scene presented by the Court assembled in the park :—"A space had been cleared of trees and underwood, and made level as a bowling-green. Around this space the huge oaks and the broad beeches were hung with trellis-work, wreathed with jasmine, honeysuckle, and the white rose trained in arches. Ever and anon through these arches extended long alleys, or vistas, gradually lost in the cool depth of foliage; amidst these alleys and around this space numberless arbours, quaint with all the flowers then known in England, were constructed. In the centre of the sward was a small artificial lake, long since dried up, and adorned then with a profusion of fountains, that seemed to scatter coolness around the glowing air. Pitched in varied and appropriate sites were tents of silk and of the white cloth of Rennes, each tent so placed as to command one of the alleys, and at the opening of each stood cavalier or dame, with the bow or cross-bow—as it pleased the fancy or best suited the skill—looking for the quarry, which horn and hound drove fast and frequent across the alleys."

"King Henry's palace," says Fuller, in his "Worthies," is "most pleasantly seated on the Thames." "The palace of Shene," writes Camden, "stood a little east of the bridge, and close by the river-side, and was chiefly used as a nursery for our princes and princesses." Some of them, however, were coffined here as well as cradled; and during a portion of Mary's reign it served as the prison-house of her sister Elizabeth. Very solemn, too, were the circumstances under which death made his visits to crowned heads at Shene— epics of history, they tell the touching moral of humanity stronger than state—of natural sorrow breaking down the artificial defences of rank, and forcing kings to find their level in affliction, like common clay upon the lap of Nature. Here Edward III. died of grief for the loss of his warlike son—he of the chivalrous heart and sable armour, whose gauntlets and surcoat still moulder above his tomb in the cathedral at Canterbury. "Here also," to quote Camden again, "died the beautiful and entirely-beloved Anne, queen of Richard II., daughter of the Emperor Charles IV., and sister to Wencislaus, King of Bohemia. Upon this event he had the palace rased to the ground, as if to revenge the misery he had suffered there, or to blot out (if it may be) the reminiscences the pile awakened; but Henry III. restored it. It is said that this queen first introduced the side-saddle into England, before which period ladies sat their horses as peasant girls in the interior of Spain continue to do their mules, *en cavalier*. Her death occurred in 1394."

The palace was much enlarged by Henry VII.

Lord Bacon, in his "History" of that king, tells us that Henry here gave splendid entertainments after giving public thanks at St. Paul's for the victory of the Spaniards over the Moors in capturing Grenada, and that a knight named Parker was accidentally killed in a tournament held on that occasion in the park.

The palace seems to have undergone various vicissitudes, for in 1498 Brayley relates how the king (Henry VII.) being at Shene, a fire broke out in his lodging in the palace, about nine o'clock in the evening, and continued till midnight, a great part, especially of the old buildings, being destroyed, together with hangings, beds, apparel, plate, and many jewels. Immediate orders were given for the restoration of the edifice; and in 1501, when much of the new work was finished, the king ordained that it should in future be styled "Richmond." Another fire occurred in the king's chamber in 1506-7, when "much rich furniture was consumed"; and in July following a new gallery, in which the king and his son Prince Arthur had been walking a short time previously, fell down, but without injuring any person. In the same year (1503), Philip I. of Spain, who had been driven on the coast of England by a storm, was entertained by King Henry at Richmond, where many notable feates of armes were proved. Here Henry died, six years later, in April, 1509; and Baker tells us, in his "Chronicle," how his dead body was brought out of his "privy chamber" into the "great chamber," and thence into the hall, and finally into the chapel, in each of which places it remained for three days, whilst solemn dirges and masses were said, preparatory to its final journey, by land, to Westminster Abbey. To him might well be applied the lines of Gray, though they refer to his ancestor, Edward I. :—

> " Mighty victor ! mighty lord !
>   Low on his funeral couch he lies ;
> No pitying heart, no eye afford
>   A tear to grace his obsequies."

He left unparalleled treasure in money, jewels, and plate, locked up in its cellars and vaults. Indeed, the hoard amassed by Henry, and " most of it under his own key and keeping, in secret places at Richmond," is said to have amounted to near £1,800,000, which, according to conjectures, would be now equivalent to about £16,000,000: an amount of specie so immense as to warrant a suspicion of exaggeration in an age when there was no control from public documents on a matter of which the writers of history were ignorant. Our doubts of the amount amassed by Henry are considerably warranted by the computation of Sir W.

Petty, who, a century and a half later, calculated the whole specie of England at only £6,000,000. This hoard, whatever may have been its precise extent, was too great to be formed by frugality, even under the penurious and niggardly Henry. Henry VIII. spent the Christmas after his accession to the throne at Richmond Palace, where his eldest son, Henry, was born and died, in 1511. Fuller remarks, in his "Worthies," that the king "alleadged his untimely death with that of another son by the same queen, as a punishment for begetting them on the Body of his brother's wife." If so, one of the causes which, in the event, brought about the change of religion in England must be for ever connected with Richmond.

The Emperor Charles V., when he visited England, in 1522, was lodged at Richmond. After this date the king seems to have ceased to like Richmond; at all events, his visits to the palace became few and brief, though he "lay" there occasionally for a night. It was here that Anne of Cleves was waited on by the royal commissioners, informing her that her divorce from the tyrant Henry had been confirmed by the Parliament; and, as was only natural, she became greatly terrified, fainted, and fell to the ground. And before the commissioners departed, we are told she took off her wedding ring, to be given back to the king, whom henceforth she was to regard as a brother. Lucky, instead, that she had not to regard him as her executioner!

Ultimately she fell in with the new arrangement, for little love was lost on either side : her figure not pleasing that fastidious monarch, and she equally despising his character. She bade her attendants tell the king there should be no "womanishness" about her, and that inconstancy could not be laid to her charge, for not the whole world should alter her. Her brother, the Duke of Cleves, was very wroth at the king's proceedings, and would no doubt have made trouble for his Majesty, had not the Lady Anne, so calm and pleasant throughout this disagreeable affair, begged of him to let her "precious adopted brother" live in peace, if not for her sake, at least out of regard for his own.

Anne continued to reside here and at Chelsea after her divorce, devoting her time to rural sports and recreations, and living an easy, quiet life, free from the cares of politics and courts. She would remark to her friends, "There is no place like this England for feeding right well." She could speak no language but Flemish; she knew nothing of music or singing; and how could she expect to suit the taste of a man such as Henry VIII.?

She was still living when Edward VI. and Mary were on the throne, and during those seventeen years received honour and respect from all who knew her, and was much beloved by the princesses Mary and Elizabeth. After the divorce had been satisfactorily settled, Henry paid her a visit, and was so "delighted by her pleasant and respectful reception of him, that he supped with her merrily, and not only went often again to see her, but visited her at Hampton, whither she went, not at all troubling herself that another was playing the queen." Very possibly she was of opinion that

> "When evil men hold sway
> The post of *comfort* is a private station."

In 1554 Queen Mary, with her newly-wedded consort, Philip of Spain, removed from Windsor to the palace at Richmond.

"During the summer of 1557," writes Miss Lucy Aikin, "Queen Mary invited her sister Elizabeth to an entertainment at Richmond, of which some particulars are recorded. The princess was brought from Somerset House in the queen's barge, which was richly hung with garlands of artificial flowers, and covered with a canopy of green sarcenet, wrought with branches of eglantine in embroidery, and powdered with blossoms of gold. In the barge she was accompanied by Sir Thomas Pope and four ladies of her chamber. Six boats attended, filled with her retinue, habited in russet damask and blue embroidered satin, tasseled and spangled with silver, their bonnets cloth of silver, with green feathers. The queen received her in a sumptuous pavilion in the labyrinth of the gardens. This pavilion, which was of cloth of gold and purple velvet, was made in the form of a castle: in allusion, perhaps, to the kingdom of Castile; its sides were divided in compartments, which bore alternately the *fleur-de-lis* in silver and the pomegranate, the bearing of Grenada, in gold. A sumptuous banquet was here served up to the royal ladies, in which there was introduced a pomegranate tree in confectionery work, bearing the arms of Spain. . . . There was no music or dancing, but a great number of minstrels performed. The princess returned the same day to Somerset House : striking indications of the preference given by Mary to the country of her husband and of her maternal ancestry over that of which she was a native and a queen in her own right. There was no masking or dancing, but a great number of minstrels performed. The princess returned to Somerset Place the same evening, and the next day to Hatfield."

It was on an occasion of less honour that

the princess was brought hither from the Tower in the charge of Sir Henry Bedingfield, her harsh custodian, to Richmond, and here she received the offer of her freedom, on condition of exiling herself from England by marrying the Duke of Savoy—an offer which she had the firmness to refuse, preferring the reversion of the English crown. On this refusal being communicated to Queen Mary, the poor princess was ordered to be removed to Woodstock. "On crossing the river at Richmond on this melancholy journey," writes Lucy Aikin, "she descried from the other side certain of her poor servants who had been restrained from giving their attendance during her imprisonment, and were anxiously desirous of seeing her again. 'Go to them,' she said to one of her men, 'and say these words from me : *Tanquam ovis*, like a sheep to the slaughter.'"

Richmond was a favourite residence of Queen Elizabeth, who here entertained Eric IV., King of Sweden, when he visited England to make her a proposal of marriage. Whilst the king was in England he paid frequent visits to Dr. Dee, the astrologer, at Mortlake, whom he employed as a spy, and of whom we shall have more to say presently, when we reach that place.

An amusing and characteristic anecdote is told of Elizabeth in connection with Richmond. A carter had three times been at Richmond with his cart, to carry away, upon summons of a removal from thence, some part of the stuff of Queen Elizabeth's wardrobe ; and when he had repaired thither once, twice, and the third time, and they of the wardrobe told him the third time that the removal held not, the queen having changed her mind, the carter, clapping his hand on his thigh, said, "*Now I see that the queen is a woman as well as my wife ;*" which words being overheard by her Majesty, who then stood at the window, she said, "*What a villain is this!*" and so sent him three angels to stop his mouth.

The well-known story of Queen Elizabeth's jest with her cousin, Henry Cary, which we have recorded in our account of Hampton Court,* is sometimes said to belong to Richmond Palace.

It is well known that Elizabeth was so vain that no ambassador or courtier succeeded in his suit with her except by addressing her as a goddess. Anthony Rudd, Bishop of St. David's, incurred her displeasure by preaching before the Court at Richmond, in 1596, on the infirmities of old age, and at the same time applying his remarks to the queen, observing how "time had furrowed her face, and

besprinkled her hair with meal." Even then, at the age of sixty-two, Elizabeth did not dislike to be complimented on her personal charms ; and she never forgave those who accused her of growing old. Bishop Rudd was never promoted.

In a note in Walpole's "Royal and Noble Authors," however, we read an anecdote, which it is to be hoped for the queen's sake is true, in part at least :—"The Archbishop of Canterbury, who attended the queen in the last moments of her life, endeavoured to console her by saying that she had everything to hope from the mercy of the Almighty for her piety, her zeal, and the admirable work of the Reformation which she had so happily established. The queen, who had turned to the other side of the bed, interrupted the archbishop by saying, 'My lord, the crown which I wore for many years made me sufficiently vain while I lived ; I beg you will not now increase my fault in that respect.' "

It is much now-a-days to find any one who believes that Queen Elizabeth was ever young, or who does not talk of her as if she was born about seventy years of age, covered with rouge and wrinkles. It may be safely said, however, that as to the beauty of this woman there is a greater mass of testimony—and from the very best judges, too— than there is of the beauty of any personage in history ; and yet it has become the fashion now to deny even that.

After Mary Stuart—perhaps, indeed, not second even to her—there is no female character in English history surrounded by such a halo of interest and fascination as Elizabeth. Every inch a queen, and every inch a woman—in her strength and in her weakness—the maiden queen appeals to our chivalry, our sentiment, and our admiration. There are writers who maintain that in mere personal beauty, in her youth and middle age, she was able to hold her own against her beautiful cousin and rival.

Charles Kingsley says :—"The plain facts seem that she was very graceful, active, accomplished in all outward manners, of a perfect figure, and of that style of intellectual beauty, depending on expression, which attracted—and we trust always will attract—Britons, far more than that merely sensuous loveliness in which, no doubt, Mary Stuart far surpassed her. And there seems little doubt that, like many English women, she retained her beauty to a very late period in life, not to mention that she was, in 1592, just at that age of rejuvenescence which makes many a woman more lovely at sixty than she had been since she was thirty-five. No doubt, too, she used every artificial means to pre-

---

* See Vol. I., p. 151

serve her famous complexion; and quite right she was. This beauty of hers had been a talent—as all beauty is—committed to her by God; it had been an important element in her great success; men had accepted it as what beauty of form and expression generally is, an outward and visible sign of the inward and spiritual grace; and while the inward was unchanged, what wonder if she tried to preserve the outward? If she was the same, why should she not try to look the same? And what

her death at last; and this no sooner was supposed to be mortal, than her courtiers hastened from her palace to make their court to the King of Scots, her presumptive heir. This threw her into a deep melancholy; and in the beginning of March, not only her limbs, but her speech, failed her very much, which made her so peevish, that she could bear nobody near her but the Archbishop of Canterbury, who gave her due attendance in prayer and exhortations. When death seemed to draw very

REMAINS OF THE OLD PALACE, RICHMOND.

blame to those who worshipped her, if, knowing that she was the same, they too should fancy that she looked the same—the Elizabeth of their youth—and should talk as if the fair flesh, as well as the fair spirit, was immortal? Does not every loving husband do so when he forgets the grey hair and the sunken cheek, and all the wastes of time, and sees the partner of many joys and sorrows not as she has become, but as she was, ay, and is to him, and will be to him, he trusts, through all eternity?"

It was at Richmond that the long life and splendid reign of Elizabeth came to a close, on the 24th of March, 1603. "At the end of January, 1603," says an old chronicle, "Elizabeth began to feel the first attacks of a distemper, which proved

near, her Council deputed the Lord Admiral to pray her to name her successor: to whom she faintly answered, 'That she had already said her throne was the throne of kings, and she would have no mean person to succeed her.' But being further desired by the Secretary to declare her pleasure more plainly, 'I will,' said she, 'that a king succeed me. And who should that be but my nearest kinsman, the King of Scots?'"

If she was not forgotten in her life, at all events in her death she was deserted by all the friends who had fawned on her Majesty, and basked in the sunshine of her royal face. Death showed to her the hollowness of earthly friendships and courtly adulation.

So true are Tennyson's words :—

> " Authority forgets a dying king,
> Laid widowed of the power in his eye
> That bowed the will."

And again he writes in the same tone :—

> " ' O cruel heart ! ' she changed her tone,
> ' And cruel love, whose end is scorn ;
> Is this the end, to be left alone,
> To live forgotten and die forlorn ? ' "

In fact, as early as the close of the previous year, another account states, she was in ailing health, but she was able to visit the Lord Admiral at Chelsea in the January, and thence she removed to Richmond, never to leave it again alive. Her distress on account of the death of Essex was so keen that she refused to take food or rest, and a fixed melancholy settled upon her, which none of her courtiers could dispel. She would not go to her bed, but sat upon cushions piled on the floor of her chamber, uttering such groans—so her kinsman, Robert Cary tells us, in his " Memoirs "—as had never before been heard from her since the death of Mary, Queen of Scots. Miss Lucy Aikin draws a picture of the Archbishop of Canterbury and her chaplains praying by her bedside, and of her raising her hand to them in token of her wish that James of Scotland should succeed to her throne.

" Between one and two o'clock of the Thursday morning, he that I left in the cofferer's chamber brought me word that the queen was dead," writes Robert Cary. There is a romantic anecdote, often told, but first published in Osborn's " Traditionary Memoirs of Queen Elizabeth," which is confirmed by Maurier's " Memoirs," where it is given on the authority of Sir Dudley Carleton, the English ambassador to Holland, who related it to Prince Maurier. It is to this effect :—The Countess of Nottingham, who was a relation, but no friend, of the Earl of Essex, being on her death-bed, entreated to see the queen, declaring that she had something to confess to her before she could die in peace. On her Majesty's arrival, the countess produced a ring which, she said, the Earl of Essex had sent to her after his condemnation, with an earnest request that she would deliver it to the queen, as the token by which he implored her mercy ; but that, in obedience to her husband, to whom she had communicated the circumstance, she had withheld it, for which she entreated the queen's forgiveness. At the sight of the ring Elizabeth instantly recognised it as one which she had herself presented to her unhappy favourite, with the tender promise that of whatever offences he might be accused, or even guilty, on his returning to her that

pledge she would either pardon him or admit him to justify himself in her presence. Transported at once with grief and rage at learning the cruel duplicity of which the earl had been the victim and herself the dupe, the queen is said to have shaken the dying countess violently as she lay on her bed, and to have flung herself out of the room. This was the cause of the melancholy which seized her on returning to her palace, and no doubt hastened her death.

" The ceremonial of Elizabeth's Court at White-hall, at Hampton, at Richmond," writes Miss Lucy Aikin, " rivalled the servility of the East ; no person of whatever rank ventured to address her otherwise than kneeling, and this attitude was preserved by all the Ministers during their audiences of business, with the exception of Burleigh, in whose favour, when aged and infirm, she dispensed with its observance." Hentzner, the German traveller whom we have already quoted,[*] and who visited England towards the end of her reign, relates that as she passed through the several apartments from the chapel to the dining-hall, wherever she turned her eye he observed the spectators throw themselves upon their knees. He also further relates that the officers and ladies whose business it was to arrange the dishes and give tastes of them to the Yeomen of the Guard, by whom they were brought in, did not presume to approach the royal table without repeated prostrations and genuflexions.

Bohun, in his " Character of Queen Elizabeth," thus describes her habits whilst at her palace at Richmond :—" First in the morning she spent some time at her devotions ; then she betook herself to the despatch of her civil affairs, reading letters, ordering answers, considering what should be brought before the Council, and consulting with her Ministers. When she had thus wearied herself, she would walk in a shady garden or pleasant gallery, without any other attendance than that of a few learned men. Then she took her coach, and passed in the sight of her people to the neighbouring groves and fields, and sometimes would hunt or hawk. There was scarce a day but she employed some part of it in reading and study. . . . She slept little, seldom drank wine, was sparing in her diet, and a religious observer of the fasts. She seldom dined alone, but more commonly had with her some of her friends. At supper she would divert herself with her friends and attendants, and if they made her no answer, would put them upon mirth and pleasant discourse with great civility She would then admit Tarleton, a famous comedian

---

and pleasant tattler, and other such men, to divert her with stories of the town and the common jests and anecdotes. . . . . She would recreate herself with a game of chess, dancing, or singing. She would often play at cards and tables, and if at any time she happened to win, she would be sure to demand the money. She was waited upon in her bedchamber by married ladies of the nobility—the Marchioness of Winchester, widow, Lady Warwick, and Lady Scrope ; and here she would seldom suffer any to wait on her but Leicester, Hatton, Essex, Nottingham, and Raleigh. Some lady always slept in her chamber ; and, besides her guards, there was always a gentleman of good quality and some others up in the next chamber, to wake her if anything extraordinary happened." The same authority, Bohun, states that she was " laudably watchful over the morals of her Court," which is good news to hear. The ladies of her Court, however, were taught to employ their minds and their hands in useful studies and accomplishments, some of them learning to write and speak both the dead and modern languages, whilst the younger ones practised the " lutes, citharnes, prick-songs, and all kinds of music," and the elder ones became " skilful in surgery and the distillation of waters."

In a curious old memoir, published in 1732 by Pierre de l'Etoile, grand audiencier de la Chancellerie de Paris, and called " Journal du Règne de Henri Quatre," I find the following article at the period of the death of our Queen Elizabeth :—" Il y a trois choses, dit le Roy, que le monde ne veut croire, et toutefois elles sont vraies et bien certaines : Que la Reine d'Angleterre est morte fille ; que l'Archiduc est un grand capitaine ; et que le Roy de France est fort bon Catholique." This tribute to our virgin queen from Henri IV. is singular, to say the least.

The queen was carried to London, and buried at Westminster Abbey on the 28th of April following. " At which time," writes Stow (Howe's editions verify), " the cittie was surcharged with multitudes of all sort of people in their streets, houses, windows, leads, and gutters, that came to see the obsequie ; and when they beheld her statue or picture lying upon the coffin set forth in royal robes, having a crown upon the head thereof, and a ball and sceptre in either hand, there was such a generall syghing, groaning, and weeping as the like hath not been seene or knowne in the memorie of man, neyther doth any historie mention any people, time, or states to make like lamentacyon for the death of their soverayne."

There is a tradition that the room over the remaining gateway is that in which Queen Elizabeth died ; but it is too small and poor to have been her chamber. Another story connected with this upper chamber over the gateway is manifestly untrue : viz., that it was the room in which the Countess of Nottingham confessed her treachery to Elizabeth. The countess died at Arundel House, London, in 1603, as appears from the parish register of Chelsea, where she was buried.

In the autumn of 1603, the year in which Queen Elizabeth died, the Courts of Law were removed to Richmond, on account of the plague.

The palace was to some extent a rival of Nonsuch, which has been so recently described in these pages. Grotius, who visited England in A.D. 1615, wrote four Latin epigrams on the four suburban palaces of the English king, " Nonswich," " Hamptincourt," " Windsoor," and " Richemont ; " and another traveller, Abraham Golnitz, in his " Ulysses Belgico-Gallicus," published some fifteen years later, draws a curious comparison between Fontainebleau and our insular palaces, reflecting sadly on the want of ordinary care in our interior and domestic arrangements, instancing cobwebs, unpolished beams and panelling, and walls scarcely water-proof.*

The furniture and decorations of the old palace are said to have been of a most lavish and costly description, " exhibiting in gorgeous tapestry the deeds of kings and of heroes who had signalised themselves by their conquests throughout France in behalf of their country.

Mrs. Goodhall, of Bridgefield, Twickenham, just over Richmond Bridge, tells me that in the winter of 1883, on some wainscoting being removed at the old palace, some dresses of Queen Elizabeth were found in a chest behind it. No details have transpired in the neighbourhood, but it is supposed that the queen has claimed them.

In 1610, the manor, palace, and park of Richmond, were settled on Henry, Prince of Wales, eldest son of James I., who was residing here in 1605, and again also in 1612, the year of his death. The king, however, liked Theobalds† better than Richmond, and spent most of his time there. In 1617 the royal estate was vested in trustees for Charles, Prince of Wales. He often lived here, both before and after his accession to the throne, and collected a large number of pictures in the palace. Ten years later, the manor, mansion, and old park, were included in the settlement made on the queen, Henrietta Maria, as part of her dower.

---

* See article by W. Bates, B.A., in *Notes and Queries*, Feb. 2, 1884.
† See Vol. I., p. 381.

"After the execution of the king, in 1649," writes Brayley, "a survey of the palace was taken by order of the Parliament, which affords a very minute description of the buildings as then existing. There was a spacious hall, with a turret, or clock case, at one end of it. The privy lodgings, three storeys high, were ornamented with fourteen turrets. There was a round edifice, called the 'Canted Tower,' with a staircase of one hundred and twenty-four steps ; and a chapel, with 'cathedral seats and pews.' Adjoining the privy garden was an open gallery (portico) 200 feet in length, with a covered gallery over it. The materials of the palace were valued at £10,782 19s. 2d."

Most of the palace was pulled down in 1649 by order of the Parliament, though enough of it remained to give a home—such as it was—for a time to the widowed queen of Charles I.

To the palace here the infant son of James II., and his consort, Mary of Modena, was sent, when only a few days old, to be brought up by hand. His life hung by a thread, and it was only by the help of a wet nurse, when his recovery had been despaired of, that he was brought through. From Richmond he was removed to Windsor.

A curious and interesting view of the royal palace as it was in 1638 is to be seen among the etchings of Hollar. It shows a forest of towers and spires rising out of the garden walls. In the distance are the houses on Richmond Green, and the parish church beyond. The view is taken from the Middlesex side of the river, moored to which is a covered pleasure-boat, a sort of "Folly."* In the front is a group of nine persons, of whom the two boys, who alone are covered, would seem to be the young princes Charles and James, and who have evidently come across the river to enjoy themselves *al fresco*.

Strype, in 1720, speaks of Richmond Palace as being "now decayed, and parcelled out in tene-ments." The palace was situated outside of the town, to the north-west of Hill Street, and between the Green and the river. On the Green, near the gateway, and almost fronting the theatre, was for-merly the ivy-clad stump of a venerable elm-tree, which is said to have been planted by Queen Eliza-beth. Its remains were removed a few years ago.

The fragment of the palace still standing bears a strong resemblance to St. James's Palace, though built on a smaller scale. A gateway still bears the royal arms of the Tudors, though now scarcely decipherable, owing to the wearing away of the stone ; besides this gateway, some of the offices

remain among residences built on the Crown lands. A part of what once formed the stables is now, by a strange irony, the depôt for the London Parcels Delivery Company.

Besides the gateway, a small portion of the out-quarters of the palace remains, a low-looking building on the left hand, but it has in it nothing remarkable. The more modern building, which stands at right angles to it, and faces the river, is thought to stand on the site of the old Guard House. It is known as the Trumpeters' House, on account of two statues of figures blowing trum-pets which once adorned its portico. It is built very much in the style of the more ornamental parts of Kensington Palace, and is fronted by one of the loftiest and most magnificent of stone porticos, which harmonises admirably with the fine red brick of the walls. One large and long room on the ground floor, now used as a drawing-room, has a ceiling exquisitely adorned with light sculptured panels, showing portraits of our national poets. This house was built by Mr. Richard Hill, brother to Mrs. Masham, Queen Anne's favourite, to whom a lease of the ground, forming part of the site of the old palace—had been granted by the queen. In the gardens is a fine cedar of Lebanon.

The house was for some years the residence of Mr. Charles Lee Mainwaring, whose collection of pictures, works of art, antique furniture, &c., includ-ing specimens of the work of Rembrandt, Teniers, Ruysdael, and other great artists, was dispersed by the hammer of the auctioneer in 1875.

In the garden behind this house, close to the river-side, is a summer-house of modern appearance, but far older than it looks. On its gates is some fine scroll-work of iron, with the Tudor rose repeated upon it. Most probably it was made in one of the forges in the Weald of Sussex. A small garden between this summer-house and Asgill House is the traditional site of the earliest palace erected at Sheen. Between the palace and this summer-house is a raised terrace planted with yews under which Queen Elizabeth may have walked. It commands a charming view of the river, looking up to Richmond Bridge.

At the river-side, just below the old palace, stands Asgill House, the seat of Mr. James B. Hilditch. It derives its name from Sir Charles Asgill, Bart., Alderman of London and Lord Mayor in 1758, for whom it was built by the distinguished architect, Sir Robert Taylor. It stands on a raised ascent at a short distance from the river-side, and is of the Tuscan order : "remarkable for its chaste and simple elegance." Externally it is heavy, though grand, somewhat in the style of Chiswick House,

The rooms inside are lofty and handsome, and irregular in plan, some of them being octagonal. They have magnificent doors and lintels, copied from those in the Mansion House, London. The principal sitting-rooms are adorned with magnificent mantelpieces of Italian marble, carved in bold relief; and one of the rooms on the first floor has its panels painted with figure subjects of classical and Italian type. In the grounds, which stretch down to the river from the palace, are one or two fine yews, a standard plum-tree of fabulous age, and a fine cedar of Lebanon, which is mentioned in the parliamentary return in the reign of Charles I.

In connection with this part of the town is told a good story, which shows that modern sovereigns cannot always get their own way in their own dominions, and even in their own neighbourhoods. All those who are acquainted with Richmond must know Asgill House, must remember the iron turnstile near it, and the swinging gate at the opposite corner, at the entrance to the path leading by the river-side to Kew. The path was formerly available to travellers on horseback; but as they were found to interfere in a manner very inconvenient with the towing-line of the barges, &c., George III. issued an order that for the future the path should be restricted to the use of foot passengers only; and, for the rigid enforcement of this order, he caused some iron turnstiles and swing gates to be set up, and a man was appointed to guard them.

It happened one day that the king himself, accompanied by one of the princes, forgetful of his own commands, rode along the path from Kew Palace towards Richmond, and coming to the gate, called out to the watchman to open it.

"Can't open this gate, sir; can't let nobody through o' horseback."

"Can't open! can't open! Then, how are we to get out?" exclaimed his Majesty.

"Which way did you come in, sir?"

"Came in at Kew, came in at Kew, to be sure."

"Then you must please to get out again that way, sir; can't let you out this."

"What! what! what! not let me out, eh? Do you know who I am?"

"No, sir; but if you were the king himself I couldn't open the gate for you. I've got my orders, and I stick to 'em."

"King! king! king! look, my good fellow, I am the king!"

"Oh, to be sure," said the man, with a knowing grin; "no doubt o' *that*; but I can't let you through, notwithstanding."

"I assure you, my fine fellow," said the prince, "this is the king, and I am the——"

"Ay, ay, sir, and you are the Emperor of *Chany*: no doubt of that, neither; but if you were the Emperor of *Rooshey* into the bargain, my orders are not to open this gate to nobody whatsomever o' horseback; so it don't signify to me."

The king, perceiving that no impression was to be made upon this rigid disciplinarian, was about to return, when a gentleman, coming up at the moment, took off his hat on recognising his Majesty, and stood respectfully still, just whispering to the gate-keeper, "The king, the king." The man, alarmed for the consequences of what he now conceived to be his misconduct, trembling and awe-struck, opened the gate.

"No, no, no; won't go through, won't go through," answered the good-natured king. "Do your duty, quite right. Home—home (giving the man a guinea); here's a picture of the king for you, that you may know him when you see him again; but don't let him go through, don't let him go through." So saying, his Majesty returned by the way he came, congratulating himself probably that he had, at all events, one faithful subject.

In the Park, near the present Observatory, at a short distance north-west of the palace, stood the monastery of Sheen, a convent of Carthusian monks, instituted by Henry V. in the year 1414. The buildings were of considerable extent, and around them grew up in course of time the hamlet called West Sheen, which has long since been swept clean away.

The history of the convent is short, but impressive. At this place King Henry, with the view of expiating the murder of Richard, by which his family had mounted the throne of England, founded the priory here for forty monks, which he denominated the "House of Jesus of Bethlehem." And upon the same principle he also founded at Sion, now the seat of the Duke of Northumberland, on the opposite side of the Thames, a convent for sixty nuns of the order of St. Bridget.* An old account in the British Museum tells us, that in these convents, by order of the royal founder, a constant succession of holy exercises was ordained to be kept up night and day to the end of time. Anthony Wood, following Beccalett, says that "at seven years of age, Cardinal Pole was sent to the monastery at Shene, to be trained up in religion and grammar amongst the Carthusians there"; and he afterwards, when about the age of twenty-five or twenty-six, "retired to his old

---

* See Vol I., p. 44.

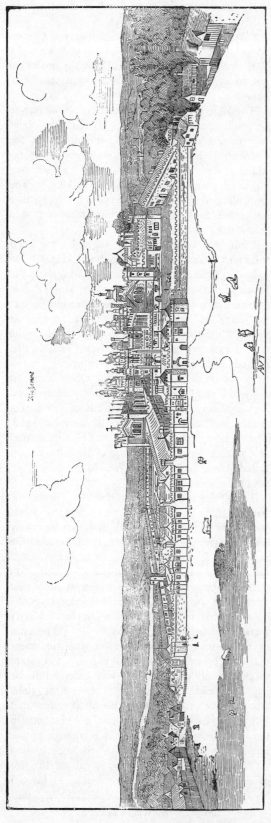

BACK VIEW OF OLD RICHMOND PALACE.

OLD RICHMOND PALACE, FROM THE RIVER. (*From Views by Antony van den Wyngaerde*, 1562.)

Cien (West Sheen).   Haravil (Harrow).   Sion.   Brentford.   Kichemont (Richmond).   S. Paolo (St. Paul's).
Aishilworth (Isleworth).

habitation at Shene, where, by the leave of the king, he had granted to him the apartment which Dr. John Colet, the founder of St. Paul's School, had a little before built (for the exercising of his learning and devotion), where he spent two years with very great delight."

The Priory was renowned for its holiness; and Protestants of these latter ages can have but a faint conception of the pomp with which Catholic worship was conducted within its walls. Perkin Warbeck made it his asylum, and Cardinal Wolsey and Dean Colet were both inmates of the Carthusian House during part of their declining years; Dean Colet, according to Wood, died at his lodgings in this monastery in 1519, of the sweating sickness. Henry V. also founded at Sheen a second house, that of the Celestines, and the son dissolved it along with sundry other priories. Cobbett, in his "History of the Reformation," states that at the dissolution of the Carthusian monastery in the reign of Henry VIII., its revenues amounted to £1,000—a large sum—now equal to £19,250. An illuminated Bible given to the convent of Sheen by Henry V. was to be seen at Paris in 1849 in the Tuileries. Queen Mary, in 1554, reinstated at Sheen the Carthusian monks who had been expelled from their house in London; but they were expelled by Elizabeth, and fled to Belgium, whence, in 1783, they migrated to Spain or Portugal.

Waller Hylton, a monk of this priory, was the author of "Scala Perfectionis" printed in English by Wynken de Worde, and of other "Pious Contemplations" in English verse.

It is stated by some authors that the head of James IV., King of Scotland, who fell, as was supposed, at the battle of "Flodden Field," fought in the reign of Henry VIII., was buried here, but this has been warmly disputed by others. "According to the generally-received account, the body of the king was found upon the field, and was conveyed to the monastery of Sheen, where it remained until the dissolution. The monastery was plundered at that epoch; and Stow says the king's corpse, "wrapped in lead," was placed in a waste room amongst old timber and other lumber, and that he saw it there. When it was in this situation, some of the workmen cut off the head, and Launcelot Young, master glazier to Queen Elizabeth, liking the sweet scent that proceeded from the medicaments with which it was embalmed, took it with him to his house in Wood Street; but, becoming careless of possessing it, afterwards gave it to the sexton of the church now under consideration, in order that he might bury it. The Scottish writers, however, contend that James was not killed at that battle, and that this head, therefore, could not be his, but was that of an individual who fought during the day in habiliments similar to those worn by the king, in order to draw off the attention of the English from James; and one writer asserts that the king escaped to Jerusalem, and died here some time afterwards. Weever, however, is quite positive that Sheen *was* the place of James's burial."*

After the dissolution the convent was granted to the Earl of Hertford, afterwards Duke of Somerset; but it seems to have carried with it a curse, for Spelman tells us in his "History and Fate of Sacrilege," that in a hundred and forty years it went to nine possessors in succession, and each of a different family, thus never once descending from father to son. This convent owned, among other properties, the manor of what is now Gray's Inn.†

A convent of Observant Friars was founded close to the southern end of the Palace at Sheen by Henry VII., about 1499. The suppression of this religious house is mentioned by Holinshed to have taken place in 1534. In the Survey of Richmond in the Augmentation Office, a building is described as adjoining to the palace called "The Friars, containing three rooms below stayrs, and four handsome rooms above stayrs." A lane, still called Friar's Lane, leads from Richmond Green to the Thames. The building here referred to is thought to have been the priory or convent of Observant Friars, which Henry VII. is said to have founded near the palace in the year 1499, and which was suppressed in 1534.

Edward II. founded a convent of Carmelite Friars "near his manor of Sheen," and endowed it with 120 marks per annum out of his exchequer. They had been settled in this convent only two years when the king caused them to be removed to Oxford.

---

* Godwin and Britton's "Churches of London."
† See "Old and New London," Vol. II., p. 553.

CHAPTER XXXIX.

RICHMOND (*continuea*)—THE ROYAL PARKS, ETC.

"Ne Richmond's self, from whose tall front are eyed
Vales, spires, meandering streams, and Windsor's tow'ry pride."—A. POPE.

Earliest Record of a Park at Richmond—The Lodge in the Little Park—It becomes a Royal Residence in place of the Old Palace—A Lease of the Lodge granted to the Duke of Ormonde—Mackay's Description of the Building—Bishop Atterbury and the Sceptic—Reception of the News of the Death of George I. by the Prince of Wales—Queen Caroline's Fondness for Richmond—George the Second's Partiality for Punch—The King and the Gardener—The Lodge Settled on Queen Charlotte—The Gardens and Ornamental Buildings—Description of Merlin's Cave—The Character of Merlin—Stephen Duck Appointed Keeper of the Grotto and Library—The Hermitage—Clarence House.

AFTER the death of Bishop Burnell, in 1292, a survey was taken of the fee of Richmond on behalf of his heirs, and in that document we find the earliest mention of a park in this locality, situated on the north-west of the present village of Richmond ; it is now incorporated with the pleasure-grounds at Kew.

In the reign of Henry VIII. there were two parks at Richmond, known as the Great and the Little Park. It was in the lodge of the latter (called also the Old Park) that Cardinal Wolsey occasionally resided after he had surrendered the palace of Hampton Court to the demand of his imperious master.*

It is probable that the two parks were afterwards united, one only, which adjoined Richmond Green, and was 349 acres in extent, being mentioned in the survey made in 1649. It was this park which, with the manor, was settled on the queen of Charles I. in 1627. After the execution of the king it was valued at £220 5s. per annum, and sold to William Brome, gent., of London, for £7,048—that is, at thirty years' purchase. The lodge, described as "a pleasant residence for a country gentleman," appears to have been afterwards in the possession of Sir Thomas Jervase, and the park in that of Sir John Trevor, and on the demolition or abandonment of the Old Palace as a royal residence, its mantle of glory seems to have descended upon this building. William III., in 1694, granted to John Latton, Esq., of Esher Place, a lease of the lodge, together with the stewardship of the manor. In 1707 Queen Anne granted a lease of it for three lives to James, Duke of Ormond, who rebuilt the house.

In 1715 Ormond was impeached, attainted, and his estates confiscated. Mackay, in his "Journey through England," thus describes the lodge :— "It is a perfect Trianon. Everything in it and about it is answerable to the grandeur and magnificence of its great master."

At the duke's table, Dr. King tells us, in his "Anecdotes of his Own Time," there arose a dispute concerning short prayers. Sir William Wyndham said that the shortest prayer he had ever heard was that of a common soldier just before the battle of Blenheim : "O God, if there be a God, save my soul—if I have a soul !" This was followed, most indecorously, by a general laugh. But Atterbury, Bishop of Rochester, who was present, addressed Sir William, saying : "Your prayer, sir, is very short ; but I remember another as short, but much better, offered up likewise by a poor soldier in the same circumstances : 'O God, if in the day of battle I forget Thee, do not Thou forget me.'" This, pronounced by Atterbury with his usual grace and dignity, was a very gentle, polite, and well-timed reproof, and was felt to be so by the entire company. The sceptic was silenced, and the Duke of Ormond, who, we are told, was "the best bred man of his day," turned the conversation to another subject.

At the Duke of Ormond's forfeiture the house was sold to the Prince of Wales, and it was here that he received the news of his father's death. Of this event Thackeray writes, in his caustic essay on "The Four Georges" :—"On the afternoon of the 14th June, 1727, two horsemen might have been perceived galloping along the road from Chelsea to Richmond. The foremost, cased in jackboots of the period, was a broad-faced, jolly-looking, and very corpulent cavalier ; but by the manner in which he urged his horse, you might see that he was a bold as well as skilful rider. He speedily reached Richmond Lodge, and asked to see the owner of the mansion. The mistress of the house and her ladies said he could not be introduced to the master, however pressing the business might be. The master was asleep after his dinner ; he always slept after his dinner, and woe to the person who disturbed him ! Nevertheless, our stout friend of the jackboots put the affrighted ladies aside, opened the forbidden door of the bed-room, wherein upon the bed lay a little gentleman ; and here the eager messenger knelt down in his jackboots. He on the bed started up, and, with many oaths and a strong German accent, asked who was there, and who dared to disturb him. 'I am Sir Robert Walpole,' said the messenger. The awakened sleeper hated Sir Robert Walpole. 'I have the honour to announce to your Majesty that your royal father, King George First, died at Osnaburg on Saturday last, the 10th instant.' '*Dat is one big lie!*' roared out his sacred Majesty King George Second; but Sir Robert Walpole stated the fact, and from that day until thirty-three years after George, the second of the name, ruled over England."

Queen Caroline, wife of George II., was very fond of the Richmond residence, and so was the king up to the date of his death, in 1760. When he reviewed the Guards here, in 1727, we are told that the three eldest princesses were present in riding-habits, with hats, feathers, and periwigs.

Walpole, speaking of the latter years of George II., says:—"Every Saturday in summer he carried a party, consisting of Lady Yarmouth, two or three of the queen's ladies, and as many of the most favoured officers of his own household, to dine at Richmond. They went in coaches and six in the middle of the day, with the heavy Horse Guards kicking up the dust before them; dined, walked an hour in the garden, returned in the same dusty parade; and his Majesty thought himself the most gallant and lively prince in Europe."

A stag hunt in the New Park, at which the king, queen, and the princesses were present— some on horseback and some in carriages—and which ended in the buck being brought to bay and killed in "the Great Pond," is described at length in the *Monthly Chronicle* for 1728, under date August 17.

George II. was also a frequent visitor and guest at Sir Robert Walpole's house on Richmond Hill. Here, too, it is recorded that the king indulged his partiality for punch to such an extent that the Duchess of Kendal enjoined the Germans who usually accompanied him to restrain him from drinking too much; but they went about their task with so little address, that the king took offence, and silenced them with the coarsest epithets in their mother tongue.

This prince seemed to have none of that love of individual and distinct property which has marked the character of many sovereigns. His Majesty came one day to Richmond Gardens, and finding them locked while some decently-dressed persons were standing on the outside, called for the head gardener, and told him, in a great passion, to open the door immediately. "My subjects," said his Majesty, "walk where they please." On another occasion the same gardener was complaining that some of the company, in their walk round the gardens, had pulled up flowers, roots, and shrubs; the king, shaking his cane, replied, "Plant more, then, you blockhead!"

"On the marriage of George III., in 1762," remarks a writer in *Notes and Queries*, "the Lodge was settled upon Queen Charlotte. In 1768 the king built the observatory close to it; and shortly afterwards the queen had the lodge pulled down, intending to rebuild it. Richmond and Kew, which join, have enjoyed the favour of royalty for several centuries, and have been noted for many palaces or royal residences, the greater part of which have now passed away. It is, perhaps, worth while to observe that Frederick, Prince of Wales, in 1730 took a long lease of Kew House, which, after his death there, in 1751, became the residence of the princess. This was pulled down in 1803, and a large stone castellated palace was built for George III., which, however, was never completed, and was in turn destroyed in 1827 by George IV. When the observatory was built in 1768, and the queen's lodge pulled down, the king used the 'old Dutch house' at Kew as a royal nursery, and there George IV. was educated as a boy, and his mother died in 1818. It is not uncommon to find these old houses spoken of as the palace.* The exact site of the lodge is shown in Rocque's large map of Surrey, 1762, and also, though not quite so well, in his map of London and surrounding country, 1745. Rocque likewise published a plan of the royal gardens in 1748, and there is an interesting account of them in 'London and its Environs,' published by Dodsley in 1761."

In 1729 the Duke of Grafton had a hunting seat near here; but it would seem to have been a poor, tumble-down sort of place, for in the Wentworth Papers his Grace excuses himself on that ground from receiving the queen and prince, who had threatened him with a chance visit.

Queen Caroline had a dairy and a menagerie in the park; and there were also in the gardens adjoining the park several ornamental buildings, including one known as Merlin's Cave. Of this latter structure we glean the following particulars from the pages of the *Gentleman's Magazine* for 1735, where, under date of June 30, it is stated that "Her Majesty has ordered Mr. Risbrack to

---

* See Lyson's "Environs of London," Brayley and Britton's "History of Surrey," and Dr. Evans's "Richmond and its Vicinity."

make the Busto's in Marble of all the Kings of England from William the Conqueror, in order to be placed in her New Building in the Gardens at Richmond. . . . A subterraneous Building is, by her Majesty's Order, carrying on in the Royal Gardens at Richmond, which is to be called Merlin's Cave, adorned with Astronomical Figures and Characters." Under date of August 21, we read :—" The Figures her Majesty had order'd for Merlin's Cave were placed therein, viz., (1) Merlin at a Table, with Conjuring Books and Mathematical Instruments, taken from the face of Mr. Ernest, page to the Prince of Wales ; (2) King Henry VII.'s queen ; and (3) Queen Elizabeth, who came to Merlin for knowledge, the former from the face of Mrs. Margaret Purcell, and the latter from Miss Paget's ; (4) Minerva, from Mrs. Poyntz's ; (5) Merlin's secretary, from Mr. Kemp's. one of his R.H. the Duke's Grenadiers ; and (6) a witch, from a tradesman's wife at Richmond. Her Majesty has order'd also a choice collection of English books to be placed therein, and appointed Mr. Stephen Duck to be cave and library keeper, and his wife necessary woman there."

The following amusing description of a visit to the royal gardens, with fuller details of the Cave, appears in the *Gentleman's Magazine* for September, 1735, quoted from the *Craftsman*, No. 491. Commencing with a humorous account of the journey up the river as far as Richmond, the writer proceeds :—" Coming to a certain place with iron palisades, my cousin so insisted upon showing us a fine garden, which he said was well worth our seeing. Being admitted at the gate by one of the gardeners, he conducted us up an avenue, leading to a house of no extraordinary appearance, and which, it seems, had nothing within to engage our attention. We were afterwards led through a great number of close alleys, with clipt hedges, without any variety or prospect, except a beautiful terras towards the river. Not having walked so much for several years, I grew weary, and expressed some impatience to be gone. But our guide told us we had not yet seen the chief curiosities of the place, which were the Hermitage and the Cave. He then led us to the first, which I found to be a heap of stones, thrown into a very artful disorder, and curiously embellished with moss and shrubs, to represent rude nature. But I was strangely surpris'd to find the entrance of it barr'd with a range of costly gilt rails, which not only seemed to show an absurdity of taste, but created in me a melancholy reflection that luxury had found its way even into the Hermit's Cell. The inside was adorned with the heads of several wise men, who have been formerly famous in their generation. As we were conducted thence to the other piece of curiosity, I observed something like an old haystack thatch'd over, and enquired of our conductor what it was. ' That, Sir, is the Cave,' said he. ' What ! a *cave* above ground ? This is still more absurd than the other. However, let us see what it is within.' We then went through a gloomy passage with two or three odd windows, which led to a kind of circular room, supported with wooden pillars. In this, too, as well as the Hermitage, are placed several hieroglyphical figures, male and female, which I cannot pretend to interpret."

In *Fog's Journal* for December 6, 1735, quoted in the *Gentleman's Magazine*, appear the following particulars concerning " Merlin and his Cave " :— " Most nations form themselves upon the model of their princes ; vice and virtue, as well as arts and sciences, flourish in proportion as the Court either practises or encourages them. For the taste of the Court is always the standard of everything but liberty to the rest of the nation. The great concourse of people that have lately flocked to view that celebrated edifice called Merlin's Cave, the universal applause it has met with, and the several humble imitations of it carrying on in different parts of the kingdom, prove the truth of this maxim, and give us reason to hope that taste in building will, from this pattern, be soon brought to its utmost perfection. I therefore thought it would not be disagreeable to your readers if I presented them with a short history of that great man to whose memory this cave is sacred, together with an account of the other figures which attend him.

" Merlin lived in the reign of Vortigern, and by his means was begot the famous King Arthur, a just and brave prince, but whose great qualities were eclipsed by his uxoriousness for his Queen Guiniver, so called, as Geoffry of Monmouth informs us, from her inordinate love of *guineas*. This avaricious and ambitious princess, after having for a long time left the king, her husband, but the shadow of power, resolved at the last to deprive him of that, too, accordingly shut him up in a cage,* and placed him to watch her chest of gold. Notwithstanding which, an old historian observes that a Prince of Wales found means to get at the treasure, and to distribute in acts of generosity what had been acquired by oppression and avarice.

" Chaucer, in his ' Wife of Bath,' gives us a remarkable instance of this queen's predominant love of power. In order to satisfy this passion,

---

* See " Don Quixote and the Knights of the Round Table."

she made use of our Merlin, whose arts and enchantments well seconded her influence over her husband, and paved the way to his future confinement. The first service by which he recommended himself to her Majesty was by his fountain, that changed love into hatred and hatred into love, so celebrated in that great poet Ariosto. He gave her a large provision of these waters, which she took care to make the king drink of on proper occasions, so that in a little while he was observed to hate all those he had loved and to love all those he had hated. The consequence of which was that he had not one friend left, those whom he loved now hating him still for his having hated them once, so that he became the helpless slave of his wife and minister.

"We have no authentic account of the birth and family of Merlin, only that he had been born a Welshman, and it is to be supposed that he was a gentleman; but of his great skill in magic history he gives us many examples; and that he had several inferior sprites at his command appears from Spencer. From which it is plain that his art was of the black, malignant kind, and employed only in wicked purposes, and that the sprites made use of by him were only of the infernal sort, but none of them geniuses to execute good designs. He was likewise a great dealer in brass, and proposed making a wall of brass for the peace and security of the nation; but though such immense sums were raised upon the people under this pretence, yet it was always doing, and never done. Having thus explained the character of the famous Merlin, and those merits which have entitled him to a place in the royal garden of Richmond, we shall now give what account we are able of the other figures. When we consider where and by whom this singular edifice is erected and these extraordinary figures placed, we cannot imagine the whole to be a mere useless ornament, nor reflect without some indignation on the indecency of those who tract it as no better than an idle whim, a painter's fancy, a gardener's gugaw, a *Salmon's Waxwork*, a Savoyard's box, a puppet show, a raree show, a pretty show, &c. On the contrary, we doubt not but that, like the works of the ancient Egyptians, frequently placed in their royal gardens and palaces, it is only hieroglyphical, emblematical, typical, and symbolical, conveying artful lessons of policy to princes and ministers of State.

"After Merlin, the first figure that presents itself is the Amazon, Britomartis, by whom (as the name seems to imply) we suppose is meant for the marshal spirit of Britannia, as we see her represented on some of our coins, half soldier half woman, formidably armed, but encumbered with petticoats. She seems to be in a very declining condition, and (being no conjurer herself) comes in the most anxious and submissive manner to enquire her fate from the mouth of that enchanter who by his skill in the black art had brought it to depend upon him. This Britomartis, or Britannia, is led by a lean elderly lady, whose name is not absolutely agreed upon, some styling her Glauce, mentioned by Spencer, others Melissa, from Ariosto, and others Mother Shipton, famous in British story; but her character and office are better known, being allowed by all to be a sort of a witch, or cunning woman, and something between a dry-nurse and governess to Britomartis, employed by Merlin in the blackest of his art, *viz.*, as his priestess, or Pope Joan. She is likewise a great pretender to sciences and diver into mysteries. Before Merlin is seated as his secretary a great boy with a pen in his hand, submissively looking up to his master for orders and instructions. A busy, dull perplexity appears in his countenance; he seems distrustful of his master's purposes, but without sense enough to understand them, or courage enough to dispute them. The next figure, which, by an unaccountable mistake, has been vulgarly called Queen Elizabeth, can by no means be supposed to have been intended for her, not only because the face is taken from a young and very beautiful lady, but because it is impossible that in the present nice and critical conjuncture of affairs a person so obnoxious to Spain should be so openly avowed and distinguished in that place."

Merlin's Cave was one of Queen Caroline's favourite "conceits," which has not survived the age of improvement and the sweeping of new brooms:—

"To Richmond come; for see, untutor'd Brown
  Destroys those wonders which were once thy own;
  Lo! from his melon-ground the peasant slave
  Has rudely rush'd, and levell'd Merlin's Cave,
  Knock'd down the waxen wizard, seiz'd his wand,
  Transform'd to lawn what late was fairy-land,
  And marr'd with impious hand each sweet design
  Of Stephen Duck and good Queen Caroline."

The above is from a poem in the *London Review* (1773), containing some curious satire on Sir W. Chambers's Dissertation on Oriental Gardening, and especially exposing the absurdity of the Chinese style, to which Sir William was strangely partial.

But how did the Queen contrive to pay for all this private and personal indulgence—this "improvement of her garden"? Walpole shall tell us in his "Reminiscences." He writes:—"The king believed that she paid for it all out of her own money; nor would he ever look at her intended plans, saying that he did not care how she flung away her own revenues. He little suspected the aids that Sir Robert Walpole furnished to her from the Treasury. When she died she was indebted

eccentric man of letters, the Rev. Stephen Duck, who was her Majesty's librarian here. Born in humble life about 1700 at Charlton, in Wiltshire, and having worked as a day labourer till fourteen years of age, he taught himself grammar and a smattering of history and science, and began to

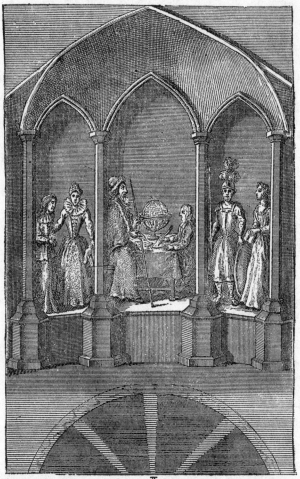

Such was the glassy globe, that Merlin made,
And gave unto King Ryence for his guard,
That never foes his kingdom might invade,
But he it knew at home, and them debarr'd.
　　　　Spens: Fai: Queen.

Fair Britomartis, to strange Love a Slave,
Glauce her Nurse conveys to Merlin's Cave;
The Martial Bradamant, a prisoner made
Was thence releas'd by sage Melissa's aid

FROM MERLIN'S CAVE.

£20,000 to the king." In all probability the patient British taxpayer really defrayed the entire cost of Merlin and his companions in the cave. Be this as it may, however, the cave and grotto furnished fruitful themes for aspirants for poetical fame in the earlier half of the last century, and even the scholars of Eton and Westminster did not disdain to issue their effusions in compliment to the royal taste in elegiac and lyric Latin verses.

The Stephen Duck above alluded to was that

write poetry. At thirty he had made the acquaintance of the Rev. Mr. Spence, who helped him to publish his effusions, which, happening to hit the fancy of Queen Caroline, led her to settle on him a small pension, and to procure his admission into holy orders. Having held the librarianship at Richmond for a few years, he was appointed to the living of Byfleet, where he proved a zealous and able country clergyman. There he rhymed and wrote sermons, and poems also, "Cæsar's Camp,"

VIEW FROM RICHMOND HILL IN 1752. *(From a Drawing by A. Heckel.)*

"Alrick and Isabel," &c. Swift indulges in much humour at the expense of Duck's poetical pretensions. His end, however, was a sad and tragic one. He fell into low spirits, and drowned himself in 1756. Though they enjoyed great popularity in his day, his poems are long since forgotten. Spence edited his poems anew, adding a memoir of his life; and his biography will be found among Southey's "Lives of Uneducated Poets."

The following caustic epigram on this reverend gentleman immortalises him with all who read the poems of Dean Swift :—

"The thrasher Duck could o'er the queen prevail ;
The proverb says 'No fence against a flail ;'
From thrashing corn he turns to thrash his brains,
For which her Majesty allows him grains,
Though 'tis confessed that those who ever saw
His poems think them all not worth a straw.
Thrice happy Duck ! employed in thrashing stubble
Thy toils were lessen'd and thy profits double."

The Thames at this spot is thus apostrophised by Matthew Green, in his poem, "The Grotto":—

"Say, Father Thames, whose gentle pace
Gives leave to view what branches grace
Your flowery banks, if you have seen
The much-sung Grotto of the queen.
Contemplative, forget awhile
Oxonian towers and Windsor's pile,
And Wolsey's pride (his greatest guilt),
And what great William since has built ;
And flowing fast by Richmond scenes
(Honoured retreat of two great queens),
From Sion House, whose proud survey
Browbeats your flood, look cross the way,
And view from highest swell of tide
The milder scenes of Surrey side."

The reference to "Wolsey's pride," and also the following line, both allude, of course, to Hampton Court Palace. Green then proceeds to apostrophise the grotto itself in the following high-flown style, which, we suppose, is allowable in a poet :—

"Though yet no palace grace the shore,
To lodge that pair you should adore,
Nor abbeys, great in ruin, rise,
Royal equivalents for vice,
Behold a grot, in Delphic grove,
The graces and the muses love
(Oh ! might our laureate study here,
How would he hail the new born year,) !
A temple from vain glories free,
Whose goddess is Philosophy.
＊　　＊　　＊　　＊　　＊　　＊
The only pilgrimage I know
Which men of sense would choose to go,
Which sweet abode, her wisest choice,
Urania cheers with heavenly voice,
While all the virtues gather round
To see her consecrate the ground."

The Grotto and Stephen Duck became the subject of much versifying and rhyming about the time when the above verses were written. They are sarcastically mentioned by Pope, in his "Imitations of Horace," in the following couplet :—

"Lord ! how we strut through Merlin's Cave, to see
No poets there, but Stephen, you and me."

In the Hermitage, another of Queen Charlotte's fanciful buildings here, were busts of Adam Clark, Newton, Locke, and other learned persons. These busts appear to have had some merit or virtue : at all events, they inspired Mrs. Catharine Cockburn (*née* Trotter) with some verses of high merit, published at length in the *Gentleman's Magazine* for May, 1737.

The following epigram is to be found in "Elegant Extracts" :—

"Lewis, the living genius, fed
And rais'd the scientific head ;
Our queen, more frugal of her meat,
Raises those heads that cannot eat."

This is followed by a repartee, or "A Conclusion drawn from the above Epigram" :—

"Since Anna, whose bounty thy merits had fed
Ere her own was laid low, had exalted your head,
And since our good queen to the wise is so just
To raise heads for such as are humbled in dust,
I wonder, good man, that you are not envaulted ;
Pry'thee, go and be dead, and be doubly exalted."

To this repartee the dean wittily rejoins :—

"Her Majesty never shall be my exalter ;
And yet she would raise me, I know, by—a halter."

In 1785 the king was empowered by Act of Parliament to unite Richmond Old Park and its gardens with Kew Gardens, by means of shutting up a long lane, or footway, called Love Lane, which had separated the park grounds from those of Kew. The entire estate now constitutes the royal demesne known as Kew Gardens. At the same time a new road a little further to the east was made by order of the king.

The entrance to the north park is in Kewfoot Lane, not far from the railway station. In this narrow thoroughfare stands Clarence House, a small and unpretending mansion of the age of William III., which was inhabited for some years by the Duke of Clarence, afterwards King William IV. Mrs. Jordan shared the house with him. The court in front of it is now occupied by an iron chapel, and small cottages have been built round it on every side, so as almost to obscure it from the view of passers-by. It has now come to be vulgarised into the "Chapel House," and is let out in tenements to the working-classes, and a charwoman occupies what once was, doubtless, the bed-room of royalty.

When the Duke of Clarence came to live here, in 1789, he became so popular that, had the place been a borough town and he had cared to offer himself as a candidate, it is said that he would have been sure to have been elected. It is amusing to learn, on such good authority that the future King of England at that time, when twenty-four years of age, " paid his bills regularly himself, locked up his doors at night that his servants might not stay out late, and never drank but a few glasses of wine." It may also interest our readers to learn that even at the early date just mentioned, and slender as his chances of the throne must then have been, the duke used to tell his brothers that he should one day be king.

The old deer-park is very level as it stretches away towards Kew Gardens, and it is occasionally used for football matches.

CHAPTER XL.

RICHMOND—THE NEW PARK.

" Miraturque novas frondes."—VIRGIL, *Georg.* ii.

The New or Great Park—Its Enclosure in 1637—The Park Seized by the Commoners in the time of the Civil War, and given to the Citizens of London—It is given back to the King at the Restoration—The Park given to the Hyde Family—A Lawsuit respecting the "right of way" through the Park—The Rangership—Extent and General Appearance of the Park—Its Natural History—Pembroke Lodge —Lord Russell—Thatched House Lodge—White Lodge.

THE present park of Richmond—called, by way of distinction, the New Park and the Great Park— is situated in the seven several parishes of Richmond, Petersham, Ham, Kingston, Putney, and Mortlake. It comprises more than 2,000 acres, and was enclosed by Charles I. That prince, like his father, being extremely fond of hunting, wanted an extensive park, well stocked with deer, in the immediate neighbourhood of Richmond and Hampton Court. But amongst the wide wastes and woods here belonging to the Crown were mingled estates of private persons and common lands belonging to different parishes, and many of the proprietors refused absolutely to give up their lands. Charles, persisting in his undertaking, carried it through, in spite of strenuous and violent opposition. Lord Clarendon relates that a great outcry was, in consequence, raised against the king, who was charged with an intention to take away the estates of his subjects at his own pleasure—though, at the worst, he did only what Harry the Eighth had done wholesale before him. " The pertinacity of the king," says Clarendon, "gave great umbrage to the people." Laud, the Archbishop, Juxon, Bishop of London, treasurer, and Lord Cottington, the Chancellor of the Exchequer, were all opposed to the king's design, " to make a great park for red as well as fallow deer " at Richmond ; and this not only for the " murmur of the people, but because the land and the making of a brick wall about so large a parcel of ground (for it is near ten miles about) would cost a greater sum of money than they could easily provide, or than they thought ought to be sacrificed on such an occasion. The Lord Cottington—who was more solicited by the country people and heard most of their murmurings—took the business most to heart, and endeavoured by all the ways he could, and by frequent importunities, to divert his Majesty from pursuing it, and put all delays he could well do in the bargains which were to be made, till the king grew very angry with him, and told him he was resolved to go through with it, and had already caused brick to be burned, and much of the wall built upon his own land ; upon which, Cottington thought fit to acquiesce." Many little compromises were, however, made in order to please the murmuring people. Roads were left open through the park for foot passengers, the right of the poor to gather firewood where they had been formerly allowed to take it was fully recognised, and the landowners were duly remunerated for the property ceded by them to the Crown.

The enclosure was completed in 1637, and Weston, Earl of Portland, was made Ranger. At the conclusion of the Civil War, the House of Commons seized on the park, as well as on other landed possessions of the Crown. In 1649 a vote was passed by the House giving the new park at Richmond to the citizens of London. On the Restoration of Charles II. the metropolitan corporation presented to him Richmond Park as a peace-offering, with the declaration—sincere or insincere, who knows?—that "the City had only kept it as stewards for his Majesty."

In the reign of Queen Anne the park was given to the Hyde family; but George II. was prevailed upon by Sir Robert Walpole to buy out the Hydes, and present the Rangership to his (Walpole's) son. But it could scarcely have been then of any great value. At all events, Lord Orford, in his "History of George II.," describes it as being at that time "a bog, and a harbour for deer-stealers and vagabonds! Sir Robert Walpole drained it, and expended great sums of money upon it; but to obtain more privacy and security, he took away the ladders on the walls, and shut up the gates, but settled keepers at them, who were to open to all foot passengers in the day-time, and to such carriages as had tickets, which were easily obtained."

Now commenced another conflict between the inhabitants of Richmond and the reigning family; but this time the people got the best of it. Lord Orford thus continues:—"Princess Amelia succeeded his son, Lord Orford, but preserved no measures of popularity. Her brother William had incredibly disgusted the neighbourhood of Windsor by excluding them from most of the benefits of the park there. The princess shut up entirely the New Park [Richmond], except by giving very few tickets. Petitions were presented to her—she would not receive them. They were printed in the public newspapers, but had as little effect. Subscriptions were formed, conferences were held, to no purpose. At last the cause was brought to trial. Sir John Phillips and the younger Beckford presented themselves, as tribunes of the people, to plead the cause, but instead of influencing the court, they confounded the rest of their counsel. The princess carried her cause against a road for coaches and carts; but some few years afterwards lost a suit commenced against her for a footway, on which she abandoned the park. The children of the crown in England have no landed appendages; they naturally covet them; rangerships for life are the only territories the king has to bestow. Both the Duke [of Cumberland] and his sister entered more easily into the spirit of prerogative than was decent in a family brought hither for the security of liberty."

This last-mentioned cause, which was tried at Kingston in April, 1758, was brought about by a Mr. John Lewis, a brewer, of Richmond, brother of Dr. Lewis, a well-known physician in his day, and author of "The Philosophical Commerce of Arts." The incidents which led up to this action are thus amusingly told in a publication which was issued soon after the events took place:—" The beauty and convenience of this terrestrial paradise were essentially impaired by having the footway shut up through Richmond Park to Wimbledon, East Sheen, and Kingston, and no passage allowed without a ticket. Lewis takes a friend with him to the spot, waits for the opportunity of a carriage passing through, and when the door-keeper was shutting the gates, interposed, and offered to go in. 'Where is your ticket?' 'What occasion for a ticket? anybody may pass through here.' 'No, not without a ticket.' 'Yes, they *may*; and *I will*.' 'You sha'n't.' 'I will.' The woman pushed; Lewis suffered the door to be shut upon him, brought his action, and was triumphant.

"The cause was tried at the Surrey Assizes, before that upright judge Sir Michael Foster. After the decree in his favour, Lewis was asked whether he would have a step-ladder to go over the wall or a door. He hesitated for some minutes, but reflecting that strangers might not be aware of the privilege of admission through a door, which could not stand open on account of the deer; considering, also, that in process of time a bolt might be put to this door, and then a lock, and so his efforts gradually frustrated; sensible, too, that a step-ladder, at the first inspection, would signify its use to every beholder, he preferred that mode of introduction. In mere spite, the steps of this ladder were set at such a distance from each other as rendered it almost useless. At a subsequent period, when the same judge happened to go the Home circuit, Lewis complained again to the court. 'My lord,' says he, 'they have left such a space between the steps of the ladder that children and old men are unable to get up it.' 'I have observed it myself,' says this honest justice; 'and I desire, Mr. Lewis, that you would see it so constructed that not only children and old men, but old women too, may be able to get up!'"

In 1727 George II. conferred the rangership on Robert, Lord Walpole, who passed much of his leisure at this place, amusing himself with his favourite exercise of hunting. He spent £14,000 in re-building the great lodge, and making improvements here. He was, from his youth, fond of field sports, and retained his attachment to them until prevented by age from following them. He was accustomed to hunt in Richmond Park with a pack of beagles. Upon receiving a packet of letters, he usually opened that from his gamekeeper first; and in the pictures taken of him, he preferred being drawn in his sporting dress.

In 1751 the appointment of Ranger was given to the Princess Amelia. Subsequently the office was held by the venerable Lord Sidmouth, more recently by the Duke of Cambridge, and now by the Duke of Teck.

The park has a circumference of nearly ten miles, and there are entrances to it in each of the six parishes above named, called according to their location. The principal entrance, or, at all events, the one most frequented by visitors to Richmond, leads direct from the far-famed Richmond Hill and Royal Terrace, so named from its having been a favourite promenade of George III.'s. The lodge and gates here were built from the designs of "Capability" Brown in 1798, and the latter bear the initials of George III. and Queen Caroline.

This gate opens upon two good carriage roads: that to the right, leading past Pembroke Lodge, and finally terminating on the Kingston Road, by Kingston Hill; the path to the left leads to the Roehampton Gate, and so on to Putney. There is great variety, both of surface and scenery, within the park itself; near the centre are two large sheets of water, called the Pen Ponds, occupying about seventeen or eighteen acres. When the new poor-house, which stands at a little distance from the park wall, was built by George III., he also directed that one of the springs near the Bog Lodge should be laid on for the use of the inhabitants on Richmond Hill, where water was then scarce.

The road to the right, on entering the park from Richmond Hill, leads more immediately to some of the most beautiful vistas and rural scenery, and within a short distance of the gate conveys the stranger's steps to the New Terrace, made in the reign of William IV. This extends about a quarter of a mile, and from it is obtained one of the most delightful views in the neighbourhood. Hence "the blending of nature and art is exquisitely grand, interspersed here and there by woods and groves, hills and dales, ever and anon catching, through some umbrageous oak or luxuriant elm, thorn or ash, chestnut or maple, the liquid current of Old Father Thames, some ancient or modern edifice or church tower here, a turreted roof there, even to the extended distance of Windsor, whence may be seen on a clear day its kingly castle, and the royal standard floating in the breeze." The foreground of this position, although originally appertaining to and within the enclosure, was for some legitimate reason sold, and was considered Petersham Park. This occurred, as we have seen in the previous chapter,* in the reign of George I. Imme-

diately adjoining, and bearing more towards Ham, is another portion of Crown land, called Sudbrooke Park, a new purchase in the present reign of about 300 acres, a tenth of which originally belonged to Richmond Park, but which, like Petersham Park, had been let or granted upon similar terms. This part of the park is richly overgrown with ferns, brambles, thorn-bushes, and horn-beams.

The view from the high ground in the park, at night-time, looking eastward, may well recall Tennyson's lines:—

" And at night, along the dusky highway near and nearer
        drawn,
    Sees in heaven the light of London flaring like a dreary
        dawn."

The timber in the park is principally oak. There are some very old and picturesque thorns, and the later plantations consist of oak, elm, beech, fir, ash, alder, poplar, and Spanish chestnut.

Mr. Edward Jesse, who, when Crown Surveyor of the parks at Richmond, resided at the farmhouse to the left, belonging to the private farm of George III., gives, in his "Gleanings," many interesting circumstances connected with natural history in respect to Richmond Park. "An amazing number of eels," he tells us, are bred in the two large ponds, sufficiently evident from the very great quantity of young ones which emigrate from these ponds every year. The late respectable head-keeper of that park assured me that at nearly the same day in the month of May vast numbers of young eels, about two inches in length, contrive to get through the pen-stock of the upper pond, and then through the channel leading into the lower pond, and thence through another pen-stock into a watercourse falling into the river Thames. They migrate in one connected shoal, and in such prodigious numbers, that no guess can be given as to their probable amount.

In the reign of George II. a large stock of wild turkeys was regularly kept-up as part of the stock of Richmond Park, and some of the old turkey cocks are said to have weighed from 25 lb. to 30 lb. They were hunted with dogs, and made to take refuge in trees, where they were frequently shot at by the king. The whole stock was destroyed about the end of his reign, in consequence of many serious affrays between the keepers and the poachers on their account.

Squirrels were formerly very numerous in the park, but they also were gradually destroyed, in consequence of the serious fights which occurred in squirrel hunts between large parties of unauthorised persons and the keepers. In addition to the herd of fallow deer, numbering above 1,600, usually

---

* See *ante*, p. 329.

kept in the park, there is generally a stock of from forty to fifty red deer, which add to the beauty of the park and forest scenery. The red deer are sometimes very difficult to hunt, but the sagacity of a fine breed of buckhounds belonging to the park is a great assistance in their capture.

At certain times of the year an assemblage of fifty or sixty herons takes place within the park, yet their stay is never permanent. In the loamy parts of the soil the black mole is abundant, but

A good story is told in "Joe Miller," *apropos* of Richmond Park. Some years ago, when his Majesty used to hunt frequently in it, such crowds of people flocked thither, that orders were given to admit none when the king was there himself but the servants of the household. A fat country parson having on one of these days a great inclination to make one of the company, Captain Bodens promised to introduce him; but coming to the gate, the keepers would have stopped him,

PEMBROKE LODGE.

a nest of cream-coloured moles has been taken near Robin Hood Gate. Both the cuckoo and the titlark abound in the park.

The park is celebrated for nightingales. Wordsworth has contrived to combine in a few lines a record of the act, with a touching allusion to the poet Thomson. He writes:—

> "The choirs of Richmond Hill,
> Chanting with indefatigable bill,
> Strains that recall to mind a distant day,
> Where haply under shade of that same wood,
> And scarcely conscious of the dashing oars,
> Plied steadily between those willowy shores;
> The sweet-souled poet of the Seasons stood,
> Listening, and listening long, in rapturous mood,
> Ye heavenly birds! to your progenitors."

by telling him that none but the household were to be admitted. "Why," said the captain, "don't you know the gentleman? He's his Majesty's hunting chaplain." Upon which the keepers asked pardon, and left the reverend gentleman to his recreation.

Several houses on the borders of the park belonging to the Crown have been given rent free to statesmen and men of science. Thus Pembroke Lodge was bestowed by her Majesty on Lord John Russell, and a house near Upper Sheen on Sir Richard Owen.

The grounds of Pembroke Lodge, which almost adjoin the New Terrace, are tastefully and skilfully laid out in such a way as to appear more extensive than they really are. Forming part of the pleasure-grounds is a little artificial hill, known as King Henry the Eighth's Mount, on which it is said that monarch stood to see the signal gun fired from the Tower of London which announced the execution of Anne Boleyn. Tradition also asserts that it was from this elevated spot that Oliver Cromwell viewed one of the battles between his troops and the Royalists. In 1834, as some of the park labourers were digging gravel near this mound, they discovered the skeletons of three persons, who had been buried side by side, about three feet below the surface. The house itself, or rather, its predecessor, was originally known as Vermin Killer's Lodge, until it became the residence of the Dowager Countess of Pembroke, who was one of the Court favourites of George III. Since that time it has been called Pembroke Lodge. On the death of Lady Pembroke, the house was given by William IV. to one of his daughters by Mrs. Jordan, the Countess of Erroll.

EARL RUSSELL.

The lodge was, for the last few years of his life, the residence of the distinguished statesman, John, Earl Russell, who died here in 1878. The youngest son of the sixth Duke of Bedford, his lordship—who was better known as Lord John Russell—was born in London in 1792, and was educated at Westminster School and at Edinburgh University. At the age of twenty-one he entered the House of Commons as member for Tavistock, of which borough his father had the disposal; and "faithful to the hereditary Whiggism of the House of Bedford, he attached himself at once to the Opposition, who were then maintaining Whig principles against the powerful ministry of Liverpool and Castlereagh." He soon acquired a leading position among the Whig politicians, and took a foremost part in bringing about parliamentary reform. Lord Brougham, after speaking of the great services rendered to the cause of reform at that time in Parliament by Lord Grey, Sir Francis Burdett, Lord Durham, and others, says:—"But no one did more lasting and real service to the question than Lord John Russell, whose repeated motions,

backed by the progress of the subject out of doors, had the effect of increasing the minority in its favour, in so much that, when he at last brought it forward in 1826, Mr. Canning [then Castlereagh's successor as Foreign Secretary in the Liverpool Cabinet], finding that he could only defeat it by a comparatively small majority, pronounced the question substantially carried. It was probably from this time that his party perceived the prudence of *staying* a change which they could not *prevent*." The Bill, the proposal of which had this important effect, was one for disfranchising certain rotten boroughs, and for enfranchising large and important towns in their place. At this time Lord John was no longer member for Tavistock, but for Huntingdonshire, which he had represented since 1820.

In 1830 Lord John Russell (who had vacated his seat for Huntingdonshire, and now sat for Bandon Bridge) accepted a not very arduous office as Paymaster of the Forces in the ministry of Earl Grey. Parliamentary reform was now the one question of paramount interest, and the new ministry had been formed expressly because the country wished them to carry it, and upon Lord John Russell devolved the main portion of the work in framing the Bill. This, the first Reform Bill, was introduced in March, 1831. After debates of unparalleled violence, it passed the second reading by a majority of *one*; on going into committee, however, the Bill was thrown out by a majority of eight, and a fresh appeal to the country became necessary. In this general election Lord John Russell was returned for Devon, and with the new Parliament the passage of the Bill through the House of Commons was at once triumphant, but it was rejected by the Lords on its second reading. A vote of confidence in the Commons, however, saved the ministry the necessity of resigning, and this was followed by a sharp conflict between the Lords and Commons; but the former yielded, and on the 7th of June, 1832, the Reform Bill became the law of the land. In 1835 Lord John Russell took office as Home Secretary in the Melbourne Administration, and with it became the ministerial leader in the House of Commons; four years later he exchanged the post of Home Secretary for that of Colonial Secretary, which he held while the ministry lasted. His lordship had in the meantime been returned for Stroud, which borough he represented till 1841, when he was elected as one of the representatives of the City of London. In 1846 his lordship assumed the reins of government, as the successor of Sir Robert Peel, and he held the office of Premier till March, 1852, when his administration was shipwrecked by his paltry Ecclesiastical Titles Bill. In the following December Lord John took office as Foreign Secretary in the Aberdeen Coalition Cabinet, but resigned it shortly afterwards. In 1854 he accepted the post of Lord President of the Council, and in that year he introduced a fresh Reform Bill, which, however, he was obliged to abandon, in consequence of the breaking out of the Crimean War. After serving for a short time under Lord Palmerston as Colonial Secretary, and having gone on a mission to the Vienna Conferences, whilst the Russian war was in progress, his lordship retired from office in June, 1855, but on the return of Lord Palmerston to power, in 1859, he resumed office as Foreign Secretary, with a seat in the cabinet. His lordship remained as one of the representatives of the City of London in the House of Commons till 1861, when he was raised to the peerage as Earl Russell. After the death of Lords Lansdowne and Palmerston, he became "the Nestor" of the old Whig party. Pembroke Lodge had been allotted to him by her Majesty as a residence as far back as 1847, and here, in peace and retirement, he spent the declining years of his eventful life. His lordship is not unknown to fame as an author. Between 1819 and 1829 he wrote a "Life of William, Lord Russell, with some Account of the Times in which he Lived"; "An Essay on the History of the English Government and Constitution, from the Reign of Henry VII. to the Present Time"; "Don Carlos, or Persecution, a Tragedy in Five Acts"; "Memoirs of the Affairs of Europe from the Peace of Utrecht." Later on he published a "Selection from the Correspondence of John, Fourth Duke of Bedford"; "Memorials of Charles James Fox"; and the "Memoirs and Correspondence of Thomas Moore." Lord Russell lies buried in the family vault of the Duke of Bedford at Chenies, in Buckinghamshire. It is to be regretted that there is not as yet a stone or a tablet erected to commemorate the public services of Lord Russell, though several years have passed since his remains were carried to their last resting-

place. Perhaps the Russells, as having been the leaders of the popular party in the State for three centuries, consider, like Pericles, that "the whole earth is the tomb of illustrious men," and when asked to point out the memorials of their forefathers, would exclaim with good old Sir Christopher Wren, "Si monumentum requiris, circumspice."

Beyond Pembroke Lodge the road leads through some forest-like scenery on the one hand, and open on the other, until it arrives at cross-roads and a public footpath from Richmond to Kingston. The road to the right leads to Ham Gate, passing through one of the most picturesque and charming nooks in the park. The left-hand road is a direct route to the Robin Hood Gate, in the Kingston and Wandsworth Road; other roads branch off to East Sheen and Roehampton. The road, going straight forward to Kingston Gate— gradually ascends, and winds through a very wild and romantic part of the park. A little to the right stands the Thatched House Lodge, a building which, in Richardson's "Survey of the Park," is described as Burkitt's Lodge, after a former occupant, a Mr. Burkitt, who held some appointment connected with the park, either as a forester, ranger, or keeper, and who died there in 1769. After Burkitt's death the Thatched House Lodge was held by appointment by Mr. Medows, grandson of the last Duke of Kingston (whose father was then Deputy Ranger). Later on the lodge was occupied by Sir Charles Stuart (afterwards Lord Stuart de Rothesay, and a well-known diplomatist of the present century). Upon the death of his widow, Thatched House Lodge became the residence of General Sir Edward Bowater, who died here in 1861.

Leaving Kingston Gate to the right, and following the line of roadway to the left, we soon arrive at the highest point of land in the park, namely, Bloomfield Hill and plain. The footpath which crosses just here, and terminates but a few yards to the right by a ladder-stile opening upon Kingston Hill, is the "right of way," which was fully established by one Lewis, a brewer, of Richmond, as above mentioned, in the law proceedings which he instituted against the Princess Amelia, the then Ranger. The road now passes on the descent through some fine old oaks, &c., towards the Robin Hood Gate, leading to Coombe, Kingston, Wimbledon, and Putney.

The Roehampton Gate opens upon private property, and for the privilege of using this entrance the authorities of the park pay a quit-rent, or compensation, in the form of venison. At the corner of the cross-roads near here there is a flourishing plantation of trees. The road to the right leads direct to East Sheen Gate and Mortlake. From the first-mentioned gate there is a right of way by a footpath to Ham.

The White Lodge—the favourite residence of Queen Caroline—is situated near the middle of the park, at the end of a splendid avenue, nearly a mile in length, called the Queen's Walk, from its having been Caroline's favourite promenade, and which opens upon the gateway forming the entrance to the park from Richmond Hill.

The White Lodge was the scene of very many of her munificent acts. Her favourite walk was along the path leading to Richmond. Hither, as readers of Sir Walter Scott's works will remember, the confident yet trembling steps of the heroine of the Heart of Midlothian—"Jeannie Deans"—were directed. It was to Richmond that the kind Duke of Argyll took Jeannie Deans in his carriage, when she walked from Scotland to London to plead the cause of her sister, Effie Deans, and to save her from the gallows; and we are introduced by Sir Walter Scott, in the twelfth chapter of his novel, to Richmond Park. They entered it by a "postern door" in the brick wall, passed through a small iron gate, the door of which was kept carefully locked. Inside they found themselves in a "deep and narrow valley, carpeted with the most verdant and close-shaven turf," and "screened from the sun by the branches of lofty elms . . . like one of the narrow side aisles of a Gothic cathedral." Here, thanks to the good offices of the duke, she was brought to the presence of Queen Caroline, who was attended by "her good Howard," Lady Suffolk. There Jeannie Deans pleaded her sister's cause with such native eloquence that the queen's heart was touched, and she promised to intercede with the king on her behalf—with how much success is known to all readers of the "Wizard of the North." At the end of the interview the duke and his Scotch *protegée* left the park by the same postern gate, they entered the duke's carriage, and returned to the great metropolis.

In the year 1760 the rangership of the park was bestowed on the Earl of Bute, who retained the office and resided in the White Lodge till his death, in 1792, when the king gave the appointment of Deputy Ranger to the Countess of Mansfield. When Mr. Addington (afterwards Lord Sidmouth) accepted the office of Premier, in 1802, the king gave him the post of Deputy Ranger, which he enjoyed for forty years. It was at the White Lodge that Pitt had his last interview with Lord Sidmouth, in September, 1805, little more than three months before his own death. Lord Sidmouth was

the son of a physician at Reading, who attended the family of Lord Chatham, and was brought forward into public life by Mr. Pitt. He first entered Parliament in 1784 as member for Devizes, and in 1789, through the friendship of Mr. Pitt, was elected to succeed Mr. Grenville as Speaker of the House of Commons. His talents were moderate, but his good luck was great, as, having been for a short time Speaker, he at last held the office of Prime Minister, when Pitt quitted the helm to make way for the negotiations of peace in 1802. When the war was resumed, Pitt found himself unable to displace his own nominee without the aid of the Grenvilles; this, however, was then accomplished, and Addington was raised to the peerage. At that time the following epitaph was made for him :—

"Sous ce marbre, passant, le Sieur Addington gît,
Ministre soi-disant, Médecin malgré lui."

The allusion in the concluding words, of course, is to the fact that he was the son of a physician, and was called in to prescribe for the Constitution on the retirement of William Pitt. Even at that date he was ridiculed in the papers and squibs of the day as "The Doctor."

Lord Sidmouth subsequently filled several important offices, especially that of Secretary of State for the Home Department, which he held from 1812 until 1824, when he retired from active life. He died here in 1844. We shall see Lord Sidmouth's tomb when we come to Mortlake, but it is almost needless to add that we shall not find the above inscription upon it. A portrait of his lordship, painted in water-colours by George Richmond, may be seen in the National Portrait Gallery.

From about the time of the appointment of Lord Sidmouth to the Rangership the present improved condition of the park takes date; and upon the death of his lordship, the White Lodge was given to the Duchess of Gloucester, who succeeded as Ranger. Before his marriage, the lodge was for some time a residence of the Prince of Wales. It is now occupied by the Duke of Teck and the Princess Mary.

The White Lodge contains some fine pictures, which are regarded as heirlooms. Among them are portraits of George III. on horseback, and of Queen Charlotte, presented to Lord Sidmouth by the king himself. Here also (says Brayley) is preserved with much care a small table, upon which in an after-dinner conversation, whilst taking wine with Lord Sidmouth, and shortly before resuming his command of the noble fleet which achieved the battle of Trafalgar, Lord Nelson traced with his finger his plan of attack, and the manner in which he proposed to break the enemy's line.

The Bog Lodge, the residence of the head-keeper of the Park, has no fewer than six good springs near it, although its site is perfectly dry. A short distance to the south of White Lodge, at the foot of a gentle slope called Spanker's Hill, was the original head-keeper's lodge. That building was enlarged by the addition of wings for the occupation of Sir Robert Walpole, and from that period known as the Ranger's Lodge. The house, however, was taken down about the year 1840. Its site is marked by two fine oak-trees, which stood on the lawn before it. The situation was not perhaps so good for a house as that of the White Lodge, but it nevertheless commanded a fine view, the beauty of which was heightened by the two large sheets of water known as the Penn Ponds.

Another lodge, towards East Sheen, was formerly the head-gamekeeper's lodge, and was at one time the residence of Sir Frederick Adam. Another house, nearly adjoining this, has been for the last quarter of a century, by royal favour, the residence of Professor (now Sir Richard) Owen.

A native of Lancaster, Sir Richard Owen was born in 1804, and at the age of twenty-two became a member of the Royal College of Surgeons of London. He was appointed Hunterian Professor and Conservator of the Museum of the College in 1835. He was an active member of the commission of inquiry into the health of towns, as well as of the metropolis, which resulted in the appointment of a Sanitary Commission; and also of the commission of inquiry into Smithfield Market, which resulted in the abolition of the latter nuisance. Professor Owen served as president of one of the juries of the Great Exhibition of 1851, and, at the request of the Government, he went to Paris and acted as president of the jury of the same class of objects in the Universal Exhibition of 1855. Professor Owen has been President of the Microscopical Society, of which institution he was one of the founders; and he is a fellow or associate of most of the learned societies and scientific academies at home and abroad. He has also been lecturer on palæontology in the Government School of Mines, in Jermyn Street, Vallerian Professor of Physiology in the Royal Institution of Great Britain, and was for many years Superintendent of the Natural History Department in the British Museum. On his retirement from the last-named post, in 1883, he was nominated a Knight Commander of the Order of the Bath. Besides preparing the "Descriptive and Illustrated Catalogue of the Specimens of Physiology and Comparative Anatomy," for the Museum of the Royal College of Surgeons, and also the "Catalogue of Natural History," that of the "Osteology," and that of "The Fossil Organic Remains" preserved in the Museum, Sir Richard Owen is the author of several books and lectures on palæontology and comparative anatomy. Of his larger works may be mentioned his "History of British Fossil Mammals and Birds," "History of British Fossil Reptiles," "Odontography," "Memoir on a Pearly Nautilus," "Memoir on a Gigantic Extinct Sloth," and "Principles of Comparative Osteology." He has also communicated numerous papers to the Transactions of the Royal, Linnæan, Geological, Zoological, Microscopical, and other learned Societies. Professor Owen has long been held in the highest esteem by his learned and scientific brethren, to whom he has become endeared by his kindly manners.

CHAPTER XLI.

RICHMOND (continued)—THE TOWN

"Loveliest of hills, that rise in glory round,
With swelling domes and glittering villas crowned."—MAURICE.

THE town of Richmond in itself, notwithstanding the world-wide reputation of the beauty of its situation and its surrounding prospect, has but little to attract the visitor apart from its historical associations. Its public buildings are few and unimportant, and its shops are of the ordinary kind to be met with in country towns of moderate size. It has the advantages of good railway communication with the metropolis by way of the South-Western line to Waterloo, and also by way of Hammersmith. The North London Railway has also a station here, with running powers over a portion of the South-Western line; the town can also be reached by the London and North-Western, the Midland, and the London, Chatham, and Dover Railway branches. Croydon excepted, there is probably no other town near London which has such frequent communication with the metropolis; and then there are omnibuses constantly in summer. There is also the silent highway of the Thames, which, in the summer months, becomes a crowded thoroughfare for pleasuring folk.

In 1845 an Act of Parliament was passed authorising the construction of a railway from the terminus at Nine Elms to Richmond, with power to raise a capital of £260,000 in £20 shares, and it was opened for public use about twelve months later. At that time the railway had a separate proprietary, which has since been amalgamated with the South-Western Company. The intermediate stations are Vauxhall, Wandsworth, Putney, Barnes, and Mortlake.

Access to London by the railway, or even by road, it need hardly be said, is now far more speedy than it was in the reign of Henry VIII., when we read that Cardinal Wolsey did his Majesty a mighty good service by carrying some dispatches abroad with extraordinary speed. Having taken leave of the king at Richmond about noon, he reached London at four o'clock the same day, in time to proceed to Dover the same evening, and so to catch the next day's passage boat to Calais.

Of late years the population of the town has largely increased. According to the census returns for 1871, its inhabitants then numbered about 15,000, which had increased to over 19,000 during the next decade.

The main thoroughfare, George Street, runs north to south for about a mile, and the town is nearly a mile in width, sloping gradually up the side of the famous hill, on whose summit is the entrance to the park, and also the well-known "Star and Garter" Hotel.

The Green, in the north-west corner of the town, was in former times an important adjunct to the old palace, for on its broad smooth surface jousts and tournaments were wont to be held. Here, in 1492, Henry VII. held a grand festivity, lasting about a month, the entertainments being carried on sometimes within the palace, and some-times "upon the Greene, without the gate of the said manor. In the which space," as we learn from Stow's "Annals," "a combat was holden and doone betwyxt Sir James Parker, Knt., and Hugh Vaughan, Gentleman Usher, upon controversie for the arms that Garter gave to the sayde Hugh Vaughan; but he was there allowed by the king to beare them, and Sir James Parker was slain in the first course."

Philip I., King of Castile, during his sojourn in England in 1506, after having visited Windsor Castle and London, was entertained by the king with great magnificence at Richmond, "where," as Holinshed, writes in his "Chronicles," "were many notable feates of armes proved both at the tylt and at the tourney and at the barriers."

In the statement drawn up by the Parliamentary Commissioners in the time of the Commonwealth the Green is described as containing "20 acres more or less . . . well turfed, level, and a special ornament to the place." It is also added that there were "113 elm trees, 48 whereof stand altogether on the west side, and include in them a very handsome walk." The old elms have greatly diminished in number, but of late years fresh trees have been planted in their place.

On the Green, Horace Walpole tells us, Lord Lonsdale, Lord Bath, and other members of the West End London clubs took a house where they could play cards in quiet on the dull English Sundays, which bored them so much.

The Green is now a large square, nearly surrounded by houses as well as lofty elms, which form a wide avenue on the north side. Its centre, a wide turf, marked by cast-iron posts, and bearing the initials of William IV., is used for cricket matches, bowls, &c. It is evident, from Lilly-white's "Cricket Scores," that Richmond had a good cricket club as late as 1827. Matches were still played in 1839, in which year Mitcham Union Club played East Sheen at cricket on Richmond Green.

On the Green is one of the Russian guns captured in the Crimea in 1855.

Richmond has its Free Public Library on the Green. It is a handsome building, and contains several thousand volumes. It may perhaps be worthy of note that this library, which was founded in 1881, was the first Free Public Library instituted within the area of "Greater London," and that its success has been so great that within the first three years of its existence five neighbouring towns have followed suit, and availed themselves of the Public Libraries Act, and many more are about to do likewise.

The library was publicly inaugurated and opened in June, 1881, by the widow of Lord Russell, whom we have mentioned as residing in Richmond Park. A bust of the earl himself looks down upon the readers as they sit poring over the books of reference, history, travels, and biography; and a medallion of Lord Beaconsfield on another wall serves to remind them that literary toilers of all and every shade of politics are equally welcome. In the interior all the various library." * It certainly is one of which the good people of Richmond may well feel proud. That they appreciate it is proved by the fact that in proportion to the population of the town the Richmond Library can boast of a larger issue of books and attendance than any other library in the kingdom, the issue averaging 350, and the readers in the news-rooms over 1,200 daily.

At the north-west corner is the theatre, built in 1766, under the superintendence of Garrick, by

RICHMOND GREEN.

departments have been furnished with the latest approved fittings and appliances. An indicator, the invention of the librarian, Mr. A. Cotgreave, and now used in many public and private libraries, shows at a glance what books are in or out, saving much time and trouble both to the borrowers and the staff. This ingenious contrivance reveals in a moment the dates of issue and return of each book borrowed, the several persons who have borrowed it, the books taken out by every borrower, and those overdue; so that Professor Stanley Jevons was scarcely guilty of any exaggeration when, in speaking of the *rationale* of Free Libraries in his Essay on "Methods of Social Reform," he called this place "the beautiful little

Mr. Horne, for his relation, James Dance, the celebrated Falstaff of his day, who played under the name of Love. Quick, Mrs. Jordan, Mrs. Siddons, Kean, and many other celebrated actors, have performed here. George III., when living at Kew, sometimes honoured this theatre with his presence. It was here that Charles Mathews the elder made his *début* as an actor, in September, 1793, in the character of "Richmond" in *Richard III.* Edmund Kean—the greatest of our tragic actors since the days of Garrick—in his later years was lessee of this theatre, and it was in a small room attached to it that the great actor died.

* See *Contemporary Review*, March, 1881

Kean had one weakness common to the members of his precarious profession : he was often heard to declare that he was born upon St. Patrick's day (*i.e.*, 17th March), 1787. Yet, latterly, he as positively affirmed that his birth took place in November, 1790! His parentage was also continually questioned by himself ; and he frequently, to many persons who were not particularly in his confidence, affirmed his belief to be that Mrs. Carey was not his mother, but that he owed his

reciting Satan's "Address to the Sun," and occasionally acting "Shylock," &c., but who concluded his efforts by a failure in "Richard III." at Covent Garden Theatre, in September, 1815. Edwards was only five or six years older than Kean, and the "boy" was so much "elder than his looks" that they became constant companions. Edwards to his death affirmed that "he had taught Kean all he knew:" this was but the idle expression of a clever but disappointed man ; how-

"MAID OF HONOUR ROW."

existence to a lady who through life assumed the title of his aunt ; that lady was, towards the end of the last century, under the protection of the Duke of Norfolk, and was introduced by him to Garrick, who gave her an introduction to the then managers of Drury, where she appeared soon after the death of the British Roscius.

About 1800, at the Rolls Rooms, Chancery Lane, young Kean, then described as "the infant prodigy, Master Carey," gave readings ; amid other things, he actually read the whole of Shakespeare's "Merchant of Venice." Many of the persons who were then stage-struck were attracted by the singularity of a child making such an attempt ; among others, one Edwards, who at one time appeared at various benefits in the metropolis,

ever, it is worthy of remark that Edwards, in common with all others who knew Kean intimately as a boy, always declared that he was then "a splendid actor, and that many of his effects (at the age of fourteen) were quite as startling as any of his mature performances." Byron, who mingled at the time in all ranks of theatrical society, says, "Kean began by acting 'Richard the Third' when quite a boy, and gave all the promise of what he afterwards became." * That such was the case there is abundant evidence. Cobham, an actor long known at the minor theatres, who was a playmate of Kean, remembered hearing all the amateur or private actors of the time (1802) say that "Carey

---

* See Moore's "Life of Byron."

was the best amateur then extant." He had little means of bearing part in the expenses, yet the *leading characters* were assigned to him at a private theatre then existing in Lamb's Conduit Street : this is an extraordinary fact when the reader is told that in these places he who pays the highest price (*maugre* his incapability) has the right of playing first-rate parts. Mr. Roach, an old theatrical bookseller, who lived many years in the court running from Brydges Street to Drury Lane, often spoke of Kean's acting "Richard" in his (Roach's) garret, with a Scotch lassie for his Lady Anne ; her *patois* was a terrible grievance to little Kean, who was teaching her English, and mimicking her Scotch from morning o night. In requital for his initiating her into che mysteries of the vulgar tongue, he made her teach him the dialect of Sir Pertinax Macsycophant, a part in which he appeared for a few nights at Drury towards the close of his career. I think it was considered to be a failure by his best friends.

In the year 1833 Edmund Kean was engaged at Drury, and played "Othello" to Macready's "Iago." He had promised to play "Iago" also, and had a new dress made for it. About this time he had the Richmond Theatre, and played there three nights per week. For his last benefit he acted there "Penruddock" and "Paul." Being in embarrassed circumstances, he requested a loan of £500 ; this, it was said, the management of Drury Lane hesitated to advance, and he engaged himself at Covent Garden. On the 25th March, 1833, he appeared as "Othello"; "Iago," Mr. Charles Kean; "Cassio," Mr. Abbott; "Desdemona," Miss Ellen Tree. The elder Kean came to the theatre in company with Mr. John Lee and Dr. Douchez; it was with difficulty he made up for the character, the nauseous process of browning his face occasioning sickness. He went languidly through the first two acts, but rallied in the third ; he spoke the "Farewell" exquisitely, but at the passage—"Villain ! be sure thou prov'st my love," &c., his energy failed him ; he essayed to proceed, and then sank on the shoulder of his son. Mr. Payne, who played "Ludovico," came on, and, with Mr. C. Kean, assisted the great actor from the stage, which he never again trod. It was singular that he should end his career in the arms of his son, and that that son's future wife should be "Desdemona." He was taken to the "Wrekin Tavern," Broad Court, too weak to even bear the operation of having the paint removed. In a few days he sufficiently recovered to go to Richmond ; here he was sedulously attended by Mrs. Tidswell, said to be his aunt. Mr. Lee, Mr. Hughes, and

Dr. Douchez, were constantly with him. He flattered himself that he was recovering, commenced studying "Master Walter," and was underlined for it at the Haymarket, but his memory had gone for ever. On the 15th May, 1833, he expired. Kean did not know his birthday ; though he kept it on the 17th of March, many of his early friends affirm that he was born in November. The year, as well as day, is doubtful. Kean himself said 1787. Mrs. Carey, who claimed to be his mother, died in the same week in the same house.

"On the 25th of March in this year" (1833), writes Mr. J. R. Planché, in his "Recollections," "I had witnessed at Covent Garden the closing scene of a great genius. I was present at the last performance of Edmund Kean. He acted 'Othello' to the 'Iago' of his son Charles. In the third act, having delivered the fine speech terminating with, 'Farewell; Othello's occupation's gone !' with undiminished expression, and, having seized 'Iago' by the throat with a tiger-like spring, he had scarcely uttered the words 'Villain, be sure !' when his voice died away in inarticulate murmurs, his head sank on his son's breast, and the curtain fell, never to rise again upon that marvellous tragedian. He expired at Richmond on the 15th of May following."

The above-mentioned mystery about the parentage of Edmund Kean is thus solved by a writer in *Notes and Queries* :—"The descent of Edmund Kean from the great Lord Halifax is well known. The latter left an illegitimate son, who, as Henry Carey, became famous as the author of operas, ballads, and pantomimes. His lyric, 'Sally in our Alley,' is still held in estimation. The authorship of 'God save the King' is also assigned to him, but upon no very satisfactory evidence. To Henry Carey was born a son, George Savile Carey, who chose the stage for a profession, and, in conjunction with Moses Kean, delivered imitations of popular actors, and a series of lectures upon mimicry. This Carey had a daughter Nancy, from whose intimacy with Edmund, the brother of her father's theatrical partner, resulted the birth of the tragedian. At his first appearance at Sadler's Wells, in June, 1801, he is described in the bills as Master Carey.' "

Richmond has been the home of other actors besides Edmund Kean.

There George Colman the younger was living in 1797, and from his house here he addressed the following humorous invitation to dinner to a friend : it is given by Mr. Planché, in his "Recollections " —

"Come to Richmond to-morrow to dinner, or
you will have lost your *Kew* for pleasing everybody here.　　　　　　　　　　　"G. C."

"The dinner's prepared and the party is met.
　　The dishes all ranged—not one is for show ;
Then come undismayed, your visit's a debt ;
　　A debt on demand, and we won't take a 'No.'

"You'll fare well, good sir, you can't fear *a dew*,
Contented you'll sleep, 'twill be better for you,
And sleeping, we know, is the *rest* of our lives,
And this way we'll try to please both of our wives.

Garrick is said to have superintended the construction of Richmond Theatre, and it enjoyed
the reputation of being one of the best little
theatres in the kingdom ; for many years, however, it has had but a precarious existence, and
it has been at various times considerably altered
in appearance.

"In the early part of the last century," writes
Dr. Evans in his book on Richmond, "there was
a place of entertainment here much frequented,
called Richmond Wells. The following advertisement is copied from a newspaper of the year
1730 :—' This is to give notice to all gentlemen
and ladies that Richmond Wells are now opened,
and continue so daily, where attendance is given
for gentlemen and ladies that have a mind either
to raffle for gold chains, equipages, or any other
curious toys, and fine old china ; and likewise
play at quadrille, ombre, whist, &c. And on
Saturdays and Mondays during the summer
season there will be dancing as usual.'—*Craftsman*,
June 11. Penkethman also, of facetious memory,
opened a 'new Theatre' at Richmond, June 6,
1719, and spoke a humorous prologue on the
occasion, alluding to the place having been formerly
a *hovel for asses !* This theatre was probably
the same that stood on the declivity of the hill,
and was opened in the year 1756 by Theophilus
Cibber, who, to avoid the penalties of the Act of
Parliament against unlicensed comedians, advertised it as 'a Cephalic Snuff Warehouse !' *The
General Advertiser*, July 8, 1756, thus announces
it :—'Cibber and Co., *Snuff Merchants*, sell at
their Warehouse at Richmond Hill most excellent
Cephalic Snuff, which, taken in moderate quantities
(in an evening particularly), will not fail to raise
the spirits, clear the brain, throw off ill humours,
dissipate the spleen, enliven the imagination,
exhilarate the mind, give joy to the heart, and
greatly invigorate and improve the understanding !
Mr. Cibber has also opened at the aforesaid
Warehouse (late called the Theatre) on the Hill,
an *histrionic* academy for the instruction of
young persons of genius in *the art of acting ;*

and purposes, for the better improvement of
such pupils, and frequently with his assistance,
to give public rehearsals—without hire, gain, or
reward !'"

"Last night," writes Horace Walpole to Lord
Strafford, under date August 12th, 1790, "the
Earl of Barrymore was so humble as to perform a
buffoon dance, and act the part of ' Scaramouch' in
a pantomime at Richmond, for the benefit of
Edwin, jun., the comedian ; and I, like an old
fool, but calling myself a philosopher that loves
to study nature in all its disguises, went to see the
performance."

Dr. Evans, in 1824, speaks of the present
theatre as having " a neat appearance, with the
king's arms in front blazing forth with all the
splendour of royalty ;" and adds :—" Mr. Klanert,
the respected manager, has exerted himself to
please by introducing good actors, and even the
novelties of the London theatres, the house is
frequented by the inhabitants of Richmond and
its vicinity far and near, as well as by their royal
highnesses the Duke and Duchess of Clarence,
his Majesty's box having been elegantly fitted up
for their reception. The theatre has undergone
great improvements. Towards the close of the
season (from July to November) the boxes are
lined with scarlet moreen curtains bordered with
velvet, which adds to the beauty of the house,
whilst it greatly augments the comfort of the
audience."

The theatre has become the very picture of
decay and desolation, and has lately been purchased by a private resident. It never could have
been a handsome structure ; but now, with its
tiling loose, its old porch, and its windows blocked
and boarded up, and notices pasted over its walls
to the effect that the place is to be sold or let,
there can be no doubt that it will soon be taken
down, and pass away out of mind. Alas, for the
memory of Edward Kean !

Near the theatre is the entrance gateway to
the Wardrobe Court of the old palace, which has
now the appropriate appellation of Old Palace
Yard, and from the lower end a narrow roadway,
called Palace Lane, leads to the water-side. In
the adjoining grounds is an old yew-tree, mentioned
in the report of the Parliamentary Commissioners
in 1649. It is still in vigorous growth ; the trunk
is upwards of ten feet in circumference, and the
branches occupy an area of from sixty to seventy
feet in diameter.

Fitzwilliam House, which stood on the site now
occupied by Pembroke Villas, close by the Green,
was, when first built, the seat of Sir Charles

Hedges, Secretary of State to Queen Anne, and was afterwards the residence of Sir Matthew Decker, Bart. "At the commencement or early part of the last century," writes Mr. Crisp, in his "History of Richmond," "this gentleman was one of the founders of the parochial school in this town, and until a comparatively recent period the boys in the said school wore Sir Matthew's livery. There was in the mansion a fine suite of apartments leading from one to the other, after the style of those in the palace of Hampton Court; one of these, a noble room, had been erected by Sir Matthew Decker for the purpose of receiving and entertaining in it his Majesty George I. A kitchen of extraordinary dimensions was likewise built at the same time, which, with its enormous range for cooking, and other accompaniments in the same proportion, would have put to shame the insignificant-sized offices for similar purposes in the present day. It was in the large apartment above referred to that George II. was dining with Sir Matthew on the day when he was being proclaimed king throughout the country.

A part of the royal entertainment above referred to consisted of a pine-apple, of which there is a painting, mentioned by Lysons, with a Latin inscription beneath it, stating that "this pine-apple, though worthy of a royal feast, was raised at the expense of Sir Matthew Decker, and produced by the skill of Theodore Netscher, Esq." It has often been said that this was the first fruit of the kind raised in England, but this is erroneous, for Lord Orford, at Strawberry Hill, had a most curious picture of Rose, the royal gardener, presenting the first pine-apple raised in England to Charles II., who is standing in a garden." * Mackay, in his "Tour through England," about 1724, says that "in Sir Matthew Decker's garden was the longest, the largest, and the highest hedge of holly that he ever saw."

"The courtyard of this old mansion," observes Mr. Crisp, "was of very considerable size, and was paved in a rather singular fashion throughout, being laid with Dutch bricks in the form of an immense star, encircled by smaller stars, somewhat similar to an ancient Roman pavement; it presented a remarkable appearance, and was at one time considered a great curiosity. It was in this courtyard that the Richmond Volunteers of the period were allowed to exercise, by the permission of the noble owner of the house.

* It is said that the first pine-apple was grown at Dorney Court, near Windsor, the seat of the Palmers, where there is a duplicate of this picture.

"The Lord Fitzwilliam who for many years was a resident here was an eccentric, but kind-hearted and humane man. He had ever been a most liberal patron of the fine arts; he had travelled much, and consequently had enjoyed frequent opportunities of making selections from the old masters of various schools, of which his house on the Green became the depository. This valuable collection was, by his lordship's permission, at all times open for inspection, and was very frequently visited by the neighbouring nobility, gentry, and all whose taste or inclination led them to do so. . . This nobleman lived for nearly the last twenty years of his life in the most perfect seclusion; he would see none but certain members of his own household, and during this period refused even to receive the king, who, as he always held his lordship in high respect, called frequently to make inquiries after his health, but the interview was always avoided by Lord Fitzwilliam, on the plea of nervous affection. Strange to say that from this retired and secluded life he suddenly emerged, and resumed the keeping of a splendid equipage with four horses, in which he generally travelled. This was not more than two years prior to his death, which took place February 5th, 1816. His lordship was buried in the family vault close to the tower of the old Richmond Church, in which lie the remains of his ancestor (relative), Sir Matthew Decker. His lordship's library was, equally with his collection of pictures, of a rare and costly character, consisting of nearly 8,000 volumes, 600 volumes of valuable prints, and 140 fine old missals, curiously and elegantly illuminated. It was to the University of Cambridge that this magnificent collection of pictures and scarce volumes was bequeathed, along with the sum of £100,000 in South Sea Annuities, to erect a building in which they might be stored, and for the purpose of maintaining and supporting it in perpetuity. The museum to which we refer at Cambridge bears his lordship's name." Lord Fitzwilliam's proof prints were upwards of 10,000, and drawn by the first artists; his library included a very scarce and curious collection of ancient music, among which were the original "Virginal book" of Queen Elizabeth and many of the best compositions of Handel in his autograph. His house here was pulled down about the year 1840.

It is said that when the Prince and Princess of Wales (afterwards George II. and Queen Caroline) were living at Richmond, they found that there was but scanty accommodation for the ladies about the Court, and that in consequence this row of houses, called Maid of Honour Row, was built for their reception by command of the king.

The last house in Maid of Honour Row, before we reach the gateway of the palace, is that which was occupied, in the early part of the last century by John James Heidegger, Master of the Revels to George I. and II., and who died here in 1749. Heidegger was born at Zurich in 1659, and came to England in 1708, when, obtaining the direction of the Italian Opera and its masquerades, the ingenious Swiss (who, by the way, wrote operas with wonderful facility) contrived to derive from it a fortune of £5,000 per annum. The lover of pleasant gossip will perhaps remember Heidegger's magnificent masquerade at the opera-house, described in *Mist's Weekly Journal*, February 5th, 1718. When Heidegger grew rich he took on lease the manor-house at Barn Elms, which stood in a small paddock at some distance from the Thames; and here he got up the famous surprise *fête* of light out of darkness, at which the second Guelph "laughed heartily."

Heidegger was extremely liberal to artists for the opera; and he commissioned his best scene-painters to decorate his house after his removal to Richmond. Under his direction they painted the panels of the principal room, or hall, with a series of views in Italy and of Heidegger's native country, Switzerland, including Mount Vesuvius and the Bay of Naples, the Falls of the Rhine at Schaffhausen, and the curious bridge at Basle, which are extremely accurate; the whole are beautifully executed, and, although painted some 150 years since, they are in perfect preservation, the house having been in the possession of persons of taste, who did not object to the appropriation of a large room, that the pictures might remain intact. The general ornamentation of the room is likewise pleasing, and the paintings are well worth the inspection of the curious.

Heidegger died at the great age of ninety. He was noted for being the ugliest man of his day, which earned his features commemoration by Mrs. Salmon, of wax-work celebrity. However, the Master of the Revels left a more enduring fame than many of Mrs. Salmon's beauties could boast of: he was a benevolent, hospitable, and charitable man, and made his way in the world to wealth and good society; and any memorial of so estimable a character is worthy of record and respect.

Besides those in Maid of Honour Row, many other houses on the Green are fine specimens of the style of Queen Anne, as attested by their carved cornices and lintels externally, and by their panelled walls and fine staircases within. Among the finest are those near the corner of Friars Lane, which are built on the old grounds of the Friary: notably Abbotsdene, the residence of Mr. John Cockborn, and the adjoining house on either side. Mr. Cockborn has on the walls of his billiard-room two copies of the old palace in its glory under Henry VIII. They are taken from an engraving in the Bodleian Library by Van den Wyngaerde, and dated 1562. These views, kindly lent to our pages by Mr. Cockborn, giving respectively the river front and that looking towards the Green, show the palace to have been quadrangular, turreted and embattled, and surmounted by short spires, not unlike those represented in our illustration of Nonsuch. At either end of the palace is a garden, laid out in formal flower-beds and gravel paths: on the south side the walls are lined internally with a series of low apartments, little more than "lean-tos," evidently for the servants and guards.

The front towards the Green is low and meagre in appearance, quite in keeping with the central gateway, which remains, and which opened into the courtyard fronting the palace itself. In this drawing the arms over the gateway are distinctly shown. A glance at this drawing will serve to show the most poetical and romantic of visitors that Queen Elizabeth could not have died in the small portion which still stands quite distinct from the central structure. The rooms in the remaining portion of the palace are low, but comfortable in the extreme. The floors are of oak, almost black with age, and some portion of the dark oak panelling and, above all, a magnificent oak staircase may well serve to remind us of the days of the Tudors. Two of the attics still go by the name of the pages' rooms; but apparently the pages in those days were not as well lodged as servant-maids are now. There can be little doubt that it is only the poetic imagination which has identified the room over the old gateway with that in which the interview took place between the Virgin Queen and the Countess of Nottingham. It is a small, narrow apartment, with a modern bow-window thrown out.

The garden is small; in it many traces of old walls and other fragments of the building can be discerned.

The Green and the rest of the lower parts of the town are subject to floods. As Akenside writes:—

> " With sordid floods the wintry urn
> Hath stained fair Richmond's level green,
> Her naked hill the Dryads mourn."

There are at Richmond four or five churches belonging to the Establishment, and several

Dissenting chapels, besides a Wesleyan Collegiate Institution of an important character.

The living, anciently a chapelry to Kingston, was, in 1769, constituted, together with Kingston and the hamlets of Ham and Hatch, a separate and distinct vicarage, "by the name of the Vicarage of Kingston-upon-Thames and Sheen, otherwise Richmond." The increase of population which has taken place since that time, however, has made it necessary to build a district church in

£2,000 was spent upon it in improvements and embellishment. The interior, which is low, but spacious, comprehends nave, with side aisles and chancel. There are four Doric columns on each side, and the nave opens to the chancel by a wide Tudor arch, over which is a large gilt carving of the royal arms, and the initials G. R. At the west end is a fine organ, built by Knight in 1770, the expense being jointly defrayed by their Majesties George III. and Queen Charlotte,

STAIRCASE IN PALACE GATEWAY.

each of the places above-mentioned. The patrons are the Provost and Fellows of King's College, Cambridge, to whom the right of presentation was sold by George Hardinge, Esq., the lay impropriator, in 1786.

The old church, dedicated to St. Mary Magdalene, stands in a central situation between George Street and old Paradise Row. A chapel at "Schene" is mentioned in a record of as remote a date as 1339, but it was probably built much earlier, the tower being evidently of more ancient construction. It is very massive, embattled, of stone and flints, and has a clock and good peal of eight bells. The body of the church, which is of brick, has been erected at different periods. It was much enlarged in 1750, and in 1823

and by a subscription of the parishioners. The church was restored in 1866, at a cost of £4,000. The registers, begun in 1583, are said to be perfect from 1682, except that of marriages from 1751 to 1754.

The monuments are very numerous. Amongst the most interesting are, on the north side of the chancel, a mural monument inscribed in memory of "the late vertuous and religious ladie, the Lady Dorothy Wright, wife to Sir George Wright, Knt., who died in 1631 "—the "ladie" and her husband are represented by small figures, under an arch, kneeling at a desk, over bas-reliefs of their three sons and four daughters; a tablet to the memory of the Rev. George Wakefield, "nine years Vicar of Kingston, and minister of this parish," father of the Rev. Gilbert Wakefield, who is buried in the churchyard, with a memorial affixed to the east wall of the south aisle, and who was eminently distinguished for his attainments in biblical and classic literature, as well as for his exertions in the cause of religious and civil liberty during a time of feverish excitement consequent on the revolutionary war with France. He was imprisoned for two years in Dorchester gaol for his "Reply to the Address of the Bishop of

"In the earth below this tablet are the remains of James Thomson, author of the beautiful poems entitled 'The Seasons,' 'The Castle of Indolence,' &c., who died at Richmond, Aug 22nd, and was buried here the 29th, 1748, O. S. The Earl of Buchan, unwilling that so good a Man and sweet a Poet should be without a Memorial, has denoted the place of his interment for the satisfaction of his admirers, in the year of our Lord 1792.

RICHMOND CHURCH.

Llandaff to the People of Great Britain." His health suffered so much during his incarceration that he died shortly after his release. Thomas Wakefield, his brother, who, "for thirty years" was "the minister, guide, and friend" of the parishioners of Richmond, is also interred here.

Thomson was buried in the north-west corner of the church, "just where the christening-pew now stands." He was followed to the grave by his friend Robertson, by the actor Quin, and his brother poet, David Mallet. A plain stone was the only memorial of his grave till Lord Buchan, in 1792, put up a brass tablet, with an inscription, to mark the spot. It is affixed to the wall at the west end of the north aisle, and is thus inscribed:—

"Father of Light and Life! thou good Supreme!
Oh! teach me what is good. Teach me Thyself!
Save me from Folly, Vanity, and Vice,
From every low pursuit, and feed my soul
With knowledge, conscious Peace, and Virtue pure:
Sacred, substantial, never-fading Bliss."

Of Thomson we shall have more to say presently, when we come to his house in Kew Foot Lane.

It would appear that they who knew Thomson best loved him most. "He was one of the best and most beloved of my friends," writes Lord Lyttelton to Doddridge. "I was as much shocked at his death as if I had known and loved him for a number of years," writes Shenstone, who, though his acquaintance with him was but slight, erected an urn to his memory at the Leasowes.

A bust and tablet on the south side of the church commemorate Mr. Robert Lewis, "a Cambro-Briton, and a barrister-at-law," who died in 1649, not "from length of days," as the inscription (in Latin) somewhat whimsically states, "but from being such a studious lover of peace, that when a contention sprung up between life and death, he immediately yielded up his spirit to end the dispute."

Mrs. Mary Ann Yates, the celebrated tragic actress, who died in 1787, is buried here, together with her husband, Mr. Richard Yates, a comedian of considerable talent. Manning says that Mr. Yates "died of passion, in consequence of disappointment of his dinner."

Amongst the monuments against the outer walls is a large one near the entrance on the north side, in memory of Richard Viscount Fitz William,* who died in 1776; the father of Richard, seventh Viscount, the munificent founder of the Fitz William Museum at Cambridge, was also interred in the same vault in 1816. At the west end, near the tower, is a handsome tablet of white marble, in memory of the inimitable actor, Edmund Kean, who, as already stated,† died at his house, adjoining the Richmond Theatre—of which he was then proprietor—in 1833, and was buried here with great solemnity. For many years no "storied urn or animated bust" recorded his talents or his name. His son Charles, however, with filial piety, at length, in 1839, caused tablets to be placed on the walls of the church. The Rev. Mr. Richardson, in his amusing "Recollections," tells a story of the members of a dramatic club, "The Owls," endeavouring to put up a rival inscription, which was rejected by the vicar of the parish on the score of bad grammar and worse taste.

Joseph Taylor, an eminent actor, who died in the year 1652, is said by Wright, in his "Historica Histrionica," to have been buried at Richmond. According to Downes, he was instructed by Shakespeare to play "Hamlet," which he did "incomparably well." He was appointed Yeoman of the Revels to Charles I. in 1639.

Another person of much note in the same profession was also interred in a vault in the churchyard, namely, Heidegger,‡ Master of the Revels to George I., and for many years Director of the Italian Opera. Mr. James Fearon, of the Theatre Royal Covent Garden, also lies here. He died in 1789.

In the new burying-ground is interred Dr. John Moore, who died at Richmond in 1802. He was the author of "Zeluco" and other novels, which were favourites in their day. In early life he had been an army surgeon, and afterwards was surgeon to the Embassy at Versailles. Dr. Moore was a voluminous writer : "Views of Society and Manners in Italy, France, Switzerland, Germany, &c.," "Journal of a Residence in France," &c. He was the father of the gallant general, Sir John Moore, who fell at Corunna.

The accomplished Lady Di (Diana) Beauclerc, wife of the Hon. Topham Beauclerc, the friend of Dr. Johnson, who died at Richmond in 1808, is also buried in the new ground. She was the eldest daughter of the second Duke of Marlborough.

Mrs. Barbara Hofland, one of the most prolific of authoresses, and the friend of James Montgomery, Miss Edgeworth, and Miss Mitford, died at Richmond in November, 1844, from the effects of a fall. She was the author, *inter alia*, of the letterpress account of the Duke of Marlborough's *description* of his gardens at White Knight's, near Reading, and she was never paid by the duke for her labours.

According to Brayley's "Surrey," the registers of this church date from the year 1583, and are said to be perfect from 1682, with the exception that the entries of marriages between 1751 and 1754 are missing. Among the baptisms, under the date of 1605, is entered that of "Thomas, son of Sir Charles Lyttelton, and Dame Anne, his wife," of West Sheen. He succeeded to the title, and was one of the Commissioners of the Admiralty, and father of George, the first Lord Lyttelton. Among the burials are noted those of "Sir William Segan, buried in 1633"—he had been appointed Garter King-at-Arms in 1606 ; "Edward Gibson, painter, living in the Savoy le Strand, in 1701 ;" and "William Gibson, gent., of the parish of St. Giles-in-the-Fields, in 1703." The former was supposed by Walpole to be the son of Richard Gibson the dwarf, a pupil of Sir Peter Lely, who taught Queen Anne to draw ; the latter, his nephew, was an excellent copyist of Lely, but chiefly practised in miniature : he bought a great part of Sir Peter's collection.* The following extraordinary instance of longevity is also recorded :—"Susanna Waterman, aged about 103, mother to the parish clerk, buried in 1803." There are many other entries of the burials of persons aged from ninety to ninety-seven years. The baptism of Swift's Stella, namely, "Hester, daughter of Edward

---

Johnson," is recorded in one of the old registers, under the date of " March 20, 1680-1."

From Crisp's " Richmond and its Inhabitants " we glean the following quaint and singular extracts from the register :—"July 24, 1596. Laurence Snow was buried, wch Laurence was executed at Kingston, and by his wife brought to Richmounte to be buried." " Nov. 12, 1599. Mrs. Elizabeth Ratcliffe, one of the maides of honor, died, and her bowells buried in the Chancell at Richmont." "July 24, 1600. Sir Anthony Paulet, Knight, died at Kew, whose bowells were interred at Richmounte.'' In 1624 the number of " Christianings " amounts to sixty-nine. Under date of February 25 of that year are recorded the names of " Nazareth, the base-born daughter of Joane Maskall ; Joane, the base-born daughter of Ann Franklin ; and Will Evans, sonne of Ryce Evans, a travailing stranger, whose wife lay in at Sheene, christened May 8th." Under date of November 13th, 1634, we learn of the death of " John Smyth, ye Bird-catcher ; " and in 1671 is recorded the fact that " Matthew, a Blackamoor," was " buried May 20." In 1636 and 1637 are recorded the deaths of two "crisom " children ; and the register for 1654 tells us how that one " William Sauley and Mary Austin had ye publicacon of their marriage published on the 12th, ye 19th, and ye 26th day of February, and were married by Richard Graves, Esqr., ye 26th day of March, 1654, in ye presence of Walter Symmes, Robert Warren, and others."

In 1839 the new ecclesiastical parish of St. John's was formed. The church, situated in the Kew Road, was built a few years previously, having been begun in 1831, and finished in 1836. It was erected from the designs of Mr. Lewis Vulliamy, architect, of London. It is built of brick, with stone dressings, in the modern Gothic style, enriched with buttresses, pinnacles, quatrefoils, and other ornaments, but it is a poor structure at the best.

Above the principal entrance, in the centre of the western front, is a large window of three lights, with flowering tracery above, and on the gable of the roof is an ornamental bell and clock turret.

The Church of St. Matthias, situated on the hill at the end of Friars' Stile Road, is a chapel of ease to the parish church, and was built in the year 1858, from the designs of Sir Gilbert Scott. It presents a fine contrast to the meagreness of St. John's. It is a handsome stone building, and has a spire nearly 200 feet in height. Holy Trinity is an ecclesiastical parish, formed in the year 1870.

The church situated in Marshgate Road was built at a cost of about £5,000. It is a plain stone building, consisting of chancel, transepts, nave, and aisles. Christ Church, in Parkshot, was formerly a Nonconformist meeting-house, but is now licensed by the Bishop of Rochester as a place of worship for members of the Established Church.

The Roman Catholic and Independent chapels stand peacefully and lovingly near each other, on the hill, in the district called the " Vineyard." The former, which is dedicated to St. Elizabeth, was opened in the year 1824, having been built by Mrs. Elizabeth Doughty, a friend and connection of the Tichborne family, who long resided on the Terrace. It is a large brick building in the Italian style, and an open tower or turret, surmounted by a large gilt cross, crowns the roof. The interior is handsomely fitted up, and the altar window is enriched with a beautiful painting of the Annunciation.

The Independent Chapel was erected in 1830, from the designs of Mr. John Davies, architect, of London. Its total cost was over £2,500. There are several other chapels and meeting-houses for different denominations of dissenters in different parts of the town.

The cemetery, which is on the south-east side of the town, consists of about four and a half acres ; it was laid out in the year 1855, and has two mortuary chapels.

Important for its size, and not for its size alone, the Wesleyan Theological Institution is a building that would not discredit either of our universities. It stands near the upper part of Richmond Hill, on ground sold to the Wesleyan body by the executors of the late Mr. Thomas Williams. The entire plan is two hundred and forty-eight feet by sixty-five in its greatest depth, and that portion of the front which is between the wings is one hundred and sixty-five feet. The chief or public rooms are on the ground floor, and are very lofty. Besides class-rooms and some others on this floor, are the refectory and lecture-room, and the governor's apartments. Beyond the entrance-hall, which has a groined ceiling, is the principal staircase, branching off right and left. This leads to the library, which is the only public room on the first floor, all the rest of it being divided into studies or separate sitting-rooms for the pupils. The library is lighted by a lofty oriel over the entrance. The next floor consists entirely of sleeping-rooms for the students, corresponding with their sitting-rooms on that beneath it ; and of each sort of rooms there are from sixty to seventy in number. At the top of the building is another room, intended to be used as an observatory, and commanding a singularly fine prospect, including Windsor Castle in one direction and Greenwich and Shooter's Hill in another. Upon the ground floor there yet remains to be noticed the corridor, or ambulatory, extending nearly the entire length of the building, forming a walk two hundred and thirty feet in extent. The wings contain several additional rooms, on a mezzanine floor over the ground one. The exterior is of Bath stone.

The College stands in grounds of about thirty acres, and is shut out from view by the houses on Richmond Hill and its Terrace. The dining-hall is a very fine room, adorned with portraits of John Wesley, and also of several presidents of the Wesleyan Conference and other friends of the cause. Here stands the pulpit originally occupied by Wesley himself when he preached at the Foundry, in Moorfields—an honoured and treasured relic, as may be supposed; for the worship of relics, in some shape or other, is a part of the poetic nature, and will assert itself in one shape or another. Up-stairs on the first floor are the sitting-rooms of the students, and above their little bed-rooms, all plainly furnished, though some slight room is allowed for individual tastes. Each student has a sitting-room and a bed-room to himself. The students are generally about seventy in number, and they do not enter here until they are twenty-two or twenty-three years of age—in fact, until they have been "accepted" as preachers by one congregation or another. Adjoining the college are houses for the principal and his assistants; and there is a chapel also, in the Gothic style, within the grounds.

When the Wesleyan societies had existed one hundred years, "it was resolved by the Conference, at their annual meeting, held in Bristol, to celebrate their original foundation, in 1739, under the instrumentality of the venerated John Wesley, whose name, in association with the Scriptures, will descend from age to age, 'until time shall be no more.'"

The primary object of this celebration was religious and devotional, and solemn public services were held in all the chapels throughout England and Ireland, and at the stations occupied by their foreign missions. In connection with the primitive design, it was deemed expedient that a general pecuniary contribution should be made, both in the congregations and personally, or in families, as a practical thank-offering to the Almighty for the benefits which the Christian world had derived from the labours of Mr. Wesley, his coadjutors and his successors, during the century

then ended. The result was unexpected, the total sum collected amounting to nearly £220,000. A part of this sum was devoted to the founding of two colleges, with appropriate establishments, for the training of the rising Wesleyan ministry. One of these was built at Didsbury, near Manchester, but is different in its style of architecture from the institution at Richmond, which is a Decorated composition, partly in the Pointed or Perpendicular Gothic, and partly in the Elizabethan style.

Richmond is apparently well off for almshouses. Besides those of Queen Elizabeth and Bishop Duppa, and Michel, in the Vineyard, there are three—the Church, Hickey's, and Houblon's—in Marshgate Road; altogether accommodating upwards of seventy inmates. Hickey's almshouses enjoy an income of over a thousand pounds yearly. A small chapel is attached to Hickey's almshouses, to which the public are admitted.

The Hospital, in Kew Foot Lane, was formerly the residence of the poet Thomson. We shall have occasion to speak of it more at length presently. It is a large institution, to which the Princess Mary Adelaide, Duchess of Teck, opened new wards in 1882. The new buildings form a block 70 ft. in length and 30 ft. in width—exclusive of separate wings for lavatories, bath-rooms, &c.—and rise to a height of over 40 ft. On the ground floor is a male ward, containing seventeen beds, and on the first floor a female ward of similar dimensions. The greatest care has been taken with regard to the sanitary and ventilating arrangements.

The inhabitants of Richmond, however, on the whole enjoy the blessings of good health; witness Dr. Armstrong, who in his poem entitled "Health"—recommending a salubrious place of residence—has these lines:—

> "See! where enthroned in adamantine state,
> Proud of her bards, imperial Windsor sits;
> There choose thy seat in some aspiring grove
> Fast by the slowly-winding *Thames*—or where
> Broader she laves fair Richmond's green retreats—
> Richmond that sees a *hundred villas* rise
> Rural or gay!"

It would seem that Richmond is a public-spirited place, or at all events that its inhabitants know how to combine in order to promote athletics, art studies, and social improvement. At all events, the town has its cricket, bicycle, football, bowling, and rowing clubs, and an archery and lawn-tennis club; its school of art, in connection with South Kensington Museum; its philanthropic, musical, piscatorial, and horticultural societies; its Vocal Union, its Church Choral Association; its

Rifle Volunteer Corps; its "afternoon dances," the latter held during the winter every other Saturday at the "Star and Garter" Hotel; its Dispensary, and, as we have shown above, even its Hospital. Its Public Free Library has been already mentioned. Richmond can also boast of a coffee palace, several branch banks, a permanent benefit building society, and a Liberal and a Conservative Association. The Baths and Washhouses Act having been adopted by the vestry, a swimming-bath has been opened in Parkshot. Richmond has also a public and a private club, the latter, of course, rather exclusive. A Mechanics' Institute was established here in 1838. The building, consisting of a theatre, or lecture-room, for 300 persons, a museum, a library, &c., is in the Italian style. The cost was defrayed by donations of the gentry of Richmond, and by subscriptions from the members.

The civic and municipal affairs of Richmond are managed by a "Select Vestry," of which the vicar and the local magistrates are *ex-officio* members. They divide themselves into committees for roads and drainage, for the regulation of schools, fire brigade, recreation grounds, public library, buildings, burial grounds, &c.

"Great bodies," however, proverbially "move slow;" and perhaps that is the reason why the vestry has now spent seven years and upwards of seventy thousand pounds upon a well without yet having come to water. This is all the more strange, perhaps, seeing that the first artesian well dug at Richmond, in the grounds of the Duke of Buccleuch, where the boring was chiefly through a hard blue clay, the water was met with at a depth of 254 feet. Opposite Spring Grove stands an ancient conduit, whence the town was partly supplied with water during difficulties with the Waterworks Company a few years ago.

One of the penalties of the rapid growth of Richmond, one of the most increasing suburbs of London, has lately been a deficiency in the water supply. The artesian well was already pierced to a depth of 1,279 feet, or 845 feet below the original boring. The deficiency is ascribed to a reduction in the amount of rainfall, and the large quantity of water used for trade purposes. Measures have, however, been taken to supply the deficiency.

Richmond, in fact, in common with other London suburbs, has suffered for some time from a deficiency in the water supply. The monopoly of the companies on the one hand, and the incompetency of local authorities on the other, have brought it to such a pass that for days together the supply entirely ceased, and that in the hottest part of summer. The Southwark and Vauxhall Company have offered to provide water at a high charge, but it is full time that measures should be taken by Government to prevent the recurrence of such an event. Mr. Frederick Senior, the vestry clerk, in a letter to the *Times*, in March, 1884, with reference to the water-supply of Richmond, writes:—"The vestry, when they undertook the water-supply of the town, had to purchase premises and erect pumping machinery and a reservoir, and lay mains, &c., which works cost altogether some £46,000; but the parish derives an income of nearly £6,500 per annum therefrom (being the produce of a 1s. water rate, assessed on the rateable value of the houses supplied, and certain minor receipts), whereof £2,500 per annum defrays all working expenses, &c., and the £4,000 per annum balance goes in repayments of the principal and interest of the money borrowed on the authority of the Local Government Board to construct the works, and repayable in thirty years; while in other respects Richmond rates are now as follows:—Poor rate, 1s. 6d. per annum; highway and general rate, including free library and every other expense, 2s. 2d. per annum—grand total, 3s. 8d. per annum."

The drainage system of the town was perhaps quite adequate to the wants of the population when it was first carried out; but the speculative builders have done their best to spoil this once charming suburb by erecting so many houses, that the underground arrangements for the carrying away of the sewage are already too small for the requirements of the place.

Of water, however, under other circumstances, the inhabitants of Richmond have sometimes enough and to spare. They are occasionally in the case of the *Ancient Mariner*, with

> "Water, water, everywhere,
> And not a drop to drink."

We read in one of the daily papers that "the Surrey side of the Thames, between Richmond and Kew, was considerably overflown by the tide of this morning, and hundreds of yards of the raised footpath was half carried away into the ha-ha of the Old Deer Park, which now resembles a lake, over one hundred acres being under water." That Richmond is subject to these floods is a well-known fact.

Richmond Bridge, which connects this shore with that of Twickenham, consists of five semi-circular stone arches, and is an elegant and substantial structure. It was built from a design by Paine, was finished in 1777, and cost £26,000. The river here is about 300 yards in breadth. The average rise of the spring tides here is about three feet ten inches ; at Kew it is seven feet, and at Teddington only one foot four inches. The time of high water here is about an hour and a quarter later than at London Bridge. The bridge itself stands nearly sixteen miles by water above London Bridge, and about twelve above Chelsea Hospital.

There was originally on the spot a ferry belonging to the Crown, as an appendage to the manor of Richmond. The increase of population rendered this mode of passage extremely inconvenient, and

as seen from the railway bridge, has a charm and richness peculiarly its own. The mansions, mingled with lofty trees and sloping gardens, are set off by all the garniture of rural scenery. Maurice, in his admirable poem, gives the following lines on Richmond Bridge :—

" Mark where yon beauteous bridge, with modest pride,
     Throws its broad shadow o'er the subject tide,
     There Attic elegance and strength unite,
     And fair proportion's charms the eye delight ;
     There, graceful while the spacious arches bend,

RICHMOND BRIDGE.

an application was made to Parliament in 1773, and an Act obtained for building the bridge.

A view of the bridge was painted by Turner whilst he lived at Twickenham. The picture is in the possession of Mr. Ruskin, who tells us that Sandycombe Lodge, on the Twickenham side of the bridge, was bought by Turner in 1808, and that he resided there till 1827.

From many points in the surrounding country the bridge forms an impressive feature, and the views from it, both looking up and down the river, are very beautiful.

The view up the river, however, is especially charming ; we see it dotted with its willow-clad eyots, and with Richmond Hill and the groves of Ham in the distance. The view of the hill, also,

     No useless glaring ornaments offend ;
     Embowered in verdure heaped unbounded round,
     Of every varied hue that shades the ground.
     Its polished surface of unsullied white,
     With heightened lustre beams upon the sight !
     Still lovelier in the shining flood surveyed,
     'Mid the deep masses of surrounding shade !
     Glittering with brilliant tints and burnished gold,
     Above the cars of luxury are rolled,
     Or commerce, that upholds the wealthy Thane,
     Guides to Augusta's towers her cumbrous wain ;
     Below, refulgent in the noontide ray,
     While in the breeze the silken streamers play,
     A thousand barks, arrayed in gorgeous pride,
     Bound o'er the surface of the yielding tide."

There was no bridge at Richmond, or probably we should find more about its park and scenery in Pope's letters, for he was on friendly terms with both Thomson and Gay; its surroundings, however, were as bright and sylvan then as now, for, as Pope writes to a friend—" I have seen no scenes of Paradise, no happy bowers, equal to those on the banks of the Thames."

What a delightful ornament to a country is the of the ancients (the modern Po) has been celebrated by Virgil, Claudian, and Lucan; Denham and Pope have immortalised the Thames; and even the rivers in savage climes, that roll their immensity of waters through vast solitary wilds, have neither been neglected nor unsung by descriptive poets.

THE TERRACE, FROM THE RIVER.

winding course of a river! How much more exquisitely enchanting does it render the most beautiful landscape! And of what an unspeakable variety of benefits is it productive to the countries through which it flows! Hence rivers, in all their diversities of scenery, ever appear a favourite theme in poetical composition. Homer seldom mentions the country of any of his great personages without introducing the principal river that waters it by some distinguishing characteristic. The Eridanus

The river hereabouts, in summer time, is in high favour alike with lovers of aquatic amusement and with that soberer and more pensive class who love quiet English scenery.

Horace Walpole describes a regatta on the Thames here in August, 1776 :—" I have since been at the regatta at Richmond, which was the prettiest and the foolishest sight in the world, as all regattas are. The scene, which lay between the Duke of Montagu's and Lady Cowper's, is so beautiful, that with its shores covered with multitudes, and the river with boats, in the finest of all evenings, nothing could be more delightful. The king and queen were on a stage on their own terrace."

Collins thus refers to our river in his "Ode on the Death of Thomson":—

> "Remembrance oft shall haunt the shore
> When Thames in summer wreaths is drest,
> And oft suspend the dashing oar,
> To bid his gentle spirit rest."

Wordsworth, again, composed "upon the Thames near Richmond," in 1789, the following lines in "Remembrance of Collins":—

> "Glide gently, thus for ever glide,
> O Thames! that other bards may see
> As lovely visions by thy side
> As now, fair river, come to me,
> O glide, fair stream! for ever so,
> Thy quiet soul on all bestowing,
> Till all our minds for ever flow
> As thy deep waters now are flowing."

It is said that Richmond has the credit of having invented those modern pleasure canoes which now flit about the Thames on every reach from Oxford to London. General Rigaud, in *Notes and Queries* for 1884, writes:—"More than forty years ago Mr. Julius, the son of a gentleman living in the Old Palace Yard, Richmond, was the champion sculler, and held the prize known as the 'diamond sculls' for some seasons. This gentleman," he adds, "built the first light pleasure canoe that I ever saw or heard of." There is nothing new under the sun, and the canoe of the reign of Queen Victoria is but a revival, with some modifications, of the coracle of our British and Saxon ancestors.

At a short distance below the bridge, at the eastern boundary of Kew Gardens, the Thames is spanned by a railway-bridge on the Windsor and Staines branch of the South-Western line. During the summer months the space betweeen the two bridges, and also for some distance "above bridge," towards Twickenham and Kingston, is alive with gay boats of "all sorts and conditions," that float upon the surface, or continue moored for the purposes of angling. The anglers are well provided for here; at all events, the Station Hotel, and the "White Cross," and the "Three Pigeons" all lay themselves out specially for the accommodation of the disciples of Isaac Walton.

When races are rowed here, the courses usually chosen are from Sion House to Richmond Bridge— a little under two miles, or from Cross Deep, Twickenham, to the same, about a mile and a half; but generally the favourite course is from Mortlake to Richmond.

Adjoining the premises of the Richmond Waterworks stands a large embattled mansion, enveloped in ivy. This was inhabited by William IV. when Duke of Clarence. The grounds slope to the river, and are tastefully planted. A small white house beyond this, built in the Gothic style, was once tenanted by the celebrated Madame de Staël.

On the lower side of the Petersham Road, adjoining the meadows, is Devonshire Cottage, once the abode of the celebrated beauty and queen of society, Georgiana, Duchess of Devonshire. It was previously the home of Lady Diana Beauclerc, whose accomplishments were so highly eulogised by Lord Orford. Lady "Di," as she was familiarly styled, was the wife of Topham Beauclerc, Dr. Johnson's friend and correspondent.

We will now wend our steps to Richmond Hill, the praises of which have been sung in book and ballad. The approach to it is by a gentle rise from the western end of the town, near the bridge, the roadway leading upwards to the park gates, close by the "Star and Garter" Hotel, which stands at the top of the hill. On the slope of the hill, on the left hand as you ascend, lies a district called the Vineyards—doubtless from the fruit of the vine having been successfully cultivated here, as in many other parts of the southern counties, in the olden time. Here the Roman Catholic chapel and the Independent chapel stand side by side.

Another house on the hill belonged for many years to the Marquis of Lansdowne. It was occupied in the summer of 1851 by the two Miss Berrys, whose grave we visited so lately in Petersham Churchyard.* At other times they lived in Mr. Lamb's house here.

The upper part of the town, with its splendid terrace, always looks gay and cheerful, even in winter, and is thought to wear something of the appearance of a foreign boulevard. What with the carriage folk who drive from every village round to enjoy the prospect, the ladies sitting basking in the sun or screening themselves under the elms and evergreens, and the nursery-maids and children strolling about in delightful confusion, Richmond Terrace, on a fine day, is about the most enjoyable place, and one of the prettiest suburbs of London.

On this terrace lives a Mr. Cook, whose gallery of paintings and other art treasures is a sight to

---

* See *ante*, p. 326.

be envied. Almost adjoining is a house which was long occupied by Mrs. Fitzherbert whilst she was privately married to George, Prince of Wales.

From the terrace which surmounts the meadow steep, formerly overgrown with brushwood, and called Richmond Common, the view begins to open in all the beauty so poetically described by Thomson. The terrace is a fine gravelled walk, furnished with seats, and is separated from the road by an avenue and row of fine elms.

The picturesque scenery of Richmond Hill must have increased in beauty since Thomson sang of it. Drawings not one hundred and thirty years old represent the land as divided into open fields, where now it is covered with masses of beautiful foliage. This may account, possibly, for the fact that no allusion to the scenery of Richmond is made by Shakespeare—who must often have been here with the court of Elizabeth—by his contemporaries, or the earlier poets, unless, indeed, we fix upon Sheen as the locality to which Chaucer was indebted for some descriptive passages in his poem of " The Flower and the Leaf." Other poets also, besides Denham and Thomson, have sung the praises of the Thames at Richmond; among others, Thomas Maurice, early in the present century, and Charles Crawford, towards the close of the last.

The scene around, as viewed from the terrace, is thus described by Sir Walter Scott in " The Heart of Midlothian." The Duke of Argyle and Jeannie Deans were on their way to see Queen Caroline at the lodge in the old park :—" The carriage rolled rapidly onwards through fertile meadows, ornamented with splendid old oaks, and catching occasionally a glance of the majestic mirror of a broad and placid river. After passing through a pleasant village [Petersham], the equipage stopped on a commanding eminence, where the beauty of English landscape was displayed in its utmost luxuriance. Here the duke alighted, and desired Jeannie to follow him. They paused for a moment on the brow of a hill, to gaze on the unrivalled landscape which it presented. A huge sea of verdure, with crossing and intersecting promontories of massive and tufted groves, was tenanted by numberless flocks and herds, which seemed to wander unrestrained and unbounded through the rich pastures. The Thames, here turreted with villas and there garlanded with forests, moved on slowly and placidly, like the mighty monarch of the scene, to whom all its other beauties were but accessories, and bore on his bosom a hundred barks and skiffs, whose white sails and gaily fluttering pennons gave life to the whole. The

Duke of Argyle was, of course, familiar with this scene; but to a man of genius it must be always new. Yet, as he paused, and looked on this inimitable landscape with the feeling of delight which it must give to the bosom of every admirer of nature, his thoughts naturally reverted to his own more grand, yet scarcely less beautiful, domains of Inverary. ' This is a fine scene,' he said to his companion, curious perhaps to draw out her sentiment. ' We have nothing like it in Scotland.' "

Well might Vancouver, after making the round of the known world, have been entranced at the loveliness of this prospect, and exclaim, as he is said to have exclaimed, " I have travelled over the world, and this is the most beautiful place that I have ever seen." He added, " Here I will live, and here I mean to die." A tablet in the parish church at Petersham, which we have so lately visited, shows that the grand old voyager was " as good as his word."

The house now known as the Wick, at the end of the Terrace, stands on the site of an old alehouse, called the " Bull's Head," which was surrounded by a tea-garden. The inn was pulled down about 1775.

The Duke of Buccleuch's house, between the terrace and the water-side, was built for the Duke of Montagu, and passed to the family of the present owner towards the end of the last century. It is often thought, because his Grace is Duke of Queensberry as well as of Buccleuch, that this house came to him from " Old Q ;"* but such was not the case. The site of the Duke of Queensberry's house is still immortalised by Queensberry House, a common-place looking villa between the old palace and the bridge. The present mansion was built by Sir William Dundas, Bart., son of Sir David Dundas, Sergeant-Surgeon to his Majesty George III., partly with the materials and on the grounds attached to the villa of the Duke of Queensberry. In front are two or three low terraces, with flights of steps.

The Duke of Buccleuch's house came to him by descent or bequest from another ducal connection, the " merry " Duke of Montagu. It was at this delightful summer residence that the Duke and Duchess of Buccleuch gave a magnificent entertainment to her Majesty Queen Victoria and Prince Albert, in 1842. Amongst the company were the King and Queen of the Belgians, the Dowager Queen Adelaide, the Duchess of Kent, the Duke and Duchess of Cambridge, with their children, Prince George and Princess Augusta, several

---

* See " Old and New London," Vol. IV., pp. 286, 334.

German princes, and other persons of exalted rank and fashion.

Maurice thus immortalises this favoured spot :—

" Loveliest of hills that rise in glory round,
  With swelling domes and glittering villas crowned,
  For loftier tho' majestic Windsor tower,
  The richer landscape's thine, the nobler bower,
  Imperial seat of ancient grandeur, hail !
  Rich diamond ! sparkling in a golden vale,
  Or vivid emerald ! whose serener rays
  Beam mildly forth with mitigated blaze,
  And 'mid the splendours of an ardent sky
  With floods of verdant light refresh the eye :
  Richmond ! still welcome to my longing sight,
  Of a long race of kings the proud delight !
  Of old the sainted sage thy groves admired,
  When with Devotion's hallowed transports fired,
  From Sheen's monastic gloom thy brow he sought,
  And on its summit paused in raptured thought,
  Stretched to the horizon's bound his ardent gaze,
  And hymned aloud the great Creator's praise."

A Frenchman who was brought by some patriotic John Bull to gaze at and admire the view is said to have exclaimed in a depreciating tone, " Take away the trees and the villas, and it would be hardly worth gazing at." This view is never more beautiful than when, as Tennyson sings—

" The charmed sunset lingers low a down
    In the red west."

From this point, amongst others, was flashed the announcement of the approach of the Invincible Armada. According to Macaulay :—

" The sentinel on Whitehall Gate looked forth into the night,
And saw o'erhanging Richmond Hill the streak of blood-red light."

There is a quaint comic drawing of Richmond Hill as it was about 1770-80, by Bunbury. It shows the character of the conveyances in vogue, as well as the costumes of the visitors, male and female.

Richmond Hill is so closely, though wrongly, associated with one of our most favourite popular songs, that it seems a pity not to make mention of it here. The following stanza is known to almost every one, but its meaning is a matter of dispute.

" On Richmond Hill there lives a lass
    More bright than the May morn,
  Whose charms all other maids surpass,
    A rose without a thorn.
      This lass so neat,
      With smiles so sweet,
    Has won my right good will.
      I'd crowns resign
      To call her mine,
  Sweet lass of Richmond Hill."

Many speculations are extant as to the origin of this favourite ballad. It has been declared that Mrs. Fitzherbert, the once beloved, though morganatic, wife of a Prince of Wales, was the heroine of the song, and there is some degree of probability attaching to this idea in the couplet—

" I'd *crowns* resign
    To call her mine."

But the lines would equally apply, however, to the account given in Leigh Hunt's " Court Suburb," in which Lady Sarah Lennox is stated to be the original lass, and another Prince of Wales to be implicated in the authorship.

Again, it is stated that a wealthy London merchant, named Croft, residing at Mansfield House about a hundred years since, had a beautiful and highly-accomplished daughter, who, having formed an attachment for a young cavalry officer, gave her father some uneasiness from apprehension that she might elope with him. Being closely confined, she was brought to a state of despair, and precipitating herself from an upper window of her father's house, gave rise to a melancholy interest which has taken the above lyrical form.

Maurice, in his " Richmond Hill," alludes to this young lady in the following melancholy strain :—

" Well, Richmond, might thy echoing shades bemoan
    Their glory darkened and their pride o'erthrown ;
  For she was fairer than the fairest maid
    That roams thy beauteous brow or laurel shade."

Dr. Evans, in his " Richmond and its Vicinity," gives the following as the story of the " Lass of Richmond Hill " :—" The tale. . . . is said to be founded on a narrative of facts well known in the neighbourhood of Richmond. A young lady, equally accomplished in mind and body, the daughter of a merchant of immense wealth resident on Richmond Hill, had consented to receive the addresses of a young officer of exemplary character and respectable parents, but—*poor !* He belonged to a regiment of cavalry quartered at Richmond. But his offers were rejected by her father on account of that poverty. Apprehensions of a clandestine marriage being entertained, the officer was forbidden the house, and *the young lady* was strictly confined within its walls. Continued grief led her, in a fit of despair bordering on insanity, to precipitate herself from an upper window of her father's house, and she was dashed to pieces on the stone steps that led up from the garden into the house ! The unfortunate young man afterwards served in America, and was shot at the head of his company."

Who was the "Lass of Richmond Hill," and who composed the song and the words of it, are questions which have been often asked, and not very satisfactorily answered, although many versions have been given, especially by some of the old inhabitants of Richmond. Among others, Mr. Edward Jesse tells us, in an article on the subject in *Once a Week*, a certain pretty Miss Smith, who lived on Richmond Hill, and was herself a writer of poetry, was thought to be the *Lass*, and for this reason : having one day made some purchases at a shop in Richmond, she was asked where they should be sent. She gave her name and address, but added, " I am better known as the ' Lass of Richmond Hill,' " an answer probably arising from a little poetic vanity.

"The lass of Richmond Hill," adds Mr. Jesse, "was one of the most popular of songs in the days of our grandfathers, and it has been ascribed to various authors—amongst others, to the Prince of Wales, who is said to have composed it in praise of Mrs. Fitzherbert, then a resident in this charming suburban neighbourhood. But, independent of the absurdity of calling a woman of thirty, and a widow to boot, a lass, there are plenty of inconsistencies in the story itself. Firstly, the real scene of the ballad was not Richmond in Surrey, but Richmond in Yorkshire. Secondly, the heroine of the ballad was not a wealthy and fashionable widow, but a plain country damsel in her "teens," a certain Miss I'Anson. Thirdly, the author and composer was not the heir to the British crown, but a briefless Irish barrister, who had only half-crowns, and perhaps but a few of them, to give to or for the object of his worship."

The following anecdote, related by Sir Jonah Barrington, in his " Personal Sketches," is amusing enough, but it must be added that what he tells us is not always to be depended on. If it were so, he has cleared up the difficulty as to the identity of the Lass of Richmond Hill. He informs us that on the trial of Roger O'Connor, on a charge of robbing a mail coach, a distinguished Irish barrister was engaged, Mr. Leonard McNally, author of a work on the " Law of Evidence," and also of the song of " The Lass of Richmond Hill." He was a great poetaster, and having fallen in love with a Miss I'Anson, the daughter of a very rich attorney, of Bedford Row, London, he wrote on her the celebrated song of " The Lass of Richmond Hill," her father having a house in that place. The young lady could not withstand this, and returned his flame. She was absolutely beautiful, but quite a slattern in her person. She likewise had a turn for versifying, and was therefore altogether well adapted to her lame lover, particularly as she never could spare time from her poe·y to wash her hands—a circumstance in which McNally was sympathetic. Her father, however, notwithstanding all this, refused his consent, and consequently McNally took advantage of his dramatic knowledge by adopting the precedent of Barnaby Brittle, and bribed a barber to lather old I'Anson's eyes as well as his chin, and with something rather sharper than Windsor soap. Slipping out of the room whilst her father was getting rid of the lather and the smart, this Sappho and her limping Phaon (for McNally was lame) escaped, and were united in the holy bonds of matrimony the same day. She continued making, and McNally correcting, verses till they were called out of this world. This curious couple conducted themselves both generally and towards each other extremely well after their union. Old I'Anson partly forgave them, and made some settlement on their children.

"We regret," adds Mr. Jesse, "that only a portion of this anecdote is true. Mr. I'Anson certainly had a house at Richmond, and Mr. McNally married his daughter, but the rest of the story may be considered as the result of the propensity of Sir Jonah Barrington to substitute fiction for truth—a second Sir Nathaniel Wraxall. The fact is that Mr. Upton wrote the song of ' The Lass of Richmond Hill,' and the music of it was composed by Mr. Hook, the father of Theodore Hook, although it was for a long time popularly ascribed to George IV., then Prince of Wales, who was a fine musician."

The name of Mr. McNally is known in the sister island as the advocate of the Irish rebels in '98, and as the author of " The Claims of Ireland," and also of a comic opera, " Robin Hood," and some ten or dozen forgotten plays and fugitive poems.

The " Star and Garter " Hotel is too prominent a feature of Richmond not to be treated with due importance. The house occupies a fine position on the summit of the hill, near Richmond Park, on the edge of an open piece of common land, nearly covered with forest oaks and underwood.

Its history may be briefly stated as follows :—Of old, although they flocked to Richmond in great numbers, visitors had to be contented with way-side inns, which does not say much for the enterprise of the time. The High Walk on the Green was the favourite promenade, to which all the fashionables flocked, the hill being then an open spot, with one or two unpretending little inns dotted about it, one of which was the " Star and Garter," which we will now describe.

Early in the eighteenth century a portion of Petersham Common was leased to John Christopher by the Earl of Dysart, lord of the manor; and it was on this ground, the rental of which was forty shillings a year, that the original "Star and Garter" was built, in 1738. It had a common wooden pent-house, as it is termed, for the entrance doorway, and a sign-post, with a large sign attached to it, standing in front of the inn, which sign-post and board were plainly visible from any part of Cholmondeley Walk by the river-side, so perfectly

hotel. In course of time the house was rebuilt in a substantial manner, and we find that in 1780 it possessed two storeys, with a porticoed entrance, while next door, on the west side, was a house which was afterwards added to the hotel.

In 1803 a large piece of ground, on which a part of the hotel was long afterwards built, was leased to Richard Brewer by the Earl of Dysart, at a rental of sixty shillings a year, on condition that the view from Sir Lionel Darell's house opposite, or from the lodge at the new Park gate, should not

THE "STAR AND GARTER."

destitute of trees was all that part of Richmond commencing from the present bridge and walk in the direction of the Duke of Buccleuch's to its summit at the entrance of the park; and it is recorded that so limited was the accommodation at the old "Star and Garter" that at no time could a visitor stay the night there, for the simple reason that not the slightest accommodation in that way was ever attempted by the proprietor!

The fact that the house was well known, and constituted a landmark of the time, is attested by the circumstance that an important view of Richmond, dated 1794, is officially described as "taken from the sign of the 'Star and Garter' on the hill." A drawing, by Hearne, of the original comparatively insignificant building is still kept, and shown at the

be impeded. No legal agreement, however, was made to this effect, and the condition was found not to be obligatory. Crisp, in his work on Richmond, remarks that this evasion must be deplored by every inhabitant; but, as a local enthusiast, he can scarcely be trusted to represent the views of the visitors. The sharp practice of Brewer, however, seems to have brought its retaliation in due course, for we find that he was shortly obliged to close the hotel, and that it remained shut up for five years.

In Miss Berry's "Diary," under date "Sunday, June 12th, 1808," is the following entry:—

"The door of the 'Star and Garter' (now shut up as an hotel) being open, we walked in, and a civil quondam servant of the house showed us the rooms.

Dismal history from the woman of the foolish man who made these great additions to the former house, ruined himself, and died in prison! His wife, seeing that all was going wrong, became insane, and died before him."

When the deserted house was at its worst, and there was hardly a whole pane of glass left in any of the windows, Christopher Crean, cook to the Duke of York, took it, and after renewing its appearance, he opened the hotel with some *éclat*

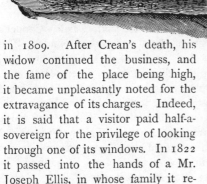

in 1809. After Crean's death, his widow continued the business, and the fame of the place being high, it became unpleasantly noted for the extravagance of its charges. Indeed, it is said that a visitor paid half-a-sovereign for the privilege of looking through one of its windows. In 1822 it passed into the hands of a Mr. Joseph Ellis, in whose family it remained till 1864, when it was turned into a limited liability company. The new company at once erected a large building, from the designs of Mr. E. M. Barry, R.A., by the side of the old hotel, which still remained. In February, 1870, the whole of the original "Star and Garter" was destroyed by fire, and now a palace has arisen upon its site. The hotel has been for many years the favourite resort of all classes, and there are few persons but have found themselves at some time under its roof. Its nearness to London and the beauty of its situation has pointed it out as a peculiarly suitable place for wedding-parties and for the dinners of the Bank of England directors, as well as for those of all the great City companies.

The fire which destroyed the original "Star and

Garter" left untouched the new hotel towards the park, and also the large dining-room towards the town, now turned into a grand concert hall. For several years afterwards the site was a mass of ruins; in 1872, however, all this was cleared away, and an important building, the Pavilion, was reared, uniting this hall to the Hotel. The Pavilion is 116 ft. by 70 ft., and has for its principal feature a ball-room, 80 ft. by 61 ft., with windows facing the terrace and river on one side, and the main road on the other, and affording dancing or dining accommodation to 400 persons. It is 33 feet high in the centre, and has a counter-ceiling of ground glass, from which depends a gas chandelier of 96 lights. At a height of 16 ft. from the floor an open loggia runs round the hall, opening out of which are thirteen rooms for private parties, all having a charming prospect.

THE OLD "STAR AND GARTER."

There is also an orchestra for a band of fifty performers.

An octangular vestibule forms a junction with the hotel, and, fitted up with ferns and plants, affords a pleasant lounge. The entrance next the large banqueting-hall can be closed off from the restaurant, so that two public dinners or private parties are frequently held at the same time without in any way interfering with each other.

The new Pavilion is Italian Romanesque in its architecture; it has two storeys of open loggias towards the road, while towards the gardens it has three storeys, the basement being occupied by a central kitchen, &c. On this lower floor is a billiard and smoking room, opening out upon a level with the terrace gardens. The ample kitchen and other accommodation will enable as many as 1,000 persons to dine in the several parts of these vast buildings, in separate or large parties, at the same time without inconvenience.

The hotel proper is essentially the residential portion of the establishment, and is, in fact, the occasional *séjour* of, it might almost be said, the entire aristocracy of the country.

It would be impossible to recount in half-a-dozen pages the celebrated persons who have dined at the "Star and Garter" in their day, and who are described at greater length in almost every book of anecdote and of social life in England. There have been bucks and dandies innumerable, M.P.'s, Lord Tomnoddies, Sir Mulberry Hawks, country parsons up in London for a spree, popular actresses, to whom a "Star and Garter" dinner is a votive offering from sighing admirers, and maiden aunts, who think it slightly wrong, but like it all the same. Many royal and other distinguished personages have not merely dined but lived here for longer or shorter periods. For instance, Marshal Soult was here in 1838, when he came over to England to represent France at her Majesty's coronation; and the Princess Lieven took up her residence in the hotel for some time. She was visited by the fashionable and official worlds, and many a piece of political intrigue was concocted in her apartments. Louis Philippe lodged here, with all his family, for six months in 1848-9, and was visited here by the Queen, and by Guizot and others of his friends. He was about to spend a second visit here when death struck him down. The ex-king had great faith in the healthiness of Richmond, and when his system needed restoration he was glad to seek change of air upon its lovely hill. After her husband's death, Queen Amelie stayed at the "Star and Garter" for a time; and among other visitors to the hotel we may mention Victor Emanuel when King of Sardinia, Napoleon III., the Archduke Maximilian before he went to Mexico as Emperor, the Crown Prince of Prussia, the Duc d'Aumale, the Empress of Austria, the Empress Eugenie and the lamented Prince Imperial, Prince Leopold, the King and Queen of the Netherlands, the Duke and Duchess of Teck, besides the greater part of the entire aristocracy, the *personnel* of the foreign embassies, and the *élite* of the foreign visitors of each London season. At one time the original "Four in Hand" Club made a practice in the summer of driving down from town every Sunday, and dining at the "Star and Garter"; and many

celebrated historical characters have been as fond of it as Vancouver, who, as before stated, came to anchor hard by after all his travels.

Even in its former state the hotel is thus mentioned in Evans's "Richmond and its Vicinity" (1825) :—

"A little beyond the terrace is the renowned tavern and hotel, the 'Star and Garter,' more like the mansion of a nobleman than a receptacle for the public, looking down with stately aspect upon the adjoining valley, and seen to advantage from every part of the horizon. Hither, in the summer season, crowd visitants from the overgrown metropolis, to inhale the pure air and exhilarate their spirits by contemplating a wide-spreading circumference of rural scenery !"

The terrace at the back of the house, from which the view was to be seen, led to a plantation which opened out upon Petersham Common, and thus an agreeable walk was always within reach of the visitors. Mr. Ellis built largely on the descent of the hill, so that the hotel contained much greater accommodation than appeared at first view.

From the western windows of the hotel is a splendid view over the intervening flat country to the distant height of Stokenchurch, Maidenhead Thicket, Windsor Forest and Castle, Cooper's Hill, St. Anne's Hill, and other points. The grounds at the back of the house are well arranged in gravelled terraces, interspersed with flowering plants and evergreens. Connected with the establishment there is an artesian well made at an outlay of £2,000, the source of which is 495 feet from the surface. The water is raised by a steam-engine of two horse-power, likewise employed in giving motion to machinery for various other domestic operations.

The sign of "Star and Garter," more frequently abridged into the "Garter," and so designated by Shakespeare in his "Merry Wives of Windsor," refers to the insignia of the Order of the Garter, and therefore most naturally we should expect to find it in the neighbourhood of a place which has been the residence of the Court. There was actually a "Garter" Inn at Windsor, on the site of the present "Star and Garter": this is proved by Mr. J. O. Halliwell in the second volume of his folio Shakespeare. The "Star and Garter" at Richmond, however, as we have seen, can boast no such venerable antiquity; it dates only from the early part of the last century. There was also a "Star and Garter" in Pall Mall, and another in "the Five Fields, near Chelsea," now better known as Belgravia.

In spite of its lying off any of the longer and greater high roads of the kingdom, Richmond would seem always to have had its fair share of inns and hostelries, as the "Feathers," the "Red Lion," the "Castle," the "Talbot," the "King's Arms," and the "Rose and Crown," have all, like dogs, had their day. The "Star and Garter," however, owes its superiority to them all to its attractive and commanding position.

About the year 1825, when the late Mr. Ellis proposed to widen Black Horse Lane—then quite a country lane—into a road, the inhabitants strongly objected to his design, as they thought that visitors would come down from London, and make their way to the "Star and Garter" and the terrace, without going into the town at all. This, however, has proved not to be the case, though Black Horse Lane has now blossomed into the "Queen's Road."

The house next to the "Star and Garter," on the same side of the road, but cut off from it by a piece of common, was originally built by Sir William Chambers for Sir Joshua Reynolds, the site chosen by the painter being occupied by a small cottage. In 1769 he employed Thomas Hickey, the Irish attorney, who is immortalised in Goldsmith's "Retaliation," to purchase the ground for him, and one of the few landscapes he ever painted was a view from the window of his drawing-room. The house has been much altered and enlarged since Sir Joshua's time.

The favour with which the summit of the hill has always been regarded has caused the historic associations so to gather, that we cannot hope to do justice to the interest with which they abound. One of the houses on the terrace, for instance, was that which elicited the *bon mot* of George III. "Whose house is that?" inquired the king, when, one fine morning, he was riding past it on horseback. The gentleman appealed to informed him that it had been built by Blanchard, his Majesty's "card-maker." "Blanchard the card-maker," said the king; "why, all his cards must have turned up trumps!"

Bishop Duppa's Almshouses, which were built in 1661, stood on ground now used as a kitchen garden to Downe House until a few years ago, when they were pulled down and re-built in the Vineyard. It was at this Downe House that Sheridan once lived.

Opposite to the "Star and Garter," and close by the park gate, is a large, heavy, and dull-looking house, which was formerly the shooting-box of the Duke of Ancaster, and still bears his name. It is now the residence of Sir Francis Burdett. It was for many years the residence of Sir Lionel Darell. George III. made a practice of coming over every week to stay here, and the hotel stables were fitted up to hold ten of the king's horses. If his Majesty were still among us he could scarcely be presumed to recognise the old "Star and Garter" of his acquaintance in the present palatial pile, where he could with ease be accommodated with stabling for a hundred and fifty.

Ancaster House was given to Sir Lionel by the king, who staked out the ground himself. Miss Darell, Sir Lionel's daughter, lived in the house for nearly sixty years after her father's death. She kept Sir Lionel's room closed, and when it was opened, everything was found just as the old baronet had left it. There, on the table, was his cocked hat, and a copy of the *Times* newspaper for 1804, ready for his perusal.

There was once a well at Richmond, but it never became fashionable, and little is known about its medicinal properties. It still exists in the grounds of Cardigan House, on the slope of the hill. Adjoining the well, in 1730, were a house and assembly-room for music, card-playing, dancing, and raffling, "gold chains, equipages, or any other curious toys, and fine old china," being put up as prizes. Lysons says that "Assemblies were advertised here as lately as 1755, but the place was then much on the decline." The premises were eventually purchased and annexed to the Cardigan estate in order to get rid of the noise and tumult attending a resort of the kind, the Wells house having been pulled down in 1774 or 1775.

A visit to Richmond would be incomplete if the pilgrim should not turn into a confectioner's shop, and lunch on the delicious cheesecakes for which it is so famous, called "Maids of Honour," though the early history of the delicacy is lost, like the Earldom of Mar, in the haze of a venerable antiquity. It is said that either George II. or George III. so named the cakes because they were introduced to the royal table by some of the queen's maids of honour. George III. had his tables at Windsor and Kew regularly supplied with these cheesecakes. Probably they have reigned at Richmond longer than the House of Brunswick.

The report that a thousand pounds was asked, and given, for the recipe for making these delicacies created some sensation, and gave occasion to the wags of the time to air their wit, as may be judged from the following epigrams :—

" Some recipes are rather dearly bought,
    Such as quack remedies for all diseases ;
Powders and pills with such rare virtue fraught,
    That no man needs to die unless he pleases.

" But let us speak of him, that man of sweets,
    Of buns and tarts, preserves, and patties savoury,
Who gives the folks at Richmond luscious treats ;
    He really must have been a man of bravery.

" For lo ! he gave for one small recipe—
    And sure he must be deemed a splendid donor—
A sum that well might solace you or me :
    One thousand pounds to make a *maid of honour*."

Another writer expresses his opinion in the following strain :—

" Who can believe that this bright scene
    Of seeming loveliness and joy,
Has in it men of horrid mien,
    Who follow most unbless'd employ ?

" Men of good reputation, too—
    At least, regarded so by many—
Who sell, ye gods ! it is too true,
    A *maid of honour* for a penny ! "

It is well known to every reader of Theodore Hook's novel of "Gilbert Gurney," as well as to every visitor to the place, that the cheesecakes here are called " Maids of Honour ; " and the former, at all events, will not forget the amusing pages which describe Daly's hoax on the poor lady who is a stranger to Richmond. " Don't you know that this is so courtly a place, and so completely under the influence of state etiquette, that everything in Richmond is called after the functionaries of the palace ? for instance, a capon here is called a 'Lord Chamberlain,' a goose is a 'Lord Steward,' a gooseberry tart an 'Usher of the Black Rod,' and so forth." The lady convulsed the whole party presently by asking the servant, in the blandest of tones, to bring up an " Usher of the Black Rod," if they had one cold in the house.

"The Maids of Honour" have been for a couple of centuries the subjects of numerous jests and riddles. Among the best of these is a conundrum by Lord William Lennox :—" Where would a soldier choose to be quartered at Richmond ? Answer : " At Billet's, for there he would be sure to meet with an excellent *Billet* among the Maids of Honour."

The institution of maids of honour dates from the Tudor times. They figure largely in Gram-

mont's " Memoirs." They were a riotous lot under the Stuarts, and once or twice there was a talk of abolishing the office. In fact, it was abolished in France, and their place was supplied by " Dames d'honneur."

The post of a "maid of honour" is the height of ambition to most young ladies who happen to have been placed by the accident of birth among titled families ; but at all events, in the days of our great-great-grandparents the position was not universally coveted, and it was acknowledged that there were two sides to the question. For example, in discussing the matter with a fair correspondent, Pope writes, certainly with a little banter, and perhaps with a little exaggeration :—" We all agreed that the life of a maid of honour is of all things the most miserable, and wished that every woman who envies it had a specimen of it. To eat Westphalia ham of a morning, ride over hedges and ditches on borrowed hacks, come home in the heat of the day with a fever, and, what is worse a hundred times, with a red mark on the forehead from an uneasy hat : all this may qualify ladies to make excellent wives for fox-hunters, and to bear abundance of ruddy-complexioned children. As soon as they can wipe off the sweat of the day, they must simper an hour, and catch cold in the princess's apartment. From thence, as Shakespeare has it, to dinner with what appetite they may, and after that till midnight, walk, work, or think, which they please."

The Richmond "Maids of Honour" may be supposed to have been a favourite with the ladies of the Tudor court, and they are manufactured at almost all the confectioners' shops in the town. It is not certain now who became possessed of the original patent or recipe for their composition, but whoever was the fortunate inheritor two centuries ago, the patent appears now to be thrown open to the enterprise of all the *cuisinières* of the town, and it is "quite the correct thing" for a visitor not to leave Richmond without tasting one of these little delicacies. At all events, they conspire with " Maid of Honour Row " upon Richmond Green to keep alive the memory of the bygone glories of the place.

CHAPTER XLII.

RICHMOND (*continued*)—EMINENT RESIDENTS.

" See ! sylvan scenes, where art alone pretends
To seek her mistress, and disclose her charms :
Such as a Pope in miniature has shown ;
A Bathurst o'er the widening forest spreads ;
And such as form a Richmond, Chiswick, Stowe."

Sir Robert Dudley—The Duke of Clarence—The Duchess of Queensberry—The Duke of Queensberry, "old Q."—James Thomson the Poet—Thomson's Alcove—His Character—His Death and Burial—Rosedale House—Pagoda House—The Selwyn Family—The Herveys—Lord Marchmont—Nicholas Brady—Bishop Duppa—Lichfield House—Mrs. Maxwell (Miss Braddon)—Egerton House.

AMONGST the natives of Sheen, or Richmond, who have obtained celebrity was Sir Robert Dudley, son of Lady Douglas Howard, the widow of John, Lord Sheffield, by the Earl of Leicester, the great favourite of Queen Elizabeth. He was born in 1575. The connection between his father and his mother was of a mysterious nature, in consequence of the earl's wish to keep his alleged marriage a secret from the queen. He always treated his son as illegitimate, and when he was about five years old Leicester openly married Lettice, Dowager-Countess of Essex. The youth seems, however, to have been treated by him with kindness and attention, and at his death, in 1588, he bequeathed to him the reversion of Kenilworth Castle and other estates, after the death of his uncle, the Earl of Warwick. He was distinguished in his youth for his learning and accomplishments, and he more especially studied mathematics and navigation. Anthony Wood, in enumerating his numerous accomplishments, says :—" He was the first who taught a dog to sit in order to catch partridges." Soon after attaining his majority he was anxious to undertake a voyage of discovery, and being refused assistance from the Government, he fitted out a squadron at his own expense, and cruised, with some success, against the Spaniards off the coasts of South America. He afterwards served with credit under Lord Essex, at the capture of Cadiz. In 1605 he made an attempt before the Star Chamber Court to establish his legitimacy, and obtain possession of the titles and estates of his father, but he was opposed by his stepmother, and was unsuccessful. Disgusted with this result, he obtained permission to travel, and went to Florence, where he was well received by Cosmo II., the Grand Duke of Tuscany, in whose service he remained for the rest of his life. He produced a plan for draining a morass between Pisa and the sea, and projecting the free port of Leghorn. The Duke of Tuscany rewarded him with a pension and the title of a Duke of the Holy Roman Empire and he was ennobled by Pope Urban VIII. He

built for himself a noble palace at Florence, where he lived in magnificent style. He had also a castle near that city, where he died in 1649, and was buried at Boldrone. He wrote an account of his voyage to the Isle of Trinidad and the coast of Paria in 1594, and a work on hydrography, besides tracts on politics and finance. Sir Robert Dudley married Alice, daughter of Sir Thomas Leigh, who remained in England when he emigrated, and was created by Charles I. Duchess of Dudley for life.* The legitimacy of her husband was avowed in the patent. She died in 1679.

Horace Walpole records in a letter to the Miss Berrys, dated September 4th, 1789, the fact of the Duke of Clarence having just taken Mr. Henry Hobart's house at Richmond, "point blank over against Mr. Cambridge's, with Mrs. Jordan as the Eve of his paradise." Mrs. Jordan afterwards became Mrs. Ford, and died in France in great distress in 1816, though she was the mother by the Duke of Clarence, afterwards King William IV., of a large family, the late Earl of Munster and the rest of the Fitz-Clarences.

The Duchess of Queensberry lived at Richmond till 1777. She was by birth Lady Katharine Hyde, and she "set the world on fire" by marrying his Grace. Her sister, Lady Jane Hyde, of whom Prior makes her jealous, married the Earl of Essex. She is thus mentioned by Pope :—

" Yonder I see the cheerful duchess stand,
For friendship, zeal, and blithesome humour known."

The *coterie* of which their Graces of Queensberry formed the centre, as Goldsmith writes, in his " Vicar of Wakefield," would " tattle of nothing but high life and high-lived company, with other fashionable topics, such as pictures and taste."

Here for several years lived the simple poet Gay, making his home in the house of his warm-

---

* See " Old and New London," Vol. III., p. 158.

hearted friends and patrons—the Duchess, as need hardly be added here, being, in the well-known words of Prior,

> "Kitty, the beautiful and young,
> And wild as colt untamed."

A higher compliment surely was never paid by one poet to another than that to Gay by Pope :—

> "Of manners gentle, of affections mild ;
> In wit a man ; simplicity a child ;
> With native humour temp'ring virtuous rage,
> Formed to delight at once and lash the age ;
> Above temptation in a low estate,
> And uncorrupted ev'n among the great :
> A safe companion, and an easy friend,
> Unblamed thro' life, lamented in his end.
> These are thy honours ! not that here thy bust
> Is mixed with heroes, or with kings thy dust ;
> But that the worthy and the good shall say,
> Striking their pensive bosoms—Here lies Gay."

And again—

> "Blest be the great ! for these they take away,
> And those they left me, for they left me Gay :
> Left me to see neglected genius bloom,
> Neglected die, and tell it on his tomb.
> Of all thy blameless life the sole return
> My verse, and Queensberry weeping o'er thy urn !"

Another noted individual who had a villa here was the Duke of Queensberry, the "old Q." who is commemorated in the pages of OLD AND NEW LONDON.   He had, however, no eye for the beauties of nature and fine scenery.   Mr. Wilberforce tells us how, when a young man, he once dined here with his Grace in the company of Pitt, George Selwyn, and other men of rank and fashion. "The dinner was early, in order that some of the party might be ready afterwards to attend the Opera.   The views from the villa were enchanting, and the Thames in all its glory ; but the duke looked on with perfect indifference.   'What is there to make so much of,' he said, 'in this Thames ?   I am quite tired of it.   There it goes, flow, flow, flow, always the same.'"   The jaded old sinner was always on the look-out for change, even in his pleasures.

Here, in a house with a garden, long known as Rosedale, and constantly visited by the admirers of his poetry, James Thomson resided after he had become famous by his poem on " The Seasons." The house is in Kew Foot Lane, a thoroughfare leading from the Green to the Kew Road.   It has since been converted into the Richmond Hospital.

The author of " The Seasons " was the son of a minister of the Kirk of Scotland, and was born in 1700.   He was intended for the ministry, but

the professor of Divinity objecting to his poetical style, he gave up all thoughts of that career, and came to London, where, he was told, "merit is almost sure of meeting its reward."   The sale of his " Winter " was his first means of supplying his necessities, the most urgent of which was a pair of shoes !   He obtained twenty guineas from the gentleman to whom it was dedicated ; and so modest was the poet, that he declared to a friend, " the present was larger than the performance deserved !"   "Winter" was published in 1726. "Summer" and "Spring" were published in the two succeeding years.   " Autumn," which completed "The Seasons," did not appear till 1730.

Thomson travelled in Italy with the son of Lord Chancellor Talbot, and on his return published a poem upon Liberty.   His tragedy of " Tancred and Sigismunda " was produced in 1745.   His latest poem was the " Castle of Indolence."

In May, 1736, just after the publication of his poem on "Liberty," Thomson removed from London hither, finding himself in such easy circumstances as to be able to have a country residence. " He established himself," writes his biographer, Mr. Robert Bell, " in a cottage in Kew Foot Lane, looking across to the Thames, and commanding the distant landscape, with a pretty garden behind. The cottage has long since been absorbed into a handsome villa, of which what was once the poet's sitting-room now forms the principal part of the entrance-hall.   His writing-table, with an inscription, is still shown, and the alcove in the garden, removed to the extremity of the grounds, under the spreading branches of a chestnut-tree, has been carefully preserved, with poetical tributes hanging on the walls, and a tablet to inform the pilgrim visitor here that—

> 'Here Thomson sang " the Seasons " and their change.'

This is not quite correct, as 'The Seasons' were all published six years before he went to live at Richmond.   Here, however, he revised and enlarged them, and carried them through three successive editions, in 1738, 1744, and 1746 ; so that the above may, with propriety, be said to be associated with the work."   He was occasionally visited by Pope whilst engaged in this revision.

Evans, in his " Richmond and its Vicinity " (1830), describes a visit to Rosedale House and its alcove, and adds : "The table formerly belonging to the poet, and on which he is said to have completed the 'Seasons,' being old and decayed, is placed in the summer-house, its place in the alcove being supplied by another of rustic form.   On a board suspended over the back seat is the annexed memorial.

"'Within this pleasing retirement, allured by the music of the nightingale, which warbled in soft unison to the melody of his soul in unaffected cheerfulness, and genial, though simple elegance, lived James Thomson. Sensibly alive to all the beauties of nature, he painted their images as they rose in review, and poured the whole profusion of them into his inimitable "Seasons." Warmed with intense devotion to the Sovereign of the Universe, its flame glowing through all his compositions, animated with unbounded benevolence, with the tenderest social sensibility, he never gave one moment's pain to any of his fellow creatures, save by his death, which happened at this place on the 27th of August, 1748.'"

The summer-house stood in an 'alcove' in the garden. It was a plain semi-circular structure, painted green, with white pillars, but had no very striking features.

Here Thomson passed the latter part of his life in his own house, reading in his garden, writing in his summer-house, communing with nature, and listening to the song of the nightingale. He was constitutionally so indolent that "he was often seen" (says Leigh Hunt) "eating peaches off the trees whilst his hands were in his waistcoat pockets. But his indolence did not hinder him from writing. He had the luck to obtain the occupation of which he was fond; and no man perhaps in his native country, with the exception of Shakespeare, has acquired a greater or more enviable fame. His friends loved him while he lived, and his readers love his memory."

Thomson was naturally very indolent. He was once found in bed at two o'clock in the day, and upon being asked why he was in bed at that hour, "Mon," he replied, in his Scotch accent, "I had no motive to rise." In Watkins's "Anecdotes" it is recorded that Thomson was occasionally embarrassed in his circumstances, and with his disposition, it would be a wonder if he were not. At one time he was in a spunging-house, from whence he was relieved by Quin, the actor.

JAMES THOMSON.

The following is the picture of the poet as drawn by his barber, one William Taylor:—"He had a face as long as a horse, and he perspired so much that I remember after walking one day in the summer, I shaved his head without lather by his own desire. His hair was as soft as a camel's. . . and yet it grew so remarkably, that if it was but an inch long, it stood upright on end from his head, like a brush. He was corpulent, and stooped rather forward when he walked, as though he were full of thought. He was very careless and negligent about his dress, and wore his clothes remarkably plain. He always wore a wig, and very extravagant he was with them. I have seen a dozen at a time hanging up in my master's shop, and all of them so big that nobody else could wear them. I suppose his sweating to such a degree made him have so many, for I have known him spoil a new one in walking from London to Richmond." It is well known that, whilst careless in the rest of his costume, Thomson was always very particular in the cut and appearance of his wig, in respect of which he was as great a dandy as any young lordling could have been. "He was also a great walker," continues the barber. "He used to walk from Mallock's (Mallet's) at Strand-on-the-Green, near Kew Bridge, and from London, at all hours of the night; he seldom got into a carriage, and never on horseback. He kept much company with persons 'of the writing sort.' I remember Pope, and Paterson, and Mallock (Mallet), and Lyttleton, and Dr. Armsbury, and Andrew Millar, the bookseller, who had a house near him in Kew Lane. Pope visited him very often, and so did Quin and Paterson. When he was writing in his own house, he frequently sat with a bowl of punch before him, and a large one, too. He sat also much in his garden, in an arbour at the end of it, where he used to write in summer-time. I have known him lie along by himself on the grass near it, and talk away as if three or four people were with him. His papers used to lie in a loose pile upon the table in his study. . . . He was very affable in conversation, very free in his conversation, and very cheerful, and one of the best-natured men that ever lived. He was seldom over-burdened with cash. . . . but when he had money, he would send for his creditors, and pay them all round." Though soft, and even foolish, Thomson was a truly "honest man."

The same barber is our authority for the cause of the poet's death. "He had had a 'batch' of drinking with Quin, when he took a quantity of cream-of tartar, as he frequently did on such occasions, which, with a fever, carried him off."

From what has been said, it may readily be inferred that Thomson was inclined to be social in his habits. His friend Mr. Robertson said that he "used to frequent the 'Old Orange Tree' in Kew Lane with Parson Cromer, and Taylor, his wig-maker;" and he remembered the poet's housekeeper expressing her regret at the late hours which Quin, the actor, induced him to keep, for they would both come home from the "Castle" together at daybreak. The truth is that the easiness of his simple nature made him conform to the habits of the company in which he chanced to find himself.

Collins, the author of the well-known ode of the "Death of Thomson," Hammond, the author of some Love Elegies—

"Hammond, the darling pride,
The friend and lover of the tuneful throng—"

and David Mallet, were among Thomson's frequent visitors. Pope often came over from Twickenham to see him, and was always admitted, whether Thomson had other company or not, but he was never a very cordial friend. In his youth Thomson was considered handsome, but as he grew in years he became fat, and stooped, and his portrait may be seen in his own "Castle of Indolence."

Dr. Johnson has done but scanty justice to Thomson in his "Lives of the Poets." He says that Savage "lived much with Thomson;" and on his authority adds that he was "a great lover, a great swimmer, and rigorously abstinent." In all probability, however, the learned doctor here has formed a rash judgment, for though Savage lived for a short time in or near Richmond, being a sort of literary jackal to Pope, and therefore had doubtless opportunities of meeting Thomson, yet his name is "nowhere to be found among the associates and visitors of the poet of the Seasons;" and his erratic habits render it very unlikely that any constant or frequent intercourse took place between them. "Poor Mr. Savage," Thomson writes to his friend, Mr. Aaron Hill, "would be happy to pass an evening with you, but where to find him requires more intelligence than is allotted to mortals."

Dr. Joseph Warton's character of Thomson and his writings is well worth transcription in this place :—

"Thomson was blessed with a strong and copious fancy; he hath enriched poetry with a variety of new and original images, which he painted from Nature itself, and from his own actual observations: his descriptions, therefore, have a distinctness and truth which are utterly wanting to those of poets who have only copied from each other, and have never looked abroad on the objects themselves. Thomson was accustomed to wander away into the country for days and for weeks, attentive to 'each rural sight, each rural sound;' while many a poet who has dwelt for years in the Strand has attempted to describe fields and rivers, and generally succeeded accordingly. Hence that nauseous repetition of the same circumstances, hence that disgusting impropriety of introducing what may be called a set of hereditary images, without proper regard to the age, or climate, or occasion, in which they were formerly used. Though the diction of the 'Seasons' is sometimes harsh and inharmonious, and sometimes turgid and obscure, and though in many instances the numbers are not sufficiently diversified by different pauses, yet is this poem, on the whole, from the numberless strokes of Nature in which it abounds, one of the most captivating and amusing in our language, and which, as its beauties are not of a transitory kind, as depending on particular customs and manners, will ever be perused with delight. The scenes of Thomson are frequently as wild and romantic as those of Salvator Rosa, varied with precipices and torrents, and 'castled cliffs,' and deep valleys, with piny mountains and the gloomiest caverns !"

Lord Lyttelton's testimony to Thomson is expressed most truthfully in the following lines, which he "laid like a garland of bays on his own copy of the 'Seasons :'"—

"Hail, Nature's poet ! whom she taught alone
To sing her works in numbers like her own
Sweet as the thrush that warbles in the dale,
And soft as Philomela's tender tale.
She lent her pencil, too, of wondrous power
To catch the rainbow, and to form the flower
Of many-mingling hues ; then smiling said—

*   *   *   *   *

'These beauteous children, though so fair they shine,
Fade in my seasons ; let them live in *thine*.'
And live they shall, the charm of every eye,
Till Nature sickens and the seasons die."

Sweeter stanzas were never penned in the English tongue than those written on Thomson by Collins.

The scene of the following stanzas is supposed to lie on the Thames, near Richmond :—

> " In yonder grave a Druid lies,
>   Where slowly winds the stealing wave,
> The year's best sweets shall duteous rise,
>   To seek its poet's sylvan grave.
>
> " And oft as ease and health retire
>   To breezy lawn or forest deep,
> The friend shall view yon whitening spire,
>   And 'mid the varied landscape weep.
>
> " But thou, lone stream, whose sullen tide
>   No sedge-crowned sisters now attend,
> Now waft me from the green hill's side,
>   Whose cold turf hides the buried friend.
>
> " The genial meads assigned to bless
>   Thy life, shall mourn thy early doom !
> Their hinds and shepherd-girls shall dress
>   With simple hands thy rural tomb.
>
> " Long, long thy stone, and pointed ciay
>   Shall melt the musing Briton's eyes,
> ' Oh, vales and wild woods,' shall he say,
>   ' In yonder grave your Druid lies ! ' "

It is said that Thomson married in early life a domestic servant, but that when he became intimate with Lady Hertford and other titled folks, he would not acknowledge her as his wife, though he kept her in his house as a drudge. But the story, though told by George Chalmers, " lacks confirmation." [*]

One summer evening it is recorded, having overheated himself, Thomson took boat, by which he caught a cold that threw him into a fever ; he recovered from the first attack, but imprudently exposing himself to the evening dews, brought on a relapse, which carried him off on the 27th August, 1748.

After Thomson's death his cottage was purchased by a Mr. George Ross, who enlarged both it and the grounds ; it afterwards passed into the hands of the Hon. Frances Boscawen, who put up the inscription relating to the poet. It afterwards became the property of the Earl of Shaftesbury, and received the name of Rosedale House—originally Rossdale—after Thómson's successor. The old Countess of Shaftesbury died here in August, 1865, in her ninety-first year. It was converted into the Richmond Hospital, in 1866, under the patronage of the Duke and Duchess of Cambridge and the Princess Mary of Teck, as stated above. [†]

As may be supposed, the house has undergone great changes. A large wing has been built on to the north side, and the garden has been cut in two, the lower part being almost entirely built over. The lawn on which Thomson's summer-house once stood is there, and a pleasant place it is for the convalescents to walk about upon ; but, alas ! the treasure is gone. When the house was purchased for a hospital from the executors of Lady Shaftesbury, it was agreed to buy the summer-house also ; but some of the roughs of the town made an entry into the garden by night, carried it off, and sold it for firewood ! The poet's table, however, is still preserved as a precious relic by Lord Shaftesbury.

One of the rooms on the ground floor and another on the first floor are shown as those which tradition ascribes to the poet's use ; but the mantelpiece and fireplace of the upper room have been altered and modernised; the Dutch tiles which lined its hearth are no longer *in situ ;* and even the brass plate on the door which marked the room as Thomson's own has disappeared. The dining-room, drawing-room, and entrance-hall, remain pretty much as they were in Lady Shaftesbury's time ; and the floors of the finest polished oak show that the house was substantially built. It now looks bright and cheerful ; and it is satisfactory to note that the institution is very generally supported by the inhabitants of the town and neighbourhood ; but we understand that with larger funds it could easily enlarge its sphere of work. It overlooks the old Deer Park, and its gardens formerly reached quite down to the high road between Kew and Richmond, which is now traversed by a tramway. The room in which Thomson died, on the left as you enter the hospital, is now the surgeon's room ; his sitting-room was on the right. It was small, and apparently well suited to a poet's means; and the house in his time had no wings, and was not larger than an average country vicarage. The garden was beyond the lawn, on which stood a fine spreading cedar. At that time there was *no* carriage-road from Richmond to Kew.

There is a second Rosedale near the hospital ; it was formerly a school, and the house, though old, has no pretence to having been connected with Thomson.

Near the new church in the Kew Road is Pagoda House, the seat of the Selwyn family. Of this family was George Augustus Selwyn, the celebrated wit. [*] His father, Colonel John Selwyn, aide-de-camp to the great Duke of Marlborough, was treasurer both to Frederick, Prince of Wales,

---

and the Duke of Cumberland, as well as to the Princesses Amelia and Caroline. Another member of the family was Mr. William Selwyn, Q.C., a man of high legal and social standing in his time. The Prince Consort read Constitutional Law with him on his first arrival in this country. Mr. Selwyn died in 1855. He was the father of Dr. George Selwyn, the first Bishop of New Zealand, and afterwards Bishop of Lichfield, and also of the late Lord Justice Selwyn. The judge lived at Pagoda House; but the outlying grounds of the estate towards Kew have been laid out since his death for building purposes, under the name of Selwyn Court, and have been spoken of in a Society journal as one of the most charming estates, the villas being pitched in the midst of orchards, and having apple, pear, and plum trees standing, not only in the front gardens, but in the very highways of the estate. At the junction of the Mortlake and Kew Road is a drinking-fountain erected to the judge's memory.

"It was at Richmond," write Grace and Philip Wharton, in their "Queens of Society," "that Lord Hervey first met his wife, the charming Lepel, among the brilliant, rather than respectable, ladies who thronged about the Princess of Wales, such as Mrs. Howard, Mrs. Selwyn, Miss Bellenden, and Miss Howe. With these ladies Pope,

'The ladies' plaything and the Muses' pride.'

as Aaron Hill wrote of him, was a great favourite. The Herveys became intimate with him, and thus with Lady Mary Wortley Montagu. This fashionable circle, as we have seen, gradually moved its centre a little higher up the Thames and on the opposite bank, Lady Mary becoming at Twickenham what the Princess of Wales had been at Richmond.

Another noted resident of Richmond in former times was Lord Marchmont, the friend of Pope, who lived to be eighty-six, and had such physical health and strength that he rode on horseback less than a week before he died. Sir John Sinclair, who knew him well, once asked him for a receipt for longevity, and what do our readers think was his prescription? Simple enough, he "never mixed his wines," but stuck to the same bottle. For many years before his death he drank a bottle of claret daily; after eighty he exchanged claret for Burgundy.

Nicholas Brady, the joint author, with Tait, of the well-known metrical version of the Psalms, lived for some time at Richmond, and at the solicitation of the parishioners, served as their curate in 1696. Dr. Brian Duppa, Bishop of Winchester, chaplain to Charles I. and tutor to his children, lived here occasionally. After the execution of his royal master, Bishop Duppa retired hither, and lived in retirement. After the Restoration, he was promoted to the above see, and also made Lord Almoner. He died at Richmond in 1662, having been visited when on his death-bed by Charles II. In the year before his death he founded an almshouse for ten poor women, unmarried, and of the age of fifty and upwards, for whose support he settled the rental of a farm and other premises at Lower Halliford, by Shepperton, Middlesex. In addition to lodging, each of the almswomen is allowed £1 monthly, and a further £1 at Midsummer and Christmas, "together with a gown of substantial cloth, called Bishop's blue, every other year." They have each also "a Christmas repast of a barn-door fowl and a pound of bacon" secured to them by the lease of the farm at Shepperton. The original almshouse, an old-fashioned pile of building, of red brick, stood by the side of the road, near the terrace, with the following inscription on a stone tablet over the entrance, "*Votiva Tabula*. I will pay my vows which I made to God in my trouble." The house was taken down a few years ago, and a new one erected in the Vineyard.

Lichfield House, on the north side of Marshgate Road, which leads into the Upper Road to Sheen and Mortlake, is so called from having been the abode of a former bishop of Lichfield. It is now the residence of Mrs. Maxwell, the novelist, better known by her former name of Miss Braddon. On the opposite side of the road is Egerton House, the name of which also calls back associations of a noble family, by which it was once occupied. Heron Court, in Hill Street, was for some time the residence of the distinguished diplomatist and author, Lord Dalling. Spring Grove, in Marsh Gate, was built at the beginning of the last century by the Marquis of Lothian. He resided there for some years.

By way of a conclusion to this chapter it may be added that Richmond figures in the "Index Villaris," published in 1700, as a place which contains the seats of a baronet, a knight, and more than three "gentlemen of coat armour."

CHAPTER XLIII

KEW.

"So sits enthroned, in vegetable pride,
Imperial Kew, by Thames's glittering side,
Obedient sails from realms unfurrowed bring
For her the unnamed progeny of Spring."—DARWIN.

Situation and Soil of Kew—Its Etymology—The Village—Suffolk Place—Kew House—Sir Henry Capel's Orangery—Kew House taken as a Royal Residence—Its Demolition, and a New Palace built, which was also pulled down—The Present Palace—Bubb Dodington at Kew—News of the Death of George I. brought to the Prince of Wales—Feud between the King and the Prince of Wales—Death of George II.—Seclusion of George III.—Queen Charlotte's Christmas Trees—The King's Insanity—The King and the Artist—Death of Queen Charlotte—Attempt to Assassinate the Duke of Cumberland—Marriage of the Duke of Clarence and the Duke of Kent—Kew Observatory—The Parish Church—The Graves of Zoffany, Meyer, and Gainsborough—The Rev. Richard Byam—Stephen Duck—Caleb Colton—Granville Sharpe—Sir Arthur Helps—Francis Bauer—Sir John Puckering—"The Pilgrim" Inn—The River Thames—Kew Bridge.

"How fresh the meadows look above the river," writes Tennyson; and nowhere are his words more true than here. The Thames takes a sweep from Barnes to Richmond, which produces a peninsula of meadow-land, at the extremity of which is the pleasant village of Kew. Kew was formerly a hamlet belonging to Kingston, but included within the royal manor of Richmond. In 1769 it was constituted by Act of Parliament a distinct parish. It is bounded on the north and east by the River Thames, on the south-east by Mortlake, and on the south and west by Richmond. The soil is chiefly a light porous sand, and the greater part of the land is occupied by the Royal Gardens, the remainder being appropriated to the purpose of raising asparagus and other vegetables for the London markets.

Its name has been variously spelt as Kayhough, Kayhoo, Keye, and Kewe, whence, as Lysons observes, "its situation near the waterside might induce one to seek for its etymology in the word Key, or Quay." Kew has to contend with all the disadvantages of a flat surface; like Versailles, too, the soil was once swampy and ungrateful : the wealth of a nation drained and fertilised both.

The village itself consists of a collection of shops and private houses, with one or two inns of moderate size, built about the margin of a green some dozen acres in extent, near the centre of which stands the parish church, and, close by, on the west side, the principal entrance to the gardens. A large number of houses have been built of late years on the Richmond Road, which runs southward from the corner of the green, and forms all along the eastern boundary of the gardens. The houses hereabouts have been mostly built since the opening of the Kew Gardens railway station, from which there is access to Ludgate Hill, Waterloo, and nearly all the other London termini. Just over the bridge is the station for the South-Western loop line trains. The area of the parish is about 350 acres, and the population, according to the latest census returns, is about 1,700, showing an increase of 700 during the preceding decade. Kew has its local institutions, its fire brigade, its cricket club, its Kew Gardens Public Rights Defence Association, and its Educational Institute, &c.

Leland, in his *Cygnea Cantio* ("Itinerary," Vol. IX.), notices Kew as the abode of the Dowager Queen of France, the Princess Mary of England, widow of Louis XII. of France, and the sister of Henry VIII. She married, *en secondes noces*, Charles Brandon, Duke of Suffolk, whose third wife she was. Leland describes Kew as a handsome town or village—"*villa elegans.*"

A mansion called Suffolk Place is mentioned in a court roll of Queen Elizabeth as having been pulled down and destroyed. This was probably the place of residence of the Duke of Suffolk. Leland says that the duke's house was erected in the reign of Henry VII., not many years before he wrote, and, according to report, by a steward of the royal household.

The original Kew Palace figures constantly in "Bubb Dodington's Diary" as the head-quarters of the party who hung about Frederick, Prince of Wales; the prince lived there chiefly when in the "country," and not at Leicester House or Carlton House, and the princess resided there in her widowhood, and here she brought up her son, afterwards George III., and his brother, Prince Edward. Here the young king and his brothers were taught riding and fencing by Signor Angelo.

The royal family were very fond of the place, and took a keen interest in laying out the grounds. Dodington writes in February, 1749 :—"To dinner at Kew . . . . worked in the new walk at Kew. All of us, men, women, and children, worked at the same place—a cold dinner." On another occasion he records having walked with the princess and her ladies in attendance round Richmond Park Gardens, as well as those of Kew. "Plays," says Bubb Dodington, "were acted here every evening."

The Richmond Lodge, where, as we have related in a previous chapter,* George II., then Prince of Wales, was living when news was brought to him of the death of his father, George I., was really in Kew. Domestic affection was decidedly not this prince's strong point. He was living in alienation from, and even in hostility to, the king, his father; the two courts of Kew and St. James's maintained no communication with each other, and it was with

It is stated as a fact that when the prince died, a messenger was sent to inform the king of the circumstance. He was at the time playing at cards with a large party at the palace; with true German *sang froid*, he continued the game to the end, and then communicated the intelligence to his mistress, the Duchess of Kendal, who was playing at another table, calmly telling her that Fritz was dead, but made no motion to interrupt the amusements; the duchess, however, with more feeling and delicacy, broke up the assembly. The following letter was given to me as one in the handwriting of the king, but I have reason to

OLD KEW PALACE (THE DUTCH HOUSE), SHOWING ALSO PART OF THE CASTELLATED PALACE BEGUN BY GEORGE III.

difficulty that he could be persuaded to rise from the sofa where he was lying, and to go to London to see his ministers.

Later on, the quarrel between himself and his son Frederick was carried on by the king with a rancour, descending to personality, unknown to the modern disputes of royalty. The ill blood is supposed to have been caused by the countenance which the Prince of Wales gave to the party in opposition to the measures of Government. "The prince had a separate establishment at Norfolk House, which was," says Mr. William Hone, "the chief resort of the disaffected to the party in power; no persons visiting the prince were allowed to come to the court of the sovereign.

* See *ante*, p. 344.

doubt the truth of the allegation; nevertheless, it bears the marks of being a rough draft of it, being altered and interlined, and, from its apparent age, there is no doubt of its being written at the time of its date (1737). There are some grammatical errors, which may possibly arise from its being the production of a foreigner :—

"'The professions you have lately made in your letters of your particular regard to me are so contradictory to all your actions, that I cannot suffer myself to be imposed upon by them. You know very well you did not give the least intimation to me or to the Queen that the Princess was with child, till within less than a month of the birth of the young Princess; you removed the Princess twice in the week, and immediately preceding the day of her delivery, from the place of my residence, in expectation, as you voluntarily declared, of her labour; and both times, upon your return, you industriously concealed from me and the Queen every circumstance relating to this important affair ; and you at last, without giving any notice to me or the Queen, precipitately hurried the Princess from Hampton Court in a condition not to be named ; after having thus, in execution of your own determined measures, exposed both the Princess and the child to the greatest perils, you now plead surprise, and your tenderness for the Princess, as the only motive that occasioned these repeated indignities offered to me and the Queen, your mother. This extravagant and undutiful behaviour, in so essential a point as the birth of an heir to my crown, is such an evidence of your premeditated defiance of me, and such a contempt of my authority, and of the natural right belonging to your parents, as cannot be excused by the pretended innocence of your intentions, nor palliated or disguised by specious

These unhappy family circumstances may have been, in true measure, responsible for the apparently ill-advised system of education pursued by the Princess-Dowager in bringing up her son, afterwards George III.

Sir N. W. Wraxall writes, in his " Historical Memoirs " :—" During nearly ten years which elapsed between the death of his father, early in 1751, and the decease of his grandfather—a period when the human mind is susceptible of such deep impressions—he remained in a state of almost absolute seclusion from his future people, and from the world. Constantly resident at

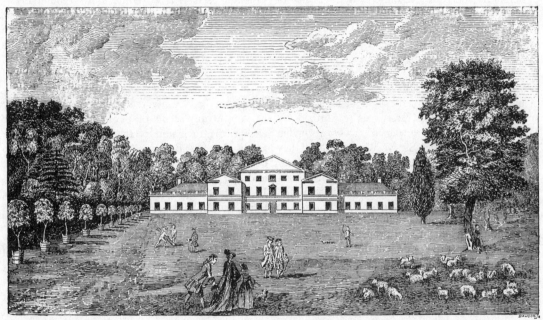

OLD KEW PALACE (PULLED DOWN IN 1802).

words only ; but the whole tenour of your conduct for a considerable time has been so entirely void *to* all real duty to me, that I have long had reason to be offended with you, and until you withdraw your regard and confidence from those by whose instigation and advice you are directed and encouraged in your unwarrantable behaviour to me and the Queen, and until you return to your duty, you shall not reside in my palace, which I will not suffer to be made the resort of them who, under the appearance of attachment to you, foment the division you have made in my family, and thereby weaken the common interest of the whole ; in this situation I will receive no reply ; but when your actions manifest a just sense of your duty and submission, that may induce me to pardon what I at present most justly resent. In the mean time, it is my pleasure that you leave St. James's, with all your family, when it can be done without prejudice or ill-convenience to the Princess. I shall for the present leave to the Princess the care of my granddaughter, until a proper time calls on me to consider on her education. 'G. R.'

'*Hampton Court, September* 10*th*, 1737.' "

Leicester House, or at Carlton House, when he was in London ; immured at Kew, whenever he went to the country ; perpetually under the eye of his mother and of Lord Bute, who acted in the closest unity of design : he saw comparatively few other persons, and those only chosen individuals of both sexes. They naturally obtained, and long preserved, a very firm ascendant over him. When he ascended the throne, though already arrived at manhood, his very person was hardly known, and his character still less understood, beyond a narrow circle. Precautions, it is well ascertained, were even adopted by the Princess Dowager to preclude, as much as possible, access to him—precautions which, to the extent of her ability, were redoubled after he became king. It will scarcely be believed, but it is nevertheless true, that in order to prevent his conversing with any persons, or receiving any written intimations, anonymous or otherwise, between the drawing-room and the door of Carlton House, when he was returning from thence to St. James's or to Buckingham House, after his evening visits to his mother, she never failed to accompany him till he got into his sedan-chair."

"What could be expected," asks Horace Walpole, "from a boy locked up from the converse of mankind, governed by a mother still more retired, who was herself under the influence of a man that had passed his life in solitude, and was too haughty to admit to his familiarity but half-a-dozen silly authors and flatterers?"

Before he succeeded to the crown, as Prince of Wales even, he had made Lord Bute his intimate friend, and the companion of his daily walks, rides, and drives; and the two were riding together along the road in the neighbourhood of Kew Bridge on the 25th October, 1760, when the news of the sudden death of George II. reached them—having been brought by a groom—intelligence which was soon afterwards confirmed by Mr. Pitt, then Premier, in person. "On receiving the information," writes Sir N. W. Wraxall, "they all returned to the Palace (at Kew), where the new king remained during the whole day, and passed the night also, not going up to St. James's till the following morning. Mr. Pitt having presented him a paper containing a few sentences which he suggested it might be proper to pronounce on meeting the Privy Council, the king thanked him, but replied that he had already considered the subject, and had drawn up his intended address to be delivered at the Council Table. The minister, who perceived that Lord Bute had anticipated him, drew the unavoidable inference. It was, indeed, sufficiently obvious that however his administration might nominally continue for a time, yet his influence and authority were already eclipsed and superseded." In fact, the walls of Kew Palace on that occasion witnessed the establishment, we might almost say, of a new dynasty.

According to Horace Walpole, the first moment of the new reign afforded a symptom of the prince's character: of that cool dissimulation in which he had been so well initiated by his mother, and which comprehended almost the whole of what she had taught him. Princess Amelia, as soon as she was certain of her father's death, sent an account of it to the Prince of Wales; but he had already been apprised of it. He was riding, and received a note from a German *valet-de-chambre* attendant on the late king, with a private mark agreed upon between them, which

certified him of the event. Without surprise or emotion, without dropping a word that indicated what had happened, he said his horse was lame, and turned back to Kew. At dismounting, he said to the groom, "I have said this horse is lame; I forbid you to say the contrary."

Sir N. W. Wraxall opens his gossiping "Memoirs" by complaining that, whereas even the dull reign of George II. had afforded material for anecdotes of court and social life, the first twenty or thirty years of the reign of George III.—in fact, nearly down to the date of his first mental attack—were spent at Kew and at Windsor in almost Oriental seclusion. "While still a young man," writes Wraxall, "he neither frequented masquerades, nor engaged at play, nor passed his evenings in society calculated to unbend his mind from the fatigues of business and vexations of state. All the splendour of a court was laid aside, or exhibited only for a few hours, on a 'birthday.' Rarely during the first twenty years after his accession did he join in any scene of public amusement, if we except the diversion of the theatre. Still more rarely did he sit down at table with any of his courtiers or nobility. His repasts, private, short, and temperate, never led to the slightest excess. Hence his enemies endeavoured to represent him, not unjustly, as affecting the state of an Asiatic prince, scarcely ever visible except on the terrace at Windsor, or in the circle at a levée."

Certainly the well-ordered and decorous court of the third George must have presented an immense contrast to those of his two predecessors, and even to those of Queen Anne and of King William at Kensington Palace, to say nothing of Whitehall between the Restoration and the Revolution of 1688. George III. was too happy in his own family circle and in his own homely tastes to need to have recourse to fashionable gatherings in order to drive away the spleen or *ennui*. He and Queen Charlotte "played Darby and Joan" at Kew, whilst the leaders of fashionable society were crowding the *salons* of Devonshire and Carlton Houses, or turning night into day at Ranelagh.

During a long period his Majesty lived at Kew about three months in every year, besides visiting it on alternate Tuesdays in the autumn, and staying three days each time. The king, true to his character as the "farmer," would dine here on boiled mutton and turnips. Madame d'Arblay—then Miss Burney—speaking of the life of the royal family at Kew, says:—"It is very different from that at Windsor. There is no form or ceremony here of any sort. The royal family are always here in so very retired a way, that they live as the simplest gentlefolks. The king has not even an equerry with him, nor the queen any lady to attend her when she goes her airings. All the household are more delicate in inviting or admitting any friends here than elsewhere, on account of the very easy and unreserved way in which the family live, running about from one end of the house to the other without precaution or care. All the apartments but the king's and queen's, and one of Mistress Schwellenberg's, are small, dark, and old-fashioned. There are staircases in every passage, and passages in every closet."

The following amusing anecdote concerning George III. and his life at Kew Palace is told in the "Reminiscences of Henry Angelo," but it will bear repeating. Alexander Gresse, to whom the story refers, was an artist of celebrity in his day, teacher of drawing to the queen and the princesses, and a great favourite of the king. "Though a good-natured and friendly-hearted man," writes our author, "Gresse was very irritable, and could not patiently endure the least observations upon the stupendosity of his figure. This, indeed, is verified in a story of his late Majesty and the too sensitive painter, which happened whilst my father was in attendance upon the royal family.

"Gresse, on his first introduction as a teacher at the royal palaces, had been told by Muller, page to the then young Prince Edward [afterwards Duke of Kent], that the etiquette was, if by accident he met the king, or any member of the royal family, within the palace, to stand respectfully still, let them pass, and take no notice, unless those great personages condescended to notice him.

"It happened, that during his many professional visits at Buckingham House, at Kew, and at Windsor, during the first two years' attendance, he had never by any chance met the king. One day, however, whilst waiting to attend the queen, and amusing himself in looking at the painted ceiling in the great audience chamber, a door suddenly opened, and by a side glance he perceived himself in the royal presence. It was no less a personage than his Majesty King George the Third, who entered alone.

"Struck, no doubt, with the extraordinary bulk and general contour of the figure of the artist—for he stood with his hands behind him, grasping his cocked hat, and his legs straddling wide, with his head thrown back—the king advanced to the middle of the room, and eyed him with apparent surprise. Gresse, remembering the point of etiquette, dropped his head to its natural position, and stood stock-still. After his Majesty had taken this survey he walked round, whilst Gresse, wishing

a trap-door to open under his own feet, remained, nothing short of a waxen figure beneath a tropical sun. At length the king, unconscious, we may reasonably suppose, of the misery of the sensitive artist, walked to some distance, and, turning round, took a view of him right in front. Gresse, determined to show the king that he really was not a statue, regardless of further etiquette, made to the sovereign a most profound bow, which the king understanding, as it is supposed, he immediately retired."

Here, or at Buckingham Palace, Queen Charlotte, as we learn from the Hon. Amelia Murray's "Recollections," true to her German associations, regularly had a Christmas-tree dressed up. "It was hung," writes the authoress, "with presents for the children who were invited to see it ; and I well remember the pleasure that it was to hunt for one's own name, which was sure to be attached to one or more of the pretty gifts." Christmas-trees are common enough in almost every household now-a-days, but such was not the case half a century ago.

It was at Kew that George III. was shut up when suffering from his first attack of mental malady. George Selwyn, who is generally regarded as a selfish wit, used to say : "Old as I am, I would stand bareheaded all the day, and open the gate on Kew Green, if I could be sure of seeing any one who came from the palace with good news of my royal master." The poor king was "allowed," writes Sir Nathaniel Wraxall, to walk out, as often as the weather permitted, in the gardens, accompanied by his keeper, Dr. Willis, and one of that physician's sons.

All sorts of amusing stories are told concerning the life led by the unfortunate king during his residence here. One day Miss Burney was walking in the gardens at Kew, when she saw his Majesty, whom she supposed to be very insane, coming towards her. To avoid meeting him, she ran off at full speed. But the king was not to be disappointed in his chance of meeting a pretty woman, and so ran after her. The king's attendants were alarmed, and ran after him. But the king proved the swiftest runner, and soon caught up with the charming queen's maid, and, throwing his arms around her, kissed her. He then informed her that he was as well as ever he had been in his life, and that he wished to talk with her on affairs of state. Miss Burney was at first terribly frightened, but soon gained her self-possession, and enjoyed one of the most pleasant interviews with the king that she ever had while in the service of the royal household. Another time, as the king was breakfasting at Kew, the great scarcity of beef which was then prevailing in England became the subject of conversation.

"Why do not people plant more beef?" asked the king. Upon being told that beef could not be raised from the seed, he seemed still incredulous. He took some bits of beef-steak, and went into the garden and planted them. The next morning he went out to see if they had sprouted, and found there some snails. Thinking they were oxen, he was heard calling out, "Here they are! here they are, Charlotte, horns and all!"

The following anecdote, which exhibits King George III. in a most kindly character, belongs to Kew Palace. A person named Goupy attended as an assistant drawing-master at the palace of his royal Highness Frederick, Prince of Wales. When he was one day there, his Majesty George III., being then a very little boy, for some trifling fault was compelled to stand behind a chair as a prisoner. Goupy was ordered to go on with his drawing. "How can I," replied the artist, "make a drawing worthy the attention of your royal Highness when I see the young prince standing under your displeasure." "You may return to your seat, sir," said the good-natured Prince of Wales; "but remember that Goupy has released you." As Goupy grew old, he became infirm and poor; at the accession of George III. he was eighty-four. Soon after that period, walking in pensive mood and piteous plight on the Kensington Road, the royal carriage passed, and he pulled off his hat. The face of the old man caught the king's eye; he ordered the coach to stop, called the friendless artist to the door, and asked him how he went on. "Little enough, in truth," replied the old man, "little enough; but as I was so happy as to take your Majesty *out of prison*, I hope you will not suffer me to go into one." "Indeed I will not, my dear Goupy," replied the good-natured monarch, casting on the poor old man a look brightened with the tear of sympathy, "indeed I will not." And he immediately ordered him a handsome allowance weekly, which the forsaken artist enjoyed to the last day of his life.

The following anecdote of an incident which happened at Kew is quoted from "Our Great-grandmothers" in *Fraser's Magazine*:—"The beautiful Miss Port (her grand-niece and adopted child, and subsequently the mother of Lady Llanover), sitting one day writing in Mrs. Delany's drawing-room at the Lodge, heard a knock at the door; she of course inquired who was there. 'It is me,' replied a man's voice, somewhat ungrammatically; but grammar appears to have been much disdained in our great-grandmothers' days. '*Me* may stay where he is,' answered Miss Port; on which the knocking was repeated. '*Me* is imper-

tinent, and may go about his business,' reiterated the lady; but the unknown party persevering in a third knock, she rose to ascertain who was the intruder, and, to her dismay, found it was no other than King George himself she had been unwittingly addressing with so little ceremony. All she could utter was, 'What *shall* I say?' 'Nothing at all,' replied his Majesty; 'you *was* very right to be cautious who you admitted.' The royal disregard of grammar seemed to have furnished a precedent for that of the court and of society in general."

Here, like Dr. Johnson at Buckingham House, Dr. Beattie attended by command of George III., to be presented to his Majesty, after he had published his famous "Essay on Truth." "I never stole a book but once," said the kind-hearted king, "and that was yours: I stole it from the queen to give it to Lord Hertford to read." A more delicate and graceful compliment can scarcely be imagined.

Kew House, or the Old Palace, as it was afterwards called, was taken down in 1802-3. A building for a palace was commenced by George III. on a site near the Thames, in Richmond Gardens, but, as stated in a previous chapter, was never finished internally, although a large sum of money had been expended on the stone exterior. After the death of the king it was pulled down, and the materials sold piecemeal by his successor, George IV.

Mr. Martin F. Tupper writes:—"Kew was an abortive attempt at a palace; and the Fourth George scarcely ever did a better deed in all his life than when he pulled down to the ground that 'castellated structure of carpenter's Gothic.' Its exotic gardens, with the conservatories and all their choice natural treasures, may well be suffered to bloom on; 'whether every temple and ruin which Sir William Chambers created is equally worthy of perpetuity may be questioned; but one, at any rate, is appropriate, useful, and ornamental.'"

The house now called the Palace, but originally known as the Dutch House, is an old structure of red brick, probably built in the time of James I. by Sir Hugh Portman, the Dutch merchant, who is mentioned in a letter among the Sydney Papers, dated 1595, as "the rich gentleman who was knighted by her Majesty (Queen Elizabeth) at Kew." It is about 100 or 150 yards from the original palace, or Kew House, which the king inhabited, and is a solid substantial building, heavy and Dutch in style, with stabling on the one side and a court with out-quarters on the other. It is one of her Majesty's private possessions, and is now quite unoccupied, the lady who has charge of it for the queen living in a small house in the adjoining garden. It is three storeys in height. On the ground-floor are the old king's dining-room and drawing-room, and another small dining-room, which was used by the young princes. In some of the rooms the panelling and some ornamental fireplaces remain ; and here and there a few pieces of antiquated and lumbering furniture serve to recal the fact that less than a century ago these rooms had tenants. In one of the upper bed-rooms are still a few specimens of the ingenuity and industry of the princesses. The bed-room in which old Queen Charlotte died is at the top of the staircase on the second floor.

The whole place has an air of desolate grandeur. Till lately there was on the walls a small collection of pictures, but these were lately carried off by order of the queen to Buckingham Palace and Holyrood. The rooms in which the poor old king was confined by his physician, Dr. Willis, adjoined the central portion of the house, and were pulled down, by order of the queen, about the same time.

The adjacent grounds are quite flat and level, but are flanked on either side by fine trees. In hot and dry summers the outlines of the foundations of the old palace may be traced on the lawn in front.

The owner of the "Dairie House," Queen Caroline, when making her improvements in Richmond Gardens, in George II.'s reign, took a long lease of this house, which had not expired in 1781, in which year the freehold was purchased from the then proprietors, in trust for her Majesty Queen Charlotte, who had previously used it as a nursery for the royal offspring. Later on the house was called the Queen's Lodge ; and although the apartments are small and inconvenient, the retirement which it afforded made it a favourite place of residence with the younger branches of the family. It is not a little singular that all notice of Kew is omitted by Mr. Pyne in his magnificent and otherwise complete history of our royal residences. Over the doorway appears the date 1631, with the initials " F. S. C."

The present palace belonged to Richard Bennett, Esq., from whom it descended to the Capels, through the marriage of Dorothy, his daughter and heiress, with Sir Henry Capel, K.B., afterwards Lord Capel. Under date of March 24th, 1688, Evelyn writes, in his " Diary ":—" From thence we went to Kew, to visit Sir Henry Capel's, whose orangery and myrtetum are most beautiful, and perfectly well kept. He was contriving very high palisados of reeds to shade his oranges during the summer, and painting those reeds in oil."

Lady Capel survived him, and resided at Kew until her death, in 1721. The property next devolved on Samuel Molyneux, Esq., who had married Lord Capel's grand-niece. This gentleman was secretary to George II. before his accession to the throne, and resided here. He devoted himself to scientific studies, especially astronomy, and he erected a telescope with which, in 1725, Dr. Bradley, afterwards Astronomer-Royal, made the first observations which led to his great discoveries, and of which we shall have more to say presently. Mr. Molyneux died in the year 1728, and his widow married the notorious empiric, Nathaniel St. André (the patron of the infamous Mrs. Toft, the rabbit producer, of Godalming), who was accused of having hastened the death of Lady Elizabeth's first husband in order to marry her.

Mackay, in his " Tour through England," speaks of Mr. Molyneux's fine seat at Kew and excellent gardens, said to have been furnished with the best fruit trees in England, " collected by that great statesman and gardener, Lord Capel."

About 1730, Frederick, Prince of Wales, obtained a long lease of Kew House from the Capel family. After his death, in 1751, the Princess Dowager of Wales continued to reside here, and took great interest in the improvement of the gardens. George III. eventually bought the fee-simple of the estate from the Countess Dowager of Essex.

At this palace, in 1818, died Queen Charlotte, leaving whatever it was in her power to bequeath to her four unmarried daughters. " This," says the Hon. Miss Murray, in her " Recollections," " consisted principally of her jewels, for there was so little money that some of her personalty was sold to pay a few outstanding debts."

Throughout the metropolis and the country in general the indications of sorrow at the queen's death were unusually general and sincere. In consequence of the queen's declining health, two amendments had been made in the Regency Bill during the last session of Parliament : the first empowering her Majesty to add six new members, resident at Windsor, to her council, in the event of her absence from the palace ; and the second repealing the clause which rendered necessary the immediate assembling of a new Parliament in the event of the queen's death. These amendments were very opportunely made, as, after a lingering illness of six months, which was sustained with great fortitude and resignation, her Majesty expired at Kew Palace on the 17th of November, in the seventy-fifth year of her age. She had been blessed by nature with a sound and vigorous frame, having until within two years of her decease enjoyed an almost uninterrupted state of health. Her remains were interred in the royal vault at Windsor on the 2nd of December. George III. survived his queen only about fourteen weeks.

At Kew, the Prince of Wales, afterwards George IV., was educated, under the superintendence of Dr. Markham, afterwards Archbishop of York, and here the childhood and boyhood of the young Dukes of Cumberland, Sussex, and Cambridge, were chiefly spent.

o'clock, at which hour the queen was conducted into the drawing-room, and was followed by the Duke and Duchess of York, the Duke and Duchess of Cambridge, the Duchess of Gloucester, the Princess Augusta, the Princess Sophia of Gloucester, the Landgrave of Hesse-Cassel, the Duchess of Meiningen, the Lord Chancellor, the Earl of Liverpool, Viscount Sidmouth, Count and Countess Munster, &c. The Duke of Clarence and his intended bride, and the Duke and Duchess of Kent, being introduced into the room in due form,

KEW GREEN.

Here the Duke of Kent was re-married, July 11th, 1818, to the Princess Victoria of Saxe-Coburg, the mother of our most gracious Queen. A contemporary thus announces the double marriage of the two royal dukes, Clarence and Kent, on the same day :—"The most important circumstance we have to record since our last is the marriage of two of our princes, his royal Highness the Duke of Clarence and his royal Highness the Duke of Kent, which took place on Saturday, the 11th instant, when a temporary altar was fitted up in the queen's drawing-room, which looks into Kew Gardens, on the first floor. The royal pairs, other members of the royal family, and the persons who were to be present, had all arrived before four

and having taken their station at the altar, the Archbishop of Canterbury, assisted by the Bishop of London, performed the marriage ceremony." The scene of this special service was probably the drawing-room.

The king was constant in his attendance on both public and private worship. But in Miss Burney's "Diary" we read :—"There is no private chapel at Kew Lodge; the king and queen consequently, except by accident, as now, never pass the Sunday there. The form, therefore, stands thus :—Their majesties and the five princesses go into an inner room by themselves, furnished with hassocks, &c., like their closet at church. By the door of this room, though not within it, stands the clergyman at his desk, and here were assembled Mrs. Delany, Mr. and Mrs. Smelt, Miss Goldsworthy, Miss Gomme, Miss Planta, Mlle. Montmoulin, M. De Luc, and I. The pages were all arranged at the end of the room, and in an outer apartment were summoned all the servants, in rows according to their station."

It may be mentioned that the locks on the doors of the principal rooms in the palace are of brass, and engraved with the Prince of Wales's

palace, but at a distance of about 200 yards, is an old sun-dial, standing on a stone pedestal, at one end of which is a tablet thus inscribed :—

"On this spot, in 1725, the Rev. James Bradley made the first observations which led to his two great discoveries, the aberration of light and the nutation of the earth's axis. The telescope which he used had been erected by Saml. Molyneux, Esq., in a house which afterwards became the royal residence, and was taken out in 1803. To per-

KEW CHURCH—INTERIOR.

plumes, the Garter, and crown, and the initials F. P. W., for Frederick, Prince of Wales.

The following epigram, engraved on the collar of a dog which Pope gave to his Royal Highness Frederick, Prince of Wales, father of George III., has been often quoted, but may bear repetition here :—

> "I am his Highness' dog at Kew;
> Pray tell me, sir, whose dog are you?"

This is taken from Sir William Temple's "Heads designed for an Essay on Conversation." "Mr. Grantam's fool's reply to a great man that asked whose fool he was—'I am Mr. Grantam's fool —pray tell me whose fool are you?'"

On the lawn immediately in front of the present

petuate the memory of so important a station, this dial was placed on it in 1830, by command of his Most Gracious Majesty King William IV."

It seems, after this episode, quite according to the fitness of things that Kew should be the seat of the great observatory of which, probably, the Rev. James Bradley sounded the first note, just as Lord Capel's taste for gardening proved the germ of the Botanic Gardens, which we shall describe presently. The Observatory stands in the park, away from all other buildings about half-way between Kew and Richmond.

"The report of the Kew Committee for the year ending October 31st, 1879," says a daily contemporary, "has been published by the Royal

Society. It contains a statement of the work done in the two departments of magnetism and meteorology, and a notice of certain of the instruments. It appears that 196 barometers and 4,828 thermometers have been verified during the year. Besides these last, 53 deep sea thermometers have been tested, the great number of which were subjected, in the hydraulic press, without injury, to strains exceeding three and a half tons on the square inch." These figures may be taken as an average of the work done here annually.

The following is an extract from a paper by Mr. C. Murray, in the "Companion to the British Almanack" for 1884:—"The so-called Kew Observatory was built for George III. by Sir William Chambers, for the purpose of studying astronomical science, with special reference to the Transit of Venus in 1769. The situation is low, but otherwise well situated both for its original and its present work. It stands in the old Deer Park, Richmond, some little distance above Kew Gardens, near that part of the bend of the Thames which faces Isleworth, a little more than 900 feet from the water-side. . . . To show how characteristically isolated this building is from the ways of the world, the only open entrance to it is through a farmyard, and along an ankle-spraining 'prairie path' of cinder-slag, little more than a foot in breadth. The park is the property of the Crown, and the stewards of the Crown have well doubled the saying of 'no royal road to learning' by maintaining there shall be no 'royal road' to Kew and its science . . . . For many years Kew may be said to have quietly glided into a long winter of hybernation, being under the careful guardianship of a curator and reader. However, in 1841, Sir Robert Peel 'disestablished' it, and bestowed such instruments as it had among several learned bodies. The Royal Society, as a body, refused the building, from lack of funds in its corporate capacity; but several private members of that society and of the British Association, headed by Lord Northampton and Lord Francis Egerton, under sanction of the Government, raised subscriptions among scientific persons to establish a physical observatory, where it was decided that meteorology, electricity, and magnetism, were to form the subjects of observation. Much opposition was raised, and at one time it was proposed that the observatory should be closed and discontinued; but a committee of the leaders of the world of science—Herschel, Sabine, Wheatstone, and others—reported in favour of its maintenance, and accordingly it pursued for several years 'the even tenor of its way.' In 1855

the Board of Trade accepted its assistance with respect to meteorological work, and when, on the death of Admiral Fitzroy, the meteorological department of the Board of Trade was transferred to a committee nominated by the Royal Society, Kew was made a central station, from which outlying observatories at Aberdeen, Armagh, Falmouth, Glasgow, Stonyhurst, and Valentia, were controlled, its superintendent being their examiner and reporter. A grant placed at the disposal of the committee — now called the Meteorological Council—is the only sum of public money given for its support. In 1871 the annual grant of the British Association was withdrawn, and a sum of £10,000 being placed in trust in the hands of the Royal Society by Mr. Gassiot for the maintenance of its magnetic observations, it passed into the hands of a committee selected by that body." It would be impossible here to describe in minute detail the marine barometer—which serves also as a barometer on land—the thermometer, the hypsometer, the barograph, the thermograph, the anemometer, and the other instruments used here to work out the several branches of meteoric science practically. Enough to say that barometers, thermometers, sextants, &c., are tested here; that all instruments so verified leave the Kew Observatory with the letters " K. O." stamped upon them, and with a registered number. To our list of these instruments may be added the "Sunshine Recorder," which marks the number of hours and minutes during which the sun is visible. Mr. Murray thus describes it :—
" It is a sphere of glass mounted on a polar axis, which rests in a suitable framework and stand. This axis can be set to coincide with the polar one at the place of inclination, whilst a graduated circle will adjust it to its working latitude. The supporting frame has movable card-holders, adapted to receive straight cut strips of card all to fit, so that when one is done with another can be instantly put in its place. These cards are cut from Bristol board, tinted with Prussian blue, and divided into slips thirteen inches long by three-quarters of an inch wide. The large-sized card-holder is used in the instrument during the months of May, June, July, and August, and the smaller-sized during the rest of the year. Each ray of sunshine passing through the glass globe leaves its path along the card, and the hours are marked by a pencil from hour to hour." In fact, so perfect is the command of man over Nature, that it is a matter of common boast that almost without exaggeration the sun is now made to photograph his own face as he rises every morning !

The Crown obtained the patronage of Kew-cum-Petersham, by an exchange with the Provost and Fellows of King's College, Cambridge, in 1867. Service was performed at Kew in a small chapel as early as 1522 ; but it would seem that it was not till 1769 that Kew was separated from Kingston and constituted a distinct vicarage.

The present church stands on the open area of Kew Green, on a plot of ground granted by Queen Anne. It was built by subscription, headed by the queen, and was completed and consecrated as "the Chapel of St. Anne, of Kew Green," on the 12th of May, 1714. It then consisted of little more than a nave and north aisle, with a school-room on the south ; and after several alterations, as the population increased, its character was completely changed in the years 1837 and 1838, when it was enlarged into its present state, under the direction of Sir Jeffrey Wyattville. "This was accomplished," says the "New History of Surrey," "through the considerate munificence of his late Majesty, William the Fourth, who, on his last visit to Kew, in April, 1837, had the plans and estimates prepared by the architect submitted to him for approval ; and after his decease, on the 20th of June following, the requisite funds (amounting to nearly five thousand pounds) were found to have been scrupulously set apart by the king for the completion of the work." In reference to his intentions, the following inscription, dictated by himself, and engraven on brass, has been affixed to the front of the royal gallery :— "King William IV., in the year 1836, directed 200 free seats to be provided in this church at his expense, for the accommodation of the poor of the parish and of the children of the King's Free School, to be for ever appropriated to their use." The walls bear several very interesting monuments.

The royal gallery, at the western end of the church, contains seats for about sixty persons. It was originally built by George III. in 1805, and on the re-opening, the king, the queen, and nine princes and princesses, their children, attended divine service. In front, besides the inscription already given, are the arms of William IV., and several small hatchments of royalty, including those of the late Duke of Cambridge, and of Ernest, Duke of Cumberland, afterwards King of Hanover.

On the vestry walls hangs a series of prints—portraits of George III. and his numerous sons.

In a recess eastward of the altar (constructed for its reception) is a small richly-toned organ, which is said to have belonged to Handel, and was a favourite instrument of his Majesty George III.,

by whose successor (George IV.) it was presented to the church in 1823.

On the south wall of the church is a monument to Lady Capel, which ends with a hope that other persons will follow her steps. It is devoutly to be hoped that her steps were heavenward. On the north wall is a medallion profile of Sir William Hooker, erected by his nephew, Mr. Francis Palgrave.

A contemporary, in 1882, states that "the queen has promised a subscription of £100 towards the fund for the enlargement of the royal church at Kew. It is proposed to increase the accommodation to 737 sittings, and in every way to improve the church. The scheme has been unanimously approved at a public meeting of the inhabitants of Kew, presided over by the Duke of Cambridge, who has also subscribed £100. The subscription list further includes the names of the Duchess of Teck, and the Grand Duke and Duchess of Mecklenburgh-Strelitz. The work, it is estimated, will cost £5,500." The Princess Mary Adelaide of Teck also organised a morning concert at St. James's Hall in aid of the same object.

As a result of these subscriptions, a new chancel, with a mortuary chapel beyond it, with a dwarf cupola, in the Dutch or Queen Anne style, has been added (in 1883-4). In this mortuary chapel rests, above ground, the body of the late Duke of Cambridge ; room is left for other members of the family. The interior of the chancel will afford a spacious apsidal sacrarium. The "wagon" roof of the nave has been raised : and as the pews and seats will be also lowered, much height will be gained in the interior.

In this church, if we may accept the story in the *Monthly Magazine*, George III., then Prince of Wales, married Hannah Lightfoot, the fair Quakeress, of whom some mention will be found in the pages of OLD AND NEW LONDON."* Other versions, however, identify the locale of this apparently well-authenticated union with Dr. Keith's chapel in Curzon Street,† May Fair.

It is said—though the assertion is doubtful—that Queen Charlotte was so much grieved and shocked on finding out the relations which had existed between her husband and the fair Quakeress Hannah Lightfoot, that she insisted on being re-married in 1765, the ceremony being performed in the presence of Lord Chatham at Kew by the Rev. Dr. Wilmot, whose daughter became the wife of Henry Frederick, Duke of Cumberland, and the mother of the Princess Olivia of Cumberland.

---

* See Vols. IV., p. 207 ; V., pp. 27, 477 ; VI., p. 289.
† See "Old and New London," Vol. IV., pp. 347, 349.

For many years there was no monument in the church to Gainsborough; but in 1875 a mural tablet was erected to his memory on the south wall by Mr. E. M. Ward, R.A. There are monuments in the church to the Aitons and to Mr. Bauer.

The churchyard, which is merely separated from the green by a dwarf wall, is crowded with tombs. Here, in kindred graves, lie Meyer, Zoffany, and Gainsborough, the painters—the latter one of the founders of the English school. Here, too, rest Joshua Kirby, the architect, father of the famous Mrs. Trimmer;* William Aiton, the gardener, of whom we shall have more to say on reaching Kew Gardens; Francis Bauer, the microscopist; &c.

Kew has been the burial-place of a few noted individuals. Zoffany, the portrait painter, was interred here in 1810. He was a native of Germany, and came when young to seek his fortune in England. Under the powerful patronage of the Earl of Barrymore, who was a leader of fashion, he soon found his way to fame. We found Zoffany at Strand-on-the-Green and at Brentford.† Zoffany lived in a cottage at Strand-on-the-Green, and here he would entertain his friends, much to the disgust of his wife, who doted on her home and her nursery, and hated strangers. One of his most celebrated pictures is a group of the members of the Royal Academy assembled in their hall, near St. Martin's Lane, on a drawing night, with portraits of West, Reynolds, Chambers, Bartolozzi, &c.

At the invitation of the Grand Duke, he visited Florence, where he met the emperor, who, admiring his works, asked him his name. Zoffany told him. "What countryman are you?" asked the emperor. "An Englishman," was the reply. "Why, it sounds German," said the emperor. "True, sir," answered the artist; "I was born in Germany, but that was an accident. I call that my country which has given me shelter and protection."

Near Zoffany's tomb other of his relatives are buried, and not far off is the grave of Mr. R. Ford, "Genealogist." Another artist buried here is Jeremiah Meyer, R.A.; he, too, like Zoffany, was a German, a native of Tubingen, in the Duchy of Wirtemberg. Born in 1735, he came to England at fourteen, and studied art with great success under Zincke. He was for many years "Painter in Miniature and Enamel to George III."

He died in June, 1789. On the north wall of the church is a tablet to his memory, showing the Muse of Painting in mournful contemplation beneath his medallion bust in white marble. It bears the following lines from the pen of Hayley:—

"Meyer! in thy works the world will ever see
How great the loss of Art in losing thee.
But Love and Sorrow find their words too weak,
Nature's keen sufferings on thy death to speak.
Through all her duties what a heart was thine!
In this cold dust what spirit used to shine!

"Fancy, and Truth, and Gaiety, and Zeal,
What most we love in life, and losing feel,
Age after age may not one artist yield
Equal to thee in Painting's nicer field;
And ne'er shall sorrowing earth to heaven commend
A fonder parent or a truer friend."

It must be owned that the feeling which prompted these lines does Hayley more credit than the lines themselves, which scarcely rise above commonplace.

In the churchyard lies Thomas Gainsborough, the well-known landscape artist. His tomb having fallen into decay, it was repaired and restored, and surrounded with a light iron railing, the inscription being at the same time re-cut, at the cost of the late Mr. E. M. Ward, R.A., a few years ago. The inscription states that Thomas Gainsborough died August 22nd, 1788, aged 62, and that his wife, Margaret, who lies beside him, died December, 1798, aged 71. Gainsborough was a most accomplished man, being not only the best landscape painter of his time, but scarcely inferior even to Sir Joshua Reynolds as a painter of portraits.

Thomas Gainsborough was born at Sudbury, Suffolk, in 1727, and while at school in his native town began to develop that artistic talent which in the end raised him to the highest pinnacle of fame. In his twelfth year he already began painting landscapes. Two years later he came to London, and became the pupil of Francis Hayman, who, like himself, was one of the original members of the Royal Academy. At nineteen he began painting portraits on his own account, and settled first at Ipswich, and afterwards at Bath, where he began painting portraits at the low price of five guineas for a three-quarter canvas, but was soon so successful as to be encouraged to raise his price to eight guineas. In 1774 he returned to London, and found an early friend and admirer in Reynolds. This was the more generous, as he was to some extent the rival of Sir Joshua himself. His last prices in London were forty guineas for a half, and one hundred guineas for a full length.

Gainsborough was liberal and hospitable to an excess; but he had a terribly shrewish and stingy wife, about whom many amusing anecdotes are related in Angelo's "Reminiscences." He was a great favourite with King George III., who preferred him as a portrait painter even to

Sir Joshua Reynolds, and who used often to say, "I hope you have not entirely left off landscape painting."

No object was too mean for Gainsborough's pencil; his habit of closely observing things in their several particulars enabled him to perceive their relations to each other, and combine them. By painting at night, he acquired new perceptions: he had eyes and saw, and he secured every advantage he discovered. He etched three plates: one for "Kirby's Perspective;" another an oak tree with gipsies; and the third, a man ploughing on a rising ground, which he spoiled in "biting in." The print is rare.

In portraits he strove for natural character, and when this was attained, seldom proceeded farther. He could have imparted intelligence to the features of the dullest, but he disdained to elevate what nature had forbidden to rise; hence, if he painted a butcher in his Sunday coat, he made him, as he looked, a respectable yeoman; but his likenesses were chiefly of persons of the first quality, and he maintained their dignity. His portraits are seldom highly finished, and are not sufficiently estimated, for the very reason whereon his reputation for natural scenery is deservedly high. Sir Joshua gave Gainsborough one hundred guineas for a picture of a girl and pigs, though its artist required only sixty.

Gainsborough had what the world calls eccentricities. They resulted rather from his indulgence in study than from contempt for the usages of society. It was well for Gainsborough that he could disregard the courtesies of life without disturbance to his happiness from those with whom manners are morals.

He derived his grace and elegance from nature rather than manners; and hence his paintings are inimitably true and bewitching.

Gainsborough resembles Watteau in his landscapes. His pictures are generally wrought in a loose and slight manner, with great freedom of hand, and using very little colour, with a great body of vehicle, which gives to his works great lightness and looseness of effect, properties extremely valuable in a picture, and too easily lost in the endeavour to give more strict and positive resemblance of substance. Sir Joshua Reynolds, in his fourteenth lecture, says of this hatching manner of Gainsborough, that his portraits were often little more than what generally attends a dead colour as to finishing or determining the form of the features; but "as he was always attentive to the general effect or whole together, I have often imagined (says he) that this unfinished

manner contributed even to that striking resemblance for which his portraits are so remarkable. At the same time, it must be acknowledged that there is one evil attending this mode: that if the portrait were seen previously to any knowledge of the original, different persons would form different ideas, and all would be disappointed at not finding the original correspond with their own conceptions, under the great latitude which indistinctness gives to the imagination to assume almost what character or form it pleases."

In the same lecture, which principally treats of the acquirements of Gainsborough, and which was delivered at the Royal Academy soon after his death by its truly exalted president, it is said of him, "that if ever this nation should produce genius sufficient to acquire to us the honourable distinction of an English school, the name of Gainsborough will be transmitted to posterity in the history of the art among the first of that rising name.

"Whether he most excelled in portraits, landscapes, or fancy pictures, it is difficult to determine: whether his portraits were most admirable for exact truth of resemblance, or his landscapes for a portrait-like representation of nature, such as we see in the works of Rubens, Ruysdael, or others of these schools. In his fancy pictures, when he had fixed upon his object of imitation, whether it was the mean and vulgar form of a wood-cutter or a child of an interesting character, as he did not attempt to raise the one, so neither did he lose any of the natural grace and elegance of the other: such a grace and such an elegance as are more frequently found in cottages than in courts. This excellence was his own, the result of his particular observation and taste. For this he was certainly not indebted to any school; for his grace was not academical or antique, but selected by himself from the great school of nature, where there are yet a thousand modes of grace unselected, but which lie open in the multiplied scenes and figures of life, to be brought out by skilful and faithful observers.

"Upon the whole, we may justly say that whatever he attempted he carried to a high degree of excellence. It is to the credit of his good sense and judgment that he never did attempt that style of historical painting for which his previous studies had made no preparation."

Nothing could have enabled Gainsborough to reach so elevated a point in the art of painting had he not had the most ardent love for it. Indeed, his whole mind appears to have been devoted to it, even to his dying day, and then his principal regret seemed to be that he was leaving his art, when, as he said, "he saw his deficiencies, and had endeavoured to remedy them in his last works." Various circumstances in his life exhibited him as referring everything to it. "He was continually remarking to those who happened to be about him whatever peculiarity of counte-

pieces of looking-glass, which he magnified, and improved into rocks, trees, and water: all which exhibit the solicitude and extreme activity that he had about everything relative to his art; that he wished to have his objects embodied as it were, and distinctly before him, neglecting nothing that contributed to keep his faculties alive, and deriving

GAINSBOROUGH.
(From the Original Picture, painted by himself, in the Council Room of the Royal Academy.)

nance, whatever accidental combination of figures, or happy effects of light and shadow, occurred in prospects, in the sky, in walking the streets, or in company. If in his walks he found a character that he liked, and whose attendance was to be obtained, he ordered him to his house; and from the fields he brought into his painting-room stumps of trees, weeds, and animals of various kinds, and designed them not from memory, but immediately from the objects. He even framed a kind of model of landscapes on his table, composed of broken stones, dried herbs, and

hints from every sort of combination." He was also in the constant habit of painting by night, a practice very advantageous and improving to an artist, for by this means he may acquire a new and a higher perception of what is great and beautiful in nature. His practice, in the progress of his pictures, was to paint on the whole together; wherein he differed from some, who finish each part separately, and by that means are frequently liable to produce inharmonious combinations of forms and features.

Gainsborough was one of the few artists of

eminence this country has produced who was indebted to foreign travel for his improvement and advancement in painting. Some use, indeed, he appears to have made of foreign productions; and he did not neglect to improve himself in the language of the art—the art of imitation—but aided his progress by closely observing and imitating some of the masters of the Flemish school, who are, undoubtedly, the greatest in that particular and necessary branch of it. He frequently made copies of Rubens, Teniers, and Vandyke, which it would be no disgrace to the most accurate con-

Hardcastle's *Somerset House Gazette*, shows how accurate Gainsborough was in his execution:— "There resided in the same neighbourhood with Gainsborough's father a respectable clergyman, named Coyte. With the sons of this clergyman young Gainsborough and his brothers passed much of their time. . . . The parson's garden having been plundered of a great quantity of wall fruit, much pains were taken, but without effect, to discover the thief. Young Gainsborough having, one summer morning, risen at an early hour, and walked into the garden to make a sketch from an old elm, seated himself in an obscure corner, and had just taken out his chalk to begin, when he observed a fellow's head peeping over the wall of the garden next the road, apparently to 'see if the coast was clear.' Upon a rough board he made a sketch of the head of

KEW CHURCH—EXTERIOR.

GAINSBOROUGH'S TOMB.

noisseurs to mistake for original pictures at first sight. What he thus learned he did not, however, servilely use, but applied it to imitate nature in a manner entirely his own.

The subjects he chose for representation were generally very simple, to which his own excellent taste knew how to give expression and value. In his landscapes, a rising mound, and a few figures seated upon or near it, with a cow or some sheep grazing, and a slight marking of distance, sufficed for the objects: their charm was the purity of tone in the colour, the freedom and clearness of the touch, together with an agreeable combination of the forms; and with these simple materials, which appear so easy as to be within every one's grasp, but which constantly elude the designer who is not gifted with his feeling and taste, does he always produce a pleasing picture. In his fancy pictures the same taste prevailed. A cottage girl, a shepherd's boy, a woodman, with very slight materials in the background, were treated by him with so much character and elegance that they never fail to delight.

The following anecdote, taken from Ephraim

the man; and so accurate was the likeness that he was instantly known to be a man from a neighbouring village, who, on closer inquiry, proved to be the very fellow who had robbed the garden."

Gainsborough was a man of great generosity. If he took as model an infant from a cottage, all the family generally participated in the profits of the picture, and some of them frequently found a home in his house. Needy relatives and unfortunate friends always received help from him. There were other traits in his personal character less amiable. He was very capricious in his manners, and rather fickle and unsteady in his social connections. This was sufficiently evinced by his general conduct towards the Royal Academy, and by his whimsical behaviour to Sir Joshua Reynolds. Soon after he settled in London, Sir Joshua thought himself bound in civility to pay him a visit. Gainsborough, however, took not the least notice of him for several years, but at length called upon him, and requested him to sit for his picture. Sir Joshua complied, and sat once, but being soon after taken ill, was obliged to go to Bath for his health. On his return to London, perfectly restored, he sent Gainsborough word that he was returned. Gainsborough only replied that he was glad to hear that Sir Joshua Reynolds was well; but never afterwards desired him to sit.

When the Royal Academy was founded, Gainsborough was chosen among the first members; but being then resident at Bath, he was too far distant to be employed in the business of the institution. When he came to London, his conduct was so disrespectful to the members of the Royal Academy that he never complied with their invitations, whether official or convivial. In 1784 he sent to the exhibition a whole-length portrait, which he ordered to be placed almost as low as the floor; but as this would have been a violation of the bye-laws of the Academy, the gentlemen of the council ventured to remonstrate with him upon the impropriety of such a disposition. Gainsborough returned for answer that if they did not choose to hang the picture as he wished, they might send it back, which they did immediately. He soon after made an exhibition of his works at his own house, which did not, however, afford the expected gratification; and after this circumstance he never again exhibited.

Among his amusements, music was almost as much his favourite as painting. This passion led him to cultivate the intimacy of all the great musical professors of his time (one of whom, Fischer, married his daughter); and they, by their abilities, obtained an ascendency over him greater than was perhaps consistent with strict prudence. Of Gainsborough's musical performance some have spoken highly. His biographer, Mr. Jackson, however, says, that though possessed of ear, taste, and genius, he never had application enough to learn his notes.

Of the former, Angelo observes that "the circumstances of his life were as various as the style, manner, and practice of his art. Some of his humours, however," he adds, "were as nearly allied to tomfoolery as those of his superiors in rank who were the subject of his sarcastic remarks."

Sir George Beaumont relates that Gainsborough had an uncontrollable propensity for laughing; so much so, that at times, when painting grave portraits, he was obliged to deprecate the sitters from taking offence.

Barry and Gainsborough, at one period, were intimate friends. They used occasionally to compare notes, and laugh at the affectation and whimsicalities of the higher orders.

Many anecdotes of both Gainsborough and Zoffany are to be found scattered up and down the amusing "Reminiscences of Henry Angelo."

The story of Gainsborough's death-bed has been often told, but it will bear telling again. He died at Schomberg House, in Pall Mall, on the 2nd August, 1788.* Reynolds in some way or other had previously offended him; but when Gainsborough found that his end was approaching, he sent for Sir Joshua, who came across from Leicester Fields without delay, and, full of emotion, heard the last words of his friend, "We are all going to heaven, and Vandyck is of the company."

Gainsborough's death was caused by a cancer. He knew that death was approaching, and he prepared himself for his end with cheerfulness and composure. He desired to be "buried near his friend Kirby in Kew churchyard, and that his name only should be cut on his tombstone." He died August 2nd, 1788, in his sixty-first year.

A handsome tablet, designed by Mr. F. T. Palgrave, has been placed at the eastern end of the church, to the memory of his uncle, Sir William J. Hooker, Director of the Royal Gardens, who died in 1865, and of whom we shall have more to say in the next chapter.

On a flat stone at the entrance of the church, under the porch, is the following curious epitaph:—

"Here lyeth the bodys of Robert and Anna Plaistow, late of Tyso, near Edg. Hill; died August 28th, 1728.

"At Tyso they were born and bred,
And in the same good lives they led,
Until they came to marriage state,
Which was to them most fortunate.
Near sixty years of mortal life
They were a happy man and wife.
And being so by nature tied,
When one fell sick the other died;
And both together laid in dust,
To wait the rising of the just.
They had six children born and bred,
And five before them being dead,
Their only one surviving son
Has caused this stone for to be done."

George III. lived at Kew so long, and on such intimate terms with his neighbours, that plenty of stories are still current about the "Farmer King." Here, for instance, is one which shows that he valued those who were not ashamed to follow the dictates of their consciences. When the king was repairing his palace, one of the workmen, who was a pious man, was particularly noticed by his

---

Majesty, and he often held conversations with him of some length upon serious subjects. One Monday morning the king went, as usual, to watch the progress of the work, and not seeing this man in his customary place, inquired the reason of his absence. He was answered evasively, and for some time the other workmen avoided telling his Majesty the truth; at last, however, upon being more strictly interrogated, they acknowledged that, not having been able to complete a particular job on the Saturday night, they had returned to finish it on the following morning. This man alone had refused to comply, because he considered it a violation of the Christian Sabbath; and, in consequence of what they called his obstinacy, he had been dismissed entirely from his employment. "Call him back immediately!" exclaimed the king. "The man who refused doing his ordinary work on the Lord's Day is the man for me. Let him be sent for, and brought back again."

Here is another story, which reflects equal credit on the king :—In the severe winter of 1784-5, his majesty, regardless of the weather, was taking a solitary walk on foot, when he was met by two boys, the elder not eight years of age, who, although ignorant that it was the king, fell upon their knees before him, and, wringing their little hands, prayed for relief. "The smallest relief," they cried; "for we are very hungry, and have nothing to eat." The father of his people raised the weeping supplicants, and encouraged them to proceed with their story. They did so, and related that their mother had been dead three days, and still lay unburied; that their father, whom they were also afraid of losing, was stretched by her side upon a bed of straw, in a sick and hopeless condition; and that they had neither money, food, nor firing, at home. This artless tale was more than sufficient to excite the king's sympathy. He, therefore, at once ordered the boys to proceed homeward, and followed them until they reached a wretched hovel. There he found the mother dead, apparently through the want of common necessaries; the father ready to perish also, but still encircling with his feeble arm the deceased partner of his woes, as if unwilling to survive her. The sensibility of the monarch betrayed itself in the tears which started from his eyes, and leaving all the cash he had with him, he hastened back to the palace, related to the queen what he had witnessed, and sent an immediate supply of provisions, clothes, coals, and everything necessary for the comfort of the helpless family. Revived by the bounty of his sovereign, the poor man soon recovered, and the king, to finish the good work so kindly begun, educated and provided for the children.

The Rev. Richard Burgh Byam, who held the joint livings of Kew and Petersham for a period of forty years, commenced life as a private tutor at Eton, and was for several years occupied in classical tuition. In 1816 he went out to Antigua to take possession of the property known as "Byams," which came to him from his elder brother, William Martin Byam; he resided there five or six years, and was some time a member of council. On his return to England he was appointed tutor of King's College, Cambridge, and soon afterwards one of the Whitehall preachers, and an Examiner in Classics at Cambridge. In 1827 he was presented by his college to a living in Devon, which he exchanged in the following year for the united benefices of Kew and Petersham.

During his residence at Kew, Mr. Byam was introduced to various members of the royal family, and became an especial favourite with the late Dukes of Cumberland, Cambridge, and Sussex, by the latter of whom he was appointed domestic chaplain. In 1852 he removed from Kew to Petersham, appointing a curate in residence at the former parish, but still maintaining the friendship of the royal family, and his personal influence as vicar. Mr. Byam died in 1867, at the age of 82. The Duchess of Cambridge, the Duke, and the Princess Mary (at whose marriage with the Prince Teck he acted as one of the officiating clergy), entertained a most sincere regard for him to the very last.

The National Orphan Home at Petersham, of which we have already spoken, was one of those public institutions in whose welfare Mr. Byam was especially interested, and its foundation was in a great measure due to his practical charity and influence. In private life he was no less beloved than in his ministerial character.

Amongst other celebrities connected with the village of Kew was Stephen Duck, the author of the lines inscribed on Joe Miller's tombstone in St. Clement Danes. He was born here, and was in early life employed as a thresher on a farm in the village, when, having picked up a smattering of learning, he turned rhymester, and attracted the notice of Queen Caroline, the wife of George II., who settled on him a small pension, made him one of the Yeomen of the Guard, and, as we have seen in a previous chapter,* installed him as keeper of Merlin's Cave. The queen further procured his admission into holy orders, and appointed him minister of Byfleet, in Surrey, where he became a

---

popular preacher, the lower orders being attached to him as "the Thresher Parson."

Duck's head was at length turned by the folly of the Court party, who set him up as a rival to Pope; but not finding the world formed so high an estimate of his poetry as he did himself, he fell into a morbid, melancholy state, and died by his own hand—drowning himself at Reading—a victim to his vanity and to disappointed ambition.

After his best fortune, Duck's friends cautioned him against becoming vain. He said he did not well understand what was meant; and being told it was that he should not speak too highly in favour of his own poems, he replied, "If that was all, he was safe : that was a thing he could never do, for he could not think highly of them. Gentlemen, indeed, might like them, because they were made by *a poor fellow in a barn ;* but he knew as well as anybody that they were not really good in themselves."

Another unhappy story is that of Caleb Colton, some time vicar of Kew and Petersham, one of those eccentric parsons who were met with oftener, it may be hoped, in the days of George IV. than now, and of whom we have already had occasion to speak in our account of Petersham.[*]

Colton was the author of "Lacon, or Many Things in Few Words." In that book he writes : —"The gamester, if he die a martyr to his profession, is doubly ruined. He adds his soul to every other loss; and by the act of suicide renounces earth to forfeit heaven." Yet the man who wrote that awful sentence was himself a gamester. Though a beneficed clergyman, and a man of acute and cultivated mind, he spent a great part of his time in the gambling "hells" of London, until he fled, in order to avoid his creditors; afterwards he became a regular frequenter of the gambling-houses of Paris, often winning large sums of money.

He did not care to live at Kew, as he would have to keep up a house and the character of a clergyman, and he thought it pleasanter to live a bachelor life in Prince's Street, London. "It was too expensive to keep up proper appearances in his parish," writes Mr. Cyrus Redding, in his "Recollections"; and Mr. Redding continues :— "He could live in London unobserved for a sixth of the expense, and he acted accordingly, transporting his gun and fishing-rod, and half-a-dozen books, De Foe's 'History of the Devil' among them, to a two pair of stairs lodging overlooking the burying-ground of St. Anne's, Soho. I had

once visited him at Kew on a Sunday, in time for the morning service. The congregation was not large. The Duke and Duchess of Cumberland were present. The sermon was above the average in matter, and correctly delivered, with a slight touch of mannerism. We were leaving the church when a servant of the Duke of Cumberland came up, and said his royal Highness wished to see him. I walked on. I saw the duke and duchess cross the green to Kew—where was the parson? Presently he returned at a quick rate. 'What did the duke want of you?'

"'Nothing of moment—an invitation to dine with him at Kew on Wednesday.'

"'How uncanonical you are—you went into the pulpit in grey trousers. I wonder if the duke remarked it? You will have a rebuke from the bishop. Half a man's importance in courtly eyes centres on costume.'

"'I don't care; the duke might have seen it—he might tell me of it. What then?—I should reply, your royal Highness will have the goodness to remember that the efficacy of the sermon of a Christian clergyman does not depend on the colour of his breeches.'"

Mr. Redding draws the following picture of Mr. Colton's lodgings in London :—"His sitting-room was carpetless; a common deal table stood in the centre, and a broken phial placed in a tea-saucer served for an inkstand, surrounded with letter covers and paper scraps. Four common chairs, one or two rickety, a side table holding a few books, half a quire of foolscap paper, and some discarded pens, on one side of the room, composed nearly all the furniture, fishing-rods and gun excepted. Here he indited 'Lacon.' His copy was written on scraps of paper, blank sides of letters, and but rarely on bran-new paper. It is untrue that his rooms were as bad as some penny-a-line scribbler made out in a newspaper sketch of him. They were always clean. . . . . He dined at an eating-house, and sometimes cooked a chop for himself, from inveterate bachelor habits. He placed excellent wine on the table, though he had not then opened a wine-cellar, which he did afterwards in the name of another person, under a Methodist chapel in Dean Street, Soho, where I once found him among casks and sawdust. Descending the steps, he called out, 'Come down— *facilis descensus Averni !*' There I tasted some of his choice growths. He was a temperate man in wine, but very choice.

"'You have methodism, heterodoxy, over your head, Colton. I wonder your wine does not turn sour, belonging as it does to a son of the Church.'

---

* See *ante,* p. 325.

" 'Wine is reconciling, Redding ; there is no fear of the two doxies disagreeing in the cellar. The pulpit is the place for pulling caps.'

" This wine-dealing fit did not last long—he was soon tired of it. There was much of the spoiled child in his composition, going from thing to thing and unsettled. He published all sorts of things in rapid succession : now a poem on ' Hypocrisy,' another on the ' Burning of Moscow,' a Latin version of Gray's ' Elegy,' and last of all, his ' Lacon.'

" Though fond of a Bohemian life, still he was no associate of low characters, of the ignorant and vulgar, but he would steal into a house where there were public tables, and play, where he probably knew no one, as he played against the tables from pure avarice. His gambling here was in Spanish bonds, by which he thought he had ruined himself when he had not, and in the alarm embarked for America. He next returned to France. Then he came over to England, and appeared for a moment at Kew, to prevent the lapsing of the living from his college, which, however, soon after appointed his successor. He went again to France, where he is said to have cleared £25,000 by gambling ; and then—strange to say—blew out his brains at Fontainebleau. This was in 1832. Such was the end of the man who, when reproached with being no credit to his clerical profession, replied, most laconically, ' Oh, we parsons, after all, are only finger-posts ! ' "

Graham, in a letter to Cyrus Redding, says :— " Have you heard of Colton ? He is missing. ' *Absit, excessit, evasit !*' . . . Empty is thy pulpit, O Kew ! and the voice of the preacher shall no more be heard in thy high places."

A pleasanter memory is that of James Thomson, the poet.* It was here, at the residence of his old friend, Mr. James Robertson, surgeon to the royal household, that Thomson first met with his " Amanda," a daughter of a Captain Gilbert Young, from Dumfries-shire. The lady, however, never became his wife.

D'Israeli tells us, in his " Curiosities of Literature," that amid the severity of his philanthropic labours and studies, Granville Sharp found social recreation in keeping here on the Thames a barge, which was frequented by his friends, who were hospitably received and entertained on board of it. His little voyages to Putney, to Richmond, &c., and the literary intercourse which they fostered, were singularly happy events, and added much to his popularity.

* See *ante*, p. 384.

Sir Arthur Helps, the distinguished essayist, lived for some years in one of the queen's houses on Kew Green. On the north side of the green Sir Peter Lely had a copyhold house, in which some of his family were still remaining about the middle of the last century, but it has long ago been pulled down.

A large mansion on Kew Green, once belonging to the King of Hanover, is now a herbarium attached to the royal gardens. It contains a library of botanical works—in that special branch of science, it is believed, the finest in the world. The Duke of Cumberland was by far the least popular of all the sons of George III., and the unpopularity which attended him in public life followed him to his country-house at Kew. He took no interest in the parish or in his neighbours, and they cared as little for him as he did for them. His chief friends, or rather acquaintances, were Lord Eldon and Sir Charles Wetherell, who used to dine with him here, and with whom he shared those high Tory ideas which were so little in harmony with the spirit of the nineteenth century. Besides, there had long clung to him an ugly rumour that he had assaulted his valet, and tried to take his life, not wholly in self-defence. He lived on at Kew till the death of his brother, King William, when he went off post haste to Hanover, to claim the crown of that kingdom, which, by its laws, could not devolve on a female. The English nation were heartily glad when the marriage of Queen Victoria and the birth of the Princess Royal and the Prince of Wales rendered it, humanly speaking, most improbable that the duke should ever succeed to our throne. His house at Kew was, and is, a dull, heavy structure, and one which always wore a sinister and forbidding look.

Among other lesser stars of the Tory party, Theodore Hook, as the editor of *John Bull*, was honoured with the special notice of the late Duke. At his royal highness's small Sunday dinners at Kew he was for years an almost constant attendant, in company with a few other stout *Brunswickers* of the same school of opinion. The duke was a great musician, a member of the Glee and Catch Club, &c. His concerts at Kew Palace, however, were very unpopular, because only German performers were employed. As King of Hanover he took the side of repression, and was not much beloved by his subjects. He rarely visited England after his accession to the Hanoverian throne. He died in 1851.

At one time, indeed, there was an Orange plot to change the succession, by placing the duke on the throne of England; but this was brought to the light of day by Mr. Joseph Hume, and the affair was hushed up.

The Honourable Amelia Murray writes thus, in her amusing "Recollections":—

"It was about this time (1815) that Sellis, an Italian servant, concealed himself in the Duke of Cumberland's bed-room, and tried to assassinate him. The man rushed back to his own room and cut his throat when he found that he had not

" Scarce half I seem to live, dead more than half.
Oh dark, dark, dark, amid the blaze of noon ;
Incurably dark, total eclipse
Without all hope of day ! "

Cambridge Cottage, on Kew Green, belongs to her Royal Highness the Duchess of Cambridge. It is a plain brick building, partly screened from the roadway by an ivy-covered wall, and the entrance is by a *porte cochère* extending across the footway. It contains some pleasant rooms, and the

CAMBRIDGE COTTAGE, KEW GREEN.

succeeded in killing his master. I know there have been a great many cruel insinuations upon these points : it is my belief that they are wholly false. The man Sellis was always an ill-looking fellow ; he might have his reasons for determining to wreak his vengeance upon the duke, who, being the most unpopular member of the royal family, was accused of many actions worse than those of which he was really guilty."

Here Prince George of Cumberland, afterwards the blind King of Hanover, was born. His queen paid a visit to the spot of her husband's birth when she was in England in June, 1853. The king would have accompanied her, but, alas ! he could only exclaim with Milton—

grounds are well laid out ; but neither externally nor internally does it offer material for further remark.

The venerable Francis Bauer, whose name and talents are indelibly associated with the Botanic Gardens at Kew, long occupied a house on Kew Green, and died there in 1840. He was remarkably skilful in microscopic investigations, and talented as an artist in representing the most minute details both of vegetable and anatomical structure. A native of Felsburg, in Austria, he was, by the generous liberality of Sir Joseph Banks, and with the sanction of his Majesty, permanently attached as a draughtsman to the establishment at Kew. Sir Joseph took upon himself the payment of his salary, not only during his own life, but also, by a provision in his will, for its continuance until the death of Mr. Bauer.

It is worth a passing note that photography was discovered at Kew, for, according to the "New History of Surrey," "M. Nièpce, sen., the original discoverer of the photographic art, afterwards advanced to perfection (but by entirely new processes, and under different views) by Daguerre, and thence called the 'Daguerreotype,' resided at

entertainment, 14 August, 1594, drawn up, apparently, by Sir John's steward. It enumerates, under seventeen heads, things to be considered if her majesty should come to my lord's house."

Rowland White, in a letter to Sir Robert Sydney, dated in 1595, and published in the "Sydney State Papers," writes thus:—"On Thursday, her majestie dined at Kew, my lord keeper's house. Her entertainment for that meal was great and exceed-

KEW BRIDGE.

Kew in 1827; and in the month of December in that year he submitted a paper on the result of his experiments, with several sketches on metal, to the Royal Society, by the intervention of Mr. Bauer. His communications, however, made but little impression at the time upon that learned body."

Sir George Jessel, some time Master of the Rolls, was at a private school at Kew before entering at University College, London.

Sir John Puckering, Lord Keeper of the Great Seal in the reign of Elizabeth, was an inhabitant of Kew, and here he appears to have entertained Her Majesty, since in the Harleian Library at the British Museum is a manuscript, entitled, "Remembrances for furnyture at Kew, and for her majestie's

ing costly; at her first lighting, she had a fine fanne, with a handle garnisht with diamonds. When she was in the middle way, between the garden gate and the house, there came running towards her one with a nosegay in his hand, delivered yt unto her with a short, well-pened speech; it had in yt a very rich jewell, with many pendants of unfirled diamonds, valued at £400 at least; after dinner, in her privy chamber, he gave her a faire paire of virginals. In her bedroom, he presented her with a fine gown and juppin, which things were pleasing to her highnes; and to grace his lordship the more, she, of herself, tooke from a salt, a spoone, and a forke of faire agate."

"It must be confessed," quietly and quaintly

remarks Miss Aikin, "that this was a most usual mode of gracing a courtier peculiarly consonant to the disposition of her Majesty." She might have been pardoned if she had said that it looked very much more like a bit of freebooting, or "levying black mail," than an act of grace. Her Majesty, in fact, seems to have been just as ready to carry off some of the family plate here as she showed herself at Nonsuch.*

In the "Index Villaris," published in 1700, Kew figures as a place containing the seats of a knight, a baronet, and more than "three gentlemen of coat-armour," that is, esquires.

In Kew Lane, there is, or was lately, an inn known by the sign of "The Pilgrim." Mr. Larwood tells us that "in 1833, a figure of a pilgrim was placed on the roof of this house, which by concealed machinery was made to move to and fro, like the Wandering Jew, doomed to wander up and down until the end of the world; it was, however," he adds, "of contemptible workmanship, and very soon got out of order." The name of the inn, however, remains.

The Thames hereabouts can scarcely be better pictured than by Tennyson's lines :—

"A slow broad stream,
That, stirred with languid pulses of the oar,
Waves all its lazy lilies, and creeps on,
Barge-laden, to three arches of a bridge
Crowned with the minster towers."

"That many-winding river" is an epithet used by Shelley of an imagined stream, but might easily be applied to the "silver-winding" Thames, as it bends in graceful curves from east to west, or, as

here, from north to south. The poet perhaps had the Thames in view when he wrote :—

"A swan was there,
Beside a sluggish stream among the reeds:
It rose at his approach, and with strong wings."

The original Kew Bridge was built about the year 1757, by Robert Tunstall, gent., the owner of a ferry between Brentford and Kew. It consisted of eleven arches, partly of brick and partly of stone. In 1782, Robert Tunstall, Esq., the son of the above, applied to Parliament for authority to build a new bridge in place of that put up by his father, and which required extensive repairs. In the same year an Act was passed under which the present bridge was built, from the designs of Mr. Payne. It consists of seven arches of stone, spanning the river, and several small arches of brick on the low ground of the Surrey shore. There is much simplicity in the design, and the effect of the bridge from the water is good, but the curve is too high, and the approaches, in consequence, too steep.

In 1873 Kew bridge was opened free to the public, the rights in the bridge having been bought over by the joint committee of the Corporation of London and the Metropolitan Board of Works. The original claim for compensation in respect of tolls was set down at £73,832; but the sum at which it was finally settled was £57,300.

In the meadows a little to the east of Kew Bridge we are nearly opposite to Strand-on-the-Green, the place from which we started on our pilgrimage at the commencement of this work.*

CHAPTER XLIV.

KEW GARDENS.

"So sits enthroned, in vegetable pride,
Imperial Kew, by Thames's glittering side;
Obedient sails from realms unfurrowed bring
For her the unnamed progeny of spring."—DARWIN's *Botanic Gardens*, Canto IV.

Sir Henry Capel's Garden in the Seventeenth Century—The Pleasure Grounds of Kew House began by the Prince of Wales—Improvement of the Gardens under Sir Joseph Banks—The Gardens taken in charge by the Commissioners of Woods and Forests—Appointment of Sir William Hooker as Director and Mr. John Smith as Curator—Transformation of the Botanic Gardens—Formation of the Museum of Practical or Economical Botany—Additions to the Pleasure Grounds—Extent and Condition of the Gardens in 1840—General Description of Kew Gardens—The Entrance Gateways—The Old Orangery now Museum No. 3—The Temple of the Sun—The Herbaceous Grounds—Museum No. 2—The Temple of Æolus—The Tropical Aquarium—The Victoria Regia—The Orchid House—The Succulent House—Tropical Fern House—The Great Palm House—Museum No. 1—The Old Arboretum—The Pleasure Grounds—The Chinese Pagoda—The Ruin—The Temple of Victory—The Pantheon—The Flagstaff—The Temperate House, or Winter Garden—Miss North's Collection of Paintings—The "Queen's Cottage"—Mr. William Aiton—William Cobbett—Sir William Jackson Hooker—Sir Joseph D. Hooker—The Herbarium—The Jodrell Laboratory.

To Lord Capel, already mentioned,† is due the original foundation of Kew gardens, which, starting from his comparatively small beginning, have

become famous throughout the whole civilised world. He had a passion for plants, and we hear of his paying £40—which represented a much

---

larger sum in those days—for two mastic trees from France for "his garden at Kew," and £5 each for four variegated hollies. John Evelyn, in his "Diary," under date of August 30th, 1678, writes:—

"Hence I went to my worthy friend Sir Henry Capel (at Kew), brother to the Earle of Essex: it is an old timber house, but his garden has the choicest fruit of any plantation in England, as he is the most industrious and understanding in it." And again, in 1688:—"From thence we went to Kew, to visit Sir Henry Capel's, whose orangerie and myrtetum are most beautifull and perfectly well kept. He was contriving very high palisados of reeds to shade his oranges during the summer, and painting those reeds in oil."

These gardens were the nucleus of the Royal Gardens at Kew. Their subsequent history is soon told.

It was about 1730 that the Prince of Wales, father of George III., having a long lease* of Kew House, began to form the pleasure-grounds which surrounded it.

In George III.'s reign, while Mr. W. Aiton was gardener, and under the auspices of Sir Joseph Banks, the gardens were greatly improved, and the extensive orangery, a large stove, and other buildings, erected from the designs of Sir William Chambers. Until the death of George III., the collection of exotics and the number of plant-houses were continually on the increase, and the gardens had then acquired great celebrity. After this period, and until the year 1840, little or no progress was made, and the collection was chiefly remarkable for the great size and richness of many of its specimens. At that time, however, public attention having been drawn to the subject, and a commission of inquiry, headed by Dr. Lindley, having been formed to report on the state of these gardens, her Majesty Queen Victoria, in the most liberal spirit, relinquished her title to the garden and pleasure-grounds; the Commissioners of Woods and Forests happily took them under their charge, and appointed Sir William Hooker —so distinguished as a botanist—to be director, and Mr. John Smith—previously well known as a careful and intelligent cultivator, and long connected with Kew—as curator.

Under the management of these gentlemen, and by the aid of liberal parliamentary grants, the Botanic Gardens have undergone a complete transformation, and have become unrivalled as a school of horticulture and botany, more especially since the foundation of the Museum of Practical or Economical Botany, to commence which Sir William Hooker generously devoted his own valuable collections.

By the addition of a large tract from the pleasure-grounds, and by the destruction of all the old kitchen gardens, the space has been extended from eleven acres to seventy-five acres. An immense stove, with accompanying flower-gardens, has been prepared; many new and superior plant-houses have been erected, museums founded, a pinetum planted, and, what is of great national importance, the whole has been thrown freely open to the public for their unrestricted instruction and enjoyment. So celebrated indeed is the place for floriculture, that Sir William Hooker gave to his "Journal of Botany" a second title as the "Kew Miscellany."

The following is an account of the extent and condition of the grounds at the time when Dr. Lindley made his report on Royal Botanical Gardens in 1840, at the request of a committee of the House of Commons:—

1. *The grounds immediately about the existing Palace of Kew*, which were of small circuit, lying near the river, and consisting mainly of those attached to the great palace begun by Mr. Wyatt in the reign of George III., and soon afterwards pulled down,* and those around the present palace. The boundary is the river on the north side, the pleasure-grounds on the south and west, and the Botanic Garden on the east.

2. *The Botanic Garden proper*, which contained at the time in question eleven acres, or thereabouts, of very irregular outline; bounded on the north partly by the gardens of those residences, mainly Crown property, which stand on the south side of Kew Green, in part by the Green itself, from which it was separated by a handsome railing, and in part by the gardens of his late Majesty the King of Hanover; westward, by the grounds of the Palace above-mentioned; eastward, by what were then the Royal Kitchen and Forcing Gardens (now a part of the Botanic Garden); and south by the pleasure-ground.

3. *The Royal Kitchen and Forcing Gardens*, situated between the Botanic Garden and the Richmond Road, comprising about fourteen acres. (This portion has been, as just observed, added to the Botanic Garden.)

4. *The Pleasure-ground*, or *Arboretum*, comprising 270 acres of wood, shrubbery, and lawn, lying to the south of the Botanic Garden, and

bounded by the Richmond Road on one side and the river on the other.

Dr. Lindley's report, as we learn from the authorised "Guide to the Gardens," has reference only to the second of these divisions, namely, the *Royal Botanic Gardens*, which are stated to "include many fine exotic trees and shrubs, a small collection of herbaceous plants, and numerous specimens of grasses." Ten stoves and greenhouses then existed, most of which have since been either pulled down or so greatly altered as to be no longer recognisable from Dr. Lindley's description.

It would be altogether unnecessary to attempt in these pages anything like a detailed account of the gardens and their contents. We will, therefore, refer merely to a few of the most important objects, and take notice of the general beauty of the grounds.

It must be remembered that Kew Gardens are not, like the Horticultural Gardens at the Regent's Park or at South Kensington, devoted to the collection, study, and dissemination of ornamental trees, flowers, and fruits, and therefore the same kind of effect must not be looked for. Rather, like the old "physic" gardens at Chelsea, they are intended strictly to aid the study of natural history and science, though in a slightly different manner.

"The gardens here are well wooded; superb beds of scarlet pelargoniums, crimson roses, delicately lemon-coloured calceolarias, deliciously scented heliotropes, and hosts of other half-hardy plants, border the chief walks; all the finest flowering trees and shrubs are to be found scattered about the grounds; the richest floral treasures of China, Japan, Brazil, and Australia have their place in the different glass erections that stud the gardens; but still, one sees at a glance, Kew is not devoted to flowers, but to botany. You may go into a house filled with plants that shall have cost an incalculable expenditure of time, talent, energy, and money to bring together, and see perhaps scarcely a dozen blossoms in some seasons of the year. But look closely; use your guide-book well; and not a step will you move without feeling a high interest awakened, that will make you glad of your visit to Kew.

"Look at those large pines, in pots, on your left, a little within the entrance gates. What noble outlines! what distinct characters! Think what effect they will have on English scenery when they shall have become everywhere distributed, as will certainly be the case in a few years with the hardier kinds. Look especially at that *Araucaria excelsa*, with its most elegant pyramidal layers of foliage tier above tier, spread out like so many giant ostrich plumes level on the air; imagine it grown to the height of a forest tree, remember it is evergreen, and judge what must be the effect of such glorious vegetable structures scattered over their native plains. Or look again at its brother Araucaria—the imbricated one—less handsome, but more extraordinary, and perfectly hardy, which you will find planted out in the open ground in front of some of the houses further on; what magnificence and variety will not that tree, which is being planted in thousands and tens of thousands, give to our own winter scenery! Or, if you prefer drooping forms, look at the sacred Hindoo pine, the deodar. What the cedar of Lebanon is to Christians, from its associations with the gates of Solomon's Temple, to say nothing of more modern ones, is the deodar to the Hindoo, in connection with the Temple of Somnauth, the gates of which, so famous in our Affghanistan history, were constructed of the deodar wood. Or look at another drooping pine—to our eyes the most beautiful of all—the *Pinus excelsa*, from Norfolk Island, also hardy, growing to an immense height, and becoming rapidly cheaper and cheaper in the flower market."

Here the results of British gardening, scientifically arranged, exhibit in a very small compass the accumulated great uses of the flora of our own islands and of foreign countries. Pleasant as it is to roam abroad and collect indigenous flowers in their various rural homes, yet even this exercise grows wearisome at last; and perhaps there are few botanists who do not at the last prefer resorting quietly for the purpose of study and comparison to the gardens of the Regent's Park or of Kew.

Apparently King George was of the same opinion with Mr. Loudon, that something would be gained for the happiness of the human kind if all men were agreed that wherever there was a habitation, whether for an individual family or for a number of persons, strangers to each other, such as hospitals, workhouses, prisons, asylums, infirmaries, and even barracks, there should be a garden, and that a dwelling without a garden ought not to be allowed to exist throughout all his dominions.

The picturesque variety of the grounds here are perhaps unsurpassed by any public garden in England. The lawns and walks are everywhere diversified by rare and beautiful trees, shrubs, and flowers. The general effect, as seen from the broad walk near the entrance gates, may be expressed in Tennyson's words :—

> " The garden stretches southwards.　In the midst
> A cedar spreads his dark green layers of shade.
> The garden glasses shine.''

Not wholly inapplicable to these gardens, too, are the bantering lines of Tennyson's well-known poem, " Amphion," some of them perhaps suggested by a visit here :—

> " But what is that I hear? a sound
> Like sleepy counsel pleasing.
> Oh Lord ! 'tis in my neighbour's ground
> The modern Muses reading.
> They read botanic treatises,
> And works on gardening thro' there,
> And methods of transplanting trees
> To look as if th y grew there.

> " The withered Muses ! how they pose
> Oe'r books of travelled seamen,
> And show you slips of all that grows
> From England to Van Diemen.
> They read in arbours clipt and cut,
> And alleys, faded places,
> By squares of tropic summer shut,
> And warmed in crystal cases.

> " But these, though fed with careful dirt,
> Are neither green nor sappy ;
> Half-conscious of the garden-squirt,
> The spindlings look unhappy.
> Better tone the meanest weed
> That blows upon the mountain,
> The vilest herb that runs to seed
> Beside its native fountain."

The above lines are quoted just " for what they are worth," and from their insertion here it must not be understood that, in our love for wild flowers, we entertain anything short of an intense respect and regard for the scientific horticulture of Kew Gardens.

The principal entrance to the Botanic Gardens is at the north-west corner of the green, by handsome wrought-iron gates ; another entrance is by the Cumberland Gate, in the Richmond Road, within a short distance of the Kew Gardens station on the London and South-Western Railway.　The entrances to the Pleasure-grounds are in the Richmond Road, by the Queen's Gate and the Lion Gate, near the Pagoda.　There is also an entrance to the grounds at the south-west corner, facing Isleworth, and another at the north-east angle, opposite Brentford.

The chief entrance to the Botanic Gardens was formerly by a narrow alley from the side of Kew Green, along which the visitor proceeded, as it were, by stealth.　A bold and highly appropriate entrance, however, has since been made at the end of Kew Green, where massive and enriched piers, gates, and open railing extend across the end of the green.　They are from the designs of Mr. Decimus Burton.

The main walk, on entering from the principal gateway, takes a westerly course.　To the right of this pathway, but a few yards from the gate, is a stone building, set apart for aroids, tropical tree-ferns, palms, and other trees requiring a more humid atmosphere than can be maintained in the great Palm Stove.　This conservatory was brought hither from Buckingham Palace.　Though a good architectural feature, however, it was built at a period when the requirements of plants were little understood or little cared for ; and hence it is far more heavy, and lofty, and dark, than modern cultivators would approve.　Turning to the left, the walk continues to the Ornamental Water near the Palm Stove, leaving Kew Palace and the grounds immediately surrounding it to the right.　The broad pathway here, one of the most favourite promenades in the grounds, is bordered on each side with large clumps of rhododendron and ornamental trees.　A large house to the left, immediately after entering this walk, is the old Orangery, which was erected in 1761 by Sir William Chambers, and now called the No. 3 Museum, in which are exhibited specimens of timber from various countries, chiefly from the colonies, and including examples of remarkable trees too large to be shown in the cabinets of the other museums.　This building was originally intended for and occupied by orange trees, most of which were removed to Kensington Palace in 1841.　From this date to 1862, it was filled with tender pines and evergreens, since removed to the New Temperate House in the Pleasure-grounds.　A large proportion of the specimens here exhibited was derived from the International Exhibition of 1862.

Eastward of this building, and separated from it by verdant lawns and delightful walks bordered with flowering plants, is an ornamental structure of the Corinthian order, bearing the fanciful name of the Temple of the Sun, near which are some of the most beautiful trees in the gardens, particularly an Oriental plane and a Turkey oak.　Another tree near here to which a certain interest is attached is a weeping willow, an offshoot from that over Napoleon's tomb at St. Helena, and the general parent of all those bearing his name in the country.　Further eastward, extending to the extreme north-east corner of the Gardens, are the several greenhouses and the Herbaceous Grounds.　The numerous beds in this portion of the garden are occupied by hardy plants, and arranged in the natural orders to which they belong. "As a principal object is to illustrate the botanical character of the various groups," remarks Mr. Oliver, in his very admirable "Guide to the Gardens" (1878), "the plants are brought together solely with a view to their relationship or *affinity*, as determined chiefly by the structure of their flowers and seeds, upon which important organs the characters of the natural orders adopted by botanists are based. Hence each bed presents, as might be expected, much uniformity in the plants which occupy it, the same bed seldom including species of more than one order, excepting in cases where the orders are small."

Here, close by, is Museum No. 2, or the Old Museum, which is set apart for specimens and products of monocotyledonous plants, or Endogens, of which palms and grasses form the typical examples. From this museum a pathway winds southward, through what is called the Rock Garden, to Museum No. 1, passing by a mound on which is an ornamental building, called the Temple of Æolus.

Half-way along the promenade, extending southward from the No. 3 Museum, and opposite the Turkey oak above referred to, a walk to the right describes a semicircle, enclosing a wide area to the north, west, and south of the Palm Stove. This walk follows the wire fence separating the Botanic Garden from the Pleasure-grounds, and, crossing the Cedar, Syon, and Pagoda Vistas, is continued to the wall of the Richmond Road, bordering the Garden on the east, where, turning northwards, it reaches the Ornamental Water near to the campanile, which forms a conspicuous object, terminating the view to the south from the principal promenade. A considerable part of the area enclosed by this semicircular walk, north and west of the Palm Stove, is occupied by a collection of hardy pines and other coniferous trees. Another pathway to the right from the termination of the principal promenade at the Ornamental Water leads to the Palm Stove and Tropical Aquarium, or Water-lily House. This is a T-shaped building of recent construction, replacing eight of the old stoves, and intended to meet, as far as possible, the double requirement of space and other needful conditions for the growth chiefly of tender and tropical plants, and accommodation for a large number of visitors. The division into compartments serves both to secure different climatic conditions and to protect the plants from the draughts, which are so prejudicial to them, caused by the ingress and egress of visitors. The head or principal part of the building, is called the Victoria Tank, being set apart for the *Victoria regia*, the wings on either side being devoted to temperate tropical orchids and economic plants, and the lower part, or stem of the T, containing Cape heaths, &c. "This building is filled almost exclusively with Orchidaceous plants, the division next to the Victoria tank with tropical species, the outer division with those which require cooler treatment, chiefly species introduced from greater or less elevations on intertropical mountain chains, where altitude compensates in climate for latitude."

The *Victoria regia*, one of the largest examples of the lily tribe, comes in for a large share of admiration from visitors, and is eagerly sought for. These gardens have the honour of having first raised this extraordinary plant from seed, and distributed it throughout the country. And although it first flowered at Chatsworth, and next at Sion House, the plant here has since bloomed abundantly. It was first discovered by Sir Robert Schomburgk in British Guiana, in 1837. Drawings were exhibited and seeds repeatedly brought over; but as these did not germinate, the idea of a plant with leaves from 5 to 6 feet across, and flowers 15 inches in diameter, began to be reckoned among those travellers' stories which men who go out of the beaten track are supposed to have a peculiar facility in concocting. At length, however, in 1849, Dr. Rodie, of Demerara, sent fresh seeds to Kew Gardens, and the plant is now cultivated here in a high temperature, with a fresh supply of water slowly, but constantly, running through the tank. The flowers are large and very fragrant, streaked and stained with deep pink towards the centre. Other aquatic plants are grown in the corners of the tanks with the *Victoria*, and contribute much to improve its appearance. When the leaves begin to turn up at the edges, it becomes more interesting, the extraordinary veins and spines on the under surface of the leaves, and their deep crimson colour on that side, imparting to it a much more striking character than when the upper surface alone is visible.

Leaving the Orchid House by the front entrance, and turning westward, a specimen of the paper mulberry, from the bark of which the Tapa cloth of Polynesia is fabricated, will be noticed on the lawn by the path leading to the Cumberland Gate. Not far distant may be observed some fine specimens of the willow oak and tulip tree from the United States, and also a large example of the Chili pine, introduced in the year 1792.

The Succulent House, a building some 200 feet long by 30 feet wide, is, as the guide-book

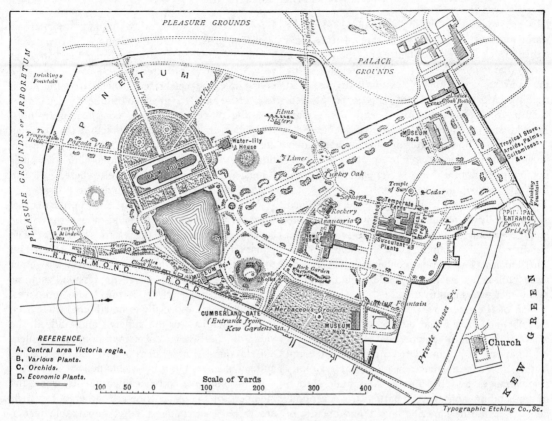

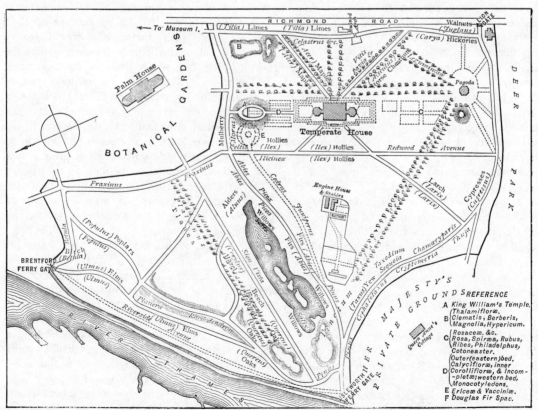

PLANS OF KEW GARDENS.

tells us, "devoted principally to those plants of warm and arid countries which are characterised either by excessive succulence of the stem or leaves (the '*plantes grasses*' of the French), or by the converse condition of extreme dryness and rigidity. Most of these are natives of Mexico, Central America, South Africa, and the Canary Islands, and require a similar treatment under cultivation. Though corresponding in habit, they include plants widely removed in respect of botanical relationship, as a comparison of their flowers serves readily to show."

Another T-shaped building near here is devoted almost wholly to ferns of temperate climates, and another greenhouse (No. IV.), a large cruciform building, contains a number of Australian plants. The Tropical Fern House contains a collection of ferns both extensive and valuable, including many rarely met with in cultivation.

One of the finest views of the great stove is that obtained from about the end of the long walk, where it is seen in perspective. Regarded as a whole, it cannot be considered a great architectural feature. The semicircular heads of the two lofty side entrances, and the attic in the middle portion of the building, appear to us particularly exception-able. But in the superior height and breadth of the central part, in the adaptation of the whole to its intended object, and in the mechanical arrange-ments for ventilation, and for painting, repairing, &c., there is much to admire. Looked at pic-torially, the building suffers—as everything of the same size would—by being so entirely unsupported. At present it stands alone, in a comparatively naked plain, with not a tree anywhere near it to enter into a composition with it. This extreme nakedness and rawness—which the transparency of the material of which it is composed renders all the more glaring—are among its most defective characteristics, pictorially viewed.

The plants brought together in this large stove are all more or less interesting, and many of them very deeply so. Fortunately, the visitor to whom such things are not familiar will easily be able to gather the required information from the labels which are attached to each plant, and which gener-ally give the common as well as scientific name by which they are known. Here, besides the stately palms, some of which are superlatively fine, are most of the rich tropical fruits, together with plants which produce spices, gums, or other articles known in commerce. Here, also, in a small basin on the eastern side of the house, is the Egyptian *Papyrus* from which paper was first made; many of the plants mentioned in Scripture; the *Vallisneria*

spiralis, also in water, where it uncoils its curious stems in proportion to the depth of the water in which it is placed; the sugar-cane, the cocoa-nut palm, the bread-fruit tree, the chocolate tree, the coffee tree, the celebrated banyan tree, the sensi-tive plants, and a great multitude of equally in-teresting objects. As more conspicuous features, the palms are extremely striking, and the bananas are also fine, and fruit well. Many of the palms flower and fruit abundantly; and numerous other things, which are rarely seen elsewhere, except in a small state, regularly blossom and fruit here.

Among the more elegant and peculiar orna-ments of this stove, the tree and other ferns will be sure to rank high in the visitor's esteem. The remarkable grace and beauty of their forms and the tender green of their foliage convey altogether a most pleasing and novel impression, such as scarcely anything else in the house produces. These ferns are especially to be admired when seen from the staircase or the gallery; and, indeed, the view of the whole collection from the gallery affords quite a new idea of tropical vegetation, and should by all means be obtained.

In an old stove, in two compartments, where the members of the Aloe tribe are gathered together, are to be seen, amongst other remarkable plants, two extraordinary specimens of the Old-man Cactus (*Cereus senilis*), pointed out on account of their unusual size. They are actually from 12 to 15 feet high, but clothed only at the summit with the white bristly hair which gives its common name to the plant. Judging from the ordinary rate of growth in this species, Sir William Hooker sup-poses these specimens may probably be as much as a thousand years old! If this be really the case—and we know how careful Sir William is in putting forth such statements—it gives a new and double significance to the name of the plant.

Here also occurred the remarkable vegetable phenomenon in connection with the *Fourcroya gigantea*—belonging to the Aloe family—related by Sir William Hooker.

Two plants of this kind "had been," says Sir William, " in the royal gardens, first of Hampton Court and then of Kew, probably from the earliest introduction of the species into Europe, upwards of a century ago (in 1731). On one and the same day, in the summer of 1844, each was seen to produce a flowering stem, which resembled a gigantic head of asparagus, and grew at first at the astonishing rate of two feet in the twenty-four hours. So precisely did the twin plants keep pace with each other, that at the very time it was found necessary to make an aperture in the glass roof of the house for the emission of one panicle of flowers (twenty-six feet from the ground), a similar release was needed by the other. The rate of growth then most sensibly diminished ; still, in two months the flower-stalks had attained a height of thirty-six feet ! The flowers were innumerable on the great panicles : they produced no seed, but were succeeded by thousands of young plants, springing from the topmost branches, and these continued growing for a long while after the death of the parent plants, both of which perished, apparently from exhaustion." Only young plants, therefore, are now to be seen in this collection. Here the fuchsia was first introduced in 1788. It figures in the *Magazine* of that date.

It will be remembered that these gardens gave a title to one of the poems of Thomas Chatterton, the only part of which that appeared in print shows that, young as he was, he had imbibed, and did not scruple to retail, the scandal of the day against the Princess of Wales and her favourite, Lord Bute.

The Palm Stove, or Great Palm House, as it is generally called, was designed by Mr. Decimus Burton, and completed in 1848, and is a work of great magnificence and curiosity. It is somewhat in the form of the hull of a large ship with the keel upwards, having attached to it the hulls of smaller ships, one at each end, the ribs being of cast-iron, and the intermediate spaces of glass. The building is thus described by Mr. Daniel Oliver, in his "Guide" :—"The entire length of the structure is 362 ft. The centre is 100 ft. wide and 66 ft. in height ; the wings 50 ft. wide and 30 ft. high. The sheet-glass with which the stove is glazed (about 45,000 square feet) is slightly tinged with green by the addition of oxide of copper, at the suggestion of Mr. R. Hunt, with a view to obviate the scorching effect of direct sunlight, by intercepting a portion of the heat-rays. The iron ribs are secured in large blocks of Cornish granite placed in solid concrete. A gallery runs round the central portion of the building at a height of 30 ft. from the ground, enabling the spectator to view from above the plume-like crowns of the smaller palms beneath. The interior is heated by six boilers (of which three or four are usually all that are required in winter), with which a system of over 19,500 feet of hot-water piping, four inches in diameter, is connected. The smoke from the underground flues was formerly conveyed a distance of nearly 5:0 ft., and consumed in the square smoke tower, 96 ft. in height, near to the Richmond Road. This tower communicates with the Palm Stove by an underground railway, by which the supply of coal is con-

veyed to the furnaces, and the ashes, &c., removed. It was also made available for obtaining the necessary elevation of the water supply required for the gardens and various plant-houses. These arrangements are now superseded by the flues from the furnaces being carried up within the wings of the building, and the water supply, which was formerly deficient, is now derived from tanks in Richmond Park, which are filled from the lake in the Pleasure Grounds by an engine near the Temperate House."

On the east side of the Palm Stove is a large sheet of ornamental water, at the farther extremity of which is the No. 1 Museum, which is devoted to the exhibition of vegetable economic products and preparations of scientific interest. This museum is contained in a large and handsome building of three floors, and of Italian design. It is devoted to specimens of dicotyledonous plants, or Exogens, "the largest and most varied class in the vegetable kingdom." It contains an important collection of fruits and seeds, gums, resins, drugs, dye-stuffs, sections of wood, and all curious and interesting vegetable products, especially what are useful in the arts, in medicine, or in domestic economy—such vegetable substances, in short, as living plants cannot exhibit. Nearly all the articles have descriptive labels attached, but the "Official Guide" to the Museum will greatly facilitate the examination. From this Guide we glean the following particulars concerning the origin of the museums :—

"The foundation and progress of these collections, not only by far the most extensive in existence, but the first of their kind established, may be briefly traced since the conception of their plan by the late Director of the Royal Gardens, Sir William Hooker. In 1847 the building now occupied by Museum No. 2, which up to that year had been in use as a fruit store-house, &c., was added, by command of her Majesty, to the Botanic Garden proper. Permission was immediately sought by the director to have one room of this building fitted up with suitable cases for the exhibition of vegetable products—objects which neither the living plants of the garden nor the preserved specimens of the herbarium could show. Sir William Hooker's request was liberally met by the Chief Commissioner of her Majesty's Woods and Forests, and the museum was forthwith commenced, its nucleus consisting of the director's private collection, presented by himself. No sooner was the establishment and aim of the museum generally made known than contributions to it poured in from all quarters of the globe, until, in a few years, the ten rooms of the building, with its passages and corners, were absolutely crammed with specimens. Its appreciation by the public being thus demonstrated, application was made to Parliament for a grant to defray the expense of an additional building for the proper accommodation of the objects, and the house occupied by Museum No. 1, opened to the public in the spring of 1857, is the result.

"In 1881 the extension of Museum No. 1 on the west side, containing a new and commodious staircase, was erected, at a cost of £2,000, met by a grant from the India Office, in order to supply the additional accommodation required for the Indian collections mentioned below. From the Exhibitions of 1851 and 1862, and from the Paris Exhibitions of 1855 and 1867, large additions were made to the museums, both by the presentation of specimens, and also by their purchase, aided by grants from the Treasury and Board of Trade. Many eminent firms engaged in the importation and manufacture of vegetable substances have most liberally contributed various illustrative series. By the different Government departments, by our colonial officers and foreign representatives, and by numerous private travellers also, the most important services have been, and continue to be, rendered. Besides these sources of contribution must be mentioned the reinforcement of the Indian element in the Museum, first in 1878 by the collection of forest produce presented by the Government of India (consisting of 1,113 specimens), and secondly in 1880, by the transference to Kew of the entire economico-botanical collections forming part of the India Museum at South Kensington. From these about 4,000 specimens were selected for permanent exhibition."

On the staircase, at the first landing, has been placed the stained-glass window in four lights, removed from the Guildhall, London, and presented to the Gardens in 1878 by Alderman Cotton, M.P. It represents the growth and manufacture of cotton. The collection of portraits of botanists is partly hung on wall spaces in this Museum. The nucleus of it was formed by the late Sir William Hooker, and after his death was purchased by the Government.

The more important objects exhibited in the museums are enumerated in a separate "Museum Guide."

In connection with the living specimens cultivated in the gardens, the museum collections serve to illustrate fully the sources and various applications of vegetable substances for purposes of necessary use and convenience.

The old Arboretum occupies the northern part of the gardens. "This Arboretum," as we learn from Mr. Oliver's work already quoted, "occupies about five acres, and includes several valuable trees, the more interesting of which only can be noted here. It is believed to be on the site of one of the oldest Arboreta in Europe, established by R. Bennet, Esq., an ardent cultivator of rare trees and shrubs, who possessed the property about the middle of the seventeenth century. It became the celebrated Arboretum of Kew when the grounds were purchased by the royal family, a century later. The present Arboretum occupies great part of the area outside the wire fence, formerly known as the 'Pleasure Grounds.'"

The Pleasure Grounds and the Botanical Gardens are distinct domains, though separated from each other merely by a light wire fence, through which visitors can pass freely from the one into the other. The entrances for the public are also at different places, either from the Richmond Road or at a gate at the side of the Thames. These grounds altogether have an area of nearly 300 acres. Just before the gate is reached, two or three very large elms will be noticed, one of which is said to have been planted by Queen Elizabeth, but was blown down several years ago. The stump is still preserved.

The grounds were originally ornamented with several temples, &c. (one in the Gothic, one in the Arabesque or Turkish style, and one in the Venetian), erected by Sir William Chambers. They were useless and tasteless structures, in keeping only with such buildings as the Royal Pavilion at Brighton, which sprung into being about the same time and under the same auspices. The principal of these is a magnificent pagoda, in imitation of a Chinese building. Of this erection a poet in the *London Magazine* of April, 1773, has written :—

> "Let barbaric glories feast his eyes,
> August pagodas round his palace rise,
> And finished Richmond open to his view
> A work to wonder at, perhaps a Kew."

With reference to these curious Oriental structures, Mr. Martin Tupper writes epigrammatically : —" If in the Richmond Manor Court-Rolls Kew, as we now indite the word, is indifferently written 'Kay-hough' and 'Kai-ho,'* we may almost naturally look for a Chinese pagoda in the neighbourhood ; and the rival to the Tower of Nanking, overlooking the Mortlake flats, has at least its use in raising some denizen of damp earth to storeys nearer to the healthy airs of heaven."

---

* See *ante*, p. 389.

The Alhambra, the Mosque, the Gothic Cathedral, and one or two other fanciful structures described in Sir William Chambers's work on the subject, have been taken down. The Pagoda, the most important of these which remain, is a substantial and well-built edifice, of an octagonal form, of hard grey stock bricks, and 163 feet in height. It consists of ten storeys, the staircase leading to which is in the centre of the building. The views from the different storeys are varied and expansive. Sir William Chambers says that the design of the edifice is an imitation of the Chinese pagoda described in his work on the buildings, gardens, &c., of China, published in 1757. "At all the angles of the different storeys were Chinese dragons —eighty in number—covered with thin glass of various colours, which produced 'a most dazzling reflection.'" These monstrosities, however, have been long removed. Most persons suppose, but quite in error, that the strange, tall, pagoda-looking building which towers above the gardens is the Kew Observatory, the veritable home of the Clerk of the Weather Office !

The Ruin, erected in 1760, approached by a gravelled walk, skirted with trees and thickets, represents a dilapidated Roman arch, and embowered as it is in foliage, is a sufficiently picturesque object. It is built of Act of Parliament brick, i.e., the size of which was fixed by Act of Parliament ; thus showing, as Horace Walpole quaintly remarks, that "a solecism may be committed even in architecture."

On a raised mound is the Temple of Victory, commemorating the battle of Minden, in which the allied army, commanded by Prince Ferdinand of Brunswick, defeated the French under Marshal de Contades, August 1st, 1759. Around the interior are medallions in bas-relief of the naval heroes, Rodney, Howe, St. Vincent, Duncan, and Nelson, with the names and dates of their respective victories. Near the lake is another Chinese building—a dilapidated wooden edifice of two storeys, called the House of Confucius, designed by Goupy.

Among the other ornamental buildings is a beautiful little Doric temple, called the Pantheon, designed and erected, under the superintendence of Sir Jeffrey Wyattville, for William IV. Its interior contains eighteen tablets, commemorating the dates and places of battles fought and won by British soldiers from 1760 to 1815. Here, too, are finely-executed busts of George III. and his sons, George IV. and William IV., together with that of the great Duke of Wellington. Opposite the entrance is also a large tablet, which, "on the removal of Cleopatra's Obelisk," was brought from Egypt, and presented by Lord Hill (the Commander-in-Chief) to his late Majesty. It commemorates the death of Sir Ralph Abercrombie, who was mortally wounded in a decisive action against the French, under Bonaparte, near Alexandria, in the year 1801.

The Pleasure Grounds are traversed by avenues and walks, bordered at intervals by trees and shrubs, many of which are arranged scientifically in beds in the order of their natural relationship ; and the circuit of the entire grounds may be made by following the path leading from the Botanic Garden near the chimney-shaft of the Palm Stove, adjoining the Ornamental Water. This path runs parallel to the Richmond Road, bordered by the collection of Limes, passes the Unicorn Gate, and, reaching the Lion Gate, or Richmond entrance, turns to the right, leaving on the left Richmond Old Park and a portion of the grounds surrounding her Majesty's (or, as it is generally called, Queen Anne's), Cottage fenced off from the Arboretum, and not open to the public. The path leads to the Thames, which it follows to the Brentford Gate, then turning eastward, conducts again to the Botanic Garden, through an entrance immediately adjoining the grounds of the old Kew Palace. On the line of this path, embracing the circuit of the grounds, and near to the Unicorn Gate on the Richmond Road, is the flagstaff, erected in 1861. This spar, which is believed to be the finest in Europe, was presented to the Royal Gardens by Mr. Edward Stamp. It is the trunk of the Douglas spruce (*Abies Douglasii*), a native of British Columbia. Its total length is 159 feet, nearly twelve feet resting under ground in a bricked well. The age of this tree is estimated at about 250 years.

In the middle of the avenue, which extends from the Great Palm House to the Pagoda, is the Temperate House, or Winter Garden, a large glass conservatory, built from the designs of Mr. Decimus Burton, the architect of the Palm Stove. The building consists of a central portion, with small octagonal houses at either end, and is set apart for palms, acacias, pines, &c., mostly from Australia and Tasmania. There is also to be seen here a collection of Japanese plants, which serve to convey some idea of the general character of the peculiar vegetation of the Japanese group of islands, in which the special characteristics of Chinese and East Himalayan botany is strongly brought out. With reference to this collection of plants, Mr. Oliver writes, in his "Guide to the Gardens" :—"The Japanese flora is characterised by an unusually large proportion of woody plants, many of which belong to families which are rare elsewhere so far to the north, and by the abundance of maples, laurels, hollies, hydrangeas, figs, evergreen oaks, and remarkable forms of Coniferæ. Taken altogether, it presents much affinity with the flora of the Southern United States of Eastern America. From the general similarity of the climate of Japan to our own, we owe to it many of our most valuable introduced hardy shrubs, and

rather suburban, collection of paintings which is open to the public on Sundays. That the working classes appreciate this privilege is seen by the readiness with which they take advantage of it. From 1,000 to 1,500 have visited it every fine Sunday since it was opened; and even on wet Sundays as many as 600 umbrellas have been taken at the doors."

The building in which Miss North's collection of paintings is exhibited is of red brick, and may

THE PAGODA.

the number of these will yet be, no doubt, largely increased when the island is more thoroughly opened up to foreigners."

Miss North, a daughter of the late Mr. Frederick North, M.P. for Hastings, established here in 1880-2 a fine gallery of paintings, mainly drawn from nature in all parts of the world, which she had herself explored. A substantial building has been erected to contain these paintings and treasures, which are, in the donor's words, "to be thrown open to the public upon all occasions, and at all hours on which the Royal Gardens themselves are open." "It results," observes a writer in the *Queen*, "from the wording of this deed of gift, that the North Gallery at Kew is the only metropolitan, or

be described as classical, and it was built from the designs of Mr. James Fergusson, F.R.S. The paintings are over 600 in number, and form by far the most complete and accurate series of illustrations of the flora of the globe that has ever been brought together. Miss North has wandered over the face of the earth in making her collection of drawings—to Brazil and Borneo, to Teneriffe and California, to Western Australia and Ceylon, to Jamaica and the Himalayas. The collection is not only singularly beautiful, but one of which Sir Joseph Hooker says that "it is impossible to over-rate its interest and instructiveness in connection with the contents of the gardens, plant-houses, and museums of Kew." All the paintings are highly-finished sketches in oil-colours, done upon paper, and in the case of flowers, &c., are of the size of life, and many of the sketches represent types which are either unknown, or almost unknown, in Europe, or are exceedingly scarce and difficult to reproduce even in the best organised garden. Sir J. Hooker, in the Preface to the " Descriptive Catalogue of the Paintings," writes :—" Many of the views here brought together represent vividly and truthfully scenes of astonishing interest and singularity, and

bamboos, coffee-flowers, and many cultivated flowers, all rendered with great vividness and force. In California, the giant Wellingtonia—one of which has been found 325 feet in height—exercised her pencil. Then we have the carnivorous plants of North America, such as " pitcher-plants," " side-saddle flowers," and all the others that are furnished with the means of entrapping luckless insects, as the sundew is. India and Ceylon have furnished Miss North with a very large number of

THE PALM HOUSE.

objects that are amongst the wonders of the vegetable kingdom ; and these, though now accessible to travellers and familiar to readers of travels, are already disappearing, or are doomed shortly to disappear, before the axe and the forest fires, the plough and the flock, of the ever-advancing settler or colonist. Such scenes can never be renewed by nature, nor when once effaced, can they be pictured to the mind's eye, except by means of such records as this lady has presented to us and to posterity, which will thus have even more reason than we have to be grateful for her fortitude as a traveller, her talent and industry as an artist, and her liberality and public spirit."

From Jamaica Miss North brought drawings of

subjects, from the cocoa-nut palm to the orchids of Simla. In Borneo Miss North found many a treasure hitherto unknown in Europe, notably the great pitcher-plant, to which her own name has been given. It may be mentioned as a notable instance of the eager enterprise of our floral collectors, and as a proof that anthomania is as real and potent as bibliomania itself, that in consequence of seeing this painting when it was shown at South Kensington, Messrs. Veitch, of Chelsea, " sent a collector all the way to Borneo on purpose to get the species." He succeeded in bringing home living plants.

As an accompaniment to Miss North's collection of paintings, there is exhibited a " Map of the

World, illustrating the distribution of vegetation." This has been drawn and coloured by Mr. Trelawney Saunders, and it has for its base the principal features of both land and water. The continents and islands which form the land are carefully drawn, with their mountain systems and inland waters. Upon this foundation the broadest aspects of the vegetation are distinguished by various harmonising tints.

"The fact, however, that a picture gallery so near London is open to the public on Sunday afternoons," writes the *Pall Mall Gazette*, "is worth chronicling, because it is incredible that those who now keep the other galleries closed can long resist the force of so successful an example. It is said that the concession of opening the gardens on Sunday was made in the first instance on the suggestion of the Prince Consort, in order that the foreigners who flocked to the Great Exhibition in 1851 might have some refuge from the melancholy of a British Sunday. Could not some high personage interfere now to induce the authorities at the National Gallery to throw open to our own much-tempted population on the only holiday afternoon which many of them possess the innocent seductions of Turner and Botticelli?" It is stated as a fact that more than half of the persons who visit Kew Gardens in the year go thither on a Sunday.

The Botanic Gardens are open to the free inspection of the public from one o'clock till six every day, except Sundays. The Pleasure Grounds and museums are open to the public every afternoon throughout the year, except Christmas Day. For many years they were kept apart, and were not accessible from each other; but new and more liberal arrangements have been made. The public thus have the additional privilege of taking a pleasant ramble and a scientific survey on the same day, and without the trouble of going round more than a quarter of a mile to reach the separate entrances.

It may be mentioned, that after the close of the Great Exhibition in Hyde Park, in 1851, it was at one time proposed to remove the Crystal Palace, and to re-erect it here.

Near the south-western corner of the gardens, not far from the Pagoda, and standing within the queen's private grounds, which are merely separated from the Pleasure Gardens by a light iron fence, stands a picturesque old building of brick with a thatched roof, and ivy-clad, known as the "Queen's Cottage"—a sort of "Petit Trianon" to this Versailles. It is screened from the public gardens to a certain extent by a belt of trees. It was for-merly used occasionally for pic-nics by the royal family and their personal friends. On the walls hangs a fine collection of Hogarth's engravings

Mr. William Aiton, who was gardener to George III., as mentioned above, was a Scotchman, and an eminent botanist in his day. He published a magnificent work, "Hortus Kewensis," of which a new and enlarged edition was given to the world by his son, Mr. William T. Aiton. In this work, originally issued in 1789, is given an account of the several foreign plants which had been introduced into the English gardens at different times, amounting to 5,600 in number; and so much was it esteemed that the whole impression was sold off within two years. Mr. Aiton did not long survive this publication, for he died in 1793, in the sixty-third year of his age, and lies buried in the churchyard at Kew. He was succeeded by his son, Mr. William Townsend Aiton, who was no less esteemed by George III. than his father had been, and who, besides conducting the botanical department and taking charge of the extensive Pleasure Grounds, was also employed in the improvement of the other royal gardens.

There was not much that was poetical certainly about the sturdy old Radical, William Cobbett; and yet few passages are more touching than that in which he describes his first journey on foot from Farnham to Richmond, on hearing from a man who had been working in the Royal Gardens at Kew a description of that earthly Paradise. The story has been often told, but it will bear repeating. Here it is in his own words:—

"At eleven years of age my employment was clipping of box-edges and weeding beds of flowers in the garden of the Bishop of Winchester, at the Castle of Farnham, my native town. I had always been fond of beautiful gardens; and a gardener, who had just come from the King's Gardens at Kew, gave such a description of them as made me instantly resolve to work in these gardens. The next morning, without saying a word to any one, off I set, with no clothes except those upon my back, and with thirteen halfpence in my pocket. I found that I must go to Richmond, and I accordingly went on from place to place, inquiring my way thither. A long day (it was in June) brought me to Richmond in the afternoon. Two-penny-worth of bread and cheese and a pennyworth of small beer, which I had on the road, and one halfpenny which I had lost somehow or other, left threepence in my pocket. With this for my whole fortune, I was trudging through Richmond, in my blue smock-frock and my red garters tied under my knees, when, staring about me, my eye fell upon a little book in a bookseller's window, on the outside of which was written : ' Tale of a Tub ; price 3d.' The title was so odd that my curiosity was excited. I had 3d., but then, I could have no supper. In I went, and got the little book, which I was so impatient to read that I got over into a field, at the upper corner of the Kew Garden, where there stood a hay-stack. On the shady side of this I sat down to read. The book was so different from anything that I had read before, it was something so new to my mind, that, though I could not at all understand some of it, it delighted me beyond description; and it produced what I have always considered a sort of birth of intellect. I read on till it was dark, without any thought about supper or bed. When I could see no longer, I put my little book in my pocket, and tumbled down by the side of the stack, where I slept till the birds in Kew Gardens awakened me in the morning, when off I started to Kew, reading my little book. The singularity of my dress, the simplicity of my manner, my confident and lively air, and, doubtless, his own compassion besides, induced the gardener, who was a Scotsman, to give me victuals, find me lodging, and set me to work. And it was during the period that I was at Kew that the present king (William IV.) and two of his brothers laughed at the oddness of my dress while I was sweeping the grass-plot round the foot of the Pagoda. The gardener, seeing me fond of books, lent me some gardening books to read ; but these I could not relish after my ' Tale of a Tub,' which I carried about with me wherever I went ; and when I, at about twenty years old, lost it in a box that fell overboard in the Bay of Fundy, in North America, the loss gave me greater pain than I have ever felt at losing thousands of pounds. This circumstance, trifling as it was, and childish as it may seem to relate it, has always endeared the recollection of Kew to me."

Cobbett's love of Kew Gardens ceased only with his death. It may be Mr. G. Lushington was not far from the mark when he wrote of him thus :—

" A labourer's son, 'mid squires and lords,
　　Strong on his own stout legs he stood ;
　　　Well armed in bold and trenchant wit,
　　　And well they learned that tempted it
　　That his was English blood.

" And every wound his victim felt
　　Had in his eyes a separate charm ;
　　　Yet better than successful strife,
　　　He loved the memory of his life,
　　In boyhood on the farm." *

Cobbett late in life was elected M.P. for Old-

* See the " Book of Authors," p. 363—5.

ham, but died in June, 1835, having held his seat less than three years.

Sir William Jackson Hooker, to whom, as stated above, the present condition of Kew Gardens is mainly due, was a native of Norwich, and was born in the year 1785. His father, Mr. Joseph Hooker, formerly of Exeter, claimed to be a member of the same family as Richard Hooker, the author of "Ecclesiastical Polity." From innate taste, William Hooker devoted himself to botanical studies, and these he pursued with so much success, that he was eventually appointed Regius Professor of Botany in the University of Glasgow, where he greatly endeared himself to the students, not only by his ability as a lecturer, but by his kind and genial disposition. Among these young men were many who have since achieved distinction in science, and one of their number thus wrote of him in the *Naval and Military Gazette*, on the death of Sir William Hooker, in August, 1865 :—"Many medical men of both services look back to some of their brightest days as those spent some thirty years ago, in company with their congenial companion, preceptor, and friend, the Regius Professor of Botany in the University of Glasgow, over the rugged hills in the west of Scotland, or the still more rugged mountains of Connemara, when, with knapsack on back and collecting case at side, he practically taught his pupils the science which he loved, guiding, directing, and cheering them to exertion, and ever ready to help them in all their difficulties, and with his lithe step and upright figure, at the age of fifty making himself young for the sake of the young, never allowing himself to be beaten on the mountain side by his more youthful associates."

In 1832 he was removed to a wider sphere of usefulness, being appointed Curator of Kew Gardens, which, in their present state, he may almost be said to have created. On the recommendation of Lord Melbourne, the Prime Minister, he had conferred on him the honour of knighthood in 1835, and in 1845 he received the degree of D.C.L. from the University of Oxford. Sir William Hooker was the author of " The British Flora," " a work containing a complete description of British plants; also the " Flora Scotica," the " Exotic Flora," &c. He also edited a continuation of Curtis's *Botanical Magazine*, and published a *Botanical Miscellany*, in which figures and descriptions of plants were given, especially of those which were of use in the arts, medicine, and domestic economy. This work, with the same design, was continued in the *Journal of Botany*.

Sir William Hooker's management of the Botanic Garden of Glasgow, and his extensive knowledge of plants, prepared him to do justice to his position as Curator of the Royal Gardens at Kew. From the time these gardens were placed under his direction, a continued series of improvements have taken place, and it now holds a foremost place amongst similar gardens for the variety and beauty of its collection of living plants. Under his management the large conservatory and other new houses were erected, and the museum of the useful products of the vegetable kingdom was formed under his direction. Sir William Hooker was for many years a Vice President of the Linnæan Society and a Fellow of the Royal Society, and he was also a member of many foreign scientific societies. In 1814 Sir William Hooker married the eldest daughter of Mr. Dawson Turner, F.R.S., of Yarmouth, who was almost as well known for his devotion to natural history as to antiquarian pursuits.

Sir William Hooker was succeeded in the post of director of the gardens by his son, Dr. Joseph Dalton Hooker, F.R.S., who has acquired great celebrity not only as a botanist, but also as a traveller. In 1839, on the occasion of the fitting-out of the expedition to the Antarctic Ocean, under Sir James Ross, Dr. Hooker was appointed assistant-surgeon on board the *Erebus*. "Although appointed surgeon, his real object," observes his biographer in the *English Cyclopædia*, "was to investigate the botany of the district through which the expedition passed—an object which was generously encouraged by the enlightened commander of the squadron. The result was the publication of the 'Flora Antarctica,' in which work Dr. Hooker has not only figured and described a large number of new plants, but by comparison of the species obtained in this voyage with those of other parts of the world, has succeeded in advancing greatly our knowledge of the laws which govern the distribution of plants over the surface of the earth." In the year 1848 Dr. Hooker started on another expedition; but this time his steps were directed to the Himalaya districts in India, whence he returned in 1852, the results of his labours being published in his "Himalayan Journals" (2 vols.) and a large work entitled "Flora Indica." He has since travelled for scientific purposes in Syria, Morocco, and other countries. Dr. Hooker, previous to his travels in the Himalaya, held an appointment in the Museum of Economic Geology, and for some ten years before the death of his father he was Assistant Director of Kew Gardens. He was President of the Royal Society from 1873 till 1878. Dr. Hooker was nominated

a Companion of the Order of the Bath in 1869, and was made a Knight Commander of the Order of the Star of India in 1877.

Sir William Hooker was the author of a variety of works on Ferns, entitled "British Ferns," "Garden Ferns," "Filices Exoticæ," "Species Filicum," and "Synopsis Filicum"; and Sir Joseph has published large and important works on the "Flora" of British India, "Tasmania," "New Zealand"; whilst the Flora of the Cape has been illustrated by Dr. Harvey, that of the West Indies by Dr. Grisebach, that of Australia and Tasmania, by Mr. G. Bentham, that of Mauritius, &c., by Mr. J. G. Baker, and that of New Zealand by Mr. Thwaites.

The Herbarium, or "Hortus siccus"—a collection of dried plants, preserved and arranged exclusively for the purpose of scientific study—and the Library, are contained in the building on Kew Green to the right, immediately before entering the principal gate of the Royal Gardens, formerly occupied by his Majesty the King of Hanover.* This herbarium is the largest in existence, and is constantly increasing by additions from every quarter of the globe. It embraces the collection presented to the Royal Gardens by Mr. George Bentham; that of the late Allan Cunningham, presented by Mr. R. Heward; of Mr. J. Carey, an admirable collection of the plants of the Eastern United States, presented by him in 1868; of the late Dr. Bromfield, presented by his sister; of the late Dr. Burchell, the celebrated traveller in South Africa and Brazil, presented by Miss Burchell; of the late Dr. Francis Boott, a type collection of the genus *Carex;* the Orchid Herbarium of the late Dr. Lindley, purchased by Government; the European Herbarium of the late M. J. Gay, of Paris, presented by Sir J. D. Hooker; and of the late Mr. Borrer; together with the private collection of the late Sir W. J. Hooker, acquired by Government.

"The Herbarium and Library," remarks Mr. Oliver, "are found to be an indispensable adjunct to the Botanic Gardens, as the only means of correctly naming the plants which are there cultivated, as necessary for determining and describing the novelties which are being constantly introduced from foreign parts, and, in short, for maintaining the establishment upon a scientific and really useful footing."

The Jodrell Laboratory, presented by Mr. T. J. Phillips Jodrell, M.A., intended for physiological and microscopical investigations, is placed at the north end of the Herbaceous Ground.†

---

* See *ante*, p. 407.   † See *ante*, p. 413.

In describing a visit to these gardens in 1854, the author of "Pilgrim Walks" writes :—"Kew can never be seen to greater advantage than after a visit to Sydenham. There all is art—here all is nature ; there the powers of imitation and skill are taxed to the utmost for effect—here the objects themselves produce effect unsought. Here grace of form and elegance of arrangement are the spontaneous result of Nature's mould ; no dressing, painting, gilding, or artificial aid, yet Solomon, in all his glory, was not arrayed like one of these !

"It is a beautiful provision of Nature that allows the productions of the vegetable world, seemingly fixed and immovable, to be transported by seed, root, or slip, to soils and climes far distant and far different from those they grow in. Here we see the inhabitants of other regions presented to the eye in all reality: the lofty palm, the brilliant cactus of the tropics, stands, or even grows, in the same soil beside the European myrtle and the rhododendron of fresh and temperate zones. Here we see them in their native or more than their native beauty ; for here no storms disturb, no insects disfigure, no drought impoverishes them. Here we can watch the development of leaf, flower, and fruit—observe Nature's hidden operations, and that, too, without fear of snakes and reptiles, which so wofully impede the labours of the naturalists in other lands."

CHAPTER XLV.

MORTLAKE.

" Dehinc et mortuus est lacus, superba
Villai effigies, domusque nota."—LELAND, *Cygnea Cantio.*

Situation and Boundaries of Mortlake—Population—Its Etymology—Descent of the Manor—The Parish Church—Sir John Barnard—The Catholic Church of St. Mary Magdalen—Christ Church—Boot and Shoemakers' Benevolent Institution—Oliver Cromwell's House—Sir Henry Taylor—East Sheen—Edward Jesse—Amy Robsart—Sir Robert Dudley—Sir William Temple—Dr. Pinckney's School—Lord Castlereagh—Lord Grey—Sir Archibald Macdonald—Mr. W. S. Gilpin—Dr. Dee, the Astrologer—Mortlake Tapestry Works—Potteries.

MORTLAKE, or Mortlage, as the name is spelt in the "Book of Doomsday," lies on the Thames immediately below Kew, which it adjoins on the west. Eastwards it stretches along the river to Barnes. On the south it is bounded by East Sheen and Richmond Park. It lies rather low, and its chief street runs parallel with the river, to the banks of which a few narrow, old-fashioned alleys lead down between shops, villas, and manufactories, the rest of its area being devoted to market-gardens. In 1871 the population of the parish was 5,100, which number had increased during the next decade to 6,300.

On account of its name and its low situation combined, it has often been styled by writers who are imbued with a smattering of classical learning *mortuus lacus.* But the derivation of the name, whatever be its origin, is not to be found in any of the dead languages. For instance, Leland, who lived and wrote in the reign of Henry VIII., facetiously styles Mortlake the " dead lake " in the motto prefixed to this chapter.* In the commentary on this passage, Mortlake, however, is called "villa eximie splendida." But, doubtless, what splendour it possessed must have arisen from or been connected with the Archbishop's palace ; for in other respects there could have been little to attract the eye of the traveller to what must have been at best a small, low, and unpicturesque fishing village.

But though not very attractive or picturesque in comparison with Richmond and its immediate surroundings, yet Mortlake is not wanting in that interest which always belongs to the history of the past. As Horace tells us, " the wine-cask long retains the odour which it has once imbibed."

At the time of the Doomsday Survey, the manor belonged to the Archbishop of Canterbury, by whom it appears to have been held for some time before the Conquest ; but shortly afterwards it was, with other estates, seized upon by that noted "land-grabber," Odo, Bishop of Bayeux. His claim to the property, however, was not allowed to pass unchallenged, for when Lanfranc was appointed to the archbishopric, he asserted his right to the manor before an assembly of nobles and prelates held on Penenden Heath, in Kent, and the cause being decided in his favour, Odo had no other choice open to him than to make restitution.

Brayley remarks that it is evident from the Doomsday Survey that the ancient manor of Mortlake was of great extent, and, in fact, that it not only composed the present parish, but likewise those of Wimbledon, Putney, and Barnes. For a

* See Leland's "Itinerary," published by Hearne, Vol. IX.

long subsequent period it was included in the manor of Wimbledon, at which place the original church was situated; but the principal mansion, or manor-house, was at Mortlake. This became the occasional residence of the Archbishops of Canterbury, and many of their public acts are dated "from their manor-house at Mortlake." In 1099 Archbishop Anselm here celebrated the festival of Whitsuntide, and here also he held an ordination in the reign of Henry I. Archbishop

immediate successor, Cranmer, alienated the manor to the king, in exchange for other lands. Stow, in his "Chronicle," under date of 1240, records that "Manie strange and great fishes came ashore, whereof eleven were Sea buls (seals), and one of large bignesse passed up the river of Thamis, through the bridge of London, unhurt, til he came as far as the *King's house* (possibly the Archbishop's house, then in the king's possession) at Mortlake, where he was killed."

THE THAMES AT MORTLAKE.

Corboyle was "confined to his house at Mortlake" by sickness in 1136. Archbishop Peckham died here in 1295, and here, too, died Archbishop Walter Reynolds, in 1327. Simon Meopham, who held the see of Canterbury in the early part of the reign of Edward III., having incurred the displeasure of the Pope, was excommunicated by him, and, "retiring to the manor-house of Mortlake, passed many days in solitude." Here, in 1406, in the manorial chapel, Nicholas Bubbewith, Keeper of the Privy Seal and Lord Treasurer under Henry IV., was consecrated Bishop of London by Archbishop Arundel, assisted by the Bishops of Winchester and Worcester. Archbishop Warham was probably the last prelate who resided here, as his

In the reign of Queen Elizabeth this estate was held by Sir Thomas Cecil, from whom it passed by sale to one Robert Walter, who, towards the end of the sixteenth century, conveyed it to Elizabeth, widow of Hugh Stukeley. In 1607 her son, Sir Thomas Stukeley, transferred the property to William Penn. The manor-house is supposed to have been taken down towards the end of the seventh century.

The original parish church of Mortlake could have been no older than the middle of the fourteenth century, for only about that time it would appear Mortlake was cut off from the mother parish of Wimbledon, and made a separate parochial district. Down to the transfer of the parish from the diocese of London to that of Rochester, in 1876, the living was only a perpetual curacy subordinate to Wimbledon, the latter being the mother church. In the king's books Mortlake is returned as "not in charge." From the Second General Report of the Ecclesiastical Commissioners, ordered to be printed 15th June, 1847, it appears

It was first erected on its present site after the exchange between Archbishop Cranmer and Henry VIII., about the middle of the sixteenth century (1543). The tower consists of four storeys; the three lowermost are of flint stone in chequer work, strengthened by buttresses at the angles; the upper storey is of brick, with stone dressings, and it

MORTLAKE CHURCH.

that Mortlake was formerly a "peculiar" of the Archbishop of Canterbury; but under an Order of Council made in 1845, and ratifying certain proceedings of the Ecclesiastical Commissioners, the parishes of Mortlake and Wimbledon, St. Mary's Newington, Barnes, and Putney, all peculiars of the same prelate, were added to the see of London from and after January 1st, 1846.

The present church, like most of those along the valley of the Thames, has preserved only its western tower, the rest of the edifice being built of brick, in the tasteless style of the earlier Georges.

is crowned by a modern lantern and cupola. The belfry and roof are reached by a spiral staircase, terminating in a turret. Over the window above the doorway in the tower is an inscription—" *Vivat Rex Henricus VIII.*"

The body of the church is plain and uninteresting, and has been re-built and enlarged at various periods. The ceiling is flat, divided into panels, and supported by Tuscan columns. At the east end is a Corinthian screen of oak, having in the centre a painting of the Entombment of Christ, by Vandergutch, who lived for some time at Mortlake, and by whom it was presented in 1794. The font is octagonal, and of stone, enriched with sculpture, among which are the arms of the see of Canterbury and also those of Archbishop Bourchier, by whom it was probably given to the church in the reign of Henry VI.

In this church was buried, in December, 1818, Sir Philip Francis, the reputed author of *Junius*, and the inveterate enemy of Warren Hastings, having survived only a few short weeks the man whose elevation and prosperity he did so much to destroy. The mystery of the authorship of *Junius*, linked as it is with the names of Burke and so many other distinguished personages, somehow or other seems to sleep in Francis's grave.

Another man of note who rests in Mortlake church is Phillips, the fellow actor of Shakespeare. One of the legacies which he left was "a thirty-shilling piece in gold" to his immortal friend.

In the churchyard lies buried Henry Addington, the first Lord Sidmouth, who was Premier in 1802, a man known to his contemporaries as "the doctor," and described by Lord Russell as "the incarnation of prejudice and intolerance"—politically speaking, of course. We have already seen him as Ranger of Richmond Park.* His wife, who pre-deceased him, also lies here.

Here, too, lie buried the astrologers Dee and Partridge, the latter of whom is immortalised by Swift, who ridiculed him without mercy; Sir John Temple, the father of Sir William Temple; and Mr. John Barber, a printer by trade, who became Alderman and Lord Mayor of London. He was well acquainted with Bolingbroke, Pope, Swift, and the rest of the galaxy of literary stars of that period. A monument records the fact that he was "a constant benefactor to the poor, and true to his principles in Church and State. He preserved his integrity and discharged the duty of an upright magistrate in the most corrupt times. Zealous for the rights of his fellow-citizens, he opposed all attempts against them; and being Lord Mayor in the year 1733, he was greatly instrumental in resisting the scheme of a general excise, which, had it succeeded, would have put an end to the liberties of his country." It is to Alderman Barber that the immortal author of "Hudibras," Samuel Butler, is indebted for the memorial tablet in St. Paul's, Covent Garden.†

Here also lies buried the eccentric and independent Lord Mayor of London, Sir John Barnard —the only incorruptible Member of Parliament

that Sir Robert Walpole was ever able to discover. He was a man of strong patriotic sentiments, and opposed Sir Robert in his plan for introducing the Excise. Sir John Barnard was born at Reading in 1685, and was originally one of the Society of Friends; but becoming a member of the Church of England, from conviction, was baptised by Bishop Compton. He distinguished himself by his independent conduct. He entered Parliament in 1722 as one of the members for the City of London.

Some good stories are told which show how strenuously Sir John Barnard maintained his independence in St. Stephen's. Here is one:—When Sir Robert Walpole, then Prime Minister, was one day whispering to the Speaker of the House of Commons, the latter leaning to him over the arm of his chair, while Sir John was "on his legs," he exclaimed, "Mr. Speaker, I address myself to you, sir, and not to your chair. I will be heard, and I call the right honourable gentleman to order." The Speaker, feeling the rebuke to be not unmerited, turned round, left off chatting with Sir Robert, and begged Sir John Barnard to proceed, as he was "all attention." The story was well known in Parliamentary circles a century ago.

Notwithstanding that Sir John Barnard was such a zealous opponent of the all-powerful Sir Robert Walpole, then Premier, the great Minister one day paid him a high compliment. The story is thus told:—They (Barnard and Walpole) were riding out in two different parties in a narrow lane, when one of Sir Robert's companions, hearing the voice of Sir John Barnard before he came up to the other party, asked Sir Robert who it was that was approaching. "Oh, don't you know his voice?" was the reply; "for if *you* don't, *I* do, and with good reason, for I have often felt its power in the House of Commons; in fact, I shall not readily forget it." When they met near the end of the lane, Sir Robert stopped his horse, and saluting Sir John Barnard with that courtesy which he eminently possessed, told him what had happened in a way that set both parties at their ease.

As an instance of the esteem in which Sir John Barnard was held in the House of Commons, it may be mentioned that during the time when Lord Granville was Secretary of State, if any application was made to the Minister by the merchants and commercial men of the City, he never gave an answer without first asking "what Sir John Barnard had to say on the subject, and what was his candid opinion." Lord Chatham, too—then Mr. Pitt—a man not particularly apt to be lavish of his praise of any one, gave to Sir John the dignified name of

---

* See *ante*, p. 152.
† See "Old and New London," Vol. III., p. 256.

"The Great Commoner," an appellation which, possibly with greater propriety, was afterwards retorted upon Pitt by Sir John Barnard, whose modesty led him by instinct to repudiate it.

When, by the death of Sir James Thompson, he came to stand first on the list of aldermen, he became "the Father of the City," and it was generally thought that the title was never better deserved. Sir John Barnard died in 1764. He is immortalised by Pope in the same couplet with the Man of Ross. It is mentioned as a proof of his modesty that he never could be induced to enter the Royal Exchange after his monument was set up there.

The first stone of the Catholic church of St. Mary Magdalen, which adjoins the Protestant churchyard on the south, was laid in 1851 by Cardinal Wiseman. It is a handsome church, and an ornament to the village. Portobello House, close to the railway-station, a mansion standing in large grounds, was occupied in succession by many Roman Catholic families, the Mostyns, Gerards, &c. Mass was said in a loft over its stables previous to the building of the Catholic church.

Christ Church was built in Sheen Lane, in the south-west part of the parish, in 1864, as a chapel-of-ease to the parish church. The Independent chapel close by dates from 1716, but has been since enlarged.

At Mortlake and in its immediate neighbourhood are several charitable institutions. Close to the railway-station is a handsome row of Gothic build-ings, which form a hospital for the relief of decayed master-tradesmen, manufacturers, or agents, or their widows, in indigent circumstances. These almshouses belong to the Boot and Shoemakers' Benevolent Institution. They were built in 1836, and afford accommodation for fourteen inmates, each of whom receives £35 per annum. There are also other almshouses in the village, founded early in the seventeenth century by John Juxon, for four persons, who receive a small money allowance weekly. At the Limes, close to the river side, Dr. L. S. Winslow has opened a hospital for the cure of dipsomaniacs.

This parish was till lately famous for its beds of asparagus, but of late years the market-gardens have been forced here, as elsewhere, to give place to the onward march of suburban bricks and mortar. Aubrey, in his "Surrey" (Vol. I., p. 91), says that the sand taken from the bed of the Thames at this place makes an excellent cement with a small proportion of lime, and that it is found to bind stronger than any other.

Mortlake is not without its fashionable and its literary associations, though the latter are far less in number than those of Richmond or of Kew.

At the west end of the village there formerly stood a dull and substantial house, said to have been occupied by Oliver Cromwell, though there is but little ground, it is to be feared, for the tradition. It was more probably connected with Thomas, Lord Cromwell, with whom popular ignorance often confounds the Lord Protector. It had a small park before it and an avenue of limes, and in the rear a fine summer-house, over-looking the river.

The old house said to have been occupied by Cromwell was certainly the abode of Edward Colston, the Bristol philanthropist. It is described by Mr. Samuel G. Tovey, in his "Memorials of Colston," as an "isolated picturesque old building, visible from the lower London road to Rich-mond;" and he adds that "when he visited it, in 1852, it was a solitary, deserted, melancholy house, overshadowed by tall poplars, and divided from the road by a low wall, with an ornamental iron gateway between two square columns supporting globes, and each containing a stone seat under an arched niche." He continues :—" The paved court in front was grass-grown, and in the fine old garden bordering the Thames shrubs had grown into straggling thickets, and gravel paths were hardly distinguishable from grassy lawns. A half-ruined summer-house commanded a view of the church and village of Mortlake and Barnes railway-bridge to the east, and Hammersmith Church and Chis-wick Conservatory to the north. The hall itself was an irregular building, plain, spacious, dark, and decayed, with a portico supported by four Doric columns on the north. A long, narrow, panelled room occupying the western wing was known as Cromwell's Council Chamber ; and in the gable of the roof, up two or three steps, was a small room, called 'Old Noll's Hole,' from a tradition that it had been the Protector's favourite hiding-place, though why he should have wished to hide, or why, so wishing, he should have chosen such an accessible and apparent hiding-place, is hard to conjecture." The whole story of Cromwell having lived here is doubtless apocryphal, though he may have visited it, since the assessments show that Ireton and other friends of Cromwell had houses at Mortlake. The identification of this house with Colston, however, is no mere conjecture. At the time of Mr. Tovey's visit, the blue drawing-room, in which once hung the portraits of Colston and his father, bequeathed to the hospital at Bristol, retained its distinguishing colour after the lapse of a century and a half. Painters evidently did their work honestly in those days. On the lawn stood a magnificent catalpa tree, said to have been the largest in England, besides several other evergreens planted by Colston himself, and mentioned by him in his will. Colston, who in his lifetime is said to have expended more than £70,000 in charitable gifts and institutions, bequeathed in 1720 the annual sum of £45 for twelve years towards the support of a charity school which had been founded in this village about the year 1670.

The house was pulled down about the year 1860, though its garden and summer-house by the water-side, and some of the lofty garden wall, still remain. Most of the mansions hereabouts have river-side summer-houses, and in the long evenings of June and July a century ago these summer-houses were the haunts of the " quality " and fashion. Thus, for example, Mrs. Stone, in her " Chronicles of Fashions," gives an amusing picture of the quality going up the river by boat to a " greate banquet at Mortlack," or to Richmond, accompanied by a band of music in a separate boat, and making the shores resound with mirth and revelry."

Cradock tells us, in his " Memoirs," that Mr. Bankes, Chancellor of the church (cathedral) of York, an intimate friend of Lord Mansfield, kept a pack of hounds at Mortlake in the middle of the last century; but the house is not to be identified now.

John Anstis, Garter-King-at-Arms, and author of the " Register of the Garter," &c., lived for some years in this village, and died here in 1744.

In a river-side villa here lived Sir Henry Taylor, the author of " Philip Van Artevelde," &c., and here he used to entertain his friends. His house and his gatherings here are repeatedly mentioned by H. Crabb Robinson in his " Diary." Sir Henry Taylor, who acquired some celebrity as a dramatist, was born early in the present century. His first published drama was " Isaac Comnenus ; " this was followed by " Philip Van Artevelde," which soon secured for him a place amongst the writers of his day. In 1842 he produced another drama of an historical character, called " Edwin the Fair." He had, however, in the meantime, published " The Statesman," a book containing views and maxims respecting the transaction of public business, which had been suggested by the author, as he himself states, by twelve years of official life in the Civil Service. In 1848 he issued another work, also based on his own experience, entitled, " Notes from Life," and comprising essays on such subjects as "Choice in Marriage," " Humility and Indepen-

dence," " The Life Poetic," " Children," &c. Shortly afterwards appeared his " Notes from Books," which included an essay on " The Ways of the Rich and Great," and three others on modern poets, reprinted from the *Quarterly Review*. In 1850 he published a comedy, chiefly in verse, entitled " The Virgin Widow," which was followed, twelve years later, by " St. Clement's Eve." A collective edition of his plays and poems was issued in 1863. In noticing the last-named plays the *Athenæum* concludes its quotations with the remark :—" In these and other instances we trace the mind to which we owe ' Philip Van Artevelde ; ' but the present work will bear no comparison with its predecessor in point either of art, vigour, or philosophy." Of " Philip Van Artevelde," the *Quarterly Review* wrote that it was " the noblest effort in the true old taste of an English historical drama that has been made for more than a century ; " whilst Lord Macaulay, in the *Edinburgh Review*, says it is " a book in which we have found more to praise and less to blame than in any poetical work of imagination that has fallen under our notice for a considerable time."

In a pretty rustic cottage on the west side of the road leading up to East Sheen and Richmond Park lived for many years the amiable and eminent naturalist, Edward Jesse, the keeper of his Majesty's parks* and palaces, whose name is so well-known to all young people as a naturalist. He was a son of the Rev. William Jesse, vicar of Hutton Cranswick, Yorkshire, and subsequently of Bewdley, Worcestershire, and was born at the former place in 1780. Having held for a short time a clerkship in a Government office, he was appointed private secretary to Lord Dartmouth while President of the Board of Control, and when that nobleman became Lord Steward of the Household, he obtained for Mr. Jesse the Court office of Gentleman of the Ewry. Mr. Jesse subsequently became Controller of the Copper Coinage issued by Messrs. Bolton and Watt at Birmingham. About the year 1812 he was appointed a Commissioner of Hackney Coaches, and soon afterwards Deputy Surveyor-General of the Royal Parks and Palaces. This latter post he held, together with his appointment at Court, until the year 1830, when both offices were abolished, and he retired on a pension. Mr. Jesse was the author of "Anecdotes of Dogs," " Anglers' Rambles," " Favourite Haunts and Rural Studies, including Visits to Spots of Interest in the Vicinity of Windsor and Eton," " Gleanings in Natural History," " A Summer Day

---

* See *ante*, p. 353.

at Hampton Court," "A Handbook to Hampton Court," "Scenes and Tales of Country Life," and also an edition, with notes, of Walton and Cotton's "Complete Angler," published in one of Bohn's series. The *Literary Gazette* speaks of Mr. Jesse's "Favourite Haunts" as "a pleasing and popular *omnium gatherum* about interesting architectural remains, the biography of their bygone inhabitants, country life, rural scenery, literature, natural history, &c."

Like White of Selborne, who made a small village in Hampshire one of the most interesting spots to the lover of Nature by his ample descriptions of the natural objects which he saw around him, Mr. Jesse rendered his walks a vehicle for much instruction and amusement to himself and to others. He principally confined his attention to zoology—the most generally attractive of the departments of natural history; and he looked upon the animal world with so much practical wisdom—being disposed to be happy himself and to see every creature around him happy—that there are few persons who will not read his slight sketches with improvement to their hearts and understandings. His house was a constant haunt of the learned, the fashionable, and the scientific world. He died in 1868 at Brighton, where his last act was to establish a "Fisherman's Home." One of his most constant visitors was his friend and neighbour, Professor Owen, of whom we have already spoken,* and who lived for many years at Sheen Lodge, just within the gates of Richmond Park.

East Sheen is practically a hamlet of Mortlake, situated on the Richmond Road, a short distance southward of the Mortlake railway-station. The place is not deficient in historic interest, for here the unfortunate Amy Robsart, daughter of Sir John Robsart, is said to have been married, June 4th, 1550, in the presence of Edward VI., to Lord Robert Dudley, afterwards Earl of Leicester. Her unfortunate fate at Cumnor, near Abingdon, is known to every reader of Sir Walter Scott's "Kenilworth," and of Mickle's ballad of "Cumnor Hall."

Fuller thus mentions, in his "Worthies," one distinguished native of this place, Sir Robert Dudley, a natural son of Robert, Earl of Leicester. "He became a most compleat gentleman, and endeavoured in the reign of King James to prove his legitimacy (his mother being Douglas Sheffield), and meeting with much opposition from the Court, in distaste left the land, and went over to Italy, where he became a favourite to the Duke of

Florence, who used his directions in all his buildings. Legorn [*sic*] was much beholding [*sic*] to him for its fairness and firmness, as chief contriver of both. Upon his refusal to come home to England, all his lands were seized by the king. These losses doubled the duke's love to him, as being a much meriting person, an excellent mathematician, physician, and navigator. In Queen Elizabeth's dayes he had sail'd with three small ships to the Isle of Trinidad, in which voyage he sunk and took nine *Spanish* ships, whereof one an Armada of 600 tun. Ferdinand II., Emperor of Germany, conferred on him and his heirs the title of a Duke of the Sacred Empire."

Here, too, resided Sir William Temple. This eminent statesman was nephew of Dr. Henry Hammond, and during the reign of Charles II. took an active part in the affairs of the nation. He formed the Triple League: "the masterpiece," says Burnet, "of Charles's life; and if he had stuck to it, would have been both the strength and glory of his reign!" King William often consulted him on political affairs, and visited him here. So dearly attached was this philosopher to his fascinating suburban retreat, that he lived here for seven years without once going up to London.

Another resident at East Sheen was Mr. Henry Brouncker. "I dined," writes Evelyn, in his "Diary," under date Aug., 1678, "at Mr. Brounker's, at the Abbey (*sic*) of Sheene, formerly a monastery of Carthusians; there yet remains one of their solitary cells, with a crosse." He adds that within the "ample enclosure" which once belonged to the abbot "are several pretty villas and fine gardens of the most excellent fruites," especially those of Sir William Temple and Lord Lisle.

Again, under date of March 24th, 1688, we find the following entry in the "Diary":—"I went with Sir Charles Littleton to Sheene, an house and estate given him by Lord Brouncker: one who was ever noted for a hard, covetous, vicious man, but for his worldly craft and skill in gaming, few exceeded him. Coming to die, he bequeath'd all his land, house, furniture, &c., to Sir Charles, to whom he had no manner of relation, but an ancient friendship contracted at the famous siege of Colchester, 40 years before. It is a pretty place, with fine gardens, and well planted, and given to one worthy of them, Sir Charles being an honest gentleman and souldier. He is brother to Sir Henry Littleton of Worcestershire, whose greate estate he is likely to inherit, his brother being without children. They are descendants of the great lawyer of that name, and give the same arms and motto. He is married to one Mrs. Temple,

---

* See *ante*, page 358.

who was formerly maide of honour to the late Queene, a beautiful lady, and he has many fine children, so that none envy his good fortune, After dinner we went to see Sir William Temple's, neere to it; the most remarkable things are his orangerie and gardens, where the wall fruit trees are most exquisitely nail'd and train'd, far better than I ever noted elsewhere. There are many good pictures, especially of Vandyke's, in both these houses, and some few statues and small busts in the latter."

have the gout, took Swift into the gardens, and amused him by showing him how to cut asparagus after the Dutch manner.

It was probably whilst residing here that Swift first met his Stella, the daughter of Mr. Johnson, of Richmond, Sir William Temple's steward. She followed Swift to Ireland, was privately married to him by the Bishop of Clogher, and died of a broken heart in 1727. The parish register of Richmond contains an entry of her baptism, as already stated.

EAST SHEEN.

These gardens were about as famous as those of the Carews at Beddington* for their growth of oranges.

The house has some literary history, for Swift was for nearly two years resident as a guest in Sir William Temple's house, and thus he had often an opportunity of meeting King William, who was often a visitor there. The king treated Swift with much familiarity, and offered him the command of a troop of horse, which he declined. This was, of course, before he had entered orders.

On one occasion King William, visiting Sir William Temple, who happened at the time to

Sir William Temple was hospitable and friendly, but correct and abstemious. It was this Sir William Temple who was the author of the *mot*, "The first glass for myself, the second for my friends, the third for good humour, and the fourth for my enemies." It would have been well if "lords" in the last century and "working-men" in this could have been brought to acknowledge the wit of this remark, and to act on it. The following lines are to be found in Sir William Temple's "Essay on Gardening" :—" If we believe the Scriptures, we must allow that God Almighty esteemed the life of a man in a garden the happiest that He could give him, or else He would not have placed Adam in that of Eden ; it was the state of

* See *ante*, p. 189.

innocence and pleasure, and the life of husbandry and cities came after the fall with guilt and labour."

The house was called Temple Grove, after its former occupier, Sir William Temple. It was for some years the favourite residence of the first Lord and Lady Palmerston, who here kept much company and had many fashionable and distinguished visitors, among the latter being Count Rumford. More recently it was converted into a school, kept formerly by Dr. Pinckney, and now by Mr. O. Waterfield.

Dr. Pinckney's school is probably intended by Disraeli in the first chapter of "Coningsby" as the "fashionable preparatory school to Eton," where that young gentleman "found about two hundred youths of noble families and their connections lodged in a magnificent villa, that had once been the retreat of a Minister of State."

Old Lady Brownlow, in her "Reminiscences of a Septuagenarian," records that Lord and Lady Castlereagh occupied, in 1805, a villa at East Sheen. Lord Grey was living here a little later, in November, 1831, as we learn from the "Life of Lord Macaulay," who spent a day or two with him, talking over with him, doubtless, the prospects of Parliamentary Reform.

In 1813 Sir Archibald Macdonald, Chief Baron of the Court of Exchequer, was created a baronet, being styled in the patent of baronetcy as "of East Sheen, Surrey," where he resided for many years. Sir Archibald was the youngest son of Sir Alexander Macdonald, Baronet of Slate, county Antrim, and brother of the first Lord Macdonald. Being bred to the Bar, and having attained eminence in his profession, he was successively Solicitor-General and Attorney-General, and was raised to the Bench in 1793.

At Palewell Lodge, East Sheen, lived and died, in 1843, at an advanced age, Mr. W. S. Gilpin, the celebrated gardener, and the author of various works on the picturesque. At whatever price the

I R. JOHN DEE.

world esteemed his horticultural taste, it would seem that he valued it still more highly himself; at all events, his biographer in the *Gentleman's Magazine* tells us that "when, in the course of a conversation upon the crowded state of all the professions, it was casually remarked to Mr. Gilpin that at all events members of *his* profession were not numerous, he quietly remarked, 'No; there is but one.' He afterwards, however, admitted that there was one other, a gardener in Derbyshire, named Pontet." Had he lived a little later, he might perhaps have admitted the existence of yet another, Sir Joseph Paxton.

But by far the most celebrated inhabitant of Mortlake was the quack alchemist and astrologer of the sixteenth century, John Dee, who died here in 1608, at the age of eighty. In conjunction with one Kelly, he employed himself for many years in searching after the "Elixir Vitæ" and the "Philosopher's Stone," and pretended to hold intercourse with the angelic and spiritual world. He contrived to make himself acceptable to the vanity of Queen Elizabeth, who, on one occasion, condescended to pay him a visit at his house here, to view his museum of curiosities, and when he was ill, sent her own Court physician to prescribe for him. He claimed, *inter alia*, to have found the true "Elixir Vitæ" among the ruins of Glastonbury Abbey. A full account of this impostor will be found in Dr. C. Mackay's "Memoirs of Extraordinary Popular Delusions."

But it may be well to tell the story of this arch-impostor more in detail, if it be only to show how foolish are the wisest of monarchs at times.

This Dr. Dee, a disciple and follower of Lilly the astrologer, "the cunning man hight Sidrophel" of Hudibras, was a Welshman, and educated at Oxford, where, we are told, "he commenced doctor, and afterwards travelled into foreign parts in quest of chemistry." Lilly tells us that he was Queen Elizabeth's "intelligencer," and that he had for his maintenance a salary from the Secretary of State; that he was the most ambitious man alive, and never so well pleased as when he heard himself styled "Most Excellent." In 1659 was printed in folio "A Relation of what passed for many years between John Dee and some Spirits." It begins with May, 1583, and ends with September, 1607. It was published by Meric Casaubon, son of the learned Isaac Casaubon, with a preface, in which we find the following statements. When young, he was "sought unto" by two emperors, Charles and Ferdinand, his brother and successor. Camden calls him "*nobilis mathematicus.*" In 1595 he wrote an apology for himself, addressed to Whitgift, Archbishop of Canterbury, in which he gives a catalogue of his unprinted works, some fifty in all, among which was a defence of Roger Bacon from the charge of holding conversation with evil spirits; besides these, he appears to have printed eight others, mostly on mathematical subjects. At the end of his "Apology" is a testimonial from the University of Cambridge. From Zachary Grey's notes to "Hudibras" we learn that "about the year 1578, Dee's pretended commerce with the angels began, the account of which was all wrote by his own hand, and communicated by Sir Thomas Cotton. He had a round stone like a chrystal, brought him (as he said) by angels, in which others saw apparitions, and from whence they heard voices, which he carefully wrote down from their mouths. He names at least twenty spirits: Gabriel, Raphael, Michael, and Uriel are known names of good angels; the rest are too far tastie to be mentioned. . . . . Of what kind all these were, if they were anything more than fancy, is plain from a revelation of theirs, April 18, 1587, enjoining a community of wives to Dee and Kelly —an injunction which they most conscientiously obeyed. He was so confident as to address himself to Queen Elizabeth and her council often, and to King James and his (council), to the Emperor Rodolph, to Stephen, King of Poland, and several other princes, and to the Spanish Ambassador in Germany. He had thought also of going to the Pope, had he not been banished from Germany. Dee's chief seer was Edward Kelly, from whose reports the shapes and words of the apparitions were wrote. Alasco, Palatine of Poland, Pucci, a learned Florentine, and Prince Rosemberg of Germany, the Emperor's Viceroy of Bohemia, were long of the society, and often present at their actions, as was once the King of Poland himself. After Kelly's death, in 1587, Arthur Dee was admitted to be a seer, and reported to his father what he saw in the stone, but heard nothing from it. In 1607 one Bartholomew Hickman was operator, and both saw and heard. In that year

Dee foretells what has become of stolen goods. There is no account when or how he died. In Dee's account of himself he says that he was offered 200 French crowns yearly to be one of the French king's mathematicians; that he might have served five Christian Emperors, namely, Charles V., Ferdinand, Maximilian, Rodolph, and the then Emperor of Muscovy, 'each of them offering him a stipend from 500 dollars yearly to 1,000, 2,000, and 3,000; and that his Russian Majesty offered him 2,000 pounds sterling yearly stipend, with a thousand rubles (*sic*) from his Protector, and his diet out of his own kitchen; and he to be in dignity and authority among the highest sort of nobility and privy councillors.'"

In fact, it would be difficult to determine which of the three, Lilly, Dee, or Kelly, was the greater pretender; though, doubtless, Lilly's name is the better known, and the more thoroughly identified with the occult sciences, on account of his having been the author of so many almanacs.

Butler, in his "Hudibras," Part II., cant. iii., thus writes of a conjuror :—

> "He'd read Dee's prefaces before,
>   The Dev'l and Euclid o'er and o'er,
>   And all th' intrigues 'twixt him and Kelly
>   Lescus and th' Emperor would tell ye."

Dr. Dee speaks of sundry charms and incantations practised on Queen Elizabeth, and adds, in the spirit of self-exculpation :—"My careful and faithful endeavour was with great speed required to prevent the mischief which divers of her Majesty's Privy Council suspected to be intended against her Majesty's person by means of a certain image of wax, with a great pin stuck into the breast of it, in great Lincoln's Inn Fields; wherein I did satisfy her Majesty's desire, and the Lords of this Honourable Privy Council, in a few hours, in godly and artful manner."

Similar charms were employed, as it may be remarked, by Eleanor Cobham to take off Henry VI., and by Amy Simpson and others to destroy James VI. of Scotland. A full description of this process will be found in the eighth "Eclogue" of Virgil.

Kelly himself was born at Worcester, and bred up for an apothecary. He was a proficient in chemistry, and pretended to have found the grand "Elixir," or Philosopher's Stone, which he received ready made from a friar on the borders of the dominions of the Emperor of Germany. He pretended to see apparitions in a crystal or beryl looking-glass, or in a round stone like a crystal. Wever, in his "Funeral Monuments," says that he lost his ears at Lancaster, and raised a dead body there to life by necromancy. He showed his famous glass, and explained the properties of it, to Queen Elizabeth, who was as superstitious as she was vain and imperious. In spite of his knowledge of future events, he appears to have met with a fatal accident, and to have died in Germany.

Miss Strickland writes as follows:—"At the very period of this stormy excitement Elizabeth was secretly amusing herself with the almost exploded chimeras of alchemy, for Cecil, in his Diary, has noted that, in January, 1567, 'Cornelius Lanoy, a Dutchman, was committed to the Tower for abusing the queen's majesty in promising to make the elixir.' This impostor had been permitted to have his laboratory at Somerset House, where he had deceived many by promising to convert any metal into gold. To the queen a more flattering delusion had been held forth, even the draught of perpetual life and youth, and her strong intellect had been duped into a persuasion that it was in the power of a foreign empiric to confer the boon of immortality upon her. The particulars of this transaction would doubtless afford a curious page in the personal history of the mighty Elizabeth. That she was a believer in the occult sciences, and an encourager of those who practised the forbidden arts of divination and transmutation, no one who has read the Diary of her pet conjuror, Dr. Dee, can doubt. It is probable that he was an instrument used by her to practise on the credulity of other princes, and that, through his agency, she was enabled to penetrate into many secret plots and associations in her own realm, but she placed, apparently, an absurd reliance on his predictions herself. She even condescended, with her whole Court and Privy Council, to visit him one day at Mortlake, when it was her gracious intention to have examined his library, and enter into further conference, but understanding that his wife had only been buried four hours, she contented herself with a peep into his magic mirror, which he brought to her. 'Her Majesty,' says Dee, 'being taken down from her horse by the Earl of Leicester, Master of the Horse, at the church wall at Mortlake, did see some of the properties of that glass, to her Majesty's great contentment and delight.'*

"A strange sight, in sooth, it must have been for the good people of Mortlake, who had witnessed in the morning the interment of the wizard's wife in the churchyard, to behold in the afternoon the maiden majesty of England holding conference with the occult widower under the same church wall on the flowery margin of the Thames. Nay, more : alighting from her stately palfrey to read a forbidden page of futurity in the dim depths of his wondrous mirror*—ebon framed, and in shape and size resembling some antique hand-screen— while her gay and ambitious Master of the Horse, scarcely refrained, perchance, from compelling the oracle to reflect his own handsome face to the royal eye as that of the man whom the fates had decided it was her destiny to wed. Many, however, were the secret consultations which Dee held with Queen Elizabeth at Windsor and Richmond, and even at Whitehall; and when she passed that way she honoured him with especial greetings."

"On September 17th," he writes, "the Queen's Majesty came from Richmond in her coach, the higher way, of Mortlake field, and when she came right against the church, she turned down towards my house ; and when she was against my garden in the field, she stood there a good while, and then came into the street at the great gate of the field, where, espying me at my door, she beckoned me to come to the coach side ; she very speedily pulled off her glove and gave me her hand to kiss, and, to be short, asked me to resort to her Court, and to give her to wete (know) when I came there." He had also flattered Elizabeth with promises of perennial youth and beauty, from his anticipated discovery of the elixir of life, and the prospect also of unbounded wealth, as soon as he should have arrived at the power of bringing to practical purpose his secret of transmitting the baser metals into gold.

"After years of false, but not fruitless, trickery, he (Dr. Dee) professed to have arrived at the point of projection, having cut a piece of base metal out a brass metal warming-pan, and merely heating it by the fire and pouring on it a portion of his elixir, converted it into pure silver. He is said to have sent the warming-pan with the piece of silver to the queen, that she might see with her own eyes the miracle, and be convinced that they were the veritable parts that had been severed from each other by the exact manner in which they corresponded after the transmutation had been effected. His frequent impositions on the judgment of the queen did not cure her of the partiality with which she regarded him, and, after a long residence on the Continent, she wooed him to

---

* "Diary of Dr. Dee" edited by James O. Halliwell ; published by the Camden Society.

* This identical mirror attracted much attention at the sale of Horace Walpole's collection, at Strawberry Hill, and was knocked down, after great competition, for fifteen guineas. It is now in the British Museum.

return to England, which he did, travelling with three coaches, each with four horses, in state little inferior to that of an ambassador. A guard of soldiers was sent to defend him from molestation or plunder on the road. Immediately on his arrival he had an audience of the queen at Richmond, by whom he was most graciously received. She issued her especial orders that he should do what he liked in chemistry and philosophy, and that no one should on any account interrupt him. He held two livings in the Church, through the patronage of his royal mistress, though he was suspected by her loyal lieges of being in direct correspondence and friendship with the devil. Elizabeth finally bestowed on him the Chancellorship of St. Paul's Cathedral."

The famous convex crystal which Dr. Dee had in 1582 he pretended to have received from the angel Uriel. This crystal was believed, as we have seen, to have the quality, when intently surveyed, of presenting apparitions, and even emitting sounds. The phenomena varied. Sometimes the crystal had to be turned about several ways before the right focus was obtained ; sometimes the spirits appeared upon the crystal, sometimes reflected upon parts of the room, but only one person could see the figure or hear the sounds. Hence a medium was requisite with whose testimony the inquirer was compelled to be satisfied, for he neither saw nor heard anything himself.

But Mortlake has a reputation for something better and more practically useful than astrology, necromancy, or the philosopher's stone. It figures also in the history of one of our national industries. Early in the seventeenth century Sir Francis Crane started here a manufactory of tapestry, under the auspices of royalty. The foundation of these tapestry works is thus recorded in *Anglorum Speculum*, 1684 :—" King James I., about the end of his reign, gave 2,000 pounds to Sir Francis Crane to build a house at Morelack (*sic*) for setting up a manufacture of tapestry, and one Francis Klein, a German, was the designer thereof, and united the Italian and Dutch perfections in that mystery. This Klein afterwards settled in London, where he had a gratuity of 100 pounds *per an.* till the beginning of the late Civil Wars."

Charles I. patronised this manufactory, and in the first year of his reign acknowledged a debt to Crane of £6,000 for three sets of " gold hangings." Archbishop Williams paid him £2,500 for a piece representing the " Four Seasons " ; and the more affluent of the nobility purchased of him, at proportionate prices, various rich hangings " wrought in silk."

At this factory much of the finest tapestry which still survives in our chief country mansions was made—notably that at Bramshill, Hampshire, now the seat of the Cope family. Here also five at least of the cartoons of Raffaelle were copied, under the direction of the above-mentioned Klein, by command of James II. The cartoons were afterwards hung up at Whitehall,* whence they were removed to Windsor Castle, afterwards to Hampton Court Palace, and at last found a permanent abode at Kensington. To Rubens belongs the merit of having mentioned the existence of the cartoons of Raffaelle to Charles I., and of having advised him to purchase them for the use of his tapestry weavers at Mortlake. " Five of them," remarks the Countess of Wilton in her " Art of Needlework," were *certainly* woven there ; and it is far from improbable that the remaining ones were also." In a priced catalogue of his Majesty's collections of " Limnings," edited by Vertue, is the following entry :—" Item : in a slit box-wooden case, some *two* cartoons of Raphael Urbinno for hangings to be made by ; and *the other five* are, by the King's appointment, delivered to Mr. Francis Klein, at Mortlake, to make hangings by."

There is extant a letter from Crane addressed to King James I., complaining of the non-payment of debts to him by the king and the Duke of Buckingham, and placing upon record the fact that he had expended no less than £300 out of his own pocket for certain drawings as designs for tapestry made originally for Pope Leo X. by Raffaelle, the subjects illustrated being the twelve months of the year. In the first year of the reign of Charles I. Sir Francis Crane received a pension of £1,000 a year ; and subsequently there was a grant of " £2,000 yearly for the better maintenance of the said works of tapestries for ten years."

After the death of Sir Francis Crane, his brother sold his interest in the manufactory to Charles I., by whose authority it was thenceforth known as the King's Works.

Allusions to the manufactory, while it was worked, are not unfrequent in the pages of contemporary writers. Thus Jasper Mayne, in his comedy of the " City Match," put on the stage about 1640, makes one of his characters ask :—

> " Why, Lady, do you think me
> Wrought in a loom? some Dutch piece wove at Mortlake?"

And again, John Oldham, in his " Satyr in imitation of the Third of Juvenal," written towards the

---

end of the seventeenth century, makes the following reference to these works :—

> " Here some rare piece
> Of Rubens or Vandyck presented is ;
> There a rich suit of Morelack tapestry,
> A bed of damask, or embroidery."

The manufactory, however was but short-lived.
The Civil Wars, or rather the "Great Rebellion,"
put a stop to the demand for such useless and
superstitious luxuries, and the industry came to an
end. Such an admirable patron of art is the
"sovereign people !"

Some idea may be formed of the extent of the
Works here, at that time called the Tapestry House,
from the Parliamentary Survey, wherein it is described as "a building 115 feet long and 84 feet
deep, having on the second floor one great working-
room 82 feet long and 20 feet wide, wherein are
12 looms for making tapestry work of all sorts,
and another room about half as long containing
six looms, a great room called the limner's room,
and on the third floor a long gallery divided into
three rooms."

Charles II. had some wish to revive the tapestry
manufacture at Mortlake, and even went so far as
to send for Verrio the Neapolitan, and consulted
him how his wishes could be effected. But in the
end it was agreed that the manufacture could be
carried on better at Windsor, where that artist
found scope for his genius in designing the
decorations of St. George's Hall and Chapel, and
other parts of the castle, including the well-known
picture of the king in a naval triumph. Verrio was
afterwards employed at Hampton Court, and also
at Burleigh and Chatsworth.

The Tapestry Works at Mortlake, according to
Lysons, occupied the site of Queen's Head Court.
Lysons also states that "the house on the opposite
side of the road, built by Charles I. for Francis
Cleyn (or Klein), was pulled down in or about the
year 1794."

Although tapestry-weaving has long been a
thing of the past at Mortlake, it may be added that
it has lately been revived with success at Windsor ;
and it is of interest to know that the late Duke of
Albany was really the founder of that manufactory.
At a meeting of the Aberdeen Town Council, held
shortly before the death of the duke, a letter was
read from his Royal Highness in which he referred
to the movement for the revival of the art of
tapestry-making as a connecting link between
painting and manufactures. The duke made an
appeal to all public bodies who have so warmly
supported technical education to extend the sphere
of action of the Windsor looms. He reminded them

that not only are works undertaken at these looms,
but that the beautiful specimens of ancient tapestry
which decorated so many of the great English
houses, and which time and moth are ruining, may
be perfectly repaired at them. The Duke of
Albany added :—" Tapestries have at all times
commanded the interest of the art-loving world,
and are particularly suited for the decoration of
the large halls which belong to the various cor-
porations to whom I am appealing for support. I should be pleased to have your view on
this matter, and to call a principal meeting to
discuss the subject, and talk over the means by
which a permanent national institution could be
established."

But Mortlake did not confine its artistic industry
to tapestry. Early in the present century it had
several potteries ; one of these existed down to
1831, if we may believe a writer in *Notes and
Queries.**The chief names connected with
these potteries were Price and Wagstaff. It is
said that "Toby Philpot" jugs were invented here.
The history of this branch of manufacture is thus
told :—

It appears that the older pottery here was established by Abraham Saunders about 1742-9; he
was succeeded in the business by his son, and
afterwards by Wagstaff and Co. ; then by Prior,
and then by Gurney. The manufactory stood near
the present mallings by the water-side, to the north-
west of the church. Another pottery, for the
manufacture of white stone-ware, on the opposite
side of the road, was established by a man named
Kishew, who had been employed in the older
establishment. It would seem, from the same
authority,† that "Toby" jugs were made at both
of these houses. It is not a little singular, as others
have remarked before me, that here, as at Chelsea
and elsewhere, such potteries should have passed
clean away, and left scarce a trace or a vestige
behind them.

Though its tapestry works have long since perished
and been forgotten, and its potteries are things
of the past, Mortlake can boast of a large
brewery. The brewery is historic, for it is said
to have been founded in 1487 by John Morgan,
or Williams, the ancestor of the Cromwell family,
of whom we shall have more to say when we reach
Wimbledon.

In 1883 it was proposed to make Mortlake the
site of new and extensive sewage-works, but the
suggestion was strongly opposed. The Local Go-

---

* See *Notes and Queries*, Dec. 28, 1867.
† See *Notes and Queries*, June 27, 1868.

vernment Board sought power to acquire fifty-five acres of land on the banks of the Thames at Mortlake, and there to treat the sewage by precipitation, the sludge being disposed of to the neighbouring market-gardeners or conveyed down the river in barges to some waste land at Woolwich, to

picture such as is not seen on the Seine near Paris, or on the Tagus near Lisbon, though the Thames here can boast no romantic beauty on its level banks, which bristle with osier-beds on either side.

Mortlake, however, enjoys one element of popu-

OLD SUMMER-HOUSE AT MORTLAKE.

OLD GATEWAY, CROMWELL HOUSE, MORTLAKE.

obtain which also compulsory powers were sought. If the scheme were carried out, Mortlake would become a depôt of the sewage of no less than twenty-one parishes, with a population of 120,000 and its inhabitants are not very anxious for the honour.

The walk from the west end of Mortlake to Kew, through green meadows and shady lanes, is pleasant in the summer. We keep the river in view all the way on our right hand, and across it we see the dark cedars and evergreens of Grove Park, Chiswick, to which we introduced our readers when they started with us on our present pilgrimage.* In the foreground, the skiffs, the sailing-yachts, and the steam-launches, present a

larity, which seems likely to last as long as the annual boat-race between the Universities of Oxford and Cambridge shall continue to be rowed on London waters. Here is the winning-post, just opposite to the "Ship" inn, which stands about a quarter of a mile above the church.

It would seem that this is the most appropriate place for a few remarks about this "Water Derby," this "Battle of the Rival Blues."

* See Vol. I., p. 7.

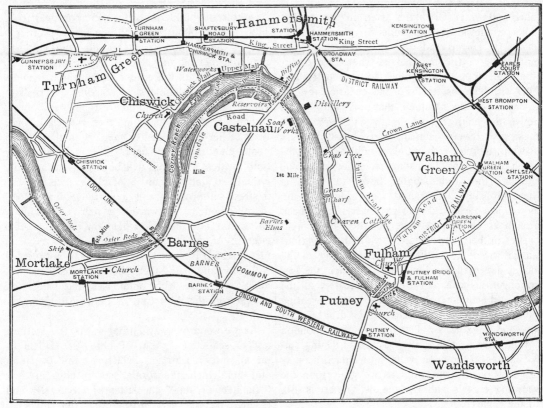

THE BOAT-RACE COURSE.

CHAPTER XLVI.

THE UNIVERSITY BOAT-RACE.

Cuncti adsint, meritæque expectent præmia palmæ.—VIRG. Æn. V.

The Crowds of Spectators brought together to witness the Race—The "Blue" Fever—Interest to Londoners occasioned by the University Boat-Race—Scenes of the Road from London on the Boat-Race Day—Popularity of the Boat-Race among the Ladies of England—Scenes on the River—The Press-Boat and the Umpire's Steamer—By Rail to the Scene of the Race—Putney and Mortlake on Boat-Race Day—Description of the Race—Past History of Rowing as an old English Amusement—The Race for Doggett's Coat and Badge—A London Regatta—The First Students' Race upon the Thames—The Earliest Race between the Universities of Oxford and Cambridge—Accounts of subsequent Races—Table showing the Results of the Race from its Institution.

IT may be easy enough to describe the general out-line of the banks of the Thames about Mortlake and Barnes, but to sketch the holiday which comes round in March or April, and the crowds of spec-tators, would require the pen of a Dickens. The surging multitude annually brought together, no matter at how early an hour in the morning, and blocks up the thoroughfares of Hammersmith, Chis-wick, Putney, Barnes, and Mortlake—diverse as are its types, infinite as are the varieties of its charac-ter—has evidently been the result of some one common object of national and universal interest. High and low, rich and poor, young and old, all seem to be swayed by one common impulse: to witness a trial of skill, strength, pluck, and en-durance between the representatives of those two universities which have been called "the eyes of England." What matters it that the sight of the

struggle can last only for a few minutes, and that, so far as concerns nine-tenths of the spectators along the banks, the race is over and past in "the twinkling of an eye?" that moment is, however, to them the most thrilling of all the year, not even excepting the "Derby" at Epsom.

For days and almost weeks beforehand London looks very "blue" indeed. The light blue of Cambridge and the dark blue of Oxford meet our eyes in the shop-fronts of half the tradesmen at the West End. If the sky is not blue above, at all events we can point to the blue bonnets and ribbons of our wives, sisters, and cousins, as an excellent substitute for its presence. As a lively writer on the boat-race remarks, "There is blue everywhere: in the silk-mercers' and haber-dashers' shops, in the shape of ribbons, and bows, and dresses; in the china shops, in the shape of 'blue and white Oriental;' even in the pastry-cooks' windows we find under a glass case an 'eight' in gingerbread propelled by blue pepper-mint oars; in the bootmakers' shops are dainty little boots topped with blue cloth, or natty little shoes with blue rosettes. For this occasion, indeed, it may be safely assumed that any lady would forgive the bold wag who might call her a 'blue stocking!' Every cabman, every bus driver, has his whip adorned with either a light or dark blue bunch of ribbons; hansoms are gay with blue curtains; the tradespeople's boys, to many of whom probably Oxford and Cambridge are un-known localities, and who may never have been in a boat or seen a race in their lives, wear rosettes in their button-holes; while in the various vehicles, from the lordly four-in-hand drag to the donkey-drawn 'flying bedstead' in which the cos-termonger, his wife, and friends are seated, all the ladies and gentlemen have some article of wearing apparel of a hue which betoken the drift of their hope and aspirations. The population of London and the surrounding country has, in fact, 'hung out' its 'banner on the outer walls,' and indeed we may well carry on the quotation as we gaze upon the swarming crowds, and exclaim: 'The cry is still, "They come!"'"

And, to speak the truth, "on they come" from every point of the compass. London has been astir from the very earliest dawn; and a view of its streets will suffice to convince the incredulous that the boat-race day is rapidly gaining upon the Derby day in popular favour. Much is to be said on its behalf. No doubt it is pleasant to see the highly-trained horses, with their sleek coats and shapely, quivering frames; but in this race it is a team of bipeds, not a number of quadrupeds, that appeal to our sympathies: sixteen stalwart youths, not goaded by the bit and spur, but voluntarily and for the mere honour of their *alma mater*, come forth to do battle for Oxford and Cambridge respectively; and it is because of this *human* interest which brains give to the contest that we feel more delight in watching the eights shoot under Hammersmith Bridge than in witnessing the scrimmage of the race-horses at Tattenham Corner, and gaze with more interest over the sweep of the river between Barnes Bridge and the "Ship" than up the "home stretch" from the Grand Stand at Epsom.

But it is time that we returned to our theme: the crowds of spectators that line the banks of the river from Putney to Mortlake. The ladies, who are up betimes, and have made their toilettes perhaps by candle-light, all do their best to reach their several destinations, no matter how long they may have to wait shuddering with cold upon the banks. Here is one young lady, a blonde, whose brother is one of the Cambridge crew, and who has sur-rendered her flowing locks to her maid to be intermingled with fluttering ribbons and streamers of the lightest possible shade of blue. Here is a young mistress of the brunette type, her bonnet, or hat, and dress equally adorned with dark blue, because her cousin or her *fiancé* is in the Oxford boat. But "light" or "dark" blue, however, to-day both mistress and maid will be intent on the same errand: to get a glimpse of "the race." The mistress will probably roll down the Fulham Road in a barouche, drawn by a pair of spanking chestnuts; and the maid will follow, a few moments later, in or on a plebeian omnibus, her "young man" seated by her side. Or, if she be not blessed with a young man, then she and the cook will quietly dispense with omnibuses and cabs, and trudge from the West End to Putney or Hammer-smith.

As we wend our way Putney-wards, the victims, not of scarlet fever but of blue fever, meet us on all sides. Carriages whisk by full of ladies and gentlemen, the former conspicuous in their "bonnets of blue," the latter with blue ties and rosettes, at the very least—from the duchess's carriage to the costermonger's cart, the prevailing hue is one and the same. And so the crowd jogs along, in the road and on the pavement, amidst the rush of wheels, the clatter of iron-shod hoofs, the tramp of shoe-leather—a ceaseless stream of vehicles, horses, mankind, all bound to see and enjoy the boat-race. We must remember that this metropolitan and suburban crowd is a material expression, as it were, of the widespread interest that is felt in the event all over the country. As a London journal truly remarks:—"The chief charm of the University Boat-Race is the general interest which it awakens. The Derby has long since ceased to be anything more than a national holiday. People go down to it as they go to the Crystal Palace on a firework night, or to the Opera when it is known that royalty will be present. But nobody, except those who are immediately interested in the matter, cares much whether this or that particular horse wins the blue ribbon of the Turf, or whether this or that particular opera is put upon the stage on the special evening in question. It is quite otherwise with those who attend the boat race. A large section of the spectators goes merely to see a sight, and is not greatly concerned as to the event; but, on the other hand, all over England, in every household where father, son, brother, or even cousin, is a member of either university, the news flashed throughout the country is waited for with the keenest interest. The boat-race is the one great link between the two old universities and the outer world, and from this point of view there is some excuse for those who have called it the modern Olympia. The university boat-race strikes a chord, the vibrations of which are widely felt. It is, as it were, the 'show day of the two universities.' The crowds 'go to see what they will see : a keen, earnest, manly contest, fought out without fear or favour ; and they will also see, if they need to be satisfied on that point, that culture of the highest kind is not incompatible with pluck and endurance, and that the civilisation of modern Europe, like that of ancient Greece, subordinates neither mind to body nor body to mind.' "

In fact, in the dense crowd which lines the banks of our river in the early morning of this annual spring festival, not a single element in English social life is left unrepresented.

The separation of political party is lost for the nonce in the division of the country into two great representative sections—the people who declare for Oxford and the people who elect to place their confidence in Cambridge. England is for this occasion more Oxonian and Cantabrigian than she is Conservative and Liberal, and there is more enthusiasm exhibited in twenty minutes along the Thames' banks from Putney to Mortlake than in the houses of the Legislature during the lifetime of half-a-dozen ministers. Moreover, antecedent to the day appointed for deciding this great aquatic contest of the year there is expressed as keen a desire to watch, note, and discuss the athletic and other qualities of the rival crews as if they had been opposing forces, on whose prowess and skill the honour of one or other of two parties in the nation was dependent. The kind of partisanship of which the Oxford and Cambridge University crews are the nucleus is as pleasant to see as it is enjoyable to share.

The better half of mankind is almost entirely answerable for this agreeable state of things. The ladies come to the fore on this innocent festival of the early year, and appear precisely in their most attractive and creditable light. Is it to be supposed that "the boat race" would be so popular or so enjoyable, so wholesome in its pleasures, or so fashionable in its accessories, were there no ladies to patronise it in their delightfully enthusiastic and emotional manner ? Not even the Ladies' Day at Epsom, nor the Cup day at Ascot, nor the charmed circle of the lawn at Goodwood, surpass—in the

popularity which they enjoy with England's daughters and matrons—

" With the light blue in their ribbons
And the dark blue in their eyes ! "

the great contest for the Academic Championship of the Thames.

To bet gloves and don the colours of blue ; to spoil new dresses, and ruin bonnets of exquisite arrangement in the cause, and vow they don't mind it ; to submit to piercing winds, iced by the face of the " King of the Floods," and, martyr-like, to bow before the chilling reception of his majesty ; to partake of cold meats when they don't want them, and to drink of too-exciting beverages of the Rhine when they hate them ; to scream, to chatter, to laugh, to flush with excitement, and pale with apprehension ; to applaud the winners and condole with the losers : all this belongs to woman, and with keen sympathy and enjoyment she bears her part. In other words, she is the life and soul of the whole affair, and were it not for the generous leadership she undertakes in this contest of university strength, once and for ever, we might bid farewell to the popularity of the Oxford and Cambridge Boat Race.

Having now given some idea of the scenes along the road, let us turn back, and see how it fares with the river, that "silent highway" which in bygone ages has witnessed so many aquatic pageants, nearly all different, itself alone unchanged. From Westminster Bridge upwards, for three hours at least before the start, the Thames is alive with craft of every size and shape, from the little coracle up to the leviathan steamer ; and all except the coracles are heavily freighted with the fairer portion of creation. All press on eagerly "to the fore"; all, and especially the ladies, are anxious to secure their promised seats.

The racing fever which prevails on these occasions is well and graphically described by one of our London journals :—

" It was not merely that everything which could be called a boat in the vicinity of London was making its way in the same direction as that which we were taking. There was an emulation which pervaded each and all on the face of the broad stream. What risks the drivers of those little steam launches ran, what perils the ladies and gentlemen who sat down to champagne lunches in the tiny saloons escaped, may never be known. But to the practised ear and eye there were signs which told of abnormal pressure and reckless speed, such as could have been the result only of a general desire on the part of everybody to reach some selected spot or other first. Nothing dawdled needlessly. Even the great clumsy coal-barges, filled, crammed with people, were going at their very best, that may possibly have not exceeded a mile an hour, probably was much less, but it was all the barge could do, as the perspiring trios who worked the sweeps abundantly testified. And as for the skiffs and shallops, the tubs and the outriggers, the indescribable craft which, despite the most palpable unseaworthiness, put off from the shore, loaded to the brim, and the canoes which bobbed in and out everywhere, generally appearing to be in the utmost peril of being swamped, but always coming out of the scrape in the end—it would be impossible to describe the manner in which they all got along. What cared their occupants for the steamers that threatened to submerge them every moment? All they cared for was the race, and the proud distinction of being in a good place outweighed all other considerations. It led occasionally to the temporary surrender of those dignified claims which it is the wont of the fairer sex to make upon men; for here and there an old lady might be seen who had laid down her umbrella and taken up the oar, and who was rowing stroke or bow, as the case might be. It overcame the attractions of music; for how could a boat's crew continue singing 'The Good Rhine Wine' when a rival 'four' was passing them? It overruled the very exchange of courtesies; chaffing was unheard; and even when a more jovial spirit held out a glass and proffered a toast to some passer-by, the response was wanting, so eager was the race. Even curiosity disappeared: a life-boat, manned by ten men, whose fantastic costume would have attracted at other times the attention of everybody on the water, was allowed to go by without so much as a glance. Steamers, crowded on deck and paddle-box, crushed by one after another; the river was literally covered with the thousands and tens of thousands who had come out on that morning to see the struggle between the Light and Dark Blues."

Yonder is a steamer with the large blue flag flying from her bows, bearing the word "Press." She is crowded with journalists and reporters of sporting papers, who, armed with chronometers and note-books, are easily recognised. There is an absence of party emblems on this boat, although among its passengers are many University men, whose hearts beat high with hope and excitement, and yearning for the success of their *Alma mater;* on the representatives of the press, however, whose business it is to be impartial and judicial-minded, we look in vain for the all-pervading colour.

Right ahead of us is the umpire's steamer; a large flag flutters towards us from her mast, but as we come up on her beam we can see that it is the Royal Standard. So we know that H.R.H. the Prince of Wales, himself an ardent and thorough sportsman, and a patron of all that is manly, is on board, standing, race-glass in hand, at the bows, and looking as if he, like everybody else, is thoroughly enjoying himself. And so we steam on past the long tower-flanked façade of the Houses of Parliament and the grey walls of Lambeth Palace, past Chelsea Hospital and Battersea Park, and aristocratic Hurlingham, until at last we see Putney Bridge ahead of us, and soon find ourselves in the thick of the fun. Here the river is alive with gigs, skiffs, wherries, punts, canoes, and every imaginable water-going thing. The edges of the stream are lined with a deep fringe of barges crowded with spectators; row-boats dart about here and there, threading their way through the floating labyrinth; little steam launches are fussily puffing about, snorting angrily now and then as they are led off by the ear shorewards by the police boats. It is a scene of indescribable animation.

So much for the river; but as there are "three R's" on the road to education, so in getting to the Boat Race; we have touched on "Road" and "River," and must now say a few words as to "Rail." There is not so much romance, perhaps, in this route as in the other two, but it combines two advantages well suited to the busy age in which we live: a saving of time and rapidity of motion. Year by year ever increasing thousands throng the railway stations; Victoria, Waterloo, and Clapham Junction are besieged from an early hour; and the Metropolitan Railway's extension to Hammersmith is a favourite route. There are few more satisfactory points of view for the boat race than from the special train which usually draws up on Barnes Bridge. The passengers are rapidly whirled to their destination, see what they went to see, and are as rapidly whisked back again. These are they for whom the "fun of the fair" has no attractions, who find no pleasure in mingling with the crowd on the banks, or following in the wake of the boats on a special steamer. Or else they are so overwhelmed with business that even for one day they cannot leave it, except for a few brief hours. But we must not forget that it is above all to the railways that we must look for an explanation of the enormously-increased attendance of late years at our national sports. The perfect organisation and system of the great lines enable them to convey tens of thousands of spectators cheaply and rapidly to and from their destinations.

And now that we have reached our destination, what spot shall we select to see the race from? Bystanders, we know, see more of a game than the players; and we may congratulate ourselves that we are not part and parcel of those two bands of rival galley-slaves, if we really wish to "see the fun." Shall we then take up our stand at Putney or at Mortlake? If we are to judge by mere numbers, Putney is the favourite spot. The head-quarters of the rival crews are there. It is here that they embark, and amid the volleys of hearty English cheers they paddle quietly up to the starting-point. At Putney, too, assemble the giants, the fat women, the jugglers, panoramas, and dwarfs, which are always found hanging on the skirts of holiday multitudes. About the streets and bar-rooms we meet famous old historic strokes and bows, who have come up from counting-room, pulpit, or professor's chair, to draw once more the breath of a score or two years ago. In short, almost all the pomp and ceremony of the race is to be seen here, but little or nothing of the race itself. Of course there are plenty of intermediate points, but they only present in dilution the con-centrated merits of the two extremities. It is undeniably delightful to be a member of a lawn party at one of the charming river-side villas, but at Mortlake such villas are wanting. The neighbour-hood is rather interesting; level meadows consti-tute the left bank of the river, while the "Ship," and a number of less pretentious buildings occupy the right. But so long as hope springs immortal in the oarsman's heart, and sympathy grows in that of the speculator, so long as oars may snap or spurts avail, so long, in fine, will Mortlake not lack patronage on the Boat Race Day.

We shall imagine ourselves, then, on the tow-path at Mortlake, wedged in among the crowd of equestrians, family carriages, country waggons, pony phaetons, sturdy pedestrians, all gathered on this strip of land, and all destined, soon after the boats and the phalanx of steamers shall have passed by, to be ducked! For presently the river, brimming with the flood-tide, but now flowing quietly at our feet, will rebel at the unwonted displacement of its waters, and encompass us with its angry waves. Retreat will be impossible, for a stone wall is behind us. But we do not think of this just now; our thoughts are bent on the river. The crowd is becoming more and more silent every moment. The time fixed for the starting has passed. A rumour buzzes through the multitude that the boats are off. "By a subsequent com-parison of times," says the writer above quoted, "I found that this news had travelled from Putney to Mortlake in rather less than five minutes: a remarkable instance of the speed of winged fame, though no doubt it can travel faster than a mile a minute on occasion." And now the swarm of boats which line the edges of the stream are forced back by the police as close in shore as possible. The watermen cease their entreaties to come on board and be ferried over, and jumping into their own boats, shove off from shore. Rolling towards us, at first with a low rumble of distant thunder, comes the roar of the vast multitude which tells of the approach of the "eights." Just at the moment when the excitement is becoming almost unendurable, the boats flash suddenly into sight from beneath the shadow of Barnes Bridge. Another moment they are level with us—past us—the pistol shot rings out sharply in the chill air, and all is over—the race has been lost and won.

It should be added that, owing to the tide and the exigencies arising from it, the race is now almost always rowed from Putney to Mortlake, and not from Mortlake to Putney, as was occa-sionally the case in the early days of the University Boat Race days, when the contest was viewed by some two or three hundred spectators, mostly old University men, and when, after the contest was over, the two crews were hospitably entertained at dinner by Sir Lancelot Shadwell at his house at Barn Elms.

It remains to give a short notice here of the past history of rowing as an old English amuse-ment. The earliest example of rowing for plea-sure would seem to belong to the Anglo-Saxon times, for we learn from history that King Edgar was rowed on the Dee, near Chester, by a crew of eight tributary princes, and doubtless all the lords and ladies of the Court crowded that river's banks to see the show. After the Norman Conquest there were water-tournaments on the Thames, and later the young men tilted at the Quintain in boats. When the river was the "silent highway" between London and Westminster, and when hundreds and thousands of Thames water-men plied for hire, we may be sure that English pugnacity showed itself in races in which the strongest arm and the coolest head won the day. In due course of time the Westminster Scholars and the young students of the Inner and Middle Temple came upon the scene as experts in the use of the oar, and gradually the "silent highway" became—at all events at times—a noisy thoroughfare. "On these occasions, and long after also, so much license was indulged in, that the 'water frolics' which sprang up came to partake of the character of a French or Italian carnival, so that modest ladies avoided appearing in pleasure-boats as much as at the play, owing to the freedom of language then prevalent, both at the theatre and on the river."

In course of time, however, an improvement came alike over the theatre and the river. One Doggett, an actor, who had removed from his native Dublin to London in the time of William III., and who retired from the stage just before the end of the reign of Queen Anne, was as fervent in his

indefinite period. But money is now given in lieu of a costume which is at present rarely even seen. The first race for "Doggett's Coat and Badge" was rowed in 1716, the course being from the "Swan" at London Bridge to the "Swan" at Chelsea. These and intermediate hostelries of the same name have since passed away, but this contest continues annually over the same course, and one of the leading regulations of the match is still retained, such being that the start shall take

THE FIRST BOAT USED BY CAMBRIDGE.

loyalty as he had been prominent in his profession. His attachment to the Hanoverian line of monarchy, coupled with his love for aquatic sports, led him to offer a prize for competition on the first anniversary of the accession of George I. It was to be rowed for by six young watermen just out of their apprenticeship. The prize consisted of a coat of antique cut, but which the actor's loyalty ordained to be of orange colour, and bearing on the right sleeve a silver badge carrying a figure of the White Horse of Hanover. The bill of the Drury Lane Theatre, in announcing the prize, stated that it was given in honour of the king's "happy accession," and that it was to be rowed for annually on the 1st of August "for ever," and Doggett left the means for supplying the annual prize for that rather

place when the tide is strongest against the rowers, so that the strength and endurance of the jolly young watermen are rather severely tested. Dibdin made this annual race the subject of one of his ballad operas. The prize is presented to the winner with some ceremonies at Fishmongers' Hall, that company being trustees of the same. In connection with this, it is interesting to state that at a banquet given by the Fishmongers' Company some years ago to the Prince of Wales, a score or so of winners of this race, in their quaint orange coats with plaited skirts, and with bright badges on their right arms, acted as a guard of honour in lieu of the usual military guard.

The next important incident chronologically in the aquatic history of the great metropolis is a regatta on a grand scale, which took place in the year 1775. Lady Mary Wortley Montagu, having written a glowing account of a regatta she had witnessed at Venice in 1740, induced the leaders of fashion in London to attempt a similar aquatic and plaster of Paris deities; nor even the crowning of the victors in the races with laurel wreaths. The "show" consisted of a procession of boats in three divisions, with the rowers dressed respectively in the three marine colours, red,

A WEARER OF DOGGETT'S COAT AND BADGE.

spectacle. But the desire to imitate the doings of the "Queen of the Adriatic" grew so slowly into action, that it was not till the date named that the London regatta actually took place; and then it was not attempted on a scale of grandeur like that which had been carried into effect at Venice. There were not, as at the latter place, any chariots of night drawn by sea-horses, changing to chariots of Aurora, nor triumphal cars, nor mythological and symbolical galleys, with pasteboard temples white, and blue, and each division led by a grand marshal. The pageant moved on Midsummer Eve from Westminster Bridge to the then noted Ranelagh Gardens, amid the booming of cannon and the cheers of a quarter of a million of spectators, who lined the river's banks, or were seated on barges or in boats, paying dearly for the privilege. At Ranelagh a Temple of Neptune had been erected, which soon became crowded with revellers. A few boat races took place in front of this temple, but the great business of the evening and night was dancing and suppering and carousing. It was broad day before the revels terminated, and then gay cavaliers and their fair partners, homeward bound, trusted themselves in boats propelled by tipsy rowers, and the result was that seven persons met death beneath the surface of the river.

The first students' race upon the Thames, at all events of any public importance, seems to have taken place no further back than the year 1818, when the best rowers of Westminster School challenged the students of the Temple to a trial of strength and skill. Much interest was excited by the match, which was bravely won by the Westminster lads. From this match the golden era of boating may be said to date. Some ten or a dozen years later there was achieved upon the Thames a remarkable feat of rowing, the story of which old oarsmen still relate with interest. A boat's crew of gentlemen rowed from Oxford to London in one day, the distance, owing to the winding of the river, being near upon, if not fully, one hundred and forty miles, and the tide being strong against them during a part of the day. The crew had little time for rest, and when they had accomplished their feat, were so exhausted that some of them had to be carried ashore.

The interest which the Westminster boys took in boating when they plied the oars more than a century ago increased as one generation succeeded another on the academic forms. In the second quarter of the present century we find them and the Eton lads occupying a position in the boating world not unlike, though less important, than that at present filled by the students of the two great universities. Before their annual matches and those of the London clubs became events of importance, few contests on the river attracted so much attention as those between the boys of the two public schools which we have named. The matches were rowed on various parts of the river between London and Windsor, and the rivals seem to have pretty evenly shared the favours of the goddess of Victory. In 1846 it was considered a great feat for Westminster to row five miles in twenty-eight minutes; but there was no humiliation in Eton's defeat, for its boat was close to that of the victors' at the end of the race. Sometimes one crew would leave their opponents eight or ten boats' lengths behind them, and the next year the luck would be reversed, so that neither school had much occasion to crow over the other. One of the last acts of William IV. was to send, one May day in 1837, for the lads who had just rowed in the match of that year from Datchet to Windsor

to come to the Castle and see him, when he conversed freely with his young visitors, asking and answering questions in his usual sailor-like fashion. In the following month half-a-dozen tars carried the sailor king to his haven of rest.

As to the race between the two universities, we find that it dates from 1829; in the February of that year the Cambridge rowers sent a challenge to Oxford to row against them on the Thames in the Easter vacation. Some correspondence took place between the lords of the Cam and those of the Isis, and eventually it was agreed that the race should be rowed not at Easter, but at the beginning of the Long Vacation. The day fixed was the 10th of June, and the course was from Hambledon Lock to Henley Bridge, a course of a little over two miles. A writer in *London Society* for 1865 thus describes this, the earliest, race between the two universities. He was evidently an eye-witness of the scene.

" Everybody who recollects the day will remember that it was as fine a day as our climate allows a June day to be. The race between the crews of the two universities was, one need hardly say, not at all what it is now. No one then looked upon it as a ' Water Derby ': such a thing had never been heard of till that year. And yet I can appeal to the memories of all my contemporaries whether they have at any time since seen the whole university itself turn itself out as it did that day. The gravest and the most unexpected men were seen riding, or even driving, on some part or other of those three-and-twenty miles between Oxford and Henley. There were gigs, tandems, pairs; and one party of friends actually approached the scene, and I believe returned in safety, in a four-horse drag driven by one of themselves. At least, I saw them safe baiting at Benson on the way back."

The chronicler of to-day would scarcely think it worth while to mention four-horse drags as a remarkable feature of the boat-race. They are to be counted now by scores. But to continue :—

" The race was rowed as evening came on; and as the time for it drew near, the whole crowd of Oxford and Cambridge men swelled down to the river-side and on the bridge, the Oxford men showing their blue favours, the Cambridge pink. I was fortunate enough to get a capital position for seeing the conclusion of the race, on the top of the little bridge house at the Berkshire end of Henley Bridge. The start was out of sight. The odds, it will be remembered, were offered and taken against Oxford. A defeat was confidently expected, even by Oxford men, so that we who wore blue on taking our stand as we could to see the end of the race were not in the highest possible spirits. At last it was known that the boats were off. And I will here set down a story which was told at the time, and generally believed. Our friendly antagonists, at starting, were said to have complained that their oars fouled in the weeds. In consequence of this complaint the start was decided not to have been a fair one, and a second was made. Then the Oxford coxswain steered his men through the same water of which the Cambridge crew had complained, and pleasantly called out to them ' Weeds, weeds !'

"I have made it my business to inquire into this story, and am able to say on the best possible evidence—the evidence of some of the crew of the Oxford boat—that it is untrue. What really happened was this : the Cambridge men, having won the toss for choice of side, chose the Berkshire shore. Then, at the start, the Cambridge coxswain steered out into the stream. If the course so steered had been acquiesced in by the Oxford coxswain, the Oxford boat would have sustained a serious loss. He held his course, and a foul ensued. The umpires decided that, there being plenty of water on the Berkshire side, both boats should be allowed to row in it. When the boats showed themselves rounding the bend of the river, all doubts as to the event were over. The first *corona navalis* was to come to Oxford . . . The Cambridge boat had no chance at any time after it was seen from Henley Bridge ; but I think scarcely sufficient justice is rendered to the skill and resolution of the Cambridge crew by the use of the word 'easily' (which is the word used by the *Times* in describing the race). However, the thing was settled ; and in a few minutes the Oxford boat came up to an arch of Henley Bridge, well ahead, and shot under to the landing-place. Never shall I forget the shout that rose among the hills. Any one who has been at Henley will recollect how well the valley lies for reverberating sound. Certainly the echo of the Berkshire hills made itself heard. It has never fallen to my lot to hear such a shout since. There was fierce applause at the installation of the Duke of Wellington a few years after, and there has been applause under a hundred roofs since, but applause that fills a valley is a different thing. I did not see the great pageant of the entry of the Princess Alexandra into London, but I had the good fortune to see her embark with the Prince of Wales at Southampton on the evening of their marriage. The quays and the Southampton water gave back no such answer to our cheers as the Henley valley gave on the 10th of June, 1829."

The following is a correct list of the crews of that year :—

OXFORD—1. J. CARTER, *St. John's* ; 2. E. J. ARBUTHNOT, *Balliol* ; 3. J. E. BATES, *Christ Church* ; 4. C. WORDSWORTH, *Christ Church* ; 5. J. J. TOOGOOD, *Balliol* ; 6. T. F. GARNIER, *Worcester* ; 7. G. B. MOORE, *Christ Church* ; Stroke, T. STANIFORTH, *Christ Church* ; Coxswain, W. R. FREMANTLE, *Christ Church.*

CAMBRIDGE — 1. A. B. E. HOLDSWORTH, *Trinity*, 10st. 7lbs. ; 2. A. F. BAYFORD, *Trinity H.*, 10st. 8lbs. ; 3. C. WARREN, *Trinity*, 10st. 10lbs. ; 4. C. MERIVALE, *St. John's*, 11st. ; 5. T. ENTWISLE, *Trinity H.*, 11st. 4lbs. ; 6. W. T. THOMPSON, *Jesus*, 11st. 10lbs. ; 7. G. A. SELWYN, *St. John's*, 11st 13lbs. ; Stroke, W. SNOW, *St. John's*, 11st. 4lb. ; Coxswain, B. R. HEATH, *Trinity.* Average, 11st. 1¾.

It may be of interest to state here that the "C. Wordsworth" of Oxford, was Dr. Charles Wordsworth, now Bishop of St. Andrew's, in Scotland, and the "W. R. Fremantle" is the present Dean of Ripon. On the Cambridge side two names, those of "Merivale" and "Selwyn," will strike the reader's attention. The former is the present Dean of Ely ; the latter is the late lamented Dr. Selwyn, Bishop firstly of New Zealand, and afterwards of Lichfield.

The following account of the race is taken from *Jackson's Oxford Journal* of June 13, 1829. "The Oxford crew appeared in their blue-check dress, the Cambridge in white with pink waistbands. The boats of both parties were very handsome, and wrought in a superior style of workmanship. In their preparation to row down to the start the men were hailed with loud acclamations. The post was marked rather more than two miles below the bridge, near a little island ; and after an agreement was made as to which side of the island they should row (the choice fell to Cambridge), the race began. The crews of both pulled gallantly, and with clever and equal stroke. There was no great difference between them till passing on each side of the island, when Oxford made a bold and hearty struggle, and, on reaching the main opening of the stream, shot ahead some distance, and then began the race in reality. Each of the boats put out the strength of their arms (!) in excellent style, and with the utmost regularity and precision ; but it was seen that the Oxford crew were the more powerful, and were gaining the victory, for the opposing crew, though coming a few strokes on them, were unable to make that head which showed a probability of success. In this way they rowed up to the bridge, among the cheers of thousands, and the contest ended in the victory of Oxford by several boats' lengths. There was a magnificent display of fireworks in the evening. It was reported that the match was for a very large sum ;

but we have authority for stating that it was by no means a gambling match, but a trial of strength and skill."

The boat in which the Cambridge crew rowed on this occasion was a heavy tub or " Noah's Ark," differing almost as much from the slight outrigger of to-day as a dapper little gun-boat at Portsmouth differs from a Chinese junk.

The next race between the two Universities did not occur until seven years later, although there was a futile attempt to arrange one in the year 1834. But in 1836 the Universities again met. The course, after some disagreements, which were happily tided over, was agreed upon, and the race rowed from Westminster Bridge to Putney Bridge on the 16th of June, and resulted in a victory for Cambridge. The Cambridge men wore "white cotton elastic rowing shirts; and the Oxford similar shirts striped blue and white, and blue handkerchiefs, the latter of which were thrown on one side previous to the start." A writer in *Bell's Life* says, that " the Red House, Lintell's, the Old Swan, Battersea, and the Baron de Berenger, at the Stadium, fired their artillery as the contending boats passed; and Avis's, the Bells, and the other houses at Putney, greeted the parties with a volley on their arrival."

The year 1837 again witnessed a failure of the negotiations for a race. In the years 1839, 1840, and 1841, over the course from Westminster to Putney, Cambridge scored three successive victories. To *Bell's Life* we are again indebted for some curious particulars as to the Oxford boat of first-mentioned year :—" She was fifty-two feet long, beautifully constructed and tastefully—nay, splendidly—'turned out.' She was painted white and blue, and pricked with gold, having the arms of the University emblazoned on the rudder, with the words, ' Dominus Illuminatio Mea.' She was named the *Isis*, and numbers of persons went to Roberts's boat-house to look at her. For the Cantabs Messrs. Searle, of Stangate, built a new boat, but they had not sufficient time to complete her painting, and she had to be launched with only a simple coat of lilac inside. Both boats seem to have been models of perfect construction, and as oak cutters had perhaps never been surpassed in lightness.

The race of 1842, over the same course, was won by Oxford; but in the next year Oxford was not able to organise a crew for Easter, and their proposal to row at Henley at Whitsuntide being declined by Cambridge, the race fell through. In 1844 again there was a failure, but the cause is not recorded.

In 1845 the race was rowed for the first time over the present course. For this race Messrs. Searle had built for the Cambridge crew a very light outrigger —then quite a novelty—but it could not be used owing to the roughness of the weather and the quantity of ice in the river. In this year Cambridge won.

In 1846 the first public trial with outriggers took place, and the "pace" was much increased. The race was from Mortlake to Putney, and Cambridge were again the winners. There was a crowd, it is true, to see the boats come to the winning post, but only one boat, an eight-oar of the Leander Club, represented the spectators. The next race did not take place till 1849, when the laurels fell to Cambridge. On this occasion we learn that Putney Bridge was crowded with carriages, and several hundred horsemen followed the race along the towing-path. This race fell to Oxford, the umpire having decided in their favour on the ground of a foul. In the year 1850 there was no race; but in 1851 the Universities met at Henley to contend for the Grand Challenge Cup, and being the only two boats entered, this was virtually a University race, Oxford winning. The chief reason for so many failures to bring about a match between the rival universities arose from the divergence of opinion as to the time of the year in which the race should be rowed, Oxford always objecting to Easter, Cambridge to Midsummer. The race of 1852 was a very fast one, and was won by Oxford by twenty-seven seconds. This race was memorable on account of the accidents caused by the swell from the steamers. Just before reaching Barnes Bridge a four-oared outrigger was swamped, and, immediately after, the *Leander* eight-oared cutter met a similar fate.

" Among the crew," says *Bell*, " was the venerable Mr. Layton, and with him Messrs. Nicholas Cocks and Wray, names well known in the annals of the University Boat Races. These were soon *nantes in gurgite vasto* with Jem Parish, their coxswain, whose position was anything but pleasant, as he could not ' swim a yard.' And here we must not omit to record an act of rare generosity and courage. The boat went down head-foremost, so that the men rowing aft could not see the danger, though the coxswain could; and the latter said to Mr. Harrison, who was rowing stroke, 'Give me your oar, sir, to hang on by, for I can't swim;' upon which Mr. Harrison generously tossed him the oar, saying, ' Nor can I '—a piece of magnanimity which speaks for itself. One of the crew, who seemed more like a water-rat than a man, sat quietly up to his middle in water on the bottom of the boat after she was turned upside down, ordering the numerous boats around him to pick up their unlucky coxswain : which done, he still kept his throne, and directed the rescue of the oars and clothes ; and even when they were collected, he still 'stuck to the ship,' and was rewarded for his trouble by bringing her to land uninjured."

In 1854 Oxford was victorious, and in 1856 the race was rowed from Mortlake to Putney, Cambridge winning by half a length. In all the contests up to this date considerable trouble had been caused by boats and barges blocking the course, the contending crews having actually to run the gauntlet, as it were, from end to end. The utmost nerve and decision was exhibited by the coxswains of both crews in the trying race of this year, the Cambridge boat narrowly escaping destruction at the hands of a pig-headed lighterman. In 1857 Oxford won, and on this occasion strenuous efforts were made to secure a clearer course. *Bell's Life* mentions the excellent behaviour of the captains of all the steamboats, " who took especial care on this occasion to keep out of the way of the umpire's and each other's boats, which, by forming a regular line across the river, and preserving it as much as circumstances would permit, not only afforded a good view of the race to all on board, but thus became themselves a magnificent spectacle when there was little else to interest." This race was remarkable as having been the first in which the present style of keelless boats and round oars were used, both Universities using the same kind of oars and boats. In fact, rowing was now becoming a *scientific* pastime. In 1858 Cambridge won, the " catching a crab " by the Oxford stroke having brought their eight to a standstill at the very commencement. The Cantabs also came to grief by fouling a barge.

In 1859 again the weather was terribly unpropitious, and the Cambridge crew were in danger of being drowned.

" It would not have been easy," wrote the *Times*, " to pitch on a more unfavourable day for an eight-oared race. The wind blew violently in raw, gusty squalls from the north-west, and raised an amount of broken water when it met the tide that boded very ill indeed for the safety of the light racing cutters. The day, too, was intensely cold, and almost every half-hour was varied by a heavy storm of hail and snow. The aspect of a muddy river under such circumstances is endurable only in one of Vanderveldt's pictures. The river swarmed with craft of all kinds, from outriggers, which were scarcely safe, to overcrowded steamers, which were very unsafe indeed. Soon after one o'clock the word was given, the oars flashed in the sun like polished steel, and with a bound that seemed to lift them from the water, both boats were off at a tremendous pace. For a short distance, until the " way " was well on them, they kept together, straining every nerve to the utmost ; but after the first 200 or 300 yards Oxford drew steadily ahead, and gained so much while their opponents were forcing by main strength their boat through the broken water, which almost swept over it, that at the end of the first mile Oxford was two or three lengths ahead. As the boats flew past, the fleet of steamers which lined the banks, and were laden almost to the water's edge with eager spectators, fell in their wake, and the race, with all its fierce excitement, commenced in earnest. The steamers rolling heavily from side to side as if they must capsize, and almost threatening to overwhelm the rival cutters, hemmed them in closely, and, with deafening cries and cheers, stimulated the losers to greater efforts. The steamers, boats, and everything in dangerous confusion, fly pell-mell under the Suspension Bridge, the steamers fouling one another, and almost unmanageable in their overcrowded state, the rival cutters just able to keep ahead of their high-pressure pursuers, which almost jeopardise the lives of the rowing crews. At Hammersmith the wind is violent, and dead in the teeth of the competitors, with an ugly stretch of broken water for the Cambridge boat. As they labour through this, it is seen at once that some of their crew are sorely distressed with this last spurt, and that the boat itself is ankle-deep in water. For the latter evil there is no remedy, and it gets worse each minute. The Oxford boat was not too dry, but the first and second oars in the Cambridge boat were almost hidden by the water, which broke completely over them, and made the boat heavier with every stroke.

" While their antagonists were thus impeded, the Oxfords improved their distance, and at last got considerably ahead, and even the steamers, in spite of the shouts and signals from the umpire's boat, in spite of all the rules of fair play, began to pass a little ahead of the poor Cantabs, leaving them to contend as they best could with their trail of broken water. Past Barnes railway bridge the water was very rough ; Oxford, now far ahead, went through it gallantly, but not so Cambridge, whose boat was almost water-logged. Wave after wave broke into it ; the track of steamers passing ahead made matters worse. Yet still, though their sinking condition was seen, the gallant crew pulled to the last, and were in the act of rowing desperately when the boat sank under them. In another minute, and amid a lot of straw hats, oars, and flannel shirts, they were all seen striking out just as manfully to gain the shore. Some were instantly picked up by the boats, others swam to land, and all escaped without any worse mishap than a ducking on a very cold day. The accident, as we have said, in no way influenced the result of the race, for even at Hammersmith the chance of Cambridge was hopeless. After the accident Oxford rowed the couple of hundred yards which yet remained to be accomplished very quietly, and came in winners amid tremendous cheering."

This exciting race found a Pindar to celebrate it in the person of Mr. H. Cholmondeley Pennell, who wrote :—

"Oxford! Oxford! she wins, she wins,
    Well they've won the toss, you see;
Whilst the Cambridge must fetch
Their boats through a stretch
    That's as lumpy and cross as can be.

"And the men are too big, and the boat's too light,
But, look, by the bridge a haven in sight,
A smooth long reach that is polished and bright,
    And Cambridge may win if she can.
And the squall's gone down, and the froth is past,
And you'll find it's the pace that kills at last."

In 1877 the race was very evenly contested, and resulted in a dead heat, though Oxford had one oar disabled when within some 200 yards of the winning-post. Oxford came off victorious in 1878, winning by nine lengths, but in the following year Cambridge once more regained her laurels.

For the next four years, however, fortune again smiled upon the "Dark Blues," but in the present year (1884) Cambridge won the race, arriving at the goal some three lengths ahead of their opponents.

The following table will show at a glance the results of the race from its institution :—

Year.	Place.	Winner.	Time.	Won by
1829	Henley, 2 m. 2 fur.	Oxford ..	14 min. 30 sec.	many lengths
1836	Westminster to Putney	Cambridge	36 min.	1 min.
1839	Westminster to Putney	Cambridge	31 min.	1 min. 45 sec.
1840	Westminster to Putney	Cambridge	29 min. 30 sec.	⅔rds of length.
1841	Westminster to Putney	Cambridge	32 min. 30 sec.	1 min. 4 sec.
1842	Westminster to Putney	Oxford ..	30 min. 45 sec.	13 sec.
1845	Putney to Mortlake ..	Cambridge	23 min. 30 sec.	30 sec.
1846	Mortlake to Putney ..	Cambridge	21 min. 5 sec.	two lengths
1849	Putney to Mortlake ..	Cambridge	22 min.	many lengths
1849	Putney to Mortlake ..	Oxford ..	— —	foul
1852	Putney to Mortlake ..	Oxford ..	21 min. 36 sec.	27 sec.
1854	Putney to Mortlake ..	Oxford ..	25 min. 29 sec.	11 strokes
1856	Mortlake to Putney ..	Cambridge	25 min. 50 sec.	half a length
1857	Putney to Mortlake ..	Oxford ..	22 min. 50 sec.	35 sec.
1858	Putney to Mortlake ..	Cambridge	21 min. 23 sec.	32 sec.
1859	Putney to Mortlake ..	Oxford ..	24 min. 30 sec.	Camb. sank
1860	Putney to Mortlake ..	Cambridge	26 min.	one length
1861	Putney to Mortlake ..	Oxford ..	23 min. 27 sec.	48 sec.
1862	Putney to Mortlake ..	Oxford ..	24 min. 40 sec.	30 sec.
1863	Mortlake to Putney ..	Oxford ..	23 min. 5 sec.	42 sec.
1864	Putney to Mortlake ..	Oxford ..	21 min. 48 sec.	23 sec.
1865	Putney to Mortlake ..	Oxford ..	21 min. 23 sec.	13 sec.
1866	Putney to Mortlake ..	Oxford ..	25 min. 48 sec.	15 sec.
1867	Putney to Mortlake ..	Oxford ..	23 min. 22 sec.	half a length
1868	Putney to Mortlake ..	Oxford ..	21 min.	six lengths
1869	Putney to Mortlake ..	Oxford ..	20 min. 20 sec.	five lengths
1870	Putney to Mortlake ..	Cambridge	22 min. ¾ sec.	1¾ lengths.
1871	Putney to Mortlake ..	Cambridge	22 min. 8½ sec.	one length
1872	Putney to Mortlake ..	Cambridge	21 min. 15 sec.	two lengths
1873	Putney to Mortlake ..	Cambridge	19 min. 35 sec.	three lengths
1874	Putney to Mortlake ..	Cambridge	22 min. 39 sec.	three lengths
1875	Putney to Mortlake ..	Oxford ..	22 min. 2 sec.	eight lengths
1876	Putney to Mortlake ..	Cambridge	20 min. 19 sec.	seven lengths
1877	Putney to Mortlake ..	Dead heat	24 min. 6½ sec.	
1878	Putney to Mortlake ..	Oxford ..	23 min. 12 sec.	nine lengths
1879	Putney to Mortlake ..	Cambridge	21 min. 18 sec.	four lengths
1880	Putney to Mortlake ..	Oxford ..	21 min. 23 sec.	four lengths
1881	Putney to Mortlake ..	Oxford ..	21 min. 51 sec.	three lengths
1882	Putney to Mortlake ..	Oxford ..	20 min. 12 sec.	ten lengths
1883	Putney to Mortlake ..	Oxford ..	21 min. 18 sec.	3½ lengths
1884	Putney to Mortlake ..	Cambridge	21 min. 39 sec.	three lengths

---

CHAPTER XLVII.

BARNES.

"Tramping o'er the breezy common."—OLD SONG.

Situation, Boundaries, and Extent of the Parish—Its Etymology—History of the Manor—Its several Lessees—The Parish Church—Dr. Hezekiah Burton—Dr. Francis Hare—Dr. John Hume—Dr. Warner—Dr. Christopher Wilson—Canon Melvill—The Rev. John Ellerton—Robert Beale—Mr. Hiam, otherwise Abiezer Coppe—Yew-trees—Barnes Terrace—Murder of the Count and Countess D'Antraigues—Mr. Bolton Corney—Lady Archer—Barnes Common—An Impertinent Hoax—Henry Fielding, the Novelist—Other Noted Residents—Castlenau—West Middlesex Waterworks—Hammersmith Suspension Bridge—The Culture of Cedar-trees carried on at Barnes—Barn Elms—Jacob Tonson and the Kit-Cat Club—Sir Francis Walsingham and Queen Elizabeth—Heidegger, Master of the Revels to George II.—Cowley the Poet—Pepys' Visits to Barn Elms—Duel between the Duke of Buckingham and the Earl of Shrewsbury—Madder grown at Barn Elms—Cobbett here cultivated Indian Corn—The Mansion of Barn Elms modernised by Sir Richard Hoare—Sir John and Lady Kennedy—Sir Lancelot Shadwell.

BARNES, whither we now direct our steps, lies to the east of Mortlake, on the right bank of the Thames, which serves as its northern boundary, whilst on the east and south it is bounded by Putney. A favourite river-side promenade, called Barnes Terrace, serves as a sort of connecting link between this village and Mortlake. The entire parish contains about 900 acres ; the soil in general is gravelly, especially towards the south-west, where it unites with Putney, but near the river is some rich meadow-land.

It is matter for conjecture whether the name of the village is derived from the Anglo-Saxon word for a barn (Berne), or whether it is the name of a family who originally held it. The name, at all events, was anciently written Bernes, or Berne.

THE BOAT-RACE: AN EASY WIN. (*See pages* 446—450.)

The manor was given to the Dean and Chapter of St. Paul's by King Athelstan. It is thus described in the "Doomsday Book" :—"The Canons of St. Paul's, London, hold Berne. In the time of King Edward it was assessed at 8 hides, which were included in the rate with the Archbishop's manor of Mortlake, as they are at present. . . . In the time of King Edward it was valued at £6, now at £7." In the taxation of Pope Nicholas, about the year 1291, the manor is valued as the property of the canons at £12. It has been held by the Canons of St. Paul's ever since, except during the period of the Commonwealth.

Edward II. granted to the canons a charter of free-warren and an exemption from the charge of purveyance. From the Patent Rolls of 10 Henry IV., it appears that the Archbishop of Canterbury was entitled to a sparrow-hawk, or 2s. in money annually, and also £2 every twentieth year, for ever, from the lords of the manor of Barnes, that they might be excused from serving the office of reeve in his manor of Wimbledon.

The estate of Barnes, as we learn from Brayley's "Surrey," has been generally let on lease for long terms. In 1467 Sir John Saye and others were lessees of this manor, which they held with the advowson, and presented to the living that year, and again in 1471 and 1477. Both the manor and advowson had been transferred, in or before 1480, to Thomas Thwayte, Chancellor of the Exchequer and of the Duchy of Lancaster. In 1504 a lease was granted to Sir Henry Wiatt, and in 1513 and 1524 Sir Henry presented to the living as patron and grantee of the Dean and Chapter of St. Paul's. About the middle of the sixteenth century the lease of the estate was held by Queen Elizabeth's favourite Secretary of State, Sir Francis Walsingham, who resided at the manor-house of Barn Elms, in the eastern part of the parish, of which we shall have more to say presently. Here he entertained her Majesty in 1585, 1588, and 1589. Previously to the queen's first visit to Sir Francis, her Majesty had taken a lease of the manor from the Dean and Chapter, to commence from the termination (1600) of the lease granted to Sir Henry Wiatt, and by deed dated in her twenty-first year she assigned her interest to Walsingham and his heirs. Frances, the sole surviving daughter and heiress of Sir Francis, was thrice married : first to the celebrated Sir Philip Sidney ; secondly, to Robert, Earl of Essex, the unfortunate favourite of Queen Elizabeth ; and, after his death, to the Earl of Clanricarde. Essex occasionally resided at Barn Elms ; and Lady Walsingham, his mother-in-law, died there in 1602, and was buried privately on the following night by the side of her husband in St. Paul's Cathedral.

Early in the seventeenth century the dean and chapter granted a new lease of the manor for twenty-one years to a Mr. John Cartwright, who, when the Church property was exposed for sale by the Parliament, purchased the estate, one Robert Shute, of London, becoming the owner of the manor and advowson. After the Restoration of Charles II., the dean and canons recovered their interest, and Mr. Cartwright, or his representatives, held it on lease as before. In the last century, Mr. Richard Hoare (a son of Sir Richard Hoare, Knt., and Lord Mayor of London in 1745) became lessee of Barnes. He was created a baronet in 1786, and was succeeded by his only son, Sir Richard Colt Hoare (known as an antiquary, and especially as the historian of Wiltshire), who enlarged the mansion and made many improvements here. Early in the present century his interest was sold to the Hammersmith Bridge Company, but it was afterwards transferred to Sir Thomas Colebrooke.

Barnes is a rectory and rural deanery in the diocese of Rochester, but the living is in the gift of the Dean and Chapter of St. Paul's.

The church is, or was, an ancient building, dating from, or even before, the time of Richard I., at which period, a hospital having been founded within the liberties of St. Paul's Cathedral by one of the canons, the dean and canons bestowed on it the church of Barnes, with the glebe and tithes. It has, however, been so much altered at different times by repairs, "restorations," and enlargements, that comparatively little of the original now remains. Towards the end of the last century the church was considerably enlarged, and further additions were afterwards made, and the walls stuccoed. The tower, of red brick with stone quoins, and repaired with cement, is supposed to have been built about the latter part of the fifteenth century, and has a staircase and turret at the south-east angle. The body of the fabric is built with stone and flint, rough-cast, and whitewashed over. In the chancel are three lancet windows, Early English, which were opened in 1852, at which time the church was restored throughout.

Near the altar is a brass of William Millebourne, who died in 1415 ; and against the north wall is a monument in white marble, representing a female leaning upon an urn, and holding a medallion of Sir Richard Hoare, Bart., who died in 1787. His second wife and relict, Dame Frances Anne Hoare, who erected this memorial, died in 1800. Another individual who was buried here, but whose tomb is no longer to be seen, was Anne Baynard, whose life appears among Ballard's "Memoirs of Learned Ladies:" she died in 1697, at the age of twenty-five. She is said to have made herself a proficient in "natural philosophy, botany, mathematics, and classical literature," and to have learned Greek for the purpose of being able to read St. Chrysostom in the original.

Near the church doorway is a mural stone, with an inscription to the memory of one Edward Rose, citizen of London, who died in the seventeenth century, and bequeathed a sum annually to the parish for ever, on condition of the railing round his tomb being maintained in repair, and roses being trained around his monument. The repairs are executed, and the bequest is still continued.

The donor is thus recorded in the columns of the *Mirror*:—"Edward Rose, by will, in 1652, directed his body to be buried at Barnes, Surrey, and bequeathed £5 for making a frame of wood in the churchyard, where he had appointed his burying-place, and ordered three rose-trees or more to be planted about the place where he was interred. He also directed the purchase of an acre of land; and out of the profits thereof, the minister and churchwardens were to keep the said frame of wood in repair and the said rose-trees to be preserved, and others planted in their places from time to time. The residue of the profits to be given to the poor."*

"Possibly," writes Priscilla Wakefield, "this worthy citizen, immured throughout life within the narrow limits of a counting-house, had, notwithstanding, a love for the beauties of Nature, and wished that this his superior taste should be known as well as admired by posterity."

A white marble tomb on the north side of the church is to the memory of Vice-Chancellor Shadwell, who died in 1850, and of whom we shall have more to say presently, on reaching Barn Elms.

Among the clergymen who have held the living of Barnes within the last two centuries have been several who have acquired a literary reputation. Among them we may mention the following:—

Dr. Hezekiah Burton, who was instituted rector in 1680, was a Fellow of Magdalen College, Cambridge, where he gained much renown as an academical tutor. Dr. Burton's sermons, published in 1684, are edited by his friend, Dr. Tillotson, with a biographical prefatory memoir.

Francis Hare, D.D., who held the living from 1717 to 1727, became a Canon Residentiary of St. Paul's, and also Dean of Worcester, and in the latter year was raised to the bishopric of St. Asaph. In 1731 he was translated to Chichester, and he died in 1740. His chief literary production was an edition of the Comedies of Terence.

John Hume, D.D., was rector of Barnes from 1747 to 1758, when he was consecrated Bishop of Bristol. He was shortly after translated to the see of Oxford, and later on to that of Salisbury. He died in 1782.

On the resignation of Dr. Hume, Ferdinando Warner, LL.D., was appointed to the living. He was the author of an "Ecclesiastical History of England from the Earliest Accounts to the Present [eighteenth] Century" (1759). He also published other works on History, and likewise on Divinity, together with a "Treatise on the Gout," with an account of a peculiar method he had adopted in his own case. He, however, died in 1768 of the very disease which he had professed to cure.

Dr. Christopher Wilson, who was presented to this rectory on the death of Dr. Warner, was a Prebendary of Westminster, and in 1785 was consecrated Bishop of Bristol, over which see he presided till his decease, in 1792.

The rectory was held from 1863 down to 1870 by the Rev. Henry Melvill, Canon of St. Paul's Cathedral, but best known in his early manhood as the most popular of London preachers, first at Camden Chapel, Camberwell, and afterwards as holder of the "Golden" Lectureship at St. Margaret's, Lothbury. At Camberwell his eloquence attracted such congregations as to render it necessary to enlarge the building, which was thronged on Sundays, not only by the people of Camberwell, but by visitors from London; and for some years it was quite the custom for country cousins, and especially country clergymen, if they stayed over a Sunday in the metropolis, to "go and hear Melvill." When he came to Barnes he was growing old, and had held the Principalship of Haileybury College during the best years of his life. Still, to the last he was regarded as "the old man eloquent," and he enjoyed great popularity as a parish minister.

Canon Melvill was a member of a family long and honourably connected with the East India Company. He was educated at Christ's Hospital, whence he proceeded as a "Grecian"* to St. John's College, Cambridge, where he graduated in 1821, and he subsequently became a Fellow and Tutor of St. Peter's College. Entering into holy orders,

---

* Further interesting particulars of this bequest will be found in the *Mirror*, vol. xvi., p., 175; a similar custom at Bletchingley and Ockley, also in Surrey, is recorded in the *Mirror*.

* See "Old and New London," Vol II., p. 375.

he was appointed, about the year 1830, to the incumbency of Camden Chapel, Camberwell. By the favour of the Duke of Wellington he was nominated in 1840 Chaplain to the Tower of London and incumbent of the church within its precincts, and he was subsequently elected to the "Golden" Lectureship at St. Margaret's, Lothbury, which he resigned on becoming a canon of St. Paul's.

The author of "Pen-Pictures of Popular English Preachers" was greatly delighted with the reverend gentleman's eloquence in his Camberwell pulpit. "Hearing Mr. Melvill," he writes, "was like walking, as did Aladdin, through avenues on either side of which were nought but glittering treasures. His style was ornamented to the utmost; yet it was evident enough that elaboration had been sedulously practised. Indeed, we have heard that Mr. Melvill writes and re-writes his sermons until they arrive at *his* standard of perfection, and a high standard it is . . . There is no sentence but what is exquisitely balanced, no period which is not elegantly rounded; every simile is perfect and apt; every descriptive passage is graphic in the extreme. Yet with all this polish, the power is not impaired: the force is not lost in the polish. Rapidly proceeds the orator, never for a moment flagging or becoming commonplace: as soon as one rainbow begins to fade, another as brilliant succeeds it :

> "'Like the waves of the summer, when one dies away,
> Another as bright and as shining comes on.'

"The fountain from whence this stream of magic eloquence springs appears to be exhaustless. For three-quarters of an hour the listeners in the solemn aisle appear spell-bound; and, indeed, they are so, for they are charmed by the so potent eloquence of a master of his art. At length the music of the preacher's voice begins to die away, and as it ceases altogether, a suppressed murmur of approbation runs through the church—a murmur which elsewhere would have burst into a shout of applause." Canon Melvill died not long after resigning the living, and his eloquence does not survive to the extent that might be expected in his published Sermons.

The Rev. John Ellerton, who was instituted to Barnes in 1876, is well known as the editor of a volume of "Church Hymns Annotated," and the author of one or two of the best of its contents.

Robert Beale, the evil messenger of death to poor, broken-hearted Mary Queen of Scots, died at Barnes, and the record of his death appears in the register. It was he who was despatched by her stony-hearted and cruel cousin, Elizabeth, with the warrant for her execution at Fotheringhay Castle. "He was a man," says Camden, "of a most impetuous and morose disposition," and it was probably on that account that he was selected for the task. Beale married a sister of Lady Walsingham, and having been introduced to Queen Elizabeth, obtained official employments, and became one of her Majesty's principal confidants. The record of his death is as follows :—"Robert Beale, Counsellor of the north, and Clark of the privy council, departed out of this life on Monday at eight of the clock at night, being the 25th of May, and is buried in London, 1601."

Another entry in the register is as follows :— "Aug. 23, 1672 : buried Mr. Hiam." "The person thus designated," observes Brayley, "was properly named Abiezer Coppe. He was a native of Warwick, and was educated at Oxford; but after having been first a Presbyterian, and then an Anabaptist, he became one of the wildest enthusiasts of the fanatical period in which he lived. He published several pamphlets with odd titles and strange contents. He was sent to Newgate in 1650 for having published one entitled 'The Fiery Flying Roll,' the writer of which apparently was a fitter subject for a madhouse than a prison. After being confined for more than a year, he was called before the House of Commons, and having obtained his liberation, he retired to Barnes, where he practised as a physician, under the name of Higham, and he preached occasionally at the neighbouring conventicles."

The churchyard of Barnes is very picturesque with its yews and dark evergreens. As in so many other churchyards about Surrey, here is a fine yew-tree of venerable antiquity. These trees are also very frequent in the churchyards of Somerset and South Wales. Their dark, sombre gloom is enough to account for their being so planted, as in harmony with the melancholy associations of the spot, without having recourse to the supposition that they were so placed in order to mark boundaries, or to encourage the growth of wood for the bows of English soldiery. It is said also that the yew is regarded as an emblem of eternity, and the very name "Yew" is but a corruption of the ancient British word which signifies "existence," or "being."

Blair has thus apostrophised the yew :—

> "Cheerless, unsocial plant, that loves to dwell
> 'Mid skulls and coffins, epitaphs and worms,
> Where light-heeled ghosts and visionary shades,
> Beneath the wan cold moon (so fame reports)
> Embodied thick, perform their mystic rounds;
> No other merriment, dull tree, is thine."

Wordsworth apparently holds to the belief that the growth of the yew was encouraged for military purposes :—

> "Not loth to furnish weapons in the hands
> Of Umfreville or Percy, ere they marched
> To Scotland's heaths, or those that crossed the sea,
> And drew their sounding bows at Agincourt,
> Perhaps at earlier Cressy, or Poictiers.
> Of vast circumference and gloom profound,
> This solitary tree ! a living thing,
> Produced too slowly ever to decay ;
> Of form and aspect too magnificent
> To be destroyed."

Facing the river, near this angle, half a mile below Mortlake, is Barnes Terrace, an irregular row of comfortable villas, each standing in its own grounds, larger or smaller, and inhabited, at all events in past years, by many fashionable and literary characters. They are occupied in the summer months by families who are fond of yachting and rowing, and of spending their days in steam-launches or fishing-punts. At the Terrace the Thames is spanned by the railway bridge over which passes the Chiswick branch of the South-Western line. The river hereabouts, having run eastwards all the way from Kew, makes a sudden bend, and turns off at Barnes Terrace to the north, in the direction of Chiswick and Hammersmith, whence it again veers southward towards Barn Elms and Putney. About the middle of Corney Reach—the stretch of river between the railway bridge and Hammersmith—is Chiswick Ferry, to which there is a pleasant roadway from Barnes Common.

The whole river-side hereabouts wears a somewhat foreign appearance. Nor is this to be wondered at, since in the early part of the present century a small colony of French exiles settled in this quiet river-side terrace, among them the Count and Countess D'Antraigues, who lived in a house near the upper end of the terrace. This house became the scene of a deplorable incident, of which the count and countess were the victims. The event is thus described in "Murray's Handbook":—"One morning, in 1812, they were about to proceed to London, and the count was following his lady down-stairs towards the coach, when his valet, an Italian, fired a pistol at him, and then struck him between the shoulders with a dagger. The count made towards his room, but fell dead on the floor. The countess, unconscious of what had occurred, turned back to see why she was not followed, when the assassin plunged his dagger into her breast. She shrieked, reeled forward, and fell dead on the pavement. The murderer fled up-stairs, and before any one could reach him had killed himself. It was said that he was led to the deed from having on the previous evening overheard the count and countess, as they were watching the moonlight on the river, speak of dismissing him from their service."

Here lived Mr. Bolton Corney, the antiquarian critic, from his marriage, in the year 1846, down to his death, in 1870. He lies buried in the Barnes Cemetery.

Here, too, lived in the last century Lady Archer, formerly Miss West, the wonder of the fashionable world, and the envy of half the ladies of the Court. Her house was furnished and decorated in the Chinese style. Her grounds, of five acres, sloped down to the Thames. The place, called St. Anne's, was afterwards the residence of Lord Lonsdale.

The centre of the parish is almost wholly occupied by an open space, tolerably level, and covered with gorse and furze, a favourite haunt of gipsies and itinerant hawkers since they were driven from the green lanes about Wandsworth, and a pleasant open recreation-ground for the Londoner of the south-western districts. It comprises an area of about 120 acres, and is known as Barnes Common. Although it has suffered greatly at the hands of the South-Western Railway Company, it is still, observes the author of Unwin's "Half-holiday Handbook," "an enjoyable spot of broken furzy ground, with mossy banks and swampy hollows, where the microscopist revels. For the rambler of this persuasion the low-lying ground on the northern boundary will be found most interesting. Here on Saturday afternoons in fine weather he is almost sure to find some members of the Queckett Microscopical Club, the South London Microscopical Society, the Lambeth Field Club, or the West London Natural History Society, at work round the pools." A sedgy ditch, backed by rank vegetation, separates Barnes Common from Putney Lower Common, where Douglas Jerrold lived in a house known as West Lodge, at the time when he wrote his inimitable "Mrs. Caudle's Lectures." This latter common is of small extent, and a portion of it is occupied by Putney Cemetery, the remainder being used as a recreation-ground.

The river-side portion of Barnes is immortalised in "Gilbert Gurney" by Theodore Hook as the scene of one of his cleverest and most amusing, but most impertinent, hoaxes, a species of wit, or rather of practical joking, in which he fairly out-Sheridaned Richard Brinsley Sheridan himself. The reader will recollect in "Gilbert Gurney" the episode of his rowing with a friend (Charles Mathews), when they read a painted board in a garden at Barnes:

"Nobody permitted to land here. Offenders prosecuted with the utmost rigour of the law." But the comedians resolved to disembark; so taking the fishing-rod as a surveyor's line, Hook, pencil and book in hand, and Mathews as clerk, with the cord and walking-stick, landed, and began to pace the lawn in front of a beautiful villa. The dining-room window was thrown up, and forth came an irritated gentleman from his dinner, inquiring how the trespassers dare invade his territory. Their

about to take their departure, as they "had engagements in town," when Hook burst into extempore song, and explained the whole in this verse:—

"And we greatly approve of your fare,
    Your cellar's as prime as your cook;
And this clerk here is Mathews the player,
    And my name, sir, is Theodore Hook."

At Barnes lived Henry Fielding, the novelist. "He resided," observes Lysons, in his "Environs of London," "in a house which is now (1810) the

BARNES CHURCH.

reply was cool and business-like. They by degrees communicated to the indignant old gentleman the pleasant intelligence that they had come to settle where a new canal company were to cut across his pleasant retreat. He grew alarmed, and the intruding officials were "never more pained than with such a duty." "Would they walk in and talk the matter over?" This they reluctantly did. An excellent dinner was on the table; they were unnecessarily pressed to stay and partake of it. They sat down, and enjoyed the repast and its accompaniments, and over half-a-dozen of claret they discussed the line of canal. The wine warmed the host's gratitude—"One bottle more, dear gentlemen"—and it was getting dark, and they were

property of Mrs. Stanton, widow of the late Admiral Stanton." The fact, too, receives a certain confirmation from a reference in "Tom Jones" (book iv., chap. ii.) to the "Toasts" of the *Kit-cat* Club.

Manning distinguishes the house as being a very old one on Barnes Green, and adds that it was called Milbourne House from a family of the name, of whom William Millebourne, Esq., was buried in the chancel of Barnes Church in 1415, and represented by an incised brass in plate armour.

Monk Lewis, the author, was for some time a resident here. It is said also that Handel, the composer, should be added to the list of the celebrities who have lived at Barnes.

To the north of Barnes, on the road leading

towards the suspension bridge, is a long row of villas called Castlenau, a modern hamlet of the parish, to the westward of which, bordering the river, and covering an area of some sixteen acres, are the reservoirs and filtering-beds of the West Middlesex Water-works Company. From these reservoirs, after filtration, the water passes under the Thames to the works at Hammersmith, whence it is pumped up to the covered reservoir on Primrose Hill.

chains, composed of wrought-iron bars, each five inches deep and one thick. Four of these have six bars in each chain, and four have only three, making thirty-six bars, which form a dip in the centre of about 29 feet. From these vertical rods are suspended, which support the roadway, formed of strong timbers covered with granite. The width of the carriage-way is 20 feet, and footway five feet. The chains pass over the suspension towers, and are secured to the piers on each shore. The sus-

BARNES TERRACE IN 1823. (*From a Print.*)

The Thames here is spanned by a handsome suspension bridge, generally known to Londoners as the Hammersmith Suspension Bridge. It was erected about the years 1827–9, and is familiar to the pleasure-loving world who come hither in hundreds of thousands in March annually to witness the university boat-race. It is thus described in the *Mirror*, soon after its erection:—"The clear water-way is 688 feet 8 inches. The suspension towers are 48 feet above the level of the roadway, where they are 22 feet thick. The roadway is slightly curved upwards, and is 16 feet above high water, and the extreme length from the back of the piers on shore is 822 feet 8 inches, supporting 688 feet of roadway. There are eight

pension towers are of stone, and designed as archways of the Tuscan order. The approaches are provided with octagonal lodges, or toll-houses, with appropriate lamps and parapet walls, terminating with stone pillars, surmounted with ornamental caps. The whole cost of this remarkable object, displaying the great superiority acquired by British artisans in the manufacture of ironwork, is about £80,000. The advantages to be derived from this bridge is the saving of distance, in that it affords a direct passage from Hammersmith to Barnes, East Sheen, and other parts of Surrey, without going over either Fulham or Kew Bridges."

The bridge was built from the designs and under the superintendence of Mr. Tierney Clarke, civil engineer. In 1825 the first stone was laid with great ceremony by his Royal Highness the Duke of Sussex, Grand Master of Freemasons, and the bridge was completed and opened in 1827, as stated above.

Of late years it has been judged by experts that the strength of the bridge is not equal to the tremendous strain placed upon it by the ever increasing crowds on the boat-race day ; and in consequence, it is closed by the order of the Chief Commissioner of the Metropolitan Police for an hour or two before and after the start.

In one respect, Barnes on a small scale enters the lists as a rival to Kew.

"About the middle of the last century," writes Brayley, " the culture of the cedar of Lebanon was carried on to a great extent at Barnes by a butcher named Clarke, who first raised his plants from the cones of the great tree at Hendon Place.* The late Mr. Peter Collinson, from whose autobiographical notes we derive this information, and who, in 1761, paid £79 6s. for a thousand of these young cedars for re-planting in the Duke of Richmond's park at Goodwood, in Sussex, says that Mr. Clarke 'succeeded perfectly, and annually raised them in such quantities, that he supplied the nurserymen, as well as abundance of noblemen and gentlemen, with cedars of Lebanon; and he succeeded not only in cedars, but he had a great knack in raising the small magnolia, Warner's Cape jessamine, and all other exotic seeds. He built a large stove for pine-apples, &c.' † Mr. Collinson further states that the weeping willow, 'the original of all the weeping willows in our gardens, was transplanted from the river Euphrates by Mr. Vernon, Turkey merchant at Aleppo, brought with him to England, and planted at his seat at Twickenham Park,' where he saw it growing in 1748."

The eastern part of the village, adjoining on Putney, is known as Barn Elms. It consists of a mansion and one or two cottages standing in park-like grounds, and it extends from Barnes Common to the river, the lofty trees which surround the house forming a delightful shady nook by the margin of the stream. Barn Elms is reached from the village by a private road to the right of the "Red Lion" inn, which stands at the angle formed by the junction of the Richmond and Hammersmith roads. It occupies the site of the old manor-house of Barnes, or Berne, whilst the addition of "Elms," as Mr. James Thorne remarks, in his "Environs

of London," "seems to point to the trees which have always been a distinctive feature of the place." Adjoining the mansion, and forming, indeed, almost a part of it, was a cottage, once tenanted by old Jacob Tonson, the venerated Secretary of the Kit-cat Club, one of the most famous booksellers of the Augustinian era of English literature. Here he built a room for the reception of its members, adorning its walls with portraits painted by the master-hand of Sir Godfrey Kneller.

Barn Elms is described by Priscilla Wakefield, in 1820, as a " pastoral spot," and as "deriving its appellation from the majestic trees by which it is surrounded." She writes :—" In an ancient mansion here, called Queen Elizabeth's Dairy, lived and died Jacob Tonson, bookseller to Pope and the other wits of that day. Here he built a gallery, at the time he was secretary, for the accommodation of those noblemen, gentlemen, and geniuses, known by the name of the Kit-cat Club, Christopher Kat being the landlord of the house where they assembled. Sir Godfrey Kneller painted the portraits of all the members which decorated the gallery : being *three-quarter-length* portraits, those of that size are known by this appellation."

Sir Richard Phillips, in his " Morning Walk from London to Kew," thus describes the place as he saw it in 1816 :—" A lane in the north-west corner of the common brought me to Barnes Elms, where now resides a Mr. Hoare, a banker of London. The family were not at home, but on asking the servants if that was the house of Mr. Tonson, they assured me with great simplicity that no such gentleman lived there. I named the Kit-cat Club as accustomed to assemble there ; but the oddity of the name excited their ridicule, and I was told that no such club was held there ; 'but perhaps,' said one to the other, ' the gentleman means the club that assembles at the public-house on the common.' Knowing, however, that I was at the right place, I could not avoid expressing my vexation that the periodical assemblage of the first men of the age should be so entirely forgotten by those who now reside on the spot ; when one of them exclaimed, 'I should not wonder if the gentleman means the philosopher's room.' ' Ay,' rejoined his comrade, 'I remember somebody coming once before to see something of this sort, and my master sent him there.' I then requested to be shown this room, when I was conducted across a detached garden, and brought to a handsome structure, in the architectural style of the early part of the last century—evidently the establishment of the Kit-cat Club. A walk, covered with bushes, thistles, nettles, and high grass, led from the remains

---

* See Vol. I., p. 279.
† See "Transactions of the Linnæan Society," Vol. X., pp. 274-5.

of a gateway in the garden wall to a door which opened into the building, Ah! thought I, along this desolate avenue the finest geniuses in England gaily proceeded to meet their friends; yet within a century, how changed, how deserted, how revolting! A cold chill seized me as the man unfastened the decayed door of the building, and as I beheld the once elegant hall filled with cobwebs, a fallen ceiling, and accumulating rubbish. On the right, the present proprietor had erected a copper, and converted one of the parlours into a wash-house; the door on the left led to a spacious and once superb staircase, now in ruins, filled with dense cobwebs, which hung down from the lofty ceiling, and seemed to be deserted, even to the spiders which had woven them. The entire building, from want of ventilation, having become food for the fungus called the dry-rot, the timber had lost its cohesive powers. I therefore ascended the staircase with a feeling of danger, to which the man would not expose himself; but I was well rewarded for my pains. Here I found the old Kit-cat room nearly as it had existed in the days of its glory. It is eighteen feet high and forty feet long, by twenty wide. The mouldings and ornaments were in the most superb fashion of its age, but the whole was falling to pieces from the effects of the dry-rot. My attention was chiefly attracted by the faded cloth-hanging of the room, whose red colour once set off the famous portraits of the club that hung round it; their marks and size were still visible, and the numbers and names remained as written in chalk for the guidance of the hanger. Thus was I as it were, by those still legible names, brought into personal contact with Addison, and Steele, and Congreve, and South, and Dryden, and with many *hereditary* nobles, remembered only because they were patrons of those *natural* nobles; I read their names aloud; I invoked their departed spirits; I was appalled by the echo of my own voice. The holes in the floor, the forests of cobwebs in the windows, and a swallow's nest in the corner of the ceiling, proclaimed that I was viewing a vision of the dreamers of a past age: that I saw realised before me the speaking vanities of the anxious career of man! On rejoining Mr. Hoare's man in the hall below, and expressing my grief that so interesting a building should be suffered to go to decay for want of attention, he told me that his master intended to pull it down and unite it to an adjoining barn, so as to form of the two a riding-house; and I learn that this design has since been executed. The Kit-cat pictures were painted early in the eighteenth century, and about the year 1710 were brought to this spot, but the room and house I

have been describing was not built till ten or fifteen years afterwards. They were forty-two in number, and were presented by the members to the elder Tonson, who died in 1736; he left them to his great-nephew, also an eminent bookseller, who died in the year 1767. They were then removed from this building to the house of his brother at Water Oakley, near Windsor, and, on his death, to the house of Mr. Baker, of Hertingfordbury, near Hertford, where they now remain, and where I lately saw them, splendidly lodged and in fine preservation." So far Sir Richard Phillips.

It may be satisfactory here to add that the Kit-cat Club pictures still (1884) hang on the walls of Mr. W. Baker's house in Hertfordshire, and are well cared for and reverentially preserved.

But Barn Elms has even older memories than that of Jacob Tonson to boast of. Here, as stated above, lived Sir Francis Walsingham, the trusty servant and friend of Queen Elizabeth, and here he entertained his mistress on more than one occasion. Queen Bess, it is related, loved to take her pleasure by the river-side, whether at Greenwich, or at Richmond, or at Barn Elms. She was wont to issue her commands to Sir Francis Walsingham to prepare for her entertainment here, and—worse luck for the minister—she invariably took her whole Court with her. We admire the stout-heartedness of the virgin queen, and her unswerving faithfulness to the country's good, but her meanness was such as to sully her reputation. It is said that Walsingham died so poor—in consequence mainly of her majesty's visits—that he was buried privately, and that no mention of his death is to be found in the records of the Herald's College. Walsingham died at his house in Seething Lane, London, in 1590; and, as Stow relates, " he was, about tenne of the clocke in the next night following, buried in Paul's church without solemnitie."

Here it was that Heidegger, who, as we have already seen,* had made a fortune as " Master of the Revels " to King George II., gratified his Majesty in a somewhat singular manner. One day he received from the king a message to the effect that he should sup one evening with him before long, and that he would come to Barn Elms from Kew by water. Now, Heidegger's profession was to create surprises. The king's attendants, who were in the secret, took care that he should not reach Barn Elms before dark, so it was with difficulty that he found his way up the avenue to the door of the house. Coming to the door, and finding all dark,

---

he was angered at so uncourtier-like a reception. Heidegger quietly suffered his Majesty to vent his displeasure to the full, and affected to make some apologies more or less awkward, when in an instant the house and the entire avenue were in a blaze of light! Lamps artfully disposed were suddenly lit up at a given signal, as if by magical incantation. The king himself—a man not to be trifled with generally—laughed heartily at the device, and went away well pleased with the entertainment devised by his servant.

James Heidegger, of whom this and other amusing stories are told, was a native of Switzerland, and died in 1749, at the advanced age of ninety years. The nobility had such an opinion of his taste, that all splendid entertainments given by them, and all private assemblies, were submitted to his direction. After a successful speculation, he has been known to give away several hundreds of pounds, saying to a particular acquaintance, "You know poor objects of distress better than I do; be so kind as to give away this money for me." He was, indeed, for a long period the *arbiter elegantiarum* of England; and yet Heidegger was a very ugly fellow, but was the first always to joke about it. His face is introduced into more than one of Hogarth's prints. Heidegger once laid a wager with the Earl of Chesterfield that within a certain given time his lordship would not be able to produce so hideous a face in all London! A woman was found whose features, at first sight, were thought stronger than his, but upon clapping her head-dress upon himself, he was universally allowed to win the wager. Another time a well-known tailor, carrying his bill to a noble duke, his Grace, for evasion, said, "Hang your ugly face! I will never pay you till you bring me an uglier fellow than yourself." The tailor bowed and retired, wrote a letter, and sent it by a servant to Heidegger, saying his Grace wished to see him next morning on particular business. Heidegger attended, and the tailor was there to meet him; in consequence, as soon as Heidegger's visit was over, the tailor received his payment. He made £5,000 a year by his wits.

Another eminent resident at Barn Elms, though only for a short time, was Abraham Cowley the poet, who lived here just previous to 1665, but not finding this place to agree with his health, he removed to Chertsey, where he spent the best years of his life, and where he died.

John Evelyn, amongst other friends, visited him here more than once. He writes in his "Diary":—" 14th May, 1663. Dined with my Lord Mordaunt, and thence went to Barnes to

visite my excellent and ingenious friend Abraham Cowley."

And again, " 2nd January, 1664. To Barne Elmes to see Abraham Cowley aftr his sicknesse, and returned that evening to London."

It may be remembered that, in his imaginary dialogue between Milton and Cowley, Macaulay introduces to us the latter as having just come up to the " Bowling Green" in Piccadilly, that most fashionable haunt of the quality, whilst his house at Chertsey was being prepared for his reception.

It was to John Evelyn that he most appropriately addresses his " Essay and Poem on a Garden."

On his death, in 1667, he was buried in Westminster Abbey, and being carried thither by water, his corpse must have passed within sight of his former home.

Dr. Spratt tells us, in his "Life of Cowley," that he always loved solitude, and chose Barn Elms on that account, but that in his haste to be gone away from the tumult and noise of the city, he had not prepared so beautiful a situation in the country as he might have done; and he states that he never quite recovered from a "dangerous and lingering fever," which he contracted during his residence here. In the grounds of Barn Elms was erected a rustic temple to the memory of Cowley.

Judging from the records of the visits of Pepys to Barn Elms about this time, the "solitude" of the place was occasionally disturbed by light-hearted visitors who enjoyed a pic-nic beneath its shade. Under date of May 26th, 1667, Pepys writes:—" After dinner I went by water alone to Westminster to the parish church, and there did entertain myself with my perspective glass up and down the church, by which I had the great pleasure of seeing and gazing at a great many very fine women; and what with that and sleeping, I passed away the time till sermon was done. Then away to my boat, and up with it as far as Barn Elms, reading of Mr. Evelyn's late new book against Solitude, in which I do not find much excess of good matter, though it be pretty for a bye discourse. I walked the length of the Elms, and with great pleasure saw some gallant ladies and people come with their bottles, and baskets, and chairs and forms, to sup under the trees by the water-side, which was mighty pleasant; and so home."

The genial secretary seems to have been very fond of Barn Elms; at all events, there are several entries in his " Diary " of visits which he paid to the spot, sometimes alone, and at other times in the company of his friends. Under date of August 21st, 1668, he writes:—"(Lord's Day). I, my wife and niece up by water to Barn Elms, where we walked by moonshine;" and again on the 15th September (another "Lord's Day"), he tells us how he "walked from Putney to Barn Elms, reading of Boyle's Hydrostat, which are of infinite delight. Walked in the Elms a good while; then to boat, and leisurely home, with great pleasure to myself."

On the 23rd March he writes:—"At noon came Mrs. Pierce and Mrs. Manuel (the Jew's wife), and Mr. Corbett, and Mrs. Pierce's boy and girl. After dinner I had a barge ready at Tower Wharfe to take us in. So we went all of us up as high as Barn Elms; a very fine day, and all the way sang. Mrs. Manuel sings very finely, and is a highly discreet, sober-carriaged woman, that both my wife and I are highly taken with her. At Barn Elms we walked round, then to the barge again, and had much merry talk and good singing." And again on Lord's Day, May 9th, he writes:— "Took boat, and up all alone as high as Barn Elms."

Hereabouts, though the exact spot is not known, was fought, on January 16th, 1667-8, the cele-brated duel to which Macaulay alludes between the Duke of Buckingham and the Earl of Shrews-bury, when the wife of the latter stood by dressed in the habit of a page, holding the duke's horse. This lady was Anna Maria, a daughter of Robert Brudenell, Earl of Cardigan, and had married firstly, Francis, Earl of Shrewsbury. She after-wards married George Rodney Bridges, Esq., of Keynsham, Somerset, and died in 1702. Her son by her second husband lived till 1751. "This woman," says the Count de Grammont, "is said to have been so abandoned as to have held, in the habit of a page, the horse of her gallant the duke, while he fought and killed her husband, after which she went off with him to his house, stained with her husband's blood."

Pepys refers to this infamous transaction in terms rather of contempt than of censure; he writes in his "Diary," under date January 17th, 1667-8:—

"Much discourse of the duell yesterday between the Duke of Buckingham, Holmes, and Jenkins, on one side, and my Lord of Shrewsbury, Sir John Talbot, and one Bernard Howard, on the other side: and all about my Lady Shrewsbury, who is at this time, and hath for a great while been, a mistress to the Duke of Buckingham. And so her husband challenged him; and they met yester-day in a close near Barne-Elmes, and there fought; and my Lord Shrewsbury is run through the body, from the right breast through the shoulder; and Sir John Talbot all along up one of his armes; and

Jenkins killed upon the place, and the rest, all in a little measure, wounded. This will make the world think that the King hath good councillors about him when the Duke of Buckingham, the greatest man about him, is a fellow of no more sobriety than to fight about a mistress. And this may prove a very bad accident to the Duke of Buckingham, but that my Lady Castlemaine do rule all at this time as much as ever she did, and she will, it is believed, keep all matters well with the Duke of Buckingham; though this is the time that the King will be very backward, I suppose, to appear in such a business. And it is pretty to hear how the king had some notice of this challenge a week or two ago, and did give it to my lord Generall to confine the Duke, or take security that he should not do any such thing as fight; and the Generall trusted to the King, that he, sending for him, would do it, and the King trusted to the Generall; and it is said that my Lord Shrewsbury's case is to be feared that he may die too, and that may make it much the worse for the Duke of Buckingham: and I shall not be much sorry for it, that we may have some sober man come in his room to assist in the Government."

The earl died from the effects of his wounds on the 16th of the following March. The Sir John Talbot and the Bernard Howard, who are mentioned as seconds in the duel, were respectively —the former M.P. for Knaresborough and a gentleman of the King's Privy Chamber, and the latter a younger son of Henry Frederick, Earl of Arundel, father of Thomas, who was restored by Charles I. in blood as Duke of Norfolk.

The old chatterbox Pepys recurs to the subject in his "Diary" on the 15th of May:—"I am told . . . that the Countesse of Shrewsbury is brought home by the Duke of Buckingham to his house, where his Duchesse saying that it was not for her and the other to live together in a house, he answered, 'Why, Madam, I did think so, and, therefore, have ordered your coach to be ready to carry you to your father's,' which was a devilish speech, but, they say, true; and my Lady Shrews-bury is there, it seems."

In the reign of Charles I. a man named Shipman, gardener to the king, planted and cured madder on a large scale at Barn Elms, and so far succeeded with his works as to find a large market among the London dyers. He failed, however, to reap a fortune by his enterprise, owing to the troubles of the times. It was again attempted by the patriotic Sir Nicholas Crispe, of Hammersmith.*

---

* See "Old and New London," Vol. VI., p. 537

To come to more recent times, Barn Elms is connected with other names which the world would not willingly allow to die : for instance, with William Cobbett, who here cultivated his Indian corn, his American forest-trees, his pigs, poultry, and butcher's meat, all which he pronounced to be the best that were ever beheld. Cobbett, at the same time that he occupied the farm here, lived also at Kensington ;* but the aristocratic suburb, we are told, did not prove a congenial soil, and he quitted it a bankrupt.

and so bethought him of the high road to England, which, as Dr. Johnson sarcastically remarks, 'is of all prospects the most pleasing to a Scotchman.'

"With that 'canniness' which is attributed to us of the 'North Countrie,' Sir John availed himself of this supposed opening to preferment, and crossed the border in the train of his royal master, in search of a beautiful and well-endowed bride. Unfortunately for the poor Scottish gentleman, it

BARN ELMS.

After Barn Elms came into the hands of Sir Richard Hoare, as above stated, the mansion was modernised, and considerably enlarged by the addition of wings. In his time some fine old pictures graced the walls of the dining and drawing-rooms, amongst them being some fine examples of the works of Gaspar Poussin.

"The occupants of Barn Elms in the reign of King James I.," writes Miss Guthrie, in her interesting account of the place,† "were a Sir John and Lady Kennedy. Sir John, like many others of his countrymen, was a

'Penniless lad wi' a lang pedigree,'

befell him, as it did another brave gallant from beyond the Tweed—

'There was an English lady bright,
    The sun shines fair on Carlisle wall ;
And she fell in love with a Scottish knight,
    For love will still be lord of all.'

"The enamoured fair one on this occasion proved to be no less distinguished a person than Elizabeth Brydges, daughter of Giles, Lord Chandos, 'King of the Cotswolds,' whom the northern knight successfully wooed and won, to the no small delight of 'gentle Jamie' and his own gratification, at the same time that it enraged the new Lord Chandos, who hated the thoughts of his gay and lovely aunt wedding with a 'beggarly

Scot.' In the retirement of Barn Elms Sir John Kennedy, no doubt, expected to lead a quiet domestic life in the society of his high-born bride. . . . The old saw, 'When poverty comes in at the door love flies out of the window,' was soon verified in their case. Unable to obtain the money necessary to defray her expenses, the lady ran into debt. The husband remonstrated, but in vain. Moreover, the capricious fair one had grown weary of the seclusion of Barn Elms, of its

flaws in the contract, he was enabled in this way to get rid of his wife.

"What follows may well suffice to point a moral and adorn a tale. How long after this separation we know not, this once gay and brilliant girl, 'the light of Sudeley and Hampton Court,' came to the gate of Sir Arthur Gorges : to make use of his own words, 'in rags, her legs bare, her feet shoeless, her coarse petticoat clinging about her limbs, an old cloak on her beautiful head, begging

HAMMERSMITH BRIDGE (BOATING-MEN GOING OUT).

orchards, its gardens, and pasturage for three geldings. What charms could these possess for one accustomed, as she had been, to the glories of Sudeley ?

"Domestic feuds ensued. Still the lady pursued her mad career. Debts poured in. In her extremity Lady Kennedy applied to her nephew, Lord Chandos, who refused her any assistance. Unable to satisfy her creditors with aught save fair words, these attacked Sir John. Actions and counter-actions in the court of law nearly drove the poor knight out of his senses. Threatened with arrest, and unable to dispute his wife's debts, Sir John at length resolved to dispute his marriage, and there happening strangely enough to be some

of him to let her come in from the cold for Christian pity and love of his wife.' "

Sir Lancelot Shadwell, Vice-Chancellor of England, whilst living here, used to entertain at dinner the rival university boats' crews after the annual race. Sir Lancelot Shadwell is represented by *Punch* as bathing in the river, and "granting a *rule*" to an anxious suitor who had put off in a boat to his lordship. The truth is that he was a fine swimmer, and bathed in a pond in his own grounds daily, both winter and summer, and that on more than one occasion those who came down from London to see him on legal affairs had to talk to him whilst he was in the water, and to receive his replies as they waited on the banks.

CHAPTER XLVIII.

ROEHAMPTON.

" Jubetur
Rura suburbana indictis comes ire Latinis."—Hor. 1. *Ep.*

Situation and General Appearance of the Parish—Population—Putney or Mortlake Park—The Earl of Portland, Lord Treasurer—Christian, Countess of Devonshire—Roehampton Grove—Mrs. Lyne-Stephens *née* Duvernay—The Roman Catholic Convent—Lord Ellenborough—The Parish Church—Roehampton House—Parkstead—The Earl of Bessborough—Manresa House—A Jesuit Community—Lord Rockingham—Lord Giffard—Lord Langdale—Sir J. L. Knight-Bruce—Royal School for Daughters of Military Officers—Mount Clare—Dover House and Devonshire House—Roehampton Gate.

FEW villages near London are more pleasantly situated than Roehampton. Lying as it does between Richmond Park and Putney Heath on the south, and Barnes Common on the north, it is open and breezy and healthy, and disfigured by few or none of those squalid hovels which abound in other suburbs ; it has always been a highly aristocratic village, and more than "respectably" inhabited. It is described by Miss Priscilla Wakefield, in 1817, as "a hamlet in the parish of Putney, abounding in handsome villas of the nobility and gentry, and a neat chapel." The name has nothing whatever to do with fallow "roes" or other members of the deer tribe ; indeed, two centuries ago it was often written Rowhampton.

The village lies about a mile to the south of Barnes Common, stretching away from that station on the Richmond branch of the South-Western Railway. The entire parish has a population of about 2,000 souls.

A great part of what is now known as Roehampton—indeed all that lies to the west of Putney Park Lane—formed a portion of Putney or Mortlake Park, for it was known at different times by each name. The park, though it has never been inhabited by a sovereign, was called "royal," being used occasionally by royalty for the purposes of the chase.

We find one Sir Robert Tyrrwhitt appointed keeper of this park in Mary's reign, and the post was afterwards conferred by James I. on Sir Charles Howard. Charles I. had not been long upon the throne when he alienated the park to his Lord Treasurer Weston, Earl of Portland, who took up his residence here. He is said to have lived here in great state and magnificence. In 1632, on May 26, as we learn from the diary in his "Autobiography," Dr. Laud, the Bishop of London, consecrated in his mansion a private chapel, in which shortly afterwards his son and heir, Jerome, was married by Laud to Lady Frances Stuart, daughter of the Duke of Lennox, a lady nearly allied to the royal house. The bride was given away by the king in person.

On this occasion Ben Jonson wrote the "Epithalamium," in which occur the following verses, which will be found in his "Underwoods" :—

" See the procession ! what a holy day,
　Bearing the promise of some better fate,
Hath filled with caróches all the way
　From Greenwich hither to Roehampton gate.
　　When looked the year at best
　　So like a feast ?
　　Or were affairs in tune,
By all the spheres' consent, so in the heart of June ?"

And then, after exhausting all the classical and romantic epithets and similes and conceits that could be crowded into some two hundred lines, some of them not over delicate, he continues :—

" See ! now the chapel opens, where the king
　And bishop stand to consummate the rites ;
　The holy prelate prays, then takes the ring,
　　Asks first, ' Who gives her ?' ' I, Charles.' Then
　　　he plights
　　One in the other's hand,
　　Whilst they both stand
　　Hearing their charge ; and then
The solemn choir cries ' Joy !' and they return ' Amen !' "

This Lord Treasurer obtained from the king, two or three years later, leave to enclose some 450 acres more, and to join them on to the park ; but he had scarcely been put into possession of them when death "laid his icy hand" upon him, and he died. Sons do not always carry out the ideas of their fathers, and the new Lord Portland was no exception to the rule, for instead of adding to his demesne, he set to work to sell it and his mansion, and many, though not all, of his broad acres passed into the hands of one of the most celebrated ladies of her age, Christian, Countess of Devonshire. She had great talents, and the art of using them ; and in a corrupt age she lived a pure and virtuous life. In fact, she seems to have been resolved to make the best use of both worlds ; at all events, we are told that "she was of considerable celebrity for her devotion, hospitality, her great care in the management of her son's affairs, and a patroness of the wits of the age who frequently met at her house." Her house was the rendezvous of the choicest spirits of her time, and the haunt of all men of learning and women of repute and character. Poets and philosophers were free of her society, and were hospitably entertained here. Royalty was often among her visitors ; and it is on record that Charles II. and the queen-mother, Henrietta Maria, often came over hither from Hampton Court to dine at her table. A daughter of the noble Scottish house of Bruce, she was a woman of great celebrity, and a very singular character. In her opposites were strangely combined, for although extolled for her devotion, she retained Hobbes, the freethinker, as tutor to her son ; and though famed for her hospitality, yet by judicious economy, whilst acting as guardian of her son, she extricated the Cavendish estates from debt and from (it is said) thirty lawsuits. She ingratiated herself so with the judges, that Charles II. said to her in jest, " Madame, you have all my judges at your disposal." The duchess deserves remembrance as the associate of most of the wits of her time. Waller frequently read his verses to her, and Lord Pembroke wrote in her praise a volume of verses, which were afterwards published, and dedicated to her by Dr. John Donne. She herself was a writer of no mean merit, having left a pleasing monument of her taste in a poem on " The Passage of Mont St. Gothard," which was translated into French by Delille. General Monk corresponded with her, and, it is said, at a time when his conduct was most mysterious, to have made known to her by a private sign his intention of restoring the king. Her loyalty led her into correspondence with half the statesmen of her time to promote the restoration of monarchy. Her " Life " was written by Pomfret. Among her most constant visitors here was good John Evelyn, who, writing of her in his " Diary," under date August, 1662 :—" Came to see me the old Countesse of Devonshire, with that excellent and worthy person, my lord, her son, from Rowhampton." And again in February, 1677 :—" I went to Roehampton with my lady Dutchesse of Ormond. The garden and perspective is pretty, the prospect most agreeable."

Of her sons, one fell in the civil wars fighting for his king, and the elder, who became earl on his father's death, was the father of the first Duke of Devonshire.

Having passed through several intermediate owners, Roehampton Park became the property of a member of Parliament, of foreign extraction, Mr. John Vanneck, afterwards Lord Huntingfield, who dismantled the house, and pulled it down to make room for a smaller one, called Roehampton Grove, which for the last thirty or forty years has been the residence of Mrs. Lyne-Stephens, better known to older readers as Mademoiselle Duvernay, the cele-

brated *danseuse* of the reign of William IV. This lady, Yolande Marie Louise Duvernay, was the daughter of Mons. Jean Louis Duvernay, and was born in France about the year 1815. She made her first appearance in England, with a considerable reputation, at Drury Lane Theatre in 1833, in a ballet called the " Sleeping Beauty." Her reception was highly encouraging, and soon afterwards she performed in the " Maid of Cashmere," a ballet opera by Auber. In December, 1836, was produced the ballet of " The Devil on Two Sticks," which met with great popularity. In this ballet Mlle. Duvernay introduced to the English public the graceful dance with castanets, " La Cachuca," with which her name has been more especially identified. Her charming execution of this dance established the lady as the worthy compeer of Cerito, Taglioni, and Fanny Elssler. In 1845 she retired from the stage, having married Mr. Stephens Lyne-Stephens, of Lynford Hall, Norfolk, and of Roehampton, formerly M.P. for Barnstaple, but was left a widow in 1860.

On the site of a portion of the park now stands a large Roman Catholic convent belonging to the Sisters of the Sacred Heart. The buildings include schools for the poor and a school for young ladies of the higher classes.

Previous to being devoted to its present uses the mansion was occupied by the late Earl of Ellenborough, some time Governor-General of India. His lordship was the eldest son of the first Lord Ellenborough (many years Chief Justice of the King's Bench), whom he succeeded in the barony in 1818. He held the post of Lord Privy Seal in the Duke of Wellington's administration in 1828–29, was President of the Board of Control during the short-lived Peel administration of 1834–35, and was appointed, on the return of Sir Robert Peel, in September, 1841, to the same office, which he relinquished a month afterwards for the post of Governor-General of India. Lord Ellenborough was recalled from the latter office by the East India Company in 1844. He had previously received the thanks of both Houses of Parliament for his " ability and judgment " in supporting the military operations in Affghanistan. His administration in India, however, had given rise to severe criticism in some quarters. His biographer in " Chambers's Encyclopædia " says :—" He was charged with reserving his favour for the military, and inflicting undeserved slights upon the civil servants of the Company. He made showy progresses ; addressed proclamations to the rulers and natives of India which appeared to sanction idolatry ; and, finally, in his proclamation concern-

ing the sandal-wood gates of the temple of Jugger-
naut, when brought back from Ghuznee, he reached
the climax of a series of extravagances which induced the directors of the East India Company to
recall him. The Ministry, however, stood by him,
and he was created by the crown an earl and a
viscount, and he also received the distinction of a
G.C.B." Lord Ellenborough subsequently held
office as First Lord of the Admiralty under Sir
Robert Peel, and Minister for India in the Derby
administration of 1858. Having permitted a
despatch to see the light, in which he had administered a severe and caustic rebuke to Viscount
Canning, Governor-General of India, an outcry was
raised against him, which threatened the existence
of the Derby government. To avert this result
Lord Ellenborough resigned. His lordship died in
1871.

The chapel, mentioned above as having been
consecrated by Laud, was removed about the year
1728, in order to make way for a larger structure,
built of brick, in the " Hanoverian " style of ugli-
ness ; and that, again, its accommodation not being
equal to the requirements of the village, was superseded by the present edifice, which was designed by
Mr. B. Ferrey, and dates from 1841-2. It is of the
Decorated period of Gothic architecture. In 1845,
when the hamlet of Roehampton was converted
into an ecclesiastical parish, cut off from the civil
parish of Putney, this chapel was enlarged, so as to
serve as the parish church. The church itself is
cruciform in plan, consisting of a nave, transepts,
and chancel, with vestry and organ-chamber at the
north-east corner. The church was altered and
enlarged in 1862, and again in 1883-4. The
structure occupies nearly the whole of the churchyard, which is square in shape. Adjoining it is a
huge mausoleum, in the Classical style, erected by
the Lyne-Stephens family, and consecrated by Dr.
Tait when Bishop of London, in 1864.

The fine houses and seats in Roehampton parish
are extremely numerous in comparison to its
acreage and population, the pleasantness of its
situation and the nearness of Richmond Park
having rendered it from a very early period a
favourite place of residence. Two of these seats
will be found depicted in the " Vitruvius Britannicus." The first of these is Roehampton House,
now the seat of Lady Leven, but formerly of Lord
Albemarle. It is a plain, heavy, and substantial
red-brick structure, somewhat after the style of
Kensington Palace. Sir James Thornhill painted
the ceiling of the grand saloon or drawing-room
with a representation of the gods at a banquet on
Mount Olympus. The house itself was erected

in 1712, from the designs of Thomas Archer, to
whom belongs the credit of having designed also
the ugliest church in Westminster, St. John's,*
Millbank. The other mansion, once the seat of
Lord Bessborough, was formerly called Parkstead.
It was built, somewhat later than its neighbour, by
Sir William Chambers, for Lord Bessborough, who
was a connoisseur in works of art, and who had here
a fine collection of paintings, sculpture, coins, and
other classical antiquities. The *Gentleman's Magazine* for April, 1801, gives a long list of these
"curiosities," including Roman and Greek statues,
busts, cinerary urns, inscriptions, vases, and also
some treasures brought from Egypt.

William, second Earl of Bessborough, who made
these collections, held the title during nearly the
whole of the latter half of the eighteenth century.
He was a man of pleasure as well of taste, and he
married Lady Caroline Cavendish, a fair daughter
of the house of Devonshire, who was a great beauty
in her time. His son and successor, Frederick, the
third earl, married a daughter of the first Earl
Spencer, and lived here till the early part of her
Majesty's reign.

The place now belongs to the Jesuit community,
who have given to it the name of Manresa, after
one of the houses in Spain which are connected
with incidents in the life of their founder St.
Ignatius Loyola. It now forms one of the novi-
ciates of that Order. In the garden facing Richmond Park is an alcove or summer-house, now
turned into a little oratory, in which the tradition
is that Lord Bessborough used to spend the long
afternoons in playing cards for high stakes with
the Prince Regent. The Fathers have here a private printing press, where many Roman Catholic
publications are set up in type by their lay brothers,
and by others who are trained to the work of com-
positors. Here they have also received several
members of the Jesuit body who have been expelled from France, Germany, and other countries
on the Continent, on account of the jealousy and
hatred felt against the ministers of religion by the
anti-clerical party.

It was to Roehampton that Lord Rockingham
retired in 1782, on resigning the seals of office ;
and here he died. " Junius " pays him a higher
compliment than perhaps he deserves when he
speaks of his "mild but determined integrity."

Lord Rockingham was a man who, though of
very moderate abilities, still contrived to leave his
mark upon the history of the eighteenth century.
In 1765 he succeeded George Grenville as First

---

* See "Old and New London," Vol. IV., p. 3.

Lord of the Treasury, but held the Premiership for only a single year. From that time he was the leader of the Opposition in the House of Lords until restored, in 1782, to his former post as head of the Government which is known as the Rockingham administration, and in which Charles James Fox and Edmund Burke held places. Under his auspices was commenced a pacific communication with the revolted States of North America, but he did not live to see his project carried to a completion. He died within a few months after his return to power, when the bulk of his large property and estates passed to his nephew Lord Fitzwilliam.

Lord Gifford lived here whilst Master of the Rolls in the reign of George IV.; and so did his successor, Lord Langdale, some ten years afterwards; and Vice-Chancellor Sir James Knight-Bruce for many years occupied the Priory, now converted into a private asylum for lunatics. In fact, Roehampton would seem to have been a favourite abode of legal celebrities; and it may be worth mentioning that a lane leading from Barnes Common towards the Roehampton Gate of Richmond Park is, according to a writer in *All the Year Round*, known from that circumstance as "Chancery Lane."

The Right Hon. Robert Gifford, Lord Gifford, was the son of a respectable tradesman at Exeter, where he was born in 1779. At an early age he came to London, and entered his name as a student of the Middle Temple. He was duly called to the Bar in 1808, and his earliest professional efforts were made at the Exeter sessions, and from that time his advancement was a rapid one. In 1817 he was appointed Solicitor-General, and two years later he succeeded to the post of Attorney-General. This appointment led to the most remarkable event in his professional career, the prosecution, in 1820, of Queen Caroline. In 1824 he was raised to the peerage, and was appointed to the office of Lord Chief Justice of the Common Pleas, and soon afterwards, on the death of Sir Thomas Plumer, he was made Master of the Rolls. Previous to his elevation to the peerage, his lordship sat in the House of Commons as Member for Eye. At the commencement of the Session of 1824 he was appointed Deputy-Speaker of the House of Lords, an office then first established. His lordship died at Dover in 1826.

The Right Hon. Henry Bickersteth, Lord Langdale, lived for many years at Templeton House. He was the son of a country surgeon and apothecary of some repute, Mr. Henry Bickersteth, of Kirkby Lonsdale, Westmoreland, and he was an uncle of the late Dr. Bickersteth, Bishop of Ripon.

Lord Langdale first saw the light in 1783, and was educated at the free grammar-school of his native town, under the mastership of the Rev. J. Dobson. He commenced life with the view of following in his father's profession; and it is stated that he was professionally consulted in his father's house so late as the year 1807. He had, in the meantime, travelled on the Continent in the capacity of medical attendant of the Earl of Oxford, whose daughter he long afterwards married. It is said to have been with the encouragement of his noble patron that Mr. Bickersteth was enabled to enter himself of Caius College, Cambridge, where, in 1808, he graduated as Senior Wrangler and first Smith's prizeman. He was called to the Bar at the Inner Temple three years later, and at once became engaged in the arduous duties of the legal profession. In 1827 he became a King's Counsel and a bencher of his inn, and subsequently filled the office of treasurer. Mr. Bickersteth rose to great eminence in the Equity Courts, to which he confined his practice. In 1835 he was offered by Sir Robert Peel a seat on the bench, which was afterwards occupied by Mr. Serjeant Coleridge, but he declined the proffered honour. In the following year, however, he was appointed to succeed Lord Cottenham as Master of the Rolls, and at the same time he was called to the House of Peers and sworn a member of the Privy Council. By an unusual exception to the course of high legal preferment in this country, Lord Langdale had thus risen to one of the most honourable and important posts in his profession without having mingled in active political life, and without having either sat in the House of Commons or held the office of a legal adviser to the Crown. Lord Langdale died in 1851, having by his marriage with Lady Jane Harley, the eldest daughter of the Earl of Oxford, left an only daughter; his title, therefore, passed away from the roll of existing peerages, but his memory as a lawyer will not soon be forgotten.

Sir James Lewis Knight-Bruce was the youngest son of Mr. John Knight, of Fairlinch, Devon, and was born in 1791, his mother being the only child and heiress of Mr. William Bruce, of Duffryn, Glamorganshire, whose name he assumed. He became a student of Lincoln's Inn in 1812, and after his call to the Bar attended the Welsh circuit for a short time, when he exchanged the Common Law for the Equity Bar, where his great talents and industry soon secured a large practice. In 1831 he entered Parliament as member for Bishop's Castle, a borough which was disfranchised at the passing of the Reform Bill in 1832. In January, 1842, Sir James Knight-Bruce, who had just been

made a Vice-Chancellor, was sworn a Privy Councillor, and he thus became, in virtue of the Act
constituting his office, a member of the Judicial
Committee of the Privy Council and of the Final
Court of Appeal for the courts of India and of
the colonies, and from the ecclesiastical and admiralty jurisdictions of this country. Nine years
later, in 1851, on the creation of the Court of
Appeal, he was selected as one of the first Lords
Justices. Of the numerous judgments delivered

who succeeded to the business and "the sauce"
complained that the brother who had not inherited
it was nevertheless vending "Burgess's Sauce," the
Lord Justice, deciding against the complainant,
commenced as follows :—"All the queen's subjects
are entitled to manufacture pickles and sauces, and
not the less so that their fathers have done it
before them. All the queen's subjects are entitled
to use their own names, and not the less so that
their fathers have done it before them." The con-

HIGH STREET, ROEHAMPTON.

by him, those which are likely to be referred to as
settling or elucidating the law are few and far
between ; yet there are some few which are remarkable not only for their sparkling cleverness and
power, but as examples of legal reasoning, and as
settlements of vexed and intricate legal questions.
Sometimes, too, there was a certain irrepressible
humour even about his gravest judgments, which
was eminently characteristic of his general mode of
getting through the otherwise dull and prosaic
transactions of the court in which he sat. Thus, in
a case which came before him, known as the
" Burgess's Anchovy Case," in which two brothers
named Burgess, sons of the original inventor of the
sauce, were the litigants, and in which the brother

clusion followed, of course. Sir James Knight-
Bruce died at Roehampton Priory in 1866.

At Clarence Lodge, situated in Clarence Lane,
which was at one time inhabited by William IV.
before he came to the throne, was established, in
1864, the Royal School for Daughters of Military
Officers.

Mount Clare, situated near Roehampton Gate,
Richmond Park, was built a little more than a century ago, and named after Claremont, already mentioned as the seat of the great Lord Clive. It was
afterwards the abode of a Scottish baronet, Sir
John Dick, who introduced into the structure
some Italian details ; more recently it was occupied by the gallant admiral, Sir Charles Ogle, who

died in 1858. He had been one of Nelson's captains.

Downshire House and Dover House, both named after noble lords who formerly owned them, are now the seats of merchant princes. In the earlier part of the present century, when occupied by Lord Dover, the latter house was famous for its social and literary gatherings. Charles Greville tells us in his "Memoirs" that he spent two or three "uncommonly agreeable" days here in the company of Tommy Moore, Sir James Mackintosh, Sir William Grant, Master of the Rolls, and other pleasant acquaintances.

Roehampton Gate, the entrance to Richmond Park on the east, has long been closed to the public. The question of the purchase of its approach, by the Crown or otherwise, in order to secure it for the use of the public, has been brought forward in Parliament, it being admitted that this gate would be the easiest way of access to the park for the inhabitants of the metropolis; but up to the present time nothing definite has been decided upon. In April, 1884, on the question being sub-

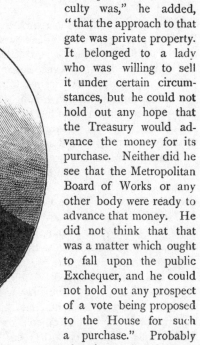

SIR J. KNIGHT-BRUCE.

mitted by Mr. Alderman Lawrence to the First Commissioner of Works, the latter replied that he thought it would be a great advantage to the public if Roehampton Gate were open. "The difficulty was," he added, "that the approach to that gate was private property. It belonged to a lady who was willing to sell it under certain circumstances, but he could not hold out any hope that the Treasury would advance the money for its purchase. Neither did he see that the Metropolitan Board of Works or any other body were ready to advance that money. He did not think that that was a matter which ought to fall upon the public Exchequer, and he could not hold out any prospect of a vote being proposed to the House for such a purchase." Probably what is required is some "village Hampden" to rise up and assert his right to enter the park by that particular gate, in the same manner that the Richmond brewer, Mr. John Lewis, did some century ago, as described in a previous chapter of this work. By that means the difficulty might be got over without a parliamentary grant.

CHAPTER XLIX.

WIMBLEDON.

"Let the great world spin for ever
Down the ringing grooves of change."

Situation and Boundaries of the Parish—Its Etymology—Early History of the Manor—Burstow Park—The Cromwell Family—The Cecils—Queen Elizabeth at Wimbledon—Visit of James I. to the Earl of Exeter at Wimbledon—Queen Victoria at the Manor House—The Viscountcy of Wimbledon—The Manor bought by Queen Henrietta Maria—It is afterwards owned by General Lambert, but again reverts to Queen Henrietta Maria—Thomas Osborne, Earl of Danby, afterwards Marquis of Carmarthen and Duke of Leeds—The Manor House rebuilt by Sir Theodore Janssen—The Park formed by Lord Spencer—The present Manor House—An Artesian Well—Description of the original Manor House.

WIMBLEDON is a very extensive and scattered parish, and one that is not devoid of historical interest. From Barnes and Roehampton, and Putney and Wandsworth, on the north, it stretches away to Merton and Cheam on the south; Kingston adjoins it on the west; and the river Wandle, which forms one of its eastern boundaries, separates it from Mitcham and Wandsworth. The living was formerly a "peculiar," in the gift of the Archbishop of Canterbury, together with the adjacent parishes of Putney and Mortlake. Wimbledon, in fact, was anciently a portion of the manor of Mortlake. Though it lies so very near to London that it is yearly threatened with the fate of annexation to the great metropolis, yet it is more famous in early history than most of the suburban districts.

If the early chroniclers are to be trusted, a place bearing the name of Wibbandune was the scene of a fierce battle between Ceaulin, King of Wessex, and Ethelbert, King of Kent, as far back as A.D. 568. Ethelbert, who had aspired to the dignity of Bretwalda, or chieftain of Britain, was defeated, and besides losing two of his great generals, his army suffered terrible slaughter, and he was forced to retreat within his own dominion. In witness of this battle, there is still to be seen at the south-western corner of the common an all but circular encampment, covering about seven acres, and locally known as Bensbury. The tradition of the neighbourhood is that Julius Cæsar encamped here during his invasion of Britain, B.C. 54. Of the encampment we shall have more to say presently.

In Camden's "Britannia" we find :—"Wibbandune, now commonly called Wimbledon, stands on the other bank of the Wandle [*i.e.*, from Beddington, which he had been describing], where, when long prosperity had produced civil wars among the Saxons after their wars with the Britons were ended, Ethelbert, King of Kent, first sounded the alarm against his countrymen ; but Ceaulin, King of the East Saxons, fortunately defeated him with great slaughter, having slain his generals, Oslac and Cneben, from which last, probably, the fortification to be seen here was called Bensbury, for Cnebensbury."

Gough, in a note on Camden, writes :—" Dr. Salmon will not allow Bensbury camp, or, as the common people call it, *The Rounds*, at Wimbledon, to have had the use which Camden assigns to it, nor can he satisfy himself of its Romaneity "—that is, in common English, of its being of Roman design and execution.

Although the variations in the spelling of the name of the parish may perhaps not have been so numerous as in some other parishes in England, there have been, at all events, about a dozen different examples of its orthography handed down to us, namely :—Wibbandûn, Wibbandune, Wipandune, Wymbaldon, Wymbeldon, Wymbledon, Wymbylton, Wimendon, Wibleton, Wimbleton, Wimbledon. The name is thought to have been derived from that of "some Saxon proprietor named *Wymbald*, and *dun*, or *dune*, a hill in the Saxon language, possibly an adoption from the British ; hence the appellations *Wymbaldon* and *Wymbeldon*, by which this place is distinguished in old records."

A writer in *Notes and Queries* (July 15, 1882) says that "it is believed that the earliest mention of Wimbledon is in the Anglo-Saxon Chronicle, under date A.D. 568, where we find that Ceaulin, King of Wessex, and his brother Cutha, fought against Ethebryght, King of Kent, defeated him, and slew two of his ' ealdermen,' Oslaf and Cnebban (Cnebban) at Wibbandune." He adds :— "There appears reason to think that this Wibbandune is the present Wimbledon, particularly as the word is found in the transition form of 'Wymbaldune.'" The writer owns that he is quite at a loss as to the etymology of the first part of the word. In this, however, another writer, Professor Skeat, of Cambridge, comes to the rescue in the same publication (July 29, 1882) with the following interpretation of its etymology :—" *Wibbandúne*," he writes, "is the dative of *Wibbandún*, meaning ' Wibba's down.' Next, *dún* is not a true Anglo-Saxon word, but borrowed from Celtic, as explained in my ' Dictionary,' the equivalent English word being *tún*, modern English *town*. A *down* meant both a hill and a hill-fort. Thirdly, *Wibba*, like all masculines in -*a*, is of the form which may be called *agential*, as it denotes an agent. The word literally means ' one who wriggles about,' or (to use a word from an allied root) *wabbles* about, and the secondary sense is ' beetle,' or ' grub'—not a very complimentary name. . . . The very form *wibba* occurs in one of our old glossaries, which gives ' *Scarabeus*, *scærn-wibba*, *i.e.*, sharn-grub, or dung-beetle.' "

" The manor of Wymbledon, or, as it is generally named, Mortelage, or Mortlake," writes the Rev. W. A. Bartlett, in his history of the parish, "was one of the many estates belonging to the see of Canterbury which were seized by Odo, Bishop of Bayeux." Domesday Book makes no mention of Wimbledon ; but it has been considered by most of the county historians that at the time of the Conqueror's survey it was included, as it certainly was at a later period, in the great manor of Mortlake, then held by the Archbishops of Canterbury. In a record made during the time of Archbishop Reynolds, 1327, and preserved at Lambeth Palace, Wimbledon is described as a grange, or farm, belonging to Mortlake. On the impeachment of Archbishop Arundel, in 1398, his estates, including Wimbledon, were seized, and in the inquisition then taken, the manor of Wimbledon is mentioned as "a member of the manor of Croydon (also belonging to the see of Canterbury), consisting of a house and buildings, containing two acres, worth nothing beyond reprises ; 100 acres of arable land at 3d. = £1 5s. ; 21 of meadow, at 6d. =

10s. 6d. ; four of several pasture, 2d. = 8d. ; assised rents of five tenants, 4s. ; divers works done for 48 virgates of land, at 3s. = £7 4s. ; and 200 courts, worth per annum, with the common fine, £1 13s. 4d. ; in all, £10 17s. 6d." Of this entry Manning has given the following explanation :—" This account could not mean the manor of Wimbledon as now comprehending Mortlake and Putney, to which belong rents and services to a much greater amount. In fact," he adds, " there were two capital houses belonging to the manor of Mortlake—one, with a park, at Mortlake, the other at Wimbledon. The former was frequently the residence of the archbishops, and occasionally that of the king in a vacancy of the see. The latter was rather a grange, or farm. When, therefore, this is called in the inquisition the manor of Wimbledon, nothing more was meant than a mansion, with part of the demesne lands (as has been found in many instances), to which, in this case, certain services of the tenants due to the manor properly so called were attached, as well for the convenience of the tenants who resided in that part of the manor as of the lord, the owner of the house and land."

" The general conclusion, therefore," remarks Mr. Bartlett, " at which we may arrive seems to be this : That the manor of Mortlake, or Mortelage, described in Domesday, included the parishes of Mortlake, Wimbledon, Putney,* and probably East Sheen ;† and that during the tenure of the archbishops this manor sometimes went by the name of Mortlake, and sometimes by that of Wimbledon." Although the mansion of the manor of Mortlake was in that parish, the church, as we have already seen, was undoubtedly at Wimbledon.‡ Then, again, the manor of Barnes, or Barn-elms, called in the Domesday Survey *Berne*, was associated in early times with the manor of Wimbledon, as is proved by the fact that " the Dean and Chapter of St. Paul's formerly paid a sparrow-hawk yearly, or, in lieu thereof, two shillings, to the Archbishop of Canterbury, as lord of the manor of Wimbledon, to be exempted from serving the office of reeve or provost within that manor."

Burstow, or Burstow Park, was also in early times comprised within the manor of Wimbledon. In the reign of Henry VIII. (1531), " William [Warham], then Archbishop of Canterbury, de-

mised Burstow Park to Sir John Gage [then the owner of Burstow Court Lodge] for eighty years." " Whether the archbishop afterwards granted it to the king, or directly to Thomas Cromwell," writes Mr. Bartlett, " we do not know ; but Cromwell had the manor of Wimbledon, and Burstow Park as an appendage to it. On his attainder it was seized by the king, and remained in the Crown till 32 Elizabeth, when the queen granted to Sir Thomas Cecil the manor of Wimbledon, with its members in the county of Surrey, and rents of free tenants—namely, amongst others, ' for lands or tenements in Bristowe, *alias* Burstowe, £6 17s. 4d. ; and all those our lands in Bristowe, *alias* Burstowe, parcel of the same lordship of Wimbledon, called the *Parke*, demised to Sir John Gage, Knt., by indenture under the seal of William, late Archbishop of Canterbury, dated March 11th, 22 Henry VIII. (1531), for eighty years, rent £11, all late parcel of the possessions of the late Archbishop of Canterbury, after of Thomas Cromwell, Knt., late Earl of Essex, attainted of high treason.' " This property was subsequently conveyed by Sir Thomas Cecil to Sir Thomas Shirley the elder, of Wiston, in Sussex, from whose time it passed altogether away from Wimbledon.

The rise and the fall of Thomas Cromwell, who obtained the manor of Wimbledon about the year 1539, are matters of history. It was not a little singular that in middle life he should have been lord of the manor upon which his father had carried on the trade of a blacksmith at the time of his birth. " The site of his birthplace," writes Bartlett, in his " History of Wimbledon," " as pointed out by tradition, agrees with a survey of the manor taken in 1617, which describes upon the same spot ' an ancient cottage called the smith's shop,' lying west of a highway leading from Putney to the Upper Gate, and on the south side of the highway from Richmond to Wandsworth, being the sign of the ' Anchor.' "

Some interesting particulars of the Cromwell family are given by Mr. J. Phillips, in the *Antiquarian Magazine*,* from which we learn that Thomas Cromwell, who had spent his early manhood in travel, returned from Antwerp about the year 1514 ; that " he then settled as a wool and cloth merchant, and practised as a lawyer, accountant, and scrivener, by Fenchurch, in Fenchurch Street, London." This Thomas Cromwell's wife was the " widow of Thomas Williams, of Wales." The family of the Williamses was of Llanishen, in Glamorganshire, but members of it

---

* Putney belonged to Wimbledon when Queen Elizabeth granted the manor to Sir Thomas Cecil.

† East Sheen was not enfranchised from Wimbledon till the reign of Henry VII., at which time it was the property of the Welbecks ; it had previously been the estate of the Dyneleys.—See Lysons' " Environs," i., 267.

‡ See *ante*, p. 426.

* See Vol. V., p. 171, April, 1884.

had been long connected with Wimbledon and Putney. "From 1492 to 1502, when he died," writes Mr. Phillips, "John Williams was overseer and collector of the revenues of Wimbledon Manor, which included the parishes of Wimbledon, Putney with Roehampton, and Mortlake with East Sheen. His father, whose name was Thomas Williams, was an attorney, accountant, and scrivener in the parish of St. Helen's, Bishopsgate. He died January 16, 1495, and was buried in St. Helen's Church, where his effigy in brass may be seen in the floor of the chapel south of the chancel. The likeness of him as depicted on the brass remarkably resembles the extant portraits of Oliver Cromwell, the Lord Protector. This may well be so, for he was great-uncle to Morgan Williams, who was the great-great-grandfather of the Protector Oliver. . . . . In Wales he was called Morgan ap William, and was brought up there to his father's profession as a lawyer and accountant, but became an ale brewer with his uncle, John Morgan, of Cardiff. In 1487 John Morgan was induced to start two ale breweries on Wimbledon Manor at Mortlake and Putney, for supplying with ale the king's household, yeomen of the guard, and their families, nearly all of whom, like the king himself, were Welsh, and who resided in Richmond, Mortlake, and Putney. Morgan Williams also had a brewery and inn called the 'Crooked Billet,' at the south-west part of Wimbledon Green, and he held, by copy of Court Roll, a cottage contained in half an acre of land in the middle of the west side of the Green, and half an acre of pasture land at Hanery Cross, in Wimbledon. In 1513 he surrendered this property 'to the use and behoof of Walter Cromwell and his heirs,' who from this time until he died, in 1516, resided at this cottage on Wimbledon Green, and carried on the brewery and inn, called the 'Crooked Billet,' close by, for Morgan Williams. Hall, Holinshed, and Stow, say that Walter Cromwell was 'in his latter days a brewer.' The fact is, he was a brewer, not only for a few years until he died at Wimbledon, as we have seen, but in Putney from 1474, when he is first mentioned in the Court Rolls of Wimbledon Manor. Three tenements, with gardens, outbuildings, and a row of cottages behind them, now occupy the site of the cottage on Wimbledon Green given to Walter Cromwell by his son-in-law, Morgan Williams."

When a boy Thomas Cromwell attended a school at Putney, and in his fourteenth year he was articled to John Williams, overseer of Wimbledon Manor, to be brought up as a lawyer, accountant, and steward or manager of estates. "His father," continues Mr. Phillips, "was then a well-to-do

brewer, fuller, and sheep farmer in Putney, having eight virgats (120 acres) of copyhold land there. This land gave him right of grazing on Putney and Roehampton Commons for two hundred sheep, forty beasts, and eight goats. John Williams resided at Mortlake, in a large house he had built between the Lower Richmond Road and the Thames, just above where the Oxford and Cambridge boat races terminate. This house was known long afterwards as 'Cromwell House.' Until John Williams died, in 1502, and from that date until 1504, Thomas Cromwell was collector, first for him and then for his own father (who was appointed temporary overseer, in succession to John Williams), of the revenues of Wimbledon Manor. The intention was apparently that he in two or three years should succeed his father in the overseership of the manor; but early in 1504 he met with some mishap, for which he was put into prison for a time. Probably he got into bad company, and lost or was robbed of the manor rents which he had collected. Whatever the mishap was, it caused a bitter feud between him and his father, which the latter never forgave. We infer from a succession of circumstances related in the Court Rolls of the manor after this date that his father neglected his business, and became reckless and a tippler; and finally, in 1514, all his copyhold lands and tenements, consisting then of five of the six virgats at Roehampton, which had been given to him on October 17, 1499, by Archbishop Morton, the lord of the manor, were seized by Archbishop Warham, the then lord of the manor. We have seen that in 1513 Morgan Williams, evidently in anticipation of this seizure, had provided him with the cottage on Wimbledon Green for his future residence. Thomas Cromwell, being the only son, was the next heir to the lands seized from his father; but as he did not appear after proclamation at three successive Manor Courts to claim them (owing, probably, to his being debarred from doing so), on October 6, 1514, 'William Wellyfed, and Elizabeth his wife, the youngest daughter of Walter Cromwell,' claimed and were admitted to the lands; and when Walter Cromwell died, in 1516, the cottage on Wimbledon Green and the land at Hanery-cross, in Wimbledon, devolved on them by the custom of the manor."

It is recorded in history that Cardinal Wolsey, who proved to be Thomas Cromwell's friend and patron, first discovered him when he was travelling in France, and made him his secretary. After Wolsey's fall, Cromwell was introduced to the notice of the king, "as the fittest person to manage the dispute between his Majesty and the Pope." For these and other public services Cromwell was raised to the peerage as Baron of Okeham, in Rutlandshire, and subsequently created Earl of Essex, and appointed Lord High Chamberlain of England. His honours, however, were but of short duration, for almost within a twelvemonth of his elevation to the earldom he was arrested for high treason, and a bill of attainder having been quickly passed through Parliament, he was executed on Tower Hill. His estates were, of course, confiscated, and Wimbledon became once more the property of the Crown, by whom it was settled on Queen Catherine Parr, the last of the six wives of Henry VIII. On her death, this manor and estate again reverted to the Crown, and, with the exception of being held for a short time by Cardinal Pole in the reign of Queen Mary, remained in the hands of the Crown through the greater part of Elizabeth's reign, when Sir Christopher Hatton had a grant of the house and surrounding grounds for a short time. In 1576 the mansion-house was sold to Sir Thomas Cecil, whose father, Sir William Cecil, afterwards Lord Burleigh, had a small grant of land in the parish during the reign of Edward VI. From Bartlett's "History of Wimbledon" we learn that during this reign and the greater part of the next he resided in this parish, most probably at the rectory-house. Here he appears to have suffered a severe and dangerous illness ; at all events, amongst the Harleian MSS. in the British Museum is preserved a letter "from Sir William Cecyll, Secretary of State, to the Lord Treasurer, Earl of Bedford," addressed "From my poore house at Wibleton." Thomas, his son and heir, succeeded his father in the estate here in 1598, and subsequently the manor was granted to him by Elizabeth, as above stated.

Queen Elizabeth honoured Wimbledon with her presence on more than one occasion. In an entry made in the register during the year 1597, and quoted by Nichols, in his "Progresses of Queen Elizabeth," we read :—"In this year the bells of Fulham were rung, when the queen went to the Lord Burleigh's house at Wimbledon," and also when "she went to the Lord Admiral's at Chelsea." Again, in an entry under date of August 1, 1599 :— "Mr. Chamberlain informs us that the Queen removed from Greenwich the 27th of last month, and dined the same day at Monsieur Caron's, and so to the Lord Burleigh's, at Wimbledon, where she tarried three days, and is now at Nonsuch." Travelling in those days was no easy matter, in consequence of the bad condition of the roads, which seem to have been continually out of repair. There is a curious entry in the churchwardens' books at Kingston, made during this "royal progress" in 1599 :—"Paid for mending the wayes when the Queen went from Wimbledon to Nonsuch, 20d."

Mr. Bartlett, in his history of the parish, quotes from the "Finetti Philoxenus" the following account of a visit paid by James I. to Wimbledon :— "On the 21st of June, 1616," says Sir John Finett, "the king, being invited by the Earl of Exeter to hunt and dine at Wimbledon (as was also the French Ambassador), killed a brace of staggs before he came to the house. Then I demanded when it would be his Majesty's pleasure to give accesse there to the Ambassador, whom he had not yet seen. It was assigned him for after dinner. The Ambassador dined with the Lords and Ladies at a table placed in the midst of a faire roome, he seated in a chaire at the upper end, at his right hand the Earle of Arundel, the Earl of Montgomery, the Lady Elizabeth Hatton, the Lady Rosse, &c. At his left were the Lady of Exeter, the Lady Anne Tuffton, the Marquis de L'Isle, uncle to the Duke of Retz (new come to England, and to that feast, in company of the French Ambassador), the Lord Haye, Sir George Villiers, and others. After dinner, the Ambassador going to see the House, he attended in the gallery the king's coming, and had there an houre's entertainment of discourse with his Majesty."

Under date of 28th June, 1619, is this entry :— "The king knighted, in the morning at Greenwich, Sir Charles Smith, and in the afternoon at Wimbledon, Sir Samuel Rolls."

It may not be out of place to record here that in the summer of 1838 our present sovereign, Queen Victoria, honoured Wimbledon with her presence, as the guest of the Duke of Somerset, then a resident at the manor-house.

The title of Viscount Wimbledon formerly existed in the Cecil family, having been conferred in 1626 on the Honourable Edward Cecil, youngest son of Sir Thomas Cecil, first Earl of Exeter, and grandson of William, Lord Burghley, Lord Treasurer to Queen Elizabeth. Entering the army, and having served with distinction in the Netherlands, he was made by Charles I. Marshal and General of the forces sent against Spain and the Imperialists. Already, in 1625, he had been created Lord Cecil of Putney. Walpole mentions in his "Noble Authors" that in the king's library are two manuscript tracts drawn up by this nobleman, on the subject of war and the military defence of the nation ; and he also mentions that a manuscript was found by the Earl of Huntingdon in an old chest, purporting to be a warrant of King Charles I., directing, at the instance of Lord Wimbledon, the revival of the old English march, so famous in all the honourable achievements and glorious wars of this kingdom in ancient times, but which by neglect had been nearly lost and forgotten." His lordship died at his house here in November, 1638, and was buried in the church, where a monument has been erected to his memory, as we shall see presently.

Queen Henrietta Maria, the consort of Charles I., bought the manor of Wimbledon on the death of one of the eleven major-generals appointed to administer justice in the several districts of England. When Cromwell began to ally himself with the nobility, and exhibit signs of securing the succession in his own family, "Lambert," as we learn from the "Memoirs of Col. Hutchinson," "perceiving himself to have been all this while deluded with hopes and promises of succession. . . fell off from him, but behaved himself very pitifully and meanly, was turned out of all his places, and returned

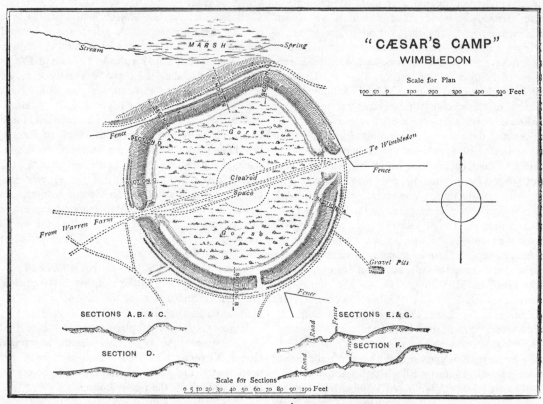

PLAN OF CÆSAR'S CAMP.
(*From the Journal of the Archæological Institute.*)

Lord Wimbledon. Charles himself seems to have taken some delight in the gardens of the manor-house, for only a few days before he was brought to trial "he ordered the seeds of some Spanish melons to be planted there." In the inventory which was taken of jewels and pictures belonging to Charles I., Wimbledon is mentioned as belonging to the Crown ; and when the Crown lands were put up for sale by order of the Parliamentary Commissioners, this manor was purchased by Mr. Adam Baynes, of Knowstrop, in Yorkshire. He, however, did not long retain possession of the estate, for in 1652 the house—then called Wimbledon Hall—was bought by General Lambert, who, under the Protectorate of Oliver Cromwell, was again to plot new vengeance at his house at Wimbledon, where he fell to dress his flowers in his garden, and work at the needle with his wife and his maids, while he was watching an opportunity to serve again his ambition, which had this difference from the Protector's—the one was gallant and great, the other had nothing but an unworthy pride, most insolent in prosperity, and as abject and base in adversity." When the final separation took place between Lambert and Cromwell in 1656, Lambert "retired to his garden," says Clarendon, "as unvisited and untaken notice of as if he had never been in authority, which gave great reputation to the Protector that he was entire master of his army."

"Lambert," writes Mr. Bartlett, "probably continued to reside at Wimbledon till after the death of Oliver and the succession of Richard Cromwell to the Protectorship, when he again became the leader of the opposition ; and, joined by a council of officers, forced that weak man to dissolve the Parliament, April 22nd, 1659. This act virtually expelled Richard. He soon after signed his own demission."

After the restoration of Charles II., Wimbledon estate of Wimbledon was conveyed, in 1677—8, to Thomas Osborne, Earl of Danby, Lord High Treasurer of England. The house was no doubt very fine at that time, but Evelyn speaks with great contempt of the library. In his "Diary," under date of December 20th, 1677, we read :— " Carried to my Lord Treasurer an account of the Earl of Bristol's librarie at Wimbleton, which my lord thought of purchasing, till I acquainted him that it was a very broken collection, consisting

ON WIMBLEDON COMMON.

was given back to the queen-mother, Henrietta Maria, together with other of the dower lands ; but the place seems to have lost its charm for her, and it was very soon after sold to the Earl of Bristol, who appears to have consulted John Evelyn with reference to the laying out of his grounds. Under date of Feb. 17th, 1662, Evelyn writes in his "Diary :"—" I went with my Lord of Bristoll to see his house at Wimbledon, newly bought of the Queene Mother, to help contrive the garden after the moderne. It is a delicious place for prospect and the thicketts, but the soile cold and weeping clay. Returned to London that evening with Sir Henry Bennet."

Upon the death of the Earl of Bristol, the much in books of judicial astrologie, romances, and trifles." And again he writes, two months later, Feb. 18th, 1678 :—" My Lord Treasurer sent for me to accompany him to Wimbledon, which he had lately purchas'd of the Earle of Bristol ; so breaking fast with him privately in his chamber, I accompanied him, with two of his daughters, my Lord Conway, and Sir Bernard Gascoyne, and having surveyed his gardens and alterations, returned late at night."

In 1689 Lord Danby was created Marquis of Carmarthen, and later on advanced to the Dukedom of Leeds. He died in 1712, having by his will devised Wimbledon to the Earl of Abingdon and others, as trustees, who, under a decree of

Chancery in 1717, sold the estate to Sir Theodore Janssen, one of the South Sea directors. The next owner of Wimbledon was Sarah, Duchess of Marlborough, who purchased the manor after the failure of Sir Theodore Janssen and his bubble company. The mansion here became her favourite residence, and here she died, at an advanced age, in 1744, leaving her estate to her grandson, Mr. John Spencer, the youngest son of Charles, Earl of Sunderland. The mansion and estate descended to his only son, John, who was created in 1761 Viscount and Baron Spencer, and in 1765 was raised to the earldom. The property continued in the possession of the Spencer family down to 1846, when it was purchased by Mr. J. A. Beaumont.

It does not appear that much alteration was made in Wimbledon House from the time when it was built by Sir Thomas Cecil till it came into the possession of Sir Theodore Janssen. It was then pulled down and rebuilt, probably on a smaller scale. The work, however, was scarcely finished, when the failure of the South Sea scheme put a stop to Sir Theodore's design, and the estate was sold, as above stated, to the Duchess of Marlborough. She pulled down the house which Janssen had built, and erected a new one, from designs by the celebrated Earl of Burlington,* on the north side of the knoll on which the present mansion stands; but not liking the situation, she soon after caused it to be pulled down, and a second house built further to the south. In 1785 this house was accidentally burnt down. The ruins were cleared away, and the grounds levelled and turfed, so that scarcely a trace of its foundation was visible. The present house was finished in 1801.

Lord Spencer formed here one of the finest parks in England. Miss Priscilla Wakefield, writing at the commencement of the present century, says:—" It contains twelve hundred acres, adorned with beautiful declivities and fine plantations. Here is also," she adds, "a sheet of water of many acres, which always adds to the beauty of any rural scene. From eminences in the park no less than nineteen churches may be counted in the prospect, exclusive of those of London and Westminster. Here are many other mansions of the gentry and the nobility." The grounds of the park were laid out by " Capability " Brown. The house was for many years occupied by the Duke of Somerset, and it was here that the late Sir Joseph Paxton began life as under gardener to

his brother, then head gardener in these grounds. Allusions to Lord Spencer's residence here are very rare in the books which record the social life of a century ago; and accordingly, only a very few anecdotes have been preserved relating to the place, though its noble owner was a leader in society, and doubtless entertained his Parliamentary friends here during the Parliamentary season. One such anecdote, however, may well be recorded here, as almost an English version of the celebrated French story of the Dog of Montargis.

When Thomas Grenville was a boy, he was dining, he would say, at Wimbledon, with Lord Spencer, when George Pitt, afterwards Lord Rivers, who was one of the company, declared that he could tame any animal, however fierce, by looking at it steadily and without shrinking. Lord Spencer suggested that he should try his powers on a mastiff in his stable-yard, who was the terror of every stranger. Pitt agreed to do so. The company went down to the courtyard, and a servant held the mastiff by a chain. Pitt knelt down at a short distance from the animal, and stared him sternly in the face. At a given signal the mastiff was let loose, and rushed furiously towards Pitt. The company stood shuddering, but the mastiff, on seeing him staring without flinching, seemed confounded, and checked her pace, and then turned tail and bounded off.

The total area of the estate when purchased from Lord Spencer was over 1,200 acres. Of this, about 500 acres on the Putney side have already been sold and built upon by a wealthy class of residents; and the whole park, when completed on the same principle, will form one of the most charming spots in England—a perfect arboretum and garden within the very neighbourhood of London.

The situation and character of the district is proverbially healthy, owing to its high position, genial and bracing air, and dry gravelly soil; and the charming scenery of the park, with its magnificent timber and luxuriant shrubs, adorning the rich pastures' that encircle the lake, presents a combination of green-sward, wood, and water, while the distant views are unequalled in extent and surpassing interest.

The lake in the centre of the park is used as a Private Subscription Water by the residents for fishing, boating, and skating. It has been restocked with a large number of fish, so that, doubtless, it will henceforth afford abundance of sport for anglers.

The manor-house, now the residence of Mrs. W. Bertram Evans, was built early in the present cen-

---

* See " Old and New London," Vol IV., p. 263.

tury, and stands on the site of the one occupied by the Duchess of Marlborough. It is a large stone-built mansion, and has about twelve acres of pleasure-grounds reserved with it ; and handsome villas of the Queen Anne type, each in its own grounds, are now springing up on all sides around it.

Standing, as it does, so high, the village of Wimbledon has never had an overflowing supply of water, and accordingly the late Lord Spencer had caused to be sunk on the Wimbledon Park House Estate an Artesian well, which is upwards of 560 feet in depth.

Lord Spencer is still lord of the Manor of Wimbledon. In this manor the custom of "Borough English" prevails : namely, lands descend not to the eldest, but to the youngest, son or daughter.

Having spoken thus far of the manor of Wimbledon and its successive owners, we will now proceed to give an account of the magnificent mansion which was once the glory of the place, but all traces of which have long since passed away.

From a " Survey of the Manor of Wymbledon, *alias* Wimbleton," made in 1649, read before the Society of Antiquaries in 1792 by Mr. John Caley, F.A.S., and printed in the " Archæologia," Vol. X., Wimbledon Hall would appear to have been a very large and well-built mansion. The " survey " begins with a minute description of the various domestic offices " below stairs," such as the kitchen, the larder, the " landrie roome," the " foulding roome," the " sweetmeate roome," the still house, scullery, the common beer cellars, wine cellars, steward's chamber, &c. The gardener's chamber and the " lower Spanish room " are then described : the latter was " floored with white paynted tyle, waynscotted round, the most part of which waynscote is varnished greene, and spotted with starrs of gould, seeled over head, and fitted for the present with boxes, wherein oringe and pomegranat trees are planted. . . . One other roome, called the Stone Gallery, floored with squared stone, one hundred and eight foot long, seeled overhead, pillored and arched with gray marble, lying on the east end of the said manor-house, waynscotted round with oaken waynscot, varnished with greene, and spotted with starrs of gould, and benched all along the sides and angles thereof." The middle part of this gallery is described as fitted with six windows, or " leaved doors," of wainscot and glass. The grotto, placed in the middle of the stone gallery, was floored with painted tile, and in the arch and sides were " sundry sorts of shells of greate lustre and ornament, formed into the shapes of men, lyons, serpents, antick formes, and other rare devices,"

&c. The great hall is described as wainscoted round eight feet high, the upper part being " spotted with starrs of gould." At the lower end of the hall was an arched screen of double wainscot, on which were " three chalices or brass boles well guilt." Then follows a description of the parlours and other chambers. The two staircases, " twenty foote square," were " topped with turrets of a great height, covered with blue slate, on the middle pinacles whereof stand two faier gilded weathercockes, perspicuous to the countrie round about." The east stairs led from the marble parlour to the great gallery and the dining-room, and the west stairs led principally to the rooms on the second floor. The staircases were adorned with a large picture of Henry IV. of France on horseback, with " landskipps of battayles, anticks, Heaven and Hell, and other curious worke." Under the stairs was " a little compleate roome, called the den of lyons, floored with paynted deale cheker worke, wherein is one ovall marble table, in a frame of wood: this roome is painted round with lyons and leopards, and is a good ornament to the staires and the marble parlor, severed therefrom with rayled doors." Other rooms and galleries are then described, together with two courts, one lying twenty-six steps higher than the other ; and the survey continues thus :—" The scite of this manor-house being placed on the side slipp of a rising ground, renders it to stand of that height that betwixt the basis of the brick wall of the sayd lower court, and the hall door of the sayd manor-house there are five several assents, consisting of threescore and ten stepps, which are distinguished in a very graceful manner ; to witt, from the parke to a payre of rayled gates, set betwixt two large pillars of brick ; in the middle of the wall standing on the north side of the sayd lower court is the first assent, consisting of eight stepps of good freestone, layed in a long square, within which gates, levell with the highest of those eight stepps, is a pavement of freestone, leading to a payr of iron gates, rayled on each side thereof with turned ballasters of freestone, within which is a little paved court leading to an arched vault neatly pillowred with brick, conteyning on each side of the pillers a little roome well arched, serving for cellaridge of botteled wines. On each side of this vault are a payre of staires of stone stepps, twentie-three stepps in assent, eight foote nine inches broad ; meeting an even landing-place in the height thereof, leading from the aforesayd gates unto the lower court and make the second assent ; from the height of this assent a pavement of Flanders brickes thirteene foot six inches broad, leading to the third assent, which stands on the south side of the lower courte, consisting of a round modell, in the middle whereof is a payre of iron gates rayled as aforesayd, within which is a fountayne fitted with a leaden cesterne fed with a pipe of lead; this round conteynes a payre of stone stayres of twenty-six stepps in assent, ordered and adorned as the second assent is, and leades into the sayd higher courte, and soe makes the third assent; from the height whereof a pavement of square stone, nine foote broad and eightie-seaven foote long, leads up to the fowerth assent, which consists of eleven stepps of freestone very well wrought and ordered, leading into a gallery paved with square stone, sixtie-two foote long and eight foote broad; adjoyning to the body of the sayd manor-house towards the south, and rayled with turned ballasters of stone towards the north; in the middle of this gallery, the hall-doore of the sayd manor-house, the fabrick whereof is of columns of freestone very well wrought, doth stand, into which hall from the sayd gallery is an assent of two stepps. From the forementioned first assent there is a way cut forth of the parke, planted on each side thereof with cloves and other trees, in a very decent order, extending itself in a direct line two hundred thirty-one perches from thence quite through the parke northward unto Putney Common, being a very special ornament to the whole house."

The hall was adorned with "a border or fret, having set therein eleven pictures of very good workmanship. The ceiling was of fret or parge work, in the very middle whereof was fixed one well wrought landskip, and round the same in convenient distances seven other pictures in frames, as ornaments to the whole roome; the floor was of black and white marble." Near the hall was the organ room, "adorned with a fayre and rich payre of organs." Close by was the "greene chamber," so called from the colour of its walls. The chapel was "well adorned with pulpitt, reading desk, and handsome seates or pewes, with a pavement of black and white polished marble;" the ceiling, a "quadrate arch," was painted with landscapes, as were also the side walls above the wainscot. The lower parlour was wainscoted with oak "adorned with stars and cross patees of gould," whilst in the middle of the arched ceiling "hung one pinnacle perpendicular garnished in every angle with coates of armes well wrought and richly guilt." The Lord's Chamber, the Queen's Chamber, the withdrawing-room, and other apartments, were on this floor. The Stone Gallery, 62 feet long by 10 feet wide, was "floored with square tile, handsomely lighted and seeled, upon the walls whereof are writt many compendious sentences." The Great Gallery, on the second floor, 109 feet long by 21 feet broad, was "floored with cedar boards casting a pleasant smell, seeled and bordered with fret-work well wrought, very well lighted, and waynscotted round with well wrought oake 13 foote 6 inches high, garnished with fillets of gould on the pillars, and starrs and cross patees on the panes, in the middle whereof is a very fayre and large chimnie-piece of black and whyte marble, ingraved with coates of armes adorned with several curious and well-guilded statues of alabaster, with a foot-pace of black and whyte marble." On this floor was an apartment called the Summer Chamber, which was also floored with cedar, and it was "well seeled with fret-work, in the middle whereof a picture of good workmanship representing a flying angel." Among the rooms on this floor were "the Duchess's Chamber," the "Countess of Denbigh's Chamber," and others named after Mr. Willoughby and Mr. Cecill.

The whole house is described in the survey as having been constructed of "excellent good brick; the angles, window staunchions, and jawmes all of ashlar stone;" and the leads and battlements of the roof are said to have been "a great ornament to the whole house."

"Wimbledon House," says Miss Lucy Aikin, in her "Court of Queen Elizabeth," "seated on the side of a hill, was remarkable for the magnificent disposition of steps and terraces, well worthy of an Italian villa," thereby illustrating and explaining what honest old Fuller states in his "Worthies," to the effect that even Nonsuch itself—to the beauties of which the reader has lately been introduced—* is "exceeded by Wimbledon in point of a real situation." The original mansion, in fact, would seem to have been magnificent, if we may judge from the two curious and scarce views of it engraved by Winstanley.

The gardens would seem to have been planned and laid out on a scale of great magnificence. They contained mazes, wildernesses, alleys, knots, &c., and are mentioned in the survey as comprising a great variety of fruit-trees and some shrubs, particularly one "faire bay-tree," and a "very fayer tree called the Irish arbutis, very lovely to look upon." Above one thousand fruit-trees are enumerated, among which appear the names of almost every kind now cultivated.

The " orangerie " contained forty-two orange-trees in boxes, valued at £10 each; one "lemmon-tree, bearing greate and very large lemmons," valued at £20; one "pomecitron tree," valued at £10; six "pomegranet trees," valued at £3 each; and eighteen young orange-trees, valued at £5 each. At the end of the kitchen-garden was a "muskilion ground," "trenched, manured, and very well ordered for the growth of muskilions."

Of the second Wimbledon House—that built by the Duchess of Marlborough—there is a view in the fifth volume of the "Vitruvius Britannicus." The building was of brick, with stone dressings and other ornaments, and the principal front was enriched with a portico and pediment, supported by four Ionic columns.

In the "Life of Hannah More" is printed a letter from that lady, in which she describes a visit paid to the mansion in 1780. She writes :—"The Bishop of St. Asaph and his family invited me to come to Wimbledon Park, Lord Spencer's charming villa, which he always lends to the bishop at this time of the year. I did not think there could have been so beautiful a place within seven miles of London. The park has as much variety of ground, and is as un-Londonish, as if it were an hundred miles out; and I enjoyed the violets and the birds more than all the marechal powder and the music of this foolish town. There was a good deal of company at dinner; but we were quite at our ease, and strolled about or sat in the library, just as we liked. This last amused me much, for it was like the Duchess of Marlborough (old Sarah), and numbers of the books were presents to her from the great authors of her time, whose names she had carefully written in the blank leaves, for I believe she had the pride of being thought learned as well as rich and beautiful."

CHAPTER L.

WIMBLEDON (continued)—THE CHURCH, ETC.

General Aspect of the Parish—Its Population—The Beverley Brook—Site of Walter Cromwell's Fulling Mill—The old Village—The Parish Church—The old Parsonage—Christ Church—Other Churches and Chapels— The Cemetery—Local Board of Health—Working Men's Club and other Public Institutions—Wimbledon Green—The London Scottish Golf Club—The Wimbledon Sewage Works—Eminent Residents—Pitt—Schopenhauer—John Horne Tooke—Joseph Marryatt—Sir H. W. Peek—Lady Anne Barnard—Captain Frederick Marryatt—The Countess of Guildford—Lord North—General Sir Henry Murray—Sir Francis Burdett—Mr. William Wilberforce—Sir John Richardson—Mr. John Murray—Mr. William Giffard—Mr. James Perry—Mr. Lyde Browne—The Duke of Cannizaro—The Marquis of Rockingham—Copse Hill—Cottenham Park—The Earl of Durham—Convalescent Hospital—Miss Eliza Cook—Jenny Lind—Sir Bartle Frere.

SINCE the "disparking" of the lands belonging to Wimbledon Manor House, the whole aspect of the parish may be said to have been altered, particularly on the south-east side, between the railway and Merton, where, within the last few years, an entirely new town, called New Wimbledon, has sprung up, whilst the population has, of course, proportionately increased. In 1871 the number of the inhabitants was just over 9,000, whilst according to the census returns for 1881 it amounted to close upon 16,000, of which number about half were located on the south side of the London and South-Western Railway, which passes through the parish.

Part of the eastern boundary of the parish is formed by the River Wandle, of which we have already spoken,* whilst a narrow brook, called the Beverley, forms its western boundary, separating it from Kingston. The latter stream takes its rise at Sutton, and after flowing near Cheam Common, Lower Morden, Wimbledon, and Richmond Park, empties itself into the Thames at Barnes. "The derivation of this name (Bever-lea)," writes Mr. Bartlett, "throws some light upon the early natural history of our parish. When the unsparing hand of the builder shall have fringed its banks with suburban semi-detached villas, their inhabitants will still be able to recognise in the name of the little stream which flows through their neatly-trimmed gardens the original "beaver's haunt." Alas! how changed is its nature and appearance, though its name remains.

It has been ascertained that there was a fulling mill on the Beverley brook, in Coombe Valley, just below Cæsar's Camp (as it is called), on Wimbledon Common; and there is not the slightest doubt that this mill belonged to Walter Cromwell,* that is, that he made and started this mill when the lease of his father's fulling mill on the River Wandle expired, about 1473 or 1474.

* See ante, p. 183.

* See ante, p. 472.

The course of the race which led out of the brook to the mill can still be easily traced. Of the mill, however, no vestige remains. It is referred to, however, in a survey of the manor taken in 1617.

The old village of Wimbledon lies along the high ground which runs to the west of the park,

place to modern villas and houses of a less pretentious class.

The parish church, dedicated to St. Mary, stands at the eastern end of the village, near the Manor-house. It is said to have had its origin in the Saxon times; but of the church mentioned in

WIMBLEDON MANOR HOUSE.   (*See page* 477.)

and on the south-eastern side of the common. Of late years it has extended considerably in all directions, particularly along the Ridgeway, on the Kingston Road, and down the hill southwards towards the railway-station. With this growth of its area, its rural character is fast disappearing; whilst many of the old red-brick mansions which in former times stood proudly surrounded by their "tall ancestral elms" have already given

"Domesday Book" not a vestige remains. With the exception of the chancel, supposed to be the work of the fourteenth century, the church was entirely rebuilt in 1788. Its predecessor consisted of a nave, chancel, south porch, and a small bell-turret, surmounted by a light spire. On the south wall, in Aubrey's time, was a tablet inscribed:—"This church was repaired and beautified in the year A.D. 1703. Thomas Knight,

John Fenton, churchwardens." Over the south door was the date 1637, and over the west door 1687. This old church having become sadly out of repair, some futile attempts were made to "restore" it, and at the date above mentioned it was determined to rebuild it, and the greater portion of it was pulled down. The chancel, however, being under the control of the Court of Arches, could not be interfered with. The new church was fitted up in the Grecian *box*, which occupied an upper storey formed in the eastern half of the old chancel, the lower storey being used as a robing-room! The nave was supported by columns painted to represent Sienna marble, the capitals being gilded. The ceiling was vaulted and ornamented. There were two side aisles, over which ran galleries, with roofs domed into three divisions, arched in front, the four corners of each dome having medallions in *chiaro obscuro* of Adam, Noah, the Apostles, &c." The church

WIMBLEDON PARSONAGE.

style. The contributions of the inhabitants for this purpose, we are told, "were so liberal, that the whole was completed without any application to Parliament, Mr. Levi, a Jew, being one of the most generous subscribers."

As the Early Perpendicular work of the old church and the Grecian could not be expected to harmonise, "the fine old chancel," writes Mr. Bartlett, "must be shut out from the rest of the building by the erection of a semi-circular apse, running in the form of a niche into the chancel. Into this apse," he continues, "were crowded the altar, *above which crowded the pulpit*, the reading-desk, and the clerk's desk! Above the altar were the *lights* or *windows* of Lord Spencer's *pew*, or

was built of white brick, and at the western end was a circular projection, from which rose a square wooden tower, with Gothic pinnacles of artificial stone, and a tapering spire covered with copper.

In 1812 the pulpit was removed from its towering position, and a few years later the semi-circular apse was taken away, and the old chancel thrown into the building, galleries being at the same time erected in the two side aisles.

The church remained in this condition till 1833, when the body of the fabric was rebuilt in the Perpendicular style, from the designs of Messrs. Scott and Moffatt; and in 1860 the chancel was restored by the Ecclesiastical Commissioners. It is a poor specimen of Sir Gilbert Scott's work, considering that it was erected before the real principles of Gothic architecture were fairly grasped. The present church consists of chancel, nave, aisles, and a western tower with lofty spire, containing six bells and a clock striking the hours and chiming the quarters, by Messrs. Gillett and Bland, Croydon. There is on the south side of the chancel a small mortuary chapel, erected by Lord Wimbledon in the early part of the seventeenth century, containing an altar-tomb of black marble to the Cecil family, some painted glass with arms of the Cecils in the windows, and some armour. In the churchyard is the tomb of one Hopkins, a usurer, mentioned by Pope as " Vulture Hopkins." The living is a vicarage, in the gift of the Dean and Chapter of Worcester.

The old parsonage, near the western end of the church, is a picturesque and interesting building, and almost the only old house in the place. It is thought to have been the home of Sir William Cecil during his residence in the parish. In the survey taken by order of Parliament in the seventeenth century, it is described as containing a considerable number of rooms, and having " two coachhouses, stabling for fourteen horses, and a hawks' mew." One other building is mentioned as adjoining it, containing " two rooms above stairs and two below stairs, wherein," continues the survey, " the minister of Wimbledon, the French gardiner of Wimbledon orange-garden, doe live." At the northwest side of the building is a circular staircase terminating in a turret. The stairs were formed of solid blocks of oak. The exterior of the building was restored in 1863 by Mr. J. A. Beaumont. The building was sold in 1883 to a Mr. Willson, who has fitted it up with due regard to its antiquity of style, though not perhaps with any great regard to strict uniformity of plan.

Wimbledon would seem to be very well off in respect of churches and chapels. Besides the parish church, there is Christ Church, on Copse Hill, which was built in 1869, and much enlarged in 1881. It is in the Early Decorated style, and consists of nave, side aisles, chancel, and a tower at the east end, and will hold nearly 700 worshippers. The Church of St. John the Baptist, on Spencer Hill, is a smaller and less pretentious building, mostly of brick, and in the Early English style, and capable of accommodating an equal number. Near the railway-station is St. Mark's, also of brick; it is as yet unconsecrated, and is used for occasional services. The district south of the railway has been formed into a separate ecclesiastical parish, and has its own church—in the Early Decorated style—Holy Trinity, with sittings

for nearly 800 more. It is a good specimen of Gothic design.

Wimbledon has also three other Episcopal chapels; the Wesleyan, the Congregationalists, the Baptists, the Primitive Methodists, are all represented in the list; and the Roman Catholics have a chapel in Cottenham Park Road, dedicated to St. Jerome and St. Agnes. In addition to these, there are three or four mission-halls and Christian Associations. There are also parochial schools for both North and South Wimbledon, with nearly 2,000 children on their books.

The cemetery, situated in the eastern part of the parish, is about twenty acres in extent. It reaches nearly to Tooting and Merton.

Wimbledon has also its Local Board of Health, its Fire Brigade, its Fever, Cottage, and Convalescent Hospitals, its Village Club and Lecture Hall, its Croquet Club, its Working Men's Club and Institute, its Benefit Building Societies, its Horticultural and Cottage Garden Society, its Musical Society, its Coffee Taverns, its Industrial Training School for Girls, its Parochial Library, its Medical Dispensary, its Art and Benevolent Society, and associations almost beyond number for helping the working-classes and encouraging habits of thrift and temperance. With such advantages, and with plenty of rich persons to support these various charities, surely Wimbledon ought to show an exceptionally good bill of health, moral as well as physical, and its local bench of magistrates ought to have an easy time of it.

Wimbledon Green was occasionally used for cricket matches. In Lillywhite's book on the noble game, it appears that a match was played here, at the commencement of her Majesty's reign, against the Kennington Surrey Club, by the united parishes of Wimbledon, Mitcham, Wandsworth, Esher, Richmond, and Kingston-on-Thames; so it is clear that cricket was a favourite pastime with the natives of the parishes which we have been lately visiting.*

For many years the " royal and ancient game of golf" has been played on Wimbledon Common, where the London Scottish Golf Club has expended large sums of money in maintaining the spaces of smooth sward known as " putting-greens," or golfing-lawns, and surrounding the small holes or pockets into which it is the golfer's aim to play his ball. " Golf," remarks a writer in the *Times*, " has some peculiar advantages which entail peculiar difficulties. It is the most outdoor of outdoor games. Lawn-tennis can be played in any fair-

* See ante, p. 359.

sized garden, while cricket or football requires at most a moderate patch of meadow. These are games not only compatible with the commonplaces of civilisation, but actually demanding their assistance. Golf, on the contrary, brings men into contact with unadulterated nature. . . . . It must be plain that the game is admirably suited to Wimbledon, and Wimbledon to the game. Nowhere else within practicable distance of London can we find in equal perfection the space, the quietude, and the ruggedness of surface which are as essential to the golfer as to the blackcock. It would surely be hard to deny him the enjoyment of these things, and to attempt this becomes most unreasonable when we remember what manner of man he is. It is not to rash and adventurous youth that golf recommends itself; it is the game of sedate middle age, of hale old age, and of bookish men of all ages, who have learned for themselves, without blazoning the fact in the newspapers, that only a very big candle can be burnt at both ends, and only very vigorous constitutions can undertake heavy brain work together with exacting forms of physical exercise. If Wimbledon Common is to be anything more than a private riding-ground for the inhabitants of the parish of Putney and the immediate vicinity of the common, surely nothing could be less objectionable than a game so played by such players. It is suspected that some notion of a right to exclusive possession has been fostered by the constitution of the Wimbledon Conservancy, which is mainly composed of gentlemen elected by the local ratepayers; but I need hardly point out that the surest way to get the common placed under the control of the Metropolitan Board of Works is to display a jealousy of the rights of the general public. It is on these rights that the Golf Club takes its stand; and I feel sure it will have a vigorous public opinion upon its side the moment it becomes understood that what the conservators object to is the intrusion of Londoners. The plea that golf is dangerous is, of course, too absurd to bear a moment's examination. It may serve as an excuse, but it cannot be the motive of the conservators' action. Golf is played upon a narrow strip, nowhere more than 150 yards wide. Every ball is played with a deliberation which I have not exaggerated in the least; and though it would undoubtedly be awkward for a rider to stop one in mid-volley, he can hardly do so without actual premeditation, or carelessness equally culpable. But perhaps the best practical answer is that during the twenty years that golf has been played at Wimbledon not a single injury of any kind has been inflicted upon a passer-by."

Among the low-lying fields on the banks of the Wandle, skirted on the one side by the Merton road and contiguous to the cemetery, is an extensive range of buildings used as sewage-works. The buildings were designed and erected under the superintendence of Mr. W. F. Rowell, the engineer to the Wimbledon Local Board; they consist of a substantial and by no means unsightly edifice, containing the engines, boilers, mixing machinery, and stores, flanked by two tasteful cottage residences, detached from the main building. In front of the engine-house, but covered over so as easily to escape observation, is the artesian well, 400 feet deep, which supplies water both for the boilers and the mixing. Adjacent to the engine-room are two mixing cylinders of wrought-iron. By a self-acting arrangement it is ingeniously contrived that the supply of water from the artesian well to these cylinders shall be regulated by the speed of the engines, so as to furnish a quantity of disinfecting liquid proportionate to the volume of sewage. The disinfecting liquid thus prepared goes into the sewage contained in the pumping reservoir beneath. A pump, also driven by the main engines, forces a portion of the disinfecting liquid into the tanks provided for the treatment of the high level sewage. The action of the pumping-engines lifts the low-level sewage from the reservoir under the engine-house, and forces it into a mixing-well outside the building. The middle level sewage is likewise lifted into this well. The sewage mingled with the disinfecting liquid is here tossed about as it is forced up from the rising main, and a perfect blending of the whole is obtained. From this well, which is, in fact, a species of circular tank of brickwork raised above the ground, the prepared sewage runs off into one or other of two precipitating tanks, each capable of holding about 400,000 gallons. In the space of three hours the precipitating process is accomplished, and the purified sewage is discharged through an overflow pipe or channel on to the filter bed, or else drawn off through valves at the bottom of the tank into open stoneware carriers for irrigating the land, about forty acres being provided for this purpose.

The overflow from the precipitating tanks leads into a long, open bricked channel, whence the purified sewage overflows on to the filtering area. This is one acre in extent, and holds about 12,000 cubic yards of burnt ballast, with an average depth of four feet. A 12-inch pipe at the opposite end of this filter leads the finally purified sewage into the Wandle, opposite the silk-works, where the stream looks so black and foul that all the purifying process carried on at the Wimbledon works seems to be at once neutralised.

The high-level sewage, before being used on the land, is treated in a separate tank about 200 yards from the engine-house. The disinfecting liquid for admixture with this sewage is forced up a 3-inch pipe to the tank by the action of the engines.

Besides those individuals whose names we have already mentioned, Wimbledon has at different times numbered among its residents several men who have left their mark on history. Here, in the words of Lamartine, Pitt buried himself in his little house, a solitude where, in the bosom of nature and friendship, he could restore his courage, attended by his niece, Lady Hester Stanhope, "an Egeria placed near that great statesman, as though to connect him to earth by something human without distracting him from the political studies in which his existence was absorbed." Here her tender care softened his last days in the midst of the ruin of his power and fortune ; for here she closed his eyes, January 23rd, 1806, one month and a few days only after the battle of Austerlitz, from the effects of which he died.

Pitt died at his house on Wimbledon Common, near the spot where Canning and Castlereagh fought their duel, and in a very neglected state, none of his political friends being with him at the time. "One who was sincerely attached to him," writes Mr. Edward Jesse, "hearing of his illness, rode from London to see him. Arriving at his house, he rang the bell at the entrance-gate, but no one came. Dismounting, he made his way to the hall-door, and repeatedly rang the bell, which no one answered. He then entered the house, wandered from room to room, till at last he discovered Pitt on a bed—dead, and entirely neglected. It is supposed he had not been able to pay the wages of his servants, and that they had absconded, taking with them what they could." Can this story be true ?

Mr. Cyrus Redding, in his "Recollections," observes : "The sight of Pitt's person was not calculated to strengthen his cause with his youthful advocate—for such I was then. His countenance, forbidding and arrogant, was repellant of affection, and not made to be loved, full of disdain, of self-will, and as a whole destitute of massiveness ; his forehead alone was lofty and good. He walked with his nose elevated in the air ; premature age was stamped upon his haggard features. It was said he had no affection for the female sex, whence the joke, ' He loved wine, but not a woman.' "

Wimbledon has other recollections of literary and political celebrities. Here, for instance, the German philosopher, Schopenhauer, went to school from July to September, 1803. His master's name, the Rev. Mr. Lancaster, is recorded by Miss H. Zimmern, in her life of that philosopher.

It was at Wimbledon that John Horne Tooke ended his days in retirement ; and here late in life he gave his political dinners or picnics.

"The political career of John Horne Tooke," writes Mr. J. T. Smith, in his "Book for a Rainy Day," "is well known, and the fame of his celebrated work, entitled ' The Diversions of Purley,' will be spoken of as long as paper lasts. In the year 1811, a most flagrant depredation was committed in his house at Wimbledon by a collector of taxes, who daringly carried away a silver tea and sugar caddy, the value of which amounted, in weight of silver, to at least twenty times more than the sum demanded, for a tax which Mr. Tooke declared he never would pay. This gave rise to the following letter :—

" ' To Messrs. Croft and Dilke.

" ' Gentlemen,—I beg it as a favour of you, that you will go in my name to Mr. Judkin, attorney, in Clifford's Inn, and desire him to go with you both to the Under Sheriff's Office, in New Inn, Wych Street. I have had a distress served upon me for taxes at Wimbledon, in the county of Surrey. By the recommendation of Mr. Stuart, of Putney, I desire Mr. Judkin to act as my attorney in replevying the goods ; and I desire Mr. Croft and Mr. Dilke to sign the security-bond for me that I will try the question. Pray show this memorandum to Mr. Judkin.

" ' John Horne Tooke.

" ' Wimbledon, May 17th, 1811.'

"As Mr. Croft and Mr. Dilke were proceeding on the Putney Road, they met the tax-collector with the tea-caddy under his arm, on his way back with the greatest possible haste to return it, with an apology to Mr. Tooke—that being the advice of a friend. The two gentlemen returned with him, and witnessed Mr. Tooke's kindness when the man declared he had a large family.

"On the 10th of March (1812) Mr. Tooke died, at his house at Wimbledon. He was buried at Ealing,* his executors objecting to inter him, as he had wished, in his own ground."

A portrait of John Horne Tooke, painted by Thomas Hardy, is to be seen in the National Portrait Gallery.

Besides the "great house," the parish in former times contained the residences of several distinguished persons, some of which have been entirely swept away, whilst the memory of others is preserved in the names of streets or houses.

---

* See Vol. I., p. 21.; also *ante*, p. 141.

It figures in the "Index Villaris," published in 1700, as a place containing the seat of one earl—this must have been Wimbledon House, the seat of the Earl of Danby, already described*—and also those of "a baronet, a knight, and more than three gentlemen entitled to bear arms."

The mansion now known as Wimbledon House stands about a quarter of a mile to the west of the church. It was built about the middle of the last century, and was for some time the residence of Sir Henry Bankes, alderman of London, who died in 1774. The estate afterwards became the property of Mr. Benjamin Bond Hopkins, who inherited the accumulated wealth of Mr. John Hopkins, the usurer, commonly known as "Vulture Hopkins," whose tomb is to be seen in the neighbouring churchyard.† Early in the present century the Prince of Condé took up his abode at Wimbledon House; and in 1815 the mansion was purchased by Mr. Joseph Marryatt, an eminent West India merchant, and parliamentary speaker on West Indian affairs. He was for some time M.P. for Sandwich, and was the author of several pamphlets, some published anonymously, and others bearing his name; among the latter being his "Speech in the House of Commons on Mr. Manning's motion respecting Marine Insurance," "Observations on the Report of the Committee on Marine Insurance," and "Thoughts on the Expediency of Establishing a New Chartered Bank." Mr. Marryatt died suddenly in the year 1824, and his widow continued to reside here till 1854, devoting much time and money to the cultivation of her beautiful gardens, which were considered among the finest in the neighbourhood of London. "Here flourished," writes Mr. Bartlett, "some of the rarest flowers; whilst the park contained, besides fine old oaks and beeches, a large cork-tree, a very fine Ligustrum lucidum, some large evergreen oaks, a red cedar, a Rhododendron ponticum, Magnolia acuminata, Pinus serotina, and other American trees, which were originally planted in these grounds when first introduced into England." A detailed description of these gardens is given in Loudon's "Suburban Gardener." The present possessor of Wimbledon House is Sir Henry William Peek, Bart., late M.P. for Mid-Surrey.

Gothic House, near the Ridgeway Road, was formerly the residence of Lady Anne Barnard, the authoress of "Auld Robin Gray." She was the eldest child of James, Earl of Balcarres, and wife of Mr. Barnard, son of Dr. Barnard, Bishop of Limerick. The house, later on, became the abode of Captain Frederick Marryatt, the author of "Peter Simple," "Midshipman Easy," "Frank Mildmay," and some half-dozen other novels illustrative of the life led by a blue-jacket in the last generation. He was by profession at once both sailor and novelist, and had a frank, dashing genius, and, as Lord Lytton said, "he splashed about in the water in good style." Few writers have done more than he to make the life of a British sailor intelligible to the multitude of land-lubber readers. It is said that he was refused promotion in the navy by William IV. because he wrote against the impressment of seamen. Here he farmed, collected curiosities, &c. Besides his novels, Captain Marryatt wrote some works on naval affairs, and also a "Diary in America." He was the son of Mr. Joseph Marryatt, M.P., mentioned above, and he died in August, 1848.

On the brow of Putney Hill lived for many years the Countess of Guilford, daughter of Mr. Thomas Coutts. At her house Fuseli the painter breathed his last, in April, 1825. Later on the house became the residence of a daughter of the Countess of Guilford, Susan, in her own right Baroness North, who died March, 1884, having succeeded in 1841 to the barony, on the termination of an abeyance of nearly forty years. She was a granddaughter of the second Earl of Guilford, so long known as Lord North, having been Prime Minister from 1770 to 1782. The house has lately been offered for sale.

Lord North is memorable as the most indolent and most good-tempered of statesmen, and as the minister who most strongly maintained both the justice and expediency of the war between Great Britain and America, contending that the English Parliament had the right of taxing our colonies on the other side of the Atlantic, and still persisting in that policy at the bidding of George III., long after he became convinced that it was necessary to make peace with the revolted colonies, and to recognise the United States. Lord North was blind even before he succeeded, late in life, to his father's earldom. For most of his personal and domestic traits the world is indebted either to the gossiping pages of Sir N. W. Wraxall, or else to his own daughter, Lady Charlotte Lindsay, who appends a long letter on that subject to Lord Brougham's "Historical Sketches of Statesmen." "It is an interesting trait in Lord North's character that he would never allow himself to be called 'Prime Minister,' always saying that there was no such thing in the British Constitution."

Bristol House is so named after its former owner, the Marquis of Bristol, and stands on Putney Heath, overlooking Roehampton. It is a large, old-fashioned mansion, brick-built and stucco-fronted, consisting of a centre and wings, and standing in well laid out grounds, in which are some fine cedars, &c. The house dates from the latter half of the last century, but has been much altered and enlarged at different periods. After the death of Lord Bristol, in 1859, the house passed to Lord Alfred Hervey; and about 1870 it was sold to Thomas D. Galpin, Esq., its present owner.

have occasion to speak presently. Sir Francis was born in 1770, and entering Parliament for the first time in 1796, speedily attained high distinction as an orator in the foremost Opposition ranks. Lord Byron, writing in 1813, expresses his admiration of Burdett's "sweet and silvery" tones, and adds that he seemed to be "the greatest favourite" in the House of Commons.

He was returned for Westminster by a great majority immediately after his encounter with Paull. On the publication of a letter in 1810, in Cobbett's "Political Register," denying the power of the

GOTHIC HOUSE, WIMBLEDON.

Wimbledon Lodge, on the south side of the Green, was built towards the end of the last century by Gerard de Visme, an eminent merchant of Lisbon, on whose death it was inherited by his daughter, afterwards the wife of General the Hon. Sir Henry Murray, K.C.B., a distinguished Peninsula officer, who ended his days here in 1860. The fourth son of the second Earl of Mansfield, he was born in the year 1784; he entered the army at an early age, and served in the Peninsula, and at Waterloo, &c. His remains are interred in Wimbledon Church, where there is a monument to his memory.

The next house east of Wimbledon Lodge was formerly the home of Sir Francis Burdett* at the time of his duel with Mr. Paull, of which we shall

House to imprison delinquents, he was committed to the Tower, and remained in confinement nearly three months—the last of the long series of State prisoners. Having become late in life a Conservative, he declined standing for Westminster at the general election in 1837, but was returned for Wiltshire, and retained his seat for that county till his death, in 1844. There is a portrait of Sir Francis in the National Portrait Gallery, painted by Phillips in 1834, and presented by his eldest daughter, Lady Burdett-Coutts.

The next house to Wimbledon Lodge, on the west side, overlooking the Green, was long the property and residence of Mr. William Wilberforce, the philanthropist. His uncle, of the same name, had lived there before him; and on the death of his father, in 1768, young Wilberforce was placed under his uncle's care. Most of his holidays were

* See "Old and New London," Vol. IV., pp. 171, 281.

spent at his uncle's house, and here he imbibed from his aunt his first religious principles. "In 1777," writes Mr. Bartlett, "by the death of his uncle, he became possessed of the Wimbledon villa. Here was matured his friendship with Pitt which had begun at college, and had been strengthened by occasional intercourse afterwards. As he was the only member of the set into which he had fallen (consisting for the most part of young, but talented and aspiring, statesmen) who possessed a villa within reach of town, his house was much visited by those who enjoyed the sweets of country after a hard day's work in the House of Commons. His villa, with some trifling alterations, gave him the command of eight or nine bed-rooms; and here Pitt, to whom it was a luxury even to sleep in country air, not unfrequently took up his residence, their easy familiarity permitting him to ride down late at night and occupy his rooms, even though the master of the house was kept in town. In one spring Pitt resided there four months; and he repaired thither when, in April, 1783, he resigned his official residence to the Coalition Ministry. "Eliot, Arden, and I," wrote Pitt one afternoon, "will be with you before curfew, and expect an early meal of peas and strawberries. Bankes, I suppose, will not sleep out of Duke Street; but he is not yet (half-past four) apparent in the House of Commons."

Numerous short entries in Mr. Wilberforce's "Diary" show us the happy freedom of his Wimbledon life at this period. "One morning," so Wilberforce writes, "we found the fruits of Pitt's earlier rising in the careful sowing of the garden beds with the fragments of a dress-hat with which Ryder had come down from the opera."

"Feb. 29th, 1782.—Morning frosty, but extremely fine. Church—Lindsays—the chariot to Wimbledon. Pitt, &c., to dine and sleep."

"April 3rd.—Wimbledon, where Pitt, &c., dined and slept. Evening walk; bed a little past two."

"4th.—Delicious day; lounged morning at Wimbledon with friends, *foining* at night, and ran about the garden for an hour or two."

"Sunday, May 18th.—To Wimbledon with Pitt and Eliot—at their persuasion."

"Sunday, July 6th.—Wimbledon. Persuaded Pitt and Pepper to church."

It may be observed that neither Pitt nor the lawyer Pepper Arden, afterwards Lord Alvanley, was particularly fond of church-going.

Again, in 1785:—"Sir G. Beaumont and Lady Phipps, &c., to dine with me at Wimbledon. Phipps's chat from Locke to New Testament."

The last entry shows the natural bent of Wilberforce's mind, though his biographer says "these thoughts were as yet entirely speculative, exercising no apparent influence upon his conduct." Yet his feelings gradually deepened, and in the latter part of the session of 1786 we find him escaping from the gaieties of town, and sleeping constantly at Wimbledon. Yet "thinking it an unfavourable situation for his servants, a needless increase of his personal expenses, and a cause of some loss of time, he determined to forego in future the luxury of such a villa." And thus his associations with Wimbledon were brought to a close.

Mr. Wilberforce's house, later on, was occupied, about 1819–20, by Dr. William Van Mildert, Bishop successively of Llandaff and of Durham. He died in 1835.

Further westward, in the house opposite the south-east corner of the common, lived Sir John Richardson, sometime Justice of the Court of Common Pleas. He resided here from 1821 to 1823.

Mr. John Murray, the friend of Byron and of Scott, and founder of the *Quarterly Review*, lived for some years close by the "Crooked Billet," near the north-east corner of the common, the first editor of the *Quarterly*, Mr. William Giffard, being one of his near neighbours. Mr. James Perry, the well-known editor and proprietor of the *Morning Chronicle*, lived at Wandlebank House. He died in 1821, and was buried in the parish church, where a tablet to his memory was erected by the Fox Club, "in testimony of the zeal, courage, and ability with which he advocated the principles of civil and religious liberty, and of the talent and integrity by which he mainly contributed to convert the daily press into a great moral instrument, always devoted by him to the support of the oppressed and the promotion of public and private virtue."

Another resident of Wimbledon in the latter part of the last century was Mr. Lyde Browne, one of the Directors of the Bank of England, who here formed an extensive collection of antiquities, statues, &c., most of which were purchased by the Empress of Russia for £22,000. His house here, later on, was occupied by Lord Lyndhurst, thrice Lord Chancellor of England, and subsequently by Robert, second Lord Melville, whose father, Henry Dundas, the first lord, lived for some time in the mansion now called Cannizaro House after a later resident. Dundas held office in the administrations of Lord North, Lord Rockingham, and Lord Shelburne. "After the overthrow of the North and Fox coalition," writes Mr. Bartlett, "Mr. Dundas became a strenuous supporter of Mr. Pitt, being chairman of the select committee which preceded the introduction of Pitt's India Bill. A warm intimacy sprang up between them, and Pitt was now as constant a visitor at Wimbledon, in the house of Dundas, as he had been a few years before in that of Wilberforce. Indeed, a room was specially set apart as 'Mr. Pitt's room.' Great, therefore, was the grief when, in 1805, Dundas, by that time Lord Melville, was impeached for the maladministration of public money, more especially as Wilberforce, though from high conscientious grounds, spoke in favour of the motion. His trial, however, in 1806, resulted in his acquittal of every charge. During his reverses he lived in a small cottage opposite Gothic House, which he called Duneira Cottage, after the family property in Scotland."

The Duke of Cannizaro, after whom, as stated above, Lord Melville's house was named, was a later occupant. He was originally Count St. Antonio, and coming to England as a refugee, married a rich heiress, and became immortalised in one of the "Ingoldsby Legends."

Near the junction of the High Street and Church Street, opposite the back premises of the "Dog and Fox" inn, formerly stood a large house, the country seat of the Marquis of Rockingham, the political opponent of Pitt. He died here in 1782, being at that time premier, at the head of a coalition ministry. After his death, the mansion became for a time the residence of Charles James Fox, who resided here whilst Secretary of State.

Copse Hill, to the west of the park, recalls the memory of a time when Wimbledon still could boast of sylvan scenery, and had its copse and woodlands.

Cottenham Park, which stands on a portion of Copse Hill, is so named after Lord Chancellor Cottenham, who lived there for some years. The second son of Sir William Weller Pepys, Bart., he was born in 1781, and entered Parliament in July, 1831, as member for Higham Ferrers. He represented Malton from the following October down to 1836. In February, 1834, he was appointed Solicitor-General, and he became Master of the Rolls in the September following. His lordship was First Commissioner when the Great Seal was in commission in 1835; and he filled the office of Lord Chancellor under Lord Melbourne from 1836 to 1841, and again under Lord John Russell from 1846 to 1850.

Before Lord Cottenham's coming to reside here the house had been the residence of the first Earl of Durham, who was some time Ambassador to the Court of St. Petersburg, and afterwards High Commissioner in Canada. His name is perpetuated in Lambton and Durham Roads. After the death of Lord Cottenham, in 1851, the house was pulled down, and much of the estate was cut up for building purposes. About twenty acres, however, were bought by the trustees of St. George's Hospital, who have erected a convalescent hospital on the south side of Copse Hill nearly opposite the cottage hospital.

Miss Eliza Cook has resided at Thornton Hill, on the southern slope of Wimbledon, for many years, and her "Musings in Wimbledon Churchyard" are among the most popular of her poems with the educated classes. She was born about the year 1818, the daughter of a respectable tradesman in Southwark. At an early age she began to contribute to various literary periodicals, including the *New Monthly*, *Metropolitan*, *Literary Gazette*, &c. In 1840 she published a volume of poems, which at once attracted the attention of the public, and stamped her as a writer of great merit and deserved popularity. She more than sustained this favoured position in the "Journal" which bore her name, and which was published weekly from 1849 until 1854, when it was given up, owing to her failing health. More recently, her "Poems" have been reprinted in a collected form, and have passed through numerous editions. In 1860 a beautifully illustrated Christmas volume of her poems was also issued; and four years later was published a new volume of poetry from her pen, entitled "New Echoes and other Poems." In 1864 she obtained a literary pension of £100 a year. She retired here soon after giving up her "Journal."

Jenny Lind lived between the Park and the Common for many years after her marriage with M. Otto Goldschmidt. The "Swedish nightingale," as she was called, is a native of Stockholm, and was born in the year 1821. She came to England in 1847, and caused a perfect *furore* in London by her singing in the character of Alice in the opera of "Robert le Diable," the *rôle* in which she first obtained popularity in the opera-house of her native city. She subsequently gained great triumphs at Paris, Dresden, Frankfort, Cologne, and Vienna, and in 1845 sang at the fêtes on the Rhine during the visit of Queen Victoria to Berlin. In 1848 she sang for the first time in a sacred oratorio, "Elijah," which was given at Exeter Hall for the purpose of founding musical scholarships in honour of Mendelssohn. Later on she visited New York, but shortly after dissolved her engagement prematurely, and returned to England. In the same year (1851) she married M. Goldschmidt, an eminent musician, and retired from the stage. She re-appeared, however, in 1855, and again in

1861, in 1863, and in 1864, for a limited period. Madame Goldschmidt is well known for her generous disposition, which has been the means of adding many thousands of pounds to the charitable institutions of every country which she has visited.

The following anecdote of the great songstress is related by Miss Logan, in her interesting volume, " Before the Foot-lights and Behind the Scenes":— " A lady in whom I have the fullest confidence relates as an actual fact the story of Jenny Lind and the Hoosier. She tells me that during her march of triumph through America, and after her visit to Cincinnati, where she captivated all hearts, Jenny Lind found herself one evening in the (then) small town of Madison, Indiana, where Mr. Barnum had made an arrangement with the captain of the mail steamer which plies between Cincinnati and Louisville, to have the boat lie by on the Indiana shore long enough for the divine Jenny to give a concert at Madison. The largest building in the town having been prepared for her reception, an auction of the tickets took place in the hall on the morning of her arrival. The capacity of the building was fully tested by the anxious Madisonites. 'Coming through the Rye' was given first. This was followed by 'Home, Sweet Home;' and who can describe the marvellous effect of that song, as rendered by Jenny Lind? The famous 'Bird Song' was then the popular air of the country, and it was given as the concluding piece on the evening in question. The last line of the song ran thus : 'I know not, I know not why I am singing,' and Jenny gave it with her full power. At this moment a genuine Hoosier, indigenous to the soil, rose up in the auditorium, and thus delivered himself : 'You don't know why you are singin', eh ? Gosh ! I know, if you don't ! You're singin' to the tune of five dollars a head, and I reckon dad's hogs will have to suffer for my ticket !' "

Sir Bartle Frere, many years one of the most notable of Anglo-Indian statesmen and administrators, died at his residence here, Wressil Lodge, on the 29th May, 1884. A nephew of the Right Hon. John Hookham Frere, "the friend of Canning," he was born in 1815, and having received his education at Haileybury College, entered the Bengal Civil Service in 1833. He was appointed in 1842 Secretary to the Governor of Bombay. From 1846 to 1850 he held the post of Resident of Satara, after which he became Chief Commissioner of Scinde, and for his services there during the Indian Mutiny he was created a Knight Commander of the Order of the Bath, and was twice thanked by Parliament. He was senior member of the Supreme Council of India in 1859, President of the Council during the absence of the Governor-General in 1860, Governor of Bombay and Chancellor of Bombay University from 1862 to 1867, and a member of the Council of the Secretary of State for India from 1867 to 1877, during which period he acted for a short time as Envoy Extraordinary on a special mission to Zanzibar and Muscat. In 1875-6 he accompanied the Prince of Wales to India, and was entrusted with the duty of acting as a mentor on all questions of Indian policy and history. In 1877 he was appointed Governor of the Cape of Good Hope and Her Majesty's High Commissioner for South Africa.

Sir Bartle Frere's stewardship in South Africa was unfortunate for him in every way, and he is said to have returned to this country after four years' absence a considerably poorer man than when he went out. In 1867 Oxford University conferred upon him the honorary degree of D.C.L., and in 1874 he received the degree of LL.D. at Cambridge. He was sworn a member of the Privy Council in 1873, created a Knight Grand Cross of the Order of the Bath, and honoured with a Baronetcy. The remains of Sir Bartle Frere were interred in St. Paul's Cathedral.

CHAPTER LI.

WIMBLEDON *(continued)*—THE COMMON.

Extent and Boundaries of the Common—Its Management—General Description of its Scenery—The Windmill and the Roman Well—Rare Birds— The Gibbets—Jerry Abershaw, the Highwayman—Duels between the Duke of York and Colonel Lennox, Mr. Pitt and Mr. Tierney, Mr. James Paull and Sir Francis Burdett, Lord Castlereagh and Mr. Canning, Mr. George Payne and Mr. Clarke, the Marquis of Londonderry and Mr. Henry Grattan, Prince Louis Napoleon and Count Léon, and the Earl of Cardigan and Captain Tuckett—The Earthwork commonly called "Cæsar's Camp."

A BRIEF and incidental mention of Wimbledon Common has been made in the pages of "Old and New London,"* but it will be desirable to describe its features now at greater length. This broad stretch of open country, about 1,000 acres in extent, has long been one of the favourite "lungs of London." It adjoins Putney Heath, Kingston Common, and Richmond Park on the north and

* See Vol. VI., p. 500.

west, and on the south and east it merges upon Wimbledon Green and the slopes of Wimbledon Park. The actual division between Wimbledon Common and Putney Heath was for many years the subject of hot dispute between the two parishes, but was at length settled by reference to the Tithe Commissioners, and the common is now under the management of a Board of Conservators. The Select Committee on Commons and Open Spaces have agreed to recommend that no portion of Wimbledon Common shall be enclosed, or sold, or dealt with in any manner that may interfere with its free and unrestricted use by the public.

Roads and pathways intersect the common in all directions, whilst the views on all sides are most picturesquely varied, the undulating nature of the ground leading the eye continually to new vistas.

"The common," writes Mr. George A. Sala, "has about it a look of real nature. There are parts of it in which, as you wander amongst the furze, you might well imagine the huge city fifty miles away; and we do not want to have these nooks and glades and sunny spots of open turf arranged with mathematical precision in monotonous order. The common is English now—English in its free and breezy uplands, in its broad expanse; English in the groups of cricketers who make it merry on a holiday; English even in its gipsies, donkeys, tramps, mud-heaps, and swamps. As for the 'butts,' they are English too, for the old archer spirit of the Plantagenets and Tudors is unimpaired amongst the riflemen of Queen Victoria. A place where the artist can study—where the lover of nature can refresh his jaded eyes with glimpses of a beauty which needs a certain wildness for its charm—where children can gambol on the green without fear of 'trespass,' and without being abruptly summoned to 'keep off the grass'—such is Wimbledon at present."

The furze on the common was a special subject of delight to Leigh Hunt, who commemorates the beauty of the common in his agreeable "Table Talk," much lamenting when he saw it advertised that part of Wimbledon Park was to be sold or let for building purposes. He writes:— "This very Wimbledon Park was once occupied by a cultivator and even a painter of flowers, whom nobody that did not know him, and did not behold all his gentle tasks, would have suspected to be General Lambert, one of the boldest and most independent of the officers of Cromwell. He lived in the interval between his rival's elevation to power and the return of Charles II., and was famous for the ab-

surdly large sums which he gave for his pinks and tulips."*

Wimbledon, like Norwood, has for many a long year been celebrated for its hordes of gipsies, who encamp on its open common at their own sweet will, and in larger numbers since their old haunts at Wandsworth have been built over.

"The wrinkled beldame there you may espy,
And ripe young maidens with the glassy eye;
Men in their prime, and striplings dark and dun,
Scathed by the storm and freckled with the sun;
Their swarthy hue and mantle's flowing fold
Bespeak the remnant of *a race* of old!"

This open breezy space, in fact, has all the attributes of the country, even to its windmill, one of which structures has stood here for more than a hundred years. A noted spring on the common, called the "Robin Hood," or sometimes the "Roman" well, was enclosed with brick early in the present century. Rare specimens of the feathered tribe are occasionally to be met with here, such as the night-jar, or fern-owl, the nightingale, and cuckoo; whilst near the banks of the Beverley Brook, the woodpecker and the kingfisher have been observed from time to time.

Horse-races were held here at the beginning of the last century.

Miss Priscilla Wakefield speaks of this common as "a spacious tract of ground, on which highwaymen used formerly to perpetrate their midnight depredations. Hence," she adds, "like Hounslow Heath, on the opposite side of the river, it was once deformed by a hideous range of gibbets, the reproach and disgrace of a civilised country. The last poor wretch whose body was here suspended on the ignominious tree, as unworthy of heaven and of earth, was one Abershaw, who, by his depraved deeds, had been the terror of the metropolis and its vicinity."

Jerry Abershaw was executed in August, 1795, on Kennington Common. The daring spirit which he manifested on his way to the gallows was the subject of general conversation. Near his gibbet, Cyrus Redding remembered seeing, on his first arrival in London, posted up close by the side of the swinging carcase, a caricature of Pitt and his duel with George Tierney. The latter, levelling his pistol at the spare form of the premier, was represented as exclaiming, "It's as well as to fire at the devil's darning needle." Wimbledon, as we have seen, was Pitt's favourite suburban haunt; the joke ran that he chose it out of sympathy, for that "Jerry took purses with his pistols, and Pitt

* See *ante*, p. 479.

with his Parliaments," the one instrument being not much better than the other. But the highwaymen did not confine themselves to midnight depredations.

A writer in Sharpe's *London Magazine* in 1846 thus records one of his earliest reminiscences of the feats of highwaymen. "Some fifty years ago I unconsciously witnessed from the drawing-room window of a friend's house at Wimbledon a highway robbery, committed in open day on the late Lord Onslow. About eleven o'clock on one fine morning in the summer, I saw his lordship's carriage stopped by two highwaymen on horseback, within the sight and call of several labourers who were at work in the adjoining field, and who, like me, must have believed it impossible that a robbery should be committed in a public place, and at such an hour. No doubt they thought, as did I, that the young man in the red jacket who was at the window of the chariot was the post-boy with Lord Onslow's letters. In this case the highwaymen owed their safety and impunity to their hardihood, and to the good generalship which led them to effect their retreat easily from the apparent impossibility of the undertaking."

The common and its neighbourhood were the scene of many "hostile encounters" in the old days of duelling. Here, in 1789, was fought the celebrated duel between the Duke of York and Colonel Lennox (afterwards Duke of Richmond), of which an account will be found in the first chapter of "Fifty Years' Reminiscences," by Lord William Lennox. The seconds on the occasion were Lords Winchilsea and Hastings. "During an inspection of the Coldstream Guards, in the parade in St. James's Park, in the spring of 1789," writes Lord William Lennox, " one of the captains was observed to leave his position, walk up to the commanding officer, and in a firm voice demand an explanation of certain words of an offensive nature which his Royal Highness had been heard to utter in reference to him. The officers within hearing were filled with consternation, and the Duke of York was evidently taken by surprise. He contented himself with ordering the offender back to his post. His Royal Highness, however, knew that he had completely placed himself in the wrong, and that after so public a display of spirit by the person he had insulted, one course only was left to him. After the parade, when in the orderly-room at the Horse Guards, he sent for the young captain, and, in the presence of his brother officers, thus addressed him :—

" ' I desire to derive no protection from my rank as a prince, or my station as commanding officer. When not on duty, I wear a brown coat, and shall be ready, as a private gentleman, to give you satisfaction.'

" It should be borne in mind," continues Lord William, " that the social status of the two presented not quite so strong a contrast as their military positions. The captain, who was a lieutenant-colonel in the army, was heir to a dukedom, and his ancestor had worn the English crown not much more than a hundred years before. The offence which the second son of George III. had committed would have placed him on a level with any private gentleman, had it been directed against him, and had he resolved to resent it. This was so perfectly understood, that there was no difficulty in obtaining seconds for either party, and when they were selected, an apology or a duel became an imperative necessity. The former not being forthcoming, a meeting was arranged to take place at Wimbledon. Pistols were the weapons employed, and one was handed to each of the combatants, who were to fire together at the usual signal.

The narrative of the duel, as related in Chambers's "Book of Days," is to the effect that Colonel Lennox, being of Tory predilections, and having proposed the health of Mr. Pitt at a dinner-party, the Duke of York, who agreed with his brother in politics, determined to express his resentment against his lieutenant, which he did in the following manner :—At a masquerade given by the Duchess of Ancaster, a gentleman was walking with the Duchess of Gordon, whom the duke, suspecting him to be Colonel Lennox, went up to and addressed, saying that Colonel Lennox had heard words spoken to him at D'Aubigny's Club to which no gentleman ought to have submitted. The person thus addressed was not Colonel Lennox, as the duke supposed, but Lord Paget, who informed the former of the circumstance, adding that, from the voice and manner, he was certain the speaker was no other than the Duke of York.

The ground where the duel was fought was measured at twelve paces. The signal being given, Lennox fired, but the Duke of York refused. Lord Rawdon (Lord Hastings), the duke's second, then interfered, and said he thought enough had been done. Lennox observed that his Royal Highness had not fired. Lord Rawdon said it was not the duke's intention to fire; his Royal Highness had come out, upon Colonel Lennox's desire, to give him satisfaction, and had no animosity against him. Lennox pressed that the duke should fire, which was declined, with a repetition of the reason. Lord Winchilsea then went up to the Duke of York, and expressed a hope that his Royal Highness would have no objection to say he considered Colonel Lennox a man of honour and courage. His Royal Highness replied that he should say nothing; he had come out to give Colonel Lennox satisfaction, and did not mean to fire at him; if Colonel Lennox was not satisfied he might fire again. Lennox said he could not

but without effect. The second fire was attended with the same result, when the seconds interfered, and declared that sufficient satisfaction had been given. In Lord Holland's "Memoirs of the Whig Party," his lordship writes :—"Mr. Pitt's irritability to Mr. Tierney was very near involving more fatal consequences. Mr. Tierney, I have been told, annexed a meaning to Mr. Pitt's words which they were not meant to convey; but the latter's imperious manner of refusing all explanation, when called upon by a member (Mr. Wigley), made it

WIMBLEDON COMMON (THE WINDMILL).

possibly fire again at the duke, as his Royal Highness did not mean to fire at him. On this, both parties left the ground.

It is this Colonel Lennox of whom honourable mention is made in the pages of the Rolliad :—

"And thou, too, Lennox, worthy of the name!
　The heir to Richmond and to Richmond's fame !"

The duel between Mr. Pitt and Mr. Tierney was fought on Putney Heath on Sunday, May 27th, 1798. The latter had sent a challenge to the Minister, in consequence of some angry words in the House of Commons. Pitt was attended by Mr. Dudley Ryder (afterwards Lord Harrowby), and Tierney by Mr. George Walpole. Standing at twelve paces, each fired at the same moment,

difficult for Mr. Tierney not to resent his language. The circumstances of the duel are well known. It was fought on a Sunday, a circumstance which gave a handle to much vulgar abuse against Mr. Pitt. He did, indeed, urge the necessity of fighting immediately, if at all, because it was not proper for one in his situation to maintain any protracted correspondence on such a subject. Never did two men meet more ignorant of the use of their weapons. Mr. Pitt, on being cautioned by his second to take care of his pistols, as they were 'hair triggers,' is said to have held them up and remarked that 'he saw no hair.' They fought near a gibbet on which the body of the malefactor Abershaw was yet suspended. . . Mr. Tierney's second, General Walpole, leaped over the furze bushes or joy when Mr. Pitt fired in the air. Some time, however, elapsed, and some discussion between the seconds took place, before the affair was finally and amicably adjusted. Mr. Pitt very consistently insisted on one condition, which was in itself reasonable : that he was not to quit the ground without the whole matter being completely terminated. On Mr. Tierney's return home, he related the event to his wife. That lady, who was much attached to her husband, although she saw him safe before her,

"But," writes Mr. Bartlett, " Mr. Paull having advertised Sir Francis as the chairman of a public dinner without his consent, as was asserted, the latter sent his brother instead with a message to the assembled guests, disclaiming the honour which had been paid him. At this Mr. Paull took offence, and challenged the baronet to mortal combat." The duel resulted in their both being wounded, and returning—ludicrously enough—in the same carriage (Mr. Paull's) to London.

THE ROMAN WELL.

fainted away at the relation—a strange, but not uncommon, effect produced by the discovery of events which, known at the time, would have excited strong emotions. The danger to Mr. Tierney had indeed been great. Had Mr. Pitt fallen, the fury of the times would probably have condemned him to exile or death, without reference to the provocation which he had received, and to the sanction which custom had given to the redress which he sought."

In Coombe Wood, near Wimbledon, the duel between Mr. James Paull and Sir Francis Burdett took place in 1807. The two combatants, it appears, had been on terms of the greatest familiarity with each other, in consequence of the exertions of the former at the Westminster election.

In September, 1809, took place on Putney Heath a like "hostile encounter," between Lord Castlereagh and Mr. Canning, when the latter was slightly wounded in the thigh at the second fire. This duel, it is stated, originated out of an alleged deception on the part of Mr. Canning, which was afterwards proved to be a mere misconception.

In the following September, Mr. George Payne, a gentleman of fortune, was mortally wounded in a duel he fought on the common with a Mr. Clarke, with whose sister he had been too familiar. Payne died at the " Red Lion " at Putney a day or two afterwards.

In June, 1839, the Marquis of Londonderry

and Mr. Henry Grattan, M.P., had a hostile meeting here, when the latter, after receiving his opponent's fire, discharged his pistol in the air, and so the affair ended.

A memorable meeting which took place here was one between the Prince (afterwards Emperor) Louis Napoleon and Count Léon. It was happily bloodless. They met at seven a.m. on the 3rd of March, 1840. "When on the ground, the count refused to fight with swords," says Mr. B. Jerrold, in his Life of the Emperor, "but he found the prince as ready to give him satisfaction with pistols. The delay caused by this change of weapons, however, gave the authorities time to scent the impending breach of the peace, and before the seconds could put their men in position the police came up." The affair ended at Bow Street, when all four were bound over to keep the peace. Count D'Orsay was the prince's "second" on this occasion.

Among the latest duels fought here, or indeed anywhere in England, was one between the Earl of Cardigan and Captain Harvey Tuckett. It took place on the 21st of September, 1840, when the captain was severely wounded by a shot beneath the ribs. The earl was "tried by his peers" in the House of Lords in February, 1841, when, in consequence of the singular tactics of his counsel, who had "discovered a deficiency of proof as to the identity of the wounded man with the Captain Tuckett named in the indictment," a verdict of Not Guilty was returned, although, of course, actually speaking, there could be no doubt of the fact. Another duel about the same time was interrupted by the sudden rise of a cock-pheasant at the moment when the principals were about to fire, and the affair of honour was turned into a jest; and one of the principals in a third duel being a linen-draper's assistant, duelling was voted low and vulgar, and ceased to be fashionable. Even the greatest reforms, however, have their drawbacks, and it may be doubted whether the abolition of duelling has not tended to make men less regardful of the feelings of their neighbours, and encouraged in cowards a tendency to gratuitous insult.

In a previous chapter* we have spoken of the ancient stronghold, or earthwork, on the southwestern side of the common, generally known as Cæsar's Camp. "This circular entrenchment," remarks the author of " Pilgrimages in London," " is not only a romantic and curious object, but derives additional interest from the mystery hanging over the traditions of its origin, occupants, and purposes. It remains a monument, perhaps a

tomb, not of individuals merely, but of nations long since passed away; and all that antiquaries or topographers can do is to surmise by whom when, and why it was shovelled up from the bosom of Mother Earth."

It has been ascribed by different authors to British, Roman, Saxon, and Danish hands; indeed, seeing that the plough has passed over it, and destroyed many of those features upon which a fair conclusion might be built, it would, no doubt, be a hopeless task to endeavour to settle definitively the period to which these remains may be referred. The final syllable of Wimbledon, as we have already shown, will at once suggest a British origin for the name, if not for the camp itself. Brayley, in his " History of Surrey," gives it as his opinion that probably it was originally a British stronghold, subsequently occupied by other nations in succession. Mr. W. D. Saull, in a paper read before the Ethnological Society in March, 1848, speaks very decidedly in favour of the British origin of this earthwork, and even goes so far as to distinctly refer it to the " Fourth, or Pastoral Period" of British history, "when our rude forefathers kept their herds in enclosures of small extent—but numerous—upon the highlands." But there appears to be no reason why this writer might not, with equal propriety, have referred it to his " Fifth Period," when, as he describes it, large and strong encampments were formed on the downs, superseding the small hill camps. Mr. Saull, on the supposition that it belongs to his " Fourth Period," refers Wimbledon to the same date as the enclosures at Edge Hill, in Warwickshire, at Brailes, at Hooknorton Heath, and at Madmarston and Nadbury Camps. As examples of the " Fifth Period," to which Wimbledon would seem more properly to belong, Mr. Saull cites the earthworks on St. Catherine's Hill, near Winchester, the camp on the downs near Folkestone, and a very fine example at Danesfield, near Stockbridge.

Mr. Saull is not alone in his decided opinions on this subject. The Rev. Thomas Hugo, at a meeting of the London and Middlesex Archæological Society, in February, 1856, stated that " a large collection of hut circles was distinctly visible on Wimbledon Common a short time ago;" and suggested that Wimbledon was "the fortified fastness to which the Romans pursued Cassivelaunus."

Mr. Walter H. Tregellas, in an interesting paper on this subject in the " Journal of the Archæological Institute," No. 67, says:—"In a letter to myself, Mr. Hugo writes that the hut circles to which he referred were numerous and conspicuous some

* See ante, p. 470.

fifteen years ago, in a line between a windmill and the 'camp,' especially on the brow of the high ground on the north, over against the camp. They were round, and about four feet or five feet deep, the edges overgrown with brake, and at the bottom of each was a mass of large stones. Mr. Hugo was then fresh from some investigations which he had been making into similar remains on Worle Hill, Somersetshire, and is quite clear as to having correctly attributed the pits at Wimbledon. But no recent investigations, either by Mr. Hugo or by myself, have resulted in a discovery, or rather rediscovery, of these remains."

Mr. A. J. Kempe, F.S.A., in a paper in the *Archæologia*, Vol. XXXI., p. 519 (1846), in speaking of this encampment, observes that its construction is somewhat peculiar, and that "the indications which still exist of a second or outer *vallum* occasioned the erroneous conclusion, formed by some authors, that there was a double fosse." He remarks that writers on British military antiquities have considered that it was one of the principles of British tactics to use concentric rings of ramparts, rising one above the other, and he finds such an arrangement faintly indicated here.

From the paper by Mr. Tregellas above referred to, we gather the following details of the earthwork : —" Constructed with the gravelly soil obtained from the excavation of the fosse, it consists of an entrenchment which would have been quite circular, but for the rapid fall of the ground on the north side : on that side it follows the contour of the surface— an arrangement which seems to indicate that much importance was attached to the occupation of this precise site. The fosse is deeper and bolder at some parts than at others, but its average depth may be stated at about twelve feet, and the height of the vallum at from ten feet to twenty feet above the ground immediately beyond it. The outer *vallum* to which Mr. Kempe refers is more easily to be traced on the southern side than on any other ; but the outworks noticed by Brayley are now almost, if not entirely, erased : they also were probably on the southern side, where the ground is, from a military point of view, not so strong as on the northern side. The interior has been ploughed, and any traces which might formerly have existed of huts, &c., are of course gone ; there is consequently little left beyond its form and situation, and the conflicting pages of late writers, to give a clue to its origin. . .   . . Bearing in mind, then, that the earthwork is situated on an elevated spot commanding an extensive view—is of a circular form—is near springs of water, and was

probably in former times surrounded by a forest (a supposition strengthened by the presence of the oaks which still grow on its ramparts), we cannot deny that the *situation* and *form* of Wimbledon Camp fulfil most of the characteristics which Cæsar and Strabo give as distinguishing the *oppida* of the ancient Britons.

"Its *form* certainly does not belie the supposition that the entrenchment is of British origin. In looking through the Ordnance Maps, it is very noticeable that along the Roman roads, and in their immediate vicinity, there is, as might be expected, a marked tendency towards the rectangular outline which distinguishes almost invariably the camps of the Romans. But it must not be forgotten that square camps are also to be met with occasionally in the fastnesses of Cornwall and North Wales, though generally the 'camps' in these parts are either circular or elliptical ; nor, as is well known, are instances wanting both of undoubtedly British and Roman works, when the advantages of a strong and irregular position superseded the ordinary practice, and the *vallum* followed more or less closely the figure of the ground on which the camp was formed. Such, then, appears to be the evidence in favour of the British origin of the camp at Wimbledon. Let us now examine what has been urged in favour of its having been a Roman work.

"It will be remembered that Surrey was long held by the Regni, and was probably governed by a Romano-British king ; and that it also lay in the line of march between the south-east coast of England and the passage of the Thames.

"Gale, in his 'Antonini Iter Britanniarum,' argues in favour of a Roman road having passed through Wimbledon ; and his views seem to have been accepted by Mr. W. Hughes, who, in his Map of Roman Britain, published in 1848, gives Wimbledon as the site of a Roman camp.

"Dr. Roots, the well-known collector of the Roman antiquities found at Kingston Hill and in the bed of the Thames,[*] was of opinion that Cæsar occupied this entrenchment, if, indeed, he did not form it, whilst preparing for his conflict with Cassivelaunus on the banks of the river ; and he urges in support of these views the Roman remains which have been found in the neighbourhood. The great objection, however, to this theory," remarks Mr. Tregellas, "appears to lie in the *circular form* of the enclosure."

Of its claim to Saxon parentage we have already had occasion to speak in treating of the

---

[*] See *Archæologia*, Vol. XXX., p. 490, and Vol. XXXI., p. 518

etymology of Wimbledon.*　Camden says of "Wibbandune, now commonly called Wimbledon," that "it is possible the military fortification I saw here, of a circular form, called Bensbury, might take its name" from Cnebben, who was slain here.　Cnebben, it will be remembered, was one of the generals in the army of Ethelbert, King of Kent, in his conflict with Ceaulin, King of the West Saxons.

"So far as we are acquainted with the earthworks of the Saxons," continues Mr. Tregellas, "there is little in the camp at Wimbledon which conflicts with the received notions on the subject. Fosbrooke, quoting Strutt, ascribes to the Saxons those earthworks with a raised interior surface, surrounded with a broad ditch, and encompassed with an earthen vallum; and he instances the small, double-trenched circular work at Mount Caburn, near Lewes, as a perfect specimen. High *valla* and deep ditches may generally, he thinks, be referred to the Saxons; and the profile of the ramparts at Wimbledon may perhaps be considered bold enough to fulfil these conditions. It now only remains to consider the probabilities of the Danes having constructed this encampment. Aubrey, in his 'Natural History and Antiquities of Surrey,' Vol. I., p. 16, says it was made by the Danes, 'as appears by the Chronicle.' It certainly appears that after Surrey passed into the hands of the West Saxons, this part of the country was much ravaged by Turkill and Swaine, Danish warriors, but I have not succeeded in finding the authority for Aubrey's positive statement; and the only other evidence that occurs to me as bearing, however remotely, on the Danish origin of this entrenchment is the statement in Spelman's 'Life of Alfred,' that 'the Danish camps were always round, and with one entrance:' a statement the accuracy of which would (not to multiply instances) be sufficiently disproved by the harp-shaped camp at Bratton, Wilts—one of the best ascertained of the Danish positions. Perhaps the utmost that could be said on this part of the subject is that, so far as I am aware, there is nothing in the form of the work to entirely preclude the possibility of its being of Danish origin.

"In concluding these remarks, it may not be out of place to notice that the earthwork now under consideration has at different times borne for its name the various forms of the word Wimbledon which have already been mentioned; that Camden knew it as Bensbury; and that Mr. Kempe tells us that in 1846 it was called

Warren Bulwarks.　Of course it is also sometimes called 'The Rounds;' and, equally of course, its most usual name is 'Cæsar's Camp.'"

Allen, in his "History of Surrey" (Vol. I., p. 475), describes it as "a round camp surrounded by a double ditch, including about seven acres," the inner trench, in his time, being deep and perfect.　The true area of the enclosure is about fourteen acres.

Whether Wimbledon Camp was originally merely the scene of a fortified village and cattle-enclosure of the ancient Britons, or an encampment of Roman legions, or a fortress of either Saxon or Danish warriors, or whether it has been the stronghold of each in succession, it is obviously a site round which historic suggestions richly cluster; and it is to be hoped that in making any future arrangements for the allotment of the common and its vicinity, this interesting piece of antiquity may be judiciously conserved.　About the year 1865 the earthwork was threatened with destruction; but in 1873 steps were taken by the Corporation of London with the view to its preservation. Nevertheless, about 1880 it was wantonly ploughed over and partly destroyed by its owner, Mr. Erle Drax; and again, about two years later, it was proposed to carry a roadway, and even a railway, through it.

In Douglas's "Nenia Britannica" is given a description of twenty-three barrows which existed up to 1786 on Wimbledon Common, about a mile to the north of the camp.　The only relic actually discovered here by Douglas appears to have been a small earthen vessel; but it is probable that these barrows had been opened by Dr. Stukeley a few years previously.

At a meeting of the British Archæological Association, in 1881, Mr. Loftus Brock gave a description of several ancient British relics found in the neighbourhood of Coombe Hill, close by the common, and which had been lent for exhibition. The relics consisted of a pre-historic vessel of clay, known as a food-vessel, such as are commonly found in early British graves, a clay mould for casting bronze implements, a bronze celt, a dagger, and a fragment of bronze in an unworked state. These relics point to the existence not only of a burial-place, but to the presence of the living, and afford evidence, perhaps, of the people who constructed Cæsar's camp.

Mr. Tregellas, in his paper on Wimbledon Camp above quoted, writes that he had been favoured with a communication from Mr. Albert Way, who told him that he had a note of a singular relic, possibly a sling-shot, found some years ago *at the*

Camp, consisting of a large perforated object of baked clay. It was shaped like a cheese, was 5¼-in. in diameter, 3¾-in. thick, and the hole was ¾-in. in diameter.

Mr. Tregellas concludes his paper with a description of some cruciform tumuli in Somerset and other parts of the country, and adds:—" Nothing, so far as I am aware, seems to be known positively, at present, of the origin or history of these singular remains, except that they are doubtless of great antiquity. It is interesting to know that there is some reason for supposing that an example existed, not very many years ago, near Wimbledon Camp; and it is to be hoped that any fresh light which may be thrown upon cruciform tumuli *generally* may also cast a ray upon the now obscure history of the Camp at Wimbledon."

Though now so lonely and desolate, yet once this old camp must have been a busy haunt of men, and the soldiers of Britain and of Rome must here have met in deadly conflict. So true are the words of Shelley—

> " From the most gloomy glens
> Of Greenland's sunless clime,
> To where the golden fields
> Of fertile England spread
> Their harvest to the day,
> Thou can'st not find one spot
> Whereon no city stood."

CHAPTER LII.

WIMBLEDON (*continued*)—THE VOLUNTEER ENCAMPMENT.

> " Oh, forthwith repair to yon ground,
> For many brave youths will be there
> To guard all the rights of the crown,
> With sword and fuzee to a hair.

> " Fine hats and rich plumes *militaire*,
> Blue coats, red collars, all the rest,
> From the head to the foot we appear.
> All gentlemen soldiers confest."—OLD LOYAL SONG.

Formation of the First Volunteer Association for the Defence of the Country—First Royal Volunteer Review at Wimbledon—Numerical Strength of the Volunteers of Old—Fiery Enthusiasm of the Country at the beginning of the Present Century—Patriotic Songs, &c.—A Defence of the Volunteer System—Revival of the Volunteer Movement in 1859—Formation of the Force—Captain Hans Busk—The First Volunteer Review by Queen Victoria—Inauguration of the National Rifle Association at Wimbledon—Camp Life at Wimbledon—Prizes, &c.—The Elcho Challenge Shield—The Ashburton Shield—The Butts—Concluding Remarks.

As far back as the year 1797—so, at least, we learn from Bartlett's " History of Wimbledon"—the local vestry took into consideration " the formation of an association towards the defence of the country." A meeting was accordingly held, which was attended by a large number of the parishioners, among them being Mr. John Horne Tooke. Two corps, one of horse and one of foot, were then formed. The leading cavalry volunteers were Earl Spencer, the Right Hon. Henry Dundas, Mr. James Meyrick, Mr. Francis Fowke, and other leading inhabitants. The first chairman of the association was the Rev. Septimus Hodson. The leading infantry volunteers were Mr. W. Rush, Mr. Thomas Eden, and Mr. Gerrard de Visme. Mr. Benjamin Patterson, who acted as lieutenant, succeeded Mr. Hodson as chairman. " The association," remarks Mr. Bartlett, " was maintained for some years with great spirit, a spirit which the ladies of Wimbledon seem thoroughly to have shared, as we find them opening a ladies' subscription for furnishing flannel waistcoats to the Infantry Wimbledon Volunteers, the waistcoats to be made by the lady subscribers; the highest subscription to be 10s. 6d., the lowest, 2s. 6d."

The example of Wimbledon was speedily followed in other localities, and the rapid progress of the movement is shown by the fact that a twelvemonth later, namely, on the 5th of July, 1798, a Royal Volunteer Review was held on Wimbledon Common, and it is notable as being the first of any importance held there. The following account of the review is quoted from Mr. T. Preston's " Patriots in Arms " (Whittaker, 1881), where a reproduction is given of Rowlandson's rare picture of the scene :—" The corps reviewed was the London and Westminster Light Horse Volunteers, under the command of Colonel Herries. The strength of the regiment was altogether 616, composed of 411 mounted men, divided into six troops, and 205 dismounted men, divided into three troops. They were reviewed by his Majesty George III., who expressed his high approbation of the state of efficiency of the regiment, and of its appearance and discipline.

The corps went through a variety of manœuvres in a very soldier-like manner, 'following the rules laid down by his Majesty's orders for the formation and exercise of cavalry. Every movement was correctly and rapidly made; the troops charged well, keeping well up in a compact, well-preserved line. The dismounted part of the corps performed their manual and platoon exercise correctly, and moved in correspondence with the cavalry with precision, steadiness, and a soldier-like manner.' This extract from the general order issued by the Adjutant-General immediately after the review will puzzle many readers, who will naturally wonder what sort of men they could have been to have been able to 'move in correspondence with the cavalry.' The following description of the dismounted part of the corps will explain the matter, and also show the use of the six-horse cars which are seen in the background of Rowlandson's picture. 'The seventh, eighth, and ninth troops of the London and Westminster Light Horse are dismounted, and act as riflemen, carrying a rifle-barrelled gun of a new construction, which will do execution at a great distance; and their broadswords are so contrived as to serve occasionally as bayonets. *Cars,* or *expedition carriages,* are always ready to convey the dismounted men at the same pace as the cavalry may march.' With reference to this curious picture, it has been observed that the carriage wheels are none of them round. This certainly is remarkable, but it is a peculiarity observable in all wheels in Rowlandson's pictures."

It would be impossible to trace the gradual growth of the volunteer movement; it is enough to say here that it woke up into new life the " train-bands" of half a century before, and that as long as there were fears of an invasion of our shores by the great Napoleon (who figures in contemporary prints as "Boney" and the "Corsican"), it continued to spread until the volunteers numbered their hundreds of thousands.

From a return made at the War Office in November, 1803, some idea of the strength of our "volunteers of old" may be gleaned. The account stood thus:—Volunteer infantry, 297,500; volunteer cavalry, 31,600; volunteer artillery, 6,207; total, 335,307. Compared in numerical strength with the French armies, a contemporary journal observes:—"If to these be added our regulars and militia, we too may boast of our 500,000 fighting men;" and taking the volunteer return merely, it exhibits — at a period, too, when the population was not more than a half of what it numbered in 1859, when the present

volunteer movement was started—a muster-roll seven times greater than that of 1859.

The efforts that were made towards organising a system of national defence in 1859 were not to be compared to the fiery enthusiasm that animated the Old England of 1803 and 1804. "At that period," observes a writer in *Chambers's Journal,* "a feverish state of anxiety and vigilance was everywhere apparent. At Folkestone, whenever the wind blew from the French coast, sea-fencibles patrolled the town all night, repeating the usual challenge at every post. 'Something decisive may be expected,' writes a gentleman in a private letter, dated 1st of September, 1804. 'At this moment the Corsican has everything in his favour: a strong flood-tide, the wind fresh and fair for crossing the Channel, and a very hazy fog, so that we cannot see two miles from shore. All the men-of-war in the Downs ready to slip or cut their cables at an instant's notice. Clerks at Admiralty said to be in attendance all night. Everything indicates on the part of the Government the utmost vigilance. A heavy firing, heard from darkness to sunrise, towards France; and on the following day, in the direction of the Cornish coast, twenty reports were counted in the space of a minute.' Yet all this terrific hurly really seems to have delighted those most interested in its momentous results. A mounted dragoon, his horse all foam and mire, dashes through the streets of Southampton, the bearer of an express from the Duke of York—for the electric wire was destined for a later generation. Two thousand four hundred men got under arms in less than an hour. The men of eight adjacent villages, where orders arrived at noon, are marching by four o'clock. The aspect of the town resembles a gala-day. Loyal songs, inspired by the supposed imminent aspect of encountering the enemy, resound through the streets. However homely the composition of those patriotic lyrics, they were calculated to sustain the popular enthusiasm, as will appear from the following fragment, sung to a well-known popular air :—

> " 'Fathers ! be of cheer ;
> Britons are no drones, sirs ;
> Should Bonaparte appear,
> Soon we 'll part his bones, sirs.
> And if on our shore
> Should he land his scums, sirs,
> When that he comes o'er,
> Soon he 'll be o'ercome, sirs.' "

Gilray and Rowlandson, the two most famous caricaturists of the day, were actually retained in the public service by Mr. Pitt in aid of the cause,

THE VOLUNTEER CAMP, WIMBLEDON—"OUTSIDE THE COTTAGE."

and their comic productions, no doubt, helped to fan the enthusiasm that then prevailed.

The following are two verses from a song called the "Volunteer Boys," to the tune of "Let the toast pass," published in 1801 :—

> " Here 's to the squire who goes to parade,
> 　Here 's to the citizen soldier ;
> Here 's to the merchant who fights for his trade,
> 　Whom danger increasing makes bolder :
> 　　Let mirth appear, union is here,
> 　　The toast that I give is the Brave Volunteer.
>
> " Here 's to the lawyer who leaves the bar,
> 　Hastens where honour doth lead, sir,
> Changing the gown for the ensigns of war,
> 　The cause of the country to plead, sir ;
> 　　Freedom appears, ev'ry heart cheers
> 　　That call for a health to the Law Volunteers."

A Scotch song, published at Glasgow about the same time as the above, and called "Britain's Contest," contains the following verse :—

> " The French they say are coming o'er,
> 　To kill our king, an' a' that ;
> They 'll kiss our sweethearts and our wives,
> 　And slay ourselves an' a' that—
> 　　And a' that, an' a' that ;
> 　　But gin they come we'll crack their crowns,
> 　　An' send them hame to claw that."

The following witty "Macaronic" lines on the same subject, supposed to be said or sung by a newly-enlisted volunteer dating from this period, have been ascribed to the pen of no less a scholar than Professor Porson :—

> " *Ego nunquam audivi* such terrible news,
> 　As at this *tempus præsens* my senses confuse ;
> I am drawn for a *miles*, and must go *cum Marte*,
> 　And *comminus manu* engage Bonaparte.
>
> " Such *tempora nunquam videbant majores*,
> 　But then their opponents had different *mores ;*
> But we will soon show to the Corsican vaunter
> 　That though times may be changed, Britons *nunquam mutantur.*"

A poem "On the Fashionable Rite of Consecrating Military Colours, particularly those of the brave Volunteer Bands," contains the stanza quoted as the motto to this chapter.

In 1806 was published "A Defence of the Volunteer System, in opposition to Mr. Windham's idea of that Force; with Hints for its Improvement." In it the writer observes :—" It has been the custom of those writers who have intended to deprecate the value of the volunteers to adduce instances from history of the inefficacy of raw troops to contend with veterans ; but these illustrations have seldom given much strength to their arguments, as, upon inspection, they will be found to bear but little analogy to the political feelings and military situations of the country. . . . It would not, however, be very difficult to select other examples from the history of any age of troops inferior to our volunteers, who have honourably distinguished themselves against old and highly-disciplined soldiers. But who that has read the history of the American War and the French Revolution, in our own time (1806), can want conviction on this head ? . . . . In estimating our means of defence, a strange infatuation seems to have laid hold of some men's minds, that, as one battle has decided the fate of nations on the Continent, so it must necessarily do ours. The brilliant actions of Bonaparte seem to have dazzled and confounded their imaginations. A battle of Marengo or of Austerlitz may put an end to a Continental war, or to the independence of a nation solely relying upon a standing army, but never can conquer a country like England, constitutionally defended . . . . . . In a country defended by the voluntary efforts of its own children, under judicious guidance, every inch of ground gained by an enemy will prove to him a sanguinary conquest. That general should be considered as guilty of little less than treason who suffered an enemy on English soil an hour's repose by night or day till he was conquered. The fresh troops that would every moment flock to his standard would enable him to undertake hourly enterprises. A war of this description would necessarily have a speedy termination. An enemy thus incessantly harassed, when it became judicious to attack him on all points, must fall an easy prey. . . . In forming a plan for the defence of the country, the worst possible circumstances that can happen should be provided against. With us, the confidence placed in our navy should be put entirely out of the question, and we should be prepared for the attack of an enemy as if no such formidable opposition to him existed. There should be no check on the exertions of our fleets : they should be ready, if necessary, to quit our shores to a ship, without fear of the consequences. . . . The question is not now whether we shall become a military nation— that is already decided—but what sort of a military nation ?—whether we shall encumber ourselves with and entail on our posterity an enormous growing expense, the natural consequence of an ever-growing military establishment ; or whether the same end shall be accomplished by the voluntary efforts of the people, under a plain, systematic form, conducted at a comparatively trifling charge, and which, when the country shall be no longer in need of their services, it is in the power of the Legislature to extinguish in an instant."

Since then the volunteer movement has progressed steadily and surely, and its prospects soon became more settled, with yet growing numbers, and "with a firm conviction in the minds of Englishmen of its vital importance to the country." "Lord Overstone showed that the immigration to this country of any portion of the French surplus fighting population would be productive of the most disastrous results ; and some events occurred which gave rise to a suspicion that although the Empire itself might be filled—paved, if that expression be allowable—with the best and most peaceable intentions, the eagles which that Empire nourished had an unpleasant habit, and a still more restless desire, of 'flying from victory to victory.'"

"It is easy, of course," remarks the *Dublin University Magazine*, " to say that untrained enthusiasm will never stand before thorough discipline, and that volunteers have only been successful against blundering commanders, or troops absurdly overmatched. Yet volunteer levies fought like veterans at Edgehill against the experienced soldiers of Lord Essex. Volunteer armies cleared France of the formidable hosts who thought to take vengeance for the cruel treatment of her king. A nation of German volunteers, under Garibaldi, harassed and defeated the Austrian troops on the skirts of Lombardy in the war of 1859 ; and yet, later telegrams told us how another army of volunteers, led by the same great hero of our day, beat off the last despairing efforts of a powerful Neapolitan force to bring back to his forfeit capital the king who had accompanied them into the field."

The volunteer movement which marked the war against the great Napoleon had all but passed away out of the memory of the living generation, when suddenly it was revived, in 1859, by Captain Hans Busk and others. It was at once received with the utmost enthusiasm ; through the influence of Lord Bury, Lord Elcho, and other members of the two Houses of the Legislature, the approval of the Government and the patronage of her Majesty was secured for it. The Volunteer movement, however, went through its share of ridicule at first, as the pages of *Punch* and the other comic journals of the period can testify ; but it has outlived this and all other weaknesses incident to infancy, and now the brave defenders of our homes are toasted along with the army and the militia forces at every public dinner.

The movement seemed to grow almost spontaneously out of the strong irritation against France which was aroused throughout England by the braggadocio utterances of some French colonels, who were, or professed to be, angry because this country did not show, as they thought, sufficient energy in punishing the authors of a dastardly conspiracy, hatched in the happy region of Leicester Square, to murder the Emperor of France by bombs. Dr. Simon Bernard had been arrested in his lodgings at Bayswater on a charge of complicity with Orsini, and the law was being put into motion to vindicate our Imperial ally. But our English law, like all great bodies, is slow in its motions, and was far too slow to satisfy the impulsive colonels who wore the French uniform. Their impatient utterances naturally "put up the English monkey," and for weeks and months the anti-Gallican feeling was growing stronger and stronger, both in London and in the provinces.

In the next year the public indignation became less unreasonable, but it still maintained its strength, though not its heat ; and, worked upon by persons of patriotic feelings and military tastes, it gave rise to one of the most important movements which ever left their mark on the social and political history of any nation. " The militia," writes Mr. Thomas Archer, in his " Life of Gladstone,"* " had already been strengthened and recognised ; but now came a steady and determined renewal of former proposals by competent men for the formation of volunteer regiments. . . . Many thousands of volunteer riflemen, whose happily-chosen motto was soon declared to be ' Defence, not Defiance,' were rapidly enrolled under officers who at all events had plenty of energy and enthusiasm, and were not deficient in ability."

But the movement received a further impulse in the same year (1859) through the interference of the Emperor of the French with the affairs of Northern Italy, which threatened to set half Europe in a blaze, in which it was feared that ultimately even England might become involved. At this moment the formation of the Rifle Volunteer force came at once into full play. Their numbers grew with the utmost rapidity, and they soon were formed into a regular body. " Volunteer corps," wrote the Prince Consort to Baron Stockmar on the 8th of December, " are being formed in all the towns. The lawyers in the Temple go through regular drill. Lords Spencer, Abercorn, Elcho, &c., are put through their facings in Westminter Hall by gaslight, in the same rank and file with shop-keepers.

* See Vol III., p. 284.

Close on 50,000 are already under arms." The prince was shortly afterwards called on to take a prominent part in the public demonstrations of this force, which kept on growing at once in numbers and in efficiency; and "when the Government decided to authorise the formation of rifle corps, as well as of artillery corps and companies in maritime towns with forts and batteries, the Prince applied himself to the study of the means of organising these bodies in such a way as to make them a permanent means of defence, on which the country might rely upon on an emergency. The results were embodied by him in an elaborate series of 'Instructions to Lord-Lieutenants,' which he sent to General Peel, as Secretary for War, on the 20th of May, 1859. It was found by him to be so complete, that he submitted it three days afterwards to the Cabinet [of Lord Derby], by whom it was adopted, and ordered to be issued forthwith. Accordingly it was printed and sent out to the Lord-Lieutenants throughout the kingdom on the 25th of the same month, and formed the code for the organisation and working of these volunteer corps." *

The earliest and most strenuous advocate of the volunteer system, when in abeyance, was the above-mentioned Captain Hans Busk, the author of "The Rifle and how to use it," "Volunteers, and how to drill them," &c., and it was by him that it was aroused to fresh life.

In 1837 (when an undergraduate at Cambridge) he strongly urged upon the Government of that day the importance of sanctioning the formation throughout the country of rifle-clubs, with a view to the subsequent organisation of an army of volunteers as the most legitimate, constitutional, and surest defence of the realm; and on receiving from the then Prime Minister a reply, indicative of apprehension at the idea of putting arms into the hands of the people at large, he formed a model rifle-club in the university. To show that the materials of which it was composed were of the right sort, it may be mentioned that several of its original members subsequently obtained commissions, and not a few of his most cordial coadjutors have since died gloriously on different battle-fields.

Captain Hans Busk continued lecturing and writing and counselling upon the subject until the revived volunteer movement became an established fact. For a period of nearly twenty years he continued on every occasion strenuously to advocate the establishment of a volunteer army, but with little effect, until the publication of his treatise on the rifle, into which he again introduced an earnest appeal in favour of the volunteer cause —a subject that had been in complete suspense since 1803. In order to demonstrate, however, the urgent necessity for increased exertion, and to prove the extent of the war preparations making by France, and the growing increase of her fleet, he visited in succession each of her ports and naval arsenals, publishing, on his return, the only authentic French navy list that had appeared for sixteen years.

Not long after he was solicited by an influential deputation from the University of Cambridge to address the undergraduates with a view to the formation of a corps, which he was subsequently requested to help in organising. Such was the success consequent on the appeal then made, that from all parts of the country other invitations daily arrived, earnestly requesting him to aid in the promotion of a cause which—to quote the expression ordinarily used by his correspondents— "he had been first to originate." He died in 1882.

In May, 1860, the whole force reached 124,000 men, and on the evening of the first great volunteer review held by the Queen in Hyde Park, on the 23rd of June, the Prince Consort was able to boast, in a speech made at the Trinity House dinner, that its numbers were in excess of 130,000.

The volunteers had now climbed up to the highest point of popularity, and it was thought by some that such popularity was likely to prove both short-lived and injurious to the force itself. The 2nd of July marked an epoch in the progress of the movement. On that day the first meeting of the National Rifle Association was held on Wimbledon Common. The weather was bright, and a brilliant assembly had gathered to witness the proceedings. "The first shot at the targets was fired by the Queen herself; and Mr. Whitworth had so adjusted one of his rifles as to secure a good score for her Majesty at the 400 yards range. An address was presented to the Queen on her arrival at the camp by Mr. Sidney Herbert, as president of the association; after which, her Majesty, accompanied by the Prince, advanced to a tent in which had been fixed the rifle which was to open the competition. A touch of the trigger was followed by a flutter of the red-and-white flag before the target, an intimation that the 'bull's eye' had been hit, and that her Majesty, in accordance with the rules of the Association, had scored three points. For six successive days the competition for the prizes for the best shooting

* T. Archer's " Life of Gladstone," Vol. III., pp. 324, 325.

continued. The number of volunteers who entered for the regulated prizes was 292, while 494 competed for those open to all-comers. The first Queen's Prize of £250, with the gold medal of the Association, was won by Mr. Ross, of the 7th York, who, in the determining contest, made eight points at 800, seven at 900, and nine at 1,000 yards. About £2,000 was taken for admission to the camp."*

" If we look for the very root and spring of the present volunteer movement," observes a writer in *Once a Week*,† " we shall find it possibly in the celebrated letter of the Duke of Wellington, with which he rudely awakened Englishmen from the dream they had dreamed since Waterloo and Trafalgar, that our isle would be inviolate ' come the four corners of the world in arms to shock us.' The Saxon mind from that time slowly took alarm, and since the establishment of the French Empire the whole nation has turned in upon itself, as it were, to consult its own deep instincts as to what should be done. The *Times*, appreciating the blind instincts of the people, first shaped and moulded the movement in the direction it ultimately took ; but it was to the voice of song that we owe the rapid and splendid development of peaceful citizens into armed battalions ready for the field. The philosopher who notes the shapeless grains of seed grouping themselves into regular forms when influenced by the vibrations of certain sounds, could in the volunteer movement see an analogous movement in the moral world, when the poet laureate's stirring song ' Riflemen, Form !' thrilled through the land, and at a stroke organised into serried lines the mobs of panic-stricken citizens. We question if any section of the nation has been taken so much by surprise by this movement as the military caste. Having experience of the lowest station only of the population of our own country, and of the National Guards on the Continent, it did not believe that the office, the chamber, and the shop, could turn out, at six months' notice, regiments worthy to be brigaded with regular troops, forgetting that in the Great Rebellion the shopkeepers of London marched to Gloucester, and there and then decided for ever in England the contest between despotism and liberty. Those, again, who remembered, with a supercilious smile, the National Guard of Continental nations—middle-aged gentlemen, fat and frowsy, who do duty on compulsion—should not have confounded their capabilities with the picked

youth of this country : athletes, with bone, muscle, and pluck enough to go anywhere and do anything."

The writer then proceeds to comment on the review by the queen which was held in 1860 :—" Among the many hundred thousands who crowded Hyde Park on the 23rd of June," he remarks, " jammed tight between two guardsmen in the purgatorial space before the stands, we noticed the long and sombre line of England's home army slowly pass before the queen. Across the green sod this sombre riband of men came on and on, their ranks ruled as straight as lines, and the whole mass sweeping round with a movement like the spokes of a wheel. For an hour and a half came the tramp, tramp, unbroken by a sound save by the distant music, their own feet, and the occasional cheers of the spectators, for it was perhaps wisely ordered that none but the queen's band should play during the review. Persons accustomed to the reviews of regular troops were struck by the exceeding simplicity of the uniforms. There was no holiday attire here. Grey and green made up the long column, save that, like a lance, at its head fluttered the brilliant scarlet of the Artillery Company and the bright tunics of the Huntingdonshire Mounted Rifles. It was impossible to avoid drawing comparisons between the different corps as they marched past ; indeed, the line of military spectators who fringed the reserved standings were very demonstrative indeed in their professional criticisms, and it is but just to say that in no instance was there the slightest shade of professional jealousy evinced by them. ' What splendid horses !' we heard a guardsman involuntarily exclaim, as the Huntingdonshire Mounted Rifles went past ; ' her Majesty don't mount our men like that.' Every horse perhaps was a valuable hunter, and the man that rode him was warranted to do some cross-country skirmishing if called into the presence of the enemy.

" The Honourable Artillery Corps again puzzled the people mightily, and we believe to this hour numbers went away with the idea that a battalion of her Majesty's Grenadier Guards led off the review. But we confess that, to our unprofessional eye, the most active and soldierly-looking set of men were the Inns of Court Corps. The greyish-brown dress possibly tended to give the men size, but it was impossible not to remark that the ' Devil's Own' carried off the palm for setting-up and athletic proportions. When we consider that these young lawyers are many of them just drafted from the Universities, where physical training is

---

* T. Archer's " Life of Gladstone," Vol. IV., p. 45.
† See July 14, 1860. Vol. III., p. 81.

perhaps better attended to than among any other assemblage of young Englishmen, it is not surprising that they should make such splendid young soldiers. That the use of their brains does not militate against the use of their legs, the repeated cries of ' Bravo, Devil's Own !' as they marched past, fully testified. Indeed, a good many could not help remarking that here, as in a good many other places, his sable majesty took excellent care of his children. It was observable in this review —such splendid beards, worthy of Titian, and such fine faces ! Imagine some dirty little scrub of a Frenchman picking off his Stanfield, or potting a Millais, in an affair before breakfast ! But there would be plenty of Englishmen left to avenge them, and to paint good pictures afterwards. Then there were the Scottish, Welsh, and Irish corps, each distinguished by some national badge or costume. The kilted company of Scotchmen certainly marched admirably, and fully justified the excellence of the

SHOOTING FOR THE QUEEN'S PRIZE.

that the spirit which leads us to stick to what is termed in the army the regimental system also obtains most fully amongst the volunteers. Each corps felt a pride in itself, which doubtless will tend to excellent results if the volunteers are ever called into the field on active service. ' Look at the Robin Hoods !' said a soldier near to us ; ' every man of them looks as though he had shot with William Cloudeslie, and could pick off the Sheriff of Nottingham at a thousand paces ;' and most certainly, if there is any reliance on manly bearing, that old idea, that we thought had perished with Merry Sherwood, lives and moves in the breasts of the brave men in Lincoln green from Nottingham. Not less admired was the little company of Artists costume for that exercise ; and the Irish, in their green uniforms, looked, we must confess, very like their own constabulary ; and we could not pay them a better compliment. . . . If Mr. Bright or any of the ' peace party at any price' were present, it must have galled them to have seen the Manchester corps, 1,600 strong, move along its dark green mass, forming with the Robin Hoods a brigade of themselves. The Lancashire lads, it is clear, are not inclined just at present to beat their swords into pruning-hooks. Neither must we forget the Durham corps, brought to the metropolis by the munificence of Anne, Marchioness of Londonderry. Up to a late hour on the previous Friday these citizen soldiers toiled in the deep mine, in the

counting-house, and behind the counter, then don-
ning their uniform, travelled all night, and appeared
on the ground as fresh as daisies, and after a hard
day's reviewing, hurried northward, and were home
again by daybreak. We question if campaigning
would be much harder work than this.

"The Bristol corps, a regiment of stalwart
Saxons, in like manner came from the other side of
the island; and indeed from all parts the volunteers were drawn to air themselves for a few hours
in the eyes of their sovereign. And her Majesty

Instruction,' 'marching and manœuvring can do no
more than place the soldier in the best possible
situation for using his weapon with effect.' How
are our volunteers to become good marksmen?
Blazing away at a target without any preliminary
instruction is a mere waste of powder and ball;
this fact they have long found out at Hythe. The
public cannot understand this, and there has been a
loud cry in the papers for ball-cartridge practice; but
General Hay will tell you that to begin with ball
practice is to begin at the end. Before a man can

VOLUNTEER REVIEW AT WIMBLEDON IN 1798. (AFTER ROWLANDSON.)

was justly proud of their devotion, and was so
moved that at one time she actually shed tears—
precious tears. What other monarch in Europe,
for such a cause, could shed them? It may be
that we see with partial eyes, but we question if
any country in Europe could send forth such an
army of picked men as defiled before the Royal
Standard on that occasion; and some of the
Parisian journals were handsome enough to say
almost as much. As the French Ambassador, Per-
signy, watched the last volunteer march past him,
he turned to an English friend, and said, 'This is
indeed the handsomest compliment you could have
paid us.' But to drill well and to make good
marksmen are two very different things; or, to use
the language of the 'Hythe Manual of Musket

shoot effectively with a rifle, he must know how to
hold it. At short ranges he can shoot standing;
but when it comes to a thousand yards, he requires
a rest of some kind, and the kneeling position will
give him a natural rest, if he is instructed how to
take it. We question if many of those portly riflemen to be seen in every corps are at all aware of
the trifling knot they must tie themselves up into
ere they can accomplish this position. In the book
of instruction the position drill for long ranges is as
follows :—'When kneeling, the right foot and knee
are to be in the right position, and the body (*i.e.*,
buttock) is to rest firmly on the right heel.' If any
rifleman who has lost his waist will have the goodness to try this position, we would recommend him
to have some assistance at hand to help him up

again! Again, we are told that before a man can take aim with his rifle, he must be able to fire a cap without winking—no such easy matter, as any man may easily prove to himself; and when this difficulty is got over, there is the very necessary exercise in judging of distances. Nothing is so deceptive as distance, especially in level places, where you see the ground foreshortened. All these things are taught at the Hythe School of Musketry, and we are glad to find that a number of volunteers have undergone the musketry drill there with exemplary patience. Nine-tenths of the volunteers are, however, perfectly guiltless of having gone through this preliminary instruction, and we cannot, therefore, expect that until they do any large number of first-rate marksmen will issue from their ranks. But we want a large number of good shots rather than a few first-rate ones; and somehow or other, this we must have. The volunteer rifleman has entered upon a new exercise, in which he cannot afford to take a second rank. He must be with his rifle what his forefathers were with the long-bow; and the only manner in which he can accomplish this is to make rifle-shooting as scientific a pastime throughout the land as cricket.

"Every village and hamlet must have its butts as of old, and village must compete with village. Thus trained, our annual gathering on Wimbledon Common will set in the shade the Tir Fédéral of the Helvetian Republic. The one great quality necessary to form a rifleman is eminently an English quality—steadiness. Strength is another quality almost as indispensable. The weak-armed man has little chance, for his muscles will tremble before he can take deliberate aim. Look at the Swiss rifleman: his chest and arms are models of capacity and power, and we do not think that in these particulars we have to fear even the mountaineers. It is thought by some that our familiarity with the fowling-piece ought to give us a decided advantage over every other nation, but the experience of the Government school at Hythe appears to be altogether adverse to this notion. The best rifle shots declare that the mere sportsman has, in fact, a great deal to forget before he can handle the rifle properly: that the kind of instinctive aim taken at a flying bird is a very different thing from the deliberate aim required for target-shooting: and that the best riflemen are invariably found among persons who had never previously fired a shot. That this dictum required some little modification, however, will, we believe, be proved by the recent competition at Wimbledon Common, for to our knowledge, some of the largest scores have been made by keen sportsmen.

The opening of our first National Rifle Match, on July 2nd, by her Majesty, gave even the used-up sightseer quite a sensation. He witnessed something of which his former experience afforded him no inkling. It was neither a Derby Day, nor a Review Day, nor a Fair Day, and yet in a measure it partook of all three. The wide-extending heath almost prepared him for the grand stand, and the innumerable persons in uniform led him to expect a sham fight. The line of streamers and flags of all nations, and the town of booths running right and left, seemed as if the old fair had been revived for his delectation. But what was the meaning of the long range of earthworks far away on the other side of the common? Of the hundred thousand people who lined the vast enclosure, in carriages and on foot, possibly not a thousand persons could, of their own personal knowledge, have given an answer. That they were butts indeed they knew, but Englishmen must go back some three or four hundred years in order to associate such appliances with any national pastime; and therefore, their appearance seemed in some measure to revive old times, and to link that vast multitude with old days that are long, long gone.

"But whilst we look into the grey distance, and gather from the size of the target—six feet square, but not apparently larger than a sheet of note-paper—what a thousand yards' range really is, there is a motion in the gay marquee on our right; the royal flag is run up, and shortly her Majesty and Prince Albert are seen proceeding down the planked road which leads to the little pavilion. Here for upwards of an hour Mr. Whitworth, with the most nervous solicitude, has been laying a rifle on a rest, specially constructed for the occasion. But the sod is soddened, and the delicate instrument is constantly sinking with its own weight, and has to be continually re-adjusted. As her Majesty approaches, however, all is prepared; and almost before the ringing cheer with which she is received has died away, she has fired the rifle, and hit the bull's-eye, and that only one inch above the two lines which bisect each other in the very centre, on the vertical line itself, and but one inch only above the horizontal one! Thus her Majesty opened the proceedings by scoring three, the highest number that could be obtained at a single shot. Now along the whole line the firing commenced from little tents situated exactly opposite their respective targets; but, as might have been expected, the first day's firing was not very satisfactory, and many a rifleman, the pride of his own local butt, found that in the flurry of the scene he had lost his usual cunning, and loud were the complaints we heard that the five shots—the regulation allowance of each gun—were not sufficient to bring out the real stuff in a man. But with the morning air of the second day shaken nerves were restored again, and Englishmen were not found to be behind the picked shots of Switzerland. It is certainly rather fortunate that the latter should have failed to have rescued their rifles from the French Custom-house authorities; but as they well knew that they could only shoot for some of the prizes with rifles not above ten pounds in weight, they have little to complain of, we apprehend.

"The establishment of an open target, at which all comers can fire without any restriction, is a very lucky hit, and is, in our opinion, well calculated to elicit some very good shots from the crowd. Englishmen have a certain individuality which is likely to display itself in rifle-shooting as much as in other things, and a little "undress" shooting is sure to be very popular. As far as we have yet seen, the National Rifle-shooting Association has inaugurated among us a new sport, which will, we believe, rapidly take root, and place us in the foremost ranks as marksmen. It is a good sign when a nation takes to an exercise as a matter of sport, which it may be called upon to perform in grave earnest; and as long as we know how to snap the rifle, truly we may snap our fingers at the gentlemen across the water."

Mr. W. W. Fenn, in *Tinsley's Magazine* (Vol. XXVI.), recounts his amusing "Recollections of a Volunteer," showing in a pleasant chatty manner how readily a man in good health, and of moderate capacity and intelligence, may become efficiently acquainted with the use of arms, and be turned to good account for his country's defence. "Once brought into contact with the smart, upright drill-sergeant of the Guards," he writes, "taught to hold oneself properly, look to the front, keep one's head up, shoulders back and knees stiff, and generally to comport oneself as if all the world belonged to us; introduced to the 'goose-step' under the name of 'balance-step,' with or without gaining ground; instructed in the mysteries of facing right, left, and about; initiated into the recondite processes of 'fours'— 'forming fours' it was then called—and 'front forming company,' with all the rest of the successive ins and outs of the early stages of manœuvring, the martial spirit was stirred within me, and I devoted myself enthusiastically to the study of my new calling. The enthusiasm was further stimulated by the congenial company in which I found myself. Shoulder to shoulder with friends and brethren of the brush, architects, engravers, musicians, authors, journalists, actors, doctors, &c., the sociability of a club was added to the attractions of our parade; and there was very soon established a spirit of emulation and an *esprit de corps* which I am glad to know still exists, and on a much larger scale in my own regiment."

The following amusing sketch, entitled "Camp Life at Wimbledon," is quoted from *Belgravia* (Vol. III.) :—

" It was a lovely summer's afternoon when Bob Miller and I got out of the train at Putney Station, on our way to the camp. The platform was crowded with volunteers from all parts of the kingdom, who had come down with us to take part in the great national meeting. Well has the camp bard immortalised these noble men—

> " ' Some were short, some were tall,
> Some were big, some were small,
> Some were black, some were blue,
> Others of a greenish hue ; '

and, carried away by the poetic transports of his soul, concluded his strains in a mystic burst of admiration.

" Upon sallying forth from the station we were beset by a host of charioteers, all of whom eagerly professed the delight they should feel at being permitted to drive us to camp. . . . A quick drive up-hill brought us on to the beautiful common of Wimbledom. In the distance, far away across an undulating tract of heath, could be seen a long line of hoarding extending right across the common. Over it peeped the tops of the tents, gleaming snowy white in the hot afternoon sun.

" ' Pretty sight, isn't it?' said Miller, noticing my admiring glances. ' That hoarding rather spoils it, though. You see the windmill away to the left there? The Blue-bottles are camping to the right of it, where that big flag is. That long blue building is Jennings's : you know Jennings? No? He is the great refreshment man. We shall turn off here soon, and go over the common. Ah, here we are! Drive straight into the camp, cabby, and go to the quartermaster-sergeant's tent. Doesn't camp look well, eh? See, there's our post-office, and there's the telegraph station; we've got all the comforts of a town. The head-quarters are round the windmill. That's the notice-board over there, where the orders for the day are posted. Our camp is at the end of this street of tents. There's a jolly tent, isn't it? The luxurious owner has positively got a carpet and a chest of drawers, to say nothing of that small family bedstead. He's been here before, I'll bet. Closely packed those fellows are, are they not? four in a tent. It must be preciously hot and squabby. That's a pretty tent, with the rock-work and flowers outside. The man in it is an artist, perhaps.' . . . The mess-tent was a long booth-like structure, tastefully ornamented inside with flags; down it ran two tables, roughly constructed of plain deal boards, doubtless the work of the mechanically disposed members of the corps. Seated at these were some seventy or eighty men, chatting and joking gaily with each other, doing at the same time ample justice to the abundant and somewhat rude fare before them. Plates and glasses there were none; but in their stead were tin platters, ingeniously devised with a view to holding either liquids or solids, and pannikins, out of which beer, sherry, and champagne were quaffed indifferently. At one end was a table drawn across the tent, forming a kind of refreshment counter, laden with provisions; behind this stood the staff upon whom devolved the duty of administering to the wants of their friends. . . . The loud report of a gun, a signal for the re-commencement of firing, broke up the dinner-party. Some rushed off to shoot in prizes; others to try their luck at the pool or carton targets; others, who had nothing particular to do, proceeded to their tents to do it, the operation in most cases consisting in throwing oneself on a bed, and, pipe in mouth, devoting the passing hour to calm perusal of a novel or newspaper; whilst Miller and I went off to inspect our quarters, and to make the necessary arrangements for our stay."

In February, 1860, the 11th Surrey Rifle Volunteer Corps was duly enrolled, the members being furnished for the most part from the parishes of Wimbledon and Merton. The Wimbledon detachment, now known as the 3rd Surrey Rifle Volunteers, have their permanent ranges on the side of the common nearest Roehampton, as also have the Civil Service and the London Scottish Rifle Corps.

The National Rifle Association holds its meetings on the common annually for twelve days in the month of July, when a large number of valuable prizes are offered for competition. These have increased in number from 67 in 1860 to upwards of 2,000 in 1884, exclusive of challenge cups, the value of which amounts to about £9,000. The principal prize is the Queen's Prize of £250, with which is presented the gold medal and badge of the Association. Among the numerous changes which have been made of late years in the list of prizes is the institution of a series of "evening" prizes.

Considerable interest and enthusiasm are awakened among the volunteers when the competitions take place among what are known as the "champions" of England, Scotland, and Ireland, in the annual contest for the Elcho Challenge Shield. This prize was presented for competition in the year 1862 by Lord Elcho (now Earl of Wemyss), who has been many years Colonel of the London Scottish Rifle Volunteers, and it has been held at different times by the representatives of each of the countries above named. Next in interest, perhaps, is the contest for the Ashburton Shield. This, known as the Public Schools' Prize, was given in 1861 by Lord Ashburton, to be competed for by teams of eight representatives of such public schools as have a *bonâ fide* volunteer corps that is annually inspected and reported upon to the military authorities. The competition is with the Snider at 200 yards and 500 yards, seven shots being allowed at each distance, so that the highest possible aggregate score of each team of eight would be 560.

Among the other prizes may be mentioned the "Vizianagram" Challenge Cup, competed for by members of the two Houses of Parliament; the Chancellor's Plate, by members of the Oxford and Cambridge Universities; the Loyd-Lindsay Prize, for sections of four mounted men from the Yeomanry and Volunteer Horse; the Royal Cambridge Shield, for Cavalry; the National Challenge Trophy, for representatives of Great Britain, Wales, and Ireland; the St. George's Vase and Dragon Cup, restricted to efficient volunteers; and the Brinsmead Challenge Shield, for teams of six against movable targets. In the present year (1884) the entries for the Queen's Prize numbered about 2,460, and for the St. George's about 2,280, the largest numbers ever chronicled. Teams from Canada and India took part in the competition.

Although the "camp" is formed annually in July, the "butts" are permanently established here, and rifle practice is carried on all the year round. There are several of these shooting butts on the common. The communication between them is effected underground; whilst the system of "marking," as well as the squadding of competitors, is carried out upon the most approved plans.

"Apart from its undoubted value as an aid to national defence," observes a writer in the *Pall Mall Gazette*, "rifle-shooting is a manly sport, inciting to honest, sociable rivalry, and may be kept thoroughly wholesome and healthy in all its surroundings. It is pleasant, therefore, to watch its development. A quarter of a century ago there were not, besides the deer-stalkers, a hundred Englishmen who could handle the rifle; now the British riflemen number hundreds of thousands, and throughout the Queen's dominions rifle-shooting has become as much a pastime as was archery in the days gone by. In developing rifle-shooting, therefore, the National Rifle Association has undoubtedly fulfilled one of its principal functions; and not only in the British Association, but also in the numberless National Rifle Clubs which have sprung up in all parts of the world since our Queen fired the famous first shot at Wimbledon, the "Wimbledon Rules" are the basis of all conditions, and the authority for settling all disputes connected with rifle-shooting. This in itself is something to be proud of; but it is still more gratifying to know that our marksmen can now hold their own against the best shots in the world."

CHAPTER LIII.

MALDEN AND MORDEN.

Etymology of Malden—Its Situation and Boundaries—Population—Improvement in the Roads—Descent of the Manor—The Original House of Scholars founded by Bishop Merton—Worcester Park—The Parish Church—Bishop Ravis—The Rev. Edmund Hinton—Situation and Boundaries of Morden—Description of the Village—Census Returns—History of the Manor—The Garth Family—Mr. Abraham Goldsmid—Morden Park—The Parish Church—The Schools.

IT would seem not a little singular that there should be a Malden within ten miles of London on the south-west, and also another Malden—or rather, Maldon—little more than forty miles from London in the north-easterly direction. But the River Thames, as we have before remarked, was, and is, very "dissociabilis;" and doubtless nine-tenths of the East Saxons in Essex lived and died in blessed ignorance that there was another parish bearing so near an approach to the same name as Malden in the neighbouring kingdom of Sudrie, or Suthereye, among the men of the South Rie.

Anglo-Saxon authorities tell us that Malden, or, as it was pronounced, "Maeldune," denotes a cross upon a hill. In the "Domesday Book" it figures as Meldone, and it is there described as a manor, or rather, as two manors, in the parish of Kingston. Malden is a scattered village, very irregularly built, and with scarcely any main street. It is located on the east bank of the Hog's Mill River, in its course between Ewell and Kingston, where it unites with the Thames. The village lies about three miles from Kingston, which parish serves as the boundary of this on the north and north-west; well away on the west and south lie Cheam, Cuddington, and Long Ditton; whilst eastward the parish joins that of Morden.

There are still a few green lanes in the parish; but its rural character is gradually disappearing under the hands of the speculative builder. With the growth of its population, too, which had increased from about 400 in 1871 to rather over 500 in 1881, the character of its inhabitants may be said to have considerably altered; for whereas, ten or fifteen years ago, its population was for the most part agricultural, the means for such industry is now being slowly, but surely, obliterated by the erection of houses and the cutting-up of the land for building purposes. Down to about the year 1850 the main road through the parish was narrow, and almost impassable, in consequence of its deep ruts and miry condition; but on the institution of the Rev. Mr. Stapylton to the vicarage at that time, that gentleman at once set to work as a pioneer, and employed labourers to cut down hedges and trees, which were used in mending the road, with the result that it may now compare favourably with the roads in any other part of the county.

At the time of the Domesday Survey, as stated above, there would appear to have been two manors bearing the name of Meldone; one of these was included among the possessions of the Abbot of Chertsey, and the other among those of Richard de Tonbridge. One of the entries in the Domesday Book is to the effect that "William de Watevile holds Meldone of the fee of the Abbot of Chertsey, who held it in the time of King Edward. . . . . It was, and is, valued at 20s." The other entry states that "Robert de Watevile holds Meldone of Richard de Tonbridge." In the latter entry we also read:—" There is a chapel, and three bondmen, and one mill at 12s., and four acres of meadow, and every seventh hog for herbage. . . . The whole manor, in the time of King Edward, was valued at £7, afterwards at 100s., and now at £6 12s." This statement, observes Brayley, is followed by an account of the manor of Cisendone (Chessington), also held by Robert de Watevile of Richard de Tonbridge ; and it is then added that "one hide in Meldone, held by Robert de Watevile, remains in challenge ; and the jury, or men of the hundred, report that Edward de Sarisburie and Robert de Oilgi reclaimed this land from Richard de Tonbridge, and that it remained quit in the hands of the king."

Walter de Merton, who held the post of Lord Keeper of the Great Seal, and was afterwards Bishop of Rochester in the thirteenth century, appears to have purchased these estates "with a view to the

Scholars" stood on the rising ground by the south side of the churchyard, on the spot now occupied by the manor-house. "In the deed of conveyance to De Merton," it is continued, "a clause was introduced, according to the custom of that age, restraining him from transferring these manors to Jews or to religious foundations. As this clause interfered with the purpose for which they were purchased, he procured a fresh license to convey the property to 'the House of Merton' (*Domui de Merton*) ; and afterwards another, to dispose of it to 'the House of the Scholars of Merton' (*Domui*

MALDEN.

foundation of a college for students." In 1262, as we learn from Brayley's "Surrey," he obtained from Richard de Clare, Earl of Gloucester and Hereford (a descendant of Richard de Tonbridge), as lord of the fee, a deed of confirmation of the property, with liberty to appropriate it to the "perpetual support of clerks residing in schools, and advantageously applying themselves to study." A document bearing date 1263 gives us the earliest stage of the founder's benevolent intentions : it presents to us a family arrangement, placing eight of his nephews under a warden and chaplains in his manor-house, with a life-long provision entitling them "scholares in scholis degentes," and tying them to a life of study and of rule, for they were to forfeit their places should they disregard the "ordinatio" or commit any serious offence. There is a tradition in the parish that the old "House of

Scholarium de Merton). In 1264 he executed a charter of foundation, and in the same year another of confirmation. The house for students, thus established, is generally stated to have been fixed at Malden, and thence transferred to Oxford, where it became distinguished by the appellation of Merton College, from the name of the founder."

In his grants to the new establishment, the founder reserved to himself the occasional use of the manor-houses, with such accommodation for himself and his family during such visits as might be consistent with the support of the scholars. In 1264 he induced the Prior of Merton to release to the college all claims to the advowson of the church of Malden, of which he likewise obtained the appropriation. The members of Merton College appear to have possessed the estate and manor of Malden until the time of Henry VIII., who took from them 120 acres of their demesne lands here, which adjoined some of the lands which he had appropriated for the formation of the great park of Nonsuch, since known by the name of Worcester Park. Elizabeth went even further, for she *compelled* the Mertonians to grant her a lease of their manors of Malden and Chessington, with the advowson and appropriation of the living of Malden, " for the time of five thousand years, at the annual rent of £40." This lease,

that the lease should be retained for the benefit of the then holder for eighty years, and then revert to the college.

Worcester Park, which we have mentioned as having been formed out of the park at Nonsuch,* is still tithe-free, and was, until recently, extra-parochial, but is now annexed to the parish of Cuddington. On this land a number of villas have been built. The place is now rendered familiar to the Londoner by having been made

WORCESTER PARK.

however, her Majesty immediately assigned to Lord Arundel as an equivalent for Nonsuch. Malden next came into the hands of Lord Lumley,* who married a co-heiress of Lord Arundel, and he conveyed it to William Goode, physician to Mary Queen of Scots.

In 1621 the members of Merton College, dissatisfied with the terms on which they had been constrained to give up their estate for a comparatively trifling rent-charge, brought an action of ejectment against the person who then held it, and at length, in 1627, with the consent of the contending parties, the Lord Chancellor made a decree

a station on the railway between Wimbledon and Leatherhead; the station stands within the bounds of Malden parish. It may be added that an outlying portion of the parish, containing a population of nearly 150, has been severed from the mother parish and amalgamated with Chessington. This alteration was effected in 1884, under the Divided Parishes Act of 1879. We have already mentioned New Malden as a hamlet of Kingston-on-Thames.†

The living of Malden has the neighbouring chapelry of Chessington annexed to it.‡ The church, dedicated to St. John, was rebuilt in the

---

* See *ante*, p. 226.

* See *ante*, p. 238.   † See *ante*, p. 316.   ‡ See *ante*, p. 272.

reign of James I. (1610), when the original structure, of flint and stone, was made to give place to a plain piece of brickwork, which about thirty years ago was covered over with stucco. The tower, of brick, profusely covered with ivy, and with its quaint porch, has a picturesque appearance. When the church was rebuilt, the lower portion of the chancel wall, of flint rubble, in which there are some traces of Saxon work, was allowed to remain, but was repaired and altered, the walls being faced with stucco. It contains a piscina in the south wall. In 1863 the interior of the church was restored, when the plaster ceiling was removed and the timbers of the roof shown, and the old-fashioned "pews" made to give place to open benches; a bold arch of English oak—the spandrels filled with elaborate tracery—was constructed at the entrance to the chancel, and a handsome new font of polished Devonshire marble, on a base of Caen stone, was set up. In 1875, in consequence of increased accommodation being required, a new nave and chancel were erected on a larger scale in the Perpendicular style on the north side, and the original north wall being pierced with arches, the old nave and chancel were made to serve as aisle and chancel aisle.

The removal of the chancel necessitated a re-consecration of the church, which was performed by the Bishop of Winchester, the ancient site of the communion-table being marked by the retention of the reredos, and the erection of a large stone slab with the following inscription:—"Here stood the Lord's Table on Maeldune, 'the hill of the Cross,' for well nigh a thousand years, until the consecration of the new chancel, Dec. 7, 1875." The east window of the new chancel is filled with stained glass, representing the Ascension; the east window of the old chancel is also filled with stained glass, the subjects being the Nativity, Crucifixion, and Resurrection; and the west window has been erected by the parishioners, the subject being the Baptism of our Lord. A new reredos, the gift of Mrs. Chetwynd-Stapylton, has been erected; it is of stone, and consists of a framework of bold quatrefoils inlaid with mosaic, the centre compartment being occupied by a cross, with an Agnus Dei on the one side and a pelican on the other. The walls of the new chancel are decorated with mural painting, on either side of the window at the east end being angels bearing the scroll of the *Te Deum*.

In 1883 the old Jacobean pulpit was superseded by a large and handsome pulpit of Caen stone, which has been erected in memory of Mrs. Stapylton, the mother of the vicar. It contains three

beautifully carved alabaster panels, the central subject being "Christus consolator," supported on either side by St. John the Baptist Preaching in the Wilderness and St. Paul at Athens. A dwarf chancel-screen of stone, covered with carved diaper-work, was at the same time erected.

Among the few sepulchral memorials are two mural tablets in the old chancel for former lords of this manor: namely, John Goode, who died in 1627, and Sir Thomas Morley, Clerk-Comptroller of the Green Cloth under James II.; he died in 1693. A grave slab of black marble in the pavement contains the following singular inscription:—

"Here lies John Hamnet, Gent., deceast April 14, 1643. Buried in the dust and grave of his wife, Elizabeth Hamnet, deceast March 30, 1623.

"Deare Consort! well o'ertaken, twice my wife;
In death made one dust, as one flesh in life:
Living, one bedd wee had; now dead, one grave;
Thus twice made one, at last one coveringe have.
Whome God had so together joyn'd, lett none
Asunder put till th' Resurrection,
When wee shall both together wake, though thou
Twenty yeares since to bedd wents't, I but now.
Thrice espoused, why not foure times? 'Tis sed
My Wife and Parish are both widowed."

A small and decayed tomb in the churchyard commemorates Catherine, Lady Walter, wife of Sir George Walter, of Worcester Park, and daughter of Sir William Boughton, Bart. She died in 1733.

Fuller mentions, in his "Worthies," Thomas Ravis, Bishop of London, as "born at Maulden, of worthy parentage." His arms in stained glass, impaled with those of the see of London, are in the east window of the old chancel. It was "by the good means and assistance" of Bishop Ravis that the rebuilding of this church was "begun and brought to pass." On another shield are the arms of Walter de Merton, Bishop of Rochester; whilst a third displays the arms of George Mynors, "who made two pews of wainscot and the pulpit, and paved the belfry and the church porch," in 1610. The porch here referred to was on the south side of the nave, but has been pulled down, and the entrance arch walled up, the present entrance being through the tower.

Bishop Ravis is stated in his epitaph to have been of illustrious parentage (*claris natalibus*), and to have been educated as a King's scholar at Westminster. In 1575 he was admitted a student of Christ Church, Oxford, over which college he afterwards presided as Dean; and he held the Vice-Chancellorship of the University for two years following. In 1604 he was appointed one of the contributors to the common translation of the New Testament. James I., in the same year, promoted him to the see of Gloucester, where, says Fuller, "in so short a time he had gained the good liking of all sorts, that some who could scant brook the name of bishop were content to give, or rather to pay, him a good report." He was transferred to the see of London in 1607, and dying in 1609, was buried in St. Paul's Cathedral.

Another distinguished native of Malden was the Rev. Edward Hinton, D.D., who was born about 1641, as Wood in his "Athenæ Oxonienses," states that "he became a portionist or scholar of Merton College, Oxford, in 1658, aged 17 years or thereabouts." He afterwards removed to St. Alban's Hall, in the same university, where he took the degree of M.A. Subsequently he obtained the mastership of Witney Grammar School, in Oxfordshire, and in 1684 he settled at Kilkenny, in Ireland, and had the degree of D.D. conferred on him at Dublin. His translation from the Greek of "Apophthegms, or Remarkable Sayings of Kings and Great Commanders," was published in the first volume of "Plutarch's Morals" in 1684.

Morden, whither we now direct our steps, lies to the east of Malden, and on high ground, whence the name of the parish is derived, *Mordone*, or *Mordune*—as it was anciently written—signifying in Anglo-Saxon the Great Hill. The entire parish is only about a mile and a half across either way, and the hill slopes gradually into the valley of the Wandle on the one side and into the Sutton and Mitcham Valley on the other, the whole being surrounded by an amphitheatre of higher ground. From the time that we leave Worcester Park railway-station the ground rises gradually, so that by the time we gain the church and village we find ourselves at an elevation which commands a distant view across to Wimbledon, Sydenham, Epsom, and Banstead, and even to Esher and Claremont.

The village is scattered and irregular, and—like its neighbour, Malden—it possesses no regular street; the whole parish, nevertheless, wears an eminently respectable appearance, and the sides of the high road are diversified with villas and residences of London merchants.

The central part of the village—consisting of the church, and a roadside-inn the "George "—well-known to visitors to Epsom during the race-week —lies about a mile and a half south-west from Mitcham railway-station, and about a mile south of Merton, on the high road to Epsom, which in summer is one of the most dusty in the kingdom; indeed, the clouds of dust raised by the hosts of vehicles of every description on a Derby Day surpass those raised by the chariot wheels of the Roman amphitheatre of old.

The soil of the parish generally is a stiff clay, and the land partly arable and partly meadow, whilst the trees are extremely fine, particularly the oaks and other hardy kinds. Altogether, Morden is still decidedly rural in appearance; it has not even, as yet, been cut up and disfigured by a railway. On passing through the village, one can scarcely imagine himself within ten or eleven miles of the centre of "the great city." Not only is the land in the parish little utilised for building purposes, but the population, instead of being on the increase, appears to be rapidly diminishing, for whereas in 1871 the number of the inhabitants was 790, the census returns for 1881 show a falling off of about 100.

Prior to the Conquest the manor of Morden formed part of the possessions of the abbot and convent of Westminster, and it is mentioned among the monastic estates in the charter of confirmation granted by Edward the Confessor, as also in the charters of William I. and Edward I. In the "Domesday Book" it is stated that "the Abbot of St. Peter, Westminster, holds *Mordone*, which in the time of King Edward was assessed at 12 hides; now at 3 hides." For the benefit of such as take an interest in these matters, it may be added that the entry continues :—" There are 3 carucates in the demesne; and 8 villains and 5 cottars, with 4 carucates. There is one bondman; and a mill at 40s. In the time of King Edward it was valued at £6, now at £10, and yet it is worth [or produces] £15."

In the time of King John an estate here appears to have belonged to Isabella de Caron, or Carron, who, in the fifth year of that reign, obtained a "charter for the right of free warren in her lands at Mordon." There was also here, as we learn from Lysons, an estate called Spital Farm, which was granted by Henry VIII. to William Forman, and afterwards became the property of the Garths. It had been held before the Reformation by the Prior of Merton. The Prior of Leeds Abbey, in Kent, also possessed lands in this parish.

At the Dissolution, as we learn from Brayley, the manor became vested in the Crown, and so remained until the seventh year of Edward VI., when it was granted under letters patent to Lionel Duchet and Edward Whitchurch. It was purchased from them in 1553 by Mr. Richard Garth, with whose descendants the estate and manor continued till quite recently.

Sir Samuel Garth, who lived here in the last century, was a great friend of Pope, who writes of him that he was "the best-natured of men, and that he died an heroical death. If ever," he adds, "there was a good Christian, without knowing himself to be so, it was Dr. Garth."

Another member of this family, Elizabeth, the youngest daughter of Mr. George Garth, and widow of Mr. William Gardiner, left a sum of money for the foundation and support of a school for poor children belonging to the parish. Mr. Richard Garth died in 1787, leaving three daughters. He devised his estates to his eldest daughter, Clara, the wife of Mr. Owen Putland Meyrick, with remainder to her second son, and, in default of such son, with similar remainders to his second daughter, Mary, the wife of Sir John Frederick, Bart. Clara, Mr. Meyrick's wife, dying without issue male, the estate descended to Richard, second son of Mr. William Lowndes Stone, who upon his succession assumed the name and arms of Garth.

The old manor-house, about a mile eastward from the church, is now called Morden Hall, and is the property and residence of Mr. Gilliat Hatfeild, a London merchant, the present lord of the manor, which was lately purchased by him from the Garths, of whom the present representative is Sir Richard Garth, formerly M.P. for Guildford, and who, in 1875, was appointed Chief Justice of the High Court of Judicature at Bengal.

Morden Hall is mentioned by the author of the "Beauties of England and Wales," in 1800, as the seat of Sir Robert Burnett. Close by is the elegant seat of the late Mr. Abraham Goldsmid, who here terminated his life in September, 1810. Mr. Goldsmid was the head of the great commercial house which bears his name, and he had been long connected with the Stock Exchange. He was the contemporary of the great Rothschild and Sir Thomas Baring, and one of the pillars of the Stock Exchange, on which his transactions were carried on to the extent of something like a million. A sudden depreciation of some stock in which he had dealt largely having overtaken him, he committed suicide with a pistol in the Wilderness, as a part of the grounds of his mansion was called, in September, 1809. So important was this event that, we are told "expresses were sent off with the news to the king and the Prince of Wales; Consols fell in a few minutes from $66\frac{1}{2}$ to $63\frac{3}{4}$, and Omnium declined from about $6\frac{1}{2}$ to $10\frac{1}{4}$ discount. "A hundred fortunes," writes Mr. F. Martin, in his "History of the Stock Exchange," "went to pieces under the fall of the most trusted pillar of the Stock Exchange."

Morden was well inhabited a couple of centuries ago; at all events, it figures in the "Index Villaris," published in 1700, as the abode of more than three esquires, or gentlemen authorised to bear arms.

It may be mentioned that when the Right Hon. Charles Yorke was raised to the Woolsack in 1770, he elected to take his title as a peer from this village, with which he must have been well acquainted, as his father, Lord Chancellor Hardwicke, lived at Carshalton.* He did not, however, live to enjoy the title, dying before the patent had passed the Great Seal. There has consequently never been a Lord Morden.

About the middle of the last century a Mr. John Ewart built a handsome house on an eminence a little to the north-west of the church. He also enclosed land for a paddock, which he held on a long lease from Mr. Garth. In 1788 he sold the property, which has since several times changed hands. The estate is now known as Morden Park, and the house stands amidst extensive pleasure-grounds, diversified by plantations, sheets of water, and other objects.

The church, dedicated to St. Lawrence, is a long and narrow structure, of red brick, dating from that dark period of ecclesiastical architecture, the reign of Charles I. The building consists merely of a nave and chancel, separated only by a raised step in the floor. Its walls have been denuded of their buttresses—if, indeed, they ever possessed any— and reduced to a Quaker-like plainness, but into them have been inserted the mullions and stone tracery of the Decorated windows of a previous church. At the west end is a low embattled tower containing three bells, but such is the insecure condition of the tower that it is dangerous to ring them. A small porch on the south side of the nave forms the principal entrance. "This church," says Manning, "appears to have been rebuilt about the year 1636, probably at the expense of Mr. Richard Garth, the lord of the manor, who restored the great tithes to the living, and was buried here in 1639." The east window is designed with flowing tracery in the upper part, and is much admired. It is decorated with stained and painted glass, of which the principal portion, namely, Moses and Aaron supporting the Decalogue, with smaller figures of St. Paul and the Gaoler at Philippi, is said to have been brought from the chapel of Merton Abbey, when that building was demolished. The dove and the cherubim in the upper part of the window were executed after the designs of Mrs. Launcelot Chambers, an accomplished lady, long resident in this parish.

The whole interior of the church is in harmony with its exterior. The upper part of the walls on either side, almost from end to end, is covered

---

* See *ante*, p. 203.

with escutcheons containing the armorial bearings of former lords of the soil who have been buried here, whilst the sculptured memorials are numerous, and some of them of an imposing character. Here are monuments, gravestones, and inscriptions in brass to the memory of the Garth, Gardiner, Leheup, Carlton, Meyrick, Lowndes, Batts, Hoare, and other families, but the inscriptions have no general interest. Indeed, the church presents, according to Mr. M. F. Tupper, "its quota of brasses and other monuments." The earliest of these memorials is a small brass in the floor of the

ornamented with quatrefoils; it was probably broken up and buried during the Cromwellian wars, and it is hoped that it will some day be restored and replaced in its original position. The altar-cloth, of crimson velvet, ornamented with gold fringe, &c., is supposed to be about 300 years old. It has been lately renovated. Hone, writing in 1831, mentions the parish church of Morden as "having no antiquity and little beauty to recommend it."

The rectory of Morden, which was once appropriated to Westminster Abbey, was granted, with

MORDEN HALL.

nave, bearing date 1609, and consequently preserved from the earlier church, which is said to have served as a chapel-of-ease to Merton Abbey.

The "sittings" afford accommodation for about 350 persons, and in a gallery at the west end, erected in 1791, is a small organ, the gift of Mr. Charles Hoare, formerly of Morden Lodge. The pulpit, octagonal in form, with a massive sounding-board, is of dark varnished oak; and the font, also of octagonal form, is of stone, with quatrefoil ornaments sunk in the panels, supported by a pedestal. It was executed by Mr. James Legrew, a pupil of Chantrey. The ancient font, also of stone, was discovered during some recent alterations in the nave: it was found smashed and buried. Like the present font, it was apparently

the manor, after the suppression of that monastery. In 1338 the vicarage was endowed with a house and garden and fourteen acres of land. In 1631 Mr. Richard Garth disappropriated the church, and converted the vicarage into a rectory by endowing it with the great tithes and fourteen acres of glebe.

The benefactions to the parish, as appears from inscriptions in front of the gallery, have been numerous.

The Free School, mentioned above as having been founded by Mrs. Elizabeth Gardiner, stands at a short distance from the church. It was built in 1731, and was intended originally for twelve children belonging to the parish, but it is now incorporated with the Endowed National School.

CHAPTER LIV.

MERTON.

Situation and Boundaries of the Parish—The Village and its Surroundings—Paper Mills and Factories—Railway Stations—Population—How the Poor are Robbed—Early Historical Events—Descent of the Manor—Merton Abbey—The Statutes of Merton—Thomas à Becket and Walter de Merton—Dissolution of the Abbey—Remains of the Monastic Buildings—Merton Church—Merton Place—Sir William and Lady Hamilton and Lord Nelson Residents here—The Fate of Lady Hamilton.

MERTON—the *Meretone* and *Meredune* of the chroniclers—is "a very ancient parish and village in the 'Mid' division of Surrey," some eight miles from Westminster Bridge, and five miles east from Kingston-on-Thames. The parish is bounded on the west by Kingston and Malden; northward it unites with Wimbledon; whilst to the east lie Mitcham and Tooting, and to the south rise the swelling uplands of Morden, which we have just left. "Merton," remarks Brayley, "appears to have derived its name from lying adjacent to a mere, or marsh, of which there are traces near the river Wandle, which flows through the parish."

Thanks to the hands of wanton spoilers and ruthless time, little enough is left of the once proud Abbey of Merton, which, standing on the banks of the clear Wandle, on the Epsom road, was once the scene of a meeting of the legislators of our land, which gave birth to the Statutes of Merton, and also to the founder of one of the proud colleges in the University of Oxford—the college which bears its name. Fifty years ago some parts of the chapel and other buildings were visible, but now desolation reigns here as complete as at Chertsey or Barking.* Fifty years ago, too, there were green meadows on every side of Merton, which was as pretty a village as could be found within ten miles of London and Westminster. But now for green fields we must journey on to its neighbour, Morden, which, as we have shown in the preceding chapter, the profane hands of the modern builder and the demon of bricks and mortar have as yet scarcely invaded.

Merton, for some reason or other, does not figure among the villages and towns mentioned in the "Index Villaris," published in 1700. The place is now rapidly extending in all directions. Lower Merton, where the Abbey stood, is on the Wandle, about midway between the parish church and Tooting, and is largely occupied by mills and factories, some of which, however, do not add to the beauty of the locality. An old undershot water-mill, which still exists here, might perhaps at one time have contributed to the picturesque charms of the Wandle. Paper-mills in the north of England, where coal is abundant, employ steam-power; but in the south they are worked by water-power: that is, they are placed on some small stream, which, being dammed up, sets the wheels in motion, as in a flour-mill. "A paper-mill moved by water-power," observes Charles Knight, in the *Penny Magazine*, "is generally a very agreeable object. It is in most instances situated in some little valley through which a little river glides; and as it is important that the water—which is used not only for turning the wheels but also for converting the rags into pulp—should be of the purest quality, the stream is generally one of those transparent ones which are so common in England —now bubbling over pebbly shallows, and now sleeping in quiet depths." The Wandle, which we have already seen at Beddington and Carshalton, is quite a stream of this description. This portion of the parish is now connected by rows of houses with Upper Merton, as that part is called which surrounds the church, southward of which lies Merton Common, but this is now being rapidly built over. The village possesses the advantage of two or three railway-stations: one called Morden station, although it is within the bounds of Merton parish, on the Croydon and Wimbledon branch of the London, Brighton, and South Coast Railway; and others at Merton Abbey and Lower Merton. Of late years the population has been slowly on the increase, for whereas in 1871 the parish numbered only about 2,100 inhabitants, in 1881 it had reached 2,500.

In the chief street, in a garden, stands a row of six cottages, which were evidently built as almshouses for the poor, as over the door of the centre one are the arms and crest of Rowland Wilson, Esq., evidently the founder, with the date 1656, and the Scripture text, "Work while it is called to-day." They have long since been diverted from their original purpose, and are sold or let like other cottages. Three of them are so much out of repair that they can only be used as stables.

Two early historical events have been appropriated to this place—namely, the murder of

---

* See Vol. I., p. 521.

Kenulph, King of the West Saxons, which happened in the year 784, and a battle between the Danes and the Saxons in 871. Lambarde, in his "Topographical Dictionary," however, doubts whether either of these events took place at Merton, in Surrey, and Lysons, in his "Environs of London," seems inclined to be equally incredulous on these points. Camden assigns the death of Kenulph to this Merton ; yet, according to Brayley, the more probable supposition is that Meretune, or

institution which in after years became famous as a home of learning and piety. The principal manor, which belonged to the Crown, was given by Henry I. to this abbey, and it continued to belong to that religious body until the reign of Henry VIII., when the monastic estates were surrendered to the king.

On June 8th, 1215, King John came to Merton, where he gave safe conduct to the Barons, who went in arms against him on their way to Runnymede, where they met a few days later.

" MERTON ABBEY."

Morden, in Wiltshire, a few miles south-eastward of Devizes, was the scene of both transactions.

"Merton," writes Mr. Martin F. Tupper, "is historically known by the murder there of King Kenulph and a battle royal between the Danes and Saxons. . . . The statutes of Merton were concocted in A.D. 1236 within the few remaining fragments of old walls which now enclose the premises of a silk-factor, a cotton-printer, and a leather-dresser." This is terse and epigrammatic, even if not literally true.

The manor of Merton, before the Conquest, was the property of Earl Harold, and was afterwards held by the king in demesne. Early in the twelfth century, Gilbert Norman, Sheriff of Surrey, founded here a convent of Augustinian canons, an

In the last year of Queen Mary (1558) the Carthusian monastery of Sheen was re-founded, and three days before her death the queen, by her letters patent, granted this manor, "with all its rights, members, and appurtenances," to that establishment. On the final suppression of religious houses shortly after, under her sister Elizabeth, the whole reverted to the Crown. In consideration of the payment of £828 8s. 9d., James I., in March, 1609-10, transferred the manor and its appurtenances to one Thomas Hunt, and his wife Joyce (with several remainders), to be held as of the manor of East Greenwich, "in free and common socage, by fealty only, and not in chief or by knight's service." The estate subsequently changed hands on several occasions, by sale or otherwise, and about the end of the last century the old manor-house was pulled down.

Concerning Merton Abbey the following account is condensed from Brayley's "History of Surrey." The original abbey, erected in 1115 by Gilbert Norman, was a wooden building, and is said to have been at the west end of the village, near the parish church; but its exact position is not now known. It was granted by the founder to Robert Bayle, a sub-prior of Austin canons. Two years later, at the latter's suggestion, the establishment was removed to a second house, whither the prior and his fifteen brethren went in procession, singing the hymn "Salve Dies." In 1121 King Henry I. granted the entire manor of Merton, with all its appurtenances, to the canons, in return for £100 in silver and six marks of gold. Here, in 1130, the first stone priory was built, the foundation-stone being laid with great solemnity by Gilbert Norman, who died the same year.

Like St. Peter's at Westminster, the abbey was a sanctuary,* and it will be remembered by readers of history that it was the place to which Hubert de Burgh, the Chief Justiciary of England, fled for refuge when he had incurred the displeasure of his fickle master, Henry III., and divers accusations had pursued the fallen minister. The king at first wished to drag him forth with an armed force, but yielded to the remonstrances of the Earl of Chester and the Bishop of Chichester, and recalled his mandate. After having several times to seek the protection of the Church, de Burgh was ultimately pardoned.

Here, in A.D. 1236, was held the Great Council of the Nation which passed the statutes of Merton, and in which the king and the pope, acting for once in concert, endeavoured to introduce the provisions of the Canon Law, but were met by the famous declaration, *Nolumus leges Angliæ mutari.*

The abbey would seem to have been the nurse of great men. It was within its walls that Thomas à Becket appears to have received his earliest training for the Church. The same was the case with Walter de Merton, afterwards Bishop of Rochester and Chancellor of England, who was a native of the village from which he derived his name, and who founded, as stated above, the college which still bears his name at Oxford. He was also the founder of the college at Malden, of which we have spoken in the preceding chapter.* Having taken holy orders, he united the clerical with the legal

profession, and speedily became eminent in the courts of law. In 1260 he was made Lord High Chancellor, a dignity to which he was appointed twice subsequently. He was consecrated Bishop of Rochester in 1274. He met his death by an accident, having fallen into a river or stream which he was attempting to ford, from the effects of which he died shortly after, in October, 1277. His tomb may be seen in Rochester cathedral.

In the Bodleian Library at Oxford are the "Chronicles of Merton Abbey," which contain the ordinances of William of Wykeham, Bishop of Winchester, for the government of the convent. These, among other restrictions, forbid the canons to hunt, or to keep dogs for that purpose, on penalty of being confined to a diet of bread and ale during six holidays. It appears, however, that this rule was not strictly observed, for we find recorded in a visitation of the abbey by Henry de Woodlock, Bishop of Winchester, his censure on the canons for not attending mass, and for carrying bows and arrows.

Nearly all the Plantagenet and Lancastrian kings in succession granted charters to Merton, and the estates belonging to the foundation were very numerous, and yielded a net annual income of £957 19s. 5½d. Among the possessions of the abbey were the advowsons of many churches in different counties.

Little is known—at all events, little stands recorded—about the history of the abbey when it was in its glory; nor is much told us about the facts which accompanied its surrender to the rapacious Tudor sovereign who "suppressed" it in 1538, and quietly appropriated its revenues, which then a little exceeded £1,000 a year. No engraving of it is known to exist. Its broad lands in Merton were about sixty acres, more or less, which were surrounded by a wall of flint and stone. Much of this wall still remains; many of its bricks are Roman.

After the resumption by the Crown of the Merton estates, Queen Elizabeth granted the buildings and site of the abbey, with the Merton lands, to Gregory Lovell, Esq., Cofferer of the Royal Household, on a lease for twenty-one years, at an annual rent of £26 13s. 4d. In 1600 the estates were granted to Nicholas Zouche and Thomas Ware, as trustees for the Earl of Nottingham, to be held by knight's service at the same rent as before; this quit-rent was afterwards settled on Henrietta Maria, queen of Charles I., as part of her dower. The estates subsequently passed through several private hands, and we find the abbey mentioned in 1648 as a garrison; for the Derby House Com-

---

* See "Old and New London," Vol. III., p. 483.
† See *ante*, p. 510.

mittee were ordered by Parliament "to make Farnham Castle indefensible, and to secure Merton Abbey and other places of strength in the same county." In 1680 Merton Abbey was advertised to be let, when it is described as "containing several large rooms and a very fine chapel."

This abbey is mentioned by Spelman, in his "History and Fate of Sacrilege," who says that in two centuries after the Dissolution it has passed into the hands of eighteen different families, and only twice in that period has descended from father to son.

In 1724 and 1752 two calico-printing works were established within the walls, and at the north-east corner a copper mill was erected, which, Lysons remarks about 1790, employed a thousand persons. These manufactories, however, have been superseded by the silk-printing works of Messrs. Littler. In the rear of these premises stands a curious old mansion, known as Merton Abbey, inhabited by Mr. Littler, the head of the printing-mills close by. It is built of a yellow-ochred brick, and its features are quite of the Dutch type. The new railway between Wimbledon and Tooting runs clean through the site of the ancient abbey, which stood by the side of the Wandle, or rather on both sides of it, the chapel and refectory, if local tradition is true, having been on the eastern bank. The site, after the Dissolution, was, as above stated, granted to Gregory Lovell, Cofferer to Queen Elizabeth, who built here a mansion after the style of the period, working up into it the materials of the dismantled structure. In the garden walls there are three curious Pointed arches, formed with tiles which may be Roman, and which probably marked the end of a cloister or ambulatory. Many of the walls, in fact, have old Roman bricks and tiles worked up into them; and it is quite possible that these may have been part and parcel of the old Roman settlement of Noviomagus, wherever that was situated.

The house is approached through a rude Norman arch, thought to be a fragment of the building erected by Gilbert le Norman about 1130, on which has been placed an Elizabethan entablature. A window of the old chapel and some portions of the exterior walls of the monastic buildings were extant only a quarter of a century ago, but the former has since that date been pulled down, and the latter have been so altered that it is scarcely possible to trace their plan. About the same time nearly half of the house itself was demolished. Of the once grand and historic abbey itself, therefore, little or nothing now remains, beyond a few pieces of its outer walls of brick and stone intermixed, and two or three oblong fish-ponds, which communicate with the river close by, as they did, doubtless, in the Norman times. In such places it is often found that the water suffers less change than the land, as Tennyson sings :—

> " For men may come, and men may go,
> 　But I flow on for ever."

The ponds, however, are now choked up and overgrown with weeds, and nearly dry in summer.

The mansion, which fronts the road, is comparatively modern. On the lawn behind it are two large cannons, which are said to have been placed there by Lord Nelson. The house and its adjoining courtyard, barns, and outhouses, are very spacious.

It is generally thought by strangers that the Abbey House is that which was the favourite residence of Sir W. and Lady Hamilton and of Lord Nelson; but this is not the case, though the tradition may easily have arisen from their having occupied it whilst Merton Place was being prepared for their reception.

The grounds have in them a fine avenue of elms, and some raised terrace walks on the south and west, but of the buildings themselves as clean a sweep has been made as in the case of the two abbeys mentioned above. And yet the abbey—for it was an abbey, and not a mere priory, as it is styled by Mr. Thorne, in his " Environs of London " —was one of the greatest and most important religious houses in England. Its abbot had a seat in the Upper House of Parliament, along with his brethren of Reading, Glastonbury, Abingdon, and St. Albans.

The parish church, which stands at the west end of the village, is a long narrow structure, mostly of the Early English period; but a Norman arch, with zig-zag moulding, apparently of the same date as that above mentioned, surmounts the north doorway. Its roof is tiled, and at the west end is a dwarf timber tower and shingled spire. The walls are cased in flint, and the chancel—recently restored and fairly well decorated—has a row of Early English arches, evidently showing that it was intended to add aisles. These, however, were never made, as is proved by the lancet windows inserted below them. On the south side is a Jacobean mural monument to Gregory Lovell, the Cofferer to Queen Elizabeth of whom we have more than once spoken.

On the walls of the nave still hang several hatchments belonging to great families once connected with the parishes; among them is that of Lord Nelson. On the floor are some slabs to the Stapyltons and others. In the north aisle is a monument to the widow of Captain Cook, the navigator, who lived at Merton for many years. The old roof of the chancel has been brought to light, but whitewash of many years' standing hides that of the nave. On the north door of the nave is some fine iron scroll-work.

In the vestry is a large and handsome picture of the Descent from the Cross, probably a copy of a picture by one of the Italian school. The parishioners desire to sell it, in order to complete the restoration of the church. Within the walls of this church Lord Nelson was a frequent attendant at service. In the church is a painted window to Mr. Richard Thornton, the London millionaire, who left a large bequest for endowing schools in this parish. This benefice, a rectory in the deanery of Ewell, was appropriated to Merton Abbey in the reign of Henry I. King Edward VI., in return for £359, granted it to Thomas Lock and his heirs, from whom it passed through various holders to George Bond and his issue. In his will this estate is described as consisting of "a royalty, the church tithes, the mansion called Merton Place, and two large farms named Merton Holts and West Barnes." The living is now a vicarage in the diocese of Rochester. The registers, dating from 1559, are imperfect. In the churchyard is the tomb of Mr. William Rutlish, embroiderer to Charles II. He died in 1687, bequeathing property of the then value of £400 for apprenticing the children of poor parishioners. In 1866 the church was restored and re-seated, and several of the windows have been filled with stained glass in memory of former parishioners who have passed away.

Besides the parish church, Merton has also a Congregational chapel in the Morden Road, and a Wesleyan chapel in High Street.

Opposite the church stands a dull, heavy Elizabethan mansion, in a square garden of several acres in extent, surrounded by a wall scarcely less massive than those of the old abbey. In front are very handsome entrance-gates of iron between two lofty pillars of brick and stone. In the rear of the house, at the other end, was another similar entrance, now blocked up, beyond which, within the memory of living persons, was a noble avenue. In front of the gates is one of those stone steps for mounting and dismounting which once were so common. The natives avow their belief that it was placed there for the convenience of Lord Nelson when he rode on Sundays to church, but it is clearly of much older date. Towards the end of the last or beginning of the present century the

house was for a time the residence of Richard Brinsley Sheridan; but later on, after being occupied for some years, it was utilised as a convalescent hospital. For the last five-and-thirty years it has been used as a school by a French family named de Chatelain. The interior of the house is almost all lined with panelling of oak and chestnut, and the beams of the roof are of massive timber. The garden is still laid out in the old Dutch fashion, with square paths.

It would naturally be supposed, from its position, that this old mansion was the original manor-house of Merton; but such does not appear to have been the case. At all events, near the middle of the village, not far from the spot where the roads branch off to Kingston and to Epsom respectively, is a farm long known as the Manor Farm. Possibly there were two manors in Merton.

Merton was a favourite abode of Lord Nelson, and is often mentioned in his "Life." His residence was called Merton Place, and he lived there, with Sir William and Lady Hamilton, from 1801 till 1803, and indeed afterwards occasionally visited it down to the time he left England for Trafalgar. Mr. Martin Tupper asserts that Merton Place was bought by Lord Nelson, and seems to think, somehow or other, that because the grounds were laid out by Lady Hamilton, "neither conscience nor memory could have there found peace."

There is still living at Merton, in possession of all his faculties, a hale and hearty man, named Hudson, over ninety years old, who well remembers Lord Nelson as a visitor here, and who stood by the door of the post-chaise in which, early on the morning of September 13th, 1805, the gallant admiral—so soon afterwards doomed to fall at Trafalgar—drove off from Sir William Hamilton's gates. He states that, as a boy, he used often to see Nelson fishing in the Wandle, near the Abbey Mill, and sauntering with Sir William and Lady Hamilton about their pretty grounds, which extended on both sides of the high road. The admiral would often stop and speak kindly to the boys who were at play in the street, and who regarded his weather-beaten form and features possibly with all the more reverence because of the fruit and the pence which he would bestow on the youngsters. Two cottages at the bottom of the Abbey Lane, he says, were built by Lord Nelson for his coachman and gardener—so entirely had a community of goods been carried out by this affectionate trio; in one of these he and his wife, a daughter of Cribb, Nelson's gardener, have lived for upwards of half a century. This cottage is marked by a mulberry-tree, which Nelson desired to be planted there. Over the mantelpiece of his little dwelling is a mirror in a gilt frame, which once formed part of the ornaments of Nelson's room in Sir William Hamilton's house, and this he and his wife treasure as their only relic of the admiral.

Merton Place itself, he told me as I sat in his room and chatted, was occupied before the Hamiltons by a family named Graves, who were in business in London; he just remembered their going and the Hamiltons' coming, so that their tenancy must have commenced about 1800. Nelson's association with the place, as may be seen by a reference to his "Life" by Southey or Pettigrew, did not begin till October, 1801, when he had just returned to England, after his magnificent exploit at the battle of Copenhagen. He continued to make Merton his head-quarters down to May, 1803, when he was ordered again to sea, but he again visited it from time to time, whenever he could be spared ashore. Hudson told me that when Nelson was away Lady Hamilton was always busily engaged in furnishing the house and improving the grounds, and that he well remembered the little streamlet which was made artificially to flow through the grounds, and which, in compliment to Nelson, she called "The Nile." It has long been filled up, and its site turned into gardens for the rows of cottages which have been built on all four sides of the estate.

Sir William Hamilton, on returning home after his first interview with Nelson, told Lady Hamilton that he was about to introduce to her a little man who could not boast of being very handsome, but who would become the greatest man England ever produced. "I know it," he said, "from the very few words of conversation I have already had with him. I pronounce that he will one day astonish the world. I have never entertained any officer at my house, but I am determined to bring him here; let him be put in the room prepared for Prince Augustus." Nelson is stated to have been equally impressed with Sir William Hamilton's merits. "You are," he said, "a man after my own heart; you do business in my own way. I am now only a captain, but, if I live, I will be at the top of the tree."

We have no space for the many stories and anecdotes that might be told concerning Nelson's life at Merton; but I may be pardoned for repeating the following:—Dr. Burney, who wrote the celebrated anagram on Lord Nelson, after his victory of the Nile, " Honor est a Nilo " (Horatio Nelson), was shortly after on a visit to his lordship at his beautiful villa at Merton. From his usual absence of mind, he forgot to put a nightcap into his portmanteau, and consequently borrowed one from his lordship. Previously to his retiring to rest, he sat down to study, as was his common practice, and was shortly after alarmed by finding the cap in flames; he immediately collected the burnt remains, and returned them to his lordship with the following lines :—

"Take your nightcap again, my good lord, I desire,
    I would not detain it a minute ;
  What belongs to a Nelson, wherever there's fire,
    Is sure to be instantly in it."

Nelson, it seems, first became acquainted with Lady Hamilton at Naples, and here the great naval hero used to visit her. It has been remarked by a writer in *Blackwood* that "of her virtues, unhappily, prudence was not one. After the death of Nelson, and the disgraceful disregard of her claims by the Government, her affairs became greatly embarrassed. Those who owed wealth and honours to Nelson, and who had sunned themselves in her prosperity, shrank away from her. In her distress, she wrote a most touching letter to one who had courted her smiles in other days, the Duke of Queensberry, imploring him to buy the little estate at Merton, which had been left to her by Nelson, and thus to relieve her from the most pressing embarrassments. The cold-hearted old profligate turned a deaf ear to the request. In 1813 Emma Hamilton was a prisoner for debt in the King's Bench. Deserted by the great, the noble, and the wealthy, abandoned by the heir of his title and the recipient of his hard-earned rewards, she, whom Nelson had left as a legacy to the country, might have died in a gaol. From this fate she was saved by one whose name is not to be found in the brilliant circle who surrounded her but a few short years before. Alderman Joshua Jonathan Smith (let all honour be paid to his most plebeian name) redeemed his share of his country's debt, and obtained her release."

After Nelson's death, the "disconsolate Emma," as she so often styled herself, lived on at Merton in her doubly-widowed condition, for her husband had died two years before. She was, however, but a bad woman of business, and this, coupled with her profuse generosity and hospitality, brought her into pecuniary difficulties, from which the ungrateful country to whose care Nelson had confided both her and her infant Horatia, did not care to extricate her, though she had helped Nelson, by her readiness of resource, when in Italy, to win one sea-fight, at all events. Even his brother, who owed him a canonry in Canterbury Cathedral, an earldom, and a pension of £6,000 a year, and who had sat and dined with him at Lady Hamilton's table two short months before his death at Trafalgar, declined to assist her with even the loan of a few pounds, and found it convenient to plead in excuse all sorts of scruples on the ground of morality, which would have been more real and more to be respected had they existed in the days of Lady Hamilton's prosperity. Her pecuniary difficulties, therefore, forced her to sell Merton, which she quitted with many a pang, to die a few years later

children of a sister, Lady Hamilton at the head of the table and Mother Cadogan at the bottom. He looks remarkably well and full of spirits. . . . Lady Hamilton has improved and added to the house and the place extremely well, without his knowing she was about it. He found it already done. She is a clever being, after all."

The sort of life led by Nelson whilst he was an inmate of the house of the Hamiltons at Merton may be gathered from another letter of the same individual, under date March 22nd, 1802 :—" I

LORD NELSON AND LADY HAMILTON.

in poverty at Calais. Such is the gratitude of great people, and, indeed, of the world at large !

By this remark it is not intended to justify in the slightest degree the relations of Lady Hamilton with Lord Nelson; but certainly it was cruelty and mockery of the reverend gentleman, who profited so largely by his brother's death, to disown in her poverty the lady at whose table he had been so willing to sit as a guest. To prove this fact it is necessary only to quote the following extract from a letter addressed to his wife by Sir Gilbert Elliot, afterwards first Earl of Minto, August 26th, 1805 :—" I went to Merton on Saturday, and found Nelson just sitting down to dinner, surrounded by a family party of his brother the Dean, Mrs. Nelson, their children, and the

went to Lord Nelson's on Saturday to dinner, and returned to-day in the forenoon. The whole establishment and way of life such as to make me angry as well as melancholy. . . . She [Lady Hamilton] and Sir William, and the whole set of them, are living with him at his expense. She is in high looks, but more immense than ever. She goes on cramming Nelson with towelfulls of flattery, which he goes on taking as quietly as a child does pap. The love she makes him is not only ridiculous, but disgusting ; not only the rooms, but the whole house, staircase and all, is covered with nothing but pictures of her and of him, of all sizes and sorts, and representations of his naval action, coats of arms, pieces of plate in his honour, the flagstaff of ' L'Orient,' &c."

Many passages might be quoted from Nelson's letters to Lady Hamilton, all showing how fondly attached he was to Merton, where doubtless he spent many of his pleasantest hours, in the company of a woman whom he so passionately adored. The following extract from one of these will serve as a specimen :—" I would not have you lay out more than is necessary at Merton. The rooms and the new entrance will take a deal of money. The entrance by the corner I would have certainly done ; a common white gate will

The house and furniture, the grounds, and all their contents, were sold about the year 1808 to Mr. Asher Goldsmid, a Jewish banker, who made the place his abode for a time. Nelson's study, as Mr. Hudson informed me, and some of the other rooms, were long preserved in the same condition as when they had been left by Lady Hamilton, and the library was not sold till about sixty years ago.

The stabling, as well as one pleasure garden and grove, were situated on the opposite side of the road, access being obtained to them by an underground tunnel which passed beneath the street. In this grove there was a mound surrounded by trees, and ending in a summer-house, in which the Hamiltons and Nelson would sit on the long

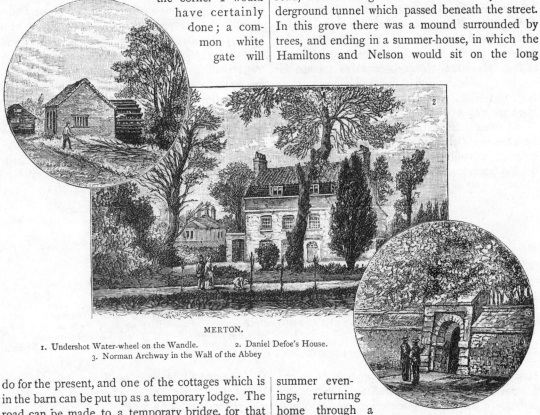

MERTON.

1. Undershot Water-wheel on the Wandle.　　2. Daniel Defoe's House.
3. Norman Archway in the Wall of the Abbey

do for the present, and one of the cottages which is in the barn can be put up as a temporary lodge. The road can be made to a temporary bridge, for that part of the 'Nile' one day shall be filled up. Downing's canvas awning will do for a passage. . . The footpath should be turned . . . and I also beg, as my dear Horatia is to be at Merton, that a strong netting, about three feet high, may be placed round the ' Nile,' that the little thing may not tumble in, and then you may have ducks again in it."

To this may be added an extract from Nelson's " Diary," given by Sir Harris Nicolas :—

" Friday Night, 13th September, 1805.

" At half-past ten drove from dear, dear Merton, where I left all that I hold dear in this world, to go and serve my king and my country. May the great God whom I adore enable me to fulfil the expectations of my country !"

summer evenings, returning home through a green gate which opened in the wall by a key from within. The stables, after having been made to do duty for a time as cottage-residences for persons of the working class, were finally pulled down in 1882, and the site in due time will be covered by houses.

The little estate occupied by the Hamiltons covered about thirty acres ; it stood just to the south of the old abbey walls, from which it was severed only by a narrow lane, called then, as now, the Abbey Road. The house was only one storey high above the ground-floor, built of plain brick, and almost surrounded by a verandah, up which the rose, clematis, woodbine, honeysuckle, and other creepers, grew freely at their own sweet will. It did not face the road, but looked south, to which side the drive-way led round from the entrance-gates, by the side of which stood a lodge-gate. This lodge is now converted into a grocer's shop, close by which is an inn, "The Nelson's Arms," still perpetuating the name of the admiral. In the bar is an original portrait of Nelson in colours, which goes as a fixture or heirloom with the house, and authenticates it. The worthy landlord values this picture greatly, and has refused very high offers for it.

"Not far from the Merton turnpike, and within a few miles of London," wrote the *Times*, August 22nd, 1849, "there is to be seen a field upon which stood the home of Nelson and of his mistress. It was left, with its debts and liabilities, to Lady Hamilton. These were large enough, for extravagance accompanied the meridian of her life, as it had characterised the dawn. The Government proving obdurate to the last, the owner of Merton was dismissed from the place. She went for a time to Richmond, and then took temporary lodgings in Bond Street. Here she was chased by her importunate creditors, and for a time hid herself from the world. In 1813 we find her imprisoned in the King's Bench for debt, but charitably liberated therefrom by a City alderman. Threatened again with arrest by a coachman, the unhappy woman escaped to Calais. Here the English interpreter gave the refugee a small and wretchedly furnished house." She died at Calais, as we have said, having been glad to accept the scraps of meat which were put aside for the dogs, and at her death her remains were placed in a deal box without an inscription, her pall being a black silk petticoat, lent by a poor woman for the occasion. As no clergyman could be found in Calais, an Irish half-pay officer read the burial service over her ; and as the cemetery in which she was buried shortly after was turned into a timber-yard, the ultimate fate of her bones is not known, and will not be known till the judgment day. Such was the end of the once brilliant, and, in spite of all her faults, patriotic lady, who a few years previously had helped Nelson to win his laurels. Alas ! for the charity of those who stood aloof from her at the last, when Christian charity was needed.

CHAPTER LV.

MITCHAM.

Etymology of Mitcham—Situation and Boundaries of the Parish—General Description of the Village—The River Wandle—Mills and Factories—The Cultivation of Flowers and Medicinal Plants—Mitcham Common—The Green—Mitcham Famous for Cricketing—Railway Communication and Population—The "King's Head"—A "Mitcham Whisper"—History of the Manor—Hall Place—Rumball's Farm—The Cranmer Family—The Parish Church—The Registers—Christ Church—Schools and Chapels—Dr. Roberts' School—Miss Tate's Almshouses—Visit of Queen Elizabeth to Sir Julius Cæsar—Sir Walter Raleigh—Dr. Donne—Mitcham Grove—A Relic of Antiquity—Mitcham a Rallying-point for Nonjurors—Defoe's House—Moses Mendez, the Poet, a Resident here.

MITCHAM, in its origin, is the same as Mickleham : the great home, or village. In Saxon times it was probably a place of considerable population and importance : hence its name.

In the Domesday Survey this parish is designated Michleham ; and in other early records, as well as in many of more recent date, it is written *Miecham*, or *Micham*. Its present mode of spelling, which is further from its etymology, observes Brayley, was not universally adopted earlier than the middle of the last century.

It is strange that there should have been a Mitcham and a Mickleham within ten or twelve miles of each other—strange, at least, on the supposition that names were given for the sake of distinction, and in that case proving how little intercourse could have prevailed between districts almost in the same neighbourhood.

The parish is environed on the north and west by Merton and Morden, whilst on the east it is bounded by Streatham, and on the south it unites with Croydon ; and locally it is divided, by a narrow thoroughfare called Wykford, or Whitford, Lane, into two portions, called respectively Upper and Lower Mitcham.

The village is very scattered. The main street extends about a mile along the high road between Tooting and Sutton, but the houses are very irregular in size and in distances.

Many old mansions, with wrought-iron gates and cedars still standing, attest that the place in former times was inhabited by not a few of the wealthier class. The River Wandle, which follows the line of the roadway through the parish, where it has not been disfigured by mills and factories adds not a little to the beauty of the level scenery hereabouts. There is a capital view of the Wandle at this point in *English Etchings* for November, 1882. Here on the banks of the Wandle are a large number of flour, paper, and oil mills; the last-named trade, it may be added, is not allowed to come nearer to London, as not being very pleasant to the olfactory nerves. People who live here have need to be addressed in the words of the Roman satirist—

"Nec te fastidia mercis
Ullius subeant ablegandæ Tiberim ultra."

The soil of the parish is principally a rich black mould, and for upwards of a century a large portion of the land hereabouts has been cultivated for the production of sweet herbs and medicinal plants. Poppies, mint, liquorice, aniseed, and chamomiles, have long been extensively grown here. One of its old horticulturists thus amusingly sung the praises of his little garden :—

"The jessamine, sweet-briar, woodbine, and rose,
Are all that the west of my garden bestows;
And all on the east that I have or desire
Are the woodbine and jessamine, blush-rose, and briar;
For variety little could add to the scent,
And the eye wants no change where the heart is content."

Mitcham, it may be stated, is remarkable for the extent to which roses and other flowers are cultivated, and, in fact, the parish has long been celebrated for its "flower-farms." In summer-time the air is perfumed by whole fields of roses, lavender, and sweet and pleasant herbs; and probably there is not in all the kingdom a single parish on which the wholesale druggists and distillers of the metropolis draw more largely for their supplies. The mulberry-tree doubtless flourished here in abundance at one time. In almost all the old gardens in the suburban districts, both north and south of the Thames, is to be seen at least one mulberry-tree, generally of a very venerable age. This is to be regarded as the consequence of an edict of the English Solomon, James I., who took it into his head that if the common people would cultivate silk-worms, and the upper-class plant mulberry-trees for their food, there would be seen a great reduction in the mass of national poverty.

Eastward of the village stretches the broad expanse of Mitcham Common, some 500 acres in extent. On the side towards the Reigate road its surface is broken up into low hills. This open, breezy spot is for the most part bare and bleak, and on it the wild gorse still abounds and the broom still blooms. This common, as we learn from Weale's "London and its Vicinity," "is an immense but not very pleasing tract, being so completely unplanted, and having very few villas on its margins. It is, however, an admirable open plot, with good views of the Norwood and Streat-ham hills on one side, and prospects of other parts of the country on the south-west. We have also found it," adds the author, "an interesting place for a botanising ramble, *Genista anglica*, *Spiræa filipendula*, and many other by no means common plants being plentifully found there. On the south side it is bounded by the plantations which screen Beddington Park.

The natives of Mitcham and its neighbourhood, it need scarcely be said, are very jealous of encroachments : for instance, when, in 1882, a portion of this common near Beddington,* hither-to used as a cricket and recreation ground, was taken for building purposes by the lord of the manor, an approach to a riot took place, which ended in the case being brought before the magis-trates at the Croydon Petty Sessions. It appears that notice-boards had been put up announcing that the land would be let or sold, and that henceforth no cricket or other games would be per-mitted. Whereupon, one James Cummings, another "village Hampden," and other commoners, in the assertion of their right, assembled, and took the liberty of clearing the ground of the notice-boards and of a builder's office which had been erected on the ground. For taking part in this attempt to establish a legal claim, James Cummings was charged with wilful damage. But the magistrates held that the accused was within his right, and dis-missed the case. Again, as recently as the present year (1884) it was rumoured abroad that Mitcham Common was being seriously encroached upon and disfigured by digging pits for gravel; and the aid of Londoners in protecting this fine open space, it is to be feared, is still urgently needed.

Over this common young Charles Mathews used to ride his pony as a boy in the early summer mornings whilst at school at Dr. Richardson's, at Clapham. Dr. Johnson, too, used often to drive along the roads about here in the carriage of his kind hostess, Mrs. Thrale, of Streatham. On one occasion Mrs. Thrale (Piozzi) records a "just rebuke" which she received from the doctor's lips. She writes in her "Anecdotes":—"After a very long summer, particularly hot and dry, I was wishing naturally, but thoughtlessly, for some rain to lay the dust as we drove along the Surrey roads. 'I cannot bear,' replied Johnson, with much asperity, and an altered look, 'when I know how many poor families will perish next winter for want of that bread which the present drought will deny them, to hear ladies sighing for rain only that their complexions may not suffer from the heat or their

* See *ante*, p. 197.

clothes be incommoded by the dust. For shame! leave off such foppish lamentations, and study to relieve those whose distresses are real'"

The village green here would be called a common elsewhere. It is a triangular space by the high road to Sutton and Epsom. It has some fine pollard elms on either side, and is well kept as a cricket-ground. Here the American and Australian teams have arranged matches for this summer (1884).

According to "Lillywhite's Cricket Scores," Mitcham is a famous village in the annals of cricket. The ground is at Lower Mitcham Green. The "Mitcham eleven" were among the most famous provincial clubs in the "good old days" when George IV. was king, and even later on, and it is still constantly in use for matches.

At the corner of the green is a small obelisk of stone, just inside the grounds of Canons. It was erected in 1822 by the Rev. Mr. Cranmer, then rector, who lived here, in order to commemorate the happy discovery of water by the sinking of an artesian well. It bears an inscription of thanks to Almighty God for the discovery, which really was a boon to the poor at that time, the village not being well supplied. Shortly after the erection of the monument, however, the supply of water failed, the inscription has been allowed to grow illegible, and the fountain has been taken within the railings of the park.

From its pleasant and rural situation, then uninvaded by railroads and excursionists, Mitcham has long been "noted for good air and choice company," as the author of "Murray's Handbook to Surrey" observes; but this is no longer the case, as the village now enjoys the advantage of railway communication with the metropolis, having a station on the Croydon and Wimbledon branch of the London, Brighton, and South Coast Railway. Of late years, too, the population has considerably increased, for whereas in 1871 it numbered about 6,500, of whom 450 were inmates of the Holborn Union Industrial Schools, in 1881 it had amounted to about 9,000.

The "King's Head" is an old inn, and could tell some stories of the past if its walls had the gift of speech, especially of those who have gone by road to the "Derby" and the "Oaks" at Epsom.

In the "judicious" Puttenham's "Art of English Poesie"—one of the first blossoms of the Elizabethan period of our literature—it is observed that the Northern men and those of the West Country, though their speech was more purely Saxon, were less polished in their talk than natives of the shires lying around London, "within sixty miles, and not much above"; and he claims for the gentlemen of Middlesex and Surrey, though not for the common herd, the best usage in talking and writing.

Hazlitt tells us, in his "English Proverbs," that "a Mitcham whisper" in Surrey denotes "a loud shout." Judging from Puttenham's standard, however, this remark would appear to apply only to the "common herd."

At the time of the Domesday Survey there would appear to have been five manors in this parish; there are now only three—Mitcham (proper), or Canon, Biggin and Tamworth, and Ravensbury. The manors of Michelham and Witford, held by the Canons of Bayeux at the time of William the Conqueror, are supposed by Manning (see "Surrey," Vol. II., p. 495) to have been retained by them until the reign of Edward III., who, on declaring war against France in 1338, confiscated all the estates belonging to alien priories and abbeys in this country, and gave Mitcham to the Priory of St. Mary Overy, in Southwark. "On the suppression of monasteries in the reign of Henry VIII.," observes Brayley, "this estate, falling into the hands of the king, was granted by letters patent to Nicholas Spakman and Christopher Harbottell, citizens of London. In 1552 they conveyed the estate to Lawrence Warren, by whom it was sold in the following year to Nicholas Burton, of Carshalton. In the year 1619, Sir Henry Burton, K.B., the grandson of Nicholas, transferred (by sale) the manor of Mitcham, or Canon, with the rectory and advowson, to Sir Nicholas Carew, *alias* Throckmorton, whose son and heir, Sir Francis, in 1645, settled it on his daughter Rebecca, on her marriage with Thomas Temple, Esq.; and in 1647, in conjunction with his son-in-law, he mortgaged the estate to Thomas Hamond, Esq. In 1656 and 1657 the parties joined in a sale to Robert Cranmer (said to have descended from the family of Archbishop Cranmer), of London, merchant, who in 1659 purchased the parsonage (or manor-house), which had been separated from the rest of the estate. Mr. Cranmer died in 1665, and his grandson, James Cranmer, Esq., left this property to his sister, Esther Maria, wife of Captain Dixon, for her life, with remainder to her son, the Rev. Richard Dixon, who assumed the name of Cranmer; and to him the Mitcham estate belonged in 1809. It is now the property of William Simpson, Esq., who, with James Bridger, Esq., is joint lord of the manor."

Hall Place is the name of a modern mansion between the church and the green. It doubtless stands on the site of an old mansion, as is clear from the old and massive range of stabling, and two rows of venerable yews which lead up to its front door from the road. At the corner of the house is a stone gateway, well-carved, with a Pointed arch and corbels, evidently not later than the fifteenth century. It is said to have formed a portion of some conventual building ; but whether *in situ* or not is uncertain.

On the west of the common, close by the Mitcham Junction railway-station, is an old farm-house, known as Rumball's or Rumbolt's, which local tradition asserts to have been a country residence of Archbishop Cranmer. The house has been so denuded of every ornament that it is impossible to fix the date of its erection, but the timbers in the upper storey are of oak, and may be three centuries old. The house has now a forlorn and woe-begone appearance, and it is approached from the railway by a very fine avenue of trees.

Mitcham is associated more closely than almost any other parish with the Cranmers. That family owned once a large mansion, still called Cranmer's, and some of them also resided at another old-fashioned mansion, known as Canons. The last of the Cranmers married a Mr. Simpson, one of the lords of the manor of Mitcham, and pastor and rector of the living, and died less than half a century ago, her maiden name, as well as her hus-band's name, being recorded on a tomb on the south side of the churchyard.

The old church, dedicated to St. Peter and St. Paul, was built chiefly of flint, and it consisted of nave, two aisles, and a chancel, with a square embattled tower crowned with a turret at the west end of the south aisle. In 1637, according to Aubrey, it was greatly injured by lightning, and had ten bells destroyed. This church remained until the present century, when, in consequence of the increase of population, it became desirable to rebuild it upon a more enlarged scale. The fabric was accordingly pulled down at the beginning of the reign of George IV., and rebuilt in the style of that most dreary period, when churchwardens and " compo " architects ran riot without fear of censure from a public which knew little and cared less about the mysteries of " the Gothic " style.

The "restorers," however, must have had a fine time of it with the monuments in the old church ; at all events, they have left few survivals in the present structure.

The new church was built exactly on the site of the old. It is, by comparison, a rather good specimen of the Gothic of the Georgian era ; and it seems to have been erected regardless of expense, both the nave and the side aisles being vaulted in stone or cement.

The monuments taken out of the old church are fixed on the walls. A very fair chancel, in the ancient style, has lately been added. The lower part of the tower is a relic of the old one. It stands at the *east* end of the south aisle of the present church, and on the right of the entrance from the south is a niche in the wall, divided into two com-partments by a shelf. In the lower compart-ment was a piscina ; in the upper a lamp was accustomed to be kept burning. The tower is now in four storeys, with octagonal buttresses, terminating in crocketed stone pinnacles, with large finials. The top is surrounded by a pierced battlement. With the exception of the lower part of the tower, the material of the new church consists of " brick and compo." The rebuilding of the church, which was completed in 1822, is commemorated by the following inscription on the north side of the chancel :—" In token of respect, gratitude, and affection to one of the most ex-cellent of mothers, Mrs. Hester Maria Cranmer, late patroness of this vicarage church of Mitcham, who died the 17th January, 1819, and with whom the rebuilding of this sacred edifice originated ; this stone was laid on the 27th of August, 1819, by the present impropriator, the Rev. Richard Cranmer, LL.B. George Smith, architect ; John Chart, builder. The boundary of this chancel extends thirty-four feet seven inches westward from the centre of this stone."

The church, as it now stands, consists of nave and side aisles, chancel, north aisle, and tower. The nave is divided from the aisles by four pointed arches resting upon columns, formed by a union of cylinders with plain capitals. The chancel, separated from the nave by a narrow Pointed arch, has a gallery on the north side. The altar-piece consists of four Pointed panels, inscribed with the Decalogue, Creed, &c.

Beneath the great west window, in a recess formed by a large Pointed arch, is a monument to Sir Ambrose Crowley, alderman of London, and his lady, the former of whom died in 1713, the latter in 1727. In the old church this monument occupied a space on the north side of the chancel. Sir Ambrose Crowley is the worthy alderman whom Steele held up to ridicule in the *Tatler* (No. 73) as having, in order to check bribery at city elections, promised, as an acknowledgment of their favour, a " chaldron of good coals gratis to every elector of Queenhithe " who engaged to poll for him.

Among the memorials in the church, chiefly of a mural character, is one in the north aisle to Mrs. Elizabeth Tate, who died in 1821 ; it was executed by Westmacott, and represents a female figure with a cup in the left hand, and pointing to the skies with the right; and amongst the tombs in the churchyard is that of Mrs. Anne Hallam, a favourite actress of the early part of the last century, celebrated for her performance of Lady Macbeth and Lady Touchwood. She died in the year 1740.

The registers are well kept, and go back to the reign of Henry VIII. Among the entries are the two following :—" Anne, the daughter of George Washford, who had twenty-four fingers and toes ; baptised October 19th, 1690." " Widow Durant, aged one hundred and three years, buried September 23rd, 1711."

In the year 1872 a new ecclesiastical district, called Christ Church, was formed in this parish. The church, with parsonage and mission-house adjoining, is situated in Merton Lane. It is constructed of brick and stone, in the Gothic style, and was built in 1874, at the expense of Mr. W. J. Harris, of Corringe Park.

The parish possesses its national and board schools, and also Dissenting and Roman Catholic chapels. On the road-side in Upper Tooting stands a large new building, the Holborn District Schools ; the managers have " annexed " a fine old mansion close by.

Early in the present century there was here a celebrated private school, kept by a Dr. Roberts ; the late Lords Derby and Carlisle, Dr. Pusey, and his brother, the scientific agriculturist, Mr. Philip Pusey, M.P., and also Sir T. D. Acland, were educated at it before passing to Eton.

In the year 1829 a row of almshouses, after the style of architecture which was prevalent in the latter part of the sixteenth century, was built, at the expense of Miss Tate, on the south side of the Lower Green. These houses were designed by the founder for twelve poor widows or unmarried women of respectable character, members of the Church of England.

Amongst those who at various times have resided here was Sir Julius Cæsar, Master of the Rolls in the reign of Queen Elizabeth, whom he had the honour of entertaining here in September, 1598, when her Majesty was on her way to Nonsuch. Nichols, in his " Progresses of Queen Elizabeth," gives the following particulars of this visit, quoted from a MS. of Sir Julius Cæsar in the British Museum :—" On Tuesday, September 12th, 1598, the Queen visited my house at Mitcham, and supped and lodged there, and dined there the next day. I presented her with a gown of cloth of silver, richly embroidered; a black net-work mantle, with pure gold ; a taffeta hat, white, with several

flowers, and a jewel of gold set therein with rubies and diamonds. Her Majesty removed from my house after dinner the 13th of September to Nonsuch with exceeding good contentment, which entertainment of her Majesty, with the charges of five former disappointments, amounted to £700 sterling, besides mine own provisions, and whatever was sent unto me by my friends."

It is said that Sir Walter Raleigh, in right of his wife, owned here a house which has not been very long since pulled down. The mansion, which in its latter years was occupied as a boarding-school, stood at the corner of Whitford Lane, and was known as Raleigh House. Sir Walter sold the property here when he went on his expedition to Guiana.

Dr. Donne,* the learned and pious Dean of St. Paul's, too, lived here for some time before he took orders. One of his letters is dated " from my hospital at Mitcham." Dryden said of Donne that he was " the greatest wit, though not the greatest poet, of our nation;" and Dr. Johnson called him " the founder of the metaphysical school of poetry." In Dugdale's " History of St. Paul's " it is stated that some time before his death, when he was emaciated with study and sickness, Donne " caused himself to be wrapped up in a sheet, which was gathered over his head in the manner of a shroud, and having closed his eyes, he had his portrait taken, which was kept by his bedside as long as he lived, to remind him of mortality. The effigy on his monument in [old] St. Paul's Church was done after this portrait." Dr. Donne died in March, 1631.

Mitcham figures as " Micham " in the " Index Villaris," published in 1700, and is described as containing the seats of one baronet, one knight, and more than three " gentlemen authorised to bear arms." And " Micham Common " had three more gentlemen of the same calibre among its residents; so, less than two centuries ago it must have been a place of some importance, and the supposition is confirmed by the handsome mansions still scattered about the parish, as shown above.

Mitcham Grove, formerly the seat of Mr. Henry Hoare, was a haunt of the Evangelical party. Mrs. Hannah More was an occasional visitor here ; and the Thorntons, Wilberforces, and Macaulays, often came over from Clapham to discuss their theological opinions. The house is now pulled down. It stood in a pleasant situation near the banks of the Wandle, and had some noble and dis-

---

* See " Old and New London," Vol. I., pp. 47 and 76 ; Vol. II., p. 414 ; Vol. III., p. 38.

tinguished owners. It was purchased by Lord Clive, and presented by him to Sir Alexander Wedderburn, afterwards Lord Loughborough and Earl of Rosslyn, in recompense for his defence of that illustrious general and statesman in the House of Commons. Lord Loughborough sold it in 1789 to Mr. Henry Hoare, the banker, of Fleet Street, and he disposed of it to Sir John W. Lubbock. More recently the house was the residence of Mr. John H. Stanton. A new mansion, the property

During the Non-juring Schism this place would seem to have been a rallying point for those who refused to give in their allegiance to the Hanoverian succession. At all events, Robert Nelson writes in 1702-3 that he finds none of " our clergy " placed nearer to his friend Samuel Pepys of Clapham than Mitcham, "where lives a Mr. Higden, who married a sister of Lord Stawell."

In this parish, not far from Tooting Junction station, and nearly opposite to " Figge's " Marsh, is

MITCHAM GROVE IN 1796. (*From an old Print.*)

of Mr. W. P. Bidder, has been erected near the site of the old house.

According to Lysons, Lord Chancellor More must have had a house here, although it is uncertain that he lived in it, as one Thomas Elrington, by his will dated in 1523, bequeathed to Alice, his wife, "his chief house at Mitcham, which was given to him by Thomas More."

Brayley says that " an object of some interest to the antiquary is an ancient house in this parish, formerly the property of Mrs. Sarah Chandler. This house, in which are the remains of a chapel, is conjectured to have been, at a very early period, the property of Henry Strete, 'who had a license for an oratory in his house at Mitcham,' in 1348. It is held under the Dean and Chapter of Canterbury, and its proprietors claim a right to the north aisle of the church."

a house, on the front gate of which is an inscription in old English characters, to the effect that " Defoe lived here in 1688." Defoe had a Presbyterian chapel in Tooting, and the minister of that chapel and many of the neighbours believe in the tradition, which is probably true, though it cannot be said to be universally accepted. The house in question is now inhabited by Mr. Bumpus, bookseller, of Holborn.

Another noted inhabitant of Mitcham was Moses Mendez, a poet of the last century, who at the time of his death, in 1758, was reported to be worth £100,000. He was the author of four little dramatic pieces—"The Chaplet," " The Shepherd's Lottery," " Robin Hood," and "The Double Disappointment," besides a poem called " Henry and Blanche," &c. Some of his productions are to be found in Dodsley's Collection.

CHAPTER LVI.

TOOTING.

The Etymology of Tooting—Probable origin of the word "tout"—The River Graveney—Doubtful Parish Boundary-lines—The Old Ermin Street—Tooting-Bec Common—Early History of the Manor—Encroachments on the Common—The Maynard Family—Sir Paul Wichcote—Sir James Bateman—The Parish Church—A Cell to the Priory of St. Mary Overy, Southwark—The Village of Tooting—Druett's School—The Jewish Convalescent Home—The Defoe Presbyterian Chapel—Biographical Notice of Daniel Defoe—Lambeth Cemetery—Summers Town—Holy Trinity Church—The Church of St. Mary Magdalene—Westminster Union Industrial School—Surrey County Lunatic Asylum—Noted Residents—Tooting Common.

THIS parish, which claims as its full designation the name of Tooting Graveney, is more commonly known as Lower Tooting. For common use, the terms Lower Tooting and Upper Tooting, as indicating the two natural divisions of this neighbourhood, are more useful than the words Tooting Graveney; but the district known as Upper Tooting is, we believe, entirely outside the boundaries of Tooting-Graveney parish, which is the smallest in area of any parish in the county of Surrey, being only some 560 acres in extent, but it has a population of about 4,000 souls, which shows an increase not far short of fifty per cent. since the census was taken in 1871; thus, it is unlike its neighbour, Mitcham, which is very extensive in its acreage.

The etymology of Tooting has been somewhat puzzling to topographers. Mr. James Thorne, in his "Environs of London," says, "it is no doubt due to the settlement here of a branch of the Saxon or Teutonic family of the Totingas. In legal documents the place is designated Tooting Graveney (properly Gravenell), the addition being derived from a family of that name who held the manor, with other property, under the Abbot of Chertsey, in the twelfth and thirteenth centuries." The first syllable of the name—*Toot*—is perhaps the same as the Welsh word "Tut," a small rising whereon beacons were placed; and the name may have been given to this district from a beacon being planted here. "'Toot,' in one of its varied forms, is not an uncommon prefix to the names of other places in different parts of England, as *Tot*nes, *Tot*ham, *Tut*bury, *Tot*hill, *Tot*tenham, &c.; and it may be added that all these places are of considerable elevation compared with the surrounding parts."* Such also is the case here, at all events in that part of the parish which is known as Tooting Bec. By some writers the name of Tooting is derived from "Theon," a slave, and "Ing," a dwelling, which would show the word to be derived from the then status of the few inhabitants of the place as villeins or churls, as the original copyhold tenants of a manor were called. In Saxon times

England was divided, as to its inhabitants, into two classes—freemen and serfs; and these latter were, to a great extent, all attached to the soil.

On more than one occasion Tooting has figured in the pages of comic literature, something in the same way as Slowborough-cum-Mud-in-the-Hole; and it may be remembered that Thackeray, in "Vanity Fair," when describing how Rawdon Crawley lived on nothing a year, mentions "the pertinacity with which the washerwoman from Tooting brought the cart every Saturday, and her bills week after week."

It is on record that during the Great Fire of London in 1666, large numbers of the inhabitants flocked to Tooting to view the conflagration, which was plainly visible hence. On the higher grounds at Tooting, and even at Morden, we are credibly informed the light was so strong that one would have sworn the fire was only in the next village.

It is worthy of note that a century or two ago, when the Court took up its quarters at Epsom, as we have already seen,* and large numbers of the wealthier classes were in the habit of going thither from London, it became customary for many of the inhabitants to station themselves at the point where the road forks off to Epsom by way of Tooting and Merton respectively, and vociferously hail or "tout" the travellers, with the object of inducing them to pass through the former village. To such a pitch had this custom grown that it became a common expression for the aristocracy as they approached this spot, in addressing one another, to say that the "toots" were upon them again. Hence, like "burking" or "boycotting," the term has become adopted into our common conversation, the word "toot" and "tout" being pronounced in the same way.

The little river Graveney, which rises in what once were meadows near Tooting Junction station, flows now with diminished flood in winter, and is all but dry in summer. The drainage of the locality no longer finds its way into its bed. Its course is marked by willows, as it wanders through the lowlands in the direction of Tulse Hill.

The parish, as we learn from a local publication

---

* See "Old and New London," Vol. IV., p. 14.

* See *ante*, p. 248.

called the *Tooting Graveney Parish Magazine*, was originally bounded by natural watercourses, but now many that were open have been covered either by drains or arches, or otherwise filled in; this makes it a difficult matter to determine the exact boundary-line in some places, and hence a bone of contention has at different times arisen between the ratepayers of Tooting and the adjoining parishes. An old inhabitant, writing in the above-named publication, remarks :—" The boundary separating the parishes on the common is properly beyond Green Lane, where formerly stood an octagonal cottage, where our pioneer used to chip a brick with his axe, and from there by a watercourse inside the present enclosure to the ditch close to the spot where Streatham Workhouse stood, which included one row of trees in the avenue and also the road. The ditch on the Streatham side was a general watercourse separating the parishes; and although our boundary post has often been put in its proper place, it is taken up again by others, and laid down. A large oak-tree was blown down there about fifty years ago, which Tooting claimed, but Streatham took it away. One field, called the 'Leg of Mutton' field, is entirely isolated from Mitcham, though rated by that parish. It is leading to Biggery Hill, towards the Wandle, and was the end field of Bell's Farm, adjoining the glebe, and surrounded by hedge and ditch, but now being only partly enclosed, great care should be taken to preserve the proper boundary. Tradition says that a corpse was found in this field, and that the Tooting officials refusing to bury it, Mitcham parish did the duty that we should have done, and claimed in consequence to rate the field, which is to this day assessed to them."

Tooting lies on the Epsom road, between Mitcham on the south and west, and Streatham on the east, Wandsworth bounding it on the north; and it is seven miles from Westminster Bridge.

The old Ermin Street ran nearly parallel to, but a little to the east of, the turnpike road through Tooting, Merton, Ewell, and Epsom, to Ashtead, and so southward to Dorking, when it went off westward to Farnham, passing to the south of Guildford. One Stane Street, branching from the Ermin Street at Dorking, proceeded southwards, through Ockley, into Sussex. Another Stane Street from London to the south passed through Streatham, Croydon, Coulsdon, Caterham, and Godstone.

At the time of the Conquest there were two, if not three, manors called Tooting—or rather, *Totinges*, as the name was then written. One of

these, forming part of the parish of Streatham,[*] came to be called Tooting-Bec, from having been held of the gift of Richard de Tonbridge by the Abbot of Bec, in Normandy. The name of this manor is now perpetuated by Tooting-Bec Common, of which we shall have more to say presently. Another of these manors is thus noticed in Domesday Book among the lands of the Abbot of St. Peter, Westminster :—" The abbot holds Totinges, which Swain, or Sweyn, held of King Edward, when it was assessed at four hides. . . . Earl Wallef obtained this land from Swain, after the death of King Edward, and he mortgaged it for two marks of gold to Alnothus the Londoner, who gave his interest in it to St. Peter, for the health of his soul. Odbert holds it of the abbot, exempt from payment of geld." This manor is supposed to have been absorbed either into the manor of Tooting-Bec or into that of Tooting Graveney.

The other estates are thus described in the Domesday Book :—" Haimo the Sheriff holds Totinges of the Abbot of Certesy (Chertsey). In the time of King Edward it was assessed at six hides, wanting one virgate : now at nothing. The arable land consists of three carucates. There is one carucate in demesne; and three villains, and two bordars, with one carucate. There is a church and four acres of meadow. In the time of King Edward it was valued at 40s.; afterwards at 20s., and now at 70s. The same Haimo holds of the abbot one hide, held of King Edward by Osward, who could remove whither he pleased. There is one villain, with half a carucate, and one acre of meadow. In the time of King Edward it was valued at 15s.; now at 10s."

Mr. S. E. Lambert, in a lecture on "Ancient and Modern Tooting," lately delivered before the Tooting and District Ratepayers' Association, observed : "It was probably in consequence of the grant to St. Peter by Sweyn that a church was erected here. At the time of the compilation of 'Domesday,' it appears that there was a church and four acres of meadow, but I have not been able to obtain any evidence that this church existed in the time of Edward the Confessor, or before the grant by Sweyn. When the land passed to the Church, as was the custom of the ecclesiastics in those times, and in order to evade the public burdens, it was assessed to them at nothing."

From the above entries it is clear that a grant of the manors must have been made at an early date to the Abbey of Chertsey; and the manor of Tooting Graveney appears to comprehend all that

---

is described in the Domesday Survey as held by "Haimo the Sheriff." It is probable that this Haimo, or some descendant, bore the surname of "de Gravenell," and gave that name to the manor, which, as shown above, has since become corrupted into Tooting Graveney. One Richard de Gravenell was witness to a deed by which the manor of Balgham (Balham) was confirmed to the Abbey of Bec. Haimo de Gravenell was owner of this lordship in the twelfth century, for in the reign of Henry II. he gave the tithes of the manor and the advowson of the church to the Priory of St. Mary Overy, in Southwark, which grant was confirmed by Richard, Bishop of Winchester. From this monastery the church was served as a vicarage down to the time of the Dissolution, when the advowson was granted to Edward Fynes, Lord Clinton and Say, and it again became a rectory. It subsequently belonged to Sir J. Bateman, Percival Lewis, Brady, Rev. Henry Allen, D.D., Barlow, Broadley, Marsden, Greaves, and others.

In 1214-15 (Charter Roll 13, Edward I., No. 40), one Bartholomew de Costello had a grant of free-warren in his land of Toting.

In 1216, as we learn from Brayley's "Surrey," "King John granted to Denis, his chaplain, the land at Tooting which had belonged to Richard de Gravenell, who had probably lost the estate in consequence of having taken part with the barons in their contest with the king. If so, however, the lands must have been shortly restored, for it is stated in the Testa de Nevill that the heirs of Richard de Gravenell held one knight's fee in Tooting of the Abbot of Chertsey."

Thomas de Lodelowe died in 1314 seized of this manor; and in 1394 the estate was held by Katherine, widow of Thomas de Lodelowe, son and heir of the above, "by the payment of a rose at the feast of St. John the Baptist." From the Lodelowes the manor passed by marriage to the knightly family of the Dymokes, who held it for about two centuries.

The following particulars of the early history of the manor were given by Mr. Lambert in his lecture above mentioned :—" In the fifth year of the reign of Edward III. (1332), a portion of the Church lands, comprising a house and 13 acres found to be held of the parish church, and described as being in Totinge Graveney, was aliened in favour of the prior and brethren of the Holy Cross next the Tower of London.

"In 1341-2 Joan, widow of Thomas de Lodelowe, was still alive, and had her dower out of the Manor of Tooting Graveney. She was seized for the term of her life of the manor of Tooting Graveney, held of the Abbot of Chertsey. There was there a capital messuage, worth nothing yearly; 42 acres of arable land, valued yearly at 10s. 7½d. ; 5 acres of pasture worth 5s., the price of the acre being 12d., and after the time of mowing they are worth nothing, because they lie in common ; also 6 acres of pasture, which is in severalty from Lady-day to August, and is worth 6s. yearly ; and from August to Lady-day it lies in common. The reversion of the dower of the said Joan belonged to Margaret, daughter and heiress of Thomas de Lodelowe (the son), but subject to the life interest of her mother, Katherine.

"In 1547, at the view of Frankpledge for Tooting Graveney, it was agreed that no cattle should be put on the common fields between the feasts of St. Mary and St. Matthew, penalty 10s. ; hogs to be yoked and ringed, penalty 10s. In 1555, several persons were fined for cutting furze off the common lands—amongst others, Richard Blake, of the Lordship of Tooting Bec, parish of Streatham. In the same year the Rector of Tooting Graveney had to make a certain gate between the highway and the common field by a certain day, under a forfeiture of 6s. 8d.

"In 1557 I find it was directed that they of Upper Tooting shall fetch no gravel within the Lordship, neither were they to fell furze. It appears that, by Upper Tooting was meant Tooting Bec, so that we can readily understand that Tooting Graveney would come to be known as Lower Tooting. In the same year it appears that the parson had encroached upon the Lord's ground and the King's highway, going to Mitcham, in making ditches beside the parson's half acre. He was commanded to fill it up within a certain time, under a penalty of 10s. Also, it was provided that the same parson suffer none of his cattell to go on the common, or in the lane, under the penalty of 3s. 4d. for every horse and cow, and 3s. 4d. for every sheep and hogge, as often as they be taken. In 1559 there was a presentment that the rector of Tooting permitted his cattell—to wit, hogs and sheep—to wander in the common, contrary to the penalty set at the last court ; therefore he forfeited 3s. 4d., but, by favour of the court, it was turned to amercement—viz., 20 pence. There was a further presentment that the aforesaid Rector of Tooting did not fill up the pit which he had dug in the highway. He was commanded to fill it up by Christmas, under a penalty of twenty shillings.

"In 1561 the Rector of Tooting was again ordered not to permit his beasts to wander in the Lord's commons or lanes, under a penalty of 4d.

each time ; and whoever took the beasts to the Lord's grounds was to have 2nd of such 4d.

"In 1565 I find the Lord's waste ground styled Tooting Graveney Common.

"In 1569 one Robert Lewesey enclosed one-fifth part of the two commons, called Tooting Common, belonging as well to the Manor of Tooting Graveney as to Tooting Bec. It was commanded that hereafter he do it not. In 1574 all persons having lands adjoining the common were to fence them, at a penalty of 12d. for every yard.

"In 1589 it was ordered that the little lane on the south-west part of the church be enclosed by the inhabitants with a gate, at their charges. There was a presentment that four elms cut in the ditch of the hedge, over against the church-yard, belonged to the lord of the manor, and not to the Rector of Tooting.

"In 1590, Robert Wymple, of Streteham, unjustly and without right, entered into the Lord's lands called Tooting Heath, and took and carried away fishes—to wit, eels—being in the ponds there."

Towards the close of the sixteenth century the lordship of the manor of Tooting was conveyed to Sir Henry Maynard, who was secretary to the famous minister, William, Lord Burghley ; and it was probably to this Sir Henry that Queen Elizabeth paid her visit when she was at Tooting in 1600, not very long before her death.

William, the eldest son of Sir Henry Maynard, was raised to the peerage, with the title of Lord Maynard ; but this estate was held possibly under a marriage settlement, as we learn from Brayley, by Sir John Maynard, his second son, who was made a Knight of the Bath at the coronation of Charles I. He sat in several Parliaments for Lostwithiel, in Cornwall, and in 1647, together with Mr. Denzil Holle, Sir William Waller, and other leaders of the Presbyterian party, was impeached for high treason, on account of his strong dislike to the proceedings of the army and his efforts to get it disbanded. Maynard was committed to the Tower, but the prosecution was eventually abandoned. On his decease, in 1658, the manor of Tooting Graveney descended to his son and heir, John, who died in 1664, leaving a daughter, Mary, wife of Sir Edward Honeywood, Bart., of Kent.

The manor was subsequently owned by the Wichcotes. In 1695 Sir Paul Wichcote obtained an Act of Parliament enabling him to grant "leases for ninety-nine years of the manor of Tooting-Graveney, and any of his messuages, lands, and hereditaments in Tooting-Graveney, Tooting-

Becke, and Streatham, in the county of Surrey, for the better improvement thereof." Shortly after we find the property in the hands of Mr. James Bateman, who was afterwards knighted, and became an alderman of London. He was Lord Mayor in 1717, and died in the following year. His funeral must have been a very sumptuous affair. He was buried by night with great pomp in Tooting Church, the *cortège* comprising twenty coaches, each drawn by six horses, a large number of mourners on horseback, and one hundred torch-bearers. His son, Mr. John Bateman, sold this manor, with his other property in Surrey, under the authority of an Act of Parliament in 1725, to Mr. Percival Lewis, of Putney, and about forty years later it was bought by Mr. Morgan Rice, a wealthy distiller, who was high sheriff of the county in 1772, and who also built the mansion called Hill House, on the rising ground above the church.

The old parish church, which is dedicated to St. Nicholas, was pulled down in 1832, when the new one was built ; it had a round tower, which was said to be the only example of a tower of that description in Surrey. The church is said to have been situated at an inconvenient distance from the population, and therefore its removal was the less regretted. But this can scarcely have been the case, the former structure having stood about the middle of the churchyard, by the present apse, where are to be seen some flat memorial stones which once lay in the principal aisle. It was a fine specimen of architecture, partly Roman and partly Saxon, with walls from four to six feet thick. The entrance to the churchyard was by a lych-gate—not unlike those which we have seen at the district of the Crays*—which led to a fine old porch. The old church was described by Lewis, in his "Topography of Surrey," published about the time of its demolition, as "an ancient structure with a circular tower and wooden spire, now much dilapidated." In former times it is said to have contained three bells, but latterly it had only one —and that the one still in use—the other two having been stolen.

The new church, dedicated, like the former, to St. Nicholas, the patron of fishermen, was consecrated in 1833, and it has been twice further enlarged. It is not a bad specimen of the Pointed style, considering the date of its erection, and has a lofty tower of four storeys, terminating in an open parapet and pinnacles. In 1873-5 an apsidal chancel, with organ chamber on the north and

* See *ante*, p. 66.

vestry on the south side, was built, from the designs of Mr. J. St. Aubyn. This chancel, which has greatly improved the appearance of the church, contains five stained glass memorial windows, with illustrations from the life of the prophet Elijah and other Scriptural subjects. The central part of the Gothic altar-screen, before the building of the new

though to the prejudice of his owne." He died in 1670. Captain Philip Gidley King, R.N., formerly Governor of New South Wales, was buried here in 1802. A more recent tablet records the death, in 1841, of Mr. Richard Alsager, M.P. for East Surrey, and one of the Elder Brothers of the Trinity House. In the churchyard are the tombs

DEFOE.

TOOTING CHAPEL.

chancel, contained a good copy of the "Salvator Mundi," by Sir James Thornhill. This, however, has now been removed. In the course of the year 1884 the body of the church was re-seated with open benches.

Among the sepulchral memorials removed from the old church, the most noteworthy is a tablet in memory of Sir John Hebdon, twice Envoy to Russia under Charles I. and Charles II., "for whose interest he spared neither purse nor person,

of Sir John Maynard and his son of the same name, who died in 1658 and 1664 respectively.

Dr. Samuel Lisle, who held the Rectory of Tooting from the years 1720 to 1729, was raised to the Bishopric of St. Asaph in 1743. He was subsequently translated to Norwich, and died in 1749.

The Church of Tooting Graveney in former times was not destitute of fitting accessories for the celebration of the Divine Office, as may be gathered from the inventory taken by the commissioners in the reign of Edward VI., when they went about the country to claim for the use of the king all plate, jewels, and articles of value, leaving only such things as they thought necessary for the continuance of public worship.   Here, however, the commissioners had been forestalled in their work of plunder, for they had to report that there had been "stowlyn out offe the Church, aboute the moneth of May," three years before, "some

Saunder, Esquiors, Comissioners of our Soveraing Lorde the King, among other to that effect these, persel of Churche goodes here after ensuing.

"Imprimis a chalice poiz X oz iiij grt.

"A cope of old red sattin and a Aulter cloth of Satin of Bridges (Bruges?) for the Communyon table.

"Also remaining in their charge to the King's use iij belles in the steeple."

OLD TOOTING CHURCH.   (*From a Drawing by Harding, Engraved by Cook*, 1827.)

crosses and candlesticks"; and they further added, "all other thynges that were in the Church att that tyme was (*sic*) taken away."

The report continues thus :—"Wyllym Hodson and Thommas Borhum were churchwardens of the said parishe Churche off Totynge Graveney" at that time; and they appear to have been in office five years.   But the next year there were fresh wardens, for Richard Kingston and Roger Marshall were wardens.   That was not long before the poor young king's death.   There was "delivered unto the Wardens there (Toting Graveney) xix day of May, Anno regni, regis Edw. VI., VII. (1553), by Sir Thomas Caswarden, Sir Thomas Saunder, Knightes, John Scott Nicholas Leigh and William

The parish registers begin in 1555, but the entries are not original until the time of James I.

In almost every neighbourhood the old "Grange," or "Manor House," if lonely and dull, is sure to be associated with a ghost; and if it has a moat or any other trace of antiquity, then the popular imagination is sure to conjure up a subterranean passage.   Tooting is no exception to the rule.   The "subterranean passage" here is supposed to have led from the church to a moated building in a field close by, which may have served as a home for a small colony of Brethren of the Holy Cross, at the time when the church was "served" by the Priory of St. Mary Overy, in Southwark.

We are told that it was a house and thirteen acres of land. The moat may have served for a fish-pond, but it also afforded protection from surprise by reckless or desperate night marauders. It stood on the edge of the wild open heath land, and there can have been no lack of needy wayfarers, ready to enrich themselves by fair means or foul. "The subterranean passage," remarks the writer of the paper in the magazine above quoted, "was no doubt constructed for the purpose of enabling the brethren to pass to and fro from the church unobserved, and, as they may have had no chapel attached to the house, of going unmolested to the vigils and services in the dark nights and mornings. It is then no great stretch of the imagination to picture on this spot the home of a small colony of the Brethren of the Holy Cross—perhaps the home of a few sent down, and changed from time to time, from the convent in the heart of London, just under the fortress walls. The brethren may possibly have had some spiritual charge in the parish. The church, as we have seen, was in the hands of the Priory of S. Mary Overie, the magnificent church of which, under the name of S. Saviour's, Southwark, still attests the splendour of the convent. And it is not unlikely that many of the services in the church here would have been conducted by the brethren from the little convent in the fields close by, even if they were not responsible to the priory for all the duties of the parish. Here, then, on the ground now in great measure covered by dwellings abutting on the road which is known as the Vant Road, stood, in what must have been the seclusion and quiet of perfect country, the moated monastery of which no known trace now remains."

The principal part of the village of Tooting lies about a quarter of a mile to the north of the church, at the junction of the Mitcham Road with that leading to Merton and Epsom. Here, in what is called the Broadway, are several good shops and houses, a large Board School, a bank, the police-station, and other public buildings. Here, too, are one or two fine old mansions with iron gates, most with extensive grounds annexed. One of these, called Fairfield House, is now, and has long been, a collegiate school. Another large house on the north side of the Broadway, called Eldon House, which has been modernised by a facing of stucco, is thought to be part of the mansion once occupied by the Maynards, and which Queen Elizabeth honoured with a visit, as mentioned above. This house, a few years ago, was occupied by a wealthy Portuguese Jew, named Salvador, and some of the contiguous property is now known as the Salvador estate. At the corner of the Merton Road and Garratt Lane is a large, square, brick-built mansion, with steep roof, called The Limes, from the trees with which its grounds are surrounded. The iron gates and red-brick piers, surmounted by stone urns, are very fine. One of these old mansions was at one time occupied by Lord Trimleston; the rich iron gates bore a coronet as part of its ornamentation. These, however, have been taken away. Sir Richard Blackmore, a city physician and poet, commemorated by Pope, had his country house here :

"Blackmore himself, for any grand effort,
Would drink and doze at Tooting or Earl's Court."

In the main street are two old inns—the "Angel" and the "Castle"—both remarkable for their low rooms and huge beams across the ceiling.

In the centre of the village, close to Tooting Corner, there stood formerly an institution known as Druett's School, devoted to the care of pauper children from some district in London in which the cholera made most fearful ravages in the year 1848, doubtless through bad sanitary arrangements. No less than 120 victims of this epidemic were buried in Tooting churchyard in the course of a fortnight. The view of the building is given in the *Illustrated News* for January, 1849.

In the Longley Road, near the centre of the village, stands the Jewish Convalescent Home, which was founded in 1869 for the reception of Jewish convalescents—men, women, and children.

The greatest and the most celebrated name connected with Tooting is that of Defoe. In the main street of the village, a few yards north of the "Angel" Inn, stands the Defoe Presbyterian Chapel, which is said to have been founded here by that reverend man of letters in 1688. The present fabric is a commonplace brick building, with the inevitable three windows and a door below; by the side of the door is a panel of stone, recording the above historical associations of the spot. On either side stand a pair of tombstones, as guardian angels, to welcome those who enter; the interior is dull and prosaic enough for the Georgian era.

When he first founded this chapel, Defoe is said to have lived at a house, no longer in existence, near Tooting Corner, close to which runs a row of small villas, called after him Defoe Road. He also resided at one time in an old-fashioned house on the road to Mitcham. It looks like a country parsonage, and has very much altered since Defoe's time; but the fact of its having been occupied by him is recorded on its front gate.

Defoe was quite young whilst he was at Tooting,

and whilst here he had written only one or two pamphlets which never rose into fame, and are now forgotten—amongst others, one on "The Young Academics" of the universities, and another on the war between Austria and Turkey. He had also only lately, through his zeal for the Protestant cause, joined in the rash and ill-concerted conspiracy headed by the Duke of Monmouth, which brought some of his companions in arms to the block. It was probably to the obscurity of his birth and name that he owed his escape from prosecution; and both here as a writer, and afterwards as a hosier in business, he lived on unmolested by the Government of James II., until the Revolution of 1688 enabled him to breathe freely. Though not a minister, he appears to have gathered around him a congregation of Nonconformists, and so to have become the founder of the chapel which is called after his name. About this time he appears to have been admitted a freeman of the City of London; and in 1695, soon after having compounded with his creditors, he was appointed a commissioner for managing the duties on glass. His "Short Way with the Dissenters," his "Moll Flanders," and his "Robinson Crusoe," on which his fame chiefly rests, were not written till a far later period of his strange and chequered life.*

Here Defoe celebrated, doubtless in a convivial manner, November 4, 1669, the first anniversary of the accession of William III. Soon afterwards he had to make good his escape, for the bailiffs were after him for debt, as the authorities of the dominant Church had been after him for his outspoken nonconformity.

It is clear that Defoe, though he read and studied for the Presbyterian ministry, was never the pastor, though he was practically the founder, of the chapel here; in fact, there is no proof that he ever was ordained at all. And it is singular that of all the "Lives" of Defoe that are published, that by Lee is the only one which mentions, and that very briefly, his connection with Tooting. Mr. Chadwick, indeed, goes so far as to say that the years 1680—88 in his life are a blank that is not accounted for, and these were the very years that he spent at Tooting.

The chapel called after Defoe was built in the years 1765-6. Probably in Defoe's time the congregation met in a small house; this was succeeded by a temporary wooden building, which in due time gave way to the present structure; which is a fair specimen of the churches and chapels of the days of Hogarth.

The following particulars of Defoe's career are gleaned from a local source :—In 1688, the year of the Revolution, Daniel Defoe, author of "Robinson Crusoe" and many other great works, lived at Tooting, founded the nonconformist church, and supplied it with a minister, upon whose teaching the educated and respectable might attend. Joshua Oldfied, D.D., the son of an ejected minister, and tutor to the family of Paul Foley, Speaker to the House of Commons in the reign of William III., was the first pastor. He was succeeded by such men as Henry Miles, D.D., F.R.S., Samuel Wilton, D.D., the Rev. James Bowden, the founder of the Surrey Mission, and the Rev. William Henry, the earnest and genial Secretary of the Home Missionary Society. In 1861 the Rev. William Anderson became pastor of the church, and in his inaugural discourse called the attention of his congregation to the brave patriot and man of genius, who in an age of persecution here lifted the banner of Nonconformity. Illustrations of old chairs and a table in our vestry, and of the house in which Defoe is said to have resided, embellish the "Life of Defoe" published by Lee in 1869. The old oak pulpit, which was occupied for many years by Thomas Goodwin, D.D., President of Magdalen College, Oxford, a member of the Westminster Assembly of Divines, and one of "the two Atlases and Patriarchs of Independency," is used by the present pastor in conducting the services. In 1874 a committee was formed for the purpose of erecting a "Defoe Memorial Manse," for the use of the minister for the time being of the Nonconformist Church. The Rev. John Congreve, M.A., the rector of the parish, co-operated in the erection of a memorial so thoroughly in harmony with the spirit and work of the far-famed Defoe. "If Daniel Defoe were alive and amongst us," said Mr. Congreve at a public meeting, "it is certain he would greatly desire to see the successive ministers of his church provided with a house suitable to their position and work." The name of Dean Stanley figures among the subscribers to the undertaking. In 1875 a freehold site was purchased from the British Land Company in the most conspicuous position in Tooting, and a manse was erected for the minister of the chapel in the Domestic Gothic style. Near the front door, between two of the buttresses, it is proposed to place a life-size statue of Defoe under an enriched canopy.

Defoe was one of the greatest of English prose writers, and the father of English novelists. His genius was at once original and versatile. He wrote over 250 works, unlike any other books in literature, besides contributing largely to periodicals.

* See "Old and New London," Vol. V., p. 537.

But from amongst his numerous works, "Robinson Crusoe" stands out the greatest of them all. Yon desolate island, where the rough-capped exile lived year after year in solitude; the goats, with their large lustrous eyes, glaring wildly through the thicket; and the parrot crying out unexpectedly, "Poor Robinson Crusoe!" beguile old, young, learned, and unlearned. From the time that "Robinson Crusoe" first saw the light it has not been possible to conceive that it would ever lose its charms. But great as Defoe was as an author, he was far greater as a man. He dared to do his own thinking in an age when independence of thought was a rare thing. For the sake of civil and religious liberty he went from his drawing-room to the prison cell, from his carriage to the pillory, and if it had been necessary, would have gone to the stake.

Nearly opposite the Defoe Chapel is a granite building forming three sides of a quadrangle, and apparently designed for almshouses. Its timbers are of solid oak, and the roof looks as if it had been designed for one of the farm-houses in Surrey or Sussex.

Close by the cemetery is Summers Town, which was made an ecclesiastical parish in 1845. The church is in the Pointed style, and consists of a chancel, nave, south aisle, and a small bell-turret. This district is really part of Wandsworth, but has been separated from it only for ecclesiastical purposes, in the same way as the Holy Trinity district, on the high ground to the east of Tooting, and has now come to be vulgarly called Upper Tooting. It has, in fact, nothing whatever to do with Tooting proper. It is simply the western side of the parish of Streatham, and still forms part and parcel of that parish for all but ecclesiastical purposes. It was formed into an ecclesiastical district in 1855. It is an extensive and rapidly increasing locality, built mostly on the hill sloping up from the Broadway, Tooting, towards Balham, and skirting the north-western side of Tooting Common, to which there is a pleasant roadway leading up from the north side of Tooting Church.

The Church of St. Mary Magdalene, in the Trinity Road, was temporarily built in 1870 as a chapel-of-ease to St. Anne's, Wandsworth. Besides this, there are chapels for different denominations of Nonconformists. The Westminster Union Industrial School, in the St. James's Road, is an attractive red-brick building, standing in extensive grounds. It was opened in 1852, and affords accommodation for 200 children, boys and girls. In Burntwood Lane, just on the border of Wandsworth Common, stands the Surrey County Lunatic Asylum. It is a large building in the Elizabethan style, and was erected in 1840, from the designs of Mr. W. Moseley. The asylum has since been enlarged, and will now hold 1,100 inmates.

Upper Tooting, like the rest of this locality, contains a large number of residences of retired merchants and tradesmen, many of which stand in their own well-wooded grounds, some of the cedar-trees which grace them being particularly fine. Here at one time lived Mr. Richard Baggallay, father of Sir Richard Baggallay, one of the Lords Justices of the Court of Appeal; the son, however, was born in the parish of Stockwell. Hill House, formerly the seat of Mr. Alderman Venables, is one of the most conspicuous mansions in the neighbourhood. It is surrounded by extensive grounds on the rising ground above Tooting Church.

Tooting Common, some sixty-three acres in extent, forms the eastern extremity of the parish, and is hemmed in on either side by portions of the parish of Streatham. It is still a delightful piece of sylvan scenery, intersected by roads and footpaths, with fine avenues and groves of elms. In some parts the surface of ground has been broken up in the process of digging for sand and gravel; in other parts it is level, but it is well overgrown with gorse and heather, and is altogether one of the most pleasant spots in the neighbourhood; but considering how great was the struggle to secure this common, it is doubtful whether the boon has been fully appreciated. Tooting Common is separated by merely a roadway from Tooting-Bec Common, which comprises about 150 acres, and the whole is now maintained as an "open space" by the Metropolitan Board of Works, the "rights" having being bought from the lord of the manor in 1875 for several thousand pounds, after an agitation extending over many months. Around the common are several good houses, both old and new, standing in well-wooded grounds; and a great portion of the land or either hand is cut up for building purposes.